D1715091

STALIN'S HOLY WAR

STALIN'S

HOLY WAR

Religion, Nationalism,
and Alliance Politics,
1941–1945

Steven Merritt Miner

The University of North Carolina Press

Chapel Hill and London

Designed by April Leidig-Higgins
Set in Minion by Copperline Book Services, Inc.
Manufactured in the United States of America

The paper in this book meets the guidelines for
permanence and durability of the Committee on
Production Guidelines for Book Longevity of the
Council on Library Resources.

Publication of this book has been supported by a
generous grant from the L. J. and Mary C. Skaggs
Foundation.

Library of Congress Cataloging-in-Publication Data
Miner, Steven Merritt, 1956–
Stalin's holy war: religion, nationalism, and alliance
politics, 1941–1945 / by Steven Merritt Miner.
p. cm.   Includes bibliographical references and index.
ISBN 0-8078-2736-3 (cloth: alk. paper)
1. World War, 1939–1945—Religious aspects.
2. World War, 1939–1945—Soviet Union.
3. Nationalism—Soviet Union.   4. Russkaëiìa
pravoslavnaëiìa ëtìserkovš—History—20th
century.   I. Title.
D744.5.S65 M56 2002
940.54'78—dc21   2002002100

07 06 05 04 03   5 4 3 2 1

To the memory of
Margaret F. Miner,
whose buoyant spirit
and intellectual curiosity
enriched the lives of all
those fortunate enough
to have known her

CONTENTS

Preface   xi

Acknowledgments   xvii

Glossary and Abbreviations   xxi

Introduction   1

Part One   The Church Redux

1   Religion and Nationality:
The Soviet Dilemma, 1939–1941   27

2   Stalin's Holy War Begins, 1941–1943   51

Part Two   Fighting the Holy War

3   A Holy Hatred toward the Enemy:
The Church as Servant of Soviet
Foreign Policy, 1942–1943   93

4   A Vatican of Sorts   123

5   The Gatherer of the Ukrainian Lands:
The Church and the Restoration of Soviet
Power in the Western Borderlands   163

Part Three   Selling the Alliance

6   You Made Me Love You:
Selling the Alliance Begins   205

7   Amplifying the Soviet Voice   245

8   Guardians of the Truth   279

Conclusion   315

Notes   337

Bibliography of Works Cited   387

Index   397

MAPS AND ILLUSTRATIONS

Maps

1. Soviet and Axis Annexations, 1939–1941   37

2. Limit of German Advance, 1941–1942, and
Number of Open Churches, 1945, by Republic   139

Illustrations

Metropolitan Aleksandr Vvedenskii, of the
Obnovlencheskii, or Renovationist, Church   281

Metropolitan Vvedenskii giving the benediction,
summer 1941   281

Soviet soldiers pose in front of the war-damaged
cathedral in Yelnia, near Smolensk   282

Worshipers in the Obnovlencheskaia Sobor'   282

Orthodox bishops, including Acting Patriarch Sergii,
conduct a service, Bogoiavlenskaia Sobor' (Cathedral
of the Epiphany), Moscow, summer 1941   283

PREFACE

In an age when literature and even history are increasingly autobiographical, when a historian who is neither a Russian nor an Orthodox Christian—nor even especially religious for that matter—undertakes to write a book that deals to a large extent with the Russian Orthodox Church and the Soviet state, his prospective reader may wish for some sort of explanation. Although the most intriguing part of the historian's art is trying to understand and explain people unlike himself as well as places and beliefs unlike his own, I did not set out to explore an unfamiliar, personally alien subject for that reason alone. Like most books, this one did not spring full-blown into the author's mind. Rather, it gestated slowly, the product of an accretion of various experiences and ideas.

My first exposure to the Russian Orthodox Church came in the 1980s, when I visited what was then still the USSR to study the language and history of Russia. The impressions I carried away from my encounters with the church at that time were contradictory, though in ways that reflected the strange and conflicting realities of religion under the late-Soviet political order. One day, I witnessed a deeply moving liturgy at Leningrad's magnificent, heavenly, sky-blue Nikol'skii Sobor'. I stood transfixed, watching the unfamiliar ceremony as it stretched over the hours, the sun streaming through the high windows, penetrating clouds of incense to pierce the heart of the dark cathedral. The deep male voices of the choir boomed impressively overhead from a choristry concealed above and behind the worshipers. The congregation was overwhelmingly female and elderly; most were old enough to have experienced the period covered by this book and so to have survived the almost unsurvivable Nazi siege of the city. They genuflected solemnly and silently at the appropriate moments, only muttering the occasional nearly inaudible "amen." Hard lives had scarred many of them; one woman, nearly bent double with a spinal deformity, had tears of emotion streaming down her face as she participated in the ceremony. Although she appeared to be in her late seventies, a life of pain, incessant hardships, and shortages had perhaps aged her prematurely. My attention was constantly drawn away from the priests with their censers and elaborately choreographed movements toward the faces of the congregation, whose etched visages testified powerfully to the sad history of a generation that had experienced two world wars, a revolution, and civil war, as well as Stalinist terror.

On leaving the church, and while still trying to sort out the profound impressions evoked by the experience, my companions and I were approached by an angry old woman, little more than half my height, who began to scream at us. Although we had been quiet and—so it seemed to us anyway—unobtrusive and respectful, she shrieked that we foreigners should not have attended the service. The woman's actions were clearly extreme, and by no means representative of other Orthodox believers, but her outburst was my first, and certainly memorable, exposure to one important facet of Russian religion that until then I had never witnessed, but which would become much more familiar over the years as I studied the subject. The Russian Orthodox Church is *Russian*— devoutly, and often xenophobically so. The ecumenical spirit is not strong among many of its clergy and laity; and of all the Christian churches, it is arguably the one most deeply linked with the history, ethnicity, and government of its people.

My second exposure to Russian religious matters, during the same stay in the USSR, was entirely different, though equally as informative, and came during two excursions to Soviet anti-God museums in Leningrad. These queer relics of Communist-atheist materialist zeal were still in operation through Mikhail Gorbachev's first months in power, though they clearly looked as though they had seen better days. My first visit, to the famous Kazan' Cathedral, managed to be simultaneously both appalling and funny. Its gloomy interior was salted with exhibits purporting to demonstrate the history of humankind's supposed ascent from the darkness of ancient superstition toward the bright beacon of scientific enlightenment, as exemplified by Soviet-Marxism. Dioramas of Stone Age peoples worshiping inanimate objects were placed side-by-side with depictions of the Spanish Inquisition. No crazed Disney cartoonist could have dreamed up more stereotypical characterizations of evil papist inquisitors. The regime that had given the world Stalin and the gulag feigned outrage over an earlier, and infinitely smaller, terror conducted in the name of dogma.

The second "museum of religion and atheism" that I visited was in Leningrad's obtrusive St. Isaac's Cathedral. A dark pile of granite with a vast gilded dome, the structure seems out of place amid the rest of St. Petersburg's graceful architecture, perhaps reflecting the dreary spirit of the autocrat Nikolai I, during whose reign it was completed. St. Isaac's had one memorable attraction: the curators had taken advantage of the vast space under the lofty dome to suspend a giant pendulum, which was supposed to demonstrate the scientific, logical, and entirely materialist principles that supposedly govern the physical order. Owing to some unexplained design fault, however, the pendulum did not work properly, and one of the "under repairs" signs that were ubiquitous during Soviet days warned visitors that the laws of the universe were temporarily in suspension.

Like my experiences at the church service, the visits to the atheist museums were highly instructive; I only wish that I could claim to have understood their full import then as I believe I do now. At that time, with Ronald Reagan still president of the United States and Mikhail Gorbachev only just elevated to the position of first secretary of the Soviet Communist Party, the Cold War was still underway, and the USSR seemed to be a permanent world presence, powerful and stable. Western scholars constantly avowed that the Soviet regime enjoyed widespread social support, some even contrasting this supposed popular acceptance of the Communist regime with the malaise pervading the post-Vietnam United States. And yet, the atheist museums were a telling omen: few people visited them; they looked neglected, tired, and forgotten. The still pendulum of St. Isaac's stood as mute testament to the larger failure of Soviet industry and technology. The new materialist faith of the Soviet regime had failed to uproot and supplant the old beliefs of Russia. It is certainly impossible to picture even a single old woman being moved to tears by a display case in an anti-God museum.

These experiences, though they lingered in my memory, did not lead me directly to study the history of the Russian Orthodox Church, or the religious question during the war. Instead, I embarked on research for what I thought would be a history of Soviet attempts to "sell" the alliance with the Western democracies during World War II. While working on my previous book, I had been struck by the fact that policy makers in the United States and Great Britain often felt constrained by a growing mood of popular enthusiasm about the USSR, which inhibited critical public comment about the nature of Stalinism. I had also noticed in American and British archives a host of files pertaining to wartime cultural relations between the Soviet Union and the Western Allies; for the most part, these rich records have been neglected by diplomatic historians more concerned with high policy. I thought that a study of cultural propaganda might shed light on how wartime enthusiasms grew, how they affected policy, and how they collapsed in the postwar era—with a boomerang effect that eventually contributed to the emergence of McCarthyism.

Western religious suspicions of the Soviet Union had been one of the more difficult cultural prejudices for Soviet propagandists and their Western well-wishers to finesse or eradicate. Nonetheless, as I began to study this question, I had not expected to find very much beyond the odd note from the archbishop of Canterbury or a prominent American cleric, perhaps addressed to the defenders of Stalingrad, Leningrad, or Moscow, commending them for their heroism and contribution to the defeat of the Nazis. I expected that at most one chapter of the proposed study would be devoted to the religious question.

As often happens with historical research, however, one begins studying a certain subject only to be led to another by the document trail. Looking at the religious question in the wartime USSR, I had always found one thing to be anomalous about accounts of the period: the explanation historians generally give for Stalin's limited restoration of the Russian Orthodox Church, and the selection of a new patriarch of Moscow which occurred in September 1943, was that the Soviet government sought to harness the power of Russian nationalism behind the USSR's war effort. Why then, I wondered, did the Kremlin wait until this late period in the war, when the tide of fighting had finally begun to flow in their favor? Why had they not acted during the more dangerous years of 1941 and 1942, when the Red Army's back was to the wall and Moscow needed to mobilize every person who could hold a gun?

One occupational hazard of researchers is that they tend to seek answers in places that confirm their preconceptions. Because I was working on alliance propaganda, I naturally assumed that the explanation for the Kremlin's new religious policy must surely lie in this direction. From 1943 on, the Red Army was steadily on the advance; Soviet forces looked set to drive the Germans from East Central Europe. The Americans and British worried that the expansion of the Soviet sphere would result in the imposition of Communist institutions—including state-dictated atheism—on the unwilling populations of the Balkans and Eastern Europe. Surely, I reasoned, this must be why Stalin restored the Russian Orthodox Church, just as he closed the revolutionary Comintern.

This seemed a plausible hypothesis, especially in an era when Soviet archives were closed to researchers. Two things happened, however, to alter my views. In the first place, I began to learn that the Soviet religious question did indeed have an important domestic component, though one overlooked by most historians. As I looked closely at the Western documentary record, and published Soviet materials, I began to notice a distinct pattern. In the wartime statements and publications of Russian Orthodox hierarchs, the overwhelming emphasis was on questions relating to the western regions of the USSR: that is, the lands seized by Moscow during 1939 and 1940, as well as the territories occupied by the Nazis following their invasion of the USSR. Only very rarely did appeals from Russian Orthodox clergy address religion throughout the USSR, and most of these were only posted in the few remaining open churches that had survived earlier Soviet atheist campaigns, or they were spread by leaflet or radio broadcast to regions behind the German lines.

While this apparently confirmed my doubts that the Soviets had brought the church back primarily in order to appeal to believers throughout the USSR, it also undercut my earlier assumption that foreign propaganda considerations alone were driving Soviet religious policy. Further digging among neglected documents, especially from British and Polish sources, suggested that Moscow was playing a much deeper game. Not only did the Soviets hope to glean foreign policy benefits by resurrecting the Russian Orthodox Church; more important, they were also using the church to assist the reassimilation of subjects who had undergone German occupation, as well as to assert central power over territories claimed by the Soviets' western neighbors. To me, this made the subject infinitely more interesting, because it suggested elements of continuity between the atheist Communist state and its Orthodox Christian tsarist predecessors; it also suggested an intersection between Soviet domestic and foreign policies.

These aspects of the story had already begun to take shape in my mind when the second surprise development occurred: the collapse of the USSR miraculously opened many Soviet archives to international researchers. As those who have worked with Soviet materials can attest, their condition is far from satisfactory. Indexes of documents are poor and sometimes unavailable. Some files are missing, and many of the most important have been withdrawn to the so-called presidential archive, which remains closed to all but a handful of privileged and well-connected native Russian scholars. The remaining documents can often be very frustrating to work with—for example, policy debates at the Central Committee level may be detailed at great length, but then no record is available of the politbiuro's final decisions.

Nonetheless, the situation for historians of Russia and the USSR is vastly better now than it was less than a decade ago. What follows below is based on a fragmentary record, to be sure, but I believe that enough documents have been made available to discern the most important features of the subject. No doubt, this work will in due course be supplanted as more records are unearthed, but this is the norm in the historical profession, and if historians were to postpone writing until every relevant document is made accessible, very few histories would ever be published. The newly available Soviet documents, taken in tandem with a careful combing of Western sources, have made possible a much more detailed and nuanced view of this subject than has ever been possible before.

ACKNOWLEDGMENTS

As with all works of this sort, this study was many years in the preparation, and consequently I have amassed a huge debt of gratitude to the many people who have assisted me in my work, either through reading and commenting on early drafts, or by assisting me during the frequent and extended travels needed to complete the research and writing. I am grateful to the Hoover Institution, where I spent a very productive year as a visiting scholar making use of their unparalleled collection of Soviet materials. I found the staffs at the British Public Record Office, at Moscow's former Party Archive near Pushkin Street, and at the National Archives in Washington, D.C., to be consistently helpful with my many and demanding requests.

A number of people have opened their homes to me during my long trips abroad. I am especially grateful to Professor Georgii Kumanev, with whom I spent the better part of a summer in his comfortable Moscow apartment; he also generously allowed me to use his own considerable personal archival collection and helped me to gain access to former Soviet archives in the summer of 1992, when that was still very much a novelty for American researchers. My parents-in-law, Doreen and James McMillan have also been very hospitable to their vexatious American son-in-law, even allowing the Miner tribe to descend on them for the better part of a sabbatical leave. They went so far as to read and make very useful comments on the final manuscript.

I have received financial assistance from my home institution, Ohio University, in the form of a John C. Baker Award; I am grateful to Bruce Steiner, our long-serving departmental chairman, for helping me to land that grand and to find other sources of funding. My colleagues at Ohio have given very generously of their time, reading portions of the manuscript and giving me valuable ideas about directions of research. I am especially appreciative of a faculty seminar organized by Ann Fidler; as a result of that stimulating exchange, a logjam in my writing was broken, and I was able to complete the manuscript. She also read almost the entire manuscript, and she was both critical where proper, and encouraging when I needed that very much. My colleagues (both current and former) Katherine Jellison, Mike Grow, Jeffrey Herf, John Gaddis, Sholeh Quinn, Alonzo Hamby, and Norman Goda all were very insightful with their comments on early drafts. Ohio University's Department of History provides a very special environment for the study of history; I am very fortunate to have such fine colleagues.

A number of graduate students at Ohio University over the years have assisted in the production of this volume, either by commenting on various drafts —and courageously delivering honest verdicts—or by helping with reproduction of articles, handling computer glitches, or tracking down obscure statistics. I would like to thank Kevin O'Connor, Marian Sanders, Jeffrey Kuhner, Bonnie Hagerman, Marc Selverstone, J. D. Wyneken, Robert Davis, Steve Remy, Jamie Fries, and Raymond Haberski.

I would like to single out my friend and colleague at the University of Washington, Professor James Felak, for his invaluable and detailed commentary that helped me to avoid a great many errors and spurred me on greatly. His were the actions of a true friend and a first-rate scholar of Eastern Europe.

As I began to assemble the materials that would provide the basis of this book, I was fortunate to take part in a series of colloquia between Russia and American scholars of the history of the Second World War. These were my first exposure to the historical profession as a newly minted Ph.D., and I learned invaluable lessons about research, writing, and historical dispute during these sessions. I thank the organizers of these meetings, Professor Warren Kimball on the American side and Academician Grigorii Sevostianov on the Soviet (and later the Russian) side. I also thank my friend and colleague Charles Alexander for getting me involved in these meetings.

I owe special thanks to my dear friends Dr. Richard Cross and Therese Cross. Their insights into religious life and politics were, along with their friendship, very valuable to me. Sherry Gillogly also added her measure of good cheer to the stressful closing stages of this work. She is a good friend and colleague.

My editors at Chapel Hill, Ron Maner and Brian MacDonald, deserve special thanks. My duties as department chair have caused unavoidable delays, and they have been patient beyond all expectation. I would also like to thank Brian for his careful editing; it is a model of care and attention. Needless to say, all mistakes that have made it through the final sieve are my own responsibility and not those of the many people who have helped me.

In closing, I want to thank my family especially: my children, Emily and Sam, have been understanding about a father with a strange set of obsessions; and my wife has remained constantly interested, supportive, and patient during a sometimes aggravating and extended process of production. She has been a model of support, and I am deeply grateful to her in more ways than I can possibly mention.

I have dedicated this book to the memory of my mother, Margaret Miner, who loved books, history, and the world of ideas. The book should, properly, be dedicated to my father Donald Miner as well, since they both supported my education through so many years and my subsequent work, even going to the unheard of length of traveling with me to Moscow one winter. On the weekends, when the archives were shut, we spent many unforgettable hours exploring the streets of Moscow on foot. Sadly, my mother did not live to see the final published result of all that effort. But it is certainly no exaggeration to say that, in this instance, the current book would have been unthinkable without her support. No mere book dedication can be adequate thanks.

GLOSSARY AND ABBREVIATIONS

CPSU	Communist Party of the Soviet Union
CPUSA	Community Party of the USA
DPSR	*Documents on Polish Soviet Relations,* published documents
FO	Foreign Office, Great Britain
FRUS	*Foreign Relations of the United States,* published documents
INF	Ministry of Information records, Great Britain
ispolkom	executive committee
NKGB	Narodnyi Kommissariat Gosudarstvennoi Bezopasnosti (People's Commissariat of State Security)
NKVD	Narodnyi Kommissariat Vnutrennykh Del (People's Commissariat of Internal Affairs)
oblast'	Soviet geographic administrative division, province
OGB	*Organy Gosudarstvennoi Bezopasnosti* (Organs of state security)
PRO	Public Record Office, London, England
raiion	Soviet geographic administrative division, region
RPTsIVOV	*Russkaia pravoslavnaia tserkov' i Velikaia Otechestvennaia Voina* (edition of wartime church documents)
RSFSR	Russian Federated Republic
RTsKhIDNI	Russian Center for the Preservation and Study of Documents of Contemporary History (former Party Archive), Moscow
Sovnarkom	Soviet Narodnykh Kommissarov (Council of People's Commissars)
TSIM	*Trudnye stranitsii istorii Moldovii, 1940–1950* (edited collection of documents from wartime and postwar Moldavia)
ZhMP	*Zhurnal Moskovskoi Patriarkhii*

STALIN'S HOLY WAR

Atheism is the core of the whole Soviet system
—Aleksandr I. Solzhenitsyn, *The Oak and the Calf*

[Religion] in its very essence is the mortal enemy of
Communism. — Leon Trotskii, *Pravda*, June 24, 1923

Introduction

During the summer of 1976, much of Western Europe experienced a severe drought that dried up vegetation and left fields a dusty brown. In that same summer, the British government happened to be conducting an aerial photography project with the intention of updating topographical maps. When these photographs were developed and analyzed, the cartographers were surprised to discover faint patterns emerging in certain country fields. On closer examination, these turned out to be the outlines of Roman forts whose locations had long been forgotten but whose foundation stones had wrought lasting changes in the vegetation covering them. The unusual change in weather conditions had disclosed ancient, previously unnoticed archaeological patterns that had survived for more than a millennium, even as passing generations of farmers unknowingly tilled the fields under which they lay hidden.

Likewise, when the tide of Communism receded in Eastern Europe at the end of the 1980s, the sudden disappearance of political structures once assumed to be durable revealed preexisting social patterns that had long been neglected, though, unlike the Roman forts, not entirely forgotten. Among such patterns emerging from the depths of pre-Communist history, perhaps the most important was the ancient gridwork of religious loyalties: the geography of confessional difference delineating Moslem from Christian Orthodox, Roman Catholic from Protestant, Greek Catholic from Ukrainian Orthodox, and so forth. As the proliferation of post-Soviet religious and ethnic conflicts has shown so strikingly, the end of Communism in Eastern Europe has not brought about an "end of history," but rather its vigorous, and often lethal, return.[1]

A fundamental conceit of the Communists had been their moral certainty that their new faith in "scientific atheism" would supplant what they believed to be mystical religious "mythologies," relics inherited from a bygone era of superstitions before Darwin, Marx, and electrification. Instead, despite the Communists' best efforts, religion outlasted the Communist era. In Russia itself, public opinion polls conducted after the fall of the Soviet state revealed that the institution most trusted by the average citizen was the Russian Orthodox Church.[2] This should not be too surprising, because the church was one of only a handful of Russian national institutions—and by far the most important one—to survive from tsarist times through the entire Communist period. Trust in the church may well dissipate with time, and interest in Orthodoxy often goes no deeper than a fascination with the color and architectural splendor of the Russian past—a beauty so manifestly lacking in late Soviet life. Certainly, public interest in Orthodoxy has not yet translated into high church attendance figures.[3] Nonetheless, the Russian Orthodox Church wields considerable political power and is even able to command overwhelming majority support in the Duma on legislation designed to restrict the activity of rival faiths.[4] The survival of religion, and its return as a publicly prominent political and social force in post-Soviet life, are in themselves sufficient grounds for a reexamination of its history.

It is the contention of this book that, despite decades of determined Soviet atheistic campaigns, religious belief, especially in combination with nationalism, remained a crucial social and political force throughout the Soviet era. This was never truer than during the war against the Nazis, when the Soviet system underwent unprecedented strains as it struggled to survive. Religion was not some marginal factor relegated to the periphery of Soviet leaders' concerns. Rather, the Kremlin was well aware of the fact that it had been unable to eradicate religious faith, and Soviet rulers continually took account of religion as a political factor while making policy in a surprisingly wide range of areas. Considerations of religion pervaded Soviet foreign and domestic policies to a degree not generally understood in histories of the USSR.

The Kremlin oligarchs did not enjoy the historian's luxury of being able to divide reality into discrete fragments; they had to deal with interconnected social and political forces as well as with rapidly changing circumstances over which they had only partial control. In order to understand the Soviet approach to religion, therefore, one must look at the problem in the widest possible context, taking into account not only Soviet rulers' intentions and actions but also the limits to their power. The image of Stalin as the master manipulator entirely dominating events, which is common in popular accounts of the Stalin era, cannot survive even the briefest acquaintance with Soviet archives.[5] Although Stalin may have enjoyed personal power greater than any other tyrant in the dictator-infested twentieth century, even he had to take account of concrete obstacles to the imposition of his will. Contrary to widespread belief, he was not free from the pressures of public opinion (even though admittedly these took quite different forms than in the United States or Britain); nor was he free of ideological blinkers. Moreover, even though Stalin wielded life-and-death power over his subjects, he could not always rely on his subordinates to enact his orders unchanged.[6] One very great barrier to his will was the persistence of religious faith among tens of millions of his mostly peasant subjects.

Stalin certainly sought to be the grand puppeteer, forcing his subjects to dance to his tune, and he succeeded in this more often than most dictators. It is a serious mistake to underestimate his power or political acumen, as so many of his rivals found to their cost. The strained efforts of certain revisionist historians to portray the dictator as almost a background figure, the impotent plaything of his advisers and of historical forces beyond his grasp, is even less persuasive than the image of Stalin-the-omnipotent.[7] This study is entitled "Stalin's Holy War," not because the dictator was in total control of events, but rather because his personality and his decisions were essential factors in the development of church-state relations during the war, something that cannot be said of any other individual.

This book is not simply a history of the Russian Orthodox Church during the war, much less a history of Soviet believers. Rather, it is an examination of the religious question in the broadest sense, as it interwove itself into Soviet politics, state security, diplomacy, and propaganda.[8] Owing to the diffuse nature of the subject, this study must be part political history, part traditional diplomatic study, and part social history. The evolution of the Soviet regime's wartime approach to religion can also only be fully understood in the context of Russian history and traditions, Soviet ideology and practice, the specific and shifting circumstances of the war against the Nazis, and the demands of the wartime alliance with the Western democracies.

An examination of the Kremlin's wartime handling of the religious question illuminates a great many crucial aspects of Soviet history. Among the more important are: the degree to which the Soviet public regarded the Communist regime as legitimate, and therefore worth defending; the shaping and definition of individual identities and loyalties among the Soviet populace; the responses of the Stalinist regime to widely held popular beliefs and social pressures; the regime's manipulation of traditional historical and religious images and the way this affected not only the Soviet public but also the Kremlin rulers themselves; the attitude of the regime to Russian and minority nationalism; the function and operation of terror in Stalinist governance; the variable balance, symbiosis, and clash between Russian traditions on the one hand and Communist influences on the other in the formation and conduct of Soviet domestic and international policy; the interaction between foreign and domestic policies; the role of morality, religion, ideology, and propaganda in the East-West wartime alliance; and the comparison and contrast between the goals and methods of the Nazi and Soviet regimes. It is argued here that religion was a significant factor in all of these areas, and a comprehensive history of religion during the war must address each of them.

This long list of important topics goes to the heart of the Soviet "experiment." It is not argued here that religion is the hitherto undiscovered key to Soviet history, the philosopher's stone that allows us to see Soviet reality in its entirety for the first time; nor do I pretend to provide definitive answers to the questions posed here. Rather, the history of religion in the USSR is more like the barium cocktail that a patient swallows before undergoing a body scan. By tracing the circulation of religious issues through the body politic of the Soviet Union, the historian can view more clearly how the Communist system operated on any number of levels. Because so many millions of common people retained their beliefs, and religious questions circulated through the major arteries as well as the veins and capillaries of Soviet life, a focus on religion provides the historian with an excellent, yet neglected, analytical tool.

The role of religion in Soviet life has seldom received its due from historians. During the Soviet years, when the USSR looked from the outside to be enormously powerful and stable, far too many Western scholars adopted unconsciously the Soviet assumption that the church was a "remarkably tenacious relic of the [tsarist] past," at best relegated to a twilight existence, at worst doomed by the powerful forces of urbanization, secular modernization, and Soviet repression.[9] In large-scale histories of the Soviet period, the church always warrants short mention but generally only as one of many victims of Soviet repression, or as just another branch of dissent, less significant than the more prominent secular forms.[10] Authors generally note, accurately enough, that the theological and institutional passivity characteristic of Russian Orthodoxy prevented it from playing the critical role that the Roman Catholic Church played in Poland; but this interpretive framework all too often causes them not to examine its history very deeply.[11] The treatment of church-as-victim is true so far as it goes, but this approach ignores the complexity of religious affairs, the nexus between religion and national identity, the intermittent congruence of interests between the Russian church and Soviet state, as well as the continuing importance of religion in the considerations of Soviet policy makers.

The relative neglect of religion may reflect in part the secular concerns of historians themselves.[12] The church is slighted even in histories of the Second World War, when the Russian Orthodox Church underwent the greatest revival in fortunes that it would experience during the seven decades of Soviet rule.[13] Fifty-seven percent of the Soviet population identified themselves as religious believers in the 1937 census, only four years before the USSR entered the war. Although accurate figures are lacking for the war years, every contemporary source indicates that the number of believers grew dramatically during this time. These facts should demand greater attention than they do from social historians.[14]

The tendency to downplay, or underestimate, the importance of religion in Soviet life is all the more striking given the fact that the Russian church defied the dominant trends of late Stalinist politics, actually growing in numbers precisely at a time when the Kremlin was circumscribing the rest of Soviet culture and intellectual life—reason enough, one might think, to spark historians' interest. Nonetheless, one recent history of "culture and entertainment" in the wartime USSR contains essays on radio, music, the stage, and the creation of "Heroes, Heroines, and Saints," among other subjects, but no chapter on—and almost no mention of—the role of religion.[15] Another new study of the "Soviet Home Front" mentions the Orthodox Church only in passing, ascribing its wartime revival to its "importance as a symbol of continuity with Russian tradition, and of its substantial contribution to mobilizing popular support for the war effort."[16] Although true enough, this is a tremendous simplification of a highly complex phenomenon; among other things, it ignores the crucial international and domestic ethnic dynamics that contributed greatly to the reappearance of the church in Soviet life.

The situation is little better in Russian-language historiography. Although many Russians have a renewed interest in the history of religion since the end of the USSR, historians trained in the Soviet era generally discount the importance of religious belief, even in accounts of the "spiritual life" of the Soviet people during the war.[17] Histories of Soviet foreign relations also ignore religious questions, despite the small but important role played by the Russian Orthodox Church in the conduct of Soviet diplomacy, especially in the critical western borderlands of the USSR, the focus of so many wartime inter-Allied disputes.[18]

Excellent histories of the Russian Orthodox Church are available, to be sure, and these studies treat religion in greater detail and seriousness than do political, diplomatic, or even social histories. Nonetheless, these works often suffer from the overspecialization characteristic of modern academic monographs, examining the history of the church as an institution while often neglecting the political, social, and diplomatic influences that shaped the Soviet state's policies toward religion.[19] Perhaps understandably, such studies concentrate on the overarching story of state persecution of the church and laity, but the more delicate questions of clergy collaboration with Soviet power are consequently neglected. If one reads the history of religion in the USSR purely in terms of the state as oppressor and the church as victim, then it is easy to overlook those instances where both sides' interests intersected, as well as how the Soviet state was itself influenced by the persistence of religion.[20]

A few outstanding studies of religion during the war exist, but these focus almost exclusively on the German-occupied regions, where churches underwent a "great revival."[21] The reason for this has been the relative paucity until recently of reliable documentary sources for the Soviet side of the front line. The only attempts to study the use of the Russian Orthodox Church for foreign policy goals were written before Soviet internal records became available, and they focus on the postwar years, mentioning the late-war period only by way of introduction.[22]

Virtually every history of the Soviet Union during the Second World War, whether scholarly or popular, mentions—if only in passing—the Soviets' adoption of a more conciliatory stance toward the Russian Orthodox Church, generally dating the change from the outbreak of the Soviet-German war in June 1941. The explanations offered for the Kremlin's change of course have varied over time. During the war, many Western observers believed that Stalin eased legal strictures against the Orthodox Church as a "reward" of sorts.[23] Although this was a widely held view at the time, it was not an accurate explanation, as informed people knew well enough. As early as 1927, Metropolitan Sergii, the patriarch *locum tenens* of the Russian Orthodox Church, had called on his followers to accept and obey Soviet power as divinely ordained.[24] This decision had been controversial at the time and was widely debated in religious circles both within Russia and abroad. Despite Sergii's pledge of loyalty, the situation of the church had dramatically worsened during the succeeding decade; so to view the wartime reappearance of Russian Orthodoxy as the result of some change in the church's attitude toward the state was misleading at best.

With the glow of wartime cooperation long since faded, and the avuncular image of Stalin a distant memory, historians are not inclined to attribute the Soviets' newfound tolerance of religion to the dictator's goodwill, or to the church's repentance of its earlier hostility to the Communist order.[25] Instead, the most common explanation holds that, whereas the Russian people would not fight for Communism, they would go into battle for Russia—the Holy Russia of Orthodox Christianity. As the great Russian author and Nobel laureate Aleksandr Solzhenitsyn writes with characteristic venom, "from the very first days of the war Stalin refused to rely on the putrid decaying prop of [Marxist-Leninist] ideology. He wisely discarded it . . . and unfurled instead the standard of Orthodoxy—and we conquered."[26] This familiar interpretation holds that, reeling from the German attack, the Soviet government immediately eased up on the church in a desperate effort to save itself.[27] Often cited in this regard is Stalin's comment at the end of the war that the Russian people fought for Russia, not "for us," that is, for the Communist Party.[28]

Some historians cite a further factor inducing the Soviet policy shift: Moscow's need to counter German propaganda. From the first days of their invasion of the USSR, the Nazis claimed to be leading a "crusade" in defense of Western civilization against Soviet atheistic atrocities.[29] Owing to institutional infighting, confusion of aims, and the sheer barbarism of Nazi ideology, however, the Germans failed to capitalize on the religious discontent of the Soviet peoples as effectively as they might have done. Nonetheless, so great was the religiously based dissatisfaction with the Stalin regime among average Soviet subjects that the Germans scored some important successes in this area almost despite themselves. A large American interview project of refugees from the USSR after the war suggested that "the church was overwhelmingly considered the sole area in which German rule brought decided improvement."[30] Certainly, Moscow knew of German-sponsored or -tolerated religious activity in the occupied territories, and this was the source of great anxiety. Many historians have therefore reasoned that Stalin's relaxation of strictures on Russian Orthodoxy resulted from the need to compete for the hearts and minds of his subjects—he "could hardly afford to be less generous than the Germans."[31]

The Soviet-era Marxist dissident-historian Roy Medvedev disagrees with such explanations. He denies that the Soviet government relaxed its repression of the church in order to tap Russian nationalism, calling this argument "mistaken." Medvedev points out that, whereas Stalin's speeches, and Soviet propaganda generally, began to feature Russian national themes immediately after the German invasion, the church did not figure in the Soviet press or propaganda until late 1943. "Nobody in Moscow gave [the Russian Orthodox Church] a second thought throughout the whole of 1942," he claims erroneously. He offers an intriguing alternative explanation for Stalin's "concordat" with the church hierarchy in 1943: this was "in effect a cosmetic operation" designed to ease American and British concerns about the Red Army's advance into the center of Europe. In the autumn of 1943, the Soviet army was rapidly recovering Ukraine and looked poised to pour into the Balkan peninsula. Many people in Britain, and even more in the United States, feared that the Kremlin would impose its own Communist system on countries in the path of the victorious Red Army. Stalin thus carefully timed the restoration of the Patriarchate precisely to still such Western fears in advance of the Teheran Conference, where the "Big Three"—Stalin, Churchill, and Roosevelt—were scheduled to meet for the first time. Although the reopening of Russian churches may well have given comfort to Russian believers, Medvedev writes confidently, "to Stalin this was of secondary importance."[32]

Other Russian historians have also made the connection between the restoration of the Moscow Patriarchate in September 1943 and the dynamics of alliance politics, though their analysis differs somewhat from Medvedev's. Stalin biographer Dmitrii Volkogonov argues that both the demands of the war effort and of international realities convinced the dictator to act. "The [Soviet] High Command," he writes, "valued the patriotic role of the church and wanted to widen its activity." But international considerations were even more important: in the months leading up to the Teheran Conference, Stalin "faced not only the task of accelerating the opening of a second front [in Western Europe] but also the increase in the quantity of military assistance." The prominence in organizations supporting material assistance for the USSR of sympathetic Western church leaders, such as the so-called Red Dean of Canterbury, Hewlett Johnson, persuaded Stalin to make the "publicity gesture" of restoring the Moscow Patriarchate. "It was not the vanity of a former seminary dropout that moved the Soviet leader," Volkogonov concludes, "but rather pragmatic considerations in relation with the Allies."[33]

The Russian Orthodox priest and historian Sergii Gordun also sees the "change in character of [state] relations with the church" as resulting from the approaching Teheran Conference and the Soviet need to bolster sympathetic forces in the West. He claims that Hewlett Johnson had long been agitating for permission from the Soviet government for a visit of a high-ranking delegation of the Anglican Church to Moscow.[34] The Kremlin finally gave its consent in

September 1943, not coincidentally only two months before the meeting at Teheran, and the archbishop of York, Cyril Garbett, duly visited the Soviet capital. In order to receive him appropriately, Gordun argues, the Russian church needed a leader of proper status; the elevation of Sergii to the patriarchal throne was the result.[35]

The historical arguments outlined here, though not entirely wrong, miss many of the subtle motives underlying Soviet religious policy. They also fail to answer certain questions and indeed raise further ones. For instance, if the Soviet government eased up on the church primarily in order to channel Russian religious nationalism into the war effort, then why did the new spirit of church-state cooperation take so long to come to fruition? Not until September 1943 did the Soviets allow the Russian Orthodox Church to select a new patriarch; only in that year did the state permit the restricted publication of church literature within the USSR, the restoration of churches, and the publication of statements by Orthodox clergy in the Russian-language Soviet press.[36] In other words, true rapprochement between church and state, insofar as it happened at all, did not come about until almost two years after the outbreak of war. The Soviets had been far more hard pressed — and thus in need of support from all domestic groups, including Christians — in the years 1941–42. And yet, during these two years, although the situation of the Orthodox Church did not deteriorate further, and may have even improved slightly, the Soviets kept religious activity on a very tight rein. The first public hints of a religious thaw appeared only after the Soviet victory in the Stalingrad campaign during the winter of 1942–43; and the church only became publicly prominent following Moscow's triumph in the battle of Kursk in July 1943. It would appear on the face of things, therefore, that the church benefited not from hard times, as historians were inclined to argue, but rather from the sharp improvement in the Kremlin's military fortunes from 1943 onward.

Furthermore, if the Soviet government's motive in reactivating the Russian church was to harness specifically *Russian* nationalism, then why did the overwhelming majority of church reopenings occur in Ukraine and other western border areas, rather than in Russia itself? Most of the regions that underwent German occupation during the war contained only minority Russian populations.[37] The non-Russian inhabitants did not always rejoice at the opening of Russian Orthodox Churches, often in places of worship that had previously housed Greek Catholic or independent Ukrainian Orthodox congregations. In addressing this paradox, it is inadequate simply to argue that the Soviets were countering German propaganda. Berlin's promises of religious freedom made their strongest impact during the opening stages of Barbarossa, before the Soviet population learned firsthand the murderous designs of the invaders. Yet, Soviet religious policy flowered from 1943 through the end of the war, at precisely the same time that German liberationist claims had lost whatever appeal they might once have exercised and as the Red Army was finally driving the Wehrmacht out of the USSR.

Nor can one accept in their entirety the arguments of those who stress foreign policy motives for the change in Soviet religious policies. Although Medvedev makes an excellent point about the diplomatic uses for which the Soviets could employ the Russian Orthodox Church, it is clearly wrong to claim that nobody in Moscow's ruling circles paid any attention to the church until 1943. Whereas the public profile of the Orthodox Church remained very low until that year, even at the time of the Nazi-Soviet partition of Poland in September 1939, and again following the Soviet seizure of the Baltic states in the summer of 1940, the church supplied important services for the Soviet state. Moscow used pliant church hierarchs, such as Metropolitan Nikolai and Archbishop Sergii (Voskresenskii)[38], to assist the forcible imposition of Soviet rule in the areas annexed to the USSR as the result of the Nazi-Soviet Pact and successive German-Soviet agreements.[39] From 1941 to 1943, although the church's role was distinctly limited, it was far from inactive; Russian Orthodox hierarchs routinely issued appeals to believers designed to meet the changing demands of the Soviet war effort.

As for the argument that the Kremlin used the Orthodox Church to allay Western fears about the export of Soviet Communism to Western Europe, this is largely true. But Moscow's international religious propaganda began well before 1943. In the summer and autumn of 1941, the Soviets worked hard to dispel the widely held—and entirely accurate—image of themselves as oppressors of religion. They did this in order to cement the anti-Hitler coalition with Britain and the United States, as well as to ensure the flow of Lend-Lease supplies from Washington. Not only did Soviet religious propaganda commence from the very first days of the war, but also Moscow employed a much wider range of tools than just the Orthodox Church to project its image overseas as the protector of Christian civilization; it deployed the full range of its propaganda apparatus, from Moscow radio to Soviet embassies abroad, to members of foreign Communist parties, leftist sympathizers, as well as moles in Western governments.

The Soviet Union's wartime religious policy is easy to misunderstand, because it was a moving target. There was no single Soviet approach to the church; rather, the Kremlin's policies continually evolved in response to developments in the war, within the alliance, and among the populace. At times, the

Soviet rulers drove events; more often events drove them. The variability of Soviet policy, as well as the complex fashion that religious considerations interacted with many other political and social factors, helps to explain the confusion and variety of historical explanations that historians have offered for Stalin's restoration of the Russian Orthodox Church. Each approach outlined here grasps only a portion of a much larger story.

The purpose of this book is to explain the complexity and subtlety of the relations between the Soviet state and religion as these changed during the war years. In order to understand the historical context, the balance of this introductory chapter briefly examines the legacy of the tsarist government's relation to the Orthodox Church, especially the ways successive tsars used the church to enhance St. Petersburg's control over the fluid western frontiers of the Russian empire, as well as to advance Russian foreign policies. Stalin's wartime religious policy would mimic this traditional pattern. It also outlines the two decades of Bolshevik antireligious policy before 1939 and how these set the stage for wartime developments.

This book is divided into three parts. The first, "Rediscovering the Utility of Tradition," (chapters 1 and 2) explores the Soviets' initial wartime use of the church during the Red Army's occupation of the western borderlands* from 1939 to 1941, as well as the limited revival of religious themes and the church during the first year and a half of the war against Germany. I argue that Moscow's religious policy at this time can only be understood in the context of Soviet security considerations, especially Moscow's concerns about the disaffection of non-Russian nationalities. The Kremlin saw the church not only, and perhaps not even primarily, as a tool for mobilizing and harnessing Russian nationalism throughout the union, but rather as one of several instruments for countering and disarming non-Russian, and anti-Soviet, nationalism. As most tsars could have told Stalin, the Russian Orthodox Church was an effective agent for the Russification of the ethnically diverse and contentious western regions.

Part II, "Fighting the Holy War" (chapters 3 through 5) examines church-state relations as these came to full fruition from 1943, when Stalin entered into his so-called concordat with the Moscow Patriarchate, until the end of the war. I argue here that Stalin decided to employ the church, and specifically to

---

*Throughout the book, I use the term western borderlands to refer to those regions the USSR seized between 1939 and 1940 in collaboration with the Nazis. These areas are the three Baltic States (Estonia, Latvia, and Lithuania) as well as eastern Poland, northern Bukovina, and Bessarabia.

reestablish the Patriarchate as a functioning institution, in order to deal with the complex political problems he and his government faced as the tide turned in the war and Soviet forces began to recover regions formerly occupied by the Germans, and later as the Red Army advanced into Eastern and Central Europe. One of the most serious tasks for the Kremlin at this time was the reestablishment of Soviet power in non-Russian areas, where anti-Soviet nationalists and guerrillas resisted the Red Army, often supported by local clerics. The Russian Orthodox Church could help the Kremlin by bringing order to the chaos of religious affairs in the region. It could tame or remove rebellious clerics while preserving the facade of religious toleration; it also assisted in the Russification of the borderlands. Additionally, the church would be used to contest the influence of the Vatican, which wielded considerable authority among the populace of the western borderlands as well as among the people of East Central Europe.

This was a masterful policy, but Moscow had not counted on the possibility of a spontaneous grass-roots religious revival among the USSR's subjects; this development is examined in the fourth chapter. As the Soviets sought to manipulate Russian Orthodoxy, as well as other Russian national symbols, they began to lose control of the process. Whereas the Kremlin restored the Moscow Patriarchate in order to keep dangerous religious forces in check, this had the unexpected and—for the Soviets at least—alarming effect of fueling the revival of active religious practice at the local level throughout the USSR. The experience of war and the revival of Russian historical themes also changed the Soviet approach to governance in important ways, causing Soviet rulers to define themselves ever more strongly in Russian national terms rather than in the "heroic" Bolshevik tradition.

Part III, "Selling Stalin's Holy War," examines the international propaganda dimensions of the Soviet religious question. The Red Army could not defeat the Germans on its own; Moscow desperately needed Western material and military assistance. (The same was true in reverse, of course, but the Soviet military situation was far more desperate than that of its Western allies.) In order to secure these things, Moscow had to overcome a deep, and entirely justified, legacy of Western popular suspicions about atheistic Communism. Throughout the war, therefore, Moscow and its agents abroad would work tirelessly to eradicate the memory of prewar Soviet religious repression and to replace it with a new image of the USSR as the defender of Christian civilization. For reasons to be explained, they proved surprisingly successful in doing so. The history of this almost entirely forgotten propaganda campaign tells us a great deal about international imaging; differences in Soviet, British, and American cultural perceptions of the USSR; the dynamics of alliance between a totalitarian state and Western democracies; the difficulties faced by reporters working in dictatorial systems; as well as the way wishful thinking, ideological commitment, careerism, and venality can shape the flow of information in wartime.

This international context is vital for a full understanding of the evolving Soviet religious policy, because at several important points religion influenced Moscow's diplomacy, and international affairs often altered Moscow's approach to religion. I argue that an examination of religion's role in the wartime USSR can help us understand the initial Soviet domestic conditions that would go far toward shaping the early Cold War. Yet, the history of the Soviet Union's wartime international use of religion has never been written, nor understood.[40]

In the conclusion I argue that the history of religion during the Second World War tells us a great deal about Soviet domestic circumstances at the outset of the Cold War, of the changing nature of Soviet identity in the postwar world, and indeed about political and social patterns that have persisted into the post-Communist period. The Soviet system passed through an intense and testing fire during the war, and the experience wrought lasting changes. The alchemy of war brought about the seeming reconciliation of opposites: it transformed the lead of Bolshevik internationalism, if not into gold, then at least into the curious alloy of Russian nationalist Communism that is such a visible presence in post-Soviet Russia. Only by first grasping this can one understand the jarring juxtaposition of clashing symbols present in contemporary Communist-nationalist public demonstrations, where people march side by side carrying portraits of Lenin next to those of Nikolai II (whose murder the former ordered), photographs of Stalin beside Orthodox icons that the dictator would gladly have thrown onto the rubbish heap.

Russian national themes had been steadily creeping into Soviet discourse since 1934.[41] But, in order to survive the Nazi onslaught, the Communist regime was forced to meld Russian nationalism with Bolshevism in a much more unrestrained fashion, creating a new, unstable compound. Soviet leaders did not abandon Communism between 1941 and 1945; instead, they tried to reconcile ultimately irreconcilable forces, aggravating the internal contradictions that would in the end help to implode the USSR. To employ Marxist terminology: if Orthodoxy and Russian nationalism were the thesis, and Bolshevik atheism and internationalism the antithesis, then the dialectical synthesis between the two, brought about by the war against Germany, was a flawed and unsteady form of National Bolshevism.

The Weight of Tradition

During the opening stages of the First World War, in that brief period when the Russian Imperial Army was advancing against its Austro-Hungarian opponent, the French ambassador to St. Petersburg, Maurice Paleologue, lamented that Russian leaders, instead of concentrating on the military task at hand, became all too easily distracted by questions of nationality and even religion. These seemingly obscure quarrels hampered military efficiency. He complained that, following the Russian entry into the Austrian province of Galicia, tsarist "officials introduce the worst practices of Russification as a sort of gift of welcome."[42]

Russian officialdom bewildered Paleologue; in the midst of a modern war, it seemed to be in the grips of an almost medieval fixation with religious questions, grasping the opportunity presented by Russian territorial gains to extinguish ancient rivals of Russian Orthodoxy. As the Russian army advanced, it brought behind it Russian Orthodox priests determined to impose their authority on the local Eastern Slavic population. The new governor-general appointed to administer the portions of Austrian Galicia occupied by Russia, Count Vladimir Alekseevich Bobrinskii, for instance, told the French ambassador: "I recognize only three religions in Eastern Europe: the Orthodox, the Catholic, and the Jewish. The Uniates are traitors to Orthodoxy, renegades and apostates. We must bring them back into the true path by force." Foreign Minister Sazonov was equally scathing, telling the French envoy, "Don't expect me to take up the cudgels for the Uniates! I respect Roman Catholics, though I regret that they have fallen into error. But I hate and despise the Uniates because they are renegades." The commander of Russia's armed forces, Grand Duke Nikolai, sympathized with Paleologue's concerns, though he could not change things; he once complained to the Frenchman that " 'I'm expecting trainloads of ammunition. They [St. Petersburg] send me trainloads of priests!' "[43]

Paleologue was an acute, sympathetic observer of the Russian scene, and his worries about misplaced Russian military priorities would be borne out by events. But in this instance his confusion betrayed his misunderstanding of the historical context of political and territorial rivalries in the long-contested plains that lie between Russia and its western neighbors. In Western Europe, where state structures have long been more stable, national identity and independence were often attained by rejection of ecclesiastical authority. In Eastern Europe and Russia, by contrast, national and religious identity have long been inextricably mixed, with the latter being the precursor and often the most important influence on shaping the former; in this unstable region, national identity was often defined by the embrace, not the rejection, of a common confession.[44]

In order to ensure the political loyalty of subject peoples in this disputed area, leaders of all the major regional powers have routinely resorted to the manipulation of religion. In the modern world—at least in the Western democracies—people have become accustomed to viewing religion as a matter of personal choice and faith, not state policy. Throughout most of human history, however, this was not the case. In Eastern Europe, where borders have rarely been firmly fixed, and where the political affinities of populations have been highly changeable, religion has been one tool, often the principal one, to ensure the loyalty, or at least submission, of subjects. In the Eastern Orthodox world, the key step toward establishing national independence, and with it political control over a given people, has been the recognition of autocephaly of the nation's church. Autocephaly confirmed ecclesiastical independence and thus a greater ability on the part of the ruler to determine religious policy within his or her domain.[45]

The fluidity of European borders, and of political loyalties, is nowhere more marked than in the region flanked on the north and south by the Baltic and Black Seas, on the west by Poland, Slovakia, Hungary, and Romania, and the east by the Russian Empire and later the USSR. In this region, which has changed hands innumerable times over the centuries, the local population has frequently endured not only political upheavals but also changes in the dominant religion, as rulers fought for control and peoples for national statehood. Historically, the principal contending religions have been Roman Catholicism, advanced by the Habsburg Empire and by Poland when that nation was independent; the Greek Catholic, or Uniate,[*] Church, the chief religion of the western Ukrainians, which the Habsburgs also often promoted, as did the Poles intermittently; Islam, the state religion of the Ottoman Empire; and Orthodoxy, most effectively championed by Russian imperial authorities. Judaism was also a significant presence, though because Jews lacked a state to protect their interests, and were vastly outnumbered by their Slavic neighbors, their religion lacked the political clout of these other confessions.

[*]Not only is religion an ancient battleground; even the names used for various confessions are hotly debated. The Greek Catholic Church, for instance is also referred to as the Ukrainian Catholic Church, the Eastern (or Byzantine) Rite Catholic Church, or the Uniate Church. Each of these names has advocates; each has detractors. I use these names interchangeably, because each appears in various documents, but I do so understanding full well that this is a contentious issue.

Russia has ancient and well-established traditions of symbiosis between church and state, which can be traced in part to the Byzantine origins of its branch of Christianity. The extent of church-state unity in Byzantium has often been exaggerated in the past, and modern historiography has reacted against this tendency.[46] Nonetheless, it remains true that the Byzantine church, to a much greater degree than its Roman rival, stressed the ideal of "symphony" between temporal and ecclesiastical authorities.[47] Roman imperial institutions and traditions survived in the East, whereas political authority in Western Europe fractured following the decline of Rome. Consequently, the Byzantine church remained a church of empire in a way that the Western Church did not.*

In addition to the Byzantine imperial inheritance, the church in Russia was vulnerable to state influence for another reason: whereas the Latin Church recognizes the preeminence of a single figure, the pope, whose authority crosses state boundaries, the Eastern Christian world is far more decentralized. The patriarchs of the East—Constantinople, Alexandria, Antioch, Jerusalem, and Moscow—have an order of precedence based on relative antiquity, which ranks the patriarch of Constantinople as the first among equals, but there is no figure analogous to the pope whose word is supreme. Orthodox writers see this as one of their church's great strengths.[48] Eastern Orthodoxy, in this view, stresses the conciliar tradition where patriarchs are treated as equals who, at least in theory, make decisions in a more consensual fashion than is customary in the Latin world. One consequence of this tradition, however, has been the fracturing of the Eastern Church's authority; split as it is into smaller fragments, it has generally been less able to contest state power than has the Vatican. To be sure, there was a "Byzantine Commonwealth," and there is an Eastern Orthodox world that commands great respect, but ambitious rulers have often been able to make use of frequent rivalries between the various centers of Eastern Orthodoxy when confronting church power.

Russia gained autocephaly in the fourteenth century and full ecclesiastical autonomy when the Moscow Patriarchate was established in 1589, at a time

---

*Ironically, Russian Slavophile writers of the early nineteenth century argued that the Eastern branch of Christianity was both more spiritual and less worldly than the Latin Church because they believed that the latter had imbibed the traditions of Roman legalism and secularism, whereas Eastern Orthodoxy had not been thus corrupted. This view entirely overlooked the fact that Byzantium, and the Eastern Church, saw themselves, with good reason, as the proud inheritors of the Roman legacy. As was so often the case with Slavophile thought, in this instance romantic *volkisch* notions were based on a curious reading of history.

when, more than a century after the fall of Constantinople to the Ottomans, the Russians were the only major Orthodox people who were no longer under the power of non-Orthodox rulers.* Although the Moscow Patriarchate was the youngest of the Eastern Orthodox world, it soon became the most important in many respects. The eclipse of Constantinople and the simultaneous rise of Russian political power changed Russians' self-image. Shortly after the fall of Byzantium in 1453, Russian church and political leaders began to speak of Moscow as the "Third Rome." Whereas both Rome and Constantinople had fallen into heresy, in this reading, Moscow had preserved the flame of true belief and had thus become the linchpin of Orthodox Christianity. Such were the origins of the Russian Messianic tendency, which is such a controversial, and easily exaggerated part of that country's history.

The century following the establishment of the Moscow Patriarchate brought the apogee of the Russian Orthodox Church's power and influence; this was the time during which relations between church and state most nearly approximated the Byzantine ideal of symphony. During the Smuta, or Time of Troubles (1598–1613), when the Russian nation nearly disintegrated under a hailstorm of external and internal blows, the church served as a rallying point, the only institution linking the disparate and warring factions of Russian society, finally helping to expel the Poles and reestablish state authority. At the end of the Smuta in 1613, when the Romanov dynasty was established, the father of the new tsar Mikhail was the patriarch of Moscow, Filaret, an ambitious man who was the real power behind the throne. During most of the seventeenth century, the church acted to restrict the penetration into Russia of foreign, heretical ideas, and it cooperated with the state to impose and secure Russian power as the country's boundaries began to expand westward, into Belorussia and Ukraine.

Peter I (1695–1725) brought an end to this period of relative church-state harmony so often idealized by Russian nationalist writers. Even before Peter, the church's position had been weakened when, during the 1660s, Patriarch Nikon tried to assert the superiority of ecclesiastical power over a wide range of areas. Nikon was defeated, and the primacy of monarchical authority

---

*The patriarch is the highest ecclesiastical ranking in Eastern Orthodoxy, there being only five figures of such standing, based in Constantinople-Istanbul, Antioch, Jerusalem, Alexandria, and Moscow. Since the fourteenth century, Russia had had its own metropolitan, the second-ranking episcopal position. The creation of a Patriarchate in Moscow gave the Russians full autonomy in their religious administration, whereas when they had only been represented by a metropolitan, the Russian church remained subordinate to the patriarch of Constantinople.

reconfirmed, even though the price of doing so was high. The church was split from within, and a large portion of the laity—the so-called "Old Believers"—defected from the ranks of the official church and, to a large degree, even from Russian society, sapping the church of much of its creative power.[49] If the church had been humbled before Peter's accession to the throne, however, he made the state's domination plain for all to see, finally codifying it in law. In his own conduct, he mocked the church and its rituals, he quarreled with Patriarch Adrian, and, when the latter died in 1700, Peter refused to name a successor. In his 1721 *Dukhovnyi reglament*, or spiritual regulation, Peter transformed the church, for all intents and purposes, into a branch of the secular state—at least in purely administrative terms. He eliminated the office of patriarch and placed the church under a governing body known as the Holy Synod, whose head was the Ober-Prokurator, a lay person appointed by the tsar, whose loyalties were invariably to the state first.[50] Priests throughout Russia were expected to act as informants to the state, notoriously even violating the confidentiality of the confessional to disclose sedition.[51]

Peter's successors, especially Catherine II, continued the work he had advanced, seizing monastic property and milking the church as a source of revenue for the eighteenth century's many wars. Much of the clergy remained a closed caste; clerics were poorly educated, badly paid, divided among themselves, and separated from their laity by their constant need to demand payment for such holy services as weddings, baptisms, and funerals.[52] It would be wrong to argue, as some have, that priests came to be seen by the population as a purely parasitic class, although this was a staple of fiction and of socialist propaganda in the nineteenth and early twentieth centuries. In reality, clerical and monastic examples of piety abounded, most Russians regarded themselves as Orthodox Christians, and the church often showed itself capable of inspiring genuine religious enthusiasm.

Nonetheless, Russian Orthodoxy suffered from the classic ills of a state church. Much of the hierarchy was corrupt. Intellectually it stagnated, as it was too easy to suppress its rivals by resorting to the power of the state rather than answering them by reasoned argument. Conservative government officials routinely thwarted reform movements within the church. Most significantly, far too many hierarchs saw little or no dividing line between the interests of the Russian Empire and those of the church. Especially along the western borders of the empire, during the last decades of the Romanov dynasty, the church cooperated with the state in the program of "Russification"—the attempt to suppress the non-Russian peoples of that region by forcing them to conform to a bureaucratic standard of Russianness.[53]

Church and state worked together to suppress churches that served as nuclei of non-Russian national feeling, especially the Greek Catholic, or Uniate, Church. This church had come into being at the Union of Brest in 1596, where the Vatican and King Sigismund III of Poland crafted an idea to recover the East for the Latin Rite. At Brest, Uniate hierarchs were allowed to retain the Eastern Orthodox liturgy, the holy days of the Eastern calendar, and other appurtenances of the Eastern Orthodox Rite. At the same time, they pledged allegiance to the pope. In this way, Rome would gain compensation for some of the losses that it had sustained in Central Europe during the Reformation, while the Uniates could retain their cherished customs. Eastern Orthodox clergy, especially in Russia, were hostile from the outset to the Uniate Church, which they saw as nothing more than a Roman-Polish plot to subvert Orthodoxy by luring believers into the clutches of Rome. Under conservative tsars such as Nikolai I and Aleksandr III, the state tried to herd Uniates back into the Russian Orthodox Church, often by force. Had Paleologue been familiar with this long history, he might have been less surprised by the otherwise seemingly inexplicable Russian obsession with the Uniates in 1914.

The Russian Orthodox Church served the interests of the empire in foreign relations as well. The Orthodox faith had for many centuries linked Russia with the rest of the Orthodox world; during the last five decades of the Romanov dynasty, however, its international role assumed an enhanced importance. From the time of Aleksandr II (1855–1881) through the outbreak of World War I, the Russians sought to position themselves as the big brother of the Slavic peoples. Orthodoxy was central to this claim, although not all Slavs were Orthodox (such as the Poles and Czechs), and not all Orthodox were Slavs (notably the Romanians and Greeks). The Russian Orthodox Church assisted the state in its program of Pan-Slavism in a number of ways: it channeled money to friendly clerics and to monasteries throughout the Balkans; it educated Slavs invited to Russia for the purpose of spreading Russian culture and influence, and it funded schools in Bulgaria and elsewhere; it provided chaplains for Russian embassies abroad, where they served as agents of Russian and Orthodox influence; it conducted propaganda throughout the Orthodox East and assisted the Slavic Benevolent Committees created by the secular authorities; and it gave moral support to Russian wars fought during the last decades of tsarist rule, especially those that could be portrayed as crusades on behalf of the Slavs.[54]

On the eve of the 1917 revolution, despite the Russian Orthodox Church's prominent position in society, its condition could scarcely be considered healthy. Its history and incestuous relationship to the tsarist state made it especially vulnerable to the Marxist-Bolshevik accusation that religion was merely a prop of the dominant exploitative order—an "opiate of the masses." This was not entirely true; the church did command the genuine loyalty of millions of people. How many is hard to determine, because the low level of Russian literacy meant that most common people left no written account of their lives and beliefs. But some idea of the extent and tenacity of religious belief can be gained from its resilience in the face of determined atheist assaults by the Communist authorities from November 1917 onward.

Once they had gained power, the Bolsheviks sought to destroy the Russian Orthodox Church—and to crush all religion throughout the empire—by a mix of means: outright suppression; the closing of monasteries, church schools, and seminaries; public mockery of clergy and church relics; propaganda; materialist education of the young; and the encouragement of nationalist-separatist and schismatic movements within the church itself.[55] Bolshevik religious repression came in waves, the three most destructive being at the end of the civil war, in 1922; during the collectivization of the farms between 1928 and 1932; and at the time of Stalin's Great Terror, 1936–39. During the first wave, the Bolsheviks sought to blame the post–civil war famine on the church, which they accused unjustly of hoarding its wealth during a time of mass starvation.[*] In fact, the famine had resulted in part from the destruction wrought by the civil war but at least in equal measure from the Bolsheviks' own ruinous grain seizure policies. Recently released documents show that Lenin himself decided to make the church a scapegoat for the famine, thereby dealing with two problems at once. In March 1922 Lenin wrote to Molotov and other members of the politbiuro: "It is precisely now and only now, when in the starving regions people are eating human flesh, and hundreds if not thousands of corpses are littering the roads, that we can (and therefore must) carry out the confiscation of church valuables with the most savage and merciless energy." Lenin was quite clear that he wanted mass executions of clergy, where the victims would be accused of hoarding church wealth as the people starved: "The greater the number of representatives of the reactionary clergy and reactionary bourgeoisie we succeed in executing for this reason, the better. We must teach these people a lesson right now, so that they will not dare even to think of any resistance for several decades."[56] Consequently, in both Moscow and St. Petersburg, the Bol-

---

[*] In fact, the Russian Orthodox Church offered to raise funds equivalent to the church treasures that the Bolsheviks sought to confiscate, and Britain's archbishop of Canterbury made a similar offer. The Soviet government refused both offers. Although the Bolsheviks were certainly eager to use church funds for their own purposes, they were even more concerned to seize and destroy church relics and treasures.

sheviks rigged show trials of church hierarchs, condemning many to death, and thousands more to internal exile or imprisonment. Lenin seems also to have considered a proposal to pay Ukrainian anarchists a bounty of 100,000 rubles per head to murder priests, calling it "an excellent plan."[57]

During the 1920s, while ceasing for the time being the more overt forms of repression that had proved to be counterproductive among the stubbornly Christian peasantry, the Bolsheviks concentrated instead on reeducating the young to reject religion while working to split the Russian Orthodox Church from within. The Kremlin encouraged the *obnovlentsy*, or renovationists, a movement that had arisen within the church even before the collapse of the tsarist order. This group began as a reformist trend but entered into schism after the revolution and received state encouragement to promote itself as an alternative to the mainstream church. Its head, Archbishop Aleksandr Vvedenskii, advocated a social gospel—a forerunner of modern "liberation theology"—that purported to see in Communist egalitarianism a realization of Christian principles. Although the *obnovlencheskii* schism was troublesome to the embattled Russian Orthodox Church, it was too obviously a creature of the Soviet state to enable it to command mass loyalty among believers, much less to supplant the mainstream church.[58]

The Bolsheviks proved far more successful in promoting nationalist splits within the church than they had with the *obnovlentsy*; in fact, they turned out to be too successful for their own interests. In order to fracture Russian Orthodoxy from within, the Kremlin encouraged, or at least did not impede, the flourishing of Ukrainian and Belorussian splinter groups such as the Ukrainian Autonomous and the Ukrainian Autocephalous churches. Whereas the former, as the name implies, sought to establish a degree of distance between Muscovite authority and the Orthodox Church in Ukraine, the latter wanted outright ecclesiastical independence from Russian authority. Both of these splinter movements quickly attracted enthusiastic adherents, soon becoming foci of Ukrainian nationalism and thus a barrier against the policies of rigid centralization promoted by Stalin as he consolidated his power during the late 1920s. As one historian of religion in Eastern Europe notes, "the greater the ethnic heterogeneity of a society, the more threatening the nationally linked religious organs will be to illegitimate regimes."[59] Stalin therefore ordered these churches closed and their priests arrested. The demons of non-Soviet nationalism proved much easier to summon up than to exorcise, however; when Soviet power in the western borderlands would be smashed by the Nazi invasion of 1941, these two Ukrainian churches, and their Belorussian counterpart, would reappear to haunt Moscow.

The second wave of violent repression against the Russian Orthodox Church was far more comprehensive and lethal than the first. When the Kremlin decided to move against peasant resistance to collectivization in 1928–32, it also struck at the church—especially in Ukraine—which the Communists rightly regarded as the fulcrum of the peasants' collective ability to resist state power. As the Soviets deliberately starved millions in the ruthless battle to impose collective farming on a resistant peasantry, the Communists closed and dynamited churches, arrested priests, and shot many of them based on fabricated charges of sedition.[60] The final wave of repression came during Stalin's political purges, between 1936 and 1938, when the clergy shared the fate of millions of other people the secret police deemed to be politically unreliable. Thousands of priests suffered arrest or execution, and even more churches were closed.

By 1939 the Russian Orthodox Church had been reduced to a shadow of its former self. Whereas before 1914 it had boasted more than 40,000 priests, almost as many nuns and monks, and more than 60,000 churches,[61] by the end of the Second World War (the first time for which we have accurate figures), in the summer of 1945, there were 10,243 working churches, and, in April 1946, 9,254 parish priests. The Soviets shut all seminaries shortly after the revolution, preventing the education and training of new priests and threatening the continuity of the priesthood. All but a handful of monasteries had been closed, the only exceptions being in the western borderlands that were only seized by the USSR in 1939–40 and where, consequently, Soviet power had not yet been fully imposed.[62]

These postwar numbers, low as they are, undoubtedly paint a more optimistic picture than that warranted by the actual conditions in 1939 for several reasons: first, the annexation of the western borderlands between 1939 and 1940 greatly inflated the number of working churches in the Soviet total; second, a great revival of religion had taken place during the war (the subject of much of the present work), which had substantially increased the number of open churches; finally, the Soviets had been forced by this wartime development to reopen seminaries, which of course swelled the number of priests.[63] In truth, the inflated numbers of 1945–46 are small enough—fewer than 10,000 priests and slightly more open churches in a continent-sized country covering more than one-sixth of the world's land mass. The situation in 1939 was thus far grimmer than even these dismal postwar figures indicate.

In the face of this savage repression, the hierarchy of the Russian Orthodox Church became complicit to some degree in its own martyrdom. For the first decade of Bolshevik rule, church leaders had tried to resist insofar as their limited means allowed. As late as June 1926, for instance, Metropolitan Sergii had declared that Communism and Orthodoxy were "irreconcilable."[64] By the following year, however, after three spells in Cheka prisons where he was subjected to unknown pressures, Sergii recanted these views somewhat, issuing a new, highly controversial declaration, which the Soviet government published in *Izvestiia*:

> We must show, not in words, but in deeds, that not only people indifferent to Orthodoxy, or those who reject it, can be faithful citizens of the Soviet Union, loyal to the Soviet government, but also the most fervent adherents of Orthodoxy, to whom it is dear with all its canonical and liturgical treasures as truth and life. We wish to be Orthodox and at the same time to claim the Soviet Union as our civil motherland, the joys and successes of which are our joys and successes, the misfortunes of which are our misfortunes. Every blow directed against the Union . . . we acknowledge as a blow directed against us.[65]

Whether Sergii made his statement owing to conviction or fear is impossible to say, although he did inject a slight—almost invisible—note of ambiguity into the Russian text.[66] Nevertheless, his appeal was rejected by virtually all Russian Orthodox believers not under the control of Soviet power, and it even split the church within Russia itself.

Sergii had no patience with clerics who refused to follow his lead. He declared that "Only impractical dreamers can think that such an immense community as our Orthodox Church with all its organizations may peacefully exist in this country by hiding itself from the Government."[67] Consequently, within the USSR he maintained that bishops who refused to accept his decision to cooperate with the state were acting uncanonically, and he also supported the Soviet government when it was attacked from abroad. In 1930, for instance, as the Kremlin renewed its violent suppression of the church, Pope Pius XI called on world Christians to pray for their fellow believers in the USSR; he was joined by Archbishop of Canterbury Cosmo Gordon Lang and by the Lutheran Church in Germany.[68] In his response, Sergii not only denied the facts of Soviet repression, he also reminded the pope of the Inquisition and questioned his and the Catholic Church's fitness to speak out against repression from any quarter.

This did not quiet the pope, who in March 1937 issued an Encyclical entitled *Divini Redemptoris*, in which he condemned Communism root and branch, especially attacking its propensity to create "front" groups designed to entice naive non-Communists into serving Communist ends. In a phrase that would trouble the consciences of Catholics who would one day wish to assist the Soviets in their war against the Nazis, Pius XI left no room for compromise or ambiguity: "Communism is intrinsically wrong, and no one who would save Christian civilization may collaborate with it in any undertaking whatsoever."[69] The pope had come to within a hair's breadth of calling Communism the tool of the Antichrist.

On the eve of the Second World War, the Russian Orthodox Church was in a parlous state. It appeared to have little future as the dwindling band of priests aged, ever more churches were shut, believers intimidated, and children taught to despise the faith of their forebears. Christians throughout the world condemned this state of affairs, and they were regularly treated to sermons delivered from the pulpit and angry articles in countless church publications denouncing Soviet Communism and expressing solidarity with its victims. In many ways, before the war the international image of the USSR among Christians worldwide was even worse than that of the Nazis. Yet, following Hitler's invasion of the USSR, the Kremlin would be forced to turn to these very same Western Christians for aid.

Before 1939 the Soviet government appeared to have no use whatsoever for the Russian Orthodox Church, and the church itself seemed little more than a hapless victim of the state. Yet, within the space of only a few years, the Soviets would execute a remarkable turnabout. Although the Bolshevik regime claimed to have made an irrevocable break with the past, the realities of geography and ethnicity, as well as the weight of tradition, dictated a return to old, half-forgotten tools to deal with domestic and foreign policy dilemmas that would have been familiar to any tsarist bureaucrat. For its part, the Russian Orthodox Church would change as well; it, too, was enmeshed in a web of traditions and conceptions—obedience to the state, identity with the Russian nation, and the desire to stamp out schism and compete with rival churches and sects—that would give it little option but to enter into unequal partnership with the very regime that had so oppressed it. Had Paleologue been in Russia to witness Soviet church policy between 1939 and 1945, he would have been astounded to discover how the atheist Communist state was engaged in many of the very same seemingly medieval quarrels that he had witnessed with such dismay in 1914. The Bolshevik Revolution, in its homicidal ferocity, had plowed and harried the fields of Russian society for twenty years, upturning the sod and wreaking havoc with the vegetation; but, despite all the sound and fury, underneath the surface the subterranean structures of history retained their ancient forms.

PART

The Church Redux

There is no such thing as an apolitical church.

—Captured German document, October 31, 1941

The Russian Church is one of the most efficient
organizations of subordination.

—Archbishop Jarema, 1997

Religion and Nationality

The Soviet Dilemma, 1939–1941

The War and Myths of Solidarity

In the years following the collapse of the USSR, visitors
to Moscow could regularly encounter small knots of drably clad people lingering about on the verges of Red Square peddling Russian nationalist and Communist newspapers. Most were older people embittered by the disappearance
of the system to which they had dedicated their careers and lives; others were
young and angry about the loss of Soviet power and what they saw as the international humiliation of their country. Many of the newspapers being hawked
featured on their covers the grim image of Stalin, invariably clad in his gener-
alissimo's uniform at the apogee of his power. These publications contained
admiring articles about the Great Leader and his supposed social, economic,
diplomatic, and military achievements. For these old-line Communists and
nationalists, Stalin remained a great man, the iconic *vozhd'*, or leader, who had
brought Russia from the wooden plow to the atom bomb in one generation.

This disturbing loyalty to one of the twentieth century's great villains was inexplicable to many Westerners who believed that the implosion of Communism had at long last freed the Russian people from an era of virtual slavery. How could there still be so many admirers of the "Kremlin mountaineer" among a people who had suffered so much at his hands? The shock was almost as great as it would have been upon discovering large numbers of modern Germans openly proud of Hitler's legacy.

The question of the Soviet people's attitude toward Stalin and his regime has long been a battleground for Western scholars, the unavailability of reliable archival evidence until quite recently making it possible to advance vastly divergent interpretations without fear of decisive refutation. According to the premier historian of the Stalinist Great Terror, the dictator maintained his regime through force and fear alone.[1] A recent generation of revisionist historians argues, however, that the Stalinist system—even with its mass arrests and campaigns against "spies" and "wreckers"—enjoyed a wide degree of social support. One prominent historian claims that at the outset of the war Stalin was "a vastly popular leader."[2] An even more extreme proponent of this view, while allowing that millions of innocent people were arrested and hundreds of thousands shot, argues that "Many citizens . . . did not experience *or even notice* the Terror except in newspapers or speeches" (emphasis added). The ostensible proof of the Soviet people's mass support for the Communist regime is said to be the loyal service of millions of common soldiers in the war against Hitler, the so-called acid test of the Stalinist regime.[3]

Certainly this was the view of the war propagated by the Soviets, beginning with Stalin himself: the defeat of Nazi Germany, he claimed, demonstrated the superiority of the Communist system and the unshakable bonds linking the Soviet peoples. On Red Army Day in 1946, the Father of the Peoples declared that the Soviet victory "is explained, above all, in that the Army is genuinely a people's army and defends the interests of its people. . . . All our people, unremittingly, day and night labored for the front, for victory."[4] The new Soviet national anthem, which replaced the revolutionary "Internationale" at the beginning of 1944, stressed both the unity of the various Soviet nationalities as well as the "leading role" of the Russian people:

Unshakeable union of free republics
Has been united by Great Rus'
Long live the country founded by the people's will,
United, mighty Soviet Union!

Despite such lavish official propaganda, the war remained a subversive memory for the regime, especially so long as Stalin ruled. Too many people were still alive who remembered the panic and disasters of 1941, the repressions and deportations, as well as the wanton waste of lives by some Soviet commanders and political commissars. The war had witnessed an abundance of genuine self-sacrifice, patriotism, and heroism, of course, but this too was a subversive memory. Too close a focus on the war threatened to elevate genuine heroes of the military, such as Marshal Georgii Zhukov, above the level of Stalin himself. This was intolerable; Stalinism was monotheistic.

At the Twentieth Party Conference of the Communist Party of the Soviet Union (CPSU) in 1956, Nikita Khrushchev would denounce some of the crimes committed by his dictatorial predecessor and mentor. During the brief cultural "thaw" that followed the speech, praise of Stalin would disappear from Soviet accounts of the war, replaced by measured criticisms of the now dead god's "cult of personality." The six-volume official history of the war that began publication in 1960 attacked Stalin for failing to foresee the German attack, refusing to accept the advice of trained subordinates, unjustly repressing military officers, and other sins great and small. Despite the more critical approach, however, this newly reworked official version of the war still maintained that a semimystical bond had united the front line with the civilian rear and perpetuated the fiction that the nationalities of the union had fought shoulder to shoulder under the unquestioned leadership of the Communist Party, with only minimal dissension by a handful of traitors or class enemies.[5] The Khrushchevite official history, and the more than 150 military memoirs published during this period, did not discuss the mass deportation of entire minor nationalities; armed resistance against Soviet power in the borderlands at the outset of the war and again at its close; the question of collaboration with the invader, both by members of minority nationalities and by Russians themselves; or the persecution, and in the case of the Greek Catholic Church the dissolution, of religions practiced by non-Russian peoples.[6]

Instead of a genuinely critical examination of such tragic wartime events, during the Khrushchev era, and even more so during the Brezhnev years, Soviet historians constructed a master historical narrative that elevated the cult of the "Great Patriotic War" to nearly religious levels. The Soviet victory over Nazism began to rival, and even to surpass, the Bolshevik Revolution as the most important legitimating event for the Communist system.[7] Whereas the creation of a Bolshevik state had triggered a fratricidal war pitting Russian against Russian, in which some ten million people had perished, the Second World War could, by contrast, be portrayed as an unambiguously positive morality tale in which the country was united against a truly evil invader. Soviet authorities sought to use the war to inculcate a Soviet patriotism that, they hoped, would supplant older national identities; they also drew on the example of the war to instill in the younger generation obedience to political and even parental authority.

Even Mikhail Gorbachev, speaking on the fortieth anniversary of the Soviet victory, echoed the themes of the Brezhnevite master narrative: in the war against Nazism, "everyone came to the defense of the native land, old and young, men and women, all national and ethnic groups." The Soviet peoples had fought as one to defend "the homeland, the socialist system, the ideas and cause of October." Nor did the new general secretary neglect his predecessor: "The great political will, purposefulness and persistence, and the ability to organize and discipline people which Stalin displayed during the war years played their role in attaining victory."[8] Gorbachev's audience of apparatchiks interrupted him with seventeen seconds of enthusiastic applause at the mention of Stalin's wartime leadership.[9] Although this outburst seemed at the time to testify to the depth of support for the dictator's memory, in retrospect it can be seen literally as the last hurrah of the Stalinist generation.

Not until the late 1980s did Soviet historians begin seriously to address the more troubling questions raised by the war, at first gingerly, then increasingly openly. Two years after Gorbachev's speech, one of the more prominent Soviet historians of World War II, A. M. Samsonov, himself a veteran, made several television and radio broadcasts calling for a franker discussion of the war's lesser-known aspects. Echoing Gorbachev's new call to explore the "blank spots" of Soviet history, Samsonov specifically suggested a discussion of Stalin's failure to anticipate the Nazi invasion, maltreatment by the Soviets of their own soldiers who had surrendered to the Germans, and the calamitous Soviet 1942 spring offensive in Ukraine.

This list of topics did not go far beyond the bounds of the Khrushchev-era debate. The public response, however, was swift and surprised even Samsonov, who was soon inundated with thousands of letters from veterans, Communist Party members, survivors of the gulag, as well as ordinary people curious about their country's history. The sharply divided nature of the letters testified strongly to the polarization of opinion about Stalin and the war among ordinary Soviet citizens. Although Stalin's defenders were in a minority, they angrily defended their hero. One veteran wrote: "My generation was born under Lenin and raised under Stalin. We stood and stand for the just cause of Stalin. We must not spit on Stalin, but study him."[10] Despite such vocal defenders of the old Soviet established truths, most of Samsonov's correspondents were highly critical of Stalin, one typical veteran of the war writing: "Many say that under the leadership of Stalin we won the war. I consider that under the leadership of Stalin we almost lost it."[11]

The correspondence showed how even a limited discussion of the war's hitherto taboo subjects threatened quickly to explode, unleashing the long-suppressed demons of the past. Many of the letters called for an expansion of the historical discussion well beyond the bounds envisioned by the cautious Samsonov, demanding the exploration of such forbidden areas as the gulag and police repression, as well as collaboration with the Nazis and the treatment by the Soviet government of minority nationalities.

These issues ran right to the heart of Soviet political legitimacy, questioning the Communist Party's fitness to rule and undermining the myths of the Soviet people's "socialist choice" and the supposed "friendship of the peoples." The instincts of Samsonov's Stalinist correspondents were right: if Soviet historians could manufacture a master narrative of the war designed to legitimate Soviet power, then the erosion of this mythical past could with equal force discredit the USSR.

In 1989 the former Soviet major general and historian Dmitrii Volkogonov did more than any other Gorbachev-era writer to demolish wartime mythology when he published his landmark biography of Stalin. In his sections on the Second World War he published for the first time selections of hitherto secret documents revealing widespread popular resistance to Soviet power.[12] Since the publication of Volkogonov's book, and especially following the collapse of the USSR, a flood of memoirs, histories, and published documents, as well as the opening of Soviet archives, have all provided the resources to reevaluate the Stalin question.

This mass of newly available information has largely undermined the revisionist interpretation of the Stalin era. Nonetheless, it does not entirely vindicate traditionalist views that underestimated the power of propaganda, myth-making, modernization, and even terror to generate a degree of loyalty in a relatively unsophisticated population, most of which was only newly literate.[13] In the light of far more detailed evidence, it has become exceedingly difficult to generalize about the Soviet people's opinions regarding the Stalin regime, or indeed about their attitude toward the Second World War. Far from providing an "acid test" from which the Soviet regime emerged vindicated, the war instead showed just how deeply crevasses ran through Soviet society, dividing people by class, educational level, nationality, religion, political persuasion, and even personal history.

Shattered Identities

The war in the East acted like a vast centrifuge separating people into categories, often independently of their will. In his magisterial novel *Life and Fate* set during the Stalingrad campaign, Vasilii Grossman, a former front-line correspondent for the military newspaper *Krasnaia zvezda*, writes that the experience of war made individual Soviet citizens more aware—sometimes even for the first time—of the groups to which they belonged. "The most fundamental change in people at this time," he writes, "was a weakening of their sense of individual identity; their sense of fate grew correspondingly greater."[14]

The cataclysm in the East overwhelmed individuals, shattering old identities, shaping new ones, and—perhaps most important—reviving ancient but latent collective loyalties that had lain dormant under the seemingly smooth surface of enforced Soviet unity. When a sledgehammer strikes a windshield, the glass shatters into hundreds of fragments, the cracks between them snaking along microscopic lines between molecules, invisible to the human eye before the blow. So too, when the Nazi invasion collided with Soviet power, at the point of impact the population fragmented along social lines that had been there all along but had been rendered invisible by the mystique of Soviet power.

For millions of Soviet citizens before the war, the Kremlin's seeming omnipotence apparently ruled out any thought of reform, much less rebellion. The Stalin-era peasantry (in the 1940s still by far the majority of the Soviet population) sullenly hated the Stalinist regime.[15] Peasants may have hated the regime, which had carried out the murderous "second enserfment" of collectivization, but they could do little to change their situation. Instead, the collective farm system bred a spirit of resentful lethargy.[16]

The war suddenly offered new possibilities for change. Most important, the Nazi invasion forced people to make choices as the unprecedented violence of the conflict rendered the citizenry's traditional political apathy untenable. The historian Nina Tumarkin, who interviewed veterans of the war, records comments by the Russian historian and former Red Army soldier Mikhail Gefter, who remarked that the first two years of the war, though the most lethal, were "paradoxically . . . also the freest." "Stalin's totalitarian system had fallen apart in the face of the invasion and occupation," Gefter noted, giving birth to "a period of *spontaneous de-Stalinization*. . . . People were suddenly forced to make their own decisions, to take responsibility for themselves. Events pressed us into becoming truly independent human beings.'"[17] Especially in the western regions of the USSR, the battleground of the Nazi-Soviet conflict, the clash of armies and ideologies compelled people to take sides simply in order to survive. Of course, the majority of Soviet citizens sided with the Moscow government for various reasons, including Communist convictions; others collaborated with the Nazis, owing to fear, desperation, opportunism, or even ideological conviction.

The choices were not, however, limited solely to the two warring sides. For a great many Soviet citizens, both Nazism and Communism were equally repugnant. For the Jewish and Slavic populations, the Nazi invaders promised only death or slavery. But the Stalinist record was scarcely less repellent: inhabitants of the western USSR had survived the successive hammer blows of civil war and repression, the homicidal collectivization campaign, political purges, and hunger. Given this history, to many people almost anything seemed better than Soviet power.

Those who rejected both Nazism and Communism gravitated toward older and deeper collective identities. The two attractive forces were religion and nationalism, often inextricably intertwined, with religion acting as both the seedbed and the expression of nationalist sentiment. Religious confession in Eastern Europe and the western regions of the Russian Empire and later the USSR had, indeed, preceded nationalism by many centuries as the locus of collective identity. It is therefore little wonder that, in the political vacuum created by the temporary smashing of Soviet political power and the advance of alien Nazism, ancient loyalties reasserted themselves.

The majority of the Soviet population stubbornly clung to its religious beliefs in the face of severe state repression. In the 1937 Soviet census, after two decades of Soviet power, 57 percent of the adult population, some 56 million people, identified themselves as holding religious beliefs; of this figure, 42 million were Orthodox Christians, the rest being Muslim, Jewish, Buddhist, and Catholic, with a smattering of Protestant Christians. As might be expected, religious faith was stronger among older people: of those in their fifties, 78 percent professed religious belief, whereas for people in their twenties the figure was 45 percent.[18] These statistics are all the more remarkable coming as they did at the height of the Stalinist terror, when avowal of religious beliefs was highly dangerous and could be interpreted as an act of political opposition. Indeed, there is every reason to assume that these census figures understate the full extent of religious belief, because a great many people would understandably have been reluctant to admit their religious faith to a Soviet census taker.

The war would witness a vast revival of religion throughout the USSR, especially in the regions that underwent Nazi occupation.[19] The reasons for the revival were complex, varying from region to region and person to person. In part, religion offered solace to a people experiencing killing and death on an unprecedented scale, and the killing was by no means limited to the front line; it was most intense in the western regions of the USSR. In Belorussia, for instance, about one-quarter of the civilian population perished from various causes: murder at the hands of the Nazis, starvation, disease, combat, partisan actions, execution by the retreating—and later advancing—Red Army, as well as other causes.[20] The war followed the earlier calamities of collectivization and Soviet repression, which had also claimed millions of victims. The ever present specter of terror and death no doubt drove many people to religion as a refuge from a daily reality too awful to contemplate.

It would be wrong, however, to explain the revival of religion purely in sociological terms as a reaction to mass death in wartime. Even in the opening stages of Operation Barbarossa (the German code name for the invasion of the USSR), before human losses had reached the astronomical proportions of the late war, and when it looked as though a German victory would be quick, people returned to religion in very large numbers. In other words, a large proportion of the wartime religious revival was a spontaneous public reaction to the apparent disintegration of the Soviet regime. Finding themselves in a political and social void, people returned to their historic roots.

Both religion and nationalism took various forms, depending on the location and population. In Ukraine, perhaps the most politically polarized region during the war, people flocked to various religions and churches, their choices reflecting their different ethnic backgrounds, political convictions, and personal histories. In the western regions of Ukraine, the Greek Catholic Church claimed the most adherents, becoming the institution most strongly identified with anti-Soviet Ukrainian nationalism. Even in those parts of Ukraine where Orthodoxy had always held sway, the population was still divided over the question of relations with Moscow. During the war, the Ukrainian Autocephalous Church would break away from the authority of the Moscow Patriarchate, believing it to be a tool of the Kremlin. Other Orthodox who still felt connected to Russia gravitated toward the Ukrainian Autonomous Church, which, despite its name, maintained ties with the Moscow Patriarchate, although doing so clandestinely for fear of drawing the wrath of the occupying Nazis.

The situation of Ukraine's Jewish population was, of course, uniquely dire. Those Jews who before the war sought to preserve their religious identities in the face of determined Soviet atheistic campaigns were treated no differently by Soviet repressive organs than other dissident religious or ethnic groups. Moscow worked to infiltrate and destroy all Jewish religious or political organizations, including those of a secular, Zionist orientation.[21] Only those Jews who were willing to shed their religious identity and accept Soviet power unquestioningly were safe, or as safe as any other Soviet subject given the capriciousness of Stalinist terror. Jack Kagan, who would eventually join a Jewish partisan band fighting the Nazis in Belorussia, writes that the Soviet occupiers, though not so homicidal as the Germans who followed them, nonetheless aimed to destroy any genuine Jewish identity: "Looking back on it now, the Russians wanted to destroy our rich Jewish culture by closing the synagogues and all Jewish institutions, and by prohibiting the use of Hebrew," he writes. "[Jewish] leaders were sent to Siberia. In the long run, we would have been Russians with the word 'Jew' only stamped in our passports."

Following the outbreak of Barbarossa, the Nazis made no distinctions whatsoever between religious, secular, or assimilated Jews. The Nazis' genocidal program quickly rendered Moscow the lesser of two evils, even for Jews who had bitterly opposed Soviet power before the war. Compounding the troubles of Jews in the western borderlands was the attitude of much of the non-Jewish local population. Anti-Semitic pogroms have a long and tragic history in the region, stretching back at least to the revolt of Bohdan Khmel'nitskii in the mid-seventeenth century.[22] In Soviet times, the local Slavic and Baltic populations all too often equated Jewishness with support for the Soviet regime, and many infamously collaborated in the Holocaust.

Despite Moscow's pretensions about the supposed "friendship of peoples" prevailing in the USSR, at the outset of the Second World War the twin problems of religion and nationalism remained intractable dilemmas for the Soviet regime. Two decades of antireligious campaigns had failed to snuff out faith among the Soviet citizenry; the Kremlin knew this, but it did not know how to deliver a mortal blow to the enemy. This was in part because the Communists misunderstood the nature of religious faith, believing it to be nothing more than a relic of the prescientific past, doomed by education and economic progress. As their repeated, unsuccessful efforts to crush religion and "bourgeois nationalism" demonstrate, they were limited by the intellectual straitjacket of their own materialist vision and by the narrow horizons of their rigid class analysis. The brutality of their methods only compounded the problem.

A Defensive Buffer

Toward the end of his long life, Stalin's foreign commissar Viacheslav Molotov reflected on the massive prewar repressions, which reached their peak in the dreadful year 1937. He was entirely unapologetic for his role in these terrible events, saying that "1937 was forced on us, so that we would not have a fifth column in the time of war."[23] Although Molotov's remarks were clearly self-serving, the fear of a fifth column within Soviet borders that might cooperate with an invader was genuine enough among Soviet authorities as the danger of war grew. In April 1941, only weeks before Barbarossa, the people's commissar of Ukrainian state security, Pavel Meshchik, wrote in an internal memorandum that "It is well known that during the conduct of wars the Germans practice a treacherous maneuver: an explosion in the rear of the warring side (a 'fifth column' in Spain, the betrayal of the Croats in Yugoslavia)."[24]

Soviet political police worked diligently to root out and extirpate any signs of disloyalty within Soviet borders, acting on the assumption that it was better for many innocent people to be sent to the camps than for one guilty person to go free. As Molotov would later admit, "innocent people were sometimes incriminated. Obviously one or two out of ten were wrongly sentenced, but the rest got their just deserts. It was extremely hard then to get at the truth! But any delay was out of the question. War preparations were underway."[25] What never seems to have occurred to Molotov, or to the other leaders of the USSR, is that the very steps they took to ensure Soviet security actually bred and fostered opposition. With each new wave of repressions, ever more people had reason to hate the Soviet regime, as their relatives, friends, and neighbors, as well as their clergy and political and social leaders, disappeared into the vast whirlwind of the gulag. The Kremlin would then have to deal with these newly generated enemies in turn—a veritable perpetual motion machine of repression.

Nowhere was this problem more acute than in the western borderlands, the territories Moscow seized in 1939 and 1940 in collusion with Hitler. These areas —the three Baltic States, eastern Poland, northern Bukovina, and Bessarabia— still contained the remnants of their pre-Soviet civil societies, which gave them the means to resist for a time the imposition of Soviet political control and Communist social and economic institutions. When the Nazi invasion struck the USSR, therefore, it did so precisely in the area most suffused with anti-Soviet nationalism, much of it religiously based.

The full reasons for the annexations have never been entirely explained, and perhaps they never will be.[26] It is quite possible that Stalin and his lieutenants never committed their reasoning to paper. Defenders of Soviet foreign policy have always emphasized the supposedly defensive nature of the annexations; less sympathetic observers have argued that they were instances of an expansionist Communist diplomacy, driven either by the dictates of ideology or by a Stalinist neo-imperialism that aimed at restoring the losses suffered by the tsarist empire at the end of the Great War.[27] Molotov himself appeared to give credence to the latter interpretation when he remarked that "I saw my task as

MAP 1. Soviet and Axis Annexations, 1939–1941

minister of foreign affairs to be the expansion of the borders of our Fatherland as much as possible. And it seems that Stalin and we did not deal badly with this task."[28]

Even if one accepts the notion that Moscow seized these western borderlands primarily for security reasons, however, the policy backfired badly. Far from enhancing Soviet security, the acquisition of the new regions presented the Communist coercive organs with a host of new military, logistical, and especially political problems that they were unable to solve before Barbarossa. The assimilation of some 20 million mostly unwilling people into the USSR would have been a tremendous political and security task even in peacetime; in the tense European situation of 1939–41, the magnitude of the undertaking overwhelmed Soviet capabilities.

The reception accorded Soviet forces when they first moved into the western borderlands varied greatly. In the Baltic states, hostility was palpable, other than among the relatively small number of Communists.[29] When the Red Army arrived in western Belorussia and western Ukraine, however, many locals at first welcomed Soviet troops. Four days after the invasion, G. I. Kulik, deputy people's commissar of defense, informed Stalin, Molotov, and Voroshilov that "The overwhelming mass of the population met the Red Army with enthusiasm. However, in large cities, in particular in Stanislavyv, the intelligentsia and merchants reacted guardedly."[30] Interwar Poland had badly mistreated its minority nationalities, especially Jews and Ukrainians, and some members of these two groups were initially hopeful that Soviet rule would lead to an improvement in their lot. Kulik noted the importance of national tensions: "In connection with the great national repression by the Poles of the Ukrainians, the latters' cup of patience is overflowing, and in particular cases there is fighting between Ukrainians and Poles, even the threat to expel the Poles. It is necessary to issue an urgent declaration of the government to the population, since this might become a big political factor."[31] Jack Kagan recalled that "Some Jews cried with joy" when the Soviets arrived. "They ran towards the tanks with flowers in their hands, blocking the way and waiting to kiss the soldiers of the Red Army." Ethnic Poles would remember this, and when the Germans invaded the region two years later, Kagan writes, the Poles "started taking revenge on the Jewish population for [having] greet[ed] the Red Army."[32]

Another group was, of course, especially delighted by the arrival of Soviet power. A Polish Communist wrote: "I think the Jews awaiting the Messiah will feel, when he finally comes, the way we felt then."[33] Although such enthusiasts existed, and were highly visible as the Red Army arrived, the mood of the majority was most probably one of "gloom and foreboding" as it anxiously awaited the imposition of Soviet institutions, not knowing what the future would bring.[34]

The Soviet occupying authorities tried to address this enormous task in the western borderlands with a system of rewards and repressions. Moscow truly sought to carry out a "revolution from abroad."[35] Kremlin policies were based on a vulgar Stalinist class analysis, which sought to decapitate the societies of the occupied regions by arresting, shooting, or deporting local elites, while simultaneously trying to appeal to the working classes and minority nationalities that had suffered under the "bourgeois" pre-Soviet governments. Although carried out vigorously and brutally, this approach—based more on an intellectual construct than on any understanding of the complex realities in the western borderland—was ultimately unsuccessful.

Loyalties, aspirations, and identities of the new Soviet subjects seldom fit into the simple class-based categories favored by Kremlin bureaucrats; they were shaped by a multitude of other influences and factors, such as nationalism, religion, shared history, and (something Marxists always had trouble understanding) the admiration for the achievements of one's social "betters" and the hope of someday joining their ranks. A Lithuanian peasant, for instance, might identify with an estate owner who was a fellow countryman, or whose management he admired, rather than with a Stalinist commissar who claimed to be liberating him from the domination of capital. Likewise, many Ukrainians valued their Greek Catholic Church far more than they did the prospect of "reunifying" with eastern Ukrainians, whose religious affiliations and historical experiences were quite alien and in some cases even antithetical to their own.

Although these ideas may seem commonsensical, even banal, they apparently eluded the understanding of Soviet occupiers. Newly released documents from the People's Commissariat of Internal Affairs (NKVD) and People's Commissariat of State Security (NKGB)[36] reveal that Soviet repressive organs never devised successful approaches to deal with opposition in the western borderlands, instead resorting again and again to the favorite Stalinist tool of repression, which only ended in squandering whatever goodwill Soviet power might initially have enjoyed. As the threat of German invasion grew in the spring of 1941, these barbaric tactics threatened to incite a genuine guerrilla war, which could only benefit the Nazi invader.

The brutality of Soviet methods in some cases even drove erstwhile enemies into each others' arms. In the interwar years, for instance, rivalry and territorial disputes had plagued relations between the three Baltic states; and the Lithuanians and Poles had quarreled over a range of issues, most notably the disposition of the historic city of Vilnius.[37] After experiencing Soviet occupation, however, these interwar rivals were often willing to shelve their differences for the time being to join arms against the invader from the east. In early April 1941, for instance, an NKVD report warned that an underground nationalist group in Latvia, Tevias Sargs (Defenders of the Fatherland), was making contact "with analogous anti-Soviet formations in Lithuania and Estonia, and took on itself the initiative for convening an illegal conference of Baltic nationalist organizations." Taking advantage of the hasty and ill-advised Soviet conscription of Latvian men, the group even managed to infiltrate the Red Army, funneling Soviet weapons to the underground. The NKVD believed that this group also established contact with the Nazis through Latvian diplomatic personnel who had been left stranded abroad by the abrupt Soviet annexation of their homeland. Moscow feared that the Germans were supplying this and other groups like it with funds, preparing the ground for an uprising timed to coincide with a possible Nazi invasion of the USSR.[38] The Soviet police managed to uncover and squelch Tevias Sargs, arresting seventy-three people in the process, but it was almost immediately succeeded by another Latvian nationalist group, Latviias Sargi (Latvian Guard), that resumed its opposition to Soviet power.[39]

In neighboring Lithuania, between July 1940 and May 1941, Soviet organs broke up seventy-five nationalist bands but had still failed to eradicate organized resistance by the time of the Nazi attack.[40] Instead, the chief result of Soviet actions was almost certainly to swell the ranks of Lithuanians prepared to collaborate with the invaders. There was certainly no shortage of enemies in Soviet demonology, and Moscow assumed that they were all working together: "In their hostile activity," the NKGB anguished, "certain leaders of nationalist formations established contact with Trotskyites [abroad] and together with them returned to the territory of western Belorussia active counterrevolutionary work uniting nationalist elements in a single platform of struggle with Soviet power."[41] Everywhere it looked, Moscow saw enemies; but in this case it stretches credulity to believe that Lithuanian nationalists, many of whose leaders were Catholic priests, had suddenly decided to make common cause with Trotskyites—or vice versa, for that matter.

Throughout the Baltics, as in occupied Poland and Bessarabia, the Soviets conducted several mass arrests and deportations of class enemies, the last occurring little more than a month before Barbarossa.[42] These were prophylactic repressions, carried out according to ideologically conceived categories, with little or no attempt to establish individual guilt. Soviet police exiled or shot such people as "former powerful landowners," "former officers of the Polish, Lithuanian, Latvian, Estonian, and [Russian] White armies" as well as other "hostile elements," such as the families of people previously repressed—including their dependent children—and even prostitutes.[43]

These arrests and deportations make a mockery even of Molotov's claim— damning enough one might think—that no more than two of ten arrests were unjustified; and they should certainly call into question the claims of historians who still write about the NKVD's ostensible "concern for gathering evidence" and about the supposed end of the Stalinist terror in 1938.[44] The terror did not end; rather, it shifted focus to the western borderlands where it resumed with renewed fury. Also, it should be remembered that the police action discussed here was only the last of several mass deportations carried out in the Baltics. Small wonder, then, that so many Balts would welcome the German invaders when they arrived. By chasing phantom fifth columns, Moscow helped to create genuine ones.[45]

The situation in Western Ukraine, which the Soviets seized from Poland in September 1939 as the Nazis invaded from the west, was, if anything, even more dire than in the Baltic states. Despite the initial hopefulness among many western Ukrainians about Soviet rule, through their occupation policies the Soviets quickly wasted this asset. Soon Moscow faced a nationalist guerrilla movement, the Organization of Ukrainian Nationalists (OUN), that was well organized, armed, and supported by large segments of the local population and already had a long history of underground resistance to the interwar Polish state.[46] The severity of Soviet repression, however, pushed even this ferocious group toward making common cause with its erstwhile Polish adversaries. The more militant faction under Stepan Bandera, the OUN-B, presented a formidable military and political challenge to the Soviets. An NKVD circular warned that, "Conducting preparation for an armed attack, the OUN is mobilizing all powers hostile to us, establishing contact with other counterrevolutionary Ukrainian and Polish nationalist organizations and the remnants of anti-Soviet politparties."[47]

The tactics employed by the OUN-B against the Soviet occupiers were themselves brutal, including sabotage, physical and material threats, and assassinations, reminiscent of other guerrilla wars of the twentieth century. The ideology of the Banderites was also repellent: semifascist in its nationalism and ardently anti-Semitic. Periodic massacres of Jews and Poles carried out by the OUN-B provide further proof, if any were needed, that victims can become victimizers in turn. The conspiratorial nature of the OUN and its liberal use of force, even against its own members if they were suspected of betrayal, made it a tough nut to crack.

Soviet methods in the war against the OUN once again proved counterproductive. While informing the party boss of Ukraine, Nikita Khrushchev, about OUN activities, the NKGB unwittingly provided proof that its own repressive methods had actually swelled the ranks of people willing to risk their lives to oppose the Communists: "By day the illegals hide themselves in the forests, wander on the roads, at night they are in the villages and gain shelter in the homes of kulaks, among families of the repressed, and in their own homes." By treating ostensibly wealthy peasants as class enemies and deporting so-called bourgeois, the NKGB clearly had increased the number of safe havens available to OUN partisans. Nonetheless, the Soviets did not draw the seemingly obvious conclusions; instead, they attributed OUN successes solely to nationalist terror tactics rather than to their own misguided actions. "The population of several villages is sufficiently terrorized [by the OUN] that even Soviet-inclined people fear handing over the illegals," Meshchik wrote. The answer, as always, was presumed to lie in more effective repression. Meshchik proposed the "liquidation of OUN bases—the [arrest and deportation of] families of the illegals, the kulaks, and families of repressed people."[48]

This approach, little short of madness, helps to explain how the self-generating whirlpool of Soviet terror could suck in thousands and ultimately millions of innocent victims: clearly the arrest of the families of those already deported would lead inexorably to the alienation of even more family members—not to mention friends—who would in turn be goaded to action by this latest wave of deportees, and so forth. Yet NKGB records show that the Soviets were trapped by the logical illogic of their crude class analysis. The Ukrainian secret police warned that the OUN was exploiting the "nationalist feelings of the backward parts of the *bedniak* [poor peasant] and *sredniak* [middle peasant] population." "As a result," they continued, "*bedniaks* and *sredniaks* are becoming unquestioning tools in the hands of the OUNites, blindly carrying out these acts."[49]

Moscow's division of the peasant population into three arbitrary economic categories, based on a simplistic Marxian blueprint, had already proved disastrous during the Soviet collectivization of agriculture a decade before and was once again leading to policies crazily mismatched to the situation. The operating Soviet assumption was that poor and middle peasants could not possibly oppose the workers' and peasants' state for their own reasons, because by definition this would have meant acting against their own presumed class interests. Rather, these simple people had to have been misled by class enemies—including the Nazi intelligence services—who were busily promoting a false class consciousness. Ruling out a priori as they did any notion that nationalism, religious affiliation, or class-crossing bonds of loyalty and basic human affection might spontaneously exist among the poorer elements, the Soviets continued to believe that if only they could eliminate the final traces of the "bourgeois" order in the western borderlands, whatever was left of society would naturally gravitate to the Soviet power.

The Directorate of the Ukrainian NKGB and NKVD proposed to employ a mix of incentives and punishments to root out OUN "illegals." On the one hand, it proposed seizing the families of partisans in the hope of inducing "illegals" to surrender; on the other hand, it suggested promising poor and middle peasants who were suspected of cooperating with the OUN that, if they ceased their underground activity, they would be allowed to cultivate their own plots of land—they did not say for how long—rather than being herded into collective farms. Furthermore, poor and middle peasants should be told that they were being "betrayed by the kulaks," who were supposedly using them as stalking horses for their own class interests. The leaders of the OUN should be arrested, the Communist police proposed; "do not arrest the underlings, because the majority of them are *bedniaks*"—and therefore presumably capable of being won over to the Soviet state.[50] These methods also proved ineffective.

The failure of local organs to crush the OUN drew a sharp reprimand from the head of the NKVD, Lavrenty Beria, and a resolution from the Central Committee calling for greater coordination between various local branches of the repressive apparat, as well as more effective class education of Ukrainian working people and greater firmness against these state enemies (as though the authorities had hitherto been too soft).[51] This resulted in yet another large-scale sweep against the OUN throughout western Ukraine, ending on May 22, 1941; this police action was part of a wider purging of all the "western oblast's of the USSR" as the threat of war with Germany loomed.[52] The NKGB arrested and slated for exile 3,110 western Ukrainian families suspected of having members in the resistance, numbering 11,476 people in all. Before shipping these unfortunates to Central Asia or Siberia, the Soviets announced that, if OUN members surrendered to Communist authorities, then their families would be spared. In the end, this gained an unspecified number of defections, but 3,073 families, or 11,329 people, were deported anyway. The remaining families were released to return home, but they remained under "careful observation" by the NKGB; in the event of any further signs of oppositional behavior, they too would be deported and their property seized.[53] In the other borderlands, Estonia, Latvia, Lithuania, and Bessarabia, a further 85,000 people were deported at the same time, each deportation carefully calculated at a cost to the state of 35 rubles and 70 kopeks per person, requiring 532 railroad cattle cars and estimated at an overall weight of 8,500 tons.[54]

Although the Soviets briefly congratulated themselves on the blow thus struck against the OUN and other centers of resistance, it did not prove to be mortal. On June 21, 1941, only hours before the outbreak of Barbarossa, even as millions of German soldiers were already moving into their forward positions,

Merkulov was still haranguing Ukrainian state security, demanding ever more decisive measures against the OUN. He ordered his forces to prepare yet another wave of arrests: "A savage and just blow must be delivered to enemies conducting disruptive work against Soviet power," he wrote, "in order to ensure calm and security for the workers of these oblast's"[55] It was already too late for such measures, however; the OUN would continue to be a thorn in the Soviet flesh throughout the war, and even after. Indeed, Stepan Bandera would actually survive Merkulov himself, who would be shot in 1953 during the purge of the NKVD-NKGB that followed Stalin's death.[56]

The Role of Religion

Histories of the Soviet occupation of the western borderlands have ignored the centrality of local churches in the process. Only with the opening of Soviet archives after 1991 has it become possible to see just what importance Soviet authorities themselves placed on undermining organized religion in their newly acquired domains. This should have been no surprise; in the USSR itself, after all, Communist authorities had been unable to extinguish Russian Orthodoxy and other religions despite two decades of repression. In the western borderlands, the religious situation was even more dangerous from the Soviet point of view. Not only were local churches still thriving, with large numbers of followers, but also they were hotbeds of anti-Soviet nationalist feeling. Furthermore, the most numerous religions in the region—Roman Catholic, Uniate, and Jewish—all had strong transborder ties. To penetrate, neuter, and ultimately subjugate these religions became a cardinal aim of Soviet occupation policy.

Religious connections were vital to the resistance in western Ukraine; especially important in this respect was the Greek Catholic, or Uniate, Church, under the leadership of the Ukrainian nationalist Metropolitan Sheptyt'sky. The deputy chief of the NKGB's Third Directorate, Ivan Shevelev, noted: "In their anti-Soviet work, the OUN widely use the aid and influence of the Uniate clergy. The leadership of the OUN is directly connected with the L'vov metropolitan Sheptitskii [sic]." The church provided the OUN with printing presses as well as safe venues for clandestine meetings. Even more important were Uniate-run schools that acted as breeding grounds for anti-Soviet nationalism: "The OUN underground pays great attention to work among the young," Shevelev wrote, "especially among schoolchildren and students, assigning their more experienced cadres of illegals for creation and leadership of 'uniatsva.'"[57]

The Greek Catholic Church and its head Sheptyt'sky enjoyed great popularity among the western Ukrainian population, as even Soviet internal documents ruefully admitted. The occupiers therefore moved methodically and deliberately against the church, banning the printing and sale of religious publications, seizing and in many cases occupying church property, and closing church-run schools and seminaries. An American Catholic priest resident in eastern Poland when the Soviets arrived describes what followed:

> The Church itself became a special target for attack. The Oriental Rite [Greek Catholic] church at our mission was closed immediately; the Latin Rite parish was allowed to function for a while for those few families who dared to attend. The rest of our mission buildings were taken over by the Red Army and used to quarter troops. A propaganda campaign was mounted against the Church and against the priests; we labored under a campaign of constant harassment and incidents large and small. And it was effective. Even the most faithful became cautious about visiting the church or seeing a priest. Young people dropped away quickly. Workers soon learned they could lose their jobs if they insisted upon attending religious services.[58]

While thus slowly strangling the church, the Soviets did not impose the full range of antireligious measures in force throughout the rest of the USSR. Children could still be given a religious education, though only in private; and congregations and clergy did not yet have to register with the state. Registration, one of the more onerous forms of harassment in the USSR, enabled authorities to identify individual believers and to take action against them at the state's convenience.[59] Despite this go-slow approach, Uniate clergy only needed to look east to see what lay in store for them. Priests were therefore natural collaborators with the nationalist resistance, even though Sheptyt'sky himself refused openly to endorse armed resistance.

Roman Catholic priests were equally inclined to join, or even lead, anti-Soviet nationalist movements. In those parts of western Belorussia that contained substantial Polish populations, the "Union of Armed Struggle" (the SVB in the Soviet acronym) sprang up to contest Soviet occupation. Composed of former officers and men of the Polish army who had somehow evaded capture by the Nazis or Soviets, this group operated a clandestine radio station and prepared for an armed uprising should circumstances become favorable. According to Soviet intelligence, the Roman church provided critical support: "The leadership of the SVB in its anti-Soviet work use the Catholic clergy, its material means and significant influence on the Polish population. Priests took and take active part in the creation and in particular the financing of anti-Soviet Polish formations, harbor illegals, organize in the churches and monasteries secret rendezvous quarters and underground printing presses."[60]

In Lithuania as well, one of the more effective leaders of the resistance was a Roman Catholic priest, Adam Stankevich, who worked to merge Lithuanian and Belorussian anti-Soviet groups in an umbrella organization, the Belorusskii tsentr v Litve. The NKGB admitted that Stankevich "has great authority among Belorussian nationalists." He had been one of the leaders of the Christian Democratic Party before the Soviet invasion, and for the time being the NKGB felt it politic not to arrest him, fearing unpredictable public reactions. Instead, they carefully monitored his activity in Vilnius, presumably hoping to net his collaborators. An NKGB memorandum said that " 'The Christian Democrats' have as their task the creation of an 'independent' bourgeois Belorussian state. As a path toward the achievement of this goal they promote a 'union of all Belorussian people on the basis of a new religion' preached by priest Adam Stankevich." In fact, this was not a new religion at all, but rather an attempt to bring together Orthodox and Catholics in the face of a common threat. Stankevich's party was especially troublesome to the Soviets, because it had strong roots not only in the cities but also in the countryside, where it was even more difficult to eradicate. Shevelev complained to Moscow that, " 'The Christian Democrats' use their earlier significant influence among the peasants of western Belorussia and had their cells in villages."[61]

As if such groups operating within Soviet borders were not headache enough, Soviet intelligence was aware that the Nazis were dabbling in Ukrainian religious and nationalist politics, hoping to exploit fissures within the USSR in the event of a future invasion. Shevelev wrote:

> The Germans widely demonstrate their support of the Ukrainian nationalist movements. The premises of clubs and theaters [in Nazi-occupied Poland] were handed over to Ukrainians. Polish churches and even the famous Kholm Orthodox Cathedral were given to Ukrainian [Uniate] churches. On the recommendation of the Germans, the former minister of education in the government of Petliura,[62] Professor [Ivan Ivanovich] Ogienko [Ohienko], was chosen to be archbishop of Kholm.

Both the Nazis and the Soviets were playing the game of *dividum et imperium*. In the Nazi case, this involved wooing Ukrainians at the expense of Poles, who were already under German domination and could therefore be abused with relative impunity. The Soviets appealed to Ukrainian national feeling by claiming that Moscow had "liberated" western Ukraine from its Polish masters and had unified Ukraine for the first time in modern history. In addition, the Soviets opened Ukrainian-language schools, a Ukrainian university in L'vov, and gave land to western Ukrainian *bedniaks* hoping to wean them away from the OUN.[63]

Such relatively small cultural and economic concessions could scarcely compensate for the full-scale war Soviet authorities were simultaneously conducting against Ukrainian society. So, in addition to direct repression of OUN activists, Moscow also sought to sever the organization's roots by moving against local churches. The arrest of nationalist priests suspected of collaboration with the underground was an especially delicate matter. During two decades of antireligious campaigning the Communists had learned the hard way that guile and tact were required in such questions. Too crude an approach could actually provoke armed resistance from otherwise intimidated villagers. The NKGB in Moscow therefore warned its local representatives to prepare arrests very carefully in order to avoid unnecessary collateral damage: "[D]uring the removal of [Orthodox] priests and Roman Catholic priests," Moscow advised, "it is necessary to think through all questions thoroughly, in order to exclude noise and excesses in the village. For this, make provision for clock and church bells."[64]

In addition to repression, even if cautiously undertaken, the Soviets employed a more subtle tool: the Russian Orthodox Church. Ironically, as one historian notes, the Nazi-Soviet Pact "probably saved the Russian Orthodox Church from extinction."[65] The newly acquired territories contained a large population of Orthodox believers whose churches were, of course, still in operation when the Soviets arrived. There were so few open churches in the USSR itself after two decades of atheist campaigns that those in the borderlands probably constituted more than 70 percent of the total by 1941.[66] The largest concentrations were in western Belorussia and Bessarabia, but there were also significant pockets of Orthodoxy in western Ukraine and the Baltic states, especially in Estonia. In the NKVD's view, each church represented a possible rallying point for resistance to Soviet rule.

The inhabitants of the western borderlands therefore witnessed the strange spectacle of the Red Army's arrival with a handful of Russian Orthodox hierarchs trailing quietly in its wake. The Orthodox prelates immediately set to work subordinating independent, or even nationalist, parishes to the authority of the Moscow Patriarchate. Even though the head of the Russian church, Metropolitan Sergii, was still only *locum tenens* and would not be elected patriarch until September 1943, nonetheless the Patriarchate itself claimed jurisdiction over most of the western borderlands. This claim was of many centuries' standing and had often been used by various tsars to enhance their foreign and do-

mestic policies along the western border of the Russian Empire. Now, the atheist Soviet state was following the example of such reactionary nationalist tsars
as Nicholas I by using the Russian church to assist the imposition of Russian
rule in the fluid borderlands.[67]

The chief ecclesiastical agent of Moscow during this process was Nikolai,
metropolitan of Kiev and Galych, a controversial figure who would become
prominent during the war as the chief executor of the church's relations with
the outside world. His lieutenant in this murky affair was the perhaps even
more controversial Sergii (Voskresenskii),[*] a comparatively young and apparently very able bishop whose rise in the church has been described as "mete-
oric." Sergii was one of only four bishops to survive the golgotha of the 1930s,
and it was widely believed in Moscow's religious circles, where he was despised,
that he had done so because of his close collaboration with the NKVD.[68] In
1939 Sergii was sent to Volhynia to subject the local Christian population to
Muscovite control. In 1940, following the seizure of the Baltic states, he was appointed metropolitan of Lithuania and exarch to Estonia and Latvia. This was
possibly an unwise and certainly a fateful choice: despite his record of compliance with the NKVD, Sergii had reason to oppose the Soviets, since his father
had been arrested and sent to a concentration camp in 1935. (Fear for his family's well-being may also explain his collaboration with the secret police.)
Whether owing to vengeful feelings toward the Soviet state or sheer opportunism, following the Nazi invasion he would ignore direct orders to retreat
with Soviet forces, instead hiding in Riga Cathedral as that city fell, only to
emerge later to cooperate with the Germans.[69]

Little is known about the mechanics of Nikolai's operation, because it seems
to have been directed by the NKVD, and the relevant documents have not yet
been made available. Nonetheless, several points emerge: despite years of severe
repression, the Moscow Patriarchate willingly collaborated with Soviet annex-
ationist aims; not only did Nikolai and Sergii (Voskresenskii) impose Muscovite control over extant Orthodox parishes, they also sought to undermine
the Greek Catholic Church through "forced conversion to Orthodoxy."[70] The
whole undertaking involved the arrest, deportation, and even liquidation of
certain recalcitrant clerics. Whether Nikolai and Sergii actually fingered those
to be repressed is unknown, but they could not have been unaware that such
things were occurring and that they were complicit.[71] This operation was
greatly enhanced by the legacy of anti-Orthodox repression by the prewar
regimes in the region. Nikolai and his confederates could not eradicate anti-

[*]Not to be confused with Metropolitan Sergii (Stragorodskii), the acting patriarch.

Soviet religious opposition, but they could and did drive wedges into the enemy camp.

On the Eve

When Barbarossa erupted, a great question mark hung over the USSR: would Soviet subjects fight for the Communist regime, for the government of Stalin that had victimized millions of the very people to whom it now turned in desperation, asking them to lay down their lives? There was ample reason to believe that many would not. Stalin himself was apparently one of the doubters. At a Kremlin victory celebration on May 24, 1945, he would admit: "Our government made not a few errors, we experienced at moments a desperate situation in 1941–42, when our army was retreating, because there was no other way out. A different people would have said to the government: 'You have failed to justify our expectations. Go away. We shall install another government which will conclude peace with Germany. . . .' The Russian people, however, did not take this path."[72] The dictator's emphasis on the Russian—not the Soviet—people was no slip of the tongue. As the experience of war would soon show, ethnic Russians were more reliable recruits for the Soviet war effort than were members of minority nationalities.

From the outset of war, Moscow could not comfortably count on the loyalty of its subjects, especially the non-Russian nationalities who inhabited the western borderlands, precisely the area that lay directly in the path of the Nazis' blitzkrieg. The largest of the republics most vulnerable to the German forces, Ukraine, had perhaps suffered disproportionately from Stalin's policies. Not only had millions of Ukrainians perished in the man-made famines of the collectivization less than a decade earlier, but also during the intervening years Moscow had waged vigorous war on any nascent signs of Ukrainian nationalism.[73] The NKVD had arrested thousands of Ukrainian political figures and prominent intellectuals suspected of "bourgeois nationalism." And Ukrainian churches had been shut down or destroyed, as had so many in Russia itself.[74] The result may have been a cowed population, but it was also one sullenly and bitterly suspicious of the Communist regime.

The situation in the other western republics was, if anything, even worse from the Soviet point of view. Here, Moscow's rule had not yet been consolidated before the outbreak of Barbarossa. In the three Baltic states, western Belorussia, and Bessarabia, Soviet occupation policies were manifest failures. Local populations continued to resist Soviet power, and religion remained an untamed and politically significant force. The program of subordinating local churches to Muscovite domination was still far from complete. Although the use of pliant Russian clerics had been designed in part to enshroud the sordid realities of the imposition of Soviet power behind the priestly stole of the Moscow Patriarchate and a gauze of spurious religious toleration, in fact very few people seem to have been deceived. Rather, as with the mass deportations, the whole affair heightened religiously based suspicions of Moscow that would redound to the benefit of the invading Nazis.

Nonetheless, Moscow seems to have judged the ecclesiastical operation in the western borderlands to have been at least a partial success, even if interrupted by the outbreak of war. The Kremlin had found, or rather rediscovered, a political use for the Russian Orthodox Church. Significantly, the limited revival of the church occurred not during the opening stages of Barbarossa, as is widely believed, but rather before war broke out. The Kremlin initially restored the church to this important, albeit quiet, political role because it required the services of a tame church to impose Soviet political and social control methodically and comprehensively over its new conquests. These facts have important implications, because they show that from the outset the Kremlin envisioned the role of the church in foreign policy and security terms, not initially as a means of mobilizing Russian patriotism within the pre-1939 boundaries of the USSR itself.

The Kremlin would not forget the services the church rendered in the western borderlands between 1939 and 1941; nor would it forget the role played by local churches in the resistance to Soviet power. The lessons of this short period would shape Soviet policy when the Red Army returned to the region in 1943–44.

The Russian People accepted this war as a holy war, a war for their faith and for their country. . . . Patriotism and Orthodoxy are one.—Metropolitan Nikolai, *The Russian Church and the War against Fascism*

"Yes," agreed Sharogorodsky. "The founders of the Comintern proved unable to think of anything better in the hour of war than the old phrase about 'the sacred earth of Russia.'" He smiled. "Just wait. The war will end in victory and then the Internationalists will declare: 'Mother Russia's equal to anyone in the world!'"—Vasilii Grossman, *Life and Fate*

Stalin's Holy War Begins, 1941–1943

The Challenge of Barbarossa

Although Soviet subjects who had endured Stalinism knew well enough what they disliked about the regime, they had very little reliable information about life on the other side of the Nazi-Soviet frontier. The Soviet press had routinely denounced Hitler and Nazism in the strongest possible terms during much of the 1930s, but these attacks ceased abruptly during the spring of 1939, when Moscow was sending warm signals to Berlin in advance of the Nazi-Soviet Pact.[1] From that time until June 22, 1941, the Soviet press maintained a strict silence about Nazi misdeeds. Less than a month before the outbreak of war, the Central Committee renewed its secret warnings to Soviet press organs to avoid any provocative anti-German critiques in their publications.[2] Even such memorable cinematic anti-Nazi propaganda as Sergei Eisenstein's *Aleksandr Nevskii* was withdrawn from viewing in order to avoid giving offense to Berlin.[3] When war broke out, therefore, many Soviet citizens were doubly surprised, because their government had regularly assured them that Soviet-German relations were on the most stable of footings.[4] Viktor Kravchenko, who during the war would defect from the Soviet embassy in Washington, D.C., later wrote that "As far as the mass of Russians was permitted to know, Soviet-Nazi collaboration was an idyl without blemish. To doubt this would have been to doubt the infallibility of Stalin."[5] Kravchenko concluded that "It took months of direct experience with German brutality to overcome *the moral disarmament* of the Russian people."[6]

After the German invasion, when Soviet propaganda suddenly reverted to attacking the Nazis, the initial output was often too crude to be believed. Nina Markovna, then a Soviet schoolgirl in the Crimea, remembers that her class was given a series of photographs purporting to show German civilians so hungry that, while standing in a food line, they captured and devoured a crow that landed nearby. When Moscow subsequently reported that the invading Nazis were massacring Jews, this seemed almost as fantastic a tale. "Our young minds were in turmoil," she wrote. "What to believe? If one were to believe the mistreatment of Jews under Hitler, then one must also believe in the crow being eaten raw by Germans!"[7]

If Moscow's propaganda was unreliable or unbelievable, most Soviet citizens could not hope to learn much about the Germans by word of mouth. In a perverse twist, the NKVD-NKGB arrested and deported thousands of people in the USSR who had experienced Nazi rule firsthand. Moscow apparently feared that the Germans were encouraging refugees to filter across their common border, lacing their numbers with Gestapo spies and saboteurs.[8] Certainly the Soviets were doing this in reverse. When, in agreement with Berlin, Moscow repatriated ethnic Germans from Bessarabia following the Soviet seizure of that province in 1940, the NKVD recruited espionage agents among those being repatriated to work for them following their relocation to the Reich.[9] Little wonder, then, that Soviet intelligence assumed that the Nazis were playing the same game. In many cases, the NKVD actually shot refugees from the Germans with little or no further evidence of their guilt than the fact of their flight.[10] Although this no doubt liquidated a number of potential German spies, it almost certainly killed even more people who would willingly have fought against the Germans; it also further insulated the Soviet population against learning about the horrors of Nazi rule.

Owing in part to its own actions, therefore, the Soviet government faced a much greater propaganda dilemma than did its enemy when the war began. Not only did the average Soviet subject know little about the nature of Nazism, but the Soviet legacy of political and religious repression was also a powerful weapon in the arsenal of the invader, imposing a heavy burden on Moscow as well. From the very outset of their invasion of the USSR, Nazi propagandists naturally capitalized on the grim Stalinist record, continually trumpeting the claim that the German army was conducting a "crusade" in defense of Western civilization against Soviet barbarism. The target of this propaganda was not only the Soviet population, but also, and perhaps even more important in Berlin's calculations, European and international Christian opinion. Given the tragic history of Soviet religious repression and the mistrust, or outright hostility, of most Christians worldwide toward the Soviet atheist regime, this was perhaps Berlin's strongest propaganda card. It certainly made more appealing propaganda than the real reasons for the invasion—race war and territorial expansion.

On the day of the invasion, German radio promised Soviet subjects that "one of the first measures of the German administration will be the restoration of religious freedom. . . . We will allow you to organize religious parishes. Everyone will be free to pray to God in his own manner."[11] Certain elements within the German high command, notably in the Wehrmacht, did indeed seek to restore some level of religious freedom to the peoples of the USSR, not because German officers had any special devotion to religious liberty as such, but rather because they believed that this might prove a potent weapon.[12] In the wake of their advances, the German armed forces often reopened churches and allowed public services, notably in the cathedral cities of Minsk and Smolensk, ensuring that German cameras were on scene to record these events for the world audience.

As in so many other ways, the seemingly monolithic Nazi government was deeply divided when it came to determining religious and nationalities policy in the East. As the foremost historian of the German occupation has noted, the Nazis might have used religion as "one more lever" for cracking Soviet authority; but Berlin proved "incapable of recognizing the available opportunities."[13] On the one hand, German leaders with experience of Russia, such as the self-appointed "ideologist" of Nazism Alfred Rosenberg (who himself came from Latvia), sought to play on the national and religious grievances of Ukrainians and other minority Soviet nationalities in order to drive a wedge between Moscow and its outlying possessions. On the other hand, such figures as Reinhard Heydrich of the SS and Martin Bormann, Hitler's dark shadow, both opposed allowing any real measure of religious liberty in the occupied regions. They were angered by the army's well-publicized opening of churches and by the Wehrmacht's sanctioning of the entry into conquered Soviet territories of Orthodox, Greek, and Roman Catholic émigré missionaries.[14] In Hitler's New

Order, these Nazi hierarchs believed, the Slavs were destined for servitude, and they should not be encouraged to believe otherwise. Nor should their national and religious aspirations be allowed any institutional focus that might enable them one day to contest German political supremacy.

Bormann, Heydrich, and other like-minded Nazis were faithfully reflecting the will of their master, Hitler, who had openly declared that "the heaviest blow that ever struck humanity was the coming of Christianity. Bolshevism is Christianity's illegitimate child. Both are inventions of the Jew."[15] Hitler was contemptuous of religion and ultimately sought to destroy it throughout the Nazi empire, though in Germany he had been cautious about confronting the churches head on, fearing their political clout. In the East he had no such qualms. He refused to allow Christian missionaries to follow the Wehrmacht into Russia, sniffing sarcastically that "If one did it at all, one should permit all the Christian denominations to enter Russia in order that they club each other to death with their crucifixes."[16] In a Führer Order of August 6, 1941, he prohibited army units from assisting churches.[17] Hitler was concerned not only about giving Slavs undue hope; he also worried that extensive propaganda in Germany about a religious rebirth in conquered Soviet lands might encourage Germans to believe that the churches had more of a future in the Reich itself than he intended. On November 14, consequently, Bormann relayed the Führer's order that "until further notice nothing should be published [in the domestic German press] about the religious situation in the Soviet Union."[18]

Although debate about the treatment of Soviet minority nationalities continued to swirl throughout the Nazi hierarchy, the matter was effectively settled by the appointment of the vicious Erich Koch to rule over Ukraine. Lacking any human virtue other than a brutal frankness, Koch announced: "The attitude of the Germans in the [Ukraine] must be governed by the fact that we deal with a people which is inferior in every respect. . . . We have not liberated it to bring blessings on the Ukraine but to secure for Germany the necessary living space and a source of food."[19]

Hitler's unwillingness to exploit religious sentiment in the conquered regions and his failure to exploit political and economic grievances of the local population by granting some measure of self-determination or eliminating the hated kolkhozes, are among the war's stranger mysteries. During his rise to power, and in his diplomacy in Eastern Europe both before and during the early stages of the war, the Führer had been adept at playing off national discontents in order to divide and conquer. Following his invasion of the USSR, however, he abandoned such subtleties in favor of an open policy of exploitation. Instead of tapping into the well of hatreds and grievances left by decades of Soviet misrule, the unashamedly tyrannical policies of the Nazi occupiers would eventually drive most of the local population into Moscow's arms, whatever their reservations about Stalin's regime. Only in the later stages of the war in the East, when German defeat was looming and a spontaneous religious revival from below presented the Nazis with a fait accompli, would the occupiers change their hostile attitude toward religion in the Soviet lands.[20] By then, however, the real nature and goals of Nazi barbarism had been revealed for all to see, and Berlin's newfound enthusiasm for religion failed to convince.

"They Are Fighting for Mother Russia"

The true nature of Nazi designs for the East would emerge only after months of war and occupation. In the meantime, it was by no means certain that the Red Army would fight effectively. Hitler, as well as the majority of American and British observers, believed that Soviet forces would prove no match for the German blitzkrieg. The legacy of Stalinist repressions, the impact of the Red Army purges of 1937–38 and the poor Soviet showing in the 1939–40 war with Finland all seemed to point to the same conclusion: the Red Army appeared to be like a man with rickets entering the boxing ring to face a heavyweight champion in fine fettle.[21]

From the first days of the war in the East, much to the surprise of prognosticators, Soviet resistance was stronger than any that the German army had hitherto encountered. By the end of the third month of Operation Barbarossa, the Wehrmacht had already sustained losses of over 500,000 officers and men. This contrasted tellingly with the 30,000 dead they had suffered during all their previous campaigns since September 1939.[22] In certain places, such as Brest-Litovsk, Red Army men held out even when they were surrounded and all hope of survival had long since vanished.[23] Wehrmacht leaders who once assumed the Soviet people to be incapable of offering any sort of vigorous defense would receive a rude shock.

If Soviet resistance was fierce in places, however, the first weeks of the war also uncovered serious shortcomings in Moscow's military machine. Some of these problems were well known even at the time, such as the damage done to the Red Army by Stalin's prewar purges. Also, the German army had two years of field experience going into the Russian war, whereas most Soviet soldiers had never before seen combat.[24] The Soviet level of technical expertise and training was thus much lower than that of their German opponents. Equipment failures, logistical bottlenecks, and the constant harassment of German air raids added to the Red Army's perils during the summer of 1941. Above all, the strategic surprise the Germans achieved during their initial attack gave them a forward momentum that would continue almost to the end of 1941.[25]

Most disquieting to Soviet rulers was the question of their soldiers' uncertain loyalty. This remains a cloudy historical subject, with very little evidence yet emerging from Soviet archives to explain the motivation of the average Red Army recruit. Nonetheless, there is ample reason to believe that the willingness of the common soldier to fight and die for the Stalinist state varied greatly from individual to individual. In the Kremlin's view, the gravest danger was the enormous number of Soviet soldiers who surrendered to the advancing Germans. During the war, more than 5.5 million Red Army soldiers would fall into the hands of the Wehrmacht—1 million more men than were in the entire initial German invasion force.[26] Most of these poor people would perish in vast, hellish German POW stockades, where the conditions were little better than outright extermination camps.

Reasons for surrender varied greatly. In large part, mass capitulations were simply the product of the swift German advance. The Wehrmacht trapped entire Soviet armies in gigantic battles of encirclement, for instance, netting more than half a million Red Army men when Kiev fell in in September.[27] Strategic encirclements do not, however, explain all Soviet surrenders. On the local level, some Soviet soldiers showed a disturbing propensity to cross the lines, unaware of the treatment that awaited them at the hands of their Nazi captors. Johnnie von Herwarth, a German cavalry officer who spoke fluent Russian and debriefed captured Soviet soldiers, recalls that NKVD troops fought well during the first hours of the war; but, he writes, "the fighting spirit of the Soviet infantry could not have been lower. If they put up any stiff resistance it was only because of the difficulty of deserting at that particular moment, due, for example, to the temporary stabilization of the front line." Not only did many soldiers desert but they also often provided their captors with "precise and reliable" information about Red Army dispositions.[28]

As evidence mounted in Moscow that many Red Army troops lacked the proper fighting spirit, on August 16 Stalin personally issued his notorious Order Number 270, decreeing that deserters be "shot on the spot" and their families to be held hostage to their good behavior.[29] In Stalin's mind, Soviet soldiers who surrendered simply ceased to exist. When the Germans offered to set up a postal exchange system for POWs, Stalin responded: "There are no Russian prisoners of war. The Russian soldier fights on till death. If he chooses to become a prisoner, he is automatically excluded from the Russian community. We are not interested in a postal service only for Germans."[30]

The dictator's new decree went into immediate, deadly effect, an orgy of executions ensuing as the high command raged impotently against its insubordinate soldier-subjects. A front-line veteran briefly on leave in Moscow complained that "One is executed for failing to carry out a military assignment, although the assignment may have been impossible to fulfill. Another is shot for desertion, but how can you implement the punishment if the whole unit deserts? The third is executed for the devil knows what, just so there are executions! The Germans are beating us and we are beating ourselves."[31] By the end of August, a Soviet writer who visited the front lines was so appalled at what he witnessed there that he decided to take the risky step of appealing to Stalin personally, noting that "here, in the 24th Army, things have gone too far. According to the command staff and political section, 480–600 men have been shot for desertion, panicking and other crimes."[32] Stalin remained unmoved, and his orders stood. Far from being shamed by accounts of such barbaric measures, the dictator actually boasted of them to American envoy Averell Harriman: "In the Soviet Army," he remarked coldly, "it takes more courage to retreat than to advance."[33]

To ensure that this remained the case, the Soviet government directed the NKVD to create units to be stationed immediately behind the front lines with standing orders to shoot those suspected of unauthorized retreat or desertion.[34] The role and numbers of these units, the existence of which official historians entirely denied during the Soviet era, is a subject that has not yet been adequately researched; but the numbers of the victims are simply staggering: 157,593 men shot for "panic-mongering, cowardice, and unauthorized abandonment of the field of battle."[35] The number of victims was equivalent to a full sixteen infantry divisions and more than half as many men as the United States lost in the entire war. It also tallies with German observations: Herwarth wrote, for instance, that Soviet "[c]aptives later reported that they had been driven forward by the political commissars and officers."[36] A recent Russian film documentary contains firsthand descriptions of how the NKVD set up machine gun emplacements behind soldiers ordered to advance, to buck up their courage.[37] This, too, was a Bolshevik tradition: Trotskii had at times resorted to the same methods, notably during his storming of the Kronstadt naval base in 1921.[38]

The part played by terror and coercion in the Soviet war effort should not be exaggerated; other motives, such as patriotism, desperation, and even Communist convictions were in play, and many of these would grow in importance as the war dragged on. Nonetheless, the continuing reliance on terror testified to the intensity of Kremlin fears about the disloyalty of its soldiers, and the mind-boggling number of victims tells its own story.[39]

These suspicions about disloyalty in the Red Army were only enhanced by images of the welcome many Ukrainian civilians and other inhabitants of the western borderlands initially extended to the invaders.[40] German propagandists eagerly photographed and broadcast such scenes, with Ukrainian peasants offering the traditional gifts of bread and salt to their "guests." Almost certainly the Germans staged many of these dramas for the newsreel cameras, though many others were spontaneous. Often, the welcomes reflected little more than the population's hope of winning better treatment by demonstrating an early enthusiasm for German rule. Nina Markovna remembers how her mother ordered her to tie down her breasts under her blouse so she would not attract the attention of German soldiers and thereby risk rape; simultaneously, her mother told her to bake bread in anticipation of the invaders' arrival. When Markovna angrily pointed out contradiction between greeting the invaders with bread and fearing rape, her mother replied: " 'Dochenka,' she began, very quietly, a bit sadly. 'So proud you are, so naive and direct. Ninochka, child, in order to survive life's upheavals, you have to learn to . . . to bend with the prevailing wind.' "[41] This attitude was probably much more widespread than was any genuine enthusiasm for the German invaders.

Still, a great deal of firsthand evidence testifies to the fact that much of the Soviet population, deprived of accurate information and not knowing yet what to expect from the Germans, at first assumed that they might well be an improvement on the Stalinist regime. In the western borderlands, and among aging veterans of World War I, folk memories lingered on of the relatively benign occupation of the Kaiser's army twenty years earlier. Wilfried Strik-Strikfeldt, a German officer of Baltic origin who had actually fought in the Russian Imperial Army in the First World War, recalls one typical scene in which an "old peasant" told his fellows that "He had . . . been taken prisoner in the 'First Imperialist War' (1914–18), and had worked on a German farm. The Germans had been good to him. . . . So he had not believed the propaganda about the 'German beasts,' and had advised his fellow-soldiers to drop their rifles and surrender."[42]

In their headlong retreat, the Soviets left in their wake further reasons for locals to rejoice in the collapse of Communist power: Stalin ordered the Red Army to practice a "scorched earth" policy, which had the effect of denying food and shelter to the invader but also left very little to sustain the remaining civilian population. According to Herwarth, Stalin's order "was viewed by the peasantry as an act of despair and only served to intensify their hatred of the dictator."[43] A Russian soldier described a typical scene, replicated thousands of times throughout the fighting zone: "When we retreat, we destroy everything left behind, even the crops, while the populace simply looks on. They beg, give it to us, don't burn it, we will die of starvation! But that would be going against orders."[44]

As if the material destruction was not enough, when the NKVD fled, it summarily executed thousands of prisoners held in regional prisons and camps—not taking time to dispose of their bodies. The Germans uncovered numerous grisly scenes, making sure that local civilians viewed the heaps of corpses.[45] Given their limited information about the Nazis, and their abundant grievances against the Kremlin, the locals' hopes of a better life under the Germans were not unreasonable, even if they proved ultimately to be mistaken.

Another large group of Soviet citizens had reason to hate the Stalinist regime and to hope for better from the Germans: deportees and inmates of the gulag. In September 1941 Wolfgang Leonhard, a young German Communist who would later become one of the leading lights in the East German Communist state after the war, was deported to the Kazakh Republic near Karaganda along with other ethnic Germans resident in the USSR. This latest round of deportations once again reflected Moscow's fears of a "fifth column."[46] Upon arriving at his place of exile, Leonhard and his fellow German Communists encountered large numbers of peasants who had been deported a decade before during the collectivization of the farms as "kulaks," or supposedly wealthy farmers. "Practically all of them were Russians," he noted, "though a few were Ukrainians or Tatars; none were Kazakhs." What struck Leonhard immediately was the fact that these people, who had lost most everything they had once owned, expressed themselves freely, unlike other people he had met during his years in the USSR.

The older deportees greeted the new arrivals wryly, saying, "we've been waiting for you for a long time. We thought from the beginning you Germans would be sent here." Leonhard and his friends explained that, though they were indeed Germans, they were antifascists and supporters of the Soviet war effort, but the peasants refused to believe that Germans could be anything other than supporters of Hitler. Leonhard was astounded to learn that, far from regarding this as a mark against the new arrivals, the peasants viewed Hitler favorably. They asked the Germans, " 'Well, how far has your Hitler got? What d'you think? Will he get as far as this and liberate us?' "[47]

Shifting patterns of loyalty were greatly shaped by developments at the fighting front. Following the Wehrmacht's failure to capture Moscow in the autumn and early winter of 1941, the Red Army launched a series of counterattacks that dramatically drove the enemy westward. The hitherto seemingly invincible Nazi armies had received their first serious check. Many Soviet leaders, including apparently Stalin himself, began to believe that the Soviet Union had not only survived the initial onslaught but also that the turning point in the war had actually been reached.[48] Unfortunately for Stalin, his optimism proved premature. When the Red Army tried to carry its momentum into the spring by launching an offensive into the eastern Ukraine, the results were disastrous. Once again a mass encirclement ensued, with more than 200,000 Soviet troops falling into German captivity and a gaping hole being torn in the southern reaches of the Soviet line.[49] Simultaneously, the last remnants of Soviet resistance in the Crimean peninsula collapsed with the capture of a further 176,000 Soviet soldiers.[50]

In the wake of these events, the Wehrmacht resumed its advance in early August, this time aiming not toward the Soviet capital but rather toward the Caucasus isthmus and the city of Stalingrad on the Volga. The offensive threatened to sever Moscow's critical lifeline to the oilfields of the Caspian basin, from which it drew more than 80 percent of its energy supplies.[51] Initially, the German advance was almost as swift as it had been the previous summer. The Red Army's successes during the winter now seemed only a distant memory, and the contrast with the disasters of the spring and the renewed German advance only served to amplify the shock in Moscow.

For the Kremlin, one positive fact stood out amid these tragic developments. During the summer and fall of 1942, there would be no replay of the mass surrenders that had marked the opening stages of Barbarossa—at least for ethnically Russian troops. In all of 1942, fewer than half as many Soviet soldiers fell into German captivity as had surrendered during the last six months of 1941.[52] The vast encirclements of Soviet troops during the spring came about owing to failed offensive operations, the product of Moscow's planning errors, not as a result of individual surrenders. As the Germans advanced toward Stalingrad, Soviet forces retreated quickly but in relatively good order; the Germans captured territory but not masses of men.[53]

To some degree this can be explained by the improving quality of Soviet military organization and unit cohesion, as well as the NKVD's terror tactics, but other factors may have been even more critical. During the Soviet winter offensives, the Red Army had briefly reoccupied areas once held by the Germans, and Russians were genuinely shocked by what they had found. No vaporings of Soviet propaganda could have prepared Soviet soldiers for the reality of Nazi occupation: evidence abounded of the vicious war against civilians; the murder of Jews; reprisals against defenseless women and even children; rapes, wanton destruction, and every other crime imaginable. As word of German atrocities spread throughout the Red Army, fighting motivation changed dramatically. Kravchenko relates that he too was swept up in the hatred of the Germans and the concomitant revival of Russian nationalism, despite his private hatred of the Stalinist system: "Hitler's hordes succeeded in inflaming Russian patriotism more effectively than all the new war cries of race and nation launched from the Kremlin."[54]

Not all was well on the morale front during the second year of the war, however; nationality problems and political grievances continued to sap the war effort. Among the non-Russian nationalities behind German lines or near the fighting zones, popular hostility to Soviet power manifested itself in particularly dangerous ways. In the Crimean peninsula, for instance, the local Tatars deserted the Soviet cause en masse. Of 130 Tatars called into the army from the village of Koush, for instance, 122 deserted; from the town of Beshui 92 of 98 returned to their village. A Central Committee memorandum noted that "Many [Tatars] went over to the service of the Germans."[55]

With the collapse of Soviet power in the Crimea during the spring of 1942, whole Tatar villages cooperated to root out pro-Soviet partisan activity. Many Tatars viewed ethnic Russians as the proximate representatives of the imperial power that had oppressed them. Their suffering during collectivization had left an indelible mark, as had the shutting and desecration of their mosques during prewar antireligious campaigns. German military successes seemed to offer an ideal opportunity to settle national and religious scores. When a Russian settlement near the Tatar village of Koush aided Soviet partisans with food and tobacco, the local Tatars, on learning of this, burned the encampment down and slaughtered the inhabitants. Only one Russian woman escaped to tell her tale. Likewise, ethnic Greeks in the village of Luki were discovered aiding the partisans; sixty armed Tatars promptly told the Greeks that if the assistance continued they would destroy the village. In March 1942, when the Greeks continued to ignore the threat, Tatar fighters razed the village and shot the inhabitants either on the spot or later after taking them to Bakhchiserai.[56]

When the Germans first arrived in the Crimea, some Tatars had actually joined the Soviet partisans, but by December 1941 Moscow's position in the peninsula deteriorated, and these few volunteers deserted. "Not one of the Tatars' populated points has given or gives any help to the partisans; on the contrary," a secret Soviet investigation continued. When Soviet partisans approached Tatar areas, they were met with "gunfire." Many Tatars at first worked with the Germans, revealing secret Soviet supply dumps and partisan strongholds. But, following the fall of Kerch in the spring of 1942, when it looked as though Soviet rule might never be restored, Tatars began to act independently. The Soviet report continued: "In general it should be said that if it were not for the treachery of the Tatar population, then the partisan movement in the Crimea would be in much better circumstances, than at the present time."[57] The Tatars' revenge against ethnic Russians was fully as brutal as the treatment meted out to them earlier by the Soviet state—again, Moscow was reaping the whirlwind.

The Tatars were not the only Moslem people suspected of hampering the Soviet war effort. When the German-Soviet front reached the Caucasus Mountains in the autumn of 1942, many local peoples refused to join or even assist the Red Army. In December 1942 the army's Political Directorate was warned that "there are instances of unfriendly relations toward the Red Army" on the part of several Caucasian peoples. This was especially true of Chechens and Ingush, but also the Osetians, Balkhars, Kabardintsy, and others showed a marked hostility to the Soviet cause. Red Army political officers admitted among themselves that Soviet soldiers were not guiltless in such clashes, because they often seized food and other provisions from the civilian population without payment; soldiers also ignored local traditions and conditions, and they did not adequately explain their "liberating mission." As ever, Soviet authorities placed great faith in more effective propaganda: "Elements of estrangement between the population and units of the Red Army doubtless could be significantly and even completely smoothed over, if appropriate work were organized both among the Red Army and the local population. By the way, there is nothing of this [at present]." Ominously, the author of this memorandum proposed: "Place before the TsK VKP(b) [the Soviet Central Committee] the question of the earned guilt of the male population of the N. Caucasus, now being drafted into the army."[58]

Stalin read these incoming documents that recounted allegations of treason among non-Russians, and he drew characteristically lethal conclusions. Infamously, in the closing stages of the war he ordered the deportation to Soviet Central Asia of all the Crimean Tatars, Chechens, and Ingush, as well as several other small nationalities.[59] Confronted in later life with his shared responsibility for these horrific actions, Molotov would defend himself and Stalin:

> Oh, so we have become wise after the event, have we? Now we know everything, anachronistically mix up events, squeeze time into a single point. Everything has its history. The fact is that during the war we received reports about mass treason. Battalions of Caucasians opposed us at the fronts and attacked us from the rear. It was a matter of life and death; there was no time to investigate the details. Of course innocents suffered. But I hold that given the circumstances, we acted correctly.[60]

Here Molotov was himself guilty of anachronistically mixing up events; Moscow did not order the deportations as a defensive measure while the alleged treason was occurring, but rather toward the end of the war, as vengeance.

More worrisome to the Kremlin than the rebellious activity of these Moslem nations—the impact of which was, after all, limited by their relatively small numbers—were the anti-Russian guerrilla groups springing up in the Baltic republics but especially in Ukraine, the most populous Soviet republic to fall to the Nazis. Soviet historiography, and far too many Westerners, have portrayed Ukrainian nationalism as wholly pro-German and fascist politically. It has long been clear, however, that Ukrainian resistance groups, like the factions fighting in the civil war, were a heterogeneous lot.[61] Some were indeed pro-German, though most were not; and the most effective, the OUN-B under Stepan Bandera, was politically close to fascism, although the Banderites opposed both Soviet and German rule.[62] It would have been miraculous if, amid the Nazi-Soviet conflict, resistance groups had not themselves adopted authoritarian ideas akin to their enemies'; the war was scarcely a hothouse of Jeffersonian democracy.

Soviet authorities were fully aware both from their own independent sources and from captured German documents that not all Ukrainian resistance groups were mere pawns of Berlin. For instance, one SS document from the Khar'kov oblast', captured and translated into Russian by the Glavnoe Razvedyvatel' noe Upravlenik, or Chief Espionage Direcorate (GRU), portrayed Ukrainian resistance as a genuine nuisance for German rulers. Writing of the organization Prosvita (enlightenment), the memorandum noted that these Ukrainian nationalists sought "to exclude all foreign influence, including German, and fight by all means for their goal of 'The establishment of an autonomous Ukraine.'"[63]

Ukrainian Orthodox clergy were proving a fertile recruiting ground for this group, the document continued.[64] And the Ukrainian nationalists successfully employed the Soviet record of repression to swell their ranks. One Banderite document declared for example: "Like a terrifying apparition stands before us the year 1933, a year of hunger and death." (This had been, of course, the year of Stalin's terror-famine.) The Banderites continued: "Down with Muscovite and German imperialism, down with Stalin and Hitler."[65] These guerrilla groups found their greatest support in western Ukraine, that supposed "defensive buffer" that the Soviets had been unable to pacify before Barbarossa, where Ukrainians vastly outnumbered ethnic Russians.

Much of the western Ukrainian clergy at first welcomed the invaders, hoping that they would act as rescuers from Soviet religious, political, and national oppression. Most notoriously, on September 23, 1941, Metropolitan Sheptyt'sky, the head of the Ukrainian Catholic Church, sent a welcoming message to Hitler. Writing "as the head of the Greek Catholic Church," Sheptyt'sky told Hitler that "The cause of the destruction and eradication of bolshevism, which

You [*sic*] yourself as the Führer of the great German Reich have adopted as the goal of your campaign, has ensured the blessings of the entire Christian world."[66] Sheptyt'sky later went so far as to bless the formation of a Ukrainian SS division, "Galicia," that would fight against both Soviet partisans and the Red Army as it began to recover western Ukraine. Within months of the Nazi occupation, however, Sheptyt'sky would become completely disillusioned with the Germans and begin to realize that Soviet oppression had been replaced by an even more pervasive and homicidal tyranny.[67]

Ukrainian opposition to Soviet rule was by no means universal. Especially in the eastern reaches of the republic, intermarriage between Ukrainians and Russians, the presence of a large ethnic Russian minority, and a less pronounced sense of Ukrainian national identity all meant that specifically anti-Russian nationalism was much weaker than in the western portions of Ukraine. From a total population of 41.3 million, about 2.5 million Ukrainians served in the ranks of the Red Army, many of them loyally and bravely; among these were 240,000 members of the Communist Party.[68] As elsewhere in the USSR, patterns of loyalties in Ukraine were deeply fractured. The situation was similar in Belorussia, where much of the population initially adopted a "wait-and-see attitude vis-a-vis the Germans."[69] Many Belorussians at first gave little or no help to Soviet partisans, but after less than year of German occupation this began to change. By war's end, according to Soviet figures, more than 440,000 Belorussians had joined the partisan ranks.[70]

Although ethnic and religious hostility among the civil population was an ongoing concern, figures from the Red Army reflect serious and widespread national discontent within the military itself. In midsummer 1942, for instance, as the German army stood poised to advance toward Stalingrad, desertions among certain national groups reached alarming proportions. According to a secret Soviet study, those most likely to desert fell into certain categories: soldiers whose families were in German-occupied areas, those in areas surrounded by the Germans (such as the Crimean peninsula before it fell to the Germans), "and also Red Army men of non-Russian nationality," especially those from the Transcaucasus and Moslems from Central Asia. In one army, along the littoral of the Black Sea, 79.8 percent of those "who have betrayed the *rodina* [motherland]" were non-Russian. In this army during the period February–April 1942, 135 Azeris, 111 Georgians, 71 Lezgins, 75 Armenians, 55 Ukrainians, and 48 members of other nationalities deserted to the Germans.[71] Clearly, not all national groups shared the official view that the USSR was their "rodina."

In one rifle division, the 345th, desertion took on a particularly threatening aspect. A group of soldiers who had already deserted to the Germans was reorganized by the Nazis into a group and sent back into Soviet lines to encourage others to follow their example. These agents targeted fellow villagers (*odnosel'chii*) and front-line soldiers (*boitsov*).[72] Even among those non-Russian soldiers who did not desert, morale was clearly low. One especially sad set of documents reveals that instances of self-inflicted wounds (*chlenovreditel'stvo*) were frequent among non-Russians, especially those who did not speak the Russian language.[73] The director of the Central Committee's agitation and propaganda directorate warned that most of those convicted of wounding themselves were unaware that the penalty for doing so was death, and he urged the Soviet Central Committee to prod the Central Committees of the Georgian, Armenian, Azerbaidjani, Kazakh, and Uzbek republics, as well as the Tatobkom, to engage in vigorous propaganda warning against self-mutilation.[74]

The relatively poor motivation and fighting qualities of non-Russian nationalities gave rise to great resentment and tensions between ethnic Russians and minorities in the Red Army. Russian recruits began to mutter that "non-Russian nationality cadres don't know how and don't want to fight." Russian recruits referred disparagingly to "sons of the Caucasus," who they believed were undependable and cowardly; only Slavs made effective soldiers, according to growing popular stereotype.[75] Distrust in the fighting qualities of national minorities combined in the minds of many Russians with the conviction that non-Russians were treated differently, with less being demanded of them by Soviet authorities.[76]

Some Soviet political officers were greatly frightened by the spread of such notions, which clearly contradicted Leninist and Stalinist dogmas about the friendship of Soviet nationalities and also threatened the cohesion of the Red Army. At the same time, however, they admitted among themselves that disparaging national stereotypes were based on all-too-real facts. Although desertion was no longer the massive problem that it had been the previous year among Slavic units, non-Russians remained problematical. An army political officer wrote: "Instances of desertion to the enemy side have not ceased, sometimes massive transfers" (*Ne prekratilis' fakty perekhoda na storonu vraga, pritom inogda massogo perekhoda*). This same memorandum continued: "Thus, a massive desertion [*perekhod*] took place in the 89th Armenian Division, that demanded the taking of a series of cardinal measures—seizing and placing under arrest the command of the division, the renewal of its staff, and so on. Other facts of desertion have also taken place in the 337th rifle division and others." Among units composed of non-Russians, "there are cases of desertion, faint-heartedness, self-mutilation." Human losses were also greater because in general their training was poorer; some non-Russians arrived at the front never having been taught to fire a weapon. Having said all this, the author then qualified his comments by admitting that many of these things were true even in units composed entirely of Russians, Belorussians, and Ukrainians; there were also instances where multinational units performed well in battle. But the clear import of his analysis was that ethnic Russians were better trained, more socialized to the Soviet cause, and far better motivated.[77]

Even after the first year of war, the problem of disloyalty was not limited to non-Russians. Some ethnic Russians believed that their first duty to their country was to rid it of the Communist regime, even if this meant collaborating with Hitler. By 1942, as it became clear to most Germans that the war against the USSR would not be the walkover they had once assumed it would be, the Wehrmacht created a unit comprising disaffected Russians for deployment against the Red Army. Calling it the Russkaia osvoboditel'naia armiia (ROA), or Russian Liberation Army, the Germans placed the captured Russian general Andrei Vlasov in command of this new force. Vlasov himself seems to have become a genuine anti-Stalinist, whose antiregime ideas gestated over a long time.[78] The motives of his recruits were more varied: some hated the Soviet system for personal or other reasons; others were opportunists, or saw enlistment in the ROA as a way to escape the lethal German POW camps.

The Vlasov Army, as it became known, never worked as its initiators had hoped. The Nazis could not overcome their reflexive distrust of ethnic Russian *Untermenschen*, and they would not allow the unit to fight against the Red Army. Ironically, the unit only went into action once during the war, not against Soviet forces but rather against SS in Prague. Vlasov's men learned the hard way that Hitler was even a worse betrayer than Stalin. As Aleksandr Solzhenitsyn writes, "fate played them an even bitterer trick, and they were more abject pawns than before." Solzhenitsyn's sympathetic but negative verdict on Russians who joined the German armed forces is well worth quoting: "[T]his was a phenomenon totally unheard of in all world history; that several hundred thousand young men, aged twenty to thirty, took up arms against their Fatherland as allies of its most evil enemy." Solzhenitsyn concluded with an old Russian proverb: "'*Well-fed horses don't rampage*.' Then picture to yourself a field in which starved, neglected, crazed horses are rampaging back and forth."[79] Fortunately for Stalin, Hitler's belated offers of fodder failed to entice most Russians.

Most Russians were fighting under Moscow's banner, and during the dangerous summer and fall of 1942—despite Vlasov and his band—they were doing so with a renewed sense of patriotism. Alexander Werth, the BBC correspondent in Moscow, later recounted the new nationalist mood that seized the

Russian people at this critical time: this was no Soviet patriotism but rather "specifically a love of Russia proper." There was an obverse side to Russian nationalism, a second motive for fighting: "The other," Werth wrote, "was hate."[80] The apostle of this hatred was the Soviet writer and propagandist Ilia Ehrenburg. In a stunningly bitter passage he penned during the opening stages of the Stalingrad campaign, Ehrenburg plumbed new depths of hatred, excluding the Germans entirely from the human race:

> [T]he Germans are not human beings. Don't let us waste time on talking, or on feeling indignant. Let us kill! If you haven't killed a German in the course of the day, your day has been wasted. If you don't kill the German, he will kill you. If you can't kill a German with a bullet, kill him with your bayonet! If you have killed one German, kill another: nothing gives us so much joy as German corpses. Your mothers say to you: kill the German! Your children beg of you: kill the German! Your country groans and whispers: kill the German! Don't miss him! Don't let him escape! Kill![81]

If Ehrenburg was the apostle of hatred, his messiah was Stalin. Hatred was one human emotion the *vozhd'* understood thoroughly and knew how to manipulate. Hatred of the Germans helped to define and fuel Russian nationalism, which in turn moved Russian recruits to fight.

Very early in the war, Stalin grasped the crucial role of Russian nationalism, perhaps as only a non-Russian leader could. In September 1941, referring to the common Russian soldier, the dictator told Harriman: "We are under no illusion that they are fighting for us [the Communists]. They are fighting for Mother Russia."[82] The fact that, following initial waverings, Russians were willing to fight led the Soviet government to revive national symbols, not as a reward but rather as an inducement for ethnic Russians to continue the struggle. Even more important, the revival of Russian nationalism provided the Kremlin with an antidote to the perceived unreliability of its non-Russian subjects.

In the army, ornamental braid and epaulettes suddenly reappeared on officers' uniforms, replacing the scruffy proletarian look affected by the early Bolshevik Red Army. In mid-1942 the British were stunned to receive an urgent request from the Soviets for tons of these seemingly frivolous materials, which took space reserved for vital war matériel in Lend-Lease shipments.[83] At precisely the same time that Western officers were becoming less formal and more "democratic"—when the anachronistic George Patton was being replaced by the "soldiers' general" Omar Bradley—in the USSR the trend was in reverse. As American and British commanders sought to look more like the working man, the military commanders of the workers' and peasants' state were assuming a new, artificially regal air. Stalin restored old tsarist Russian military orders dating from the time of Catherine the Great, that earlier non-Russian usurper. Gleaming Orders of Suvorov, Kutuzov, and Aleksandr Nevskii soon appeared on the heavily bemedaled chests of Soviet marshals.

The critical institution in this process of re-Russification, one of the last, embattled remnants of prerevolutionary Russian society, was the Orthodox Church. The church, despised and denounced by a generation of commissars, would now be conjured up to serve the cause of the Communist state. The church could help to reinforce the Slavs' martial spirit by redefining the war in Russian national, and even in specifically Christian, terms. It would work to rally Russians, Belorussians, Ukrainians, and other Orthodox Slavs to Moscow's cause, not only in the Red Army but also—and perhaps even more important—behind German lines.

The revival of Russian nationalism in late 1942 and early 1943, of which the restoration of the Russian Orthodox Church to public activity would be the most striking part, is easily misunderstood. It is insufficient simply to say, as so many historians have, that the state turned to the church in order to motivate Russians to fight, or to harness their nationalist spirit. Although true, it is even more the case that the Soviets restored the church to a limited measure of public life because Russians and other Slavs had *already* demonstrated their willingness to fight. Having survived the disasters of 1941, Moscow was concerned that during the second summer of the war all too many non-Russians were still not fully committed to the Soviet cause. At the front line and in the German rear Slavs, and especially Russians, had proved far more reliable fighters—at least in Soviet perceptions.[84] By ratcheting up Russian nationalism, as well as Orthodox Christianity, Moscow was reinforcing success. In the Red Army and in partisan ranks, Russians provided the critical leavening that bolstered Soviet fighting strength. Through the winter of 1942–43, as the Stalingrad campaign raged on and the outcome of the war remained in grave doubt, the Soviet government would swallow hard and transform its relations with the church.

"Not the Swastika, but the Cross"

Even though German actions in Russia would ultimately expose the hollowness of their liberationist pretensions, for Moscow the religious question assumed immediate urgency from the very first day of Barbarossa. German talk of granting religious freedom at first struck a sympathetic chord among certain elements of the Soviet population, particularly in Ukraine and the western borderlands—the *Schwerpunkt* of the Nazi attack. The possible defection of millions of their Orthodox subjects struck the Soviets as all too plausible, causing them immediately to silence their more strident antireligious propaganda. Within a few days of the German invasion, Soviet atheist journals ceased publication, and, in an ironic twist, the last issue of *Bezbozhnik*, the leading atheist periodical, condemned Nazi persecution of Christian churches and even called on believers to rally to the Soviet cause. The BBC correspondent in Moscow, Alexander Werth, who was quite well disposed toward the USSR, recorded his impressions about this abrupt and odd turn of events: "*Bezbozhnik's volte-face* was a bit blatant, and, in fact, this was to be its last issue. It was closed down owing to 'paper shortage.' Instead, Emelian Yaroslavsky, the 'anti-God' leader, was publishing pamphlets like the *Great Patriotic War*, in the best nationalist tradition, which they were now selling on bookstalls."[85] In addition to silencing antireligious publications, the Soviets soon reduced some of the heavy taxes they had levied in the past on churches and soon closed many of the anti-God museums that they had established in closed churches around the country.[86]

The most significant sign that Soviet religious policy would change sharply came on the first day of the war. Metropolitan Sergii, patriarch *locum tenens*, hitherto an almost invisible figure to the public, issued an appeal to Russian Orthodox faithful. Russians, he said in a nod to the Nazi-Soviet Pact, had hoped that the war would pass them by, but the fascists knew only the law of force. Sergii likened the Nazi attack to earlier invasions of Russia and warned that "The times of Baty, the Teutonic Knights, Karl [XII] of Sweden, and Napoleon are being repeated."[87] During these earlier national wars, Sergii declared, the church had always shared "the fate of the people," and it would do so now; he also recalled "the holy leaders of the Russian people, for example Aleksandr Nevskii [and] Dimitrii Donskoi," military princes and saints of the Russian Orthodox Church, who had led the Russian people against the Teutons in the thirteenth and the Mongols in the fourteenth centuries, respectively. "With the help of God," the metropolitan said, the Nazis would be defeated just as these earlier invaders had been. Sergii saved his most important points for the end of his declaration, warning believers that Orthodox clergy must not remain indifferent to the people's cause, since this would "be a direct betrayal of the motherland and their pastoral duty." As for the laity, Sergii promised that "The Church of Christ will bless all Orthodox who defend the holy borders of our motherland."[88]

There is no reason to doubt Sergii's sincerity in issuing this pronouncement. Seen in the light of more than two decades of Soviet religious repression, however, this was an extraordinary statement for the Communist authorities to authorize. In fact, the publication of Sergii's message was technically a violation of Soviet laws as they stood.[89] In a state that forbade religious education or evangelism, where ostensibly unofficial groups regularly harassed believers, and where the state-run atheist campaign enjoyed monopoly access to the media and schools, it must have astounded the average Russian to read the acting patriarch's statement that God now favored Stalin's cause.

There are several significant features of this important declaration: Sergii likened the Soviet war effort to previous *Russian* defensive wars; he did not once mention the USSR or the cause of socialism, nor did he include the Russian civil war and Allied intervention in his list of great Russian victories. He also omitted any mention of the 1914–18 conflict against Germany, which the Bolsheviks had opposed as an imperialist war before extricating Russia in a separate peace with the kaiser. This deemphasis of Communist history and themes in favor of Russian nationalism would soon become a staple of Soviet wartime propaganda, secular as well as religious. Sergii did not act on his own; although he may well have taken the initiative, the NKVD had to approve any public declaration by a religious figure.[90]

Another notable aspect of Sergii's statement was the fact that it anticipated problems. He acted early, following the Nazi attack but before any important clergy or laity could possibly have yet collaborated with the invaders. Clearly, Moscow was expecting trouble, and, as events would show, these were not idle fears. Sergii's pronouncement seems to have been directed at several audiences simultaneously. First, and most important, were domestic Christians, especially those in the western borderlands: Soviet authorities faced the nightmarish prospect that their subjects would fall prey to Nazi blandishments promising to restore religious freedom. Something had to be done to prevent disaffected Christians from collaborating with the invader. The second target group consisted of non-Russian Orthodox; throughout the summer of 1941, and during the rest of the war, the Soviets tried to appeal to ostensible Pan-Slav feeling, part of which they deemed to be religious in nature.[91] This appeal was based on the slim, and very un-Marxist, hope that fellow Slavs—Bulgarians, Poles, Czechs, Slovaks, and others—could be induced because of a supposed ethnic, historical, and religious bond with the Russians either to refuse service in Axis forces or actively to sabotage Germany's war effort. Finally, throughout the war, Soviet diplomats would give Sergii's statements the maximum possible publicity in the Western democracies in order to bolster their twin claims: that the Soviet government had never mistreated Christians and that believers wholeheartedly supported the Soviet war effort.

The very publication of this message was highly unusual in the USSR, given official state atheism and hostility to church propaganda; but it did not yet betoken a genuine thaw of antireligious repression.[92] Sergii's declaration, and others in a similar vein that soon followed, would not be printed in the Russian-language press until 1943; nor was the church allowed to issue its own publications until that same year, and clergy statements did not figure in broadcasts intended for listeners behind Soviet lines, though they received prominent treatment on shortwave broadcasts targeted for foreign audiences. Instead, the Soviet authorities broadcast such proclamations either to German-occupied or threatened areas, or had them posted as broadsheets in already open churches; in some instances, they arranged for their distribution behind German lines by clandestine means.[93] The Soviets worried more about Christians near or behind German lines than they did about believers in the hinterland.

Moscow's fears concerning the dubious loyalty of Christians proved well founded. In the first months of war, news began to filter into the Soviet capital that serious defections were taking place. This would be reflected in the increasingly desperate tone of appeals from Russian Orthodox clergy as the Nazi armies sliced deeply into the USSR, occupying vast regions and snaring millions of Soviet subjects. In October 1941 Sergii prepared a statement, to be read out and posted in churches, in which he returned to the theme of Russian historical victories. Russia's Tatar overlords were defeated in the fourteenth century under the banner of "the great God of the Russian land," Sergii said. In that war, the people and church had stood together. Sergii then made an extraordinary admission about the current war: "Rumors are afoot [*khodiat slukhi*], which one would not like to believe," that certain Orthodox clergy behind German lines "are prepared to enter into the service of the enemy of our Motherland and Church." To these unnamed turncoats, Sergii issued a stern warning: "I call to repentance all who are wavering from fear or for other reasons, but those who do not wish to repent I declare to be prohibited from holy services and [I] deliver the church's verdict for an even sterner teaching [*vrazumleniia*]. God will not be mocked."[94] As Sergii's statement suggests, clergy collaboration with the Germans was a genuine problem, and many took their flocks with them.

Throughout the first year of the war, loyal Orthodox hierarchs repeatedly warned bishops and other clergy behind German lines that failure to repent of their collaboration with the fascist powers would result in their excommunication from the church, as well as secular punishment by the Soviet state following the war—should the Red Army win, that is.[95] Especially alarming to Moscow was the defection of Bishop Polykarp Sikorskii of Vladimir and Volynsk. This renegade bishop offered his services to the Nazis as the supposed head of Orthodox believers in Ukraine.

Metropolitan Sergii singled out Polykarp Sikorskii for particular censure. "I hasten to warn the Orthodox congregation and clergy of the Ukraine against this new wolf in sheep's clothing," Sergii declared. "Sikorskii's act seems to me to be exclusively political, and not clerical. . . . He has always been a worldly cleric." Sergii then made an interesting distinction between different types of clergy opposed to the Soviet regime:

> As is common knowledge, our patriarchal Church, following the apostolic teaching with regard to the origin of state power, demands from its priests loyalty to Soviet power. Those who disagreed with this principle left their holy offices; some fled abroad. Though such irreconcilibility cannot be justified from the point of view of Christ's teaching, a certain frankness or integrity cannot be denied in those who thus surrendered their office.
>
> Sikorskii, however, did neither the one thing nor the other. He remained and prayed for the Soviet power, or at least did not refuse such prayers. Now we see that even while he did this, Sikorskii was only waiting for a suitable turn in politics to take advantage of his bishopric and turn traitor.[96]

Although the attack on Sikorskii was both harsh and personal, Sergii was walking a fine line. While condemning the traitorous bishop, Sergii was holding out an olive branch to Russian Orthodox émigré communities in Western Europe and North America who had earlier broken with the Moscow Patriarchate, believing it to be controlled by the Communists. These other Orthodox congregations might still be induced by appeals to national solidarity to support the war against Hitler; presumably for that reason, Sergii's denunciation of Sikorskii was translated and reprinted in the English-language *Soviet War News*.

Another troublesome bishop was Sergii (Voskresenskii), the metropolitan of Lithuania and exarch of Latvia and Estonia. Moscow had despatched him to the Baltic states in 1940 in order to subordinate local churches to Soviet control, but following the German attack he had remained in Riga instead of withdrawing with the Red Army when ordered to do so.[97] The three Baltic states fell quickly to the Wehrmacht during the first weeks of war, and much of the local population collaborated willingly with the Germans. Sergii continued his religious functions, working now with the newest occupiers as he had before with the NKVD; but he remained a slippery character, and the Germans never entirely trusted him. The exarch proved highly successful in organizing congregations along the Baltic littoral, almost to the gates of Leningrad, eventually bringing about 200 parishes under his jurisdiction including more than 10,000 believers.[98] He did not, however, at first make a formal break with the Moscow Patriarchate. For more than a year, much to Nazi consternation, Sergii actually seems to have restrained many local nationalist clerics who advocated an immediate rupture with Muscovite control. Sergii's relative restraint has led some historians to believe that he might have been working covertly for the Soviets while outwardly appearing to collaborate with the Germans.[99] Soviet documents suggest otherwise, however: Sergii presented a serious threat to Moscow's interests.

The Soviets knew that the Germans were successfully exploiting nationalism and religion in the Baltic region. In a major Central Committee review of the political situation in Estonia in September 1942, the authors noted gloomily that "the Germans strengthened and perfected their propaganda. They presented themselves as the defenders of religion and the churches, which the Bolsheviks supposedly wanted to destroy." (The word "supposedly" is an interesting touch.) The Nazis recruited local "fascists" and clerics to denounce Soviet religious repression, both in the USSR and in Estonia during the months of occupation. There was precious little that Moscow could do to counteract this activity, though. Not only did the Nazis occupy the Baltics, but also the German army was once again advancing, this time toward the Caucasus and Stalingrad in the south, after having been checked in the winter of 1941–42. The Soviet military position at the end of the war's second summer looked almost as desperate as it had the previous year. Many people behind German lines drew their own conclusions from the military facts, coming to believe that the occupiers were there to stay. The Central Committee's pathetic proposals to deal with the political dilemma reflected just how impotent Moscow was in the face of this political and military situation. Soviet propagandists charged with shaping Baltic opinion were ordered to "Pay special attention to the national question. Perhaps we made mistakes and did not do everything as we should, but we will correct that."[100] Once again, the bill for prewar repressions had now come due.

In early August 1942, in the midst of this desperate military and political situation, Sergii (Voskresenskii) convened a congress of Orthodox bishops in Riga, with German permission; Archbishop Iakov of Elgava as well as bishops Pavl' of Narva and Daniil of Kaunas also took part.[101] Although the congress once again refused to make a final break with the Moscow Patriarchate, the assembled bishops nonetheless affirmed their belief—accurate enough—that acting patriarch Sergii (Stragorodskii) was under Soviet control and thus not an independent figure. The rebel bishops also "sent a telegram of greetings to Hitler," wishing him good fortune in his war against the Stalin regime.[102]

Closely monitoring events in the Baltic from the other side of the front line, Deputy People's Commissar of the NKVD Bogdan Kobulov noted the bishops' willingness to remain under the Patriarchate's jurisdiction but wrote that "all the same they are trying to discredit the patriotic antifascist pronouncements of the head of the Russian Orthodox Church Metropolitan Sergii Stragorodskii, and with that goal they spread rumors." This threatened to undermine Moscow's entire religious program, in addition to worsening the already bad situation in the Baltics. The bishops' accusations were all the more devastating for being true; the Soviet transformation from atheist state to defender of the faith had been all too sudden and unbelievable.

In a letter to politbiuro member A. S. Shcherbakov, Kobulov proposed a covert operation to deal with this dangerous development:

> With the goal of unmasking the Baltic bishops who have entered into the service of the fascists, and also to strengthen in the eyes of international opinion the influence of the patriotic pronouncements issued by the church center in the USSR, metropolitan Sergii Stragorodskii and those near him, the council of bishops consisting of 14 people, will issue a special pronouncement to believers of the Baltic SSRs with special church details condemning the Baltic bishops.
>
> Covertly assisting this enterprise, which is politically useful for our country, the NKVD USSR will take measures for the reproduction of these patriotic documents by typographical means and the distribution of them on the territory of the Baltic allied republics, temporarily occupied by the Germans.[103]

Interestingly, Kobulov mentioned "international opinion" before that of domestic believers. When it came to religious matters, Soviet authorities kept foreign policy considerations constantly in the foreground.

With Kobulov's proposal accepted by the highest authorities, the Muscovite Sergii duly issued a blistering attack on his rebellious younger subordinate, the Baltic Sergii. The acting patriarch reminded the errant bishops that the Moscow Patriarchate retained legal jurisdiction over Orthodox churches in the Baltic region. Insubordination would not be countenanced: "The Ecclesiastical Court will not tolerate in the fold of the Orthodox Episcopacy those who persist in blaspheming the Church and in disregarding her voice." The metropolitan called on the younger Sergii either to confirm or deny his convening of the reported episcopal congress. If reports reaching Moscow had been correct, however, the Baltic bishops must apologize for their rebellion "so that the forthcoming Ecclesiastical Court, in finally judging the case, may have before it not only the commission of the offense, but also its rectification."[104]

In a second message, the metropolitan denounced trafficking with the Nazi enemy. "One's hair stands on end when reading about the torture by the fascists of women, children and old people," he wrote, denouncing the Baltic bishops' telegram of congratulations to Hitler. As in his earlier appeals, Sergii differentiated between opposition to the Soviet regime, manifested by many Orthodox émigrés (whose dissent he described interestingly enough as "understandable"), and collaboration with the invader of the motherland. The Nazis were the enemy not only of the Russian people but also of all Slavs: "[F]ascism is known to us as a natural and, so to speak, systematic enemy of the Russian bloodline and to that of Slavs in general; by its racial theory carried to the farthest physiological extreme, fascism is in principle hostile to Christianity, though for tactical purposes it might try to hide its hostility." As for the Baltic clergy, Sergii thundered, by its complicity with the Nazis they shared guilt for German crimes: "In order to shield themselves from such a conclusion, the Baltic hierarchs (or those who directed their hands) are trying to throw a shadow on me, as though I am compelled by Soviet power to write my statements against the fascists and summon the people to struggle against them."[105] Sergii might not have been "compelled" to issue his appeals, but he was certainly doing so at the Kremlin's behest, as Kobulov's note proves.

The rebellious Sergii (Voskresenskii) would come to a mysterious end. On April 28, 1944, he fell into an ambush while driving through the German-occupied Baltic countryside. No group ever owned up to the assassination, and the culprits remain unknown. The Germans authorized a lavish funeral for the murdered cleric, but they may have arranged his killing. Despite his break with Moscow, Sergii was no friend of the occupiers. As one who knew him would later remark: "Sergius was a determined Russian patriot. In his sermons he never mentioned the Germans, but implicitly his sermons did have a political character.... Evidently there was a denunciation of him by somebody, perhaps through a special Einsatzkommando."[106]

Historians have generally attributed the murder to the Germans, but it is equally plausible that a Soviet death squad was responsible. Only twenty-three days before his murder, Sergii had issued the so-called Riga Declaration, stating that the return of the Red Army to the three Baltic States would spell the extinction of these peoples' independent cultures. Gestapo hierarch Ernst Kaltenbrunner deemed Sergii's declaration "adequate and propagandistically serviceable."[107] As Kobulov's observations make clear, Moscow regarded Sergii as a dangerous enemy—an assessment that could only have been reinforced by the Riga Declaration—and Soviet hit teams were certainly operating behind German lines.[108] Sergii's true orientation remains a mystery: if he was a collaborator with the Nazis, or simply an opportunist, then his fate illustrated the perils of such a course. If he was a patriot hoping to forge a non-Soviet Russia between the fires of Nazism and Communism, as his defenders claimed then and now, then his assassination proved the tragic futility of such a dream in the midst of the Nazi-Soviet inferno.

In addition to issuing propaganda appeals to Soviet Christians behind German lines, and condemning collaborators real or imagined, Orthodox hierarchs also appealed to Soviet subjects in German-occupied territory to assist Soviet partisans in every way possible. On the first anniversary of Barbarossa, Sergii addressed those behind German lines: "Perhaps not everyone can enter the partisans' ranks and share their bitterness, danger, and deeds, but all can and should consider the cause of the partisans their own personal cause."[109] Six months later the metropolitan returned to this theme: "God will help those who do everything within their powers for the nation's cause with whatever is at hand. Do not let the enemy feel himself to be the master of your territory, to live there fat and secure. . . . The day is already not far, when you will joyfully meet your brothers and liberators."[110]

From the first days of the war, the Russian Church also raised relief funds. Metropolitan Aleksii of Leningrad reported that only four days after the German attack, donations from the laity were already pouring in.[111] The most visible result of such fund raising was the creation of a Red Army tank unit that would be dubbed "Dmitrii Donskoi" after the Muscovite prince and subsequent Orthodox saint who led the Russians to victory over their Mongol overlords in 1380.[112] Later, the church funded an aerial squadron called "Aleksandr Nevskii." The choice of names directly linked the cause of church and state and identified the current war with the most emotive events in Russian history. The raising of charitable funds was also a sharp break with past practice, because religious charity had been forbidden by Soviet law since early 1918.[113] By the first anniversary of the Nazi invasion, the Russian church had raised a further sum of "more than three million rubles" from believers for the supply of winter clothing for the Red Army.[114] By war's end, the church had raised a total of 150 million rubles.[115]

While raising funds at home, the church was also instrumental in motivating and publicizing donations from sympathetic Christians abroad. In June 1942 Sergii declared, "In the struggle with the fascists we are not alone." He noted that "Fifteen thousand religious societies of the USA arranged" for special days of prayer" and had promised to raise funds for the Soviet cause. Interestingly, although the Soviet authorities were reluctant to publicize Lend-Lease assistance from the Allied governments, they were more than willing to broadcast the comparatively much smaller help received from Western Christians. Whereas the former was politically problematic because it came from capitalist governments, the latter was from the common people—always assumed to be on the side of the USSR. Furthermore, the support of foreign Christians reinforced Moscow's efforts to erase the memory of their own repression of religion and suggested that even Western believers understood that the Soviet struggle was divinely sanctioned. As Sergii announced: "The best people in the free countries stand behind us and are ready to share with us the struggle of our people."[116]

As the war continued, Russian Orthodox Church leaders amplified their religious rhetoric, denouncing Nazi crimes against the Russian people, believers in particular. Most jarring, they began to claim that the war in defense of the Communist state was a "holy war." In November 1941, for instance, Sergii issued a declaration, signed by the other bishops of the church, identifying Hitler as nothing less than the servant of Satan: "The Hitlerite Moloch continues to prophesy to the world as though he has lifted the sword for the 'defense of religion' and the 'salvation' of an ostensibly desecrated faith," Sergii stated. In fact, however, Nazism sought to "establish its satanic power over the entire earth." With the invasion of the USSR, "It is clear to the whole world that the fascist monsters are the satanic enemies of faith and Christianity. . . . That is why progressive humanity has declared against Hitler a holy struggle for Christian civilization, for freedom of conscience and faith." When speaking of the Nazis, the metropolitan sounded more like an acolyte of the god of war than the Prince of Peace: "The Christian's heart is closed to the fascist beasts; it imparts only a destructive mortal hatred to the enemy."[117]

On the first anniversary of the war's outbreak, Sergii reminded believers that Hitler had justified his invasion by claiming to lead a "crusade" against the Soviet system. Instead, the fascist invaders had brought Russia only death and destruction. Who, Sergii asked, had destroyed "many tens of our Orthodox churches in Moscow, Orlov, Kursk, Kalinin and many other oblast's? Who turned the temples of God into stables[118] and torture chambers for the torment of Orthodox people? Who has killed pastors, church elders, regents, and other church people in Tula, Kalinin, and other oblast's?" Uncomfortably, of course, the answer to Sergii's rhetorical questions might well have been the Soviets themselves. But the metropolitan did not leave his listeners to draw their own unguided conclusions. The culprit, he declared, was the "Antichrist-like [*antikhristopodobnyi*] Hitler."[119]

On the war's first Easter, the most sacred holiday of Eastern Orthodoxy, Sergii's rhetoric soared to extraordinary new heights. "Not the swastika, but the cross has been called to head our Christian culture, our 'Christian home' [*khristianskoe zhitel'stvo*]," he said. Listeners unaware of conditions in the USSR might have been forgiven for believing that Sergii lived in a theocracy, where the cross, not the Red Star, was the regime's symbol. The metropolitan spoke as though atheism was an invention of the satanic Nazis: "In Germany it is claimed that Christianity has failed and that it is unsuited for the future of world progress. So, Germany, predestined to lead the world of the future, should forget Christ and follow its own, new path." These thoughts, Sergii concluded, should "open the eyes of all those who do not wish to see in Hitler the enemy of Christ."[120] The implication was clear, even if it was not the one Sergii wanted his audience to derive from his remarks: some Russians' eyes still were not opened, and many were falling prey to Nazi blandishments.

Seven years before Barbarossa, Emelian Iaroslavskii, the head of the League of Militant Godless, had mocked churches' willingness to prostitute themselves during the First World War for reasons of state: "During the war the priests conveniently forgot the command: 'Thou shalt not kill.'"[121] Now the Soviet state was doing the same thing, though even more shamelessly. The strident talk of "holy war," Sergii's call for merciless vengeance, the cynical manipulation of the clergy, and the crass attempt to paint Nazi Germany as the birthplace and home of modern militant atheism and the USSR as the defender of Christ—combined to make even tsarist practice look restrained in comparison. The appeals were all the more strident precisely because the Soviet authors who drafted and approved Sergii's statements were not themselves religious and so did not believe what they were writing.

Whether this sort of crude propaganda had the desired effect is hard to tell, given the paucity of reliable sources. We do know certain things, however: when the Germans chose to play the religious card, they were initially rewarded with significant results. As the true nature of Nazism became apparent—more so in Slavic lands than in the Baltics—any appeal that German rule might once have held out as an alternative to Stalinism rapidly dissipated. It is also clear that the gradual restoration of the Russian Orthodox Church to public life would contribute greatly to the general revival of religion that began at the outset of the war, and that many average Russians were grateful for the change. Many Soviet subjects credited Allied pressure with forcing the Kremlin to change its ways, which prevented Moscow from reaping full reward for the relaxation of state strictures on religion.[122] Nonetheless, the relative flexibility of Moscow, especially when contrasted with the contradictory and episodic German attempts to exploit religious belief, paid important political dividends to the Soviets.

Several key features stand out about Soviet religious propaganda from June 1941 through the end of 1942. As with Metropolitan Sergii's declaration on the day of the German attack, those appeals issued by Orthodox clerics during the first year and a half of the war that were not directed specifically overseas were designed either to be broadcast to or distributed in regions threatened by the Germans, or those areas already occupied. These were not broad appeals issued to the Soviet or Russian populace as a whole. Through the end of 1942, Soviet authorities still sought to use the Russian Orthodox Church in a restricted fashion to reinforce the Russian (or Orthodox) elements in the western regions, rather than to appeal to Russian patriotism throughout the USSR. Religious activity in the Red Army, for instance, still remained prohibited. Furthermore, Moscow sought to employ the church to deal with specifically religious questions, such as dealing with the defection of clerics, countering the hostility of believers toward the Soviet regime, or mobilizing those members of the laity who even before the war had been willing to brave regime disapproval by attending church under the dangerous conditions of high Stalinism. Even in the case of charitable donations, Soviet authorities did not allow publicity for church-sponsored fund-raising drives; instead, the church collected money from already extant congregations, not via public campaigns.

These facts paint a very different image of religious conditions in the USSR than the widely held notion that the Soviet government eased up on the church immediately following the German attack. As 1942 ended, the general revival of Russian nationalism, in which the slowly increasing prominence accorded to the Orthodox Church played its part, helped to keep Russians' hearts engaged in what was a long, wearying, and ever more horrific war.

A Limited Revival

Despite the activity outlined thus far, during the first two years of war the Russian Orthodox Church's role remained distinctly limited. Most important, the outbreak of war did not lead to a sharp improvement in the condition of churches, or to a relaxation of everyday restrictions on congregations in areas not directly threatened by the Germans.

In the months following the outbreak of war, Soviet authorities worried about a perceived rise in religious and superstitious sentiments, which they regarded as much the same things. G. Aleksandrov, the director of propaganda and agitation for the Central Committee, lamented the poor quality of local propaganda, saying that activists were badly trained and inferior in education. The war had created a large new demand for propagandists while at the same time the most able people were being drawn away by the needs of the front. This left a vacuum, especially outside the major cities: "As a rule," he wrote, "conversations, lectures, and speeches are not conducted in the countryside."

There was also a shortage of radio sets that could receive broadcasts from the center. As a result, in his view people were being led astray from the Communist Party line by all sorts of hucksters.[123] According to Aleksandrov, the Central Committee had its work cut out for it in combating the rise of heretical superstitions, religion included.

The strange new situation of the Russian Orthodox Church was closely watched in the United States and Britain, where state propagandists were hungry for portents that their Communist ally had changed its antireligious ways. Diplomats stationed in Moscow poured cold water on such hopes. In late July 1941, responding to a request from the British Ministry of Information to provide any available evidence of improvement in religious conditions in the USSR, the British ambassador to Moscow, Sir Stafford Cripps, who was himself both an ardent Christian and a socialist, wrote: "[T]here are no real signs of 'popular religious revival'" in Moscow. "Perhaps the few churches which are still in use . . . are slightly fuller," he continued, "but as they were always crowded this may merely mean that . . . [people who are already believers have] become more actively devout under [the] stress of wartime conditions."[124]

So delicate did Cripps believe the position of the Russian church to be that he refused to transmit a simple message of greetings and goodwill from the archbishop of Canterbury addressed to the metropolitan of Moscow. "It will not contribute anything to [the] Soviet's war effort," he wrote, "which . . . Russian clergy are supporting from necessity and choice; and it might embarrass both [the] Soviet authorities and the Metropolitan himself. [The] Latter's position is at best a very delicate one and it would do him no good to receive such a message through foreign *official* channels."[125] The archbishop of Canterbury abandoned for the time any attempt to send official greetings to Russian churchmen.[126]

Following another hopeful appeal from London on September 30 to supply any positive Soviet religious information, Cripps allowed that the Soviets had closed *Bezbozhnik*, which he called "a remarkably tedious little wrag [*sic*]," but this did not necessarily denote a significant change in course for the Kremlin. "In our opinion it is not an important sign," he wrote. "For a number of years now direct anti-religious *agitation* has been decreasing, though it still continues in numerous indirect forms and is of course implicit in the whole teaching of the Soviet schools." "The Soviet authorities have other and more direct methods of discouraging religion," he continued: "Churches continue to be closed on one pretext or another—we know of two recent cases in Moscow; and the priesthood of a religion which sets great store by outward forms and observances has long since been reduced to a state of cowering misery." Despite London's wish to discover some encouraging sign of greater religious tolerance in Moscow, the simple facts contradicted such hopes. Cripps ended his remarks with a tart comment: "'Evidence' could of course be manufactured quite easily. . . . So far, however, we have only been asked for facts."[127]

The incidents of church closings taking place *after* the German attack—and in Moscow, the Russian city most accessible to foreigners—strongly suggest that the Soviet authorities' newfound tolerance of religion had shallow roots. Such closings might have resulted from low-level bureaucratic inertia, rather than any overall state policy; on this question Soviet records are still unclear. At the very least, however, such actions suggest that no central directive had yet proscribed continued antireligious policies of this sort. In October 1942, more than a year after the German attack, Cripps, who had returned from Russia earlier in the year, still judged that the Soviet authorities had budged very little in their treatment of religion. He believed that signs of change in the Soviets' repressive religious policies were merely cosmetic: "With regard to the Soviet attitude he thought that the stopping of Buzboznik [*sic*] and the other events in the same line meant nothing except that they were intended to have a useful effect on foreign opinion, especially in America."[128]

The British Ministry of Information agreed with Cripps's negative assessment. In June 1942 the Reverend Herbert Waddams, an official in the ministry's religion section, wrote: "I do not feel that the situation regarding religion has changed very much since . . . 1.10.41." Although the British press was "as optimistic as possible about the general situation in Russia of religion," this owed more to wishful thinking and a desire to promote Allied unity than to any genuine understanding of the actual situation in Russia. Information from nearby Sweden and elsewhere suggested a less optimistic conclusion. A positive reading of religious events in Russia, wrote Waddams, "is not encouraged by the tales and sights which are reported from those parts of Karelia which have been captured by the Finns from the Russian armies. Nor do reports of events in Soviet occupied Estonia and Latvia before the German attack lead those who know to imagine that Soviet hostility towards religion has been modified. These latter facts do not often receive publicity in Great Britain." "Such facts," Waddams concluded, "do not help to dispel distrust in the minds of Christians, many of whom would otherwise be quite ready to be friendly to Russia."[129]

Although in his wartime reporting the BBC correspondent Alexander Werth did nothing to discourage overly optimistic accounts of a rebirth of Russian religious freedom, in his postwar memoirs he pointed out that no serious relaxation of religious controls followed the German invasion. As late as 1942 the limited number of Russian churches still open were, according to him, "a dismal and depressing sight," badly in need of repair. There were shortages of incense and candles, and the "whole [religious] scene" struck Werth as "drab and miserable."[130] He contrasted the sad state of Russian churches with their dramatic improvement during and after the spring of 1943.

Soviet records support the assessment of these foreign observers that during the first two years of war religion in Russia still existed under very strict limits. As late as October 1942 press censors remained vigilant against even seemingly harmless hints of religious faith that might creep into national newspapers. In one instance, the Central Committee press section complained about folk sayings printed in a series of *Pravda* articles. The eagle-eyed censors claimed to find "double meanings" in many of the sayings, as well as "outright wrecking"; others were merely "stupid." Most disturbingly, sixty-seven were about God, with many others mentioning the devil (hardly surprising given the religiously saturated world of the Russian peasantry, where many of the sayings originated). An example of a saying with a religious double meaning: "It's easy to live without truth, but hard to die without it." Other sayings carried subversive messages implying a critique of Communist dogma and cooperative socialist effort: "When two people are doing the same thing, then it's not one and the same thing"; or, "Bread eaten before work makes one lazy."[131]

It might be tempting to dismiss this incident as just another instance of stereotypical government humorlessness; but this would ignore the Stalinist historical context. Many state officials had been, and would be, arrested or even shot for "crimes" that would be seen as trivial in other times and places. The censors who reviewed *Pravda* and other national newspapers worked at the highest levels of the Soviet government and were kept informed about the latest twists in the current party line. Clearly, in late 1942, even the most oblique references in the national media to religious themes remained sternly forbidden.

A notable exception to continuing repression was the open celebration of Easter in 1942, but the curious circumstances of this celebration suggest two things: that the Kremlin feared that public religious manifestations might become uncontrollable; and that this unusual laxity toward Easter owed as much to the Soviets' need to impress Allied opinion as to any desire to placate Soviet Christians.

A Soviet writer later recounted that "Suddenly, at 6 o'clock on the morning of Saturday April 5 [1942], the morning radio, unexpectedly for all, opened with the announcement of orders from the commandant of Moscow, permitting free movement in Moscow on the night of April 5." This announcement by state authorities came as a surprise even to Orthodox hierarchs, the metropolitan of Moscow having told his flock only the previous day that they would have to observe curfew regulations on Easter.[132] Russian believers were also apparently taken by surprise. A Soviet source cites one woman headed to church who exclaimed excitedly: "'May God bless Soviet power! You may walk about the town fearlessly, it says, do all that belong to Easter and nobody will interfere.'"[133] Soviet authorities also released extra rations of sugar and flour for the baking of traditional Orthodox Easter cakes.[134]

The Soviet government had not eased up on Easter celebrations purely to sway foreign public opinion, even if this was the principal motive. The provision of extra rations and the celebrations in the midst of wartime stringency must have come as a welcome change to long-suffering Soviet Christians, accustomed as they were to both petty and major limitations on their religious liberties. Nonetheless, the abrupt announcement regarding the lifting of the Easter curfew left little time for believers to organize large-scale celebrations; it also lessened the chances that spontaneous demonstrations might spread beyond police control. Furthermore, the way the Soviet authorities managed information about the celebrations suggests an eye for the foreign, rather than the domestic, audience. Britain's ambassador to the USSR, Sir Archibald Clark Kerr, who had replaced Cripps earlier in the year, reported that the Kremlin "took credit for the religious celebrations at Easter itself by including photographs of Easter services held in Moscow churches in their distribution of photographs for publication abroad—*not* for publication at home."[135] The domestic press remained silent about the Easter services. Unlike average Soviet believers, American and British diplomats, as well as members of the Allied military missions, received ample notice that traditional Russian Easter worship would take place, they were given conspicuous seats at Moscow's main cathedral in the Kremlin, and their presence at the ceremonies received prominent treatment in TASS releases for foreign readers. An Irishman present in Moscow noted that many Russians believed that the relaxation of strictures against open Easter celebrations had been arranged by the Kremlin "to please England and America."[136] Whether true or not, it is telling that many Russians also believed this to be the case.[137]

The relatively open Easter celebrations of 1942 were the largest public indication yet that the war had begun to wrench significant changes in the Soviet attitude toward the church. But the curious circumstances surrounding the affair suggest that the Kremlin still had grave reservations about proceeding too fast. Moscow was not, however, the master of events; once again, as in 1939, during the critical year of 1943 domestic and international security considerations would compel Moscow to chart a course on which it was clearly hesitant to embark.

Rival Totalitarians

The history of religion and nationalism during the early stages of the Soviet-German war demonstrates convincingly that Nazi and Soviet ideologies, far from being mere rhetorical devices constructed to justify and mask the exercise of realpolitik, were in fact important determinants in the conduct and outcome of the conflict. The elites of the totalitarian powers, perhaps even more than their subjects, were clearly trapped by their own ideological conceptions of the world—their options, and even perceptions, being limited by the narrow bounds of their own beliefs.

On several levels, there was a great deal of congruity between the methods of the Communists and Nazis. Both were almost unimaginably brutal, willing to consign millions of people to arrest, misery, forced labor, and death to further the purposes of the party-state. Both regimes dealt with enemies by dehumanizing them and cramming them into preconceived, intellectually constructed social categories that bore little relation to complex reality: the Nazis by a twisted racial calculus that defined some peoples as masters and others as vermin, the Soviets according to an inhuman class analysis that contrasted sturdy proletarians with bourgeois "insects." Both regimes arrested and murdered millions of innocent people for no crime other than belonging to a proscribed group. Finally, the Soviets and the Nazis were hostile to religious faith for similar reasons: idealist morality represented an intolerable ideological challenge to the reigning creeds of party supremacy; and the existence of working churches, the nuclei of civil society, posed a political obstacle to party-states that aspired to dominate their subject populations completely.

If there were striking similarities between the totalitarian states, there were differences as well, and these tended in the end to militate in the Soviets' favor, contributing significantly to the eventual Soviet victory. The disparities between Hitlerite and Stalinist ideologies in action are well illustrated in their approaches to the religious-national question. If both regimes shared an animus against religion, following the German invasion Moscow proved far more flexible than Berlin on the religious battleground. There are many reasons for this. In part, the very desperation of the Soviet military situation during the opening stages of Barbarossa, the near terminal shock delivered straight to the Communist central nervous system, compelled the Kremlin to make greater concessions to domestic social and class enemies than it would have done had circumstances been less dire. As town after Soviet town fell to the invader, as millions of Red Army soldiers surrendered to the Nazis, and as droves of Soviet citizens seemed initially to accept German conquest with equanimity or even some enthusiasm, the Soviet regime either had to adapt or face destruction.

In mid-1941, by contrast, the Nazis were on a roll. With much of Europe at his feet, Hitler had lost the knack he had demonstrated so convincingly during his rise to power of being able to capitalize instinctively on the divisions among his opponents—even those he considered racially inferior. Many of his followers, especially in the Wehrmacht, wanted desperately to harness the religious and national discontents of Soviet subjects in order to destroy the USSR. Within the Nazi Party, the minister for the occupied eastern territories, Alfred Rosenberg, was the most ardent advocate of this line, but in a face-to-face confrontation with him in June 1943 the Führer decisively rejected any notion of holding out the prospect of freedom for eastern Slavs.[138] Hitler was no ordinary politician; he was an ideologue par excellence. To much of the Wehrmacht, as for Rosenberg, the object of the war seemed as obvious as it was logical: the defeat of the Red Army and the destruction of the Soviet regime. For Hitler, however, the war was never an end in itself but only a means to a larger, ideologically conceived goal: the extermination or subjugation of the indigenous inhabitants and the establishment of German *Lebensraum* in the East. His categorization of Eastern Slavs as *Untermenschen*, as nothing more than beasts of burden in this nightmarish future German imperium, prevented Hitler, and most Nazi leaders, from realizing the potentialities that lay all about them in the East for the exploitation of national and religious fissures. Had Nazi ideology been nothing more than an invented "discourse," constructed to screen the self-aggrandizing interests of power elites, or had Hitler been nothing other than an opportunist and practitioner of traditional German diplomacy, then he would surely have used these tools to unhinge Stalin's empire from within.[139]

Unlike Nazism, Leninism did not entirely blind its adherents to the dynamic possibilities present in religious and national questions. Although the Kremlin regarded nationalist elites, and the leadership of churches, to be class enemies slated for eventual destruction, in contrast to the Nazis this contempt did not extend to the common people, at least not in formal ideological terms. Whereas Nazism regarded entire races—upper classes and common folk alike— to be beneath consideration, in the Leninist view workers and peasants were not deemed to be beyond reach by their very nature. Lenin had insisted that "There are two nations in every modern nation," one the product of "bourgeois" culture, the other "democratic and socialist."[140] When the masses acted against Moscow's interests, as they often did, the Kremlin reflexively explained this as resulting from machinations of class enemies—the kulaks, bourgeois, or priests. In other words, Communist leaders made an important distinction that the Nazis did not: they differentiated between non-Communist elites and the mass of ordinary people, understanding that winning over the latter was the most important political objective in wartime. Soviet class analysis was a blunt instrument, but it was a veritable scalpel when contrasted with Nazi racism.

Before the German invasion, the Soviets' ideological division of the population into bourgeois elites and working masses had confused and distorted policy. The NKVD-NKGB's mass deportations of proscribed classes from the western borderlands, far from crushing anti-Soviet nationalist resistance, had instead resulted in its perpetuation. If ideology could confuse, however, it could also sometimes sharpen political vision. Lenin had always stressed the importance of focusing on the destruction of one opponent at a time. Before the German invasion, the target had been possible "fifth columnists." Once the war began, Moscow was in no doubt as to its primary enemy; it accordingly reoriented its propaganda and began to pose as the champion of religious liberty, Slavic unity, and even national self-determination.

The history of Leninism is replete with such abrupt policy reversals, where yesterday's enemy becomes today's friend and ally. Bolsheviks would collaborate with any political or social force—no matter how antithetical to Communism —if it was of use in defeating the primary enemy of the moment. In precisely this way Moscow denounced West European social democrats as "social fascists" in the 1920s, turned to them as fellow "progressives" when they hoped to forge anti-Nazi popular fronts after the rise of Hitler, and denounced them once again following Moscow's 1939 pact with Germany, only to call again for popular fronts after June 1941. Likewise with religion: before 1939 Soviet Communists denounced the church as one of their worst foes, the hireling of class enemies and foreign intelligence agencies; during the occupation of the western borderlands, they rediscovered a use for Russian Orthodox hierarchs and so tempered their atheistic rhetoric. Following Barbarossa, Moscow sought to portray its war effort as "a holy struggle for Christian civilization, for freedom of conscience and faith" and the Nazis as "the satanic enemies of faith and Christianity."[141]

As would become clear soon enough, Soviet Communists had by no means abandoned their fundamental ideological hostility to religion, and many religious leaders found the Soviets' change of heart simply too swift and expedient to believe. But clergy and church hierarchs were not Moscow's target audience; the laity was. Without the loyalty, or at least political obedience, of the great mass of people, Moscow could not hope to defeat the Germans. Force and terror were important tools, to be sure, and Moscow continued to use them profusely. But at least the Soviets understood that, without some appeal to the non-Communist beliefs and loyalties of the common people, a great many Red Army recruits would not fight. Soviet religious propaganda worked because so many people wanted to believe that time and the war would change the nature of Soviet power, that the alliance with the Western powers would erode the hard edges of Communism, and that the new Soviet line was a reversion to Russian tradition rather than simply another tactical shift in the party line.

None of this is to claim either that the Soviet system was somehow more "moral" than the Nazis, or that Communist leaders valued the inherent worth of human beings more highly than did the Hitlerites. The attempt to discover a "humanist" or Enlightenment core at the heart of Soviet Communism that somehow set it apart from Nazism is a project increasingly doomed to failure, undermined by each new archival revelation from the Soviet era. The Kremlin leaders condemned millions of their own people to exile and death, apparently without suffering any pangs of regret whatsoever. As the wartime Soviet use of the Russian Orthodox Church demonstrated, Moscow sought to propitiate public opinion, not by genuinely meeting popular needs but rather through the manipulation of symbols and institutions. The Kremlin did not view its subjects as individuals, each of whom possessed an inherent worth, whose material and spiritual needs must be met or respected by government, but rather as so many passive, easily led, and largely interchangeable beings. The point was to herd them in the right direction.

In the end, victory in war is determined not by which combatant ideally harnesses the available human and material resources but by which side does so better. The Stalinist record was cruel beyond description, but Moscow was fortunate in its enemies. In *Life and Fate*, Vasilii Grossman captured this idea succinctly when he had his character, the political commissar Getmanov, remark: "We're in luck. The Fritzes have done more to put the peasants' backs up in one year than we communists have done in twenty-five."[142] One can point to any number of reasons for the Nazi defeat in the USSR: inadequate planning, too few mechanized and armored units, insufficient German manpower, the wretched conditions of communications in the East, the endless spaces of Russia, Hitler's military misjudgments. These are all considerations with which German military memoirists were most comfortable, because they cast the war in technical-strategic terms, rather than focusing on the inhumanity of the entire Barbarossa concept. The most fundamental failure of the Nazis in the East, however, was not military or logistical but moral and political—their refusal to offer the local population any reason to support the war against Stalin, or even to remain neutral. Ultimately, the Nazis' problem was not that they made this or that misjudgment but that they were Nazis.

The viciousness of the invader did not mean that the Soviets could afford complacency. In the first two years of war, the Kremlin discovered that ethnic Russians were more reliable fighters than most other Soviet nationalities. The Communist authorities adjusted their propaganda and policies accordingly. A great many Red Army men fought for Stalin and Communism, to be sure, as current-day testimonies confirm; even more went into battle, though, not for their *vozhd'* but for Russia, or at least against Hitler. The Soviet state managed to mobilize this vital Russian patriotism by employing national symbols and history as well as manipulating the most important remaining Russian national institution, the Orthodox Church. The political manipulation of identities, institutions, and symbols cuts several ways, however; at the same time that the Soviets channeled Russian national feeling into the war effort, they also released unpredictable agents into the political bloodstream.

As events would soon show, the Kremlin did not always anticipate the political and social side effects of its policies. One such result was the transformation of the Soviet oligarchs' own view of themselves. As the tide turned in the war, they began to see themselves not only as revolutionaries but also as leaders in the Russian Messianic tradition. As Molotov would later remark: "Stalin had mastered the national question. He was correct in calling the Russian people the decisive force that broke the back of fascism. Like no one else, Stalin understood the great historical destiny and fateful mission of the Russian people—the fate about which Dostoevsky wrote: the heart of Russia, more than that of any other nation, is predestined to be the universal, all-embracing humanitarian union of nations.[143] Dostoevskii had indeed written that "the Russian ideal is universal wholeness, universal reconciliation, and universal humanity."[144] But the great author's vision had been explicitly Christian and Slavophile; he believed that Russia was a "God-bearing" nation, destined to carry true Christianity to the rest of the world, including the Catholic West. In his later years, he had become a bitter opponent of socialism, which he saw as a demonic force and the direct offspring of papal heresy.

During the war, Stalinist Communism assumed Dostoevskii's Messianism and national chauvinism—even his animus against the Vatican—but it drained his vision of any genuinely spiritual element. The new Stalinist mythology groaned under the weight of its contradictions: a nationalist internationalism, an atheist Messianism, a determinist voluntarism, a society of self-proclaimed abundance and science teetering on an impoverished base, and a state supposedly leading the world to a new era of freedom even as millions languished in concentration camps in wartime.[145] In order to defeat the Nazis, the Soviet state had been forced to twist itself inside out, and—in an ironic dialectic—the victorious Marxist state aggravated the very "internal contradictions" that would help to doom it in the long run.

PART 3

Fighting the Holy War

It must be noted that Stalin was not a member of the "League of Militant Atheists." He was, of course, first and foremost a revolutionary, and he continued Lenin's Line. . . . True, we sometimes sang church songs, after dinner. Sometimes even White Guard songs. Stalin had a pleasing voice.
—V. M. Molotov, quoted in Felix Chuev, *Molotov Remembers*

Some predator and human monster may very sincerely, in true veneration, worship sainthood, place candles in front of saints' icons, embark on pilgrimages to monasteries—remaining at the same time a predator and a monster.
—Nikolai Berdiaev, 1918

A Holy Hatred toward the Enemy

The Church as Servant of Soviet Foreign Policy, 1942–1943

Although the position of the Russian Orthodox Church improved spasmodically during the first two years of the war, as 1942 came to a close it still existed very much in the political and social shadows. Worship services were limited to the few remaining open churches, mostly concentrated in the large metropolitan areas; whole regions in the hinterland lacked any facilities for religious services whatsoever.[1] The Soviet press mentioned religious matters only in foreign-language publications or in radio broadcasts and Informbiuro releases targeted at audiences abroad.[2] Under the stresses of war, with violent death an ever present reality and the demand for spiritual solace clearly growing, Soviet authorities did not even allow open religious activity among the millions of Red Army soldiers. Ironically, although Soviet radio would begin to appeal to Romanians and other Balkan Christians as "fellow

Orthodox," the largest branch of Eastern Orthodoxy—the Russian church itself—remained tightly circumscribed by the Communist authorities.[3]

The winter of 1942–43 would witness sharp changes in the fortunes of Russian Orthodoxy. The reappearance of the church as a public institution, and the apparent partial reconciliation of church and state that many contemporary observers, as well as subsequent historians, mistakenly date from the opening days of the war, was in fact a development of this crucial time. The church's recovery came in stages, with Orthodox leaders first playing a more prominent role in foreign affairs and only later reassuming a larger part in domestic affairs. The transformation of Soviet policy toward the Russian Orthodox Church grew directly out of the rapidly shifting military situation. By 1943 the long-awaited turning point in the military fortunes of the Allied coalition finally arrived, following the first decisive defeats of the Nazis in North Africa, in Sicily, but more importantly at Stalingrad, where the surrounded German Sixth Army finally surrendered to Soviet forces in February. This was followed in July by the Soviet triumph in the Battle of Kursk.[4]

Along with military opportunities, the turn of the tide in the East and the recovery of German-occupied territories revived dormant international and domestic disputes. Almost two years into the war, the disposition of the USSR's postwar western borders remained undecided, the resolution of this matter threatening to drive a wedge into the anti-Hitler coalition. At a minimum, the Soviets sought a restoration of their frontiers at the time of the German attack, returning to their control the three Baltic states, almost half of eastern Poland, Bukovina, and Bessarabia, as well as the portions of Finland it had seized following the 1939–40 war. The Kremlin's coalition partners had not yet recognized Soviet sovereignty over these western borderlands; nor were large segments of the local population reconciled to the return of the Red Army.[5]

In the two years following the invasion, Stalin had neither abandoned nor forgotten his claim to these disputed territories. During his meetings with British foreign minister Anthony Eden in December 1941, the dictator stated unequivocally that the recovery of these lost provinces and recognition of Soviet sovereignty by its allies were "absolutely axiomatic." Regaining these lost provinces, Stalin claimed with more than a bit of exaggeration, was "really what the whole war is about"; this was "the main question for us in the war."[6] In the spring of 1942, Moscow tried to convince both the Americans and British to recognize the Soviet claim to the western borderlands. Although both President Roosevelt and Prime Minister Churchill had assured Stalin that they were willing to recognize Soviet sovereignty over the Baltic states, they had balked at Moscow's claim to the formerly Polish territories.[7]

The Western Allies entertained slender hopes that Moscow might prove more flexible on the Polish border question than it was on the fate of Baltic states. In the summer of 1941 Stalin had patched up relations—superficially at least—with the London-based Polish government-in-exile, whose territory the Red Army had invaded and occupied almost two years before. The disastrous Soviet military situation immediately after the German invasion compelled Moscow to make apparent diplomatic concessions in a desperate quest for allies. The text of the Polish-Soviet Agreement of July 1941 stated that "The Government of the Union of Soviet Socialist Republics recognizes that the Soviet-German treaties relative to territorial changes in Poland have lost their validity."[8] Both London and Washington hoped that this wording indicated a willingness on the part of the Kremlin to disgorge at least a portion of the territories it had seized in eastern Poland in 1939. In 1942, however, when British and American diplomats tried to negotiate a compromise with the Kremlin on the border question, they had been rebuffed.[9]

With the Red Army victories in 1943, the question of the USSR's frontiers once again occupied center stage. The strategic situation had been entirely transformed since the desperate summer of 1941. No longer were Soviet forces reeling from the German onslaught; instead, the Red Army looked poised soon to reenter the western borderlands. Whether or not the Western Allies chose to recognize Soviet territorial claims, the Soviet advance threatened to present the world with a fait accompli. The London Poles, as well as other East European exile governments, bombarded the Americans and British with increasingly alarming warnings about Soviet intentions. Would the USSR export its social system, imposing Communism by force? Would Red Army soldiers carry Soviet antireligious policies in their knapsacks?

The situation was clearly fraught with danger for Soviet foreign policy. Although the Red Army had seized the initiative against the Wehrmacht, the war was still far from over. The rapid Soviet advance, if handled badly in the diplomatic arena, could alarm the Western Allies, perhaps compromising the war-winning coalition or imperiling the all-important Lend-Lease aid. In late spring 1943 the Soviet ambassador in Washington, Maksim Litvinov, told Moscow that, regarding the USSR's western neighbors, "[President] Roosevelt won't support their claims if he finds himself facing a fait accompli." Instead, "Considering American public opinion, Roosevelt will try to present his decisions in a manner that corresponds with the ideas of 'international justice' and the Atlantic Charter." In Litvinov's opinion, though, Roosevelt was vulnerable to changes in volatile popular opinion: "If we virtually settle the problem of our western borders ourselves, there will be no major counteraction on the part of the U.S. However, since we'll need U.S. assistance for that, American public opinion will be influential."[10] In other words, the USSR could achieve its territorial aims, but careful presentation was important to avoid alarming American opinion.

The Kremlin thus faced a formidable task: the reconciliation of its territorial, security, and political aims in Eastern Europe with the need to preserve the wartime coalition. Some of the methods Moscow adopted to deal with these dilemmas were remarkably traditional, at least on the surface. Just as the Kremlin had turned to the Russian Orthodox Church in 1939–41 when trying to pacify the western borderlands, it would do so again as the Red Army reentered the region. The revolutionary Soviet state, heir to Lenin's Communist internationalism, would use a number of familiar tsarist tools in its newly crafted East European policy. The spring of 1943 saw new life breathed into themes redolent of the nineteenth century: Russian nationalism, Pan-Slavism, and Orthodoxy. In 1943, these themes would gain new and greater prominence as Moscow tried to pose once again as the center of Pan-Slavism and Orthodoxy.

"The Truth about Religion in Russia"

As Litvinov's comments indicated, Soviet diplomats and government officials were aware of the need to preserve the anti-Hitler coalition, and they understood the necessity of persuading American and British opinion that Soviet power was benign and that the advance of Stalinist forces westward was unthreatening. Popular fears in the Western democracies about the expansion of "Godless Communism" had therefore to be allayed. From the autumn of 1942 through the end of the war, the Russian Orthodox Church played an important and growing role in this propaganda operation, but the church was not an entirely passive tool of Soviet authorities; in exchange for their services in the international arena, church hierarchs sought to carve out a niche in the atheist Communist society.

In 1942 the Soviets initiated what would ultimately turn out to be one of the more successful religious-propaganda initiatives to be directed at the Anglo-American audience. On the September 16 Metropolitan Nikolai, accompanied by an unnamed bishop, appeared unannounced at the door of the British Embassy in Kuibyshev, which had been evacuated to that city during the previous October when the Germans were at the gates of Moscow. Nikolai met with Lacy Baggallay, a British diplomat with many years of service in the Soviet Union. Baggallay was understandably astonished by the archbishop's unexpected approach, which he believed "must have been the first time for many years and perhaps since the revolution that a leader of the Russian Church has visited foreign missions openly and unescorted." It was not strictly true, however, that Nikolai was "unescorted"; it would be interesting to establish the identity of his silent bishop-companion.[11]

Nikolai told his host that he was en route to Ulianovsk, to which Sergii, the patriarch *locum tenens*, had been evacuated from the capital. As a gift, he handed Baggallay several copies of a Russian-language book entitled *Pravda o religii v Rossii* (The truth about religion in Russia), saying that he had already sent several boxes of the book to the archbishop of Canterbury. In fact, he had sent ten cases, containing 700 copies.[12] After a polite discussion about the English church and the war, Baggallay later recorded, Nikolai raised "what was evidently the real object of his visit to this Embassy and perhaps to Kuibyshev." Nikolai proposed to make an official visit to Britain in order to meet with the heads of the Anglican Church: "There was a long record of friendly relations" between the Russian Orthodox and Anglican Churches, the metropolitan said, and these "should be maintained and strengthened. In particular it was desirable that each should know what the other was doing in these difficult times." Nikolai said that the Soviet government supported such an ecclesiastical exchange and "would give all facilities" to make this possible. "He said nothing to suggest that the exchange of missions would be directly concerned with the question of the union of the Churches, or with anything other than the promotion of goodwill and closer relations generally," Baggallay wrote. The British also learned that, earlier on the same day, Nikolai had visited the American and Chinese ambassadors, where he received a cool reception, and was turned away by the Japanese, who regarded him as "either an impostor or an *agent-provocateur*."

Baggallay met again with Nikolai on September 18 at "a small luncheon" held at the British Embassy. Nikolai appeared to be "anxious" to gain agreement to his proposed visit to London; he suggested that the Anglicans send a delegation to the USSR, although he was prepared to go to London even if the Anglicans felt unready to visit the Soviet Union. "In fact," wrote Baggallay, "one or two of the staff thought they detected a desire that the Russian mission should in any case precede the English one."

The British asked the metropolitan what kind of contacts the Orthodox Church maintained with other Christian churches in the USSR, but this question "met with little response." Nikolai claimed that all Russian Christians supported the war against Germany, but as for non-Orthodox Christians, "He practically stated that the Russian Church was not interested in other denominations and stated clearly that it saw no point in trying to build bridges at the present time. The Church of England was the only exception." He might have added that there were no foreign policy benefits to be gained from better relations with other domestic Christian churches.

Nikolai stressed that, when it came to Christians in the USSR, "all alike were steadfast" in their support of the war. This was true of Orthodox Christians in other countries as well, "with one exception." "This exception was the Roumanian Church. Even the Bulgarian Church was on the right side and its leaders had already suffered for their attitude." In describing the loyalties of Orthodox in German-held territory, Nikolai admitted the betrayal of only one cleric, "[t]he notorious Bishop Polycarp (Sikorski)," who had "broken with the mother-Church and been canonically deprived of his rank for treason." Nikolai claimed that "He knew of no Russian priest who had not been true to his Church and his country." Bagallay concluded that "Although he did not exactly say so, I think His Eminence was drawing a distinction between the clergy in the original territory of the Soviet Union and those in the provinces taken from the Union's western neighbors."[13] In fact, of course, defections of clergy had been a much greater problem than Nikolai allowed.

Trying to make sense of Nikolai's visits, Baggallay wrote that the only time Nikolai's "answers . . . were lacking in frankness . . . was when it was difficult to answer without seeming to criticise, however indirectly, the past or present policy of the Soviet Government. (The nearest approach to a criticism seems to have been when he told the American Ambassador that 'The Truth about Religion in Russia' described the position of the 'remnants' of the Russian Church.)" Baggallay was convinced that Nikolai could not have made his visit without "the express permission of the Soviet government and perhaps at their express wish." "The mere fact that he and the bishop stayed at the Grand Hotel is proof of this," Bagallay wrote, "for so far as Soviet citizens are concerned this is closed by the N.K.V.D. to all but a narrow circle . . . who are trusted to be under the same roof as foreigners without being led into dangerous paths." He added that the hotel's staff apparently agreed, because "they could not conceive that anyone should be a real priest and least of all that he should stay at their hotel." Furthermore, Nikolai "only put his clerical robes on [once he was] inside the Embassy."[14]

Nikolai's biographer raises the possibility that the metropolitan was working for the NKVD, although he draws no firm conclusion. At any rate, if Nikolai was indeed cooperating with, or working for, the NKVD, his access to the Grand Hotel can be easily explained.[15] Quite apart from the question of Nikolai's political masters, the metropolitan's quick change into church garb only after leaving the streets of Kuibyshev and entering the British Embassy was also rather telling; in the autumn of 1942 freedom of religion in the USSR was still something of a show for foreigners.

The book that Nikolai gave the British was a significant production given the strictures of wartime publishing, the Soviet paper shortage, and the generally low standards of Soviet book design. Bound on unusually high-quality, relatively low-acid paper, the book has an attractive layout with colorful and decorative print. In short, it was unusual both for its quality and for the fact that it was a religious tract published in the USSR. The book was printed on the presses of Iskra revoliutsiei, which for years had printed propaganda for the League of Militant Godless.[16] It was most probably the first religious publication the Soviet authorities had approved since the revolution.[17]

According to figures printed in the book itself, it had a relatively large run of 50,000 copies, although the British later learned that the real number may have been closer to 10,000.[18] The contents as well as the circumstances of its publication and distribution indicate that it was designed primarily, though perhaps not exclusively, for the foreign audience. A couple of weeks after his meeting with Nikolai, Baggallay noted that the book "has not, so far as we know, been mentioned in any vernacular newspaper," although the English-language edition of *Moscow News* printed a glowing review. Furthermore, potential Soviet purchasers could not simply drop in at the local bookstore and buy or order a copy; instead, as Baggallay wrote, "it is by no means a simple matter to buy a copy of it even through a Church. It is not an impossible matter either, but it is necessary, if the experience of one of our staff who went to the local church is any guide, to make a written application saying exactly who one is."[19] The average Soviet citizen, mindful of the hazards of open religious activity, might have been forgiven for thinking twice before making such an application for purchase. Also, the listed price for a copy was expensive, though perhaps affordable, at almost 30 rubles.[20] As with the number of copies supposedly printed, however, things were not what they seemed on the surface: the list price differed from the actual price, which was found to be 110 rubles. On learning of this particular instance of deception, one Foreign Office figure observed: "This is very amusing[,] and the prohibitive price of 110 rubles is a further guarantee that the book will not receive a wide circulation in the U.S.S.R."[21]

Acting patriarch Sergii wrote an introduction for the volume, but Metropolitan Nikolai was in charge of the production, and most observers of the Russian religious scene regarded him as the true power behind the throne. Sergii wrote that "This book is an answer above all else to the Fascists' claim of a 'holy crusade.'" "At the same time," he continued, "the book answers the general question: does our Church regard itself as persecuted by the Bolsheviks and does it ask anybody to free it from such persecution?" Of course, the answer to these rhetorical questions was negative. Only "certain well-known people who have mercenary and selfish interests at heart" could claim that Orthodox support for the Soviet war effort was the product of coercion, or that the Soviets persecuted religion at all. Sergii acknowledged that "excesses" had indeed occurred during the early years of the revolution, but such things were "inevitable during all mass uprisings." Claims by émigrés of systematic Communist repression were transparent fabrications; such people, whom Sergii labeled "church bourgeois," were only troubled by the Soviet confiscation of church lands. But "the simple Orthodox people" who remained in Russia "are inclined to see in the present change not persecution but a return to the time of the Apostles, when . . . [clergy] regarded their service as a vocation, not one of the worldly professions and a means of livelihood."

This claim would be taken up and repeated by many Soviet apologists during the war: critics of the Soviet record on religion would be accused of being concerned only with the church's loss of property and, in the case of émigrés, with their own personal fortunes. The Soviet government had actually done a favor to Soviet believers, this argument ran, by seizing the Orthodox Church's worldly possessions, thereby freeing it to return to a purer, nobler path, its true mission.[22] There is, however, another reading one can make of Sergii's analogy. If the Stalin era was indeed akin to "the time of the Apostles," the latter had been a period of the severest repression by the Roman state. Whether Sergii was in fact writing in "Aesopian" language, as later Soviet dissidents would, is difficult to guess, though it is not entirely unthinkable.

In Sergii's telling, the Bolsheviks had conferred another favor on the church: "During and after the revolution," he admitted, "the Church suffered great losses"; but this was only because "all artificial barriers that forced people to remain in the body of the Church were abolished and all nominal churchmen left us." The revolution had freed Russian Orthodoxy from its "fatal" link with autocracy and cleansed church ranks of opportunists and the faint of heart.

It should be admitted that, as with most good propaganda, there was some truth to Sergii's argument—enough at any rate to make it seem plausible. The Russian Orthodox Church had indeed suffered from too close an identification with the tsarist state, and before the revolution many people had called themselves Orthodox simply to please the authorities, or for careerist considerations (the same reasons that would later persuade many to join the new state church —the Communist Party). But the prerevolutionary church, for all its manifest faults, had shown itself capable of generating spontaneous loyalty, and, despite the Bolsheviks' persistent efforts to crush it, the church had survived two decades of sustained repression. The Soviets had hardly disestablished Orthodoxy as a favor for the church, as Sergii implied, and the Bolsheviks had done far more to discourage worship than simply seizing church property.

One historian writes that it is hard to find "a Christian message" amid the propaganda in *Pravda o religii v Rossii*.[23] This may be so; but a careful reading reveals a message important to the Orthodox Church as an institution, and from Sergii's remarks one can divine the shape of the agreement in the process of being made between the church and the Soviet government. Sergii's comments quoted earlier were all obviously of great use to Soviet propaganda, but buried in his introduction are remarks that were probably of the utmost importance to him as the head of the Russian Orthodox Church. He wrote that, during the upheaval of the revolution, the "left" of the church "[u]sed the new freedom in order to disregard the rules and traditions of the church and to arrange their personal and professional life according to their own judgment." Among those whom Sergii thus labeled as schismatics—and, given the reference to "personal life," as implied degenerates as well—was Aleksandr Vvedenskii, the head of the *obnovlentsy*, the Bolshevik-inspired "Renovationist" Church.[24] "There appeared followers of arbitrariness and every kind of schism," Sergii wrote: "In short, incredible chaos reigned in our Church." This was an oblique reference to nationalist schisms that had sprung up in Ukraine and elsewhere following the revolution.

The true Orthodox Church had saved the most important brand from the conflagration, however: "In our outward helplessness, we could only rely on the moral strength of canonical truth, which has frequently saved the Church, in the past as well, from final disintegration." He repeated: "Our Russian Church was not swept away and wrecked by the whirlwind of events. She preserved her canonical conscience unsullied, together with her canonically lawful authority."

The weary reader could easily be so benumbed by the mass of anti-German and pro-Soviet propaganda that constitutes the bulk of the book that these essential remarks might be overlooked. Sergii was in effect reiterating his controversial pledge, first made in 1927, that he would recognize the Soviet state as legitimate, would serve it in war and peace, and would even deny the truths of Bolshevik repression. In exchange for these services rendered to the Soviet state, the Moscow Patriarchate would once again become the sole voice of Orthodoxy throughout the USSR. As a result of this Faustian bargain, Vvedenskii and his church, as well as Ukrainian splinter groups, would be consigned to the rubbish heap of history.

If one gives him the benefit of the doubt for sincerity, Sergii's reasoning probably ran along these lines: the period since the Bolshevik Revolution had been a time of troubles for the church, but Orthodoxy could not assault the Soviet state head-on. The church's view is long-term, however, extending far beyond the life-span of one or two generations, and at any rate Russian Orthodoxy has never expected much from this world. Bolsheviks and other persecutors of religion come and go, but if the unity of the church can be maintained through even the worst times of trial, then the faith can regenerate when circumstances improve.

Another chapter of *Pravda o religii* directed the anti-schismatic argument against Orthodox believers outside the USSR who were wary of the Soviet state's record of religious persecution. The chapter was a reprint of an article, first published in the United States in October 1941, authored by Veniamin, metropolitan of the Aleutians and North America and patriarchal exarch in America. Most Russian Orthodox clergy in the United States rejected the authority of the Moscow Patriarchate, believing that it had lost its independence to its Soviet masters. An observer of the Russian religious scene noted that, other than Veniamin, "all the other Russian bishops in America (I know of no exception) are heartily opposed to the Soviet Union."[25]

Veniamin denounced the hierarchs of the Russian Orthodox Church in America as schismatics and, through further logical gymnastics, as traitors to boot. "He who has betrayed the Mother-Church," the metropolitan thundered, "also cannot remain true to the state." He called on Orthodox in America to obey President Roosevelt's call to assist the Soviet war effort, and said that criticism of the USSR's record of religious persecution was a betrayal of "Christian love." "As regards political rights," Veniamin wrote, "in which you see the essence of freedom. . . . At this difficult moment no one [in the USSR] has said even one word of such rights at all. And how understandable this is. Is it possible at such a time to raise these questions, which are not even existent for a Christian [*da eshche ne sushchestvennye dlia khristianina*]?"[26]

In the first stages of the war, the Soviets had limited religious propaganda to claiming that Soviet believers enjoyed freedom of conscience and unanimously supported the war effort. Now, at the direction of its political masters, the Patriarchate seized the offensive and extended its reach. In *Pravda o religii*, the Russian Orthodox hierarchs proposed the following dubious logical progression: refusal of Russian Orthodox clergy and believers anywhere in the world to accept the authority of the Moscow Patriarchate equaled schism; schism aided the Nazis and amounted to secular treason. Furthermore, Russian Orthodox believers had no business issuing any calls for greater political or religious freedom in the USSR, because such secular matters should be of no concern to genuine Christians, whose focus should be on the betterment of their souls and on the next life rather than on the affairs of this imperfect world. For the Moscow Patriarchate, the Communist Party's line was now God's will as well.

The British, to whom Nikolai had given hundreds of copies of this extraordinary book, overlooked the ecclesiastical and political subtleties of *Pravda o religii*, viewing it as little more than "a travesty of [the] facts," and "a fresh attempt by the Soviet Government to put themselves advantageously with churchmen in [the] United Kingdom and United States." The British ambassador told London that this cynical interpretation was reinforced by the fact that the book "is not in circulation here [in the Soviet Union]."[27] Following Nikolai's strange approach, Baggallay wrote: "Although this visit may be the forerunner of interesting and important developments . . . it is too early to assume that there has been any fundamental change" in Soviet religious policies. The Kremlin "must go a long way yet before religion plays in this country a part comparable with that which it played here before [the revolution] or still plays in some other countries." "Without being unduly cynical," Baggallay continued, "one may conclude the Government and the Church have come to an understanding."[28]

After some internal wrangling, the British government would eventually translate *Pravda o religii* into English, and the ecclesiastical exchange proposed by Metropolitan Nikolai would go ahead with the visit of Britain's archbishop of York to Moscow in September of the following year.[29] Even more important than the propaganda value, however, was the sketchy outline provided in the book of Sergii's proposed concordat with the state. It proved an accurate indicator of Soviet religious policy.

"Prowling Morbidly Round the Three-Year-Old Graves of Smolensk"

Whereas the production and dissemination of *Pravda o religii v rossii* was designed to address some of Moscow's problems with American and British opinion, the Soviets faced much more vexing propaganda dilemmas in Eastern Europe and the Balkans. In 1943 the Soviets already had a conduit for propaganda directed at the Slavic world. Two years earlier, in the summer of 1941, Moscow had created the All-Slav Antifascist Committee dedicated to allaying suspicions of the USSR on the part of Eastern Europe's Slavic population and to harnessing as much international popular support as possible behind the Soviet war effort.[30] Throughout the war, in an apparent return to Russian tradition, the Soviets sought to position themselves as the Big Brother of the Slavic people. Despite the vigorous efforts of the All-Slav committee, however, the past could not simply be erased. Just as 1943 promised political gain for Moscow, it also reopened gaping rifts between the USSR and its Slavic neighbors, especially the Poles.

Moscow's Pan-Slavic card was not automatic trumps, as a glance at Russian history could have told. Ever since the reign of Catherine the Great, Russian tsars had tried to exploit the aspirations of the Balkan and East European Slavs to advance their own foreign policy designs; the results of these efforts, however, invariably fell far short of inflated Russian hopes.[31] The central problem was that the Slavs were far from being an undifferentiated mass; their often conflicting interests were not always congruent with those of Russia, or with its successor state the USSR. Traditional nineteenth-century Russian Pan-Slavism was a mystical brew of Orthodoxy and linguistic nationalism. Russian views of their Slavic brethren "remained paternal, superior, and anti-Catholic."[32] Unfortunately for Russia's Pan-Slavic enthusiasts, not all Orthodox people were Slavs; nor were all Slavs Orthodox. Even worse, many Slavs rejected Russian paternalism, viewing Russia itself as backward, authoritarian, and unjustifiably condescending.

As in the nineteenth century, so too during World War II, the chief obstacle, among many, to unifying Slavic nations was Poland—Catholic Poland. Russia's claim during the previous century that it was the liberator of the Slavic peoples from Ottoman and German domination had always run aground on its determination to cling to the eastern and central Polish lands that Catherine II had seized at the end of the eighteenth century. To Poles restive under tsarist rule, Russia's liberationist claims rang hollow.

Religion, likewise, had been a Russo-Polish battleground since at least the sixteenth century, as both states contested the fluid border regions between them and sought to convert the local populations to their own confession. These disputed regions stretch from Lithuania in the north to the northern border of Romania in the south, and from Brest-Litovsk in the west to near Minsk in the east. From the eighteenth century until 1914, when the Russian Empire had controlled the region, the tsars had tried to undercut the power of the Catholic and Uniate Churches and to shepherd the Eastern Slavic population into Orthodoxy, under the authority of the Moscow Patriarchate. By contrast, when Poland ruled this region, as it had during the seventeenth and much of the eighteenth centuries, the Polish authorities had done their best to wean Eastern Slavs away from Orthodoxy, preferably directly to Catholicism but, failing that, then into the Uniate Church.[33]

During the interwar years, when Poland regained its independence from Russia following the chaos of World War I and the Russian Revolution, territorial and religious rivalry continued between the two states. In a brief war with Bolshevik Russia, Poland seized these vast territories to the East. Polish possession had been ratified by the Treat of Riga in 1921, but Moscow was not reconciled to its losses. The local population was ethnically mixed: Belorussians, Rusyns, and, most numerous, Ukrainians. Eastern Slavs were in the majority in rural areas, there was also a substantial Jewish population, for the most part centered in the cities, and an interlarding of Poles, many of whom owned large estates worked by Eastern Slavic tenants.[34] A substantial proportion of the population was Orthodox Christian. The Polish census of 1931 claimed a total of 3,762,484 Orthodox believers in Poland; 1.5 million of these were Ukrainians, 903,557 Belorussians (called White Ruthenians by the Poles, presumably to differentiate them from Soviet Belorussians), 497,290 Poles, 99,636 Russians, 21,672 Czechs, and a further 696,397 of "undefined nationality."[35]

To deal with those who could not be drawn to Catholicism or Uniatism, in 1922 the Polish government arranged for a synod of Orthodox bishops in that country, which established a Polish Orthodox Church that declared itself autocephalous. This constituted a declaration of ecclesiastical and political independence from the Moscow Patriarchate, which had to that point exercised jurisdiction over the region's Orthodox. The ostensible justification for the move was the claim that the Moscow Patriarchate, being under the political domination of the atheist Soviet state, had lost its freedom.[36] Although true, the second, unstated goal was to cement Polish political authority over its sometimes restive Orthodox subjects.

In fact, the declaration of Polish autocephaly was a disappointment from the Polish government's standpoint. The new church soon began to take on a genuinely Ukrainian character and to defend the interests of its Eastern Slav Orthodox laity against Warsaw's sometimes violent Polonizing policies. Disappointed that the Polish Autocephalous Church did not serve its intended function of neutering nationalist opposition, Warsaw began to insist on the use of the Polish language in church services and either destroyed many Orthodox churches or handed them over to the Roman Catholic Church. They also tried, though without any great success, to convert Ukrainians and other Eastern Slavs to Catholicism. Cut off from any international protection, Orthodox in Poland were "more exposed to repressive Polish policies" than were the Uniates, who could rely to some extent on the support of Rome.[37]

From the outset, the declaration of Polish autocephaly was controversial within the international Orthodox community. Of the five bishops who took part in the 1922 synod, two maintained that such a move must await the agreement of the "Mother Church," perhaps a way of diplomatically opposing the entire initiative.[38] The Moscow Patriarchate naturally refused to accept the claim of autocephaly, made without its prior consent, as did many bishops within Poland itself who had not been present at the synod. Even White Russian Orthodox émigrés in Europe, the so-called Karlowitz Synod, who were in all things bitterly hostile to the Communist regime, nonetheless rejected Polish autocephaly, seeing in it nothing more than a cover for Polish political scheming. At the same time, however, Gregory VII, patriarch of Constantinople, the most senior Orthodox hierarch in the world, accepted the Polish Synod's decision; he was followed by the patriarchs of Antioch, Jerusalem, and Alexandria.[39] Thus matters stood when war broke out in 1939: Warsaw's meddling in religious matters had only further alienated local Orthodox.

The tragic historical legacy of Russo-Polish political, ethnic, and religious conflict was only made more bitter by Moscow's thorough purging and mass deportations during the two-year Soviet occupation of the western borderlands.[40] Soviet repression had been designed to "decapitate" the local population by eliminating the ruling elite en masse, thereby ensuring that it would be unable to offer effective resistance to Soviet power in the future. In the words of a wartime British cabinet study of Polish-Soviet relations: "All the conduct of the Soviet authorities from the day of their entry into Eastern Poland in September 1939 indicates that they considered themselves to have made a permanent acquisition of territory."[41] Contemporary estimates placed the number of deportees at about 1.2 million, 50.7 percent of whom were ethnically Polish, 36.15 percent Jewish, and 13.15 percent "other Slav races."[42] The clergy, as a natural leadership caste, had suffered disproportionately.

The decapitation had failed. Neither the existence of the common Nazi enemy, nor the signing of a Soviet-Polish alliance, could entirely dispel the legacy of hatred and distrust fostered by these violent events. Residents of the western borderlands sought to learn how many of their family members, neighbors, and leaders had survived arrest and deportation. The Polish exile government in London was especially anxious to learn the fate of some 15,000 Polish army officers who had surrendered to the Red Army following Poland's defeat in September 1939. Although their Soviet jailers had at first allowed Polish officer POWs to correspond with their families, from the spring of 1940 onward, all communication had suddenly ceased. The NKVD had secretly murdered them.

These mass killings would become known as the Katyn Forest massacre after the site where roughly a third of the murders took place.[43] Like the deportations of leading members of the civilian population in the western borderlands, the Katyn slaughter was a coldly calculated move—a particularly bestial one—designed to solidify the Soviet occupation of the Polish eastern territories. The Polish officer corps, composed as it was not just of career officers but also of professional, educated, and relatively privileged people, would have provided a leadership class capable of contesting Soviet control over their newly acquired territories.[44] Those killed included not only the 14,736 imprisoned officers but also a further 11,000 people variously condemned as being subversive to the Soviet order.[45]

Between 1939 and 1943, Soviet-Polish relations whipsawed between extremes. Enemies in 1939, the two governments formally became allies in July 1941 after the Nazi invasion of the USSR unwillingly forced the Soviets and the London-based Polish government-in-exile into one anothers' arms. From the outset of this uneasy partnership, the Poles demanded an accounting of the missing officers. When in late 1941 the Polish ambassador to Moscow asked Stalin about them, the latter denied any knowledge of their whereabouts, claiming that all Polish military prisoners had been freed, though allowing that "things sometimes happen to the released men."[46] Pressed by General Sikorski a month later for a better accounting of the missing men, Stalin claimed that they had escaped "to Manchuria."[47]

Suddenly, in April 1943, news of the missing officers came from the most unlikely source: the Germans.[48] On April 11 the Nazis announced that they had uncovered a series of mass graves near Smolensk in their zone of occupation, containing what would turn out to be about one-third of the missing Poles, and they broke the story in hopes of driving a wedge into the Allied coalition.[49]

Moscow's Informbiuro immediately branded the German story "a monstrous invention of the German-Fascist scoundrels," accusing the Germans themselves of the crime.[50] The Polish Exile Government called for an impartial investigation of the killings by the International Red Cross.[51] But the Poles' attempt to obtain a truthful explanation of the killings while denying propaganda benefit to Berlin and without angering the USSR would prove an impossible mix of aims, falling victim to the demands of coalition politics and military needs. The governments of the United States and Great Britain separately undertook their own internal investigations of the killings, both coming to the conclusion that Moscow was indeed responsible. The British investigation summed up a long analysis of the Soviet occupation of eastern Poland with an unflattering conclusion: "If we compare the German and the Soviet treatment of the Poles during the period . . . [from September 1939 to June 1941] . . . the amount of human suffering inflicted by [the Soviets] on the Polish race was not less than that inflicted by Nazi Germany during the same period."[52]

Despite frank American and British evaluations of the Soviet record in Poland, both Roosevelt and Churchill ordered the suppression of news coverage of the Katyn killings; they would also bar publication of their own govern-ments' conclusions about Soviet responsibility.[53] Both leaders worried that a row over this issue could divide the alliance and weaken the war effort. One day before the British internal study judged Moscow responsible for the killings, Churchill wrote directly to Stalin, assuring him that the British cabinet would work to limit the damage caused by the Katyn revelations, which he called "Goebbels' greatest triumph," and would also muzzle the Polish-language exile press.[54] Churchill privately believed the Soviets to be guilty of the crime, but in his view the war effort outweighed claims of justice. As the prime minister wrote to Foreign Secretary Anthony Eden, "There is no use prowling morbidly round the three-year-old graves of Smolensk."[55]

Despite the fact that all members of the Allied coalition knew Moscow to be guilty of the Katyn killings, all, the Poles excepted, had reason to pretend oth-erwise. On April 25 Molotov summoned the Polish ambassador, Tadeusz Romer, accusing his government of colluding with the Nazis' "slanderous" propaganda campaign. On this pretext, the Soviet government severed relations with the Polish government-in-exile.[56] Moscow obviously knew the charges against the Poles to be false. Indeed, in what must rank as one of history's more shameless instances of diplomatic hypocrisy, as Molotov railed against the Poles' supposed betrayal, his own signature was on the execution order, though this would not be revealed for another fifty years. Both the American and British governments knew that Moscow was acting on ulterior motives and had "seized on [the Katyn revelations] as a not entirely unwelcome pretext" for severing relations with the troublesome Poles.[57]

The issues at stake were of the utmost importance to Moscow, involving both the postwar borders of the USSR as well as the composition of the future Polish government. Stalin and Molotov demonstrated their political and diplo-matic deftness by transforming the revelation of their own atrocity into an op-portunity to settle these questions to their satisfaction. The Katyn affair and the reappearance of the Russian Orthodox Church on the international scene were closely intertwined. The church could reinforce Soviet territorial claims to dis-puted Polish territory on ethnic, religious, and historical grounds; it could help to divide the local population as the Red Army advanced by appealing to Or-thodox who had resented interwar Polish repression; its hierarchs could sup-port Moscow's claim that the Katyn massacres had been the work of the Nazis; and, most important, its reappearance—seemingly free and strong—could allay fears that a Soviet victory would spell the end of religious freedom in Eastern Europe.

"Dear Brother-Slavs"

Soviet religious policy took a sharp new turn in the spring of 1943, as a central component of Moscow's attempt to deal with nationality and reoccupation questions, as well as with the rapidly shifting Soviet diplomatic position. As was so frequently the case in Soviet affairs, the shift in religious policies was first signaled by a high-level speech, in this instance delivered by the nominal Soviet president Mikhail Kalinin. Although Kalinin was a political cipher, the fact that he was chosen to speak on this matter was perhaps significant in one way: during an earlier wave of Soviet repression against the Russian Orthodox Church following the civil war, Lenin had ordered that Kalinin, rather than Trotskii, assume the public leadership of the campaign. Whereas the former was of Russian peasant background, the latter's Jewish origins would greatly complicate the planned antireligious campaign among a population traditionally disposed to anti-Semitism.[58] Perhaps Stalin emulated Lenin in this as in so many other ways.

Speaking on May 19, 1943, to Red Army political agitators, Kalinin said that, in advancing Communist propaganda among the ranks of the armed forces, "one problem sometimes crops up." Many soldiers, he said, "especially among the older generation," retained their religious beliefs. "You must remember," Kalinin warned, "that we persecute nobody for religion. We regard religion as an error and fight it with education." The Soviet president cautioned overly ardent young Communists that "we will not fight religion by jeering at it."[59]

The speech was revisionist history with a vengeance. The Soviets had, of course, jeered at religion and mocked religious beliefs and symbols from 1917 onward, and they had indeed waged a campaign of varying ferocity against Orthodox clergy and recalcitrant believers. Nor does the speech at first reading sound especially conciliatory toward religious belief; it remained, in Soviet eyes, "antiscientific," and Kalinin reiterated Moscow's intent to combat belief in the future, using the Soviet state's monopoly of propaganda. Nonetheless, seen in the context of the earlier Soviet war on religious faith, the new line sketched by Kalinin represented an important turning point, as would become clear in the coming months. Following Kalinin's remarks, conditions for the Russian Orthodox Church began to improve almost at once, though slowly.

The timing of Kalinin's speech was significant. Historians of the Russian church, concerned primarily with domestic Russian affairs, generally fail to notice that the Soviets' new religious policy—albeit still in its embryonic stages— coincided with another momentous shift, this one in the realm of Soviet foreign policy. By the same token, historians of Soviet diplomacy and military affairs overlook the connections between foreign affairs, the military situation, and the changes in church policy. Three days after Kalinin's statement, on May 22, the Kremlin announced the dissolution of the Comintern.[60] The motives for this move were manifold, but one central intention was to calm Western fears that the Soviet Union would impose Communism by force as it pursued the Nazi armies into Eastern and Central Europe.[61] A little more than a week after the announcement, in answer to a question submitted by Harold King, chief Moscow correspondent of Reuters, Stalin himself gave four reasons for the dissolution: first, it would undercut "Hitlerite" claims that Moscow sought to "'Bolshevise'" its neighbors; second, it would counter the "calumny" that "Communist parties in various countries are allegedly acting not in the interests of their people, but on orders from outside"; third, it would assist the "uniting [of] all freedom-loving peoples into a single international camp" against the Nazis; and, finally, "It facilitates the work of patriots of all countries for uniting the progressive forces of their respective countries, regardless of party or religious faith, into a single camp of national liberation—for unfolding the struggle against fascism."[62]

As Stalin's carefully weighed remarks indicated, the dissolution marked a return to the prewar policy of "united fronts," that is, a call to form coalitions of left-leading (in Soviet parlance "progressive") parties. This would allow the numerically weak but politically cohesive Communist parties of Eastern and Central Europe to place themselves at the center of broad antifascist coalitions within their countries and thus play a shaping role in the formation of postwar governments. Stalin had never thought much of the Comintern anyway, regarding it as a talking shop filled with undisciplined windbags. By this stage in the war, its well-deserved reputation for directing international Communist parties to the benefit of Moscow's narrow interests made it little more than a burden to Soviet diplomacy. The dissolution would assuage fears of a forcible imposition of Communism. Communists would continue to serve the interests of Moscow, of course, but they must not be seen to be doing so.[63] Communist parties worldwide at once felt the consequences of this new twist in policy, from Yugoslavia, where the Soviets demanded that Tito's partisans downplay Communist ideology, to the United States, where the American Communist Party actually dissolved itself in 1944.[64]

Often overlooked in discussions of the Comintern's dissolution is Stalin's reference to the importance of "religious faith." Yet, during the spring of 1943, rumors abounded throughout the Allied diplomatic community that the shutting of the Comintern presaged changes in the Soviet religious sphere. On May 27, the Washington correspondent for the New York Times, Harold Callendar, reported that "Some of those in closest touch with Russian relations believe that the dissolution of the Communist International may be followed by some gesture in the religious field calculated to allay suspicion of Moscow abroad." Although correct about this, Callendar's predictions were less accurate. He continued, "This might take the form, they say, of an understanding with the Vatican, possibly a concordat, permitting freedom for Catholic schools and monastic orders in Russia."[65]

In fact, in the near term the changes planned by the Kremlin would affect the Russian Orthodox Church rather than other denominations, because the Russian church possessed the assets the Soviets needed to deal with their political and diplomatic tasks. The first, most dramatic public manifestation of the Soviets' new religious line would occur at the Third Pan-Slavic Congress. The first two such conferences, in 1941 and 1942, had been relatively unremarkable affairs, with a steady diet of stories about German atrocities served up by leftist or Communist figures from other Slavic countries who had taken refuge in the USSR to escape the Germans. The conferences had, however, helped to shape the propaganda beamed at Eastern Europe from Moscow Radio. Before 1943, with a few notable exceptions, this had been entirely secular in character; it also tended to be rather heavy-handed. Russia, both tsarist and Soviet, was portrayed as the benefactor and big brother of the smaller Slavic nations. In mid-1942, for instance, Soviet directives for propaganda directed to Bulgarian listeners stressed that broadcasts must "show concretely in what a great debt the Bulgarian people are before the Russian people, which helped the Bulgarian people fight for their national, state and cultural independence." More cleverly, Moscow also sought to sow disunion within the ranks of the Nazi coalition by cultivating Romanian-Hungarian discord. To this end, the Directorate of Propaganda and Agitation adopted the slogan: "Romanians! Defend your land from Hungarian invasion, struggle for the return of northern Transylvania, given by Hitler to Hungary."[66]

The Russian Orthodox Church did its bit in appealing to the people of the Balkans. In two broadcasts, one on November 22 and the second on December 9, 1942, Metropolitans Sergii and Nikolai issued appeals to "Brothers in Faith! Soldiers of the Romanian Army." The metropolitans reprimanded Romanian soldiers for participating in Hitler's aggressive war against the "peaceful Orthodox Russian people" and against fellow Orthodox believers. The Nazis had fantacized about conquering the world, but "The powerful alliance of Russia, America, and England is squeezing fascist Germany and its vassals in a ring . . . and the hour of fascism's defeat is not distant." "Finally," the metropolitans declared, "the Romanian soldier must not forget that the state independence and the national freedom and existence of Romania were gained by the blood of Russian soldiers in the war of 1877–1878." The Romanian people owed Russia an eternal debt. Casting their argument in explicitly Christian terms, the metropolitans intoned: "Your military and Christian duty is not to die for the Germans, whose guilt pours out the life's blood of your homeland and subjects your people to endless suffering. Your Christian duty is immediately to desert the German ranks and to go over to the side of the Russians, thereby expiating the sin of collaboration with the criminal Germans, to take part in the sacred duty of defeating the enemy of humanity."[67]

These two appeals were carefully timed to coincide with the opening stages of the Soviet counteroffensive against Stalingrad, which was launched on November 19. Soviet radio broadcast them in Romanian, and they were printed as propaganda leaflets. The Red Army delivered the main blow of this attack against the northwest flank of the German Sixth Army, then bogged down in fruitless street fighting. Romanian divisions held this vital stretch of the Axis front line, and the Soviet offensive would quickly annihilate them, making possible the encirclement of the more powerful German forces. Unfortunately, it is impossible to know whether these appeals by Orthodox hierarchs induced so much as a single Romanian soldier to desert. The broadcasts showed two things, however: for the first time, Soviet propaganda was prepared to issue appeals to a foreign audience cast in explicitly Christian terms, and such appeals were being closely coordinated with the most critical military developments. The details of the Soviet offensive against the Romanian line near Stalingrad were not common knowledge, of course; those directing the hand of Russian Orthodox hierarchs were privy to military secrets of the highest order.

The appeals to Romanian soldiers indicated the direction that Soviet propaganda and church policy were heading; in the spring of 1943, the church's role in foreign policy would become much more prominent. On May 9, 1943, only a few days before the Comintern's dissolution, the Third Pan-Slavic Conference convened. Held in Moscow's Hall of Columns, where Stalin's earlier purge trials had been staged, the conference had a surprise in store for the participants. With no advance fanfare, several high-ranking clergy of the Orthodox Church appeared as delegates to the conference. As an anonymous informant present at the meeting later told the British: "[T]he most startling sight was the presence of some thirty-five Greek [sic] Orthodox priests in their habits and with their best Sunday-go-to-meeting crosses proudly hanging from chains of gold, silver and brass. Three or four of these crosses were magnificently jeweled. The priests . . . sat in little groups of three or four, and some had their wives with them." The spectacle was certainly an unusual one in Moscow, where it was almost unheard of for priests to appear in public, much less take part in official functions in full regalia. As the observer noted, "press photographers and cinematograph operators got busy on the audience" recording this unprecedented scene. The participants of the conference were also aware of the uniqueness of the clerics' presence; "the chief interest of the audience was focussed on the venerable Metropolitan of Kiev, in his rich deep blue cassock and two heavy gold crosses, whose bearing suggested that for the last twenty-five years he had had an honoured front seat at every national and pan-national gathering."

The audience listened politely as delegates from Poland, Czechoslovakia, Ukraine, and other Slavic nations spoke of the war and of German outrages. Midway through the speeches, most listeners seemed somewhat bored by the proceedings, which for the most part recycled routine wartime propaganda.

> Then the President called on Nicolai—Metropolitan of Kiev and Galicia [*sic*]. As he rose, the ovation broke out. I was thunderstruck! He was just cheered and cheered and not allowed to start. I looked round the hall in amazement. Everyone was expressing themselves freely, as if some great weight had been lifted from each and every heart. The cheering was not confined to the audience, but was almost as hearty, although nowhere near as prolonged, on the platform.

Given such a grand entrance, the metropolitan did not disappoint.

> Nicolai had notes, but did not refer to them. He spoke magnificently, without a falter or hesitation, for eighteen minutes straight to the audience, straight at the microphones, and one felt direct to the millions of the Orthodox Church, listening to a Christian believer's voice from Holy Moscow.[68]

Nikolai's performance was impressive, effectively exploiting his position as a clergyman to breathe new life into familiar Soviet propaganda themes. He tackled head-on the greatest single proximate threat to Slavic unity, the Katyn massacre. The previous November, Nikolai said, he had been named a member of the Soviet commission for the investigation of German war crimes, and, he vowed, he could personally guarantee that the Soviet government was innocent of the murders. As the second-ranking hierarch of Russian Orthodoxy, Nikolai was prepared to lend his church's moral authority to Moscow's claim that the Nazis had committed the atrocity. The Germans were guilty not only of the crime, he assured the audience, but also of slanderously trying to pass it off as a Soviet misdeed. By implication, the demand of the Polish government in exile for an impartial investigation of the killings could only provide aid and comfort to the enemy.

The special point of Nikolai's attack was the German appeal to religious believers. The Nazi claim to be leading a "'crusade in defense of the faith'" was hollow. Instead, Berlin had waged a "satanic struggle with the church, with Christianity." "Dear Brother-Slavs!" Nikolai continued, "All of you well know that Hitler is the most evil enemy of Christianity!" The Nazis had turned Orthodox churches into stables for their horses, they had desecrated and destroyed scores of church buildings, and they had shot priests and believers.

Russians were not the only sufferers, Nikolai said; brother Slavs—he specified Serbs, Slovenes, Croatians, and Bulgarians—had also experienced Nazi repression. "Our struggle with these enemies is the holy duty of each Christian," Nikolai declared; Slavic Christians should nurture "a holy hatred toward the enemy." Nikolai related how the Russian Orthodox Church had raised money for the Dmitrii Donskoi tank column, and he linked the current support of war effort with Russian historical tradition: "Dear Brother-Slavs! I want to tell you that our Orthodox Church, which during all of Russian history lived the same life as its people, now, in the days of the Patriotic War, gives itself completely to the service of the homeland and to the Russian people in this time of tragic experience."[69] Nikolai's was a bravura performance, but it also had interesting omissions for any speech given in wartime Moscow, as the British informant noted: "The Metropolitan did not mention Stalin, the Soviet Government, the Red Army, Navy, or Air Force." Instead, "He spoke to the Orthodox Christian believers wherever they might be, and urged them to gird up their loins to fight the forces of evil, darkness, Satan—now in the guise of Hitlerism. He and the Church blessed all those participating in the Holy War." Finishing his speech, Nikolai was met with a "deluge" of applause; "it went on and on, long after Nicolai had modestly taken his seat at the President's table. I looked round the hall. Many were crying, and most notably the clergy."[70]

Although the immediate results of such propaganda conferences tended to be limited, they were an important indication of Moscow's plans for the future, and the participants were clearly rising stars. Many of the delegates, such as the Poles W. Wassilewska and S. Berling as well as the Czechs Z. Fierlinger and L. Swoboda, would within the next few years be members of governments imposed by the Red Army as it occupied Eastern Europe. It was one sign of the importance the Kremlin attached to religious opinion, especially in Eastern Europe, that Russian Orthodox clerics should appear in such company, taking part in a government-sponsored public function for the first time since the Bolshevik Revolution in 1917—if one discounts appearances as indicted criminals in show trials. Stalin himself had identified nationalism and religious belief as two key forces that the Soviets must court in their advance into Eastern Europe; the Russian Orthodox Church accordingly fell into line.

The Missing Patriarch

Following the Third Slavic Congress, Moscow's new church policy would begin slowly to emerge in view. It neatly augmented the Soviet diplomatic offensive against the London Poles, which gained pace in the wake of the Katyn revelations. Throughout the spring of 1943, Poles in the USSR began to pick up hints that the Russian church was preparing once again to subordinate Orthodox residents of the former eastern Polish provinces to the Moscow Patriarchate's authority. The disposition of canonical power was no small matter, because, if the Moscow Patriarchate were to regain authority, it—or more precisely its Soviet masters—could decide episcopal appointments and, even more critically, excommunicate clergy who refused to cooperate with the Communist regime. Whoever controlled the selection and appointment of priests would, by exercising this power, be able to place a vast web of carefully vetted and reliable people at the local level.

This was not a new threat, of course; the Moscow Patriarchate had never sanctioned its loss of authority in this region in the first place. Up to this point, however, the Poles had always countered Moscow's claims with two persuasive arguments: first, the establishment of autocephalous churches within independent countries was long-established practice in Eastern Orthodoxy; the patriarch of Constantinople, the senior Orthodox heirarch, had recognized Polish autocephaly when it was declared in 1922, as had the patriarchs of Antioch, Jerusalem, and Alexandria.[71] They had done so after determining that the Russian church had lost its freedom under the Communist regime.

The Poles' second argument was more critical in terms of church law. As a propaganda pamphlet published in 1940 by the Polish government-in-exile put it, the Moscow Patriarchate had no right to summon canon law in its defense when "it acknowledged the irreligious Soviet regime and possessed no spiritual head able to speak with real authority in the name of the faith." "Metropolitan Sergius betrayed a woeful subservience [to the Soviet government] in his actions," the Poles claimed; furthermore, following the death of the last Moscow Patriarch, Tikhon, in April 1925, the Soviets had not allowed the election of a successor. The current head of the church, Metropolitan Sergii, was only patriarch *locum tenens*. The Poles, and rebel Orthodox clergy as well,[72] made good use of this fact, arguing that, lacking a genuine patriarch, Moscow had no firm legal basis for claiming canonical authority over them. "[T]he letter of the law demanded the election of a successor [to Tikhon]. . . . Hence all the protests of the Russian Church, as a religious institution, and still more those of the un-canonical Sergius, could not be regarded by the Polish Orthodox Church as justified."[73]

Russian Orthodox hierarchs were fully aware of this weakness in their position; the absence of a genuine patriarch handicapped their struggle with schismatics. On March 29, 1943, Sergii fired a shot across the Poles' bow, however, handing a note to the Polish representative in Moscow outlining Russian intentions regarding the Orthodox of the western borderlands. Sergii wrote that the question of the autocephalous Polish church "has been the theme of a widespread discussion" among Russian clergy. The acting patriarch then made several interrelated points. "The question of the autonomy of the Polish Orthodox Church," he declared, "can be decided legally, impartially and with good will by taking a firm stand on grounds of religious law alone and by getting rid of all political national and other influences, especially as this will be in accordance with the most excellent plan of post war reconstruction of international relations, which represents the dream and aims of all civilised nations."

This was an oblique way of saying that the Polish Orthodox Church could not claim autonomy simply on the grounds of being based in an independent state. Any final decision regarding autonomy would be made ostensibly on purely religious, not political or national, grounds. Sergii's argument that national and political considerations were not germane to church questions was disingenuous and at variance with church history, as well as with his own cooperation with the Kremlin.

Sergii's first point laid the groundwork for his second, in which he cited canon law to support his argument:

According to Holy Canons the diocese of Great Russia and the Ukrain [sic] which later formed part of the Polish State, had been a part of the Moscow Patriarchy and as such should have recognised the Patriarch of Moscow [as] their Head [law of the Apostles 34] and used his name in all church services. They could not free themselves from his jurisdiction without his consent and blessing. Friendliness of other [p]atriarchs and heads of the Orthodox Church towards the autonomy of the Polish Orthodox Church can only give proof of their good will and . . . praiseworthy intentions to cooperate in the keeping of peaceful relations between Orthodox Churches, but it can nowise be a Canonic justification of autonomy.

Sergii reminded the Poles that the Moscow Patriarchate had never recognized Polish Orthodox claims. Autocephaly had been declared "despite the strong protest of the deceased saintly patriarch Tichon [sic]" and those of his successors, Sergii included.

Sergii's fourth point was critical:

For refusing to recognise the Head of the Church, the 15th Rule of Two Congresses orders the guilty one "to remain completely strange to all priesthood." But as we have not so far summoned a general congress, which would have taken just such a decision in regard to Polish archbishops, we cannot therefore regard them as destituted, and we consider only that they are separated from a community, and are in a state of divergency with the Church. Therefore we recognise their priesthood and religious activities and do not reject these, but all their administrative decisions and judgements we declare illegal and binding to nobody.

This was the crux of the argument: Sergii was implicitly admitting that, for the time being at least, his church lacked the authority to whip the rebels into line. Unable legally to elect a new patriarch for a decade and one half, owing to its Communist masters, the Russian Orthodox Church could only toothlessly restate its protests against the Polish schismatics. Sergii's argument revealed both the Russian church's weak legal position and hinted at the direction Soviet religious policy would head during the next months.

Sergii closed his message by noting that several unnamed Orthodox archbishops in Ukraine and Belorussia—in regions that had been part of eastern Poland before 1939—remained loyal to Moscow, rejecting the autonomy of the Ukrainian-Polish schismatics. The ranks of these clerics included "some of whom had even taken part in the formation of this autonomy" but had since repented and rejoined the Mother Church. "Since those archbishops who recognise the jurisdiction of the Moscow Patriarchy, form a great majority in White Russia and the Ukrain [sic], therefore the autonomy of the Orthodox Church in those districts . . . should be regarded as non-existent and not requiring any looking into."

In closing, Sergii held out the possibility that some form of Polish autonomy might be negotiated in the future; he coyly wrote that "it is as yet too early to go into details over this matter," but "with good will on both sides by getting rid of old time prejudices, this question can be settled painlessly for both parties concerned. In the first place," Sergii continued, "the very fact that this Church will find itself within the boundaries of a sovereign state [Poland], renders it independant [sic] in all internal matters. There remains only the question of religious dogmas, essential canons, liturgical [sic] customs, etc."[74]

On first reading, Sergii's reasoning appears curious: having argued vigorously that the Polish Orthodox could not canonically claim autonomy from Moscow merely because they resided in an independent state, he then apparently seemed to admit the reverse proposition. The apparent contradiction in his argument vanishes, however, when one remembers that Sergii believed that postwar Poland would lose its eastern provinces, and with them the vast majority of its Orthodox subjects. Whatever minuscule number of Orthodox might be left to a much-reduced Poland after a territorial readjustment would not be worth arguing over.[75]

The Poles were aware of Sergii's unstated political motives. M. Wyaznski, an official in the Polish Ministry of Information, produced a twenty-seven-page polemical pamphlet, which he gave to a bewildered British Foreign Office, addressing the challenge of the Russian church, and presenting a version of the region's religious history every bit as slanted in favor of the Poles as Sergii's had been toward Russia's interests. Religion in Poland, Wyaznski wrote, "always had an internal and external aspect." "There had been several cases" in the history of independent Poland "of the Moscow Patriarchy intervening in internal affairs." The Polish Orthodox "were strongly adverse [sic] to Russian interference" as religion in Poland developed "along lines of western culture and civilisation." Orthodox in Poland were "totally different" from their brethren to the east. This reading of history ignored the fact that many bishops had opposed separating from Moscow in the 1920s; it also papered over the considerable ethnic strife that had existed within prewar Poland and the Polish government's own use of religion as a tool for political control.

Nonetheless, in his critique of Moscow's motives Wyaznski was on firmer ground. The Russians had historically used the church to support a policy of westward expansion and to consolidate their control over non-Russian areas, he wrote: "From the end of the XVIIth century right up to the Bolshevik revolution, the Russian Orthodox Church was a tool of russian [sic] policy toward Poland."[76] Another Polish message warned that Stalin was "resum[ing] the traditional policy of old Russia, which turned the Orthodox Church into an instrument of her policy towards the adjacent states and foreign religious bodies." The note reminded the British that the Communist state had used the church once before, when it annexed the western borderlands in 1939 and 1940: "the Patriarchal Church played its part with regard to Poland, the Baltic States, and Rumania by coercing the Orthodox Churches of these countries into union with Moscow. The Patriarchal Church endorsed the conquest of these lands by the Soviet Government and showed its complete agreement with the policy of the Kremlin."

The Poles had been locked in this religious-political battle with their giant eastern neighbor for several centuries, and to them the direction of Stalin's new religious policy was evident: "Today the Moscow Patriarchate . . . is necessary to the Soviet Union not only as an instrument to support its claims and extend its influence, in the lands annexed in 1939–40, but also as a means of influencing the Balkan countries and the Eastern Patriarchates. The church policy of Metropolitan Serge is but a cloak for the policy of the Soviet Union which attempts to take advantage of the Church to further the ambitions of Moscow."[77]

Unsurprisingly, given their reading of Russian motives, the Poles responded point-by-point to Sergii's memorandum. Sergii's note assumed, though it did not state this openly, that Poland would lose its eastern provinces; and yet the Soviet government had in 1918 renounced Russian claims against Poland dating from the eighteenth century. In the Treaty of Riga, Moscow had recognized Polish sovereignty over the eastern provinces. As for the Soviet invasion of September 1939, made in conjunction with the Nazis, the Kremlin had agreed in July 1941 to nullify the Nazi-Soviet territorial provisions regarding Poland. To contest Polish sovereignty now, as Sergii evidently was doing, violated these previous agreements and was an alarming indication concerning the direction of Soviet policy. Sergii's assumption that the USSR would regain Poland's eastern provinces, the memorandum argued, "now, in the fourth year of the war, is propagated only by Germany, with whom all the United Nations, and therefore also the Soviet Union, are at war."

Sergii had no right to assume either that Poland would lose its eastern provinces or to claim authority over Polish Orthodox subjects; Russian Orthodoxy "is but one of many branches of the Orthodox Church." The declaration of ecclesiastical independence had been supported by several Orthodox patriarchs, including that of Constantinople, "which," Wyaznski wrote, "for the Eastern Church is what the Pope is for the Catholic world." This was a misleading argument; although the patriarch of Constantinople was indeed the senior hierarch of Eastern Orthodoxy, there had never been an equivalent to the pope in Eastern Christianity. The argument over this very question had famously been one cause of the split with Rome in the first place.

The Poles then again fired what they believed to be their most potent weapon: "In addition the continuity of the Patriarchy was broken in 1923, and so far no General Congress for normification of conditions in the Church, has been summoned in the Soviet Union." This was clear even to the Russian clerics:

How well the Primate Serge and his councellors the Archbishops understood the weakness of their reasoning, is shown by the fact that they made no decisions concerning the application of recognised church sanctions but only gave their opinions, which are not binding to anybody. . . . Point four of the Primates['] letter cannot even deny the priesthood of the polish orthodox bishops and admits shamefully, that religious sanctions have not been brought against them only because no Russian General Congress had so far been summoned. On the other hand the representatives of the Polish Orthodox Church might inquire of the Primate Serge why such a Congress has not so far been summoned.

The Poles must have felt confident, in making this point time and again, and in such a taunting tone, that the atheist Soviet government would surely never countenance the convocation in the USSR of any such church council.

This optimism would soon prove misplaced. The Poles, and many others, believed that Soviet hostility toward religion was immutable, that the gulf between Marxist materialism and religious faith was unbridgeable, and that the legacy of Soviet antireligious repression was too well established and bitter for any regeneration of the Russian Orthodox Church, so long as a Communist government remained in power.

In one sense, the doubters were right. Moscow was not preparing a genuine rapprochement between church and state; as events would show, the Communists were prepared to use the Russian Orthodox Church to deal with the exigencies of war, but they still believed it to be an enemy in the long term. And yet, the winter of 1942–43 had been a watershed in the history of the Russian church. Until that time, it emerged only gradually from the depths into which it had been driven before 1939; it performed services for the Kremlin during the occupation of the western borderlands, and following the German attack it issued patriotic appeals and supported Soviet foreign and military policies— even when this meant denying the repression it had undergone at the hands of its political masters.

By the summer of 1943, however, looking at the revival of the church from the outside, it no longer seemed fanciful to imagine that Russian Orthodoxy had returned from the grave and would come to play a limited public role in Russian political and spiritual life. A normally cautious contemporary British observer of the Russian religious scene could write: "I do not suggest that there has been any change of heart on the part of the Soviet Government towards religion, but there has been a very remarkable change of practice. . . . Judging by their actions in recent years it is *not* the determination of the rulers of Russia to extirpate religion. Perhaps tomorrow it will be a true statement. Today it is not."[78]

The first, small shoots of a public rehabilitation began to inch through the Stalinist permafrost. Unlike the previous year, Sergii's Easter greetings were published in the Russian-language press, not only in newspapers and releases targeted at a foreign audience. The publicly announced service of Metropolitan Nikolai on the Extraordinary Commission to investigate German war crimes, and his speeches and addresses to East European Slavs, also seemed significant steps toward rehabilitation of the church.

Believers in the USSR continued to inhabit a hostile environment, for all the apparent changes taking place in their church. Children still received antireligious education in the schools, though this had been toned down somewhat; priests were forbidden to provide religious education to more than three people at a time, and there were no open seminaries; parents hoping to baptize their children still had to register with the secular authorities, thereby making themselves hostage to any future change in the current party line of tolerance. The church could not yet publish Bibles or other religious literature—*Pravda o religii v rossii* having been a singular exception. Social or charitable work, other than raising money for the war effort, remained illegal; and even the wartime fund raising received no publicity, being restricted to the few already open churches. Nor were more churches being reopened yet. In short, the changes were, so far, all from the top downward.[79]

To this point in the war, Moscow's manipulation of the church and its symbols had been adroit. It had managed to harness the power of religious faith, and its moral and political authority, to augment Soviet foreign and domestic policies. It would continue to do so, and indeed the church's profile would continue to grow during the remaining two years of the war. Until mid-1943, power flowed only in one direction—from the top down. The Soviet government was carefully using the church for its own ends while forestalling genuinely spontaneous religious manifestations. This new line, however, courted risk. As Moscow allowed the church to play an ever more public role, and as the Red Army recovered areas from the Germans where Soviet political control was as yet not firmly reestablished and where independent churches had been set up, the Kremlin would find that it no longer entirely controlled the process that it had unleashed. It would become necessary to deal with pressure from below for change, and with confusion among the Soviets' own ranks about how to manage such pressures.

Why haven't you any personnel? Where have they got to?
—Stalin speaking with Metropolitan Sergii, September 4, 1943

The new-found enthusiasm for rebuilding Christian Churches
will keep our comrades busy if they make it retrospective. Not
only Nazis have destroyed fine Byzantine churches in Russia!
—The Reverend Hugh Martin, British Ministry of Information,
  March 1942

A Vatican of Sorts

Stalin and the Patriarch

On September 9, 1943, Moscow Radio's English-language broadcast announced that on the previous day a synod, or *sobor'*, of Russian bishops had convened in the country's capital to select a new patriarch—the first to be elected since the death of Patriarch Tikhon on April 7, 1925, and only the second since Patriarch Adrian's death in 1700. The radio also reported that, before his elevation to the patriarchal throne, Metropolitan Sergii met with Stalin himself in Moscow's Kremlin. The news was widely reported in the Western press, where it came as something of a surprise to readers, who, if they thought at all about religion in the USSR, had long assumed that the Soviet state's hostility to religion would prevent such things from occurring.

Even to those close observers of the Russian religious scene who had watched the evolution of Moscow's church policy during the previous years, the announcement was unexpected. Certainly it came as a nasty surprise for the Polish government-in-exile, which had counted on the fact that the Russian church lacked a legal head able to enforce Moscow's ecclesiastical claims in the western borderlands. The selection of the patriarch "is a tactical move of great significance," the Polish Ministry of Foreign Affairs warned its legations throughout the world. "The decision that the Patriarchate should be reestablished means the resumption, one cannot say for how long, of the traditional co-operation between the Church and the Russian Government. It also . . . will facilitate the enlisting of the services of the Church in its relations with other Churches in the interests of Soviet policy."[1] As events would show, this was an uncannily accurate reading of Stalin's intentions.

Foreigners might have been forgiven for failing to predict this new twist in Soviet church-state relations; they were not the only ones taken unawares. The decision to restore the Patriarchate was made at the highest levels of the Soviet government, by Stalin in consultation with Viacheslav Molotov, Lavrenty Beria (head of the NKVD and a member of the politbiuro), and Georgii Malenkov (also a member of the politbiuro).[2] These Soviet oligarchs apparently did not even bother to consult in advance the very church leaders who would be involved.

Sergii and the remnants of the Moscow Patriarchate had been evacuated from Moscow to the Volga city of Ulianovsk in the autumn of 1941 as the Germans threatened the Soviet capital. On July 3, 1943, Vsevolod Merkulov, people's commissar for state security, wrote to Shcherbakov and the Central Committee, suggesting that the time had come to return the acting patriarch to Moscow, and Stalin approved the idea sometime before early September. Merkulov's note lays out the underlying reasoning: first, Sergii had complained that, isolated as he was in Ulianovsk, he was losing control over church affairs just as these were becoming more vital. Second, and more important, "In addition, the presence of the church centres in Ulyanovsk makes significantly more difficult the practical handling by them of a range of measures especially needed in connection with the large number of churches on liberated territory, which had been opened by the German occupiers."[3]

This was to be the church's new primary function, so far as the Soviets were concerned: to assist the reoccupation of enemy-held territory and to deal with the unwelcome consequences of the religious revival that had taken place under the Germans. It is significant that the state security organs initiated Sergii's return; they were the authorities most intimately involved in issues of reoccupation and the suppression of disloyalty. To play the critical role its Communist masters envisioned for it, the Patriarchate would have to be returned to the political center where its activities could be carefully monitored and directed by the NKVD-NKGB. Consequently, on September 3, Metropolitan Sergii and his coterie were suddenly summoned from Ulianovsk to appear in Moscow, where they would meet Stalin.[4] Upon his arrival, Sergii was greeted by Metropolitan

Aleksii of Leningrad and by Metropolitan Nikolai, who had most probably negotiated the terms of Sergii's meeting with Soviet leaders.[5]

Only a few hours before meeting with Sergii, Stalin summoned Georgii Karpov, a major general in the NKVD, to brief him on church affairs.[6] The dictator quizzed Karpov about the personal histories and characteristics of Russian church hierarchs and the current state of the church—the number of parishes, bishops, and so forth. Most of the dictator's questions, however, concerned the church's relations with foreign groups: he asked "what links the Russian orthodox church [sic] has abroad." What were its connections with fraternal Orthodox patriarchs in Constantinople, Jerusalem, and elsewhere, as well as with the Orthodox churches in Romania, Bulgaria, and Yugoslavia? Having also inquired about Karpov's own background and making sure that he was an ethnic Russian,* Stalin then ordered him to form a Soviet for the Affairs of the Russian Orthodox Church, to be answerable to the state government, not to the Central Committee of the Communist Party. "The council [soviet] will not take decisions separately," Stalin ordered, "it will report and receive instructions from the Government."[7]

At 9 P.M. on September 4, Sergii and the other two metropolitans were driven by limousine to the Kremlin and ushered into the company of Stalin, Molotov, and Karpov. After a rather nervous exchange of greetings, Stalin congratulated Sergii on the church's "patriotic work" in support of the war. He then asked his guests to "spell out any pressing questions."[8] Sergii listed three points: churches must be reopened to deal with the people's needs (most particularly in areas behind Soviet lines where the authorities had not allowed this to happen), a new patriarch should be elected, and seminaries should be opened to educate new priests. Sergii's comments elicited the following curious remarks:

> At this point Stalin suddenly broke his silence. "Why haven't you any personnel? Where have they got to?" he asked, taking his pipe out of his mouth and staring intently at the company. Aleksii and Nikolai were confused. . . . everyone knew that the "personnel' were scattered in the camps. But Metropolitan Sergius was not discountenanced. . . . The old man replied, "We lack personnel for several reasons, one of which is we train a man to be a priest, but he becomes a Marshal of the Soviet Union." A satisfied grin moved the dictator's moustache. He said, "Yes, yes, I was a seminarist. I even heard about

---

*As was the case when he made Kalinin launch the new church policy in the spring of 1943, the dictator seems to have wanted to place ethnic Russians in positions of authority in religious matters, almost certainly to avoid damaging anti-Semitic popular accusations that Jewish Bolsheviks were manipulating the Russian church.

you." He then fell to reminiscing about his years as a seminarist. . . . He said that his mother had regretted to her dying day that he had not become a priest. The conversation between the metropolitan and the dictator took on a relaxed air. After tea had been served, they talked business.[9]

As for priests still languishing in the gulag, Stalin told Sergii: "Draw up a list [of names] and we'll look at it."[10]

Following this surreal exchange, the extraordinary meeting continued for five minutes short of two hours.[11] Stalin and Molotov worked out a new set of rules for the church with their clerical guests, approving the resumption of theological education for new priests as well as the renewal of an official church publication. A second account of the meeting records an interesting remark by Stalin, which indicated the dictator's plans for the church: he told the clerics that they should "create a Vatican of sorts."[12] This could only come about, however, if the church had its own counterpart to the pope; a *sobor'* would therefore have to be held to elevate Sergii to the patriarchy. When Sergii pleaded that such a meeting would possibly require a month to organize, "Stalin, smiling, remarked: 'Isn't it possible to show a bolshevik tempo?' He turned to me [Karpov] and asked my opinion, I said if we help metropolitan Sergy with suitable transport for the speediest arrival of the episcopate in Moscow (by air), the Council could be convoked even within 3–4 days."[13] Stalin assured his guests that "the church can rely on the comprehensive support of the Government in all questions connected with strengthening and developing its organisation within the USSR." Even the hierarchs' personal comfort was not to be overlooked: they were to receive special food supplies from the state, and Sergii was to be given new, sumptuous quarters, the prewar residence of former German ambassador to the USSR, Count von der Schulenburg, which the Soviet government had confiscated following the outbreak of war. "[T]his building is Soviet, not German," Stalin assured the metropolitan, "so you can live there quite happily." To emphasize his supposed friendliness to the church, The dictator pretended to scold Karpov: "Then, turning to me, comr. Stalin said: 'Gather together two or three aides to be members of your Council and set up an office, but just remember this: first of all, you are not a chief procurator [like the official overseeing the church in the tsarist era]; secondly, stress more in your work the independence of the church.'"[14]

At eleven o'clock at night—only the start of Stalin's normal working day but a hard hour for the septuagenarian Sergii, who had only months to live—the dictator struck the pose of a respectful young seminarian: "At the end of the conversation the ancient and ailing metropolitan was exhausted. . . . Stalin took him by the arm with great care like a real subdeacon, led him down the stairs and bade him farewell in the following words: 'My Lord, that is as much as I can do for you at the present time!' And with that he wished the hierarchs goodbye."[15] The metropolitans had witnessed Stalin at his most disingenuous. As events would show, despite the dictator's assurances that the government would assist the church in every way, the Kremlin had no intention whatsoever of allowing churches to spring up like mushrooms throughout the union; Karpov's new Soviet would act to restrict the expansion of church activity to those areas where it had already taken place, for the most part under the Germans. Stalin's performance had all been a charade, from feigning that Sergii's fellow clergy had somehow vanished through a fit of absent-mindedness rather than as a result of conscious policy, to pretending to warn the NKVD man Karpov to allow the church greater independence, unlike those wicked tsarist bureaucrats. It had been no more than a cynical dictator's conjuring trick, whereby clergy was made first to disappear, then reappear at the wave of a pen. One wonders what Sergii made of it all.[16]

With Stalin's eager endorsement, the military provided scarce transport aircraft to enable a *sobor'* to gather only four days after the Kremlin meeting, on September 8. Thus assembled, the hierarchs of Russian Orthodoxy recreated a Holy Synod, electing as members Metropolitan Aleksii of Leningrad, Metropolitan Nikolai of Kiev and Galych, and four archbishops.[17] On September 12, this body duly elected Sergii as its new patriarch. Despite the significance of the congress, these meetings had not been complicated affairs to arrange, because the ranks of the clergy had been considerably thinned by decades of arrests, shootings, and other forms of repression. Only 19 hierarchs signed the *sobor'*s declaration: 3 metropolitans, 11 archbishops, and 5 bishops.[18] The small number of participants stood "in bleak contrast to the hundreds" of bishops and other clergy who had taken part in the election of Patriarch Tikhon in 1917.[19] At that earlier church council 250 bishops and clergy and 314 laity had taken part.[20]

The official documents published after this historic *sobor'* are uniformly unenlightening about the participants' thoughts. At war's end, however, Karpov wrote a survey—classified as "top secret" [*sovershenno sekretno*]—of the role religion had played during the previous four years. In this remarkable document, Karpov recounted that the Russian Orthodox clergy summoned to the *sobor'* were deeply fearful and skeptical about the government's newfound tolerance of the church. Karpov wrote, "In certain cases the clergy and believers consider the current situation of the church as a temporary phenomenon, brought about by the war, and that they may await sharp changes in the policies of the government in relation to the church" following the defeat of the

Germans. Karpov cited the remarks of "Bishop Mikhail of Kherson"[21] who "clearly expressed these feelings of mistrust in conversation with the delegate of the Soviet, about the impressions of participants of the *Pomestnyi Sobor.*" The bishop said that "'The ceremonies connected with the *Pomestnyi Sobor*' made, of course, a deep and unforgettable impression,'" but that this impression varied greatly. The bishop continued:

> [T]o me it seemed that only a small minority of the *Soborites* accepted all these ceremonies and all manner of attentions as a direct recognition by the government of the institution of the church and the establishment of complete religious tolerance, but the overwhelming majority of the clergy and laity, *almost to a man repressed in the recent past,* regarded all of this very critically and with great caution, with great doubt, and even complete distrust, considering that all of this has been brought to life by some sort of as yet unclear moment of political necessity. (emphasis added)

Many of the clergy believed that "When the war ends, the church will end." While the majority of clergy were understandably distrustful of the Soviet regime's constancy, Karpov wrote, "There are also partisans of the opinion that the existence in Russia of churches and the establishment of full religious toleration is a matter not of a temporary character, but an indisputable fact for the fundamental stabilization of the church." Karpov did not specify who these more optimistic clerics were, though they seem to have been a small minority.[22]

Small wonder that the clerics remained skeptical about the regime's sincerity. The participants of the *sobor'* had not been consulted in advance about their meeting; indeed, some seem to have been released from the camps specifically for the occasion, so they could play their allotted role before the newsreel cameras as they paid homage to their Soviet masters. It is known that, of the four Russian Orthodox metropolitans, twenty-one archbishops, and thirty-six bishops who would be alive at war's end, at least seventeen had been "repressed" before 1941.[23]

The meeting issued greetings to Stalin, in what had become a routine feature of wartime gatherings in Moscow, though in this instance the religious wording must have grated on those who recalled the Leader's recent relations with the church. The participants of the *sobor'* declared themselves "Profoundly moved by the sympathetic attitude of our country's leader, the head of the Soviet Government, J. V. Stalin, towards the needs of the Russian Orthodox Church and the modest work which we, its humble servants, are doing." *Sobor'* documents, and later accounts of the event, uniformly repeated this same careful phrasing: Stalin had met the church's request for a *sobor'* "sympathetically."[24] The impression conveyed is that the church itself approached the Soviet government, and that Stalin merely met their initiative with "sympathy." In fact, of course, the reverse was true.

The bishops also appealed to "Brother Christians throughout the world." Although "Our Motherland has borne the main blow of the German onslaught," the bishops claimed, they appealed to Christians worldwide "to bend all efforts to the holy struggle for the ideals of Christianity which Hitler has trampled underfoot, for the freedom of Christian churches, for the freedom, happiness and culture of all mankind." To Christians in Nazi-occupied countries, the hierarchs appealed for more effective partisan warfare; to Western Christians, they expressed the hope that "the long-awaited Second Front may finally be created to bring nearer victory and peace for the people."[25]

Shortly after the synod, the Soviet government announced that it would allow the church to resume publication of its official organ, the *Zhurnal moskovskoi patriarkhii*, which would have a printing of 15,000 copies.[26] And in October the creation of the Council for Affairs of the Russian Orthodox Church was announced, with Karpov being named as its new president.[27] The appointment of Karpov, a senior officer of the secret police who had taken an active part in Stalin's purges, was an important indication both that the Soviet government understood the wide-ranging political possibilities opened up by its new church policies, as well as the dangers posed by the return of the church to public prominence.[28] The creation of the new council, and the quickness of Karpov's appointment, following as they did directly on the heels of the *sobor'*, also suggest, as one historian of the Russian Church writes, that "it seems likely that these were not new creations but merely an administrative redesignation."[29] Karpov had already most probably been involved in the direction of Russian church affairs from behind the veil of police secrecy; now, many of his activities could be more open.

If the first, and most immediately visible, outcome of the *sobor'* was the issuance of familiar Soviet propaganda declarations, sprinkled this time with a little Orthodox Holy Oil, behind the scenes the resurrection of the Patriarchate betokened genuine policy changes. The participation in the Kremlin talks of Molotov, the wartime foreign commissar, was an important omen indicating that church policy was designed in part to address significant foreign policy issues; in quizzing Karpov before his meetings with the metropolitans, Stalin had focused on issues of foreign policy. During the coming months, the church's assigned tasks would become clearer: first, the newly elected patriarch was invested with sufficient legal power finally to deal with Moscow's religious opponents, renegade Poles and Ukrainians in particular; second, at the same time, the *sobor'* itself served as excellent theater, and Moscow would make the most of the occasion to broadcast to the world its newly reworked image as the tolerant protector of Slavs and Orthodox Christians. The propaganda value of the *sobor'* would be greatly enhanced by the arrival of an Anglican Church delegation, led by Britain's archbishop of York, which would arrive in Moscow only days after the meeting.[30]

Although the Soviet state was clearly manipulating the Russian Orthodox Church for its own ends, it would be wrong to assume that church hierarchs were wholly reluctant or passive participants. Unfortunately, we have few records of the clerics' private thoughts; in the circumstances of Stalin's Russia, it would have been madness for any priest to keep a private diary, and engaging in frank correspondence was risky. The Soviets certainly read letters exchanged between Orthodox clerics; intercepted mail is contained within the Kremlin's archives and was circulated in the highest ranks of the Soviet government.[31] Karpov's observations about the 1943 *sobor'* indicate that the bishops were unsure of the regime's long-term intentions, and they were in no position as yet to demand more than the state was willing to give. Nonetheless, the church did receive genuine benefits from the new party line. If the Moscow Patriarchate were to serve as the "Vatican" that Stalin envisaged, this would mean greater centralization of ecclesiastical authority in its hands, something that could only be welcomed by Orthodox clerics.

The *sobor'* and Sergii's elevation to the patriarchal throne represented the realization of the project outlined by Sergii in his introduction to *Pravda o religii*. The church would supply its considerable political and propaganda services to the government, and in exchange the Kremlin would give it the power to rid itself of its enemies and rivals: Renovationist schismatics backed in the past by the Communists, Ukrainian secessionist movements in rebellion against patriarchal authority, the Uniates whom the Muscovite church had always regarded as the worst sort of heretics, and other smaller sects. The rewards that the Moscow Patriarchate received in 1943 in exchange for services rendered to the Soviet state were in fact what the Kremlin also wanted to see: the recentralization in the patriarch's hands of spiritual and institutional authority over all the country's Orthodox.

Following the *sobor'*, the Renovationists were the first to close up shop and meekly reenter the ranks of the patriarchal church. The *sobor'* openly condemned the Renovationists: some church members, the Patriarchate announced, "walked the path of divisiveness and schism," because this "promised them greater freedom in their personal life."[32] This was a jab at the relatively lavish (by Moscow standards) life-style of the divorced and remarried Aleksandr Vvedenskii, whom the American photographer Margaret Bourke-White characterized as "witty, worldly, and a bit of a flirt."[33] Vvedenskii's family was also a source of gossip, one British diplomat resident in the Soviet capital describing the archbishop's daughter as "the nearest approach to a society girl that I have met here. She was very well dressed."[34]

During late 1943, and through the spring of the following year, one after another Renovationist priest reentered the church, begging the Patriarchate to forgive "the sin of their association with the *obnovlencheskii* schism."[35] In March 1944 Vvedenskii himself finally realized that his Soviet protectors had cut the earth from under his feet, and he reentered the Patriarchal Church.[36] He was soon rewarded for his betrayals by being appointed Archbishop of Tula and Belevsk in July 1944.[37]

The genius of the Soviets' new religious line consisted in the fact that it pushed in the same direction that its executors, the clergy, wanted to go. There may have been no trust between church and Soviet state, but for this brief period their interests ran together; at least they shared common enemies.

Nationalism and Conflicted Loyalties

The Russian Orthodox *sobor'* occurred as Soviet forces were sweeping into Ukraine, having defeated the Wehrmacht in titanic battles during the summer months. Historians who argue that the Kremlin restored the church because it needed to harness Russian national feeling behind the Soviet war effort miss this critical timing. The Russian Patriarchate was not restored as an institution as the Germans were pressing at the gates of Moscow, but rather after they had been driven back and while the Soviets were reoccupying vast areas that had fallen under German rule during the first two years of war. Soviet religious policy was evolving with the changing demands of the war: by late 1943 the services demanded of the Russian Orthodox Church had become more complex. Whereas the ending of the more overt forms of religious repression may have been a product of the Nazi attack, the restoration of the Patriarchate as a public institution came about owing to the demands of reoccupation. Soviet authorities realized in 1943 that, lacking a canonically elected head, the church could not perform its required political services. Sergii's election was the result.

Like all dictatorships, Stalin's regime was to some extent a prisoner of its own propaganda. The Kremlin had no extra regime source of information concerning the loyalty of its subjects. The NKVD-NKGB reported on signs of disloyalty to be sure, but, as Stalin told Churchill, one could not entirely trust intelligence services to tell the boss the whole truth.[38] The secret police, especially under Stalin when the consequences of being insufficiently vigilant were severe, was not above manufacturing enemies; nor was it reluctant to tell the Kremlin what it wanted to hear. In the first months of the war, however, Stalin had learned the hard way that many of his subjects were disloyal.[39] As Soviet authority returned to German-held regions, therefore, Moscow tried to divine the opinions of the local population. Unsurprisingly, the results varied tremendously, reflecting the deep regional, national, and class divisions characteristic of the Soviet Union.

When the Soviets recovered the city of Khar'kov in 1943, the Directorate of Propaganda tried to discover the opinions of educated people in that city, which had changed hands four times during the fighting. "The basic mass of the intelligentsia welcomed the Red Army with joy," I. Fomina, a director of a propaganda group wrote. But among "the intelligentsia of the old school," or those educated during the tsarist period, there had been several "serious betrayals." Some educated people welcomed the Germans at first. "However, repressions and terror, the shooting of Jews, and the compulsory mobilization of youth to Germany," in addition to public executions, requisitioning of apartments and private possessions, soon brought an end to overt pro-German sympathy. The saying spread, Fomina wrote, that "What comrade Stalin could not do in twenty-four years, Hitler did in one." That is, the Führer ruined Khar'kov and turned almost the entire population against him.

Although the Germans had alienated the educated population, this did not mean that these same people were sympathetic to, or properly educated about, Soviet realities as interpreted by Moscow. The fact that the city had been cut off from Soviet propaganda exercised "a hostile influence on the intelligentsia." In particular, *intelligenty* misunderstood the nature of the anti-Hitler coalition, seeing in it a hope that the USSR would grant greater intellectual freedoms such as those enjoyed in the Western democracies. The docent of Khar'kov University, for example, thought that alliance with the United States and Great Britain would lead to an infusion into Soviet society of "the ideas of western culture not only in the scientific-technical sphere, but also in the areas of morals and politics." A Professor Tereshchenko allegedly said that "After all we've survived the government should change its policies." He cited the agreements signed with the United States and Great Britain, the dissolution of the Comintern, and the "creation of a committee on churches" as proof that Moscow was being forced to change its ways. Another professor echoed this idea that the alliance had forced the USSR to ease its prewar repressive policies: "Freedom of religion now in the USSR can be explained by the influence of

England and America, but all the same religion in our country should die off, since it is incompatible with the creation of a communist society."

In conclusion, Fomina wrote that "fascist lies and demagogy" sowed incorrect views among the elite of Khar'kov; these people did not fully understand "the change in the correlation of forces" that favored Moscow. She drew three conclusions from her review of intellectual opinion: first, that "several bourgeois and petty-bourgeois opinions" had taken root; second, "A whole group of scholars [*uchenykh*], in the past abasing themselves before west European [political] order and culture, not understanding the nature of the anti-Hitler coalition, have fallen into apologetics for bourgeois-democratic politics and culture"; and, third, "Although the Germans were unable to raise the basic mass of the Ukrainian intelligentsia against the Russians, and the creation by them of nationalist organizations did not find support among the basic mass of educated people in Kharkov, nonetheless among the intelligentsia there are people with hostile attitudes towards all Russians."[40]

Reports from *propgruppy* (propaganda groups) that followed the Red Army into areas formerly held by the Germans repeated many of the same themes contained in the report from Khar'kov. The local population evinced great anxiety about the future. Concerns ran in several different directions: on the one hand, many people feared possible postwar conflict with the Western Allies; on the other hand, some were hopeful that the alliance would produce a softening of Soviet life. Questions most frequently asked of propaganda officers concerned the kolkhozes—would these hated institutions return after the war? Many people also asked about the revival of the church: "Was the organization for the committee for the affairs of the church connected with our relations with England and the USA?" "Why did they decide during the war to open the churches?" "Why in the period of collectivization and after did Soviet power place more limitations on religion—they closed and destroyed churches— was this not an excess [*peregib*] on the side of Soviet power?" Even more dangerously: "Will there be Soviet power after the war, or will there be such a power as exists in America and Britain?"[41] Civilian believers could now visit church; what about Christians in the Red Army?[42]

In reports such as these, one can see the seeds of postwar anti-intellectual and anti-Western campaigns, the so-called Zhdanovshchina. In the short term, however, the more worrisome threat for Moscow was the clear existence of anti-Soviet and anti-Russian feeling among Ukrainians and other minority nationalities. Such sentiments were, if anything, even stronger in rural areas than in the cities, and they were more intense the further west one went. In the western borderlands, significant partisan resistance sprang up opposing the reimposition of Soviet control, in some areas continuing well after the war, into the 1950s.

As the Red Army moved into Moldavia, the Baltic states, and western Ukraine, the high command attempted to draft local men into military service. Casualties from the first years of fighting had already climbed into in the millions, and the need for new recruits was intense if the Red Army were successfully to pursue the beaten Nazis into Central Europe; but in the western borderlands the local population evaded the draft and resisted Soviet demands by any number of means. A Red Army general major, V. Zolotukhin, informed Moscow that in the L'vov and Drogobych oblast's of western Ukraine the situation was mixed at best. A "significant part"—though by inference not a majority—of the population was "against the Germans." Such people thanked the Red Army for their liberation, willingly undertook reconstruction tasks, and exhibited anti-German feelings; when one woman gave retreating German soldiers bread, for instance, she was beaten up by other locals. At the same time, however, opposition to German occupiers did not translate directly into support for the Soviets. There was a great deal of open distrust about Soviet intentions among the western Ukrainians. One *starik*, or elder, asked whether it was true that the Red Army would kill innocent people; he decided that, even if this were true, it was better to die at home than become one of the war's numberless refugees. Zolotukhin wrote: "In several regions of the western Ukraine the city and village bourgeoisie, and also part of the chauvinistically inclined intelligentsia are hostile to Soviet power and the Red Army. They sympathize with the German-Ukrainian nationalists and give them all assistance." Even among those people who were either sympathetic to Soviet power, or at least not opposed, "the population was scared and terrorized by the nationalist bands" who, the author claimed, intimidated young men by threatening reprisals against their families if they dared to join the Soviet forces.

Many people fought the draft—some with weapons, others with whatever was at hand, such as pitchforks, shovels, and sharpened stakes. Others even tried passive resistance: "[W]omen laid themselves in the road to block the path of automobiles." One person cried out at the Soviets: "You wrote about yourselves as liberators, but in actual fact you are robbers." That unfortunate man was immediately arrested by SMERSH, the feared counterespionage unit of the Red Army, whose name was an acronym for *Smert' shpionam*, or "death to spies." It is hard to credit Zolotukhin's claim that such obviously dangerous and desperate tactics were all motivated by fears of partisan retribution; nor does his analysis convincingly explain the motives of the Ukrainian nationalist partisans themselves. They fought hard against the Red Army, as many of them had against the Germans before, using arms left to them by the retreating Wehrmacht or captured from the Soviets; they possessed automatic weapons, heavy machine guns, and even artillery. Using these, in one twenty-day period they killed 185 "party and Soviet aktivs" in the L'vov *voennyi krug* alone.

Owing to such resistance, after the Red Army first entered the region, the draft went "slowly," as young men went "to the woods and hills." There, the Banderites "frightened the population with horrors about exile to Siberia and other repressions by the Red Army." Such propaganda was, of course, all the more credible and potent because people could remember for themselves the mass deportations that occurred when the Red Army last controlled the region, between 1939 and 1941. Consequently, the number of people responding to Soviet draft calls in the two oblast's was "very low"; but, based on "incomplete figures," the Soviets believed there were 52,639 draft-age men, of whom only 3,380 answered the government's summonses. In the L'vov region, the situation was better, though even there 28.3 percent did not respond to the call.

Zolotukhin offered several explanations for local hostility to Soviet power, in addition to the influence of Ukrainian nationalist partisans: he cited the long legacy of Austrian and Polish rule, as well as "religious feelings." This latter was a problem even among those successfully drawn into army ranks. "The level of development of the replacements is low," Zolotukhin complained, painting an image of country bumpkins: "Many soldiers never once saw a movie, never heard the radio, never saw a combine and tractor, and also have troublous preconceptions of the Soviet Union and its armed forces." It is rather hard to believe that the average recruit from the plains of Central Asia—or indeed from the Russian heartland itself—was very different in many of these respects. But once these suspect Ukrainian recruits entered the army, they brought with them the danger of infection to good Soviet lads. Many were not good soldiers, Zolotukhin concluded; some were Evangelicals or Baptists, others were members of nationalist "counterrevolutionary" bands; others had served in the prewar Polish army, where they actually fought against the Red Army in 1939. Such nationalists had a detrimental effect on army morale, encouraging desertion or pacifism. The Christians even "conduct anti-Soviet agitation among the soldiers."[43]

Religion continually proved problematic in the western borderlands. As Georgii Karpov noted ruefully, "a massive opening of churches" occurred "in regions that underwent German occupation . . . in the period 1941–1943."[44] As they had done before the Nazi invasion, churches provided a natural subterranean network for the recruitment, organization, and sustenance of anti-

Soviet nationalists; after all, many of their clergy had every reason to fear the return of the Communist atheist—and Russian—order. Pavel Sudoplatov, who headed an NKVD hit team roaming through Ukraine with orders to assassinate prominent enemies of the Soviet order, writes that "the bulk of guerilla commanders came from the families of Ukrainian clergymen."[45] An intelligence document from the Moldavian Republic—which had been under Romanian jurisdiction during the Axis occupation—recorded that "materials gathered by agents" (*agenturnymi materialami*) demonstrated "that anti-Soviet church-sectarian circles" in that republic harmed Soviet interests in a number of ways. They assisted the occupiers in "the strengthening of the fascist order" by distributing "anti-Soviet nationalistic propaganda." They also "cooperat[ed] with the punitive organs of the occupiers through the betrayal of Soviet aktivs and the monitoring of the political opinions of the population." "Monastics also actively collaborated with the occupiers" by "revealing places of partisan deployment, Soviet parachutists and disclosing Red Army prisoners of war who had escaped from prison camps." Finally, religious nationalists furthered both "the Romanianization of the population by means of drawing them into the creation of nationalistic organizations [and] the use of occupationist newspapers, chiefly, readings advocating an anti-Soviet character."[46]

One should be careful, of course, about accepting the claims of such documents entirely at face value. Stalinist secret police were not fastidious when it came to identifying enemies, and they defined anti-Soviet activity with liberal flexibility. Nonetheless, it is clear both that churches represented an impediment to the reestablishment of Soviet power in the western borderlands and that Communist agents were determined either to subvert or to root them out.

The Soviets adopted three approaches toward this religious-national dilemma: first, and most successful, Soviet propaganda focused intently on branding as fascist- or Nazi-inspired even the smallest manifestations of anti-Soviet, especially non-Russian, nationalism; second, the newly revivified Russian Patriarchate excommunicated recalcitrant clerics, handing over their parishes and church property to priests loyal to Moscow and so far as possible Russifying religion in the western borderlands; finally, Soviet secret police worked to penetrate and break up politically unreliable religious centers, and Sudoplatov's band of assassins arranged the murder of key nationalist clerics who could not be suborned or intimidated into cooperation. Moscow's three approaches would prove a highly effective mix in dealing with the religious question, even in its smaller manifestations.

The most important targets of this new church-state alliance were the Ukrainian Orthodox splinter churches, the Ukrainian Autocephalous and Ukrainian

Autonomous Churches.[47] On September 12, 1943, Archbishop Grigorii of Saratov and Stalingrad delivered a "discourse" at the Church of the Epiphany in Moscow in which he condemned rebels against patriarchal authority. Greeting the elevation of Sergii, he said that God had protected the church even when it lacked a lawfully elected patriarch: "The Russian Orthodox people did not betake themselves to the Renovators, to the Gregorians, to the Josephians, the autocephalists and other self-constituted congregations, the heads of which were bishops who were greedy of power, and their tools."[48] Although the archbishop was outwardly congratulating the Russian people for not following these schismatics, his long list of rebels was an implicit admission that many believers had in fact done so.

In November 1943 Metropolitan Nikolai addressed believers in Ukraine, brandishing the newly refashioned disciplinary sword given him by the *Sobor'*. "I know the peace loving character of the Ukrainian people," Nikolai wrote. "But I also know of their fiery love of their homeland!" He called on those Ukrainians still behind German lines to assist Soviet partisans. He also called them to "Be true to the end to our Holy Mother Russian Church" and to Patriarch Sergii. Sadly, Nikolai admitted, not all Ukrainians had been loyal to the Soviet cause: "With deep grief our Russian Orthodox Church is learning that several of the Ukrainian hierarchs are cringing before the temporary fascist lords, disavowing their Mother-Church, and betraying their Homeland to Hitler, the world bandit." Nikolai was pressing the approved line: anti-Soviet nationalism of any sort equaled Nazism. Nikolai mentioned two traitorous bishops by name, Polykarp Sikorskii and Metropolitan Feofill Bul'dovskii of Kharkov, before issuing a stern warning:

> Brother believers of the Ukraine! By the resolution of the last *sobor'* of bishops of the Russian Orthodox Church, which took place in Moscow on the 8th of September this year, all those guilty of betrayal to the common cause of the church [*obshchestserkovnomu delu*] and going over to the side of fascism, as an enemy of the cross of Christ, are to be reckoned excommunicate, both bishops and clerics—and relieved of office. And let not one of you follow after pastors or archpastors who have betrayed the Mother-Church and Homeland! Do not ruin your soul eternally by fatal relations with false hierarchs and false priests that have been condemned by the *sobor'*.[49]

The newly elected patriarch himself issued a letter to "His Flock," in which he declared: "It is not for nothing that our church so urgently requires that the name of the patriarch should be commemorated in all the churches of our country. He who suppresses the commemoration of the Patriarch has 'neither part nor lot' (Acts VIII.21) with the faithful children of the Orthodox Church."[50] Schismatic, or anti-Russian, clergy were being told to submit to patriarchal authority or face excommunication.

Despite the return of schismatic clergy, the church's new role placed a great strain on its human resources, because it had lost a large proportion of its clergy during the previous decade and a half. The Soviets had long ago closed all Russian Orthodox seminaries, preventing the education of new priests and further aggravating the problem. Now, there were not enough priests to man all the working parishes. As Karpov wrote at the end of the war: "Churches and houses of prayer are distributed very unevenly. The greatest quantity are located in regions that underwent German occupation, when in the period 1941–1943 there took place a massive opening of churches." By August 1945, of 10,243 active churches in the USSR as a whole, the great majority were in the western borderlands: 6,072 were in Ukraine alone, 633 were in Belorussia, and a further 615 in Moldavia.[51] Another Soviet source closer to Moldavian affairs places the number of open churches in that republic even higher under the German occupation, claiming that there were 888 working Orthodox churches and 25 monasteries at that time; after the return of the Red Army, this number was reduced to 582.[52] The Baltic states, whose Orthodox population was only a minority, had a further 343. In Russia itself, by far the largest republic of the Soviet Union both geographically and in population, there were only 2,297 open churches and houses of prayer, with many of these also being in regions once occupied by the Germans, or in areas that had been near the front.[53] In other words, more than 70 percent of the open churches were in the non-Russian western borderlands, with only a smattering being in areas that had remained behind the Soviet lines throughout the war. Ukraine was clearly the focal point of this Orthodox revival. "In the Ukrainian SSR in the period of occupation," Karpov wrote, "1,124 buildings were [re]occupied by church societies, of these following liberation 587 were returned to their former designation," to be used by state organizations and for other nonreligious uses.[54]

The reopening, or more properly the conquest, of churches in the western regions triggered a rush of episcopal and clerical appointments as Moscow sought to replace local clergy with properly vetted clerics. A study of Russian Orthodox personnel in 1944 counted two metropolitans, as well as fifty-eight bishops and archbishops; of these, all but eight received their positions in the spring and summer of 1944—precisely as the Red Army finally drove the Germans back beyond the USSR's prewar boundaries. The others were appointed in late 1943.[55] Many priests who had been driven out of the church by the prewar repressions cautiously resumed their callings. Karpov told a Canadian dip-

MAP 2. Limit of German Advance, 1941–1942, and Number of Open Churches, 1945, by Republic

lomat somewhat misleadingly that "a number of former priests who some years ago turned to bookkeeping, teaching or other works, are beginning to return to church duties."[56]

So great was the need for new priests, and so useful were the services provided by the church, that Stalin himself promised Sergii that the church could open a seminary.[57] Consequently, on November 28, 1943, the Soviet of People's Commissars authorized the opening of a seminary in Moscow; on May 10, 1944, the same body allowed the church to begin a religious training course in Saratov. In March 1944 the Russian Orthodox Church duly opened its first seminary since the early days of the Bolshevik regime in Moscow's famous Novodevichy Convent, which had been closed before the war.[58] Understandably perhaps, given the circumstances, the religious standards for appointment to bishoprics were minimal; religious training was to be much more compressed than in tsarist times, no doubt reflecting the urgent need to train church personnel quickly in order to staff the newly recovered western parishes.[59]

By April 1946, 9,254 parish priests were at work in the USSR, a figure greatly at variance with the claim made by the Soviet authorities to foreign visitors that there were 58,442 priests in the USSR.[60] As a group they were rather old: only 7.7 percent were under the age of forty; 42.8 percent were more than sixty-one years old. Just under half, or 45.6 percent, had served in some religious capacity before the revolution; but 30.3 percent had been ordained during the war years, a reflection of the urgent need to refill the drastically thinned ranks of the clergy. Just as most of the working churches would be in the regions formerly occupied by the Nazis, so the overwhelming number of priests would be sent to parishes in these areas. Of 264 priests ordained during the war, 240 were installed in parishes that had undergone Nazi occupation.[61]

Although NKVD-NKGB records are not yet available on this matter, it is safe to assume that the political police infiltrated the ranks of these clergy. This had been police practice since at least 1921, when Chekists were ordered to resort to blackmail and bribery in order to suborn priests: "Financial and material subsidies without a doubt will tie them to us," Chekists were told, "and to a new relationship where [the priest] becomes an eternal slave of the Cheka, fearing the unmasking of his activity."[62] In most instances, these newly minted priests replaced local clergy who might have collaborated with the Germans, or who were connected with the anti-Soviet (and also often anti-Nazi) nationalist underground. The placement of these new priests in the western borderlands, therefore, served multiple functions: decapitating local nationalist resistance and establishing a network of informer-priests throughout the provinces, while also helping to Russify the region. Once again, although this whole process clearly served the security interests of the Soviet state, no doubt many Russian Ortho-dox clergy welcomed the education of new priests and the return to firm patri-archal authority of parishes in the western regions, even if this inevitably meant making compromises with state power.

Using the new powers conferred by the *sobor'*, the Russian Orthodox Church was now able to excommunicate clergy unwilling to bow to the new order, as it had been unable to do so long as Russia lacked a canonically sound patriarch. Not all clergymen thus forced back into the fold were comfortable with the new church-state relations, but with the Red Army advancing and Sergii in-stalled on the patriarchal throne, they had precious few alternatives. An anony-mous bishop from a Ukrainian splinter church remarked: "All that Metropoli-tan Sergii is doing is a very dirty business, but I want to return finally home, after all!"[63] Thus, while the outward appearance of religious tolerance was pre-served, behind the scenes, the Patriarchate and the NKGB worked to enhance the security of the Communist order.

Revival from Below

Until the *sobor'* of September 1943, the Kremlin remained firmly in control of religious developments behind Soviet lines. Power flowed overwhelmingly from the top down, and the Russian Orthodox Church recovered strength only so far as the state allowed. Following the *sobor'*, however, state controls began to break down from two directions at once: first, the chaos of war and reoccupa-tion, and the consequent temporary weakening of state authority as the front shifted from east to west, created circumstances favorable for a religious revival from below; and, second, the Soviets' new religious policy was ill-defined, and people throughout the USSR, both in and out of government, were confused about the degree of religious toleration now allowable. The Soviets' wartime dalliance with Orthodoxy unleashed furies that Moscow would find difficult to tame.

Beginning in 1943, and even more so during 1944, the Soviets faced what was, for them, an alarming growth in the numbers of spontaneous religious mani-festations; Soviet sources uniformly testify to this phenomenon throughout the USSR, both in areas occupied by the Germans and in the Soviet rear. Karpov tried to explain this: "Activities in the life of the church in the past few years: se-lection of a patriarch; the increase of the episcopate, the conduct of a *Pomest-nyi Sobor'*, the publication in newspapers of a series of church documents, the opening of new churches, theological courses, the distribution of a church journal—[all] eased the revitalization of the church." "In general," Karpov continued, "in the war years religious moods increased, visits to churches underwent a significant increase."[64] Nor was the religious revival limited to Orthodox churches; another Central Committee report noted the same trend "in all religious cults," including among Evangelicals, Baptists, Seventh-Day Adventists, and Jews.[65] Soviet authorities deemed these latter groups to be even more pernicious than Russian Orthodoxy, because they could not be subordinated to a pliant Patriarchate; many Protestant sects also had stronger evangelical traditions than did the Russian church, raising the frightening prospect of mass recruitment.

Even the patriarchal church was only a barely tolerable evil, however, since its relative freedom encouraged believers to demand ever more from the state. An NKGB document from Penza oblast', to the southeast of Moscow, illustrates this: "There are two working churches in the oblast', which basically exert a useful influence on the believing population," the police officer wrote, because they called on their congregations to give their all in the war against Germany. But, at the same time, these two churches served as centers "for agitation for the mass opening of churches. They spread such views among believers visiting the Penza church from distant villages of the oblast', from 100 and more kilometers."[66]

In trying to understand this explosion of religious activity, Soviet authorities tended to view the population as being largely passive and easily led. In the report just cited, a colonel of the NKGB attributed the widely proliferating, spontaneous religious acts in his region to public ignorance, bad propaganda work, and the manipulation of simple people by religious charlatans. Religious activities "speak, above all, of the absence of mass party-educational work among the populace," he wrote. "A vagrant element is using" wartime dislocation and public ignorance to present themselves as "*iurodivy*" (holy fools) or, "invalids." "They call for prayers and the opening of churches, they spread all sorts of rumors. Itinerant priests exert a special influence on the religiously minded, appearing in recent times in the oblast' after serving a term of punishment, from exile cities [*rezhimnykh gorodov*]." He cited two specific instances of this: the first, a Kh. T. Volokitin, served a sentence for "counterrevolutionary crimes," only to reappear in the Penza region as a wandering priest; and the second, I. V. Kalinin, returned from exile after being convicted of "anti-Soviet activity," promptly gathering prayer groups in his apartment. He even continued to do so after authorities forced him to move to another city.[67]

The dividing line between the gulag and ordinary Soviet life was far too permeable for NKGB tastes. Not only did priests return from terms of imprisonment to spread their faith; even within the "corrective labor camps," religion was a troublesome presence. One NKVD document warned that some gulag prisoners were "holding church and sectarian prayer meetings" in which anti-Soviet and supposedly "profascist" agitation was being conducted. Some prisoners were planning escapes to spread their contagion. Furthermore, the NKVD warned, "Instances have been discovered of the sentenced church people illegally setting up links with their fellow believers at liberty with the aim of receiving instructions for a.-s. [anti-Soviet] work, as well as religious literature and material help." To deal with this problem, the NKVD proposed recruiting "qualified agents among the imprisoned church people and sect members," to "unmask their illegal links with those in freedom."[68]

Noting instances throughout the USSR where spontaneous religious activity was proliferating, and where unsanctioned priests were conducting services, Karpov believed such people to be venal and self-interested: "Supernumerary, wandering [*bezmestnoe*] clergy play a well-known role in presenting applications [for the opening of churches], and even former church elders and treasurers, who see in the opening of churches a source for their personal income."

The truth, however, was more complex than these Soviet bureaucrats allowed: religious believers were making as much use of the war's chaos and the absence of stable governmental structures as they were of the Soviets' new-found religious tolerance. "The clergy is showing great initiative in the cause of revitalizing the religious mood," Karpov admitted. Some priests who, as the reports cited here noted, had earlier served sentences in the gulag were now following behind the Red Army, hoping to sow the seeds of new churches in ground upturned by fighting and the temporary weakness of political authority. Perhaps some of these clergy were opportunists; but, contrary to Karpov's attribution of ulterior motives, it is at least as plausible to view many of them as genuinely responding to a public demand for religious solace in the most tragic of wartime circumstances. After all, anyone motivated primarily by money and personal security would scarcely have chosen the church as a promising career in Stalin's USSR. The continuous threat of arrest, clandestine monitoring, betrayal, and harassment by authorities testified to in these accounts suggests a high level of determination, and even courage, on the part of these wandering clergy. Given their materialist world view, however, Soviet functionaries were unable to understand the clergy's motives as being anything other than manipulative, greedy, and underhanded.

Priests and ordinary believers often flouted Soviet law, risking severe punishment. In Kiev, for instance, as 2,000 people watched, 40 believers violated Soviet prohibitions against baptism, openly being immersed in the waters of the Dniepr River, where the legendary "baptism of Rus'" had taken place in 988. Much the same thing occurred in Khar'kov, where 150 onlookers witnessed the baptism of 45 people. Many similar incidents occurred throughout the western regions.[69] In many other areas of the USSR, believers ignored Soviet legal restrictions, creating their own churches. Karpov wrote: "In regions where there are no working churches, or where they are insufficient, there is quite a large proliferation of complete religious services and rites by priests in unregistered churches, and even by people not belonging to the clergy. In a number of places these services have a mass character." Here, as in so many other areas, the reconstituted Moscow Patriarchate was of use. During the *sobor'*, Sergii warned of priests giving services who were not properly ordained, and he told communities of believers that they were responsible for rooting out false priests.[70] The Patriarchate, with the Kremlin behind it, could identify and remove politically unreliable priests.

Despite the services of the Patriarchate, the spontaneous revival of religion posed serious political dangers for the tightly controlled Stalinist system, leading to what Soviet bureaucrats called "facts of anti-Soviet manifestations." Even defiance of Soviet law by single individuals carried the risk of snowballing. Such was the case with open acts of pacifism. One Seventh-Day Adventist medical student in the Ukrainian city of Dnepropetrovsk, for example, refused to serve in the Red Army. After he was imprisoned, six fellow students petitioned for his release. "The leader of that society [of Seventh-Day Adventists in the city] along with its members, views military service negatively." They claimed that, for each individual, military service was a matter " 'of his own conscience.' "[71] This was a deeply heretical notion to Stalinists. In Zhitomir, to the west of Kiev, Baptists and Evangelicals gathered publicly to pray for those arrested for refusing military service; they too suffered the consequences.[72]

In rare cases, the Soviets also faced communal religious resistance to governmental authority. Even when this was largely passive, the security organs reacted harshly. In January 1945 NKVD officials informed Lavrenty Beria that during the previous year they had smashed a sect calling itself the " '*istinno-pravoslavnye khristiane'* ['*IPKh'*)," or genuine-Orthodox Christians, from Orel, Voronezh, and Riazan' oblast's. The sect's members "refuse to enter into the kolkhozes, they do not recognize laws." The NKVD accused them of "parasitism," withdrew their food allowances, and sent "[e]lders and children . . . to invalid homes." When these measures failed, the remaining members were deported to various places in Siberia and Central Asia.[73] By war's end, a total of 1,212 members of the IPKh had been deported and were still living, including 102 men, 659 women, and 451 children under the age of sixteen.[74] The sources do not reveal how many more people died as a result of arrest and deportation.

Small religious demonstrations could grow if unchecked by the police. An

NKGB report told how on May 30, for example, in the village of Nikolo-Azias' "an anti-Soviet element" took advantage of a "mass" religious gathering. Following community prayers, a group of 30 women, led by Tat'iana Kolchina and Ol'ga Potapova, made a procession through the town carrying icons and singing hymns; soon they were joined by more than 100 followers. Suddenly, Potapova "supposedly in the throes of religious ecstasy, began to express anti-Soviet shouts, directed against the kolkhozes." A secretary of the Penza obkom asked angrily, "[W]hy was this performance by church people tolerated?" The local NKGB man, Zhdanov, knew in advance about plans for the procession, but he "took no [preventative] measures; he did not even inform" his superiors.[75]

These incidents, and many others like them, were certainly minor affairs, but they illustrate how the totalitarian authorities stood ready to crush even such pathetic signs of opposition for fear that they might spark a new Pugachev-shchina, the great, savage peasant rebellion of the early 1770s against Catherine II that stood as a warning to Russia's rulers of how rural discontent could spiral into mass rebellion if not suppressed at once. Both the "genuine Orthodox" affair and the Nikolo-Azias' incident, small though they were, linked two potent rural forces: religious enthusiasm and hatred of the collective farms, both of which were widespread among the peasantry. The NKGB promptly arrested Kolchina and Potapova, plus another luckless woman, and reprimanded its local agent for lack of vigilance; it also dispatched two propaganda officers to this otherwise insignificant village to undertake "mass-political work for an extended time."[76]

As already noted, spontaneous religious activity was most dangerous for the Soviets when linked with nationalism and partisan resistance to the Red Army. This was common in the western borderlands, not just in Ukraine, but also in the Baltic States and Moldavia. Sometimes it was on a small scale and broken up relatively easily by Soviet repressive organs. In 1944, for example, in Povensk oblast' a man named Mikhail Kuz'min led a group of fifty "*piatidesiatniki*"[77] into the woods to meet with Ukrainian nationalist partisans. Later, when that group had been "liquidated," Kuz'min and twelve members of his sect were arrested and brought to trial.[78] In Moldavia, NKGB records testify that, even after the war had ended, the republic's Orthodox Church continued to assist the Romanian nationalist resistance and engaged in "the inculcation of negative relations with the Soviet order."[79] This same document detailed allegations of church collaboration with the enemy during the war, condemning the republic's Orthodox clergy for its hostility to the Moscow Patriarchate.[80]

Religion and nationalism blended together throughout the western borderlands, and believers' pressure for greater freedom of worship involved sometimes oblique calls for more national independence. In Lithuania, for example, Catholics demanded religious education in the schools and told local Soviet authorities that they would "not recognize that freedom of conscience and churches exists until the time when the teaching of God's law in the schools is not forbidden. We consider this the basic question, and all the remaining is just small change, and we do not even want to discuss it."[81] Catholicism helped to define Lithuanian cultural and national independence from Russia. For the authorities to allow religious education was unthinkable, not only because this would have violated Soviet "scientific atheism," but also because it would have trained new recruits to man the ranks of the Lithuanian nationalist resistance, one of the more effective anti-Soviet partisan movements.

Demands for religious education were common among ethnic Russians as well. In part, this stemmed from a lack of clarity about how far the Soviets' new religious tolerance went. In August 1945, Karpov wrote: "Several groups of believers never had explained to them in full measure the unchangeability of the law of the division of church from the state and suppose that the changes taking place in the life of the church signify that the church has become a part of the state, and on that ground they submit a series of illegal claims."[82] "The revitalization of church life," Karpov warned, encouraged priests in some locales to demand religious training for young people. "Priests are attempting to exert their influence on children," both preschoolers and students. One such priest, in Stalinsk oblast', even tried to gain access to orphaned children in a *detdom* (children's home), giving the organization a 1,000 ruble donation as a sweetener. "The director gave him a full rebuff," Karpov noted smugly.

The most common flashpoint between believers and the state concerned church property. The Soviets had shut thousands of churches during their earlier antireligious campaigns, transferring these buildings to other uses or leaving them empty, some in a severe state of disrepair. In the areas occupied by the Germans, believers reoccupied many such churches, restoring them to their original function. When Soviet authority returned, therefore, considerable friction ensued between Soviet organs and local congregations. Karpov wrote: "Legal activities of local Soviet organs in seizing state and social buildings that were taken over for purposes of prayer by societies of believers during the period of [German] occupation are sometimes interpreted by believers as 'repression' of the church." In one such case, when a deputy of the Soviet told a priest named Vasilevskii that his church would not be restored to its true function, the priest replied, " 'Again the repression of churches is beginning; the relations will be just like they were in the past. They 'gave' societies the premises, and now they 'demand their return.' "[83] According to Karpov, disputes of this sort occupied much of his Soviet's time, with "believers arriv[ing] every day not only from Moscow oblast' but also from a number of more outlying oblast's." In pleading for the restoration of churches, believers "refer to the Constitution, to the distances to working churches, to the facts of the opening of churches in other regions, to the existence of a great many believers in certain points and to the need for prayers for family and friends who perished in the war." By July 1945 the Soviet for Russian Orthodox Affairs had received 5,770 petitions to open churches, not including duplicates, of which only 414 had been granted; 3,850 were refused by local Soviet organs, and 1,506 were still under review in August 1945. Clearly, Karpov's group was intentionally dragging its feet. Petitions were not limited only to Russian or majority Slavic republics; in Turkmenistan, local Orthodox petitioned to reopen their churches, encouraging local Moslems to follow their example.[84]

A letter from the archbishop of Tambov in July 1944, intercepted by Soviet intelligence, sheds light on the problem of church reopenings and shows that some Orthodox clergy tried to craft a Fabian strategy for patiently expanding the bounds of religious freedom as far as circumstances allowed. The archbishop lamented the spiritual state of Russia and the fact that so few people had been baptized, but, he believed, the Russian people remained Christians at heart despite years of Communist antireligious propaganda. "Slowly, intolerably slowly goes the opening of churches in villages," he wrote. The clergy must work to reclaim churches not already wrecked by fighting, neglect, or prewar anti-God campaigns. He suggested that, rather than trying to repair ruined churches, for which there were no funds anyway, believers should instead build small wooden *izby* as chapels. Russian Orthodoxy should follow the Moslem example, the archbishop wrote, where small mosques existed on every street. In the meantime, the church should ask the state to authorize the production of religious items, such as icons and prayer books.[85]

This the Soviet authorities were reluctant to allow during the war. Indeed they destroyed many religious items that fell into their hands. In March 1944 Soviet forces captured some 60,000 icons that had been manufactured in Dresden, along with other church items. The Germans produced these as part of their last desperate effort to use Slavic religious opinion for their own ends. The icons alone were worth the considerable sum of 617,509 rubles. V. N. Merkulov of the secret police wrote the Central Committee: "The NKGB SSSR proposes it to be expedient that all of these church items of German origin be destroyed by means of fire."[86]

Some believers naively interpreted the convocation of the *sobor'* as evidence that the state had bestowed sweeping new rights on church people. "An incorrect understanding of questions related to the activities of the church is leading to a number of infractions of existing laws by the clergy and believers," Karpov wrote. "After the publication of the resolutions and addresses of the *Pomestnyi Sobor*' believers strengthened their entreaties by reference to these documents."

While congregations and individual believers throughout the USSR were confused about the extent of the state's newfound religious tolerance, personnel within the Soviet apparat also became less certain how to act. The old, prewar rules had been simple enough: organized religious activity was to be crushed. Now, however, the bounds of the allowable had become fuzzy, and a state not familiar with popular movements had to learn a degree of religious toleration —or at least to affect the appearance of it. This was no easy transformation for unimaginative, middle- and low-ranking state bureaucrats. Unsurprisingly, perhaps, two opposite trends emerged: some local authorities believed that nothing had really changed in church-state relations, and they continued to treat believers' demands with utter contempt. Other local Soviets wrongly interpreted the bewildering changes at the center as constituting the reconciliation of church and state. The first tendency seems to have been more common, but the second was more dangerous from Moscow's point of view.

"Complaints frequently appear in the Soviet regarding the slowness of deciding questions about opening churches," Karpov wrote, "about the baselessness of refusals, on the rudeness of representatives of local organs of Soviet power, and even of betrayal." In some cases, the local Soviets behaved like gangsters, shaking down groups of believers for cash. In the village of Pavlovo in Iaroslavskaia oblast' to the northeast of Moscow, for instance, believers petitioned the raiispolkom to reopen their local church. The authorities promised to do so if the congregation would first pay "arrears for the taxes from 1939 to 1943 to the sum of 27,000 rubles, which was done by the believers." After payment of this huge sum, the believers repeated their appeal, only to be told that they would have to produce yet more money for repairs. After raising another 18,000 rubles, however, the local authorities still did not open the church, using it for grain storage. Pavlovo's now impoverished believers still had to travel twelve kilometers to the nearest open church.

These financial abuses of power reflected the pressure that local officials themselves were under from their superiors in Moscow. The center leaned heavily on local government organizations to raise money for war loans, and some officials turned to the most vulnerable and ready sources of cash under their control, resorting at times to blackmail. Near the city of Vinnitsa, for instance, the head of a sel'sovet ordered a priest and representatives from a society of believers to contribute to a state loan. When they refused, he sent them to prison until they changed their minds. Afterward, the victims of this scheme complained to Moscow.

Many other local disputes tell similar stories. In Kherson oblast', in southwest Ukraine, the chairman of the sel'sovet in the village of Nono-Natal'evskii "organized a demonstrative closing of a working house of prayer." He threw religious items out the door, destroying or ruining them, and he removed a cross from the building's roof, replacing it with a red flag. When believers in the village of Vershents, Kirovograd oblast', asked the chairman of the local raiispolkom, Glatskov, to allow them to reoccupy a church that had been turned into a club, he refused. When they asked him where they could pray then, Glatskov replied: "'Pray in a mud hut, or in a cellar, or anywhere you want.'" The same Glatskov was at the center of another incident. The chairman of a kolkhoz in the village of Mel'nika ejected believers from a church that had been closed and turned into a school before the war, throwing icons and other religious items into the town square. When the congregation appealed to Glatskov, the latter "did not want to listen to the believers and told them to get out of his office." Glatskov's hostility to religion was not unique; in Novgorod oblast', the head of another raiispolkom told petitioners: "While I'm chairman of the Ispolkom there will be no churches opened in my raion. Better you not write petitions."

Local Soviet bureaucrats sometimes also interfered in purely internal church matters. In a small village, also in Kirovograd oblast', a bishop removed a priest from his post for misbehavior, only to be overruled by the local Soviet. Only after the intervention of Moscow was the bishop's original order upheld.[87]

Reestablishing the Party Line

This uncooperative spirit on the part of local authorities—sometimes serious, at other times merely petty—threatened to subvert Moscow's overall designs. The Kremlin had learned during earlier antireligious campaigns that religion could not be wished away, nor could it be crushed outright; if repressed too harshly, it would only be driven underground where it would be harder to control. The last thing Moscow wanted was to herd believers into secret societies that, especially in the western borderlands, could link up with nationalist resistance. Far better to allow a measure of religious practice that could be controlled by the Moscow Patriarchate, which itself was under the Kremlin's thumb.

In the year following the *sobor'*, Moscow became concerned with the spreading disorder in religious affairs and especially with the confusion among local cadres about the allowable degree of religious tolerance. Local party workers and propagandists needed Central Committee guidance. In a long, high-level memorandum, designed for circulation among party activists dealing with religious matters, G. Aleksandrov, the head of the Central Committee's Directorate of Propaganda and Agitation, outlined the evolving party line.[88] There had been a general patriotic upsurge during the war, he wrote, and believers and the church played their part. The church prayed for victory against the Germans, raised money for the Red Army, and summoned believers to fight loyally for the Soviet state. Furthermore, "The Church condemned that part of the clergy in Soviet regions occupied by the Germans, who sold themselves to the enemy and helped the Germans smother the Soviet people."

These important steps had changed the position of the church in relation to the state, Aleksandrov argued. During the revolution and the civil war, Russian Orthodoxy had been the hireling of "anti-Soviet circles abroad" as well as the exploiting classes of Russia. As Bolshevik power was established, it had engaged in "counter-revolutionary work," siding with the White forces against the Communists. "In view of this," the state had been compelled to restrict "the activity of the churches and the rights of the clergy."

From the beginning of the war against the Nazis, however, the church had proven loyal; "that is a fact of great political significance." During the war, Aleksandrov wrote, the Soviets needed both the church's moral support and the active participation in the war effort of common believers since, "despite the enormous growth of atheism and the abandonment by the workers of religion, the church still unites within its ranks great masses of believers, tens of millions of people." It was vital that this vast influence be used in a "friendly," rather than a "hostile" fashion. This is why during the war the Soviet government had allowed the church to publish appeals, raise money, make radio broadcasts, publish documents and articles, as well as hold a *sobor*'.

Although these measures had been necessary, party members must not draw unwarranted conclusions that the Kremlin was rehabilitating religion:

> [T]his does not by any means signify that the party and Soviet power are changing their principal relation toward religion and the church. Our relations toward religion and the church, based on the teachings of Marxism-Leninism that religion is an anti-scientific ideology, remain unchanged. Therefore, all changes in the mutual relations of church and state brought about in wartime, do not break the basic line of the party on the religious question, and moreover will not change it. (emphasis in original)

Despite the new degree of religious tolerance, all Soviet laws remained in force concerning the separation of church and state, and also regarding the exclusion of religion from the schools. The correct understanding of this line was very important, Aleksandrov argued, because the church was using the circumstances of the war to extend its influence among "the masses." Clerics were spreading the notion that "'The Motherland and Church, Orthodoxy and patriotism are one'"; they also claimed that God would only reward a believing people. The church was thus exploiting the Soviet people's understandable wish to see an early end to the war to advance the idea that only prayer, the opening of churches, and the resumption of religious education would bring this about.

Aleksandrov noted with alarm the deluge of petitions to Moscow for the reopening of churches and complained that "all types of superstition and prejudice have become more noticeable" during the war. "Party organizations cannot stand aside and quietly watch as the church seizes by means of its influence thousands of Soviet people, the majority of whom are honest kolkhozniks and workers." Communists must "struggle with the influence of the church on the population by means of the development of cultural-educational and politico-enlightenment work." "Even more," Soviet authorities should crack down on clergy who tried to extend church influence "rudely breaking Soviet law in the process, and sometimes conducting under the flag of religion the opening of anti-Soviet propaganda." As examples, he cited several instances where crowds paraded with icons and prayed in public for rain.

Another manifestation of anti-Soviet influence was the spread of "lying rumors." Rumors were being spread that Metropolitan Nikolai's appointment to the Commission for the Investigation of Fascist Crimes signified a return to the old order, where the tsar and metropolitan decided policy jointly. The opening of the churches gave rise to another slanderous, unfounded rumor: that Moscow had been forced to this step as "a result of the influence of the allies." When the church's greetings to Stalin were printed in Soviet newspapers after the *sobor'*, more lies circulated, claiming that the schools would once again be allowed to teach God's law, that more churches should be restored, and "that ringing of church bells would be permitted and all arrested priests would be freed."

Such "hostile" rumors were highly disruptive and must be combated, Aleksandrov warned; they were designed "to discredit the policies of the party in the eyes of the people," and to foster "among the working masses the idea that Soviet power and the Communist Party 'were mistaken' in their negative attitude toward religion and now have abandoned their earlier views and returned to the policies of supporting religion and the churches." Soviet aktivs must counter such ideas by explaining that Moscow's policies were consistent with

Soviet law, and that the greetings to Stalin had been published, not because the party line had changed, or to meet any "mythical needs," but rather because the church was doing its "patriotic duty" in the war. Nor did the opening of churches represent any change of heart in the Kremlin, much less an admission that party policy had been wrong in the past; propagandists should explain that freedom of conscience had always been party policy and was enshrined in the constitution. The inclusion of Metropolitan Nikolai in a government commission had merely been "expedient" because the Germans had destroyed so many churches.

The selection of a new patriarch should be explained to the public as an "internal matter" of the church; the state merely placed no obstacle in the way of the process. "This testifies to the fact that in the USSR the church is accorded full freedom in its religious life. . . . The state not only does not interfere with this freedom, but, on the contrary, accords it and preserves it." Any notion that the patriarch's election signified a restoration of prerevolutionary church-state relations, or that churches would be allowed to educate children, were "provocationist inventions." A correct explanation of these questions will counter "various lying and slanderous rumors, spread by hostile elements."

Aleksandrov scolded local party leaders who, through their alleged inactivity, had allowed the church to make inroads among the masses, and who then tried to remedy their initial failure to act by resorting to "crude administrative measures." This was an "incorrect and wrecking path," because repression only had the effect of "embitter[ing]" believers. Party members should instead adopt a policy of "non-interference." They should be guided by Lenin's dictum: "to struggle with the fog of religion purely by ideas and with ideological weapons." But Aleksandrov also hinted that cadres should be prepared for future changes in tactics—meaning, perhaps, after the war when the church's support might not be so vital. Lenin had also written, Aleksandrov pointed out, that tactics against religion should change as "the concrete situation" changed.

The chief task for the party at the moment should be to mobilize "all the powers of the people for the defeat of the enemy." Therefore, it would be "politically mistaken if we were to continue to conduct antireligious propaganda in the old forms." Propagandists should cease giving lectures with titles such as "Religion—Enemy of Socialism," "Is There a God," "Did Christ Live," or "The Church and Espionage," which might cause "dissension" between believers and atheists, weakening the unity of the people in the face of the enemy.

Instead of making "intolerable" direct attacks on religion, the party's approach to the church and to patriotic believers during the war "should be especially cautious, [and] tactical." Working hard through lectures, in movie theaters and other public arenas, propagandists should give the masses "correct" explanations of natural phenomena to unmask the lies of religious superstition. Aleksandrov suggested several possible lecture topics: "where does the rain come from?" "what does the weather depend on?" "how to get a good harvest," and so forth. Such materialist, scientific lectures should wean the people away from prayers for good weather. Propaganda cadres should also explain why the Red Army was fighting. Equally important, propaganda must "unmask demagogic approaches of the fascists, directed at the betrayal of the believers (opening by them, in places, of churches, permission to ring church bells, and etc.), to show how fascism smothers freedom of conscience, victimizes believers and clergy, forcefully destroys the Christian religion, destroys temples, etc." Engaging in such campaigns, aktivs must enroll members of the Soviet intelligentsia, doctors, teachers, technicians, engineers, agronomists, and so forth.

Aleksandrov's memorandum was designed to provide guidelines for future propaganda; it was by no means accurate history. It blamed the Russian Orthodox Church for having earned its own travails by engaging in anti-Soviet activities during the early years of Bolshevism; it did not mention the party's birthright, inherited from Marx himself, of hostility to religion in all its forms. The claim that Lenin and his followers always pursued antireligious propaganda on the ideological plane alone was sheer nonsense, and the older readers of the document would certainly have known this. Nor was it true that the church had gradually earned the regime's trust during the first years of the war; the Kremlin had been the initiator at each step of the church's resurrection. Finally, Aleksandrov did not mention the foreign policy and political uses to which the church was being put by the state.

For all its shortcomings and economy with the truth, the document made several important points, if only by inference. Aleksandrov admitted that, despite the regime's determined efforts, tens of millions of Soviet citizens stubbornly retained their religious beliefs, and that for the time being this presented a significant barrier to Communist plans. The church might have to be tolerated during the war, while its services were needed, but the task of Soviet cadres should be to limit the damage; the church remained an enemy, to be restricted and undermined slowly, by cutting its roots. In particular, the party placed its bet on Soviet youth. Aleksandrov's observations also revealed another facet of religious dynamics in the USSR: the Kremlin may have succeeded in co-opting the hierarchy of the Russian Orthodox Church, but common priests constituted a dangerous political and social force as they continued to offer prayers and services throughout the country. Indeed, one of the chief attractions of collaboration between church and state, from the Kremlin's point of view, was that the Patriarchate could be used to bring these lower-ranking clergy into line.

The ideological challenges for Moscow were sharpest in the western borderlands, where the German occupation had fostered the growth of twin evils: anti-Soviet nationalism mixed with the growth of religious sentiment. To uproot these ills, Stalinist authorities evinced great faith, as always, in a combination of propaganda and police repression. At roughly the same time as Aleksandrov's memorandum, from mid-1944 through the beginning of 1945, the Soviet Central Committee issued a spate of resolutions and decisions concerning the organization of propaganda work in Moldavia, Belorussia, western Ukraine, and the Baltic states.[89] The Central Committee noted that the population of these areas had been subjected to "lying fascist propaganda" and "deprived of correct Soviet information." Soviet propagandists should recount Nazi crimes and cultivate "hatred of the enemy."[90] The Central Committee urged party organizations in Belorussia to pay "special attention" to the education of the population about the proper "socialist attitude to labor and public property," and, more ominously given the history of Stalinism, "to the strengthening of state discipline." Party members must work to counter "private property, antikolkhoz, and antistate attitudes inculcated by the occupiers in certain groups of the population."[91] The "foremost task of party organizations of the western regions of Belorussia," the Central Committee ordered, was "to be the final unmasking of fascist nationalists and their ideology." Communist cadres should therefore "explain to the population that only the Soviet government, based on the friendship of peoples, will give the workers of the western regions of Belorussia basic freedom, material well-being, and rapid cultural improvement."[92]

These orders stressed the reeducation of all people who had experienced German occupation, but especially the young. They proposed intensive training programs for propagandists, educators, and party activists in the fundamentals of Marxism-Leninism, in the "friendship of peoples" that supposedly was the norm within the USSR, and in the importance of rebuilding the economy and supporting the war effort. Moscow authorized scores of newspapers to be published in local languages, as well as the mass distribution of union papers in the Russian language. Films, posters, new school textbooks, lectures, discussion groups, and public readings were all prescribed as antidotes to anti-Soviet notions widespread in the western borderlands.

Consistent with Aleksandrov's strictures to avoid direct assaults on religion, these public resolutions never once mentioned the need to counter belief as such, using code words instead. Training for educators and common citizens alike was to contain a powerful dose of "the bases of the Marxist-Leninist world view."[93] The absence of any explicit reference to religion has prevented historians from realizing that the wartime popular religious revival was in fact the principal target of the Central Committee's new propaganda campaign. Following Aleksandrov's guidelines, propagandists were to stress themes of natural science to combat religion:

> The basic content of scientific-enlightenment propaganda should be a materialistic explanation of the facts of nature, an explanation of the achievements of science, technology, and culture. Among the population, especially in the countryside, lectures should be organized widely, conversations and readings aloud should be conducted of popular brochures and articles about the universal order, about the origin of the sun and earth, about fundamental astronomical facts, about the rise and development of life, and the origins of man, about the makeup of the human body, and the origins and life of plants and animals, about the reasons for illnesses and the struggle with them, about the scientific bases of agriculture and animal husbandry, about measures to improve harvests and the productivity of animal farming, about energy and its uses, and etc.

The Central Committee ordered public lectures, the printing of brochures and the publication of a "popular" series of books, as well as the production of films, all on these "natural-science" topics. Several journals normally targeted at teachers and agitators were also ordered regularly to print "scientific-enlightenment propaganda."[94]

These documents testify to the abiding inability of Soviet officials to understand religious phenomena. Most city-dwelling, educated bureaucrats had imbibed atheism or religious skepticism with their mothers' milk; religious belief was, for them, an artifact of peasant backwardness and poor education. The Central Committee's mandarins apparently believed that, if only peasants could be shown the scientific mechanics of rainfall, they would abandon their stubbornly held beliefs.

Before long, the Kremlin's renewed, but more subtle, propaganda campaign against faith became apparent to foreign observers. In April 1945 Frank Roberts, newly assigned to the British Embassy in Moscow following the Yalta Conference,[95] told London that "in spite of the Soviet Government's recent concessions to the Orthodox Church, the Communist Party continues steadfast in its opposition to religion and in its determination to counteract the existence of religious beliefs among the people in general." Roberts noted that textbooks used for the training of primary-school teachers still emphasized the importance for Soviet youth of "an anti-religious upbringing." These texts, assert "that religion is not only anti-scientific but a profoundly reactionary ideology and that the Soviet must give an anti-religious direction and edge to all the subjects which it teaches." The People's Commissariat for Education issued similar guidelines for secondary-school chemistry training, which said that the reason for studying that subject was to learn the proper materialist and dialectical world view. The same was true of the schools' astronomy and physics programs for 1944.

Reading between the lines of the Soviet press, it was possible to deduce that a great many teachers in the USSR had become infected during the war with politically incorrect attitudes toward religion. A long article on September 16, 1944, by a young Mikhail Suslov in the newspaper for young Communists, *Komsomolskaia pravda*, reminded readers that the Communist Party continued to regard religion as antiscientific but warned that crude tactics of suppression would only result in the "strengthening of religious fanaticism." The teachers' newspaper, *Uchitelskaia gazeta* of April 4, 1945, warned that some teachers, though happily quite few according to the author, had drawn incorrect conclusions about religion because of the church's renewed prominence during the fight against fascism. It reminded teachers that their task was to inculcate the proper materialist world view in their charges.[96]

It is little wonder that many teachers were confused about the party's newly recrafted line toward the church; it was no easy thing to master. At one and the same time, people were being told to believe that religion was unscientific, that it had been and would continue to be an anti-Soviet force, that the church had sided with Bolshevism's enemies following the revolution, and that it would soon die out. Simultaneously, however, millions of regular Soviet citizens remained believers; priests were reappearing on the streets, sometimes direct from imprisonment; churches were slowly reopening, and priests were collecting donations for the war effort; Metropolitan Nikolai appeared and spoke at state functions and served on a government commission to investigate Nazi war crimes.

Even within the Soviet apparat, there was serious confusion about religion's new role in society. In February 1945, as part of the Central Committee's effort to reintroduce proper Soviet propaganda into western Ukraine, I. Kovalev, an official in the Dorogobychskii obkom, wrote "theses" outlining the history of religion in Russian and Soviet society and explaining the position of the Uniate Church in particular.[97] Kovalev's work was designed to direct religious propaganda in his volatile region, where nationalism, both secular and religious, was as virulent as anywhere in the USSR. As his subsequent grilling would show, the party line had its limits, even though these could be hard for those outside the Central Committee to discern. The Kovalev affair is interesting not only as an illustration of how difficult it was for the Kremlin to fine tune religious propaganda, but also as a case study of how the proper ideological recasting of history—even quite distant history—could be vital in Stalin-era policy questions.

Kovalev began by echoing Aleksandrov and other Central Committee guidelines: "All religions in general," he wrote, "are the antipode to science." "Materialist science" knows no god, and the Deity did not create man in his image; "on the contrary," man created God. Marx and Darwin have supplanted "idealistic philosophy," which has "suffered a final defeat." Nonetheless, progress was under threat; religion remained a dangerous force and worked "to drag mankind back to ancient times, to the ideology of the epoch of the slaveowners." The current era was a hopeful one precisely because, rather than being subject to the natural elements as religion taught, man could now begin to master his environment.

When he turned to the history of religion, Kovalev steered into deeper waters. Although religion was clearly outmoded in the Stalinist era, he argued, this did not mean that it had always been retrogressive; on the contrary, "dialectically" it had many times been a positive force in Russian history, even though it was inherently and objectively flawed. Russia's baptism in 988 bequeathed to the Russian nation superior manners, morals, art, learning, and even a more unified state. Under Ivan III and Ivan IV during the fifteenth and sixteenth centuries respectively, the church had helped to tame the great landowners, thereby strengthening central state power. During the seventeenth century, and especially under Peter I, however, the church began to become reactionary; it surrendered its institutional freedom to the state, and it opposed the new force of capitalism, at that time deemed to be progressive in the Marxist canon.

The church remained a servant of the tsarist state until the Bolshevik Revolution erupted. With a higher clergy drawn from the landed class, Russian Orthodoxy naturally served "the white-guard counterrevolutionaries against the people." The new Bolshevik state was forced to answer the "White terror" with its own "Red terror," assaulting the church—not because it propagated a false doctrine but rather because it fought the creation of a socialist state. "Soviet power absolutely did not repress religion," Kovalev wrote; "Soviet power conducted a war against its enemies. Soviet power was not to blame if the leaders and priesthood of the Orthodox Church turned out to be among the enemies of the people." The Bolshevik government separated the church from the state, an action that, Kovalev unconvincingly explained, "was directed toward the interests of the church, not against them." Freed "from the enslaving union with tsarism," Kovalev wrote in a phrase that would cause him trouble, the Church "restored its noble face and reputation and rapidly liquidated the legacy of tsarism in its internal life." It raised millions of rubles for famine relief at the end of the civil war and ceased its hostile activities against Communism. Through such efforts, as well as by its loyal support for the war against Hitler, "the Orthodox Church and her clergy have shown the whole world that they are now on the side of the people [*idut s narodom*]."

Kovalev's treatment of the Greek Catholic Church was the most controversial portion of his "theses," especially given the political and social importance of that church in western Ukraine. The Uniate Church, he wrote, "had an entirely different historical path" from Orthodoxy, because it was always a minority church within the Russian Empire, and it had never entered into a "symbiosis with tsarism." "As the Ukrainian people conducted a historical struggle for its national liberation, the Greek-Catholic Church, despite its catholicization, was always a bulwark of the national-liberation movement in western Ukraine." This national struggle was a good thing when directed against Austria-Hungary and tsarist Russification, but over time the church "fell into the hands of the local national bourgeoisie" and developed "a bourgeois character." Church leaders opposed the Bolshevik Revolution and "sought to deliver [Ukraine] into the hands of the capitalist world" and also tried to forge closer ties with the reactionary Vatican. After the "liberation" of western Ukraine by the Red Army in September 1939, however, the clergy supposedly "recognized the mistakenness" of its earlier anti-Soviet activities.

Following the Nazi attack, most members of the church fell in line with the defense of their homeland against the invader. "The period of German occupation," Kovalev wrote, "even more opened the eyes of the Greek-Catholic clergy," who now "entered on the path of an ideological break with the Catholic West" in favor of the Orthodox East. Kovalev then reached the crux of the matter:

The bourgeois-nationalist movement in western Ukraine is regrowing now in bands of German-fascist spies, diversionists, and traitors to the homeland, in Ukrainian-German nationalists, which are now the most evil enemies of the Ukrainian working people. OUNites, Banderites, Mel'nikovtsy, utsekisty [are all fighting the Soviet state]. . . . Remnants of these bandit nationalist groups still roam about the woods and villages, mocking the people on German orders.

The task of the Ukrainian clergy consists in taking active part in the unmasking of German-fascist individuals, Ukrainian-German bandits before the wide mass of the people and to put an end to the betrayal of the mass of the people by the Nazi-demagogic bandits.

To root out these traitors, Kovalev concluded, party aktivs should cooperate with local clergy.[98]

Kovalev's religious-historical survey has a rather naive cast about it—similar in tone to the famous historical parody *1066 and All That*, where major developments in English history are all labeled Good Things or Bad Things. Clearly, Kovalev was trying to enact Central Committee directives by portraying religion as at once both antiscientific but at times also a positive force; he was also focusing on the key question by trying to drive a wedge between armed anti-Soviet nationalists and the Uniate and Orthodox churches. But he had gone too far, and the reaction to his "theses" shows how hard it was for Moscow to calibrate its new religious policies.

The organizational-instructors' department of the Central Committee reprimanded Kovalev for his excessive enthusiasm for religion, especially his call for cooperation between local party figures and Uniate clergy. "Having received these theses," an alarmed Muscovite official noted, "several raikoms of the party [in western Ukraine] took them as directives of the obkom." Acting on what they thought to be instructions from the center, local officials held meetings with clergy, discussing important political matters with them. In Turetskii raion, one such meeting took place "over a cup of tea," where invited clergy were treated to lectures on the military and international situations, the Crimean Conference of the Big Three, and other such high-level matters.[99]

Kovalev was also reprimanded for his overview of church history, which was called "rudely mistaken." Kovalev's admission that the Orthodox Church had raised money for famine relief in the early 1920s was—even if true—nonetheless inadmissible because church leaders had actually been put on trial under Lenin on trumped up charges of refusing to assist starving Russians.[100] Moscow could scarcely admit that the church had raised millions of rubles, because this would have been an admission that Lenin himself had sanctioned the unjust trial of church hierarchs and even the execution of several of them.

Over time, and despite the difficulties of enforcing a proper line, the Soviet government's measures designed to limit religion's gains had the cumulative effect of restricting religious practice while failing to eradicate it entirely. Many more churches were open than before the war, and if believers were willing to ignore the state's discouragements, and risk possible police suspicions, they could attend services—although in many regions they would have to travel long distances to do so. There are few sources describing the actual state of the churches in the closing stages of the war: Soviet records reveal very little, because government workers were not really interested in church life, being concerned only with the political and ideological ramifications of religion. And church figures were understandably reluctant to record their experiences. One invaluable firsthand account exists, however, written by a British subject in the summer of 1944 following a visit with several friends to Staryi Obriachevskii Cathedral, the sole remaining Old Believer church in Moscow.

The once beautiful and wealthy church was now in a dreadful state of disrepair. The Soviets had used it briefly during 1941 as an ammunition dump, and an explosion had destroyed part of the building. "The congregation was of course mainly female and mainly elderly," the anonymous informant wrote; he estimated that only one-sixth of the worshipers were young or male. Most interesting was the sermon, delivered by Archbishop Gerontsi, who "was only recently released after some twenty years' imprisonment." The archbishop recounted the story of the Prophet Elijah and preached against stealing. "We asked him afterwards," the visitor wrote,

> why he spent so little time on the Biblical story. He said that it would be unwise for him to dwell too long on the coming end of the world and the dissolution into Heaven and Hell, in case any N.K.V.D. people were listening. Apparently he recently took his flock to task in a sermon for not reading the scriptures themselves and for not teaching their children Christianity. He was visited a few days later by an N.K.V.D. Agent who said that, if he wished to continue to preach in his church, he had better leave children out of the question.

The archbishop showed his guests around the cathedral, showing them damage done by Napoleon's troops in 1812 as well as the more thorough destruction wrought since 1917. The Bolsheviks stripped gold from the church's icons, and they had seized marble tombstones, ostensibly to help construct Moscow's Metro. Later, wooden crosses were also taken for firewood. The congregation kept the cathedral open and repaired it so far as possible with their donations. Gerontsi himself received a "small stipend" from the state, but this was more than offset by the authorities' claim that he owed 57,000 rubles in taxes, which "he has no means of paying." This outrageous tax bill, of course, left the archbishop constantly in violation of Soviet law, assuring that if he transgressed even slightly he could be instantly arrested.

The cathedral left a sad impression on the visitor, who recounted that "the whole thing [existed] very much on [state] sufferance and in pathetic poverty."

The Old Believers evidently shared the view, widespread among the population, that what little religious tolerance the state allowed resulted from the demands of alliance politics: "Gerontsi and another cleric, as well as many members of the congregation, thanked us, as English people, for having won them back freedom of worship. They are all convinced that it is our efforts which have gained them such freedom as they have. On the other hand it is clear that this freedom is still very limited, that they are still watched very closely and know it."[101]

How representative Gerontsi's experiences were of religion as a whole is hard to tell. The Old Believer community may have been more suspect than mainstream Orthodoxy to Soviet authorities, as indeed it had been to the tsars. Old Believers created cohesive communities that cut themselves off from the wider Russian society around them, which they regarded as heretical; and Stalinists were not known for their tolerance of difference. Nonetheless, it is fair to assume that in Stalin's well-manned police state monitoring of sermons and church services was routine, and that priests never knew for certain when they were being watched. Certainly, when Averell Harriman attended a crowded church service celebrating the Orthodox Christmas in January 1944, he noted that "officers of the 'NKVD' were noticeably scattered throughout the congregation."[102] As for the Old Believers, the police warning to Gerontsi against religious education of young people squares with the Central Committee directives cited earlier. Following the *sobor* of September 1943, many outward forms of religious tolerance returned to the USSR, but the state was clearly working hard to limit the church's growth; and believers held their breath, never certain that the prewar terror would not return.

Marshal Stalin will go down eternally in history as the gatherer of the Ukrainian lands. — Father Havryil Kostel'nik, 1945

The Ukrainians avoided meeting this fate [deportation and exile] only because there were too many of them and there was no place to which to deport them. Otherwise, Stalin would have deported them also. (*Laughter and animation in the Hall*). — Nikita Khrushchev's "Secret Speech" denouncing Stalin's crimes to the Twentieth Communist Party Congress, 1956

The Gatherer of the Ukrainian Lands

The Church and the Restoration of Soviet Power in the Western Borderlands

During the last decade of his rule, Stalin's favored method for dealing with the USSR's myriad nationality problems was deportation and internal exile; it was an easy, reliable, and relatively inexpensive bureaucratic option. The repressive machinery was in place and well oiled by use, and the human cost incurred by shipping people of every age and condition east or west in cattle cars was unlikely to disturb the sleep of oligarchs who already had the blood of millions on their hands.[1] Stalin could not solve all the USSR's nationality dilemmas by such methods, however; as Nikita Khrushchev's remarks during his "secret speech" of 1956 indicate, the sheer numbers of people in Ukraine and the Baltic States rendered internal exile a logistical impossibility. Whether it wished to or not, the Kremlin therefore had to find methods in situ to disarm and manage national minority pressures in the western borderlands.

During 1943 the blueprint of Moscow's methods had been sketched out; the drawing would be filled in during 1944–45 as the Soviets consolidated their power throughout the western borderlands. The Kremlin was set to disarm religious nationalism from without and within by a combination of brute force and guile.

"We Are Not Cannibals"

In mid-January 1944 Soviet Foreign Minister Viacheslav Molotov met with the American ambassador to the USSR, W. Averell Harriman, to complain as he had done many times before about the allegedly anti-Soviet orientation of the London-based Polish government-in-exile. During the previous spring, Moscow had broken relations with the London Poles, and accusations had flown back and forth between the two sides, only becoming more heated as the Red Army looked poised to drive the Nazis out of Poland. The Poles feared that Moscow would impose Communism in their country, or perhaps even reincorporate all of Poland into the USSR as a Soviet republic. For their part, the Soviets were eagerly casting about to find sympathetically inclined Poles who might collaborate with the Kremlin in creating a Moscow-friendly Polish postwar government.

Speaking with Harriman, Molotov professed himself willing to work with the London exile government, but only if certain unspecified "Fascist elements" were first removed. Then Molotov surprised the American representative by suggesting that Americans of Polish extraction known to be sympathetic to the USSR might be substituted for members of the Polish exile government who were supposedly hostile to Moscow. He suggested three names: Leo Krzycki, Oscar Lange, and Father Stanislaus Orlemanski.

Krzycki was vice president of the Amalgamated Clothing Workers of America, then part of the CIO, and national chair of the American Slavic Congress. Of all American trade-union groups, the CIO had long been the most favorably oriented toward Moscow and was most heavily influenced by American Communists.[2] Controlled behind the scenes by the Soviets' own Antifascist Slavic Committee, which Moscow had set up during the first days of the war to unite East European Slavs against the Nazis, the American Slavic Congress had been formed at the outset of the Nazi-Soviet war to organize support for the Soviet war effort among the American Slavic community.[3] As the director of the Soviet committee noted, "It is turning out that the main attention of the All-Slav Committee is being directed at American Slavs."[4] Moscow clearly valued both the American Slavic Congress and Krzycki, who, one Soviet official wrote in late 1945, "since 1942 has taken a progressive position" regarding the USSR. Krzycki was, the document continued, "affiliated with" the Polish Communist Party; "In the past he belonged to the reactionary group of Poles, but from 1942 he changed his position, coming closer to the group of Lange [and] Orlemanski and spoke in support of the [Soviet-controlled] Polish National Committee of Liberation and the Provisional Polish Government."[5]

Molotov's second American nominee, Oscar Lange, was a professor of economics at the University of Chicago who would later serve as the postwar Polish Communist government's ambassador to the United States.[6] Lange had first gained prominence during the Katyn dispute when he issued a letter, subsequently broadcast over Moscow radio, calling on the exile Polish government to resign in favor of Poles who would "renounce the policy of preservation of dominion over the Ukrainians and Byelorussians against their will and settle with the U.S.S.R in a friendly way, the problem of the Eastern frontier."[7]

Molotov's third suggestion was certainly the most surprising: Father Orlemanski was the priest of Springfield Catholic Church in Massachusetts. This was an odd turn of events—that the foreign minister of the world's only Communist state should suggest an obscure Catholic priest as a candidate for a friendly post-Soviet Polish government.[8]

Nobody in the American embassy in Moscow had ever heard of Orlemanski, and they immediately asked Washington for background information on the three people Molotov had mentioned. Six days later, the State Department replied that all three had "been very active in recent months in connection with the setting up in Detroit of the Kosciuszko League whose program is distinctly pro-Soviet." The league had received glowing coverage in the Communist and leftist press "and it has been particularly outspoken in its criticism of the Polish Government-in-exile." As for Orlemanski, he had been born in 1889 and "had recently made an extensive speaking tour in the Middle West and Canada appealing for support in Polish communities for closer collaboration with the Soviet Union."[9]

Molotov's suggested candidates, especially Orlemanski, raised a host of questions that American diplomats would rather have avoided. Under Secretary of State Edward Stettinius wrote a worried memorandum to President Roosevelt: "These two men represent a specific and heavily slanted view of the Polish-Soviet question which is not shared by American citizens of Polish descent nor by American public opinion as a whole." Stettinius fretted that "Their visit will be widely interpreted as the first step in the abandonment by this Government of the Polish Government-in-exile." Stettinius suggested somewhat hopefully that the visit might be in violation of the Logan Act, which forbade private American citizens from engaging in diplomacy; perhaps, he suggested, this could be used as a pretext to deny the pair travel documents. At the very least it must be made clear to the press that the Americans were traveling as private citizens, not as official emissaries.[10]

Despite such hand-wringing by American officials, an express request from Molotov and Stalin to meet with American citizens could scarcely be denied. Orlemanski duly journeyed to the USSR where on May 5 he had a two-hour conversation with Stalin and Molotov. Orlemanski spoke quite frankly with his hosts, telling them that, in the United States, "Polish organizations and clergy are inclined against the Soviet Union. The goal of [his] visit to the Soviet Union is to find out how to split them." He recounted his earlier efforts to this effect, and said that many Polish Americans were troubled by "rumors" that ethnic Poles in the USSR, especially children, were "treated badly." In fact, Orlemanski said, the Polish adults and children whom he had met caused him to believe that "the Polish people should be thankful to Russia and to Stalin." The dictator modestly replied, "we are not cannibals."[11]

Afterward, the priest delivered an address in Polish over Moscow Radio in which he recounted his trip to the Soviet Union, his role in creating the Kosciusko League, and his meetings with ethnic Poles in Canada and the United States. He said he had met with Polish soldiers serving in the Red Army and visited the town of Zagorsk, site of the famed Trinity Monastery, where children of Polish exiles attended classes conducted in the Polish language and were given lessons in Polish history. "Permit me as a neutral observer and a practical American to inform you that under present conditions things could not be better than they are," he declared. "We Poles should be grateful to the Soviet Government for its good attitude and put forth our efforts to maintain this condition."[12]

Orlemanski told his radio audience that Stalin had assured him that Poland must never again be used as a "corridor" for invasion of the USSR. According to the American priest, Stalin "wished to see a great strong and democratic Poland which will know how to defend its borders effectively. Stalin does not intend to interfere in the internal affairs of the Polish state." "With reference to religion," Orlemanski continued, this "will continue to be the religion of our fathers. The affable reception of a Catholic priest by Marshal Stalin should convince you." "Unquestionably Stalin is a friend of the Polish people," Orlemanski asserted. "I will also make this historic [sic] statement: future events will prove that he is very friendly disposed towards the Roman Catholic Church." The Polish Catholic clergy must accept Moscow's proffered hand of friendship and "show its maturity in relation to world problems."[13]

On the same day as his broadcast, Orlemanski released a letter he had received from Stalin, in which the dictator answered several questions the American had posed concerning religion in general and Catholicism in particular. Stalin said that, "advocating as I do the freedom of conscience and ... worship," a "policy of coercion and persecution" against Catholicism was "precluded and inadmissible." Furthermore, he believed that "cooperation" with the pope was "possible."[14] These were odd assurances from the Soviet dictator: from which quarter was "persecution and coercion" of the Catholic Church to be expected if not from the Soviets themselves?

Stalin's vague remarks apparently impressed Franklin Roosevelt. Little more than a month after Orlemanski's visit to the Kremlin, when speaking with Polish premier Stanislaw Mikolajczyk, the president asked the Polish leader whether he had met with Orlemanski: "[H]e [Roosevelt] said that he had been told that the latter was a clean and honest man, perhaps somewhat naive, but well-meaning; he was wondering whether he should receive him." Roosevelt thought he detected an opening in Stalin's comments about freedom for Roman Catholicism in the USSR. The president's remarks were later summarized by the Polish ambassador to Washington, Jan Ciechanowski:

> Stalin [had said] that he did not oppose such freedom, but that there were so many religions that it was difficult for one to find his bearings. Should some religions be granted freedom in Russia, several others would claim the same right. Would it not be possible to bring about the merging of religions? The President said that he was much impressed by this statement as, in fact, it would be a good thing to unite the Roman-Catholic and Orthodox churches. . . . Stalin has not the ambition which the Czar had to become the head of a Church. Perhaps he would agree to the Pope becoming the head of these two churches. It would, perhaps, be useful if Orlemanski went to the Vatican and submitted this question there. The President said that he intended to bring this about.[15]

It is hard to know who was being more naive here—Orlemanski or Roosevelt. The Polish premier was well aware of the long history behind Orthodox-Catholic rivalry in his native region and also knew that Moscow had by no means abandoned notions of using the Russian Orthodox Church to advance its own political ends.[16] The suggestion that this deep historic rift could be papered over in a religious union, because it would serve Washington's passing wartime needs, may have made sense to an American leader for whom Eastern European religious questions seemed untidy, even trivial, but it must have confirmed Polish concerns that the American leadership was out of touch with the historical realities of the USSR and Eastern Europe. One must also wonder whether Roosevelt would ever have been so glib about healing religious disputes in his own country—the Protestant-Catholic divide, for instance.

Historians have generally interpreted the strange meeting between an obscure American priest and the two leading lights of the Soviet government as a bungled attempt to "improve relations with Poland, Polish-Americans, and the Catholic Church."[17] As with many of Stalin's policies, there were no doubt many considerations behind his actions, but the visit should also be seen in the context of Moscow's continually evolving approach toward religion and ethnicity. By the spring of 1944, the Red Army was poised to sweep into Eastern and Central Europe; the Soviet summer offensive, launched at the end of June, would tear a gaping hole in the center of the German line through which Soviet forces would pour into eastern Poland. Although the Russian Orthodox Church could soften somewhat the USSR's international image by appealing to fellow Orthodox in the region, large segments of the populations of Poland, Czechoslovakia, Hungary, and other countries were loyal to the Roman Catholic Church and were therefore unlikely to be swayed by appeals from the Moscow Patriarchate. Roosevelt's dismissive optimism aside, the hostility of the Kremlin and the Vatican was mutual, had a long history, and in early 1944 only showed signs of worsening. The Vatican had refused to approve the Soviet cause after the German attack of June 1941, and, although it may have briefly considered sending a diplomatic representative to Moscow, in the end this had not happened.[18] The prospect of a postwar Soviet-dominated Europe horrified the Vatican, and it was taking steps, within its limited powers, to prevent this from happening.

In a review of public opinion throughout Nazi-occupied Europe, the British Political Warfare Executive made a special note of the religious question, which, unlike Roosevelt, it regarded as a very important problem for the Red Army as it moved into Central Europe. In the British view, the reappearance of the Moscow patriarch had defused tensions among East European Orthodox, but other Christians remained suspicious of Soviet power. The Catholic Church especially viewed the Soviet record of religious repression "with a horror equal to that aroused by the anti-religious campaigns of revolutionary France. For almost a quarter of a century the Vatican has regarded 'Atheist Russia' as the final enemy." This was strengthened "by the fact that the ruling classes in Poland and Hungary, the two north-eastern bulwarks of Catholicism, were particularly hostile to Russia on national and social grounds."[19] Interestingly, a similar top secret report, which also contained British estimates as to the power and appeal of Communism and Communist parties throughout Europe, was somehow purloined by unnamed Soviet agents, translated into Russian by Soviet military intelligence, and sent directly to Stalin.[20] The Soviet leadership was aware both from its own and from British sources that the Catholic Church was braced for a confrontation in Eastern Europe.

Orlemanski was only the most visible Catholic priest being courted by the Kremlin at this time. It was not Moscow's aim, however, by making this and other contacts, to improve relations with the church as such; the Soviets rightly regarded this as impossible given the Vatican's suspicions. Rather, the Kremlin sought to find individual priests who might be persuaded to cooperate with the USSR, thereby splitting the church's power. Such were well-tried Soviet tactics in infiltrating hostile organizations in order to fracture them, or to influence them from within.

As ever, Poles posed the sharpest problem. Under the pressure of events, the Kremlin had agreed in July 1941 to the creation of Polish national armed units for service on the eastern front under the Polish General Wladyslaw Anders (the so-called Anders Army); this had the effect of assembling and arming Poles who had little love for the Soviet regime.[21] Their antipathy toward the Soviets had both nationalist and religious dimensions. In September 1941, reacting to demands from the London Poles, Moscow had allowed Catholic priests to minister to Polish soldiers, something that they did not permit Orthodox clergy to do in Red Army units.[22] But the granting of religious freedom, even on such a limited scale, spawned unwelcome side effects. Most Poles being mustered into the new Soviet-sponsored armed force were stationed in the Moslem Uzbek Republic, and the restoration of even limited religious worship among Poles encouraged locals to hope that their own situation might improve. An American bishop of Polish extraction who was well connected to the Bishop Gawlina, spiritual head of Polish forces in the USSR, wrote a letter, intercepted by British postal censorship, in which he claimed that "The Bolsheviks are questioning the bishop continually as to when he will leave Russia. The Mahommedans are demanding for themselves the same religious freedom as has been accorded to the Poles. The Soviet authorities maintain that it will take more than 20 years to make good the harm done by the religiousness of the Poles." The experiences of many of these Polish recruits had reinforced their opposition to a Soviet-dominated Poland following the war. "The morale of the soldiers is admirable," the bishop continued. "Our soldiers leaving Russia can be qualified as hyper-national and hyper-religious."[23]

Because Polish religious nationalism posed the sharpest problem, Soviet authorities focused their fire on finding Polish priests that they could coerce or seduce. Before finding Orlemanski, the Soviets had tried to suborn another Polish-American priest, Walter Ciszek, though in this instance they were unsuccessful. Ciszek was born in Pennsylvania and, after becoming a priest, had been trained in Rome at the Pontifical Russian College (the so-called Russicum) that Pope Pius XI had created in April 1929 to train priests for eventual service in Russia should this become possible.[24] Ever since the 1917 revolution, certain Catholic hierarchs believed that the creation of a Communist, atheist state in Russia represented a long-term opportunity for the conversion of Eastern Slavs to Catholicism. Ciszek was trained with this prospect in mind and was stationed in the town of Dubno in southeastern Poland, there to await his opportunity.

Following the Soviet invasion of Poland of September 1939, Ciszek and his fellow priests found that, as he would later write, they did not have to travel the USSR; it had come to them. With the hope of evangelizing the East, Ciszek and two other priests traveled under false names to the heart of the USSR, where the ever vigilant NKVD soon arrested them. After imprisoning and torturing Ciszek, the NKVD tried to lure him with visions of freedom in exchange for his promise to work within the Catholic Church as a Soviet agent. For a time, it appeared as though their work would be rewarded, as the American, in his own words, "despaired in the most literal sense of the word." According to Ciszek's account, his interrogator "offered me a Russian parish if I would break with the Pope who, he said, was on the side of the Fascists, Mussolini and Hitler. . . . He wanted me to deliver a radio address to that effect on a certain date." "[H]e suggested that, since I wanted to remain a priest, I should become a member of the Orthodox Church. He explained how easy it would be for him to arrange that." Although Ciszek was willing to entertain these offers, his jailer made an even bolder suggestion: that he "go to Rome to arrange a concordat between the Pope and the Soviet Union." Before going, he would be given "courses in radio and telegraph" so he could receive instructions and relay information back to Moscow. This proposal obviously involved the risk that Ciszek would defect following his return to Rome, but the NKVD had anticipated that danger: "Naturally, the interrogator explained, I would not be alone in Rome. . . . Should I betray this trust, those with whom I worked would see to my speedy execution." Somehow, Ciszek found the courage to refuse this offer. Tiring of their stubborn prisoner, the NKVD sent Ciszek to the gulag, where he languished until the Khrushchev era.[25]

In his account, Ciszek is vague about the timing of these approaches; he could scarcely have been expected to keep an accurate track of time in his Soviet prison cell. But apparently they took place at the end of 1943 and the beginning of 1944. Having run into a brick wall with one American Catholic priest, the NKVD seems to have turned to the more promising Orlemanski, who, unlike Ciszek, could be expected to act from conviction rather than under threat.[26] Events would soon show that Moscow had only begun its efforts to find malleable people within the ranks of Catholicism who might enable them to penetrate the Roman church.

In the looming conflict with the Vatican, the Soviets foresaw a central role for the Russian Orthodox Church. Some insight into the Kremlin's reasoning can be gained by a conversation between an American journalist and Vladimir Pravdin, outwardly the head of TASS in New York but in fact the NKGB station chief in the United States.[27] Pravdin allowed that religion was very important in Eastern Europe and the Near East and that "this factor was very often overlooked by American commentators." The Kremlin, however, understood its importance: "[F]or the first time," Pravdin said, "there would be a well-organized, dynamic and state-controlled Orthodox Church that would have great influence throughout the Balkans and Near East," capable of serving as a "force to combat the Vatican." "Protestantism," he said, "could not do this since it was too divided within itself, and [therefore] the only force capable of doing so was the Greek Catholic Church [sic] controlled by the Soviet Government." Although "the Soviet Government . . . did not intend to proselyte for the Greek Orthodox religion, [the Kremlin] would nevertheless back the Greek Orthodox Church and Greek Orthodox Christians wherever they were." Praising the wisdom of Soviet policy, Pravdin claimed that "the Vatican is sufficiently intelligent to see in the Soviet backing of the Greek Orthodox Church a much greater threat to Catholicism than Atheistic Communism had ever been."[28] Pravdin's approach supplies an insight not only into Soviet thinking about the role of religion and the Orthodox Church in foreign affairs, but also about Soviet eagerness that representatives of the American press should understand Moscow's emerging religious policy. His frank admission that the Russian church was squarely controlled by the Soviet government also flatly undercut the Kremlin's repeated assurances that it had not encouraged the revival of the church but rather had simply not placed any obstacles in its way.

Pravdin was merely reflecting the latest twist in Moscow's line. Guidelines from the Central Committee in the early spring of 1944 informed Soviet propagandists that although the pope wanted to see Hitler and the Nazi regime defeated, Soviet authorities did not believe that he wished to see a complete weakening of Germany, because this would lead to Soviet domination of the continent. To prevent such a catastrophe, the Vatican sought a "compromise peace" that would maintain some balance of power. The "sharply anti-Soviet policies of the Vatican" were evident in the actions of Catholic clergy as far away as the United States, the document continued. It pointed out that twenty-eight members of the American Catholic clergy had signed and published an appeal for an end to Allied aerial bombardment of Germany, and it accused these Catholic leaders of hypocrisy. "When the Germans bombed London," the guidelines continued, "when the aerial pirates of Hitler destroyed our cities, shot and killed our peaceful people—they were quiet. But when they began to bomb Germany, they protest."[29]

In midsummer 1944, as the Red Army offensive, launched in tandem with the Allied landing in Normandy, drove first into Belorussia and then into eastern Poland, the Soviets prepared the governmental structures needed to deal with the reincorporation of the local non-Orthodox populations into the Soviet system. On July 1 the Soviet press announced the formation of a Council for Affairs of Religious Cults, to be under the authority of the Sovnarkom. Just as the council formed after the *sobor'* of the previous September dealt with Orthodox affairs, this new organization was designed to govern state relations with other churches: the Armenian Gregorians, Old Believers, Catholics, Eastern Rite Catholics, Lutherans, Moslems, Jews, and Buddhists.[30] Ivan Vasilevich Pol'ianskii was named the head of the new council. German propaganda immediately picked up on his appointment to claim that he "formerly belonged to the Bolshevik anti-God organisation. From 1933 to 1940 he was responsible for the deaths of numerous members of the clergy in the Soviet Union."[31] Whether this contention that Pol'ianskii was directly responsible for clergy killings is true or not, like his counterpart Georgii Karpov, the head of the Council for Orthodox Affairs, he was a high-ranking officer in state security.[32] Certainly his new group enjoyed significant influence, receiving "ample office accommodation in a central building in Moscow," despite the severe housing shortage, as the British ambassador noted.[33]

American diplomats regarded the creation of this new council as a hopeful sign, believing as they did that it reflected the "more tolerant attitude" of the Kremlin toward religion. In their view, the council would give minority religions "a greater degree of recognition than heretofore accorded." The American diplomat Charles Bohlen wrote rather optimistically: "[P]erhaps it should be considered in connection with the assurances given by Stalin to Father Orlemanski concerning the Catholic Church." More accurately, Bohlen predicted that the council "is undoubtedly related with the Polish question and is probably designed to provide machinery to handle questions involving the Catholic population of eastern Poland which the Soviet government intends to incorporate in the Soviet Union."[34]

Moscow would certainly need whatever help it could get in dealing with the Poles. The Soviets had worked incessantly to create Polish army units and governmental cadres that would be under their control, but this had not been easy. In 1942 the Soviets allowed more than 30,000 members of the nationalist Anders Army to leave the USSR for the western front, hoping thereby to skim off the more nationalist, or anti-Soviet, officers and men. Subsequently, Moscow created a new, Communist-controlled force under the command of Lieutenant Colonel Zygmunt Berling. Although Berling's force was more reliably pro-Soviet than its predecessor, as the Red Army moved westward, even these Soviet-Polish units began to disintegrate.

In part, the reason for the high rate of desertions was the arrival of the Red Army in Poland, as well as contact with non-Communist Polish underground forces. In July 1944 Soviet intelligence estimated that Polish Home Army units in the path of the Soviet offensive numbered between 8,000 and 10,000.[35] Although these were formally allies of the USSR, in fact the Kremlin regarded them with great suspicion—which was returned in full measure by the Poles. Even after these men were disarmed, Soviet problems continued. I. A. Serov, deputy people's commissar of internal affairs (and a future head of the KGB), reported to his boss Lavrenty Beria that "organs of counterespionage" within Soviet-Polish units were poorly staffed and unable to deal with "hostile elements penetrating the ranks of the Polish Army." There was also the problem of "massive desertion from the Polish Army," which also required extensive intelligence work to stem. Given the bottomless demand for manpower caused by the huge casualty rates in the war, Soviet recruiters had allowed many Home Army veterans to enter Red Army Polish units "without sufficient checking," and leaders of the Polish underground were therefore able "to conduct hostile agitation" using these people as agents. According to the NKVD, this led to desertion rates of between forty and fifty officers and men daily. In the first half of October 1944 alone, 2,000 men had deserted before Soviet authorities took "decisive measures" to staunch the flow.[36]

The morale of Soviet-controlled Polish units could not have been improved by the events of the Warsaw rising. On August 1, in response to orders from the London Polish government, and having been encouraged to act by Soviet radio appeals, the Polish Home Army rose against the Nazis in the Polish capital. What followed was, along with Katyn, one of the most controversial episodes in Soviet-Polish history: the Red Army, which had reached the eastern bank of the Vistula River just short of Warsaw, did not advance to assist the Polish forces. The Nazis crushed the Polish insurgents after two months of bitter street fighting that destroyed more than 80 percent of the city. Not only did the Soviets fail to offer direct help to the Poles, they also refused landing rights to American and British planes when the Allies offered to make supply drops to

Home Army forces. The Soviets only reversed themselves when the outcome of the rising was already clear, and by that time the Anglo-American airdrops were ineffective.[37] Although no conclusive evidence has emerged from the Soviet archives, it would seem consistent with Stalin's Polish policies to assume that the Soviets refused to assist the Poles—or at least did not rush to do so—in order to allow the Germans to crush the troublesome Home Army; any Nazi casualties incurred during the fighting would also, of course, be a welcome bonus.[38]

War against the Vatican

These intense Soviet-Polish tensions were mirrored at the international level, where the conflict between Moscow and the London Poles threatened the unity of the anti-Hitler coalition. President Roosevelt, ever mindful of the religious dimension, once again approached the pope in hopes that he might agree to some formula to defuse tensions, or at least give the outward impression of doing so. Accordingly, he returned Myron Taylor to Rome as his personal emissary. Roosevelt had other concerns as well: in the upcoming presidential and congressional elections he hoped to retain the ethnic Polish-Catholic vote, which had been reliably Democratic in the past. As he told Stalin during their private conversation at the Teheran Conference in December of the previous year: "In America there are six–seven million citizens of Polish extraction, and therefore I, being a practical man, would not want to lose their votes."[39] If the close U.S. alliance with the USSR were to result in a subjugated Poland, or the imposition of Soviet antireligious policies, this might alienate a great many of America's Polish voters. Roosevelt was eager to distance himself from any Soviet-imposed solution of the Polish question at the same time that he sought to assure Stalin that the United States would not oppose steps taken to ensure Moscow's security in that country. It was an impossible balancing act.

Taylor had several audiences with the pope and with Monsignor Tardini, the political advisor to Pius XII. In Taylor's view, Tardini was especially unhelpful, since he "has very pronounced [negative] ideas on Russia and the spread of communism."[40] In his first meeting with the pontiff, on July 12, Taylor presented a draft declaration that he said resulted from conversations he had held in London with Ivan Maiskii, the Soviet ambassador to Britain. "We reached a point" in these talks, Taylor said, "where the Ambassador enquired what form of statement of assurance to be made by Marshal Stalin would be accepted" as proof of Soviet good intentions. Taylor had also conferred with Roosevelt, Secretary of State Cordell Hull, and influential members of the American Catholic hierarchy. The result was a two-point draft declaration. In the first point, the Kremlin would pledge, in conformity with article 124 of the 1936 Soviet Constitution, to proclaim "complete freedom of religious teaching and freedom of worship in all Soviet territory." Taken alone, this might have been a hopeful statement, but the second point gave Moscow a loophole the size of a Zeppelin: "Any abuse of these privileges, either to organize movements or to incite the people to overthrow the Government, will be dealt with in each case according to the law."[41] Naturally, both the pope and later Tardini "objected to item II in the formula . . . but approved item I," Taylor recorded.[42] They rightly believed that Soviet propaganda would stress the fine sentiments of the first point while the Kremlin would use the second to crush any religious activity of which they disapproved.

Taylor pleaded with the pope, but the pontiff had been engaged in this game far longer than Taylor and did not have alliance pressures or an insistent president to contend with. He was less anxious to find a face-saving formula that would mask the realities of Soviet religious repression with nice phrases. At a subsequent meeting he told Taylor that "such a statement" by Stalin "would mean very little." The pope was concerned about the fate of Catholic Poles who would find themselves east of the Curzon Line,* and thus under Soviet control. He did not trust vague Soviet promises.

The American emissary said that he had recently spoken with Aleksandr Bogomolov, the Soviet liaison to the Allied Advisory Council for Italy, who had only recently arrived in the country; Bogomolov had said that he might be prepared to enter into talks with the Vatican. Taylor pointed out to the pope that the Orthodox tsars had sent representatives to the Vatican and that "with the Polish question becoming ever more acute, that the Roman Catholic Church in Poland and the Orthodox Church in Russia might be led into a very difficult conflict in the future unless the Russian situation vis-a-vis the Church was liberalized and clarified." The pope readily agreed but again insisted that signs of Soviet good faith must precede any generally agreed statement; he pointed out that Soviet actions in the recent past, especially during their occupation of portions of Poland and the Baltic states, did not give great cause for hope. He also said that Moscow would be wrong to assume that sound relations between the

*The "Curzon Line" was so named after Britain's Foreign Secretary Lord Curzon, who during the Versailles conference at the end of the First World War attempted to delineate a boundary based on ethnicity between Poland and its eastern neighbor. The actual interwar Polish-Soviet border, established after the Treaty of Riga in 1921, was considerably to the east of the Curzon Line.

Vatican and these regions the Kremlin hoped to regain were unimportant: "[A] careful student of the European political arena," he said "must yield to the conclusion that a harmonious religious basis would promote a better political and economic understanding."[43]

The Americans made another fruitless attempt to sway Pope Pius the following month, August, as the fighting raged in Warsaw and inter-Allied tensions grew. This time the Americans drew on British support: Admiral Standley, former American ambassador to Moscow, and Hugh Wilson, a high-ranking Foreign Office official, had another audience with the pope. "Stalin," Standley said, "had recreated [sic] the Orthodox Church; had incorporated it however as a part of government administration ... Admiral Standley felt that Stalin has his vanity," and that he sought to be an even greater historical figure than Lenin. During the discussion, the pope returned time and again to the legacy of Soviet religious repression, which he said prevented good relations; but Wilson took a historical view, arguing that the Vatican had often entered into relations with nonreligious leaders such as Napoleon. The pope remained unmoved.[44]

The clearest statement of Vatican reservations about cooperation with the Soviets at this time of the war is contained in a memorandum written by Tardini, which he gave to Taylor. The condition of the Catholic Church in the Soviet Union, Tardini wrote, "does not show any substantial improvement from what it was before the war. The anti-religious Soviet legislation always remains in vigour." Although Tardini did not say this explicitly, the draft Soviet assurances on religion did nothing to weaken these existing antireligious laws. The Vatican was most concerned that "the now very few survivors of the Catholic clergy who had been arrested in Russian territory since the Soviet Revolution, were not set free, nor were they afforded any possibility of exercising their sacred ministry." Some ethnically Polish priests had been released from the gulag in 1942, when the Soviets were forming the Anders Army, and some had been able to make their way to the West. But "not all the priests, previously imprisoned and deported from Poland, were set free, nor does it appear that they were set free after this date." In particular, Tardini mentioned the unknown fate of Archbishop Edward Profittlich, the apostolic administrator of Estonia, whom the Soviets had arrested in Tallin in June 1941 "and deported towards the Urals." Nothing had since been heard of the archbishop.

Tardini wrote that the Vatican remained unconvinced by the apparently more moderate treatment of religion in the USSR "within the last two years." The Soviets' new line neither quashed antireligious propaganda nor indicated "a positive recognition of religious liberty." "[I]t is not difficult to find an explanation for it in the desire to take into account the obvious reasons of political and military opportuneness and the psychological needs of a people in a war." As for the Soviet publication, *The Truth about Religion in Russia*, Tardini was unimpressed. "The book, very widely diffused in various translations, and almost impossible to find in the U.S.S.R., is reticent, inexact, and sometimes contains falsehoods," he wrote. The Soviets had lied when, shortly after the Nazi attack, they published figures purporting to list the number of open churches in the Soviet Union; at that time Moscow claimed that 1,744 Catholic Churches were operating in the USSR. "As regards the Roman Catholic Church," Tardini wrote, "this information is completely false."[45]

Despite the closing of the Comintern in 1943, Tardini continued, Moscow continued to push the ideas of Communism throughout a Europe weakened by war. "These principles are essentially materialistic and the doctrines based on them destroy the personality of the individual to the advantage of the State, proclaim class-war, tend to the dictatorship of the proletariate [*sic*], and antagonize religion." The appeal of Soviet propaganda was especially dangerous in the chaotic political situation of Europe as the war wound to its destructive end:

> This propaganda is carried on especially in countries through which the war has passed or is passing, and avails itself of the very miserable conditions of these peoples. . . . Such propaganda is indeed very cleverly carried on, nor does it reveal to the inexperienced the erroneous principles from which it springs and on which it bases itself; in fact, it rather proclaims even a tolerance and an understanding for the Catholic Religion, respect for the Faith and religious practice and offers collaboration. Thus is renewed the policy of the "Extended Hand," already tried in other countries. However, because of the sad consequences which it has had, one cannot but entertain very serious concern.

Tardini stated that the Vatican would continue to "follow a policy of watchful expectation and reserve."[46]

Clearly, the Americans could expect no help from this quarter. Even worse, however, Taylor's mission, which had been undertaken in large part to improve relations with Moscow, had precisely the opposite effect. Soviet NKGB agents operating in Italy were highly curious about Taylor's intentions in Rome, and they were certain that the Vatican was up to no good. On July 24 the Soviet intelligence *rezident*, or chief espionage officer, informed Moscow that Taylor was negotiating a separate peace with the Germans, using the Vatican as an intermediary. The Soviet agent was obviously misinformed about a number of things: "[Cardinal] Spellman and Taylor arrived in Rome at the request of the Pope.

They met with the German ambassador to the Vatican, Weizsäcker, who represented the military group of Brauchitsch and Keitel in Germany. Weizsäcker is seen as the best diplomat who has not compromised with Nazism and is strongly anticommunist."[47] The same agent reported to Moscow on August 27 that Churchill had visited the Vatican and had also received proposals for a separate peace from Weizsäcker. "As regards the Vatican," the rezident wrote, "it stands for the prompt formation of a German government, with which to avoid during the occupation of Germany what might be a pro-Soviet government."[48]

According to one well-placed source in Lubianka, Moscow headquarters of the NKVD, the Soviet agent in Rome was Joseph Grigulevich, a person of Soviet origin who had become a Costa Rican citizen and subsequently that country's ambassador to the Vatican. According to Grigulevich's reports to Moscow, the principal cause of papal hostility to the USSR was fear about Soviet treatment of the Uniate Church as well as other East European Catholics.[49]

There is no independent verification of Grigulevich's claims that either Churchill or Taylor was engaged in negotiations with the Germans.[50] Indeed, in Taylor's case, this would have run contrary to the entire purpose of his mission, which was to work toward some form of reconciliation between the Vatican and the USSR, if only a superficial one designed largely to assuage American public concerns. The Soviet intelligence reports do not reveal the source of these allegations, which may well have been German disinformation; certainly the mention of Keitel among the ranks of supposed anti-Nazis, as well as the exculpation of Weizsäcker, make one suspicious. Despite the poor quality of the reports, however, if they were believed in Moscow as they seem to have been, they could only have heightened Soviet suspicions about their Allies' intentions and those of the Vatican. This would also go a long way toward explaining why at this time Moscow began to hint darkly about Western maneuvers for a separate peace in Rome and also why Soviet anti-Catholic propaganda became much more intense and strident during and after the summer of 1944. At any rate, the Concordat between Rome and Moscow of which Roosevelt dreamed was stillborn.

The Vatican indulged in pipe dreams about creating mechanisms to prevent Soviet domination of Central Europe. In early 1944 the OSS learned, for example, that the pope hoped to reestablish "a Habsburg Monarchy in Central Europe and plans for the re-organization of a Catholic Federation to counteract the Soviets' religious policy." These Vatican plans, the report continued, "are no secret to Moscow."[51] In fact, of course, the Roman Catholic Church, for all its reach, lacked the political muscle needed to recreate a Habsburg Empire—or, indeed, to do much to slow the advance of Soviet power.

Stalin and the Greek Catholic Church

On April 8, 1945, a controversial article entitled "Z Khrestom chy z nozhem" (With the cross or with the knife) appeared in the newspaper *Vil'na Ukraina* in Soviet-controlled L'vov; after its publication, it was reprinted two days later in *Pravda Ukrainy* and eventually in Soviet newspapers throughout Ukraine. Although it was signed by V. Rasovich, this was in fact a pseudonym for the Soviet "journalist" Iaroslav Galan. The article was a vicious attack on the highly popular Eastern Rite Catholic metropolitan Andrei Sheptyt'sky, who had died on November 1 of the previous year; the publication was the first open sign that Soviet policy toward the Greek Catholic Church was taking a new and fateful course.

Galan accused Sheptyt'sky of having served foreign interests throughout his long tenure as metropolitan, betraying the national cause of the Ukrainian people first by serving the Vatican, then later by acting as a cat's paw for the Polish government during the interwar years, and finally by collaborating with the Nazis after June 1941. According to Galan, only the Soviet government served the higher interests of the Ukrainian people, uniting all Ukrainians under a single government for the first time in their modern history.[52]

There was an element of truth to Galan's charges, though they were one-sided and ignored the narrow range of real choices Sheptyt'sky had actually faced. The Greek Catholic Church existed in an unenviable situation throughout most of its history, since its creation at the end of the sixteenth century. Wedged between Orthodox Russia to the east, the Catholic Habsburg Empire to the west, and Catholic Poland to the north and west, Uniates were regarded by Moscow as heretics and renegades and by mainstream Catholics as politically and religiously unreliable; especially in the modern period, Poles regarded them as being the hotbed of Ukrainian nationalism. When the region was under Russian rule, as much of it was from the end of the eighteenth century through World War I, the state worked to close Ukrainian Catholic churches and impose Russian Orthodoxy. When the Poles regained the region following the First World War and the recreation of a Polish national state, Warsaw sought to transfer ecclesiastical authority away from Uniate clergy to more Polonized Catholic hierarchs. With its power base in western Ukraine, the church suffered from the fact that in modern times there was no Ukrainian state that might have defended its interests. In the absence of a nation-state, the Greek Catholic Church served as the nucleus of Ukrainian nationalism. As one of the premier historians of that nation writes, the Greek Catholic Church "functioned as the national church par excellence."[53]

The prewar years had been perilous for the Greek Catholic Church. On the one hand, the Warsaw government sought to extinguish nationalism among the Ukrainians who constituted 16 percent of Poland's population. By the 1930s these Polonization policies resulted in the creation of a Ukrainian nationalist guerrilla movement that Warsaw proved unable to crush entirely.[54] On the other hand, during the late 1920s and early 1930s, to the east the Soviet regime was carrying out the murderous collectivization of the farms, which resulted in the deaths through starvation and various forms of repression of millions of Ukrainians.[55] Soviet antireligious policies also completely destroyed the negligible structure of the Greek Catholic Church in Moscow-ruled portions of Ukraine.

When western Ukraine fell under Soviet control in September 1939, therefore, Greek Catholics had good reason to fear that their church might be liquidated entirely. Sheptyt'sky himself sought permission from the Vatican to confront Soviet authorities directly and publicly, even if this meant his own death. It would be a positive thing, Sheptyt'sky wrote the pope, "if someone became a martyr in this invasion."[56] The Vatican refused Sheptyt'sky's request to die for the faith, preferring to follow a more cautious policy toward the Communist occupiers, and in fact this approach proved sounder. Although the Soviets carried out mass deportations of about 1.5 million people from their newly acquired Polish lands, they moved slowly against the churches. The Communist authorities launched propaganda attacks against religion in general, but, just like their tsarist predecessors, they were markedly more lenient to Latin Catholics than to those of the Greek Rite. Even as late as December 1939, although he complained of various antireligious policies, Sheptyt'sky informed Rome that "the clergy is still able to work in all parishes and churches."[57]

Greek Catholic leaders loved neither Warsaw nor Moscow, but of the two the latter appeared to present the greater mortal threat owing to its hostility to all forms of religious worship. For this reason, when the Nazi-Soviet war began, Sheptyt'sky and other Greek Catholic clergy briefly believed that their situation might improve. The metropolitan even entertained hopes that the destruction of the Soviet atheist regime might result in the evangelization of the Russian people and the extension of Catholicism throughout the Slavic East, effectively ending the split that had rent Christendom since 1054.

That was not to be, of course, and Sheptyt'sky soon enough learned that any hopes placed in the Nazis would inevitably be dashed. The Germans arrived not as liberators but rather as more scientific enslavers. In August 1942, in deep despair about the state of Ukraine under Nazi rule, Sheptyt'sky sent a report to the Vatican that one historian of Catholicism has called "among the most moving documents of Catholic church history." Sheptyt'sky wrote:

Today the whole country is agreed that the German regime, perhaps to a higher degree than the Bolshevist, is evil, indeed even diabolical. For half a year not a day has passed that the most horrible crimes have not been committed. The Jews are the first victims. . . . The Bolshevist regime is being continued, spread and intensified. . . . The village inhabitants are treated like colonial negros [sic]. . . . It is simply as if a band of madmen or rabid wolves were throwing themselves upon the poor nation. . . . It will take much freely sacrificed blood to atone for that shed as a result of these crimes.

Sheptyt'sky then referred to his earlier request that the pope bless his wish for martyrdom: "I believe that I lost the best and perhaps the only opportunity for [martyrdom] under the Bolsheviks. . . . These three years have taught me that I am not worthy of such a death."[58] His early miscalculations in regard to the Nazis' intentions had led the metropolitan to the edge of political and personal despair.

The Red Army reentered L'vov on July 27, 1944, and by the end of the year Soviet authority had been restored throughout western Ukraine, except in those places where it was still contested by partisans of the Ukrainian Insurgent Army (Ukrainska porstanska armiia, or UPA). Metropolitan Sheptyt'sky well understood that Moscow would not forget his flirtation with the Nazis and would possibly retaliate not only against him but also against his church. So, in a desperate move designed to ensure the survival of the Greek Catholic Church, he sent an "open letter" of greetings to Stalin and prepared to dispatch a delegation to the Soviet capital to negotiate a modus vivendi with the Communist government and the newly restored Russian Patriarchate. Unfortunately, the aged metropolitan soon fell ill and died on November 1, leaving his less experienced and less prestigious successor, Archbishop Slipyi, to steer the Greek Catholic Church through the most hazardous period in its history. Sheptyt'sky's funeral was an occasion not only for an outpouring of public affection for the departed metropolitan but also for a mass show of support for the distinct western Ukrainian national identity, which seemed in danger of being extinguished by Sovietization.[59]

Slipyi tried unsuccessfully to build bridges to the new regime, but neither side trusted the other. On November 23, he issued a pastoral letter to his flock in which he called on members of his church to cease resisting Soviet power by armed force. "A man who sheds innocent blood," he wrote, "even of one's enemy, [one's] political opponent, is the same as a murderer who kills to rob. Divine law condemns him, and the church anathematizes him." In the same letter, however, Slipyi showed where his sympathies lay: "True, not a few of them [resistance members] are guided by patriotism, their love of [their] people. But this is a wrongly understood love."[60] At any rate, Slipyi's pacific appeals had little impact on the Soviets, who continued to believe that the Uniate Church was one of the central supports of western Ukrainian partisan bands, and individual Uniate priests, to say nothing of the laity, ignored Slipyi's calls for peace, continuing their armed resistance.

The new metropolitan also adopted Sheptyt'sky's idea of sending a Greek Catholic delegation to Moscow, consisting of Metropolitan Sheptyt'sky's brother Klymentii, archimandrite (*nastoiatel'*) of a Uniate monastery, Fathers Ivan Kotiv and Budzins'kyi, as well as the controversial Havryil Kostel'nyk, senior priest (*nastoiatel'*) of the Preobrazhenskii Church in L'vov.[61] Kostel'nik had long been a proponent of closer cooperation with Russian Orthodoxy; his strong advocacy of a pro-Russian line, in addition to the role he would soon play in the dissolution of the Greek Catholic Church, have caused his many critics to view him as a Judas-like figure, the man who betrayed his mother church to Stalinist forces; indeed, in September 1948 Ukrainian partisans would assassinate him as a collaborator.[62] Sending Kostel'nyk to Moscow was both an olive branch offered to the Soviets as well as an indication of the Greek Catholic Church's desperate situation.

Clearly, the arrival of this delegation in Moscow was a matter of great governmental and even strategic importance. Before being allowed to meet with the hierarchs of Russian Orthodoxy, therefore, the group was ushered into NKGB headquarters. There it met with secret police chief Lavrentii Beria's lieutenant, General Stepan Mamulov, who headed the NKGB secretariat, as well as Pavel Sudoplatov, one of the Lubianka's specialists in political counterespionage and murder. During the prewar years, Sudoplatov had become an expert of sorts in anti-Soviet Ukrainian nationalist groups, having in 1938 assassinated the Ukrainian separatist leader Yevhen Konovalets, on Stalin's personal orders. (Sudoplatov had first ingratiated himself into Konovalets's trust before giving him a gift of a box of chocolates packed with explosives. Sudoplatov had learned that the man had a weakness for sweets.)[63] During the war, Sudoplatov led the Fourth Directorate of the NKGB, which organized partisans as well as assassination teams operating behind German lines in Ukraine.[64] That a delegation of the Greek Catholic Church should be met by such officials was a confirmation that the highest Soviet authorities viewed the church question in western

Ukraine primarily, and perhaps even solely, as a vital strategic and security issue.

According to Sudoplatov, he surprised the visitors by addressing them in the western Ukrainian dialect and then "laid out the record of the Uniate Church leadership in collaborating with the Germans. At the same time," Sudoplatov writes. "I was ordered to assure them that, provided they repented and no military crimes had been committed by church officials, they were not liable to prosecution."[65] The NKGB's assurances were hollow: within months of this meeting in the Lubianka, Moscow would move against the Greek Catholic Church. At the end of February 1945 an attempt to use the church as an intermediary to persuade the UPA to cease its armed resistance failed, and by mid-March Stalin gave his permission for the subjection of the Greek Catholic Church to the Moscow Patriarchate.[66] Soviet authorities had always been suspicious of organizations with international links, and in the Greek Catholic Church they faced, from their perspective, the worst sort of enemy. The church was not only a nucleus of anti-Russian Ukrainian nationalism, but it was also linked with the hated Vatican, which had long been an avowed enemy of Soviet Communism and was—so Soviet agents believed, with some reason—busily working to rob Moscow of the political fruits of its impending victory over the Nazis. With its closed world of priests and constant communications across state lines with the Vatican, as well as its anti-Soviet nationalist activity during the war, the Ukrainian Catholic Church was the ideal organization to serve as a focus for resistance to the reimposition of Soviet rule. The foremost historian of the Greek Catholic Church concludes that the Soviets never really sought a true compromise with the Uniates; rather, Moscow only wanted to convey the impression of flexibility in order to stall for time as the Germans were defeated and the Soviet position in the western borderlands consolidated. Since 1939, the Kremlin had planned to subordinate the Uniates to the Russian Orthodox Church, but this had been impossible owing to the weakness of the latter church, the fluid international situation, and most of all the German invasion.[67] By 1945 Stalin at long last judged the circumstances to be ripe.

When Iaroslav Galan published his April 1945 attack on Sheptyt'sky, therefore, this was only the first public shot fired against the church, but it reflected tensions that had been building for a long time. The Ukrainian Central Committee's Directorate of Propaganda and Agitation used the publication of the piece as a way of smoking out popular attitudes among western Ukrainians, as well as to discover people with whom they might work to undermine the church. Word of the article spread fast among the people of L'vov, with "big lines" forming around kiosks where it was sold or where issues of the paper were displayed. Additionally, Ukrainian Communist authorities broadcast the article over local radio on April 9–10; they also published it in pamphlet form with a print run of 10,000 copies.[68]

According to Soviet observers, the article "made a very great impression." The effect was especially marked among the "local intelligentsia" and the clergy. There was, however, no uniform response: "[T]he clergy and believers reacted variously to the article." Educated people (*nauchnyi*) also displayed differing reactions, some of them disquieting to Communist authorities. One unnamed professor described the article as "a big, powerful bomb." A number of professors at the city's university believed that the best—perhaps the only—course for the Uniates was to join the Russian Orthodox Church if they wished to remain part of Ukrainian life. Others, however, believed that the attack on the popular Sheptyt'sky would "enliven" the OUN and "strengthen propaganda against Soviet power." Many readers said openly that, far from being a Roman lapdog, Sheptyt'sky had for years been drawing away from a closer union with the Vatican, because greater papal control would have spelled complete Polish domination. An academician by the name of Kolessa said that, if Sheptyt'sky had been such a slave of papal interests, as the provocative article claimed, then how could one explain the fact that, when the metropolitan visited Rome in 1920, the Vatican had refused to allow him to return to L'vov and had in fact "interned" him there? Other readers saw the article as a Bolshevik provocation designed to sow discord among Ukrainians—which it was, of course. And a priest named Garchinskii said "'The clergy are very insulted by the article and will complain to Moscow.'" Unfortunately, of course, Moscow was fully aware of Galan's piece and had sanctioned it in the first place; Kremlin authorities were scarcely going to come to the aid of the Uniates. In one Greek Catholic seminary, there had been a public reading of the article, during which "the mood among all students and teachers was anxious and depressed." Galan's piece, they believed, constituted a "terrible accusation" against Uniates; but rather than join the Russian Orthodox Church, it was better, they believed, for each to go his own way.

Not all reactions were so equivocal or negative to Galan's article. Certain educated people, though apparently a minority, said that "at last" the Soviets were unmasking Sheptyt'sky's collaboration with the Poles and Germans. Furthermore, "there is one case [*est'sluchai*]," the Soviet monitors noted, "where a part of the Uniate clergy and believers express the wish to break with the Union and accept the Orthodox faith." As expected, the pro-Russian Havryil Kostel'nik also responded favorably. "Kostel'nik in church stated that Sheptyt'sky was 'sick to his very soul [*dushevnobol'noi*]'; however, after Kostel'nik's statement, those who support Sheptyt'sky's line, in their turn, have called Kostel'nik 'crazy.'" Undaunted by the skepticism of his fellow clergy and the laity, Kostel'nik said that the now dead metropolitan had "dreamed" of uniting with Moscow but feared that Soviet authorities would not have allowed him to remain in Kiev, and that this would have spelled the "Russification" of the Uniate Church. "Now no one is afraid of that," Kostel'nik continued, "because Ukraine is united and indivisible." He also promised that "As soon as the war ends, then he will declare war on Slepyi and work for the unification of the [Russian Orthodox and Uniate] churches and himself convert to Orthodoxy [*i sam primet pravoslavie*]."

Litvin, the author of the Soviet memorandum quoted here, closed with some general observations about the western Ukrainian public's reactions:

> All of these facts testify that the article of V. Rasovich [Ia. Galan] . . . delivered a serious blow to the prestige of the Uniate Church. The article has caused the leaders of the Uniate Church seriously to think about their role in the conditions of the western oblasts of Ukraine. The article helped a significant part of the workers, peasants and intellectuals to be convinced that the Uniate Church conducts an antipopular line [*antinarodnuiu liniiu*] and is helping the evil enemies of the Ukrainian people—Ukrainian-German nationalists and through them German fascists.[69]

Understandably, perhaps, in reporting to his bosses in Moscow, Litvin sought to put a positive coloring on the popular response to Galan's attack. Judging from his own observations, however, it is hard to see how Soviet authorities could have taken much comfort from the western Ukrainian public mood. Far from demonstrating widespread hostility toward the Uniate Church, public responses to Galan's provocation generally supported Sheptyt'sky, and, even more seriously for the Soviets, beyond Kostel'nik, very few Uniate clergy seemed ready either to accept the attack on the dead metropolitan or the idea of a union with the Moscow Patriarchate.

Not being democrats by temperament or practice, the Soviets were not going to be dissuaded by such things as the public will. They had decided to be rid of the troublesome Uniate Church and to sever the connection between Soviet Ukrainians and the Vatican, and they would do so even if it meant covering their actions with the smallest of fig leaves. Just as they had sought to do when working with Father Orlemanski, or in attempting unsuccessfully to seduce Father Ciszek, Communist authorities found a handful of Uniate clergy and laity who would cooperate with them to destroy the independence of the Greek Catholic Church from within. Galan's article had proved invaluable in winkling out pliant people. No doubt these people acted from various motives: some, such as Kostel'nik, may genuinely have believed that their church had no justification for continued independence, because Ukrainians were all now within the bounds of a single state for the first time in modern history. The other members may have acted out of fear of the Soviet authorities, or from opportunism. There is no way of knowing, but the Soviets were certainly not above using strong-arm tactics against the church, as events would show.

Whatever their motives, the work of this small group was of great interest to the most powerful figures in the Soviet Union. In May 1945 Nikita Khrushchev, the future premier of the USSR who at this time was party boss of Ukraine, wrote to Stalin: "When in Moscow, I informed you about the work underway regarding the dissolution of the Uniate church and the transfer of the Uniate clergy to the Orthodox church. As a result of this work, from among a number of the Uniate clergy an 'initiating group' has been formed." This "initiating group," consisting of Kostel'nik and two other senior priests,[70] was a pathetically small and low-ranking affair. Not a single Uniate bishop could be persuaded or compelled to take part in this Moscow-ordered charade. Instead, when the leaders of the church, including Metropolitan Slipyi, learned of the group's intention to dissolve the Greek Catholic Church from within, they addressed a letter of protest to Molotov: "Our attitude towards the action of Fr. Kostel'nyk is entirely negative," they wrote. "We condemn his action as harmful, totally anti-ecclesiastical, and contrary to the truth proclaimed by Christ."[71] Their protests, however, unsupported by military force or by any great power, could not halt the Soviet steamroller once set in motion.

According to Khrushchev's letter to Stalin, the initiating group had composed two documents: a letter to the Soviet of People's Commissars concerning the situation of the church in western Ukraine, and a letter to all Greek Catholic clergy, which he would circulate following approval of the "initiating group" by the Kremlin. Up to this point, Khrushchev continued, officials of the NKVD who dealt with denominations (*veroispovedanii*) in the Council of People's Commissars (the SNK) had conducted all relations with the initiating group. However, "all documents were composed by church people themselves," Khrushchev assured Stalin; "our people took no part in editing them." He argued that Moscow should approve the request to circulate and "after that publish these documents in newspapers of the western regions of Ukraine." "I request your order," he closed.[72]

Apparently, Stalin approved Khrushchev's work, issuing an ukaz allowing the initiating group to proceed with its plans.[73] The text of its appeal to the Greek Catholic clergy, the chief author of which was Kostel'nik, would be approved for circulation. The document provides an interesting insight into the historical arguments swirling around issues of religion and nationalism in the western borderlands.

Kostel'nik's historical survey claimed that there had always been clergy members among the Uniates who desired to join the Russian Orthodox Church, but throughout history powerful political forces had thwarted these hopes. "In our church history, the Union was initiated and brought into existence by the Poles, the more effectively and rapidly to destroy Russia." When, after the partition of Poland at the end of the eighteenth century, western Ukrainian lands had fallen under Austrian rule, the church cleansed itself of Polish influence. But then, in the middle of the next century, when, following the Ausgleich, these Ukrainians had fallen under the control of the Hungarians, authorities in Budapest instituted "Magyarization" policies designed to destroy the Ukrainian people and their church.

This dire situation persisted until the First World War, when the Austro-Hungarian empire collapsed; but even this turn of events brought the Ukrainians no relief. The recreation of an independent Polish state brought renewed pressures, this time from Warsaw again. During the period 1919–39, it became clear that neither the Polish government nor Rome supported the existence of an independent Greek Catholic Church; both wanted to impose the Latin Rite for their own reasons. The Vatican sought greater centralization and disliked the remnants of eastern Orthodox ritual in the church. Warsaw wanted to achieve the "Polonization" of the Uniates and believed that this could be furthered by transforming Uniate parishes into Catholic ones. Metropolitan Sheptyt'sky protested the seizure of Uniate churches in vain; Pope Pius XI had consistently supported the Poles. This sad history, Kostel'nik wrote, proved that only union with Russian Orthodoxy could "save us from perishing" at the hands of "the chauvinist Poles."

When war broke out in 1939, Kostel'nik argued, some Uniates briefly believed that the Germans would rescue the Greek Catholic Church from its historical dilemmas. But the Nazis had, of course, not invaded the East as liberators but rather to launch an all-out assault against all of Slavdom. In toying with Sheptyt'sky as they did, the Nazis were merely following the ancient conqueror's trick of "divide and conquer."

What course did these tragic events leave for the Greek Catholic Church, Kostel'nik asked? Since the fourteenth century, Ukrainian Christians had been linked with Western Europe, and yet the Poles had constantly betrayed their interests. "On the other hand," Kostel'nik wrote rather frankly, ". . . we could not place our hopes on the USSR, since we feared revolutionary atheism, were always alien to socialism, and, besides that, did not have trust in the outcome of the national question in the USSR, the rightness of which has been clearly shown by the victorious conduct of the war by the USSR." The war, and the co-operation of nationalities in the Red Army, had supposedly shown that "we were mistaken in [our] evaluation of Soviet reality and the historical mission of the USSR." "Under the leadership of the first marshal, the incomparable Stalin," the Soviet people had triumphed and had saved the Slavic peoples. Fur-thermore, for the first time since the Mongol invasion of the thirteenth cen-tury, the Ukrainian people were finally united in a single state: "Marshal Stalin will go down eternally in history as the gatherer of the Ukrainian lands," a ref-erence to the fifteenth-century Russian tsar Ivan III, the "Great," who built up the power of Muscovy by conquering rival princedoms and "gathering" the Russian lands. Stalin's incorporation of the last remaining portion of Ukraine into a single state constituted a feat for which Ukrainians everywhere should give "truly heartfelt thanks." Kostel'nik also mentioned the "very great services" of Khrushchev, so as not to offend the local party boss by omitting him from the roll call of glory.

With the Ukrainian people now united in one state, Kostel'nik continued, the time had come for their union within one church. Unfortunately, the let-ter continued, the Uniate bishops had not yet reoriented themselves to deal with the new religious and political situation; they clung instead to their "sink-ing ship" and their "leaderless and disorganized" church. This situation was in-tolerable; "So we, the undersigned, leading representatives of our three eparh-kies, decided to lead our church away from anarchy" and into union with the Russian Orthodox Church. Although this step must be taken, Kostel'nik wrote strangely—but nonetheless revealingly—the union must proceed slowly so as to reduce the number of "victims."[74] Sadly, the process would not be slow, and there would be a great many victims.

The initiating group's arguments contained a great deal of truth: the history of the Greek Catholic Church had indeed been a tragic one, and the Poles, Aus-trians, Hungarians, and the Vatican had all too often acted against the church's interests, and through them the Ukrainian people's, frequently resorting to outright repression. The document is more interesting, however, for what it did not say. Kostel'nik made no mention of the stormy relations between the tsars, and later the Soviets, and the Greek Catholic Church; had he chosen to do so, he could have composed a list of repression at least as long as the one his group produced. One also wonders how his call for hosannas to the very same Soviet leaders who had starved millions of Ukrainians during the collectivization would go down among those who remembered these terrible events firsthand.

Events moved swiftly following approval of the initiating group's documents. In April 1945 the Soviet government arrested all the Uniate bishops, including Slipyi, followed by the deportation of a further 500 priests. On March 8 of the next year, a majority of the remaining Greek Catholic clergy (997 priests from a total number of 1,270) issued a written statement asking to enter the Orthodox Church. This application is still cited by defenders of Orthodoxy as proof that most Uniate clergy favored union with the Moscow Patriarchate. It would be reckless, however, to assume that, in the conditions of postwar Stalinism, these priests' choices were freely made.[75] With the end of the war, and the reestablishment of Soviet power, genuine political or religious independence was impossible. Refusal to take part in the forced union with Orthodoxy would spell arrest and deportation for recalcitrant priests and perhaps even the complete extinction of their church. In the same month, the Soviets closed the church's three seminaries, arresting almost all of the instructors, and they shut a total of 9,900 primary and 380 secondary schools run by the church.[76] As priests became available from the newly reopened Russian Orthodox seminaries, they were given Uniate parishes, which served to reinforce the Russification of the border region, precisely as Sheptyt'sky had long feared. These newly minted Russian priests, many of whom no doubt had strong connections to the NKGB,[77] were both more loyal to Moscow than were local Uniate clergy, and they also were unlikely to develop ties with the Ukrainian nationalist resistance. Soviet security organs were quite pleased with the result of their work. Sudoplatov writes that "Reunification was a decisive blow against the Ukrainian guerilla resistance under [Stepan] Bandera's leadership because the bulk of guerilla commanders came from the families of Ukrainian clergymen."[78]

In helping thus to drive wedges into the Ukrainian resistance against the restoration of Soviet rule, the Russian Orthodox Church may have provided its most useful wartime service to the Soviet state. It had begun to act as an alternative "Vatican," precisely as Stalin had indicated at the time of the September 1943 *sobor*'. Again, as with the 1943 move against schismatics within Orthodoxy itself, there is no reason to believe that Russian priests had to be strongly coerced to engage in the dissolution of the Greek Catholic Church, though many must have had qualms about the fate of their brother priests languishing in the hands of the NKGB. Certainly, some reflective Orthodox writers have since had their doubts. Timothy Ware, a historian of Eastern Orthodoxy and himself a bishop in that church, has written that "The fate of the Greek Catholics after the Second World War is perhaps the darkest chapter in the story of the Moscow Patriarchate's collusion with Communism."[79] Still, the Russian Orthodox Church had always regarded the Greek Catholic Church with the greatest disdain, seeing in it little more than a Vatican-Polish alliance designed to lure simple Orthodox believers away from the true faith into the clutches of Rome. If the individual fate of arrested priests may have been troubling to the consciences of Russian Orthodox, the demise of their rival church occasioned little mourning, then or since.

As with most repressions, however, the dissolution of the Uniate Church was achieved at a price. Not all Uniates accepted their church's destruction with equanimity. Some believers—it is impossible to tell how many—went underground to create a "Church of the Catacombs."[80] Well into the 1980s, when under Gorbachev the Kremlin at last allowed the church to reestablish itself legally, reports circulated of open-air masses held in the forests, fields, and hills of western Ukraine. The Soviets constantly sought to expose and disband such groups. In 1961, during Khrushchev's renewed antireligious campaigns, for instance, Soviet authorities in Ukraine uncovered eighty-seven unregistered Greek Catholic groups.[81] When the restoration of the Greek Catholic Church finally came about under Gorbachev, endless and bitter squabbles ensued between the Russian Orthodox Church and the Uniates over the control of church property seized during the 1940s. Still, as with so much of Stalin-era diplomacy and politics, though the dissolution of the Greek Catholic Church stored up serious problems for his successors, Stalin himself could claim a success. The shattering blow the combined forces of the Soviet state and Russian Orthodoxy delivered to the Greek Catholic Church in Ukraine prevented it from playing an active, organized role in the fluctuating and dangerous political conditions at war's end.

Patriarchs of the World Unite

On May 15, 1944, Patriarch Sergii died at the age of seventy-eight. He had presided over the Russian Orthodox Church during the hardest, most dangerous period of its nearly millennium-long history. Having become patriarch *locum tenens* shortly after the death of Tikhon in 1925, Sergii had to endure the years of Stalinist terror, during which time it looked as though the Communist state might extinguish the Russian church entirely. Toward the end of his life, he saw the church experience a revival of sorts, however tenuous and dependent on the continued goodwill and needs of the Communist state it might be. The postwar future remained murky.

Soviet newspapers announced the patriarch's death prominently, giving it much greater attention than they had accorded to any other Russian religious development since the Bolshevik Revolution of 1917.[82] In itself, this was a sign of the state's greater tolerance of a degree of open religious practice. In conveying news of Sergii's death to the American public, the Moscow correspondent of the radio network NBC predicted that "throngs of worshippers" could be expected at the funeral and that the ceremony was "likely to produce a great demonstration of religious fervor."[83] The funeral took place in the Patriarchal Church of the Epiphany in Moscow's Kremlin and was attended by Georgii Karpov, among other Soviet officials.[84]

Sergii's successor was to be Metropolitan Aleksii (Simanskii) of Leningrad and Novgorod. Aleksii was born in 1877 in Moscow and had been educated in law at Moscow University; he received his religious training at the Moscow Spiritual Academy, entering the priesthood in 1903 and rapidly becoming a bishop in 1913, on the eve of the First World War and during the 300th anniversary of the Romanov dynasty's establishment.[85] As bishop of Leningrad when the Nazi-Soviet war broke out, Aleksii, already in his sixties, remained in the city during the blockade, suffering privation alongside its residents; many of his fellow priests and assistants succumbed to starvation or disease during this ghastly time. The bishop enhanced his reputation in the city by his courageous example, continuing to celebrate the divine liturgy despite the siege, and for his efforts the Soviet state awarded him the Medal for the Defense of Leningrad. He was also named metropolitan while the city was still cut off from the rest of Russia.[86]

Aleksii would not be officially elevated to the Patriarchal throne until January of the next year. The *sobor'*, which would be summoned at that time to enthrone Aleksii, was to be a first-class political and religious event, and the Soviet authorities were determined to wait until wartime conditions eased sufficiently to enable other Eastern Orthodox patriarchs to travel to Moscow, or to send their representatives. In the meantime, on May 15, 1944, the Holy Synod selected Aleksii to serve as acting patriarch until a full *sobor'* could occur.

In a further sign of the greater public role accorded to religion, Moscow Radio's Home Service—not just programming directed to the foreign audience—broadcast the news of Sergii's death and also an open letter addressed to Stalin from Metropolitan Aleksii. This document officially announced Sergii's death and told the Soviet dictator:

We, his closest collaborators, were well aware of the sincere love he felt for you, and of his devotion to you as "the wise leader of the peoples of our great Union, appointed by God." These were the terms he always used. This feeling found particularly strong expression after his personal acquaintance with you, after our unforgettable meeting with you on 4th September last year. I often heard him speak of his moving recollections of this meeting and of the high historic significance he attached to the valuable attention you gave to our ecclesiastical needs.

Aleksii vowed to continue along the course charted by his predecessor: "obedience to the canons and laws of the Church, and unflinching loyalty to the Fatherland and our Government which is headed by you."[87] As one historian of Russian Orthodoxy has shrewdly noted, although Aleksii vowed future obedience to the Soviet state, his first loyalty was to church law.[88]

On November 21, 1944, TASS announced that an assembly of thirty-nine Russian Orthodox bishops had gathered to determine a time for the convening of a *sobor'*. The bishops unanimously decided to hold their council at the end of January, declaring that they would invite the ecumenical patriarch of Constantinople as well as the patriarchs of Antioch, Alexandria, and Jerusalem all to attend the ceremony; they would also invite the Georgian Catholics.[89] The *sobor'* elevating Aleksii consequently took place between January 31 and February 2, 1945.

The convening of the 1945 *sobor'* was a significant moment not only in the development of Russian church history but also in wartime diplomacy and even Russian history in general.[90] Such councils are rare; this was only the first time since 1667, during the Nikonian controversies, that the patriarchs of Eastern Orthodoxy traveled to Moscow for a *sobor'*. Between 1700 and 1917, the Russian church had no patriarch and thus held no enthronement councils. Even though two patriarchs had been chosen since then, owing to the First World War and the Russian Revolution the Eastern Orthodox hierarchs (most of whom resided in the Ottoman Empire, then at war with Russia) had been unable to travel to Moscow in 1917, when Patriarch Tikhon was enthroned. The 1943 *sobor'* had also occurred in the midst of war. The gathering of the patriarchs is the most important and solemn event in the world of Orthodox Church politics, because the Eastern Church stresses the conciliar tradition even more than does Western Christianity. Judging from outward appearances alone, the willingness of the leading figures of the Eastern Christian world to travel to wartime Moscow and take part in the enthronement of the new patriarch seemed to impart an important blessing on the Kremlin's new policy of cooperation with Russian Orthodoxy.

As is often the case, however, appearances can be deceiving. The carefully arranged show of Orthodox unity, as it would appear to the newsreel cameras the Soviets carefully sited to record the spectacle, masked great uncertainties, disunity, and even distrust among the delegates. A British diplomat who observed the ecclesiastical visitors recorded some of the underlying tensions:

> The Oecumenical Patriarch of Constantinople did not feel able to attend in person, & only sent his Exarch in Western Europe. . . . Similarly the Patriarch of Jerusalem, on the ground of poor health, sent one of his bishops [Bishop Athenagoras]. The Patriarch of Antioch appears to have been anxious to go for political reasons, and the Patriarch of Alexandria's vacillations were ended through his desire not to be outdone by an Arab confrere. Of the newer Orthodox Churches, the Patriarchs of Serbia and Roumania alone were represented. The Serbian Patriarch Gavrilo is still in German hands, but it is not clear why Patriarch Nicodim of Roumania merely sent one of his Bishops. The Bulgarian Exarch could not have been invited, the Bulgarian Church still being regarded as being in schism by all the Orthodox except the Russians.

Of the various Orthodox groups in North America, only the reliably pro-Soviet exarch of the Moscow Patriarchate, Veniamin, attended the council, all others boycotting the event, believing Aleksii still to be under the atheist Soviet state's control.[91] Even among the delegates attending, great suspicion was common: Bishop Athenagoras had "been instructed by the Holy Synod not to take part in the election at Moscow, and to hold aloof from any patriarchal conference which may be held there under the aegis of the Russian Government."[92]

Georgii Karpov addressed the members of the *sobor'*, declaring that "In our great country . . . the victory of the new, unexampled, most equitable socialist system" had "set free and liberated our people, [and] also liberated the Russian Orthodox Church from the fetters which had hampered and constrained its internal activities." Karpov explained how his council for Orthodox affairs was "interfering in no way with the internal life of the Church." His office had already done a great deal, he said, to establish "correct relations" between church and state, and he promised that "in the future the council will take every measure to eliminate all obstacles in the way of the exercise of Soviet citizens of the freedom of conscience proclaimed by the Constitution."[93]

One should recall that, as this NKVD officer recast as benign bureaucrat spoke, the Central Committee was already deeply engaged in its campaign to counter the grass-roots growth of religion in the USSR.[94] It is hard to know whether Karpov's sugared words had much effect on the visitors; his comments might have been directed to the ears of the international audience, rather than to the assembled delegates. But certainly the Soviets spared no expense in entertaining their guests: one British diplomat noted that "the Council, with the co-operation of the Soviet Government, were at pains to interest their visitors throughout their stay by visits to churches and monasteries, concerts of church music, and other suitable activities." On the evening of Aleksii's enthronement, the Soviets arranged a banquet in the Hotel Metropole—the nearest thing to a luxury establishment in drab, wartime Stalinist Russia—"which is understood to have cost 150,000 roubles."[95] At a time when many people throughout the USSR were at or near starvation level, the contrast with the heavily laden tables at the Metropole, piled high to serve the visiting bishops, was striking.[96]

A Canadian diplomat who spoke with several of the delegates to the *sobor'* found that "They all expressed themselves as surprised and impressed with the facilities which the Church has obtained in the Soviet Union, compared with their expectations. However their private attitude is definitely reserved." Doubts remained: "The Patriarch of Alexandria said that he and the others had come chiefly because they thought it would encourage the Russian clergy and believers, who have had such a hard time during the past 25 years."[97] The British also noted that "The visiting prelates derived the clear impression that the careful attention to publicity and the repeated emphasis on the freedom of the Russian Church were intended to convince them, and the outside world at large, that the era of persecution is now over." Although the delegates "were pleasantly surprised at the extent to which the Orthodox religion appeared to be tolerated again . . . the Archbishop of Tyre and Sidon summed up the general impression by quoting, during a visit to this embassy, the Arabic saying 'We remember the past: we do not know the future.'"[98] The visitors, each of whom represented the cumulative experience drawn from centuries of religious and diplomatic conflict and rivalry, were not easily taken in; they were also concerned about the unstated international intentions behind the Kremlin's revival of the Russian Patriarchate.[99]

In addition to a positive impression on the visiting bishops and spreading the Kremlin's propaganda message throughout the Orthodox world, the council also had other vital business to transact. If the Moscow Patriarchate was to act as the "Vatican" envisioned by Stalin, it would have to enlist the aid of the assembled hierarchs in the fight against that other Vatican, in Rome. On February 7, the *sobor'* issued an appeal "To Christians the world over." This apparently only meant certain Christians, because the missive constituted an oblique attack on the Catholic Church, which at this time was calling for a compromise peace in a desperate effort to avert the Vatican's nightmare scenario—a Communist-dominated Europe. Although "There will still be hard engagements and sanguinary battles . . . the outcome of the war has been sealed," the declaration announced. The imminent Allied triumph "is evident to all on earth, both those whose arms have been blessed by our Lord Jesus Christ and those whose arms have not received such blessing; both those whose prayers have reached the Lord as Abel's sacrifices, and those whose sacrilegious invocations spread over the earth like smoke from the fire of Cain, the fratricide." The Red Army had driven the Nazis out of occupied Eastern Europe, and "the territory of Germany herself has now become a battlefield. The former dreams of world domination of the 'master race' have become a disgraceful thing of the past." With Nazism's defeat, "humanity will be able to return to peaceful labour and to the building of a happy, joyous life on earth." "The Russian Orthodox Church, the Church of the great country which has borne the brunt of the blows of bloodthirsty Fascism and has wounded it mortally in battle, through the voice of the Council of all Bishops," called on all "warrior Christians" "to strain your efforts to complete the holy struggle."

The authors then delivered their indirect attack on the Vatican. Although the crimes of the Axis were clear for all to see,

> Yet nevertheless voices are sometimes heard calling "in the name of forgiveness" to pardon the infanticides and traitors! And they come from people who have the hardihood to consider themselves Christians. . . . In the name of the triumph of the Christian and all-human principles of liberty, the Orthodox Church calls upon all Christians of the world to struggle with all their force against such monstrous distortions of the Saviour's divine doctrine. May Fascism and its inspirers "disappear like smoke, like wax melting before the fire." Christ's words, that he who raises the sword shall perish by the sword, are already being visited upon them.[100]

This explicitly Christian, theological interpretation of the world war's moral meaning was unique in Soviet history, as was the sudden and heavy Soviet domestic press coverage of the bishops' council. All this publicity provoked varied reactions among Stalinist true believers, the Canadian embassy noting that it "seems to have astounded rank and file communists in Moscow, and provoked some unhappy muttering, among others ribald wit."[101]

Although the Christian message issuing from Moscow may have been somewhat jarring to Communist ears, the church's services were simply too valuable for the Kremlin to dispense with. The Orthodox attack on Rome served to taint and isolate Greek Catholics in western Ukraine as well as to counter the Vatican's influence throughout Eastern and Central Europe. A top-secret letter from the Ukrainian Central Committee, written shortly after the 1945 *sobor'*, shows just how highly Soviet authorities evaluated the Orthodox Church's services—and also how they still viewed religion as a most dangerous enemy:

"[M]illions of Slavs inhabiting the territory of Europe" retained their Orthodox faith, so the "mobilization" effort of the church "obviously deserves approval." But the church was serving a wider function: "the Orthodox Church — as a counterbalance to the Roman Catholic Church — calls upon Christians to carry the cause of routing and crushing Germany and punishing war criminals to the [very] end. By the same token, the Orthodox Church acts against the Roman Catholic Church, which conducts propaganda for mild conditions of peace for fascist Germany."

These wartime services were indispensable, the letter continued, "But we Communists must not forget for a single minute that the church's ideology contradicts our scientific Marxist-Leninist worldview, that it [religion] is profoundly reactionary and should ultimately be overcome. Therefore, in our everyday activity we should ceaselessly carry on the struggle against the idealistic and mystic ideology of the church, against its reactionary activity." The letter closed by warning that nothing less than the ideological verdict of the war was at stake: "At this time, as the war approaches its end, as the enemy is being defeated in open battle, hostile agents are attempting to intensify their influence on the ideological front [and] seeking to deliver a blow against our worldview, realizing that our struggle and our victories represent the triumph of the materialist Leninist-Stalinist worldview."[102] Documents such as these show that, despite the traditionalist veneer covering Soviet diplomacy and religious policy at the war's end, Stalin was no "Red Tsar," and all the blather in Western newspapers about the Soviets' return to traditional Russian methods was simplistic in the extreme. For the Kremlin, the Orthodox Church was a useful tool of the passing moment, nothing more; it remained an enemy in the long view. Furthermore, materialist ideology was more than just talk; it remained the unifying principle of Soviet governance and—perhaps most important—helped to define Moscow's enemies.

In addition to firing broadsides against the Roman church, the *sobor'* attended to other business closer to home. In an article published by the Central Committee newspaper, *Izvestiia*, the bishops called for greater unity among Russian Christians and for obedience to God's laws. Praising the work of the faithful during the war, the conferees also mentioned that the previous year had brought "the gradual and now almost final cessation of disastrous schism of the 'Living Church.'" Nonetheless, the article warned, there were some "unhealthy signs" in Russian religious life. Standards were low among priests (not exactly surprising, given the shortage of well-trained clergy coupled with the great demand); marriages "of churchgoers" were occurring without grace or sacrament, fasts were not being observed, and there was a general "*decline of Christian discipline* both in church and in private life."

Of even greater concern, in some areas believers "are unable to distinguish pastors appointed according to canons and clothed in grace from impostors, alien to God's grace, self-appointed." There were two themes underlying this assertion, one religious, the other secular and political. Russian Orthodox hierarchs certainly sought to ensure that priests exercised their offices under valid canon law; the preservation of church legality was the twig they clung to in the roiling waters of war and repression. At the same time, however, it was also very much in the state's interests that "self-appointed" priests not wander the country spreading politically unpredictable messages. Far better for all priests to be subject to the discipline of the Patriarchate, which would ensure obedience in turn to the Soviet state.

Questions of discipline and church structure were very much on the minds of those participating in the *sobor'*. During its first session, on January 31, the council unanimously adopted a new church statute (*Polozhenie ob upravlenii Russkoi Pravoslavnoi Tserkov'iu*) designed to govern the organization of Russian Orthodoxy and to define the powers and modes of selection for clergy. This was an important document, being the first comprehensive reworking of church-state relations since the early Bolshevik decrees of 1918. The statute must be interpreted not only in the context of the Russian Orthodox Church's own internal needs but also as a part of the Kremlin's unfolding designs regarding the political uses to which the church could be put, tasks which required the centralization of power in the hands of Moscow-based authorities.

The resulting regulations gave much greater powers than hitherto to the Moscow patriarch; with the new church law, local clergy and even bishops could be appointed or removed almost at will by the patriarch himself. Likewise, the law strengthened bishops' powers of appointment and dismissal. According to one sensitive historian of the Russian church, the statute created a set of rules "resembling that of the Roman Catholic Church" with "an almost papist church structure," rigidly centralizing power in the hands of the patriarch himself. Guessing at the reasons for this great change in church law, the same historian writes: "Apparently, Sergii and Aleksii wanted to match the Soviet administrative structure by their church centralization, hoping that such a centralized church would be stronger and would better withstand future trials and attacks of an ideologically incompatible and hostile state."[103]

This may well have been the reasoning of Orthodox hierarchs; we simply do not know given the paucity of sources. The regulations drawn up by the *sobor'*, however, could never have been promulgated had the secular authorities not given their consent, and it was at least as much in the interests of the Soviet state—in the conditions prevailing in 1945—to concentrate power in the hands of the patriarch as it was in the church's own.[104]

If the new law conferred important powers on the patriarch, however, it did not make him omnipotent in church affairs. The new regulations for the selection of future patriarchs made it quite clear that the Council for Russian Orthodox Church Affairs would exercise the right of prior approval. In future, state authorities would carefully vet possible candidates for the patriarchal throne, leaving the church itself merely to rubber stamp the state's chosen man. One further point stands out in the statute: the state recognized the patriarch, but it did not grant the church itself legal status. Such power as was to flow within the church would emanate from the patriarch, who was to be chosen by state authorities; the church itself would not be granted its own separate legal sphere.

The statute gave the patriarch the powers he needed to wield the almost papal authority required by the Kremlin, at the same time making him answerable to the Soviet state. Aleksii would use his new powers to dismiss recalcitrant clergy, and to appoint new and more reliable priests and bishops, as he worked with the Kremlin to dissolve the Greek Catholic Church; the same bag of tools would enable him to assimilate into the patriarchal church the various Orthodox sects in Ukraine, Ruthenia, Moldavia, Belorussia, Bukovina, and elsewhere in the western borderlands. Once again, church and state interests were in proximity, but they were not identical. Although Aleksii was surely happy to see the sweeping away of schismatic movements, this came at a high price. Clearly, behind the scenes, and now with newly refashioned legal authority, the Communist state still held the whip.

Pyrrhic Victory

Soviet manipulation of the Russian Orthodox Church, adept as it was, could only work to a limited extent. Suspicions of Stalinist Communism among believers and nationalists ran very deep and could not be eradicated entirely. The very fact that the war had forced the Kremlin to make peace with its erstwhile mortal enemies, the Orthodox clergy, showed the depth of the Soviets' political predicament. The problem was at its most acute, and thus most politically combustible, in the western borderlands rather than in the heartland of Russia, because the wartime reopening of churches had been heavily weighted in favor of the areas formerly occupied by the Germans. Despite the efforts of Soviet officials to contain the phenomenon, eight years after the war Karpov was still complaining that his council was continually inundated with petitions to re-open churches. The figures tell their own story:

> The number of inactive churches throughout the USSR exceeds 19,000. Of these, more than 17,000 are in the Russian Republic because in Ukraine and Belorussia all church facilities were occupied by religious congregations during the temporary period of German occupation. Approximately 13,000 buildings have been taken over for storehouses, for cultural purposes, or even for industrial enterprises; around 3,000 buildings are in a semi-ruined condition; and more than 3,000 are vacant, with their cult fittings preserved and their keys in the possession of a church member, even though church services are not conducted.[105]

Karpov warned that popular pressure for the reopening of these churches often led to "undesirable outburst[s] among the believers and other protests." He told local authorities that it was best to move swiftly when converting closed churches to secular use, giving believers less time to organize opposition. Local officials should make no changes in the "exterior or interior" of the churches, because, if these things were untouched, "great activity by groups of believers is not aroused."[106]

NKGB records from the postwar years reveal that throughout the western borderlands secret police continually confronted anti-Soviet religious-nationalist groups, a legacy of the prewar annexations and the Axis occupation. In July 1946, for instance, a representative of central state security sent from Moscow to examine the situation in Moldavia informed his superiors that local security forces had been lax in "[t]he exposure and arrest of agents of foreign intelligence, participants of bourgeois-nationalist organizations and groups, and also anti-Soviet elements working under church cover." He complained that "On the territory of Moldavia before the war there were a number of bundist, Zionist, and clerical organizations connected with foreign centers." Many of these groups had somehow managed to survive the war and subsequent sweeps by Soviet state security. "On February 27, 1945," the same source wrote, "The second section of the MGB MSSR [Ministry of State Security of the Moldavian Soviet Socialist Republic] conducted operation 'MIRAGE' against an a/s [anti-Soviet] group of church people, with opinions against the [officially sanctioned] Russian Orthodox Church and harshly negative attitudes toward Soviet power." In his view, this operation had not been carried out with sufficient severity, and various "Zionist" groups, as well as an illegal sect called "warriors of Christ" had not yet been cracked.[107] In a further letter, he complained to

Abakumov in Moscow that the regional security forces were unacceptably slothful: "The peripheral organs, apparently, do not want to fulfil Your [sic] direct order in this serious line of work of the NKGB. It is necessary to take decisive measures in relation to negligent people."[108]

These remarks are very telling: here was an agent of Moscow complaining not only that local Orthodox believers were spreading anti-Soviet opinions but also that they were opposed to the Russian Orthodox Church and the Moscow Patriarchate. Because Soviet security forces and the church were working hand-in-glove to pacify the borderlands and to drive a wedge between ordinary Christians and anti-Soviet nationalist forces, the NKGB interpreted the rejection of patriarchal authority by ordinary Orthodox believers as a form of rebellion against the state. Soviet security organs were on the horns of a dilemma: they could not move against the Russian Orthodox Church for fear of driving believers into less easily controlled unofficial sects; by using the patriarchal church as a means of control however, this had the unwelcome effect of keeping religion a living, visible presence. The critique of local security agents was also significant: the implied suggestion is that provincial political police could not be trusted to purge Moldavia of religious-nationalist groups. The reference to "decisive measures" in the Stalinist context was especially chilling.

A year later, in 1947, the purging of local cadres and exhortations from the center still had failed to crush the Kremlin's enemies in the borderlands, or to bring the civil population into line. The situation was aggravated by the desperate economic conditions throughout the USSR, which were at their worst in the western regions, which had been the scene of the fighting. The war had destroyed homes, mines, and industrial enterprises, and the transportation network had been wrecked. The two years following the war brought an immense famine that may have consumed 5 million lives. A recent Russian study of this famine, the extent of which was unknown to the outside world until after the collapse of the USSR, concludes that, although it was initially caused by the war's destruction, it was aggravated by counterproductive, overly centralized state policies. It was also worsened by the growing East-West confrontation, which persuaded the Kremlin to place a higher priority on heavy industry and the continued production of arms than on supplying the needs of the civil population.[109]

Moldavia alone lost 230,000 people, or 11 percent of its population between 1946 and 1947, most of them to famine.[110] A letter intercepted by the NKGB, written by an Orthodox priest of Romanian nationality living in Moldavia and sent to the Romanian exarch, provides a terrifying glimpse of the desperate situation in that republic:

I hope that in the near future we will once again see our old homeland. In our area life is very bad. The authorities levy heavy taxes on the peasants, the people remain impoverished. Many have died now who have not been buried, and those who live eat what they can find: they eat cats, dogs, the dead, and even people and their children. Thanks to this regime, people have become bad and unbelieving: felons, bandits, and what have you. The church has been completely separated from the state. Many churches are closing. In Kishiniev only 6 are working, the remainder are turned into warehouses of every kind and are even used for movie theaters and dance halls. They look on us, the clergy, as beasts, they swear and even spit, but despite everything I live with the words you said to me: "patience—we'll soon meet again."[111]

This was a return to the nightmarish famine conditions that followed the civil war, or the collectivization of the farms. Understandably, in such circumstances popular opposition to Soviet power continued to simmer. "Anti-Soviet elements from among the clergy . . . conduct hostile work among the population," the NKGB reported, "inculcating in the believers nationalist, Romanophile opinions, predicting an imminent war against the USSR on the part of England and America, and prophesy the 'unavoidable destruction of Soviet power.'"[112]

This was a dangerous development: a great many Christians throughout the USSR already attributed the reappearance of the church to pressure from the Western Allies, and many had hoped that the Soviet order would liberalize after the war; now, with the threat growing that the Cold War might lead to a conflict between the former allies of the anti-Hitler coalition, at least some Christians—it is impossible to estimate how many, given the vagueness of Soviet records—were hoping that a new East-West war would result in the destruction of the Stalinist regime. Throughout the early years of the Cold War, the Kremlin could never be sanguine about the political loyalties of its restive population, least of all in the western borderlands, the very area that was most exposed to outside influence and which would have been in the front line of a conflict with the Western powers. Even the return of full-scale political and social repression in the late Stalin years could not extinguish the threat; rather, as ever, senseless repression served mainly to feed popular discontent.

The war had proved that significant numbers of Soviet citizens would, if given even a slim opportunity of success, lay their lives on the line against the Stalinist order. Soviet authorities were uncomfortably aware that religion and churches remained the foci of this hidden but ever present social and political discontent. An analytical document written only months before Stalin's death complained of this state of affairs: "The Council for the Affairs of Religious

Cults attached to the USSR Council of Ministers has materials in hand which show that among the unregistered clergy and active religious groups of registered religious communities, there are former kulaks, traders, former Vlasovites, Banderists and all kinds of bourgeois nationalists, people sentenced for anti-state and criminal lawbreaking, relatives of those repressed, speculators, etc."[113] Even allowing for the exaggeration of threats that is often characteristic of police state documents, Soviet authorities believed that their subjects were restive, that their enemies were omnipresent, and that they clustered around the churches. The war had defeated the external Nazi enemy only to disclose the existence of an internal foe that was omnipresent but intangible, which could be sensed but not exterminated. Even worse, this internal enemy could not be trusted in the looming conflict with the new foreign threat—the United States and its allies.

PART **3** Selling the Alliance

I don't like to see our gullible people misled. But in practice it is not too easy [to avoid].—Christopher Warner, British Foreign Office, September 25, 1942

It is uncanny what skillful propaganda can do, if it does not oppose but reenforces the natural aspirations of human beings. —N. S. Timasheff, *Religion in Soviet Russia*

You Made Me Love You

Selling the Alliance Begins

The Propaganda Dilemma

From shortly after the outbreak of war between Germany and Great Britain in September 1939 until June 1941, on Sunday evenings the BBC broadcast the national anthems of all the Allied powers as an affirmation of solidarity among the nations fighting against Nazi Germany. Over time, as the Germans invaded country after country, the list of anthems grew accordingly. Early on the Sunday morning of June 22, 1941, Hitler's attack on the USSR added Stalin's empire unwillingly and abruptly to the ranks of the Allies. This new twist in the war faced the BBC with a curious but revealing dilemma: the Soviet anthem at this time was still the revolutionary hymn, the "Internationale," a stirring musical summons for the workers of the world to rise against their masters and shed their capitalist chains. How could the staid BBC broadcast this inflammatory hymn without seeming to condone its revolutionary message?

A direct order from Prime Minister Winston Churchill, whose anti-Communist credentials stretched all the way back to the early days of Bolshevism, settled the question: British foreign secretary Anthony Eden was told that "The PM has issued an instruction to the Ministry of Information that the Internationale is *on no account* [*sic*] to be played by the B.B.C."[1] Worried officials from Britain's Ministry of Information, fearing that the ban might offend the Kremlin, scurried to the Soviet ambassador in London, Ivan Maiskii, to ask whether he and his government would mind terribly much if the BBC substituted Tchaikovsky's 1812 Overture, or some other well-known Russian patriotic piece, as an alternative "national song." Maiskii replied that they would indeed and "was quite firm on the subject."[2] Ultimately, the BBC abandoned the practice of playing Allied anthems altogether rather than continue pointedly to exclude only the Soviets'. The lead writer of London's *Evening Standard* caught the essence of the dilemma best when he whimsically suggested that, in place of the "Internationale," the BBC should instead play the popular song "You Made Me Love You; I Didn't Want to Do it."[3]

Stalin's Soviet Union was not a state just like any other, and partnership with the world's first Communist country posed vexing dilemmas for the Western democracies and the USSR. To much of Western public opinion, the war had seemed to be a clear-cut struggle between dictatorship and democracy, even though the democratic credentials of such stalwart Allied powers as Poland were at best unconvincing. Now the USSR—revolutionary, totalitarian, Communist, and atheist—had joined the side of the angels battling the evils of Nazism. Soviet citizens had been told consistently, by contrast, that the war was a contest between rival imperialists and that Nazism was no more pernicious than the machinations of Britain's capitalist class.

Worst of all, from the Western point of view, until the moment of the German invasion, the USSR had been partnered with Germany, following the notorious Nazi-Soviet Nonaggression Pact of August 1939. In its directives to American and British Communist parties, the Comintern in Moscow continued to the bitter end to urge members to oppose the "imperialist" war being waged by Great Britain as well as the foreign policies of President Roosevelt. As late as May 5, 1941, a secret Comintern directive called on American Communists to combat the "demagogy and influence of Roosevelt," by aiming "their chief fire against the imperialist policies of the Roosevelt government and the ruling circles of monopoly capital, [who are] rapidly pushing the USA into war on the Atlantic and Pacific Oceans."[4]

Such, at any rate, were Moscow's orders to American and British Communists. The Comintern's directives to the French Communist Party, suffering under German occupation, were quite different and suggest that the Soviets were not entirely blind to the Nazi threat, at least in the long run. Moscow urged French Communists to work for "national unity, excluding all traitors and capitulationists" in order to reestablish "national independence" by struggling against "invaders and wreckers."[5]

In the months leading up to the German attack, Moscow was thus attempting to navigate a narrow and perilous course: trying to bring an end to the war by pressuring the Western powers through the agency of their working classes, even if this meant leaving Germany in an extremely powerful position on the European continent. At the same time, the Comintern clearly hoped to keep trouble brewing in the countries occupied by the Nazis. This evenhanded approach to the combatants may have been an understandable position diplomatically, but its subtleties were not appreciated in the United States or Great Britain.

When it came to selling the new Soviet-Western alliance to people in America and Britain, and to the West European public as well, the USSR therefore began the war at an enormous disadvantage. Although public opinion in the West was greatly divided when it came to interpreting the nature of the Soviet regime, Moscow's collaboration with the Nazis, the prewar purges, the Stalinist show trials, the arrests and execution of priests, and mass deportations had all left their mark. Many of the details about Stalinist political repression would not become known for years, but enough information had leaked out to leave a malodorous residue lingering about the USSR's international image.

In both the United States and Great Britain, suspicion about the USSR was strongest among religious believers, because Western churches, especially the Roman Catholic Church, had regularly focused on Soviet religious repression during the previous decades.[6] Even the experience of alliance with the USSR did not immediately wipe away the stain of the prewar purges and repression. In July 1942, more than one year after the USSR entered the war, and when sympathy among the British public for the Soviet Union was nearing its peak, the Listener Research Department of the BBC conducted a survey of attitudes toward the Soviet ally. Among "barriers to full understanding of the Soviet Union," the survey noted Soviet religious repression as the chief obstacle. "More than any other problem," the report noted, "it has been a cause for misunderstanding and deep mistrust, and there is a genuine need for clarification, particularly on the question of persecution."[7]

The long-standing Soviet record of religious persecution taxed the ingenuity of Soviet and Western propagandists charged with selling the new East-West alliance more severely than any other issue they faced. By its very nature, religion raises fundamental questions of morality more starkly than any purely political, economic, or logistical question. Although debates over Lend-Lease assistance and the timing of the landing by the Western Allies on the European continent, in addition to a host of smaller disputes, would certainly generate a great deal of heat, the passions roused by religious suspicions about the USSR and Communism ran far deeper and were more difficult for propagandists to eradicate or finesse. Also, of course, religious antipathy to the Soviet system was not isolated from other matters of the alliance; it colored every area of Soviet-Western cooperation. Each of the three great powers that would form the nucleus of the "Grand Alliance"*—the USSR, Great Britain, and the United States —had to deal with the problems of religion and the alliance. Each did so in ways that were both shaped by and reflected the three countries' different cultures, social compositions, political systems, and state interests.

The British God Reconsiders

Up until the outbreak of the Soviet-German war, British propagandists had used the Soviet legacy of religious persecution as one of their favored weapons, portraying Britain's war effort as a crusade of Christian civilization against totalitarian materialism, both Nazi and Soviet. This had been comparatively easy to do during the period of the Nazi-Soviet Pact, when both totalitarian powers were in the same camp, or at least when British propaganda could portray them as such. In January 1940, for instance, in a broadcast targeted at Orthodox Christians in Poland and Greece and transmitted in the native languages, the BBC thundered that "the overwhelming majority of the Orthodox population in Poland, some four million, has been deliberately handed over by the German Government to Soviet rule," and consequently, "atheist propaganda is being vigorously carried on by the league of Militant Godless of which Stalin is the President."[8]

The BBC likewise denounced Soviet antireligious policies during the Soviet-Finnish War of 1939–40. Canon Douglas, who headed the Church of England Committee of Foreign Relations, issued an appeal at the behest of the Ministry of Information "to all the Churches of Christ" throughout the world to rally to Helsinki's aid in its fight against the Red Army, lest Finnish Christians "will be abandoned to bitter religious persecution at the hands of the enemies of Christ

---

*The Soviet-era term for the alliance, "the anti-Hitler coalition," has always seemed more accurate, stressing as it does the principal glue that held the alliance together, while not suggesting any community of shared values.

and of God."[9] The point of such broadcasts was clear: one of Hitler's greatest sins consisted in his pitchforking innocent Christians into Stalin's atheist Inferno. This argument resonated well, especially among Catholics. Following the Nazi-Soviet partition of Poland, the Catholic *Month* editorialized that "We have the fact that Germany . . . has handed over the larger half [*sic*] of a Catholic country to the Soviet terror. It is one of the blackest crimes ever committed against religion and civilization."[10]

The unceremonious entry of the USSR into the war blurred these starkly drawn, and comforting, moral battle lines. Now that the Soviet Union was a de facto ally, how could British religious propaganda continue to claim that God was securely on London's side alone? A great many histories have mocked the Soviets' and Comintern's abrupt reversal of their international line following the German attack, but fewer have noted that London, too, was left shamefacedly trying to explain why the British God, who it was assumed had always been most offended by Soviet atheism, now considered Stalin's sins less damning than Hitler's. British propagandists faced a dilemma: on the one hand, any attempt to portray the USSR as a bastion of religious liberty risked alienating believers who knew better; but, on the other hand, telling the truth about Soviet persecution of religion would hand a propaganda bonanza to the Nazis, who cast their invasion of the USSR as a "crusade" of Western civilization and Christianity against Bolshevism.[11]

Of the three great powers that constituted the core of the anti-Hitler coalition, only Britain was a belligerent before June 1941, which gave it an edge over its two partners in forming and dispensing wartime propaganda. Its information apparatus was extensive, well organized, and geared for the needs of the war. The United States never did develop a wartime propaganda organization to rival the British, and the Soviet propaganda machine—though extensive—was riven by departmental rivalries, shortages of resources, and a poor comprehension of the outside world.

Britain's Ministry of Information was subdivided according to region as well as subject, with great effort and expense being poured into understanding and shaping not only domestic but also international and neutral—especially American—opinion. The Ministry of Information had a Religious Affairs Division, with sections devoted to Protestant, Catholic, and Orthodox issues. British propagandists enjoyed powerful assets, the most effective and visible being the BBC, which had a worldwide reach and a staff trained to meet the demands of their international audience; they were also equipped with the necessary languages and broadcast network to spread the British message.[12] Although the BBC constantly asserted its independence from the government, in practice it worked hand in glove with the Ministry of Information and was a reliable conduit for materials originating there.

Before June 1941 the British had done very little to reach the Soviet people, although in February they had briefly considered initiating shortwave radio broadcasts in Russian directed at the USSR. At that time, Ivone Kirkpatrick of the BBC admitted that most radio sets in the Soviet Union were held communally, which enabled Communist authorities to exercise political control over the listening habits of simple Soviet citizens. Nonetheless, he wrote, "a fair number of Russians, especially from the classes from which leaders are most likely to arise, could—if they would—listen to a British shortwave broadcast."[13] The BBC had taken no decision on this matter before the Soviet-German war broke out, but in the weeks during that summer some British officials revived the idea of broadcasting to the Soviet Union. They soon decided against it. In the glowing dawn of Anglo-Soviet partnership, officials reversed their earlier reasoning and argued that there were too few privately owned shortwave sets in the USSR to justify a large-scale effort.[14] The real cause for the reversal by Britain's cautious propaganda mandarins was the fear that they might offend the Kremlin if they circumvented it in an attempt to address the Russian people directly; as one ministry document put it, "the Russian Government has asked us not to [broadcast directly]."[15] Only later in the war would the British return to the idea of issuing official information directed at the Soviets. For the British, one of the greatest propaganda problems posed by the alliance with Moscow was domestic, not international, and it had two broad aspects: first, critics of cooperation with Moscow must either be persuaded to change their views, or at the very least be marginalized. Second, information officials wanted to ensure that any enthusiasm for the USSR would be kept within acceptable bounds; they did not want to have Soviet sympathizers, or outright Communists, whipping up uncritical admiration for the USSR on ideological grounds. As ministry officials would phrase it in their internal memoranda, they sought to "steal the thunder of the Left" by posing as fair-minded champions of a sober alliance with Moscow.[16]

Almost two months after Barbarossa began, when it seemed possible that the USSR might survive the initial Nazi onslaught, the Ministry of Information decided to create yet another section, this one designed to shape British propaganda about the USSR. Designated the "Soviet Relations Branch" (later, Division), it was founded to direct and monitor all official British publicity relating to the USSR, both within the British Empire and abroad. At first, the directors of the Ministry of Information sought a "big boy" to be the director of the new section,[17] "some personage who would have some knowledge about Russia; a great deal of knowledge about England, and some political sensitivity."[18] Having failed to recruit Julian Huxley, the novelist J. B. Priestley, or the journalist Vernon Bartlett for the position, the ministry's directors finally chose Peter Smollett. This was to prove a fateful choice. Smollett, whose real name was Smolka, lacked a prominent reputation beyond the monastic halls of the Ministry of Information, but he had served ably in the Neutrals Division and turned out to have a much deeper understanding of Soviet affairs than his bosses imagined: he was a Soviet mole.[19]

From August 1941 onward, the Religious Division and Soviet Branch would together formulate policy toward religious questions relating to the USSR. Before this great union took place, however, the Religious Division had wrestled alone with the problems posed by alliance with the USSR, and on July 5 it produced guidelines for official propaganda regarding the Soviet religious question.[20] The resulting document reflects the cautious—though, as events would show, unfounded—optimism that prevailed among Britain's leaders in June 1941, the belief that, with judicious management, they could restrain the development of any undue or misplaced sympathy for the Soviet system among the British public while at the same time making a calm, rational case for aid to the Red Army.

As with other branches of Britain's propaganda apparatus, the Religious Division adopted the tone of Prime Minister Winston Churchill's June 22 radio address as its lodestar. In this famous speech, the prime minister declared that "The Nazi regime is indistinguishable from the worst features of Communism" before drawing a distinction between supporting the Communist regime and helping the Russian people: "No one has been a more consistent opponent of Communism than I have for the last twenty-five years. I will unsay no word that I have spoken about it. But all this fades away before the spectacle now unfolding. . . . I see [Russian soldiers] guarding their homes where mothers and wives pray—ah, yes, for there are times when all pray—for the safety of their loved ones." The Russians were now partners in the war; that did not mean that the British must learn to love Communism.[21] The prime minister's reference to prayer was, of course, a jab at Soviet atheism and another way of reinforcing the notion that the Russian people and the Soviet regime were not identical.

Using Churchill's speech as a blueprint, the ministry's new religious-propaganda guidelines stressed, in particular, that Hitler must not be allowed to drive a wedge between the USSR and Britain by posing "as a champion of Christianity." "Nazi Germany is utterly unfitted to take on the role of defender of Christian civilization," the authors argued. Germany had launched an "unprovoked" attack, and "Aggression is still aggression even when committed against an atheist state." As for Britain's own allegation that it was the defender of Christian culture, "This claim remains as before. We are fighting . . . to retain the spiritual heritage of the Christian West. Although [we?] may feel, especially on the Continent, that this spiritual heritage is potentially threatened by Communism, there is no doubt that it is actually threatened at the moment by Nazi Germany."[22]

The Ministry of Information's defense of its new ally was tepid at best. It was scarcely rousing propaganda to argue that Hitler was at least as guilty of religious repression as was Stalin, because this had certainly not been true before the war, when the Soviet government had been a much more ruthless persecutor of religion than the Nazis. Nor was it comforting to claim that Western Christianity was only "potentially threatened" by the very country with which London now proposed to ally.

Nonetheless, most British Protestant clergy fell loyally into line with the newly reworked demands of state. On July 17, the Right Reverend J. Hutchison Cockburn, moderator of the Church of Scotland, issued a statement on British-Russian cooperation that he wrote at the behest of the Reverend Hugh Martin of the Ministry of Information.[23] Affirming his opposition to Soviet Communism, Cockburn cited biblical precedent for collaboration between believers and heathen before declaring that "It may well be that the future will show how in our day God used even atheists and communists to help forward His cause, even against their will."[24]

Fearing that the continental Europeans might be swayed by Hitler's claim to be leading a crusade of Western civilization against the Soviet Union, the Ministry of Information prevailed upon Dr. William Paton, secretary of the International Missionary Council and joint secretary of the World Council of Churches, to prepare a radio broadcast for the French audience.[25] Paton's argument was much the same as Cockburn's, but his tone was more uneasy. He wrote that "The war has taken a very strange turn in these last days. A few days ago Germany was joined in a pact with Russia. Now we find . . . Russia is resisting the aggression of Nazi Germany along with us."

Revealing British concerns about European Christians, Paton wrote, "We know that many Christians on the Continent are wondering whether they should now line up against what they regard as the enemy of Christianity [the USSR]." Paton labeled as "utter hypocrisy" Hitler's claim to be leading Christendom against the scourge of Bolshevism. "We are not deceived," he declared. He was, however, less sanguine about the French, pleading: "All over the free world there is a terrible hardening of hearts against Nazi Germany. Is it really possible for you to believe that this wide world of free men . . . should now turn and support the Nazis because, forsooth, they are fighting against the Russians?"[26] Even to frame the question in such a way showed that Paton and the ministry were as yet uncertain of the answer.

British officials worried most about the reaction of European and British Catholics to the new London-Moscow partnership. In his encyclical *Divini Redemptoris* of March 1937, Pope Pius XI had condemned Soviet Communism in no uncertain terms, telling Catholics that they could not cooperate with Communists in any endeavor whatsoever—no matter how worthy. Although the pope had five days earlier denounced Nazism as well, the categorical papal condemnation of cooperation with Communists seemed to offer little wiggle room for Catholics wanting to support alliance with Moscow. Only two days after the Nazi attack, the British Foreign Office asked the Ministry of Information to contact editors of Catholic publications to persuade them to moderate their anti-Soviet line: "It is not to be expected of course that they will—any more than the Prime Minister has done—withdraw their condemnation of Russian Communism and its anti-religious activities. But it is important that they should get the proportion right."[27]

To encourage Catholics to rethink their doubts about partnership with the atheist state, Foreign Office officials worked busily behind the scenes to persuade Cardinal Hinsley, spiritual leader of Britain's Catholics, to issue a statement endorsing cooperation with the USSR.[28] Only six days after the invasion, the cardinal complied. Although he mentioned *Divini Redemptoris* and his church's categorical opposition to Communism, like his British Protestant counterparts he claimed that "No-one who knows how anti-Christian the ideas and practices of the Nazis are, will for one moment be deceived by Hitler's latest pose as the champion of European civilisation, or think that it has become any less vital to resist his attempt to enslave the Continent."[29] Hinsley's views were, however, in the minority among British Catholic bishops at this time.[30] Nonetheless, the Ministry of Information distributed his statement to the press association hoping that it would convey the impression to the public that Catholic clergy generally supported the USSR's defensive war.[31] Duff Cooper, then coming to the end of his term as minister of information, ordered that "the widest possible publicity [be] given this statement."[32]

Despite such important support as that supplied by these prominent Protestant and Catholic clergymen, the Ministry of Information's new religious policy was flawed from the outset. Like all official British propaganda about the USSR at the beginning of the Soviet-German war, the policy was based on a mistaken assumption. The ministry believed that "responsible" people could remain in control of shaping public opinion and that they could successfully hew to a very narrow line, arguing for the necessity of helping the USSR on strategic grounds while at the same time maintaining a principled distrust of and even disdain for the Soviet regime. In reality, however, Britain's Ministry of Information did not possess the resources, manpower, skill, or indeed the legal authority to keep as tight a rein on opinion as envisioned in such optimistic estimates. As Churchill had done in his June 22 speech, the new ministry guidelines drew a sharp line between the Russian people and the Communist state. This was the same distinction that both the Americans and British drew between the German people, who were portrayed as potentially redeemable given proper democratic institutions, and the Nazi regime, which represented evil incarnate. Just as it was impossible for Britain to make war against the Nazi regime without killing Germans, however, it would likewise prove impossible to assist the Russian people in their struggle for hearth and home without rescuing the Communist state.

A second problem with the new religious policy was that the ministry did not foresee the dramatic upswell in British public sympathy for and interest in the USSR that would occur as the Red Army began to show its powers of resistance. It is difficult to fault the ministry for this. Before June 1941, in the words of A. P. Ryan, an adviser to the BBC on home affairs, "only a handful of communists and cranks were actively interested in Russia."[33] As is so often the case with public apathy, however, when political circumstances change, it can become transformed almost overnight into a ferocious, but ill-informed and unstable enthusiasm. Britain's propagandists found that they could not simply repeat over and over again that the USSR was an associated power, useful in fighting the war against Nazism but in all other ways objectionable; the public would demand more. As Ryan continued ruefully, the flood of requests for news about the USSR "cannot simply be dammed. Whether we like it or not, the public will go on taking a more kindly interest in Soviet Russia than ever before—unless the Russians pack up."[34]

The final flaw in the program was the most serious. If the ministry could not or would not supply the rapidly growing public demand for information about the USSR, either because it lacked the information and resources or because it did not want to encourage unrealistic expectations about the situation in the Soviet Union, there were many people and groups less scrupulous about the truth who were ready to fill the void: fellow travelers, Communists, and the Soviets themselves, as well as all sorts of apologists would gladly step in where the ministry feared to tread. At the same time, the British government, checkmated by the need to promote and later preserve the anti-Hitler coalition, would find it very difficult to counteract such unofficial and misleading propaganda.

Part of the problem was that very few people outside the USSR actually knew very much about the real situation of religion in that country. The British government was almost as ignorant as the man in the street. Ryan understood the problem, even if he offered no solution: "Our own experts seem to know very little about how the wheels really go round in Russia, and in any case we could not afford to upset the Kremlin, as we certainly should if we gave any publicity, with official or semi-official blessing, to critical comments on Russian affairs."[35] Widespread public ignorance of the real conditions prevailing in Stalin's USSR allowed Soviet sympathizers, as well as outright operatives, to tout the supposedly marvelous achievements of Soviet industry and society with little fear of factual contradiction.

Although during the previous two decades enough information had dribbled out of the USSR to create a very damning portrait of religious repression, visible at least to that small number of people who paid close attention to such matters; in the rapidly changing circumstances of the war, there were few ways of speeding up this flow. In a desperate search for something to tell the public, the ministry turned first to the Soviet Embassy in London.[36] While awaiting a response from that quarter, R. R. Williams in the Protestant section of the ministry wrote that he would need to obtain "something of a confidential character from a reliable source," because whatever the Soviet Embassy supplied would no doubt be misleading. "The position [of Soviet religion] on paper," he wrote with some understatement, "may be very different from the actual state of affairs, in fact we are pretty certain this is so."[37] The ministry decided to request Sir Stafford Cripps, the British ambassador in Moscow, to supply the "latest information" about Soviet religion. "Are there signs of greater official leniency?" they asked him hopefully: "what signs of popular religious revival have been manifested? In reporting please differentiate between what should + [sic] should not be used for publicity purposes."[38]

As might have been foreseen, the Ministry of Information received two flatly contradictory reports on the state of Soviet religion from these two sources. Twelve days after the British request, on July 28, G. Zinchenko, first secretary of the Soviet Embassy, handed the ministry a memorandum purporting to describe the legal status of Soviet believers; as Williams had feared, the Soviet memorandum concentrated on constitutional formalities—never the best reflection of reality in Communist countries—but failed to say anything about how these rules were applied in practice.

"Among other democratic liberties," Zinchenko's document assured the reader, Soviet citizens were all guaranteed "freedom of conscience." Although "religious gatherings have no political rights . . . [a]ll of them, no matter what their religious beliefs, participate on general principles in elections and in the social political life according to their work and place of residence." Rather less clearly, and also more ominously, the memorandum stated: "Houses of worship can be closed only at the instigation of the predominant voice of the population, or if there are not believers who wish to take on the responsibility of the building and the property."[39] It is not difficult to guess who would interpret the public's "predominant voice" in Stalin's USSR.

Cripps's reply to the ministry's inquiry was more accurate than Zinchenko's but also less optimistic and has been quoted earlier.[40] He said that it was "impossible" for any foreigner to gauge the true state of Soviet religion, but he denied any evidence of a real change for the better.

For God and Lend-Lease

Soviet representatives abroad were perfectly aware of the magnitude of the tasks that lay before them. Although the United States was not yet a combatant, by means of the Lend-Lease program, which extended massive material aid to the Allied side, Washington was quickly becoming the "arsenal of democracy" envisioned by President Roosevelt. Moscow knew that American industrial support would be vital if the Red Army were to repulse the Nazis. But to tap into the rich sap already flowing from the American money tree, the Soviets would first have to overcome widespread American public hostility toward the USSR, or at least isolate their most committed enemies. They also understood that antipathy toward them was concentrated most dangerously among the churchgoing public and religious hierarchies.

On June 22, 1941, only hours after news of the Nazi attack reached Washington, Konstantin Umanskii, the Soviet ambassador to the United States, cabled Moscow with a report outlining opinion among American "ruling circles." In Umanskii's view, there was widespread support for the USSR's war effort among the "workers and petty bourgeois public," which was reflected in encouraging telegrams and messages already pouring into the Soviet Embassy. At the same time, however, powerful American isolationists welcomed the German attack, because this would supposedly ease German pressure on Great Britain and consequently defuse demands for American entry into the war. Prominent "reactionaries," whom Umanskii identified as Herbert Hoover and Charles Lindbergh among others, were delighted by the German invasion and could be expected to argue that "nothing should be done to assist Communism." Members of the Republican Party, as well as "certain Democrats," would adopt a similar line. Umanskii also warned the Foreign Commissariat to expect opposition from "our professional enemies of the type of [William] Bullitt and [Adolph] Berle, plus the Catholic hierarchy." In Umanskii's view, isolationist, anti-Soviet opinion would find its strongest outlet in the Scripps-Howard newspaper chain.

According to Umanskii, a war was raging for the soul of the White House, and the outcome remained unclear. There were, however, reasons for hope: "Roosevelt is fighting with these circles," Umanskii wrote. In Roosevelt's "inner circle [*neposredstvennom okruzhenii*] there are agents of this [anti-Soviet] clique, who in the recent past succeeded in strengthening [the president] in anti-Soviet positions." "In particular," Umanskii warned, "Roosevelt fears influential Catholics." At the same time, a "progressive circle," including Harold Ickes, Hans Morgenthau, and Harry Hopkins, could be expected to advance the Soviet case. "But this group, though very close to Roosevelt and weighing on him, is in a minority. Our task is immediately to use all the good relations we have with figures of this type, of course." Only by cultivating such positive ties could Soviet representatives "neutralize the influence of hostile groups within the State Department and the naval ministry," thereby easing the shipment of vital war supplies to the USSR.[41]

Umanskii understood that Americans were divided on the question of supporting the USSR, but his perception of the fault lines of American opinion was often inaccurate, and his terms were crude. Also, his claim that the American working class was staunch in its support of the Soviet cause was typical Leninist boiler plate. In fact, many working-class people, especially Catholics and many trade unionists, were suspicious of the USSR and would remain so despite the flood of wartime alliance propaganda.[42] At least Umanskii understood that religion in general, and the Catholic Church in particular, was an obstacle to Soviet hopes for aid.

Most Americans, regardless of denomination, preferred to see the Soviet Union defeat Hitler: a Gallup Poll conducted three weeks after the Nazi attack showed only a small difference between Catholics and Protestants on this question. Whereas 74 percent of Protestants favored a Soviet victory, 65 percent of Catholics did; those hoping for yet another German victory were a mere 3 and 6 percent respectively.[43] If most religious believers favored the Soviet cause, however, this did not necessarily translate into support for extending American material assistance to the Communists.

The Soviet ambassador's identification of religious opinion as a central barrier to cooperation with the United States was almost immediately reinforced when, on the following day, Under Secretary of State Sumner Welles held a press conference to address the Nazi invasion of the USSR. Speaking to press correspondents, Welles scolded Moscow, declaring "that freedom to worship God as their consciences dictate is the great and fundamental right of all peoples." Warming to his task, Welles continued: "This right has been denied to their peoples by both the Nazi and Soviet Governments. To the people of the United States this and other principles and doctrines of communistic dictatorship are as intolerable and as alien to their own beliefs, as are the principles and doctrines of Nazi dictatorship." Nonetheless, Welles said, distinctions were in order. The Nazi "plan for universal conquest" posed the gravest threat to American interests. "In the opinion of this government, consequently, any defense against Hitlerism ... from whatever source these forces may spring" was to be welcomed, since "Hitler's armies are today the chief dangers to the Americas."[44]

This was not exactly a warm welcome extended to Moscow with open arms, even though Welles's reticence can be explained in part by the domestic American political situation. In the United States, as in Great Britain, significant portions of the population believed that both Hitler and Stalin were international gangsters, that they were natural partners but that, as with thieves, there was no cause for surprise in their ultimate falling out. William C. Bullitt, who had once been the American ambassador to Moscow and had subsequently become a firm skeptic about Soviet intentions, wrote that war between the two dictators was akin to a battle between "Satan and Lucifer." And, in a frequently cited comment, the future president of the United States, Harry S. Truman, then a senator from Missouri, remarked: "If we see that Germany is winning, we should help Russia and if Russia is winning we ought to help Germany and that way let them kill as many as possible, although I don't want to see Hitler victorious under any circumstances." In private correspondence with his wife, Truman was even more scathing, likening Stalin to Al Capone.[45]

For American diplomats serving abroad, Welles's deference to domestic opinion left them with unresolved problems. They had to deal with troubling questions about the USSR's entry into the war on Britain's side, the side with which the United States was rightly identified in international opinion. In his talk with reporters, Welles had drawn the narrowest of distinctions between the USSR and the Nazi regime, but this was rather thin gruel for American diplomats trying to present the case for support of the Allied side and trying to counter German religious propaganda.

The American ambassador in Italy, Phillips, told Washington that "It would be helpful if the Department could let me have any evidence that may come to hand of religious tolerance in Russia." He asked for something more helpful than Welles's "recent statement in which we repudiated for ourselves Communist doctrines and principles." Perhaps the American government could state hopefully that, given proper Western support in the war against Germany, "the Soviet Government would abandon its attitude of religious intolerance and adopt instead more humane and liberal policies[.] Some such pronouncement would have a reassuring effect on the Holy See and Catholic countries and it seems to me on all decent people as well."[46]

Phillips was brought up short by the State Department. Welles curtly informed him that "We have received no indication of increased religious tolerance in the Soviet Union," continuing: "Although we sympathize with the spirit which prompted your suggestion, we do not believe that it would serve any constructive purpose or that it would be advisable at this time to make any statement which might be interpreted as representing any pressure on the Soviet Government to change certain of its internal policies."[47] The State Department was neither ready to issue unjustifiably optimistic propaganda about nonexistent Soviet religious freedoms, nor to exploit the USSR's discomfiture to extract promises of improved conduct.

The reaction of American Catholic opinion to the outbreak of the war in the East conformed with Umanskii's expectations and showed that the American government had reason to act with circumspection when dealing with the Soviet religious question. Before Barbarossa, the Jesuit publication *America* had warned that "While every Christian deeply deprecates the persecution of the Nazis, every American Christian must be a conscientious objector in a World War, where the United States is an ally of atheist Russia."[48] Following Barbarossa, the editors of the relatively liberal Catholic journal the *Commonweal* wrote that "The American Communists now have 'their' war." Having opposed rearmament when the USSR was still formally neutral, the Communist Party of the USA (CPUSA) was now in the forefront of those calling for American entry into the fighting.[49] The desperate, and seemingly hopeless, situation of the Red Army following the Nazi attack allowed American religious opinion to be complacent for the time being. There was little reason to debate the question of American aid to the USSR if Hitler's blitzkrieg was, as seemed likely, about to extinguish the Stalin regime. Even in late July, Helen Iswolsky, a Catholic writer who would comment on Soviet affairs throughout the war, wrote that "Nothing . . . seems less certain than a decisive victory of Stalin over Hitler." Like many other observers, Iswolski believed that the Soviet regime suffered from fatal internal weaknesses: "The Russian people, subjected for twenty-four years to a regime which breeds hatred and disgust, will scarcely be likely to offer this regime their moral support. . . . Close observers of the Soviet military and industrial organization have little doubt as to the final issue of the present invasion." Given the supposed alienation of Stalin's subjects, "it seems scarcely necessary to consider the eventualities of a communist triumph inside or outside Russia."[50]

Pessimism about the USSR's chances of survival was widespread both in the United States and in Great Britain and merely reflected mainstream military opinion.[51] Stalin's prewar purge of the Red Army, as well as the Soviets' poor showing in the Winter War of 1939–40 against Finland, confirmed the doubts of Western military analysts about Soviet staying power and to bolster the belief that the Soviet military was a poorly motivated slave army.[52]

Ironically, this very line of argument—that the USSR would collapse owing to the legacy of Communist repression and the regime's lack of popular support —would soon whip around to sting its proponents. If a defeat of the Communist state could be cited as definitive proof that the Soviet people hated their government, then when the Red Army confounded the experts by repelling the Nazis why did this not prove beyond a reasonable doubt that the masses loved their Great Leader Stalin? Every Red Army victory gave friends of the USSR another brick to toss at their opponents, as if victory in battle somehow provided the ultimate certification of a regime's political and even moral health.

One important political figure dissented from the majority's skepticism about Soviet staying power: Franklin Roosevelt. Although Roosevelt's belief in the USSR's powers of resistance was "intuitive," it turned out to be more accurate than his military specialists' estimates.[53] The American president believed that the Soviet people, whom he invariably referred to as "Russians," would fight to the end against the inhuman Hitler regime, whatever their doubts about Stalin's despotism. From the very first days following Barbarossa, therefore, Roosevelt decided that the United States must extend Lend-Lease assistance to the USSR as a means of defending America's own security, even though he recognized the domestic political risks that such a policy would entail.

In building a domestic political coalition in support of aid to the USSR, Roosevelt understood the significance and centrality of religious hostility to Communism. As the president's special emissary to Stalin, Averell Harriman, would later note, "the religious question . . . was regarded [by Roosevelt] as a matter of the highest domestic priority," because it threatened to tie the government's hands over aid to the USSR.[54] When Robert A. Grant, a congressman from Indiana, wrote to the president to complain about his stated intentions to extend Lend-Lease aid to the USSR, Roosevelt felt compelled to respond personally. Grant had written that "Much as we abhor Hitlerism and the boundless greed of the Nazi war machine, equally do we detest Stalinism and its anti-God doctrine." Grant pointed out the role Moscow had played in the destruction of Poland and said that it would be "contrary to the whole history of the United

States to now pledge all possible aid to this ruthless aggressor."[55] Roosevelt replied: "The decision to render assistance to the Soviet Union does not signify that this government condones or approves various acts and policies of the Soviet government."[56]

The president understood that Polish Americans and others who had roots in Eastern Europe were suspicious of Soviet motives and that these groups constituted a significant voting bloc. Furthermore, the overwhelming majority of them were Catholic, and Roosevelt knew that the church represented the most organized, vociferous, numerous—and therefore politically most potent—nexus of principled opposition to Soviet Communism. When it came to American opinions about the USSR, ethnicity was inextricably bound up with religious sentiment.

To deal with this problem, Roosevelt decided to go directly to the center. In August 1941 he decided to send his own "personal representative" to the Holy See, Myron Taylor. Taylor, a prominent Episcopalian, conveyed a letter from Roosevelt to the pope, and he was given the unenviable task of inducing the pontiff to make a declaration about the war in the East, differentiating between the combatants and urging American Catholics to support American cooperation with the USSR. This was a tall order given the long-standing Vatican hostility to Communism, and Roosevelt's own arguments showed that he had not yet himself thought through the implications of his intuitive belief that the Nazi and Soviet dictatorships were different in kind.

This letter to the pope deserves to be quoted at length, because it was President Roosevelt's most direct and forceful intervention in the religious question as it related to the USSR. It is also one of the best examples of the president's moral reasoning regarding cooperation with the Soviet Union, as well as being perhaps the clearest insight into his view concerning the moral differences between the dictatorships of Hitler and Stalin. Roosevelt told the pontiff that "these are matters in regard to which I feel very strongly." He continued:

In so far as I am informed, churches in Russia are open. I believe that there is a real possibility that Russia may as a result of the present conflict recognize freedom of religion in Russia, although, of course, without recognition of any official intervention on the part of any church in education or political matters within Russia. I feel that if this can be accomplished it will put the possibility of the restoration of real religious liberty in Russia on a much better footing than religious freedom is in Germany today.

Roosevelt knew that his claim regarding open churches was an exaggeration; his own State Department could not discern any improvement in the Soviet religious scene and, in fact, possessed information suggesting that 135 Catholic priests were "believed to be in Soviet prisons from 1939."[57] Roosevelt, however, tried to draw a bright moral line between the two great totalitarian dictatorships:

> In my opinion, the fact is that Russia is governed by a dictatorship, as rigid in its manner of being as is the dictatorship in Germany. I believe, however, that this Russian dictatorship is less dangerous to the safety of other nations than is the German form of dictatorship. The only weapon which the Russian dictatorship uses outside of its own borders is communist propaganda which I, of course, recognize has in the past been utilized for the purpose of breaking down the form of government in other countries, religious belief, et cetera. Germany, however, not only has utilized, but is utilizing, this kind of propaganda as well and has also undertaken the employment of every form of military aggression outside of its borders for the purpose of world conquest by force of arms and by force of propaganda. I believe that the survival of Russia is less dangerous to religion, to the church as such, and to humanity in general than would be the survival of the German form of dictatorship. Furthermore, it is my belief that the leaders of all churches in the United States should recognize these facts clearly and should not close their eyes to these basic questions and by their present attitude on this question directly assist Germany in her present objectives.[58]

Pope Pius's opinions regarding this direct approach from the American president are difficult to determine exactly; his official response was noncommittal. He simply thanked the American people for their assistance to European war victims, without mentioning the Soviet Union or addressing the central arguments of the president's note.[59] The pope did not issue the hoped-for endorsement of the Soviet war effort; he would continue to refuse to chose sides in the Soviet-German war.[60]

Some of Roosevelt's arguments must have sounded less persuasive in Rome than they might have in Washington. The claim, for instance, that Moscow restricted its interference abroad to propaganda rather than military force rang hollow in the Vatican, which was actively following events in eastern Poland and the former Baltic states, which the USSR had seized in September 1939 and June 1940 respectively. In the Polish eastern lands now under Soviet control, the number of Catholics had been considerable: among a total population of 11,965,400 people, Roman Catholics constituted 4,023,800, or 33.6 percent; in addition, Eastern Rite Catholics, who were also loyal to Rome, numbered 3,028,200, or 25.3 percent of the total population.[61] In Lithuania, 87 percent of the population was Catholic; for Latvia the figure was 25 percent.[62]

During the short period of Red Army occupation, the Soviets had not moved decisively to crush the Catholic Church entirely.[63] They allowed priests to continue serving the faithful. Nonetheless, the Soviet secret police had arrested a number of Catholic priests, had closed Catholic monasteries, and had confiscated their property.[64] In view of these and other facts, from the perspective of the Catholic Church's institutional interests, and ignoring the wider political context, Roosevelt's contention that Stalin's tyranny was preferable to Hitler's was not immediately apparent to the Vatican.

Even before receiving the pope's neutral reply, on September 11 Roosevelt met with the Soviet ambassador to assure him that he was doing all he could to counter anti-Soviet tendencies within the American religious community in order to smooth the way for aid to begin flowing from the United States to the USSR. Harry Hopkins, who had recently returned from his visit with Stalin as the president's special emissary, was present at the three and one-half hour meeting, as was Cordell Hull. It is hard to know exactly what was said at this meeting, because the two extant records differ in some intriguing ways. According to the American record of the talk,

> The President explained in some detail the extreme difficulty of getting the necessary authority from Congress [for extending Lend-Lease aid to the USSR] on account of the prejudice or hostility to Russia and the unpopularity of Russia among large groups in this country who exercise great political power in Congress. The President also referred to the fact that Russia does have churches and does permit religious worship under the Constitution of 1936. He suggested that if Moscow could get some publicity back to this country regarding freedom of religion during the next few days . . . it might have a very fine educational effect before the next lend-lease bill comes up in Congress. The Ambassador agreed that he would attend to this matter.[65]

There is a curious lack of specificity about this record of the meeting. It does not reveal who these anti-Soviet groups were whom Roosevelt believed to be responsible for sabotaging aid to Russia in the halls of Congress. Umanskii's own account of this important meeting, which he cabled to Moscow two days later, tells a rather different tale, but one that is not inconsistent with Roosevelt's diplomatic approach. According to the ambassador,

> Roosevelt complained about the anti-Soviet intrigues of the church, especially the Catholics and their people in Congress, requested that information from the USSR stress the patriotic position of the church in the USSR, said

that he sent his personal representative to the Vatican, [Myron] Taylor, once again to the Pope with the fundamental goal to neutralize the "in fact pro-fascist" influence of Catholics in the USA and bring round the Pope on the question of the USSR.[66]

It would seem from this and many other instances where Russian and American accounts of private meetings between Roosevelt and Soviet diplomats differ quite dramatically, that the president and his advisers were careful about the level of detail they chose to include in the official record. It would, of course, have been very damaging politically had it become widely known in the United States that Roosevelt was trying to establish intimacy between himself and the Soviet ambassador, and through him with the Kremlin, by labeling domestic religious groups as "in fact pro-fascist."

The president would discover the hard way how the newspapers and public would react to any direct attempt to whitewash the Soviet legacy of religious repression. In a press conference on October 1, answering a question from a journalist, Roosevelt made some ill-chosen remarks on the subject. The Polish ambassador to the United States, Jan Ciechanowski, had issued a statement on September 29, announcing that the Soviet government had agreed to allow freedom of worship among Poles in the USSR. The president optimistically fastened on this as evidence that "an entering wedge for the practice of complete freedom of religion [in the USSR] is definitely on its way." He did not stop there; he declared that "As I think I suggested a week or two ago, some of you might find it useful to read Article 124 of the Constitution of Russia." Although he had not "learned it by heart," the president assured the reporters that it guaranteed

> Freedom of religion. Freedom equally to use propaganda against religion, which is essentially what is the rule in this country; only, we don't put it quite the same way. For instance, you might go out tomorrow—to the corner of Pennsylvania Avenue, down below the Press Club—and stand on a soapbox and preach Christianity, and nobody would stop you. And then, if it got into your head, perhaps the next day preach against religion of all kinds and nobody would stop you.[67]

Roosevelt knew perfectly well that Red Square was not the Soviet equivalent of a Hyde Park corner. The Congressional debate over extending Lend-Lease assistance to the USSR was looming, however, and he was trying, albeit ham-handedly, to forestall the inevitable objections from churchpeople, and espe-

cially Catholics, against military assistance to an atheist state responsible for religious repression on a scale unprecedented in history. Not everyone in the
president's circle thought he was wise to anticipate problems rather than wait
on developments. As Robert Sherwood would later write, "There were some
impatient people [around Roosevelt] who thought that the President exaggerated the strength of Catholic sentiment, but it was his way to travel with extreme wariness wherever religious sensibilities were involved."[68]

At the same time, however, Roosevelt may have genuinely believed, or persuaded himself, that the war, and cooperation between the Western democracies and the USSR that this would entail, might act as a solvent on the Kremlin's hard-line religious policies. This may have been part of his larger belief
that the United States and the Soviet Union were on a path toward "conver-
gence," an idea widespread among Western intellectuals, which held that,
whereas Washington could learn economic planning from Moscow, American
influence might in turn liberalize the Communist political system.[69] Interestingly, many average Soviet citizens believed the same thing, hoping that alliance with the Western democracies would moderate the harsh Stalin regime—
an idea Soviet apparatchiks found heretical.[70]

Whatever his intentions, the president's remarks provoked predictably polarized reactions. Representative Martin Dies, who would later become an early
ally of Senator Joseph McCarthy, vehemently denied that religious freedom existed in the USSR; in a letter to Roosevelt, he lamented the fact that the president's assertions to the contrary were being reprinted in the Communist and
leftist press "in a manner to obscure the truth." He also pointed out that Soviet
practice was at variance with Roosevelt's own famous "four freedoms" and
called on the president to make "it unmistakably clear that the Soviet regime
is utterly repugnant to the American people and nowhere more so that [sic] in
its cruel pretense to freedom of religious worship."[71] Representative Hamilton
Fish, also an ardent anti-Communist, was even more scathing than Dies, suggesting that Roosevelt might want to follow up his remarks by baptizing Stalin
in the White House swimming pool.[72]

The Roosevelt Papers contain a number of anguished responses to the president's initiatives, not all of them so intemperate. One of the more interesting
came from Mathew Spinka, a respected scholar of the Soviet religious scene at
the Chicago Theological Seminary, who was sufficiently "disturbed" by the president's exaggerations to write him directly. Basing his objections "on a thorough knowledge of the official Russian documents in the case," he wrote to set
the record straight about the wide range of limitations on religious worship in

the USSR still in force. "Since I heartily agree with your general policy," Spinka wrote, "I feel that your advocacy of that policy is weakened by such statements as are ascribed to you."[73]

Although moderate Catholic publications responded soberly enough to Roosevelt's press conference, his remarks seem to have had the opposite effect to that intended among the Catholic clergy as a whole. The Catholic Laymen's Committee for Peace, an isolationist organization, conducted an unscientific but nonetheless telling poll of Catholic clergy below the level of bishop on the question of aid to Russia. A little more than one-third of clergy questioned, or 13,155, responded to the group's questionnaire, and of these 90.5 percent opposed sending any American military assistance to the Soviet Union.[74] Even if the poll results did not reflect overall clergy views very accurately, the large number of respondents with strong opinions shows that disquiet was widespread in the church. As the liberal Catholic writer Ruth O'Keefe wrote: "The President's statement . . . quoted without the modifying comments, brought a violent reaction from both Catholic and non-Catholic churchmen. No-one denied the truth of the statement, but from all corners of the country came hot denials that the guarantee [of Soviet religious freedom] meant anything."[75]

The mixed public reception of Roosevelt's remarks, and the frankly hostile reaction of many Catholic clergy, made some positive Soviet demonstration even more politically vital for the administration. As these events were unfolding, Averell Harriman was in already Moscow with the British press baron Lord Beaverbrook, trying to work out with the Soviets a schedule for Western material assistance, should Lend-Lease be approved by Congress. Before Harriman left for the USSR, Roosevelt had urged him to press Stalin for some public gesture on the religious question to ease passage of the legislation. Although Harriman would go through the motions, it was clear that he regarded this as an annoying distraction from what he regarded as the main issue at hand. When he first raised the religious question with the Soviet oligarchs, by his own account he "made no progress with Stalin." He then approached Molotov and Umanskii, where "He received the most profuse assurances from Oumansky and an enigmatic nod from Molotov."[76]

On October 4, only three days after the president's press conference and just after Harriman's approach, Solomon Lozovskii, of the Soviet wartime informational organization the Informbiuro, issued a statement at his own meeting with the Moscow press corps. Lozovskii thanked Roosevelt and amplified his remarks about Soviet legal protections for freedom of conscience: "The Soviet public read with great interest President Roosevelt's statement . . . regarding the freedom of religious worship of Soviet citizens," Lozovskii wrote. He confirmed that church and state were separate in the USSR, and that "this means that the State grants no privileges to one or another religion." "Religion is a private affair of every Soviet citizen," Lozovskii continued; "the Legislature of the Soviet Union does not regard it possible to compel citizens either to worship or not to worship at all." More ominously, given the Stalinist record, Lozovskii closed with the warning that "Freedom of worship presupposes that no religion, Church, or religious community will be utilized for overthrowing the existing Government recognized in the country."[77] Answering questions from Western correspondents after reading his prepared statement, Lozovskii said that "all faiths in the Soviet Union were 'speaking determinately against Nazi banditry and barbarity.'"[78]

American diplomats congratulated themselves for having prodded the Soviets to make such a public declaration. The American ambassador in Moscow, Laurence Steinhardt, told Washington that Lozovskii's "statement was unquestionably that promised by Oumansky [*sic*]" in their earlier conversations.[79] But Harriman remained skeptical about the worth of Soviet assurances. In a cable to Washington, he predicted that "religious worship will be tolerated only under closest G.P.U. [Gosudarstvennoe politicheskoe upravlenie] scrutiny with a view to keeping it under careful control like a fire which can be stamped out at any time, rather than be allowed to burn freely with the dangers of uncontrolled conflagration."[80] Nor was Roosevelt pleased with Harriman's grudging efforts or Moscow's tepid gesture. As Harriman later remarked, Roosevelt "made me feel that it was not enough and he took me to task on my return" to the United States.[81]

On November 7, the twenty-fourth anniversary of the Bolshevik Revolution, the American government formally committed itself to extend Lend-Lease assistance to the USSR. Whether this was the critical war-winning weapon many Americans believed it to be, or rather just one of many factors contributing to a shorter end of the war, this was nonetheless a critical historical moment. Even before itself being drawn directly into the war, the United States had decided to aid one continental totalitarian state in order to defeat another. The geostrategic case for doing so was overwhelming, as even many bitter opponents of Communism eventually came to recognize, and it is hard to imagine how Nazi Germany could have been defeated without Soviet military power.

It is doubtful that Roosevelt had advanced his case by his public statements about religion in the USSR. Instead, he would almost certainly have better served his cause by focusing on behind-the-scenes pressure on influential Catholic bishops, the Vatican, and other prominent doubters. His misguided attempt to explain away the legacy of Soviet religious repression had only given his critics a tempting target. This was a lesson he would learn. The president never forgot the importance of the religious issue for the Soviet-American alliance, but from this point on he would adopt a strategy of indirect maneuver rather than head-on assault.

Moscow Burnishes Its Image

The USSR entered the war with an already existing and extensive foreign propaganda apparatus. American and British leaders had long feared the power and reach of Soviet propaganda; indeed, this had been a crucial issue disrupting Anglo-Soviet relations since the early 1920s.[82] Before Washington finally recognized the Soviet government in November 1933, American diplomats demanded guarantees against both Moscow-funded subversion and the distribution of Communist propaganda in the United States. In a letter from then foreign commissar Maksim Litvinov to Roosevelt during the negotiations leading up to mutual recognition, the Soviet government had specifically pledged to refrain from any "agitation or propaganda" that might undermine the American "political or social order."[83] As the opening of Soviet archives has shown, however, these guarantees were rarely honored.[84]

Ironically, given the level of Western fears, direct Soviet propaganda was of poor quality, was chronically underfunded, and was badly organized, with warring agencies endlessly contending against one another. The reality was quite different from the notion, widely held in the West, that Soviet propaganda was the product of a well-oiled machine. Nominally, the chief prewar agency for propaganda abroad was VOKS (Vsesoiuznoe Obshchestvo Kul'turnykh Sviazei s zagranitsei). Although this group was responsible for spreading the Soviet message outside the USSR, many other organizations (among them the Comintern, TASS, *mezhdunarodnaia kniga* [international books], and the Foreign Commissariat) vied for control over ordinary propaganda; furthermore, especially sensitive operations were always dealt with by the NKVD-NKGB, with the formal propaganda agencies being entirely circumvented.

In December 1940 the head of VOKS, V. Kemenov, wrote a review of his agency's work, highlighting its many shortcomings.[85] The competition between rival agencies handling international publicity, he complained, caused "chaos and irresponsibility," duplication of effort—what he called "parallelism"—and the frequent mishandling of materials. As a result, "frequently the propaganda is of very low quality." "In the complex and tense international situation," he wrote, the problems of propaganda "have an especially responsible meaning," which demanded "strict centralization of all work."

Comparing the dissemination of Soviet propaganda with that of foreign countries', Kemenov saw the Nazi program as a model of efficiency and centralization. He also envied the British: "England is spending great sums of money on foreign propaganda," he wrote. By his estimate, based on published American sources, London had spent $550,000 on propaganda in 1940. He continued tartly: "We note that the estimate of VOKS for 1940 translated into dollars consists of $28,000, that is, 20 times lower." The British had very successfully penetrated the United States market, he argued, and had "achieved significant results in the preparation of American public opinion for a state of war." Kemenov continued:

> In comparison with foreign propaganda, Soviet propaganda abroad has an almost unorganized, haphazard character, it is atomized, with no plan or connection with foreign policy. Of course, the goal and tasks of Soviet propaganda are completely contrary to those of capitalist countries. The fact that the content of Soviet propaganda is socialism raises unavoidable problems in the conditions of capitalist countries.

In order to deal with the peculiarities of the capitalist market, Soviet propaganda needed excellent organization and a trained staff, and it must "be flexible." VOKS propagandists "must avoid all amateurishness and provincialism." This was an ironic suggestion, given the fact that, after the Soviet entry into the war, VOKS, and Kemenov himself, would be among the least flexible and most provincial of Soviet propagandists. Perhaps most surprising, Kemenov wrote that VOKS was frequently unable to purchase "even a few issues" of Soviet publications to be sent abroad, even though the agency had the means to send these materials directly to representatives in Soviet embassies. Nor was Soviet radio propaganda any better, in Kemenov's estimation; the broadcasts composed by the Radiokomitet were "boring, [and] long." Ivan Maiskii and Aleksandra Kollontai, the Soviet ambassadors to Britain and Sweden respectively, regularly complained to the center that Soviet radio programming was of poor quality and continually "demanded the organization of lively, interesting radio broadcasts."

Kemenov argued that "plenipotentiaries" of VOKS, stationed abroad in Soviet embassies, were not being used effectively. These people represented a valuable resource, because they understood the changing moods of foreign opinion and could work directly on the target market. They could also inform Moscow about the conduct of foreign propaganda. Even more importantly, VOKS men could establish "personal contact with progressive representatives of foreign culture, which has great importance for the realization of Soviet propaganda abroad." Instead of being used effectively, however, VOKS personnel could only work on propaganda matters in their spare time, because ambassadors overloaded them with routine diplomatic work and they held "insufficiently authoritative diplomatic rank" to resist these petty demands.

In the United States, VOKS had fraternal organizations in New York, San Francisco, and Philadelphia, which published the English-language *Russia Today*. These groups needed trained help, but VOKS had "not one free worker" to offer them to assist in their important work. Kemenov closed with another plea for greater centralization and for "systematic, daily orders from TsK VKP(b) and Narkomindel [NKID, or People's Commissariat of Foreign Affairs]."[86] Unfortunately for VOKS, the Central Committee issued no definite centralization orders before the outbreak of war. Confusion and redundancy continued to reign in Soviet international propaganda.

Instead of streamlining the already top-heavy Soviet propaganda apparat, when the Soviet-German war broke out, an entirely new agency, the Sovinformbiuro (or simply Informbiuro), soon supplanted VOKS as the chief agency for distributing Soviet wartime information to foreigners (although VOKS continued to function, which caused even more frequent turf wars). The politbiuro itself actually created the new body on June 24, 1941, almost certainly because VOKS had never been a high-profile operation; its personnel were of second-rate importance, and the urgency of the war clearly necessitated the appointment of better-connected officers.[87] The chief figure governing the day-to-day working of the Informbiuro throughout the war would be Solomon Lozovskii, deputy people's commissar for foreign relations. Lozovskii was deputy director under A. S. Shcherbakov, who in addition to his direction of Informbiuro also headed political and ideological indoctrination in the Red Army. Shcherbakov was one of Stalin's trusted henchmen; during the height of the Stalinist terror he had served "as a mobile purger to various reluctant provinces."[88] The high ranking of Shcherbakov in ideological circles and of Lozovskii within the foreign policy elite testified powerfully to the significance of the new propaganda body.[89]

Soviet foreign propagandists faced one great task, in addition to a host of smaller ones: they had to win over a substantial portion of public opinion in the Western democracies to the idea of an anti-Hitler coalition with the world's only Communist state. As explored already, this was no easy thing to do given the Soviet record of purges, secret police repression, and the crushing of religious freedoms. At the same time, Soviet propagandists sought to appeal to opinion in Nazi-occupied Europe, first not to support Hitler's supposed "crusade" against Godless Communism, then to rise up against their Nazi oppressors, and later, when the tide of battle had turned, to assist or at least not to hinder the advance of the Red Army into Central Europe. The greatest flaw in the USSR's newfound pose as a bastion of antifascist probity was, of course, the fact that up until the moment of the attack Moscow had been a reliable partner to Hitler's New Order and had indeed in November 1940 even offered to join the Axis alliance.[90]

If the Soviets thus began the war with something of an image problem, and if their propaganda machinery was redundant and had unclear lines of authority, this did not by any means signify that they entirely lacked assets in advancing their cause. In selling their message abroad, the Soviets enjoyed important advantages over the Western democracies. The United States and Great Britain would only make the barest propaganda inroads into the wartime USSR, given the almost hermetically sealed nature of the Stalinist state.[91] In crafting their propaganda for the Western audience, by contrast, the Soviets benefited immeasurably from the open nature of their new partners' societies. In the first place, Moscow could draw on the impressive exploits of the Red Army, which sparked a growing sympathy in the West that would grow in intensity from the fall of 1941 onward as it became clear that the USSR would survive the initial Nazi assault. Perhaps more important, the Soviets could also make use of the plurality of opinions in the West, as well as the wide array of views printed in the press; Western openness, even under the constraints of wartime, was of inestimable value to the Soviets in pressing their case.

The Soviet state's professed devotion to the ideals of socialism and the betterment of universal human welfare was its strongest card in the international propaganda game, winning it adherents and admirers throughout the world— as well as bitter enemies, of course. In terms that could apply even better in the Soviet context, Alexis de Tocqueville likened the appeal of the French Revolution to that of a religion: "it created a common intellectual fatherland," he wrote, "whose citizenship was open to men of every nationality and in which racial distinctions were obliterated." "[L]ike all great religious movements," he continued, "it resorted to propaganda and broadcast a gospel. This was something quite unprecedented: a political revolution that sought proselytes all the world over and applied itself as ardently to converting foreigners as compatriots."[92]

Hard as it may be to believe in retrospect, Stalin's Communist state likewise exercised the appeal of a new, secular religion.[93] For many left-wing Western intellectuals, Nazism and fascism were merely more aggressive species of the capitalism practiced in their own countries, and Moscow's creation of an alternative, supposedly nonexploitative, economic system more than compensated for the USSR's failings, most of which went unmentioned in any case. As Victor Gollancz, the influential editor of the Left Book Club in Britain, wrote in

January 1940: "I have had many grave differences of opinion with communists since more than a year before the war; but their single-minded devotion to the cause of human liberation is such that it should make every supporter of capitalist and fascist abominations hang his head in shame."[94] From the creation of the Comintern in 1919, following the Bolshevik Revolution, through the succeeding two decades, Moscow had worked diligently to create nests of proselytes abroad. In advancing its propaganda, therefore, the Kremlin could rely on a large number of sympathizers in the West, ranging from outright members of foreign Communist parties, through moles in Western governments, to fellow travelers like Gollancz, as well as favorably inclined leftists of various complexions.

Before employing these assets, however, Moscow would have to reorient its international message. As was the case with the British Ministry of Information and, to a much lesser degree, the American State Department, the Soviets had to shift their propaganda abruptly into reverse immediately after the German attack. Barbarossa transformed Moscow's erstwhile partner, Berlin, into Enemy Number One and its chief foe, London, into an ally. The turnaround was head-spinningly abrupt: as late as mid-May 1941 Nikolai Pal'gunov, deputy head of the NKID press department, had ordered the Central Committee propaganda directorate to instruct Soviet newspapers and radio to avoid giving any offense whatsoever to Berlin: "The conduct of the Soviet press should not give any kind of pretext for conclusions that at this moment any kind of changes have occurred in the situation of Soviet-German relations and, much less, any pretext for any sort of diplomatic representations."[95] Soviet local papers, Pal'gunov continued, should avoid any reference to "the nonvictoriousness of German arms." Instead, while they must not convey the impression that the Wehrmacht was invincible, they should stress instead that Berlin's enemies had been rotten from within and had therefore collapsed when attacked. These newspapers must not emphasize the "horrors of war," because this would be the "pacifist style." Instead, they should argue that war demanded offensive tactics and quote Lenin's work on Clausewitz: "'On foreign soil defend your own soil.'" *Pravda* must run stories outlining the "differences between the Soviet political world and pacifist-petty bourgeois and social traitors [social democrats]." Pal'gunov then told *Pravda* how to explain the Nazis' victory over France during the previous summer: "The basic thesis of the article: The capitulation of France after 6 weeks from the start of active operations on the French front was the result of attempts of the French bourgeoisie with the help of a defeat in war to forestall the realization of revolution in the country." "The fear of the French bourgeoisie before the revolutionary mass of the people" had been the true reason for the French surrender.[96] Coming less than a month and a half before the

Nazi invasion of the USSR itself, Pal'gunov's instructions fell far short of a stirring call to prepare for conflict with fascism; indeed, he significantly never even mentioned Nazi ideology. And, ironically, he was labeling as "social traitors" the very leftist political forces to whom Moscow would soon issue fraternal appeals.

Soviet diplomats abroad would have their work cut out for them in managing the USSR's transformation into an ally of the Western democracies. In their representative to Britain, at least, the Kremlin was fortunate. Moscow's ambassador in London when the Soviet-Nazi war erupted was Ivan Maiskii, the rotund, long-serving diplomat whose oval face, goatee, and high-pitched voice would become a familiar part of the wartime British scene until his recall to Moscow in the summer of 1943. Maiskii was an effective proponent of Soviet interests in Britain; he spoke English fluently and had long experience in that country, having lived there before the Russian Revolution, a young revolutionary on the run from the tsarist secret police. Following the Bolshevik seizure of power, Maiskii briefly served in a Menshevik-dominated alternative government before making his peace with Lenin's men, unlike so many of his less fortunate, or perhaps less flexible, comrades who ended up in exile, prison, or the Cheka's execution cellars.[97] Whatever the terms of his reconciliation with the Bolsheviks, they worked well enough for him, because his career prospered even as many of his fellow diplomats fell victim to Stalin's purges. Maiskii rode out this lethal storm in the safe haven of London, where he served as *polpred* (plenipotentiary) from 1932 to 1941 and then as ambassador to 1943.[98]

During his long residence in London, Maiskii successfully courted the wealthy and powerful, concentrating naturally on such left-wing notables as Sidney and Beatrice Webb and Sir Stafford Cripps, but not neglecting prominent Conservatives, such as the Canadian press magnate and war cabinet member Lord Beaverbrook.[99] During the period of the Nazi-Soviet Pact, Maiskii understandably kept a low public profile, but he remained active behind the scenes in diplomatic circles. Despite his unwavering advocacy of the Soviet cause, he well understood the reasons for British suspicions of the USSR, and so, four days after the German attack, he visited Foreign Secretary Anthony Eden to suggest approaches to overcome British popular doubts.

Maiskii discussed with Eden the task of promoting a better understanding of the USSR and its people. Eden responded, "I thought that we must proceed most carefully. The Ambassador would understand how deeply the dislike of Communism was rooted in this country. Nothing could be more unfortunate" than if the notion were to take root in Britain that the Foreign Office was "lending itself to the popularising of Communist creeds to which in fact it was strongly opposed."[100] Maiskii said he understood, and only wanted to disseminate information on "the literary and artistic plane. Also he thought that it would do the British public no harm to be given some information about the nature of the peoples that made up the Soviet Unions [*sic*], their ways of life, their traditions and so forth." A cautious program of Soviet and Russian cultural propaganda was needed to acclimatize the British people to the new alliance with Moscow.[101]

Religious propaganda was to be a significant aspect of Maiskii's proposed cultural program. This was in part a response to demand, both from the American and British governments; like Moscow, London was concerned not only about British Christians but also about believers on the continent who might see the invasion of the USSR as the righteous reward for Moscow's antireligious policies during the previous two decades. To counter this tendency, Soviet and British publicists quickly formed a symbiotic relationship, disseminating Soviet propaganda throughout the world via British media while masking its origin.

On July 16, for example, the Ministry of Information requested that the Soviet embassy supply statistics about religious freedoms in the USSR, to which the first secretary of the embassy G. Zinchenko responded twelve days later with materials VOKS had sent him.[102] The Soviet information was brazen in its denial that there had ever been religious repression in the USSR. Zinchenko supplied a second, longer document that went well beyond his initial description of legal "rights" of Soviet believers.[103] In a cover letter, he wrote Dr. Elizabeth Hill of the Ministry of Information: "I trust that all of it will be of use to you for distribution to the press."[104] In this latest document, Zinchenko claimed that the "fullest religious toleration is characteristic of the Soviet regime." Soviet religious policy was far more enlightened even than its tsarist predecessor's, the piece claimed, because "there is no privileged or governing church as there was in Tzarist [*sic*] Russia." The document also cited several Soviet clergymen who vowed that they were freer under Stalin's rule than they had ever been before 1917 and who pledged unconditional support for the Soviet government in the war against Germany.[105]

Most of the information Zinchenko supplied to the British appeared also in the August 22 issue of *Soviet War News*, a journal the Soviet embassy in London began publishing shortly after the German attack and which proved quite popular, eventually reaching a circulation of 68,000 by the end of 1944.[106] British authorities even allowed it to be distributed among their armed forces. These latest Soviet materials purported to provide recent figures for the number of active believers in the USSR, the number of open churches, mosques, and synagogues, as well as the number of clergy from various denominations. According to the *Soviet War News* article, throughout the USSR, there were a total of 8,338 open churches. Broken down according to denomination, this figure included 4,225 Orthodox churches and 37 monasteries; 1,312 Islamic mosques; 1,744 Catholic churches; and 1,011 Jewish synagogues supposedly still functioning on the territory of the USSR. As for clergy, official Soviet figures listed 58,442, though significantly they did not describe these people as still active; they also claimed a total of "28 Metropolitans and bishops," though, if true, the Soviets would inexplicably prove unable to find and assemble them all for the *sobor'* of September 1943.[107]

In itself, these figures, even if inflated, testified powerfully to the devastation wrought by the Kremlin's antireligious policies. At the turn of the century, there had been about 37,000 Orthodox parish churches, 720 cathedrals, and another 2,000 churches on public or state property. Furthermore, there had also been 440 men's and 250 women's monasteries.[108] Moscow's acquisition of the Baltic states, eastern Poland, and the Romanian provinces of Bessarabia and Bukovina between 1939 and 1940 had certainly added to the number of working churches on Soviet territory. One historian has estimated that, in the former Romanian lands alone, there were about 6 million Orthodox believers and between 3,500 and 4,000 active churches when the Red Army rolled in.[109] In the eastern Polish lands, there were a further 3,508,300 Orthodox.[110]

For those who knew anything about the Russian Orthodox Church, these new Soviet figures provided sad testimony to the attrition of the Soviet years. But, of course, few people outside Russia knew how large that country's church had been before the Communists had set to work, though a moment's reflection on the small figure of 8,338 churches in an empire covering one-sixth of the earth's land mass should have given readers pause. When British propagandists distributed these Soviet figures, however, they did not include statistics on the prerevolutionary church.

Among themselves, the Ministry of Information's Religious Division officials knew perfectly well that, even if Zinchenko's figures were accurate—and there was no independent way of verifying them during wartime—they were inflated by the Soviet seizure of the western borderlands, where the Kremlin had not yet had time fully to curtail religious activity before the German invasion.[111] Nonetheless, Elizabeth Hill was enthusiastic, thanking Zinchenko for his material, which, she assured him, "has been passed on to the proper quarters." Indeed it had. She continued: "You will be glad to know that the three articles which you sent at the same time have been circularized to 1500 newspapers and periodicals in Great Britain and overseas, so that we hope they will receive the utmost publicity." In closing, Hill wrote that she "Look[ed] forward to increasing collaboration with" the Soviet embassy in the future.[112]

Zinchenko's propaganda materials received much greater respectability and far wider circulation by being channeled through the British Ministry of Information than they ever would have done coming directly from Soviet sources. Zinchenko's "information," especially the statistics about churches and believers, appeared in a wide range of respected newspapers and magazines, as well as in those segments of the press consistently sympathetic with the USSR; most often the reader had no way of knowing that the original source was Soviet. The ministry distributed these Soviet materials despite knowing that they were at best incomplete and misleading, and quite possibly entirely false. In a letter he wrote almost five months after the publication of Zinchenko's propaganda, the Religious Division's Reverend Williams warned a Baptist correspondent against using information about Russian religion that he had obtained directly from the Soviet embassy. He should only cite the statistical information with great caution:

> The material was published by [the Soviet] press agency at a time when they were anxious to prove the existence of religious freedom. I do not think that there is any reason to doubt the truth of these statements as far as they go. The problems arise in the area which is not covered, e.g. the number of churches that have been closed, [denial of] permission to teach the young, the [denial of the] possibility of evangelism, etc.[113]

What Reverend Williams did not say was that his ministry had conveyed this very same dubious Soviet material to the British and international press during the summer of 1941 without any such disclaimer.

Despite Soviet propagandists' ability to plant such important bits of information, or misinformation, in the Western mass media, after two months of war, flaws in Soviet foreign propaganda had become apparent. In particular, the Soviets found it much harder to penetrate the United States with their message than to work in Britain. On September 4, M. Burskii, of the Informbiuro, wrote to Shcherbakov saying that "I regard it as my party duty" to explain the agency's shortcomings. Burskii had examined more than 3,000 issues of the 230 leading American journals, and he found almost no articles on Soviet life or culture. At the same time, many such pieces about Germany had appeared in the American press; the Germans had also employed numerous lecturers and were using German-Americans to advance their cause. This had created an "intolerable" situation, Burskii argued, because the Soviets had not yet started a program of speakers that might compete with the Germans; indeed, no Soviet scientists or artists had even yet been sent to the United States. "In the area of press propaganda," he continued, "our affairs are better," since the Informbiuro sent a daily short telegram to the United States written by the well-known Soviet writer Ilia Ehrenburg; they also sent a weekly despatch from the Soviet humorist Petrov and one biweekly from the writer Aleksei Tolstoi. But, even here, Moscow did not monitor the usage of these messages.

As a solution, Burskii proposed that Informbiuro undertake a "systematic" campaign to influence the foreign press; the Soviet government should also send "several hundred" of its best scientists, technicians, literary figures, and artists to the Western democracies. "Hundreds, if not thousands of articles, sketches, pamphlets, [and] feuilletons should be sent monthly from Moscow." These materials should be designed to penetrate every region of the United States and should be geared to every segment of the readership. Translators should be employed to ensure that such materials could be published not only in the United States but also in Latin America, Australia, and Canada.

Finally, Burskii wrote, Informbiuro should send leading Soviet literary figures on tours of the United States; these should be the most "energetic and self-motivated individuals" who knew the English language, could speak directly to the public and could compose their own material without needing to await instructions from Moscow. They should work to "establish close ties with influential scientific and literary-artistic societies and associations" that might prove sympathetic to the Soviet cause.[114]

Burskii's ideas seem commonsensical, even far-seeing, and many of them would soon be put into action. Nonetheless, Burskii himself did not benefit: only eighteen days after writing his letter to Shcherbakov, he resigned from Informbiuro, having failed to receive the requisite security clearance. He wrote to Shcherbakov to "demand my rehabilitation," and he indignantly continued: "It is unfortunate that during a war it is necessary to waste time and energy not on work but on a struggle with slanders."[115] Soviet documents do not reveal the reasons for Burskii's dismissal, or the slanders he complained of, nor do they disclose his fate. But, in pushing hard for sending Soviet speakers to America who would be independent and able to compose their own propaganda, he was trying to go farther than control-obsessed Moscow would allow during the war, despite repeated appeals from such prominent diplomats as Litvinov and Maiskii.[116]

Although Burskii was out of the picture, his suggestions would be taken up by higher authorities. On October 2, a crucial meeting took place at Informbiuro headquarters to reexamine Soviet international propaganda. The record of this conference, which was the key session for shaping Soviet propaganda in the West during the opening stages of the war, provides a fascinating insight into Soviet perceptions of their new Western partners.[117] Lozovskii directed the meeting, which included Informbiuro workers as well as the leadership of the Soviet press agency TASS, the Radio Committee, leaders of the Comintern, officials in charge of monitoring foreign broadcasts, as well as "our writers working for the foreign press," among them Ilia Ehrenburg. Konstantin Umanskii, recently returned to Moscow from his ambassadorship in Washington, was also present and provided a firsthand account of the American scene.

In his opening remarks, Umanskii told the assembled Soviet propagandists, diplomats, and officials that they must understand that Western public opinion was not one undifferentiated mass. "There are a number of differences between the English and American situations," he said. "It is much easier to work in England. Everything that is sent to England is published in the English press." In Britain, the molders of opinion and the public in general were more favorably inclined toward the USSR than were their counterparts across the Atlantic. He claimed that, "Amid the ruling circles in America there is a deep schism in radio production, [and] film production, between on one side the Roosevelt people, who, following his line, consider the situation in England very dangerous for them." This group was supported by the "Parliamentary majority." On the other side stood "the isolationist camp, which is deeply hostile to us." Among unfriendly press organs, Umanskii mentioned the "isolationist press of the Midwest," but singled out for special opprobrium the *New York Daily News* and the *Chicago Tribune*, which, he said, "is hostile to us to the point of hooliganism."

Umanskii said that he had encountered few difficulties in getting Soviet materials printed in New York publications; the situation in that city was more akin to British conditions than to those prevailing in the rest of the United States. "The further you go from New York," though, "the worse the situation becomes." Soviet-inspired articles printed in the East Coast leftist press (such as *PM*, the *New York Post*, and the *New Republic*) "don't reach the mass of readers." Umanskii understood one of the chief dilemmas of Soviet foreign propaganda: information and articles coming directly from the USSR did not have great credibility among most Western readers. The Soviets therefore needed to disguise the source of their propaganda either by funneling it through publications covertly funded by Moscow or, more expediently, by persuading Western writers to issue Soviet arguments under their own names. "The most effective method of acting on American public opinion is articles by Americans," Umanskii said, "American correspondents, issuing from people with famous names. We do not use these successfully enough." "This is extraordinarily important," Umanskii emphasized. He later remarked that, whereas 240 foreign correspondents were assigned to Berlin, only 28 worked in Moscow. As an example of the misuse of American correspondents, he cited the recent tour of the USSR by Ralph Ingersoll, the left-wing editor of the New York paper *PM*. The American visitor had not been given sufficient access to Soviet leaders, nor enough to do during his time in Moscow. "It seems to me that we use these foreign correspondents far from successfully," Umanskii said, offering suggestions for improvement: "Effective routes—use foreign correspondents, foreigners in general, cultivate them, work on them, reeducate them, even if they are hostile to us. They have espionage, and it is at work [*Razvedka u nikh est', ona rabotaet*].* Despite the fact that they might be drunks, still we need to use them."

Steps were being taken in the right direction, Umanskii allowed; Lozovskii's recent institution of press conferences for foreign correspondents was a "turning point" in this respect. The Soviets could learn a great deal from Roosevelt, whose own sessions with the press were masterful. Humor was also an effective tool, as the American president had shown, and Lozovskii's jokes during his press conferences went down well with Americans; Western papers reprinted them widely.[118] It was also very important for press conferences to focus on specific issues: "for example, about the churches," Umanskii asked, "Why, tov. [comrade] Lozovskii, have you not had a press conference on the question of religion?" Two days later, of course, Lozovskii would do precisely that, holding the press conference that so pleased the Americans, in which he touted Soviet religious freedoms.

Just as Maiskii had stressed the importance of Soviet cultural propaganda for the British audience, Umanskii said that more such material should be directed to the United States, though he was scornful about Americans' ability to comprehend the riches of Stalinist culture: "From the point of view of our cultural standards," he sniffed, "it is very hard to come up to them. The general cultural level in America is not high." The United States might be rich, but it remained the realm of spiritual barbarians: "From the point of view of material culture, so called, the living standard, he cannot even speak," the contrast was so great with the rigors of wartime Russia. Despite their material wealth, however, people in the United States did not even know the powerful works of more than a handful of Soviet musicians: "Of [our] composers, they know

---

*Unfortunately, given his imprecise wording, it is hard to decipher whether Umanskii was speaking of Soviet, or of Western, espionage. It would seem that he meant the former, and that the "they" meant Soviet organs. Soviets could rely therefore on covert agents to help forward their cause with American and British journalists.

Shostakovich, Shostakovich, and again Shostakovich. [Also] Prokofiev, Khacha-turian." Later in the meeting, he returned to this theme: "Our readers respect writers very much, but in America they do not elevate the writer to such a height," an observation that evoked the following interesting exchange: "Lo-zovskii: 'If it were a film star or . . .' Voice: 'or a boxing champion.'" Such re-marks indicate that the Soviet leadership had a rather inflated view of their own citizens' devotion to high culture. One can almost picture the average Rus-sian kolkhoznik, driving her tractor over the boundless steppe by day, perusing Dostoevsky by night, as the strains of Tchaikovsky wafted over the wireless.

On a more serious note, Umanskii explained that Soviet propaganda was not making effective use of American mass media. VOKS, for example, broad-cast regularly to the United States, but its programing did not reach more than a handful of listeners, because most Americans did not own shortwave radio sets: "Very rich people listened to you," he told the VOKS representative, "[peo-ple] who live in rich villas, but the people of America did not hear you." To reach these untapped masses, Soviet propaganda must penetrate the major American radio networks, using American correspondents, and especially Hol-lywood, the jewel in the American cultural crown. Umanskii suggested that the celebrated Soviet director, Sergei Eisenstein, should be enlisted to talk "with his friends in Hollywood." "We might set up a conversation with [Charles] Chap-lin, [Rouben] Mamulian, the Williamses,[119] who are well-disposed toward us." Spencer Williams, who had been a sympathetic correspondent in Moscow in the 1930s, would soon exceed all Soviet hopes when he wrote the screenplay for the movie production of *Mission to Moscow*, Ambassador Joseph Davies's wildly apologetic account of his years in the USSR and of Stalin's purge trials.[120] Whether Williams did so because the Soviets approached him, or because he was a true believer—or because the American government gave the project strong encouragement—is hard to say.

As for the Soviets' own cinematic productions, the situation was "very bad, but this is for the most part a technical problem," Umanskii believed. Once again, circumstances were somewhat better in Britain than in America, but he pointed out that a recent newsreel distributed in the United States had a voice-over "with a clear Jewish accent. We need to take Americans with a purely American accent."

Matyas Rakosi, a leading member of the Comintern who would later be one of the founders of the postwar Hungarian Communist government, raised the question of Americans with East European ethnic backgrounds and asked whether "American comrades" could not help mobilize them for the Soviet cause. Moscow should use the half-million American Hungarians, as well as the many German-Americans who did not support Hitler. Umanskii agreed, saying "we worked mostly among Slavs. . . . Now in this area there will be a[n American] Slavic Congress." Communists in the United States were also working to activate American Jews sympathetic to the Soviet war effort: "The Jewish meeting has received the biggest response. The whole press published their telegrams, even the press hostile to us." There would soon be an American Jewish Congress to match the Slavic organization, and American Czechs had so far been the most successful group in raising money for medical assistance for the Red Army. Not all American groups were so easy to direct, Umanskii complained: "With the Poles it is endless squabbles, intrigues. With the French it is very nasty—endless regroupings and no leader." As for work among American women, "Organizations are being created from church groups, women's clubs and an American women's committee is now being created and will function."

Ilia Ehrenburg asked whether any pro-Soviet materials had been distributed by American evangelicals or Baptists sympathetically inclined to the USSR. Umanskii replied that he knew of none, but perhaps this had been done during the two weeks since his return to Moscow. The only religious figure operating in the United States who was firmly controlled by the Soviets was Metropolitan Veniamin, the Moscow Patriarchate's controversial exarch to North America. "We used Metropolitan Veniamin," Umanskii said, but "he has no authority of any kind." Veniamin had instituted a number of lawsuits against Orthodox churches in the United States, arguing that the Moscow Patriarchate had a just claim to their property. American Orthodox priests and congregations almost unanimously resisted Veniamin's leadership, and they remained hostile to the USSR, under the influence of "white-guardist organizations," according to Umanskii.

Religious opinion was vital, however; Umanskii said that if American isolationists were to be defeated or at least marginalized, then religious suspicions must be countered: "First, church powers, second, Catholics, in a single basket. The pope wanted to speak out against any country that entered into alliance with us. [But] Roosevelt called the Catholics to him and stated that [their] funds would be sequestered. As you see, we have the possibility of influence [*vozmozhnost' vozdeistviia*]." How Umanskii gained this strange piece of information is anybody's guess. If Roosevelt did indeed lean so heavily on Catholic hierarchs, then no record has survived, and it is unlikely that such crude tactics could have been hidden for very long; indeed, it is not clear what church funds the executive branch would have been able to seize, given the American separation of church and state.[121] Either the story is a product of Umanskii's imagination, or—an equally plausible interpretation—an example of Rooseveltian exaggeration. Whatever the explanation, most Catholic bishops remained implacably opposed to Soviet Communism; therefore, the church was an especially important Soviet target, particularly since so many Americans of East European extraction were Catholics. Umanskii said that Soviet diplomats, sympathizers, and agents must work with Catholic clergy members, such as the bishop of Chicago, "with whom we might carry on antifascist conversations. He follows that line, but it is very important that this be popularized."

This gathering at the Informbiuro provides not only a unique insight into how the Soviet propaganda and foreign policy elite planned to influence Western public opinion but also how this elite understood its principal characteristics and hoped to take advantage of the democracies' great political and social openness. The discussion also reveals a certain self-confidence on the part of the Soviet apparat both about their ability to exploit this openness and the extent of the assets available to them in the West. Soviet propagandists could draw not only on the talents of Soviet diplomats stationed abroad, but also on members of fraternal Communist parties, sympathetic socialists, women's groups, workers, East European émigrés, and even espionage agents. Although the number of outright Communists in America or Britain might be very small, they could provide a leavening to activate these much larger sympathetic, non-Communist forces in support of the USSR.

Interestingly, although these Soviet officials discussed in great detail the various layers of Western opinion and fissures in American society, one area they did not touch was race, whether owing to oversight or some other cause is hard to say. Certainly American Communists had exploited the racial question extensively during the 1930s, and they would do so again during the Cold War. Now that the Soviets desired the United States to be a strong partner for the time being, however, they had no wish to highlight matters that might weaken, rather than strengthen American war production.

Although religious propaganda as such was a relatively small part of the overall plan outlined at this meeting, religious questions were nonetheless central to Soviet propaganda considerations, as Umanskii's comments indicate. Religiously based distrust of the Soviet system was interwoven into all American and British perceptions of the USSR. In trying to tackle this problem, the method of analysis these Soviet officials applied to Western political and social conditions was clearly Marxist and class-based. They assumed that Western leaders were serving hostile, bourgeois-capitalist class interests, but they believed the workers and common people to be actively or latently sympathetic to the Soviet cause. The Western working class could be reached, these Soviet officials assumed, by energetic and effective propaganda. Regarding religious matters, in their international as well as in their domestic analysis, Soviet officials continually underestimated the depth of genuinely held religious convictions among the "masses." Instead, they viewed the Western religious leadership as part of the exploiting class, even though certain clergy members might be persuaded to support Moscow's war effort. Religion, being the "opium of the people," promoted a false consciousness among the Western working class that could be dispelled by vigorous propaganda. Therefore, much of the cultural propaganda the group planned was designed to undercut or counteract religious skepticism about the USSR not by attacking churches head on, but rather by appealing to alternative loyalties: ethnic solidarity, shared history, class consciousness, ideological sympathy, or appreciation of Soviet artistic achievements.

All propaganda which is powerful and effective must be cumulative in character. It must increase in intensity as it proceeds,
until ultimately it reaches a tone not much removed from
violence.—Lord Beaverbrook, *The Divine Propagandist*

We have suffered much from the suppression of all public
criticism of the Russians, and if it went on it would surely
lead to disaster. For it would mislead the Russians . . . and
lead straight to a policy of appeasement.
—Christopher Warner to Balfour, January 25, 1944

Amplifying the Soviet Voice

Propaganda, both secular and religious, emanating di-
rectly from Moscow and beamed at the outside world was clumsy, almost always out of date, and for the most part believed only by committed Communists and fellow travelers. Soviet propagandists understood this and knew that
if they wanted to reach a wider audience they would have to make use of Western news outlets whenever possible as amplifiers for their propaganda. For this
trick to work, however, it was absolutely necessary to mask the Muscovite
source of the propaganda. In the period following the dissolution of the Comintern in the spring of 1943, as the Kremlin sought to recreate the era of "popular fronts" of all progressive parties, the drive to spread the Soviet word took
on a new urgency. For a host of reasons, some of them cultural, others political
and institutional, Britain would be the focal point of this propaganda offensive.

A Mole in the Ministry

As Konstantin Umanskii had noted in October 1941, it was far easier for Soviet
propagandists, both open and covert, to operate in Britain than in the United

States.[1] The more diffuse ownership and wider geographic distribution of press power in America, as well as sharp regional differences and the greater political independence of the media, in combination with much deeper popular American cultural prejudices against Communism, made it far harder for Soviet operatives to plant stories in the American press or on radio than in their British counterparts. There was nothing in the United States comparable to the London press corps; wartime Washington still resembled an overgrown small town, and the dominance of mass media, now such a prominent feature of the American capital, still lay in the future.[2] London, much more than Washington, was a front-line city, and so the international press clustered there. The BBC also had no American counterpart.

The Soviets admired, envied, and studied the British Ministry of Information. They discounted the protestations of British diplomats that their press was free of government influence and control. Instead, Moscow believed that British information organizations were simply smoother and more adept than their Soviet counterparts at concealing the hidden government hand. In Moscow's view, all British press outlets "simultaneously are organs of espionage." Soviet intelligence also envied the way that the British managed to plant stories and false rumors in newspapers, as well as shape the coverage of foreign news: "With rare exceptions," a secret Soviet evaluation declared, "the British press has no independence in the area of foreign policy evaluations."[3]

The very centralization and hierarchical organization that made the British informational apparatus so effective also made it vulnerable to Soviet penetration, and the Soviets valued British propaganda so highly that they targeted it as a priority for infiltration, proving successful in doing so beyond their wildest dreams. The man at the center of the Soviet operation was H. Peter Smollett. Smollett's real name was Smolka, and unbeknownst to the British he was an Austrian Communist who in his own words was "a frequent visitor to the Soviet Union."[4] As far as his shadowy record can be reconstructed, during the early 1930s Smollett caught the eye of the renowned Soviet agent Teodor Maly, and later Harold "Kim" Philby, the notorious British traitor and Soviet spy. After emigrating to Britain in 1933, Smollett made a modest reputation as a journalist and author. Playing on his credentials as an anti-Nazi Austrian, shortly after Britain declared war on Germany, Smollett entered the Ministry of Information working in the Neutrals Division. He also managed to befriend Brendan Bracken, the owner of the *Financial Times*, a connection that proved invaluable, because the latter was a Conservative MP and an intimate of Winston Churchill. Smollett made good use of the link.[5]

In the summer of 1941 Duff Cooper retired from the post of minister of information, and his place was taken by none other than Bracken. This was a time of great upheaval in the organization; the invasion of the USSR had changed the character of the war, and British propaganda had to be restructured to take this into account. In late August, when the new Soviet Relations Branch (later Division) was established in the ministry to handle domestic and foreign propaganda relating to the USSR, after some debate and a brief search Peter Smollett was named as its head.[6] Although Smollett was an obscure figure, he seemed a natural enough choice given his journalistic background and his relationship with the new minister. At a stroke, Soviet intelligence had penetrated the heart of the British propaganda apparatus. To adopt a religious analogy, it was as if the archbishop of York was a Soviet mole, while being a friend and close associate of the archbishop of Canterbury. The Ministry of Information's hierarchical structure, as well as its clubbish contacts with the press, schools, and civic organizations, could now be turned to the uses of Soviet foreign policy and propaganda.

Shortly after the creation of the Soviet Relations Branch, Bracken officially appointed Smollett to be his personal liaison to the Soviet Embassy in London, where the latter met regularly and in private with the first secretary, G. Zinchenko.[7] This was an almost unimaginably fortuitous position for a mole, giving him the ability to consult his handlers regularly without having to resort to subterfuge or risk arousing suspicion. It also allowed him to strike a plausible pose as the skeptical and even reluctant messenger of Soviet views. Within months of Barbarossa's outbreak, largely owing to Smollett's gentle pressure, the Soviets were given veto power over all information about the USSR composed by the ministry or circulated through official channels in Britain. A Ministry of Information meeting in November 1941 established as policy that "no statement about Russia or action to present Russia in England should be taken by [the ministry] without Mr. Smollett approving it from the angle of its suitability in the eyes of the Russian Embassy. Similarly Mr. Smollett is not entitled to approve any action to be taken without securing the approval of Mr. Parker as to its suitability from the Home angle.[8]

From his position at the center, Smollett was able to shape or influence propaganda policy in an astonishingly wide range of areas. He pretended to be intent on "stealing the thunder of the Left": that is, denying Communists and others on the extreme political left control over public rallies and propaganda in support of the alliance with the USSR.[9] Based on this pretext, the Soviet Relations Branch took charge of organizing "Anglo-Soviet Weeks" in various towns and cities throughout Britain, ostensibly to channel pro-Soviet enthusiasm into "responsible" directions but in fact to stoke public enthusiasm for the gallant new Soviet ally. Smollett worked quietly and steadily to assure that such rallies excluded anyone who might comment critically on the USSR or Communism. He specifically forbade what he called "white Russians" (non-Communist Russian émigrés) from speaking at ministry-sanctioned rallies and exhibitions "as this will give offence to the Soviet Embassy," although exceptions were allowable "in cases where we are fully satisfied that the individuals concerned, and what they will say, will not complicate our relations with the Soviet Government."[10] At the same time that Smollett was thus freezing out critics of Stalin, he worked to secure speakers from the Soviet embassy to appear at public events. He claimed, plausibly but deceptively, that Soviet officials would be under Moscow's discipline and would therefore be unlikely to make statements that might undermine the alliance.[11]

While pretending to screen participants of such rallies to exclude Communist front organizations, Smollett cleared several such groups to work with his ministry's imprimatur. Thus, owing to his advocacy, the "Society for Cultural Relations with the U.S.S.R." (the SCR) was cleared to participate in ministry activities, such as Anglo-Soviet weeks and public exhibitions, and he authorized the circulation through official channels—even to the ministry's own regional information officers—of the group's publication, the *Anglo-Soviet Journal*.[12] While Smollett allowed that the SCR was at times indulgently pro-Soviet, he claimed that it was independent of Soviet control, and indeed he argued boldly that collaborating with the SCR would actually prevent public opinion from "running off into channels that are a cause of confusion to everybody."[13]

Smollett's assurances aside, a Soviet Central Committee document from August 1942 proves that the SCR was carefully controlled, both politically and financially, by Moscow:

> Societies of cultural contacts with the USSR in England, America, Sweden, and China, publish regular journals from materials sent by VOKS and with money which in secret gift VOKS conveys for these goals to our foreign friends. Frequently some articles which are included in these journals are of a tone and character that are unwelcome to us. In such instances VOKS gives a special order [and] these mistakes are corrected in the following issue and the entire line of the journal is examined and controlled by us.[14]

Despite its unwaveringly pro-Stalinist orientation and its covert funding and control by Moscow (of which Smollett was certainly aware), the SCR was welcomed by Smollett's unknowing colleagues as a useful ally. In October 1941 an anonymous ministry official wrote that "it is to be anticipated that the Society [for Cultural Relations] will form a useful instrument of the same character as the British Council."[15]

Smollett was an influential figure behind the scenes, but he was by no means omnipotent at the Ministry of Information, much less in the government as a whole. He had to deal with a number of powerful and important colleagues and superiors who were skeptical of, or even downright hostile to, the USSR. Chief among these was Prime Minister Winston Churchill himself, who was wary of any British-sanctioned propaganda that might whitewash the Soviet record. In September 1941, in one of his many letters on the subject, he ordered Bracken "to consider what action was required to counter the present tendency of the British Public to forget the dangers of Communism in their enthusiasm over the resistance of Russia."[16] Pressure from such a quarter did moderate the occasional pro-Soviet excess, but the prime minister was far too busy to monitor the daily output of the Ministry of Information or the BBC, and the old truism that ministers propose but their secretaries dispose was certainly confirmed by the operation of the Soviet Relations Branch.

Nonetheless, especially during the summer of 1941, when many sensibilities had not yet been trained by the experience of alliance to accept the systematic falsification of the Soviet record that would soon become commonplace, Smollett occasionally suffered reverses in his attempts to promote pro-Soviet propaganda. In July, for instance, the Schools Department of the BBC, "having failed to find one of [their] experienced commentators to give this," requested that the Ministry of Information suggest a person who could compose a broadcast for schoolchildren describing the geography of Britain's new ally.[17] They turned to Smollett, who suggested that Andrew Rothstein, a British subject and Moscow's TASS correspondent in London, could write a suitable piece.

The finished product was predictably skewed. It focused on "the Soviet Republics on the western borders of the Soviet Union," precisely those regions that Moscow had seized before the war. Thus it described the "Karelo-Finnish Soviet Socialist Republic" as "one of the youngest: since it only came into being as a separate federal Republic in March of last year." No mention, naturally, of the Soviet invasion that brought this about. Likewise, the Lithuanians "only last year . . . finally decided to do without landlords any longer, and joined the Soviet Union." Rothstein described the supposed bounty produced by collective farming in Belorussia, writing surreally: "[Y]ou can imagine how the eyes of some of the simple country lads conscripted into the German army, coming from villages which have been getting poorer and poorer as the huge Nazi war machine was built up, will open when they see if they ever do—how the Belorussian peasants live." As for Moldavia, with its population of just under 3 million, from which the Soviets had deported 22,648 people during their brief period of occupation (at least two-thirds of whom were women and children):[18] "[L]ike all inhabitants of sunny lands, the Moldavians have always been accomplished singers and dancers, and their music and rhythm seem to radiate the sun. Their harvests were nearly doubled last year when they stopped working for foreign landlords, and began working for themselves—so their leaders have reported."[19]

In July 1941 this was all still a bit much, and the script was rejected for broadcast. But the upshot was instructive: the Soviet ambassador, Ivan Maiskii, immediately protested against this supposed censorship and had to be assuaged. Maiskii's stock was not yet high enough to carry all before him, but as the war dragged on the one-two punch of Smollett working within the system to generate pro-Soviet material and Maiskii operating from the outside, objecting that the alliance would be harmed when or if any favorable material was blocked, would prove a highly effective combination.[20]

By year's end, BBC broadcasts for schools were no longer so reserved as they had been in July. The schedule of travel talks for Britain's schoolchildren between the ages of nine and eleven included such innocuous-sounding topics as "Everybody's Farm: turning a whole village into one big collective farm," and "The Wandering Peoples Settle Down: teaching the Mongol nomads scientific farming and fishing." In fact, of course, collectivization had resulted in the deaths of millions, and nomadic peoples had been especially hard hit. Reviewing the list of proposed subjects, Sir Orme Sargent of the Foreign Office noted dejectedly: "[W]e find that, since the British Broadcasting Corporation naturally must now give talks on present day Russia and cannot of course expose the less pleasant side, their talks cumulatively tend to build up a picture of a Soviet paradise."[21]

Later in the war, Smollett's field of activity would grow, and he would be able to influence, among other things, the selection of reading lists distributed to British schools for courses on the USSR and Communism.[22] In an even stranger twist, when London devised a publication designed to promote Britain's image among the Soviet people, entitled *Britanskii soiuznik* (British ally), there was Smollett once again, helping to select and edit the material deemed suitable for Soviet readers.[23] It is almost enough to evoke sympathy for Smollett, as he struggled to remember who his true master was.

"Dexterity in Providing Moral Dress for the State's Political Needs"

By design, religious themes did not constitute a large portion of official British propaganda during the first two years of the alliance with the USSR, owing to the subject's extreme delicacy. In general, the Ministry of Information sought to accentuate the positive rather than dwell on points of difference with Britain's totalitarian ally; religion remained the most divisive and emotional question and was often best ignored. In September 1941, responding to one of several complaints from the prime minister about the growing British public enthusiasm for the USSR, Bracken explained his ministry's reasoning: "It is agreed that our propagandists ought not to hesitate about emphasizing the divergence between our own political conception and Communism. But we have asked that they should concentrate for the present rather upon the enduring value of our democratic way of life than upon criticism destructive of the Soviet ideology."[24]

The Ministry of Information never did decide firmly whether its job was to act as the advocate of the USSR in Britain—promoting the alliance with Moscow among a reluctant and suspicious public—or as a brake on undue popular enthusiasm for Communism and the Soviet Union.[25] The priority accorded to either of these two objectives varied from official to official. In practice, the approach outlined by Bracken meant saying nothing negative about Communism and a great deal that was both positive and inaccurate, or even untrue. Echoing Bracken's letter to the prime minister, ministry guidelines stated that "while both Russia and Britain fully maintain their very different ideals about future forms of society, and remembering clearly that they differ fundamentally over the attitude to religion," nothing was to be gained by dwelling on such differences "while Hitler and Germany is [*sic*] unbeaten."[26] When it came to the question of religion in the USSR, ministry organizers of Anglo-Soviet weeks were told that "clearly the topic is not one which we would like to bring up."[27]

Ignoring the subject of religion would not make it go away. In mid-1942, a survey of public opinion among what a Ministry of Information official quaintly but without explanation called "the more intelligent members of all sections of the population"—which he judged to be "fairly representative"—indicated "that of all those who feel that there are obstacles to a proper understanding between Great Britain and the Soviet Union, 72 per cent named the Soviet treatment of religion as the chief difficulty."[28] When the subject of religion did raise its head, the result was invariably embarrassing to the British government.

An incident in the autumn of 1941 illustrates the religious issue's tricky dynamics. On September 23, at a time when the Soviets were in the midst of their campaign to secure Lend-Lease assistance from Western Allies, Ivan Maiskii, the Soviet ambassador to Britain, delivered a speech to the American Chamber of Commerce in London in which he claimed that the Soviet record on religion was exemplary. Not only had the Communist government never repressed the Russian Orthodox Church, the ambassador declared, but also believers practiced their various faiths with the full support and protection of the Communist state. The speech was obviously intended to allay religion-based suspicions of the Soviet Union, but it had a rather different effect. Although the influential *Times* of London gave a warm endorsement to Maiskii's remarks, the religious, and especially the Catholic, press reacted negatively. On October 3, in an article entitled "Boldness Pays," the *Catholic Herald* admitted that it had to "pay a tribute of admiration to the effrontery of the Russian Ambassador's remarks."[29]

The public row over Maiskii's remarks drew in another important figure, Archbishop of Canterbury Cosmo Gordon Lang, who felt moved by the attacks on Maiskii to state that, whereas the Soviet Union might study Britain's tradition of tolerance, the British could for their part learn a great deal from Moscow about the equitable distribution of wealth and the rational planning of society and the economy. This is the same archbishop, it should be remembered, who in 1930, during the brutal collectivization of the Soviet farms and the campaign against religion that accompanied it—examples of "rational" planning gone mad, if you will—denounced Soviet Communism and called on world Christians to observe a day of prayer on behalf of the Kremlin's victims. Once again, the alliance had worked its magic.

Rebutting the archbishop's remarks, the *Catholic Herald* wrote that "When the Russian Alliance was first made we pointed out the danger lest a natural and necessary military co-operation should be allowed to develop into a moral and cultural union between Great Britain and the Soviet. We confess that even then we did not anticipate the speed and energy with which this perilous development has come about." Excusing or glossing over the Soviet record of religious repression "threatens to make a nonsense of Mr. Churchill's pledge against Bolshevism." Although they only criticized Archbishop Lang "with great regret," they believed it to be "a tragedy that the Archbishop should speak as he has done," because "nothing in the long run more certainly debases Christianity in the eyes of the people than these continual *volte-faces*, this dexterity in providing moral dress for the state's political needs." They doubted that Britain had very much to learn—in a positive sense—from Soviet Communism.[30]

The Soviets did not take British press criticism lightly. Fedor Gusev, head of the Soviet Foreign Ministry's second Western European Department and a future ambassador to London, complained not only of the Catholic papers' attacks but also of a number of articles in the British provincial press lampooning Soviet bureaucracy. Such articles, Gusev said, "were not doing the common cause any good."[31] In a more pointed complaint, Maiskii himself protested against what he saw as an "anti-Soviet campaign in the Roman Catholic Press," which "hardly corresponds to the spirit of the present relations between" Britain and the USSR. The ambassador hinted darkly that, because the articles in the Catholic papers only appeared a couple of weeks after he had delivered his speech on religion, this "inevitably suggests that the campaign referred to could not be considered as a spontaneous reaction on the part of the Roman Catholic papers but rather indicates that this has been ordered from certain quarters which are in a position to give instruction to the Roman Catholic Press in this country. This makes the campaign still more ominous."[32] Although Maiskii left the source of these supposed "instructions" unnamed, under direct questioning from Foreign Minister Anthony Eden he confirmed that in his opinion Britain's Catholics were marching to the orders of the Vatican, which was itself supposedly under Mussolini's thumb.[33]

British reaction to these Soviet complaints illustrated the immense delicacy of the religious question. From Moscow, British Ambassador Sir Stafford Cripps wrote: "I realise [the] difficulty of trying to influence [the] press in matters of [the] Soviet treatment of religion where [the] facts are unfortunately not in dispute." He added, however, that he sympathized with Gusev: "[I]t is obvious that such references *do* do [the] common cause no good," and he asked "whether there is anything you can say to" unhelpful editors to restrain their commentary in future.[34] Foreign Office officials agreed with Cripps, calling the articles "really deplorable," although they stated nothing untrue and had in fact simply restated the prime minister's position. Nonetheless, in apologizing to Maiskii, one official wrote, "we can only shelter behind the 'freedom of the press' while taking such action as possible."[35] (The inverted commas in this minute are priceless.) While unconvincing declarations in support of press freedom in Britain may have been the Foreign Office's public stance, in private it "urgently" requested the acting director general at the Ministry of Information, Radcliffe, to look into "the question of bringing pressure to bear on the three Catholic papers."[36]

At this point, Smollett gave the deliberations his own spin; drawing on his "contacts with both religious bodies and the Soviet ambassador," he claimed that Maiskii had admitted privately "that he had been ill-advised—and he did not make it clear by whom—when he made his statement about religion. M. Maisky added that it was neither useful nor indeed true to pretend that the Soviet Government was friendly to religion, and he, for his part, would be content not to raise the issue further in public." Maiskii then suggested a peculiar compromise: "His Excellency express[ed] his hope that this Ministry, on its side, would make its influence felt with the religious bodies and with the religious Press with a view to persuading them, while fully maintaining their attitude in principle, not to make the religious issue the 'pretext' for interfering with the Government's policy of aid to Russia." Smollett concluded by saying that his office was "trying to work out an appropriate line which it might be suggested religious bodies should take when defining their attitude to the present Anglo-Russian co-operation."[37]

It is unclear from the British documents whether ministry officials met at this time with the editors of the religious press as Smollett had proposed. With Maiskii's comments passing into the mist of yesterday's news, no further inflammatory articles appeared at that time in the religious papers, nor did any more evidence surface of a malevolent, Vatican-inspired campaign.[38] Nonetheless, Smollett's plan to craft new guidelines for the religious press was ominous. He would let religious editors know that, for national security reasons, explicit attacks on the USSR were unhelpful and unwelcome. The ministry may have lacked the legal authority to censor such comment, but arguments based on national security carry a great deal of weight with patriotic editors when their country is at war. Smollett's remarks quoted earlier suggested a strange compromise: Maiskii promised to refrain from lying if the British press for its part ceased to print the truth about religion in the USSR.

Incidents of the sort described here, each of which was relatively minor and passed with little or no public notice, would recur often throughout the war; it would be possible to recount scores of similar instances. Each showed just how unrealistic the prime minister's hopes had been in June when he declared confidently that an alliance with Moscow need not lead to a prettifying of the Soviet record. Over the years of the alliance, occasions such as the debate set off by Maiskii's September 1941 speech had a cumulative effect, just as water dripping on stone will dissolve even the hardest minerals. Through exchanges such as these, the bounds of allowable public discourse were defined and narrowed. The mood, or "temper" of the times, which people who lived through the period recall and believe to have been entirely spontaneous, was in some part the creation of people operating with deliberate intent behind the scenes. Spontaneous support for the USSR certainly existed and grew as people genuinely sympathized with the heroic suffering of the Soviets; people are not sheep after all, even if propagandists believe them to be. But spontaneity was only one part of the story. To a degree, the pro-Soviet mood that swept Britain, and to a lesser extent the United States, was prodded and pushed by these subterranean forces. Unfortunately, public opinion is so vast and complex that it is impossible for the historian to dissect reality in order to determine the precise extent to which covert pressures and informal censorship of the type described here shaped the public mood.

Leaders, both secular and religious, certainly helped to define the wartime mood. In this regard, the enthronement of William Temple as archbishop of Canterbury on August 23, 1942, was a significant step in the evolution of British wartime religious attitudes toward a more indulgent view of the USSR. Temple's predecessor, the seventy-eight-year-old Archbishop Lang, no doubt weary with the burdens of high office in wartime, had decided to retire. Although Lang had already moderated somewhat his prewar anti-Communist views, Temple would move his church much farther in that direction. In late Autumn 1941, even before becoming the head of the Anglican Church, while still archbishop of York, Temple spoke out forcefully in support of the alliance with the USSR.

At a diocesan conference on November 13, Anglican hierarchs discussed the moral dimensions of the new British alliance with Moscow. With good reason, Temple's speech earned a high profile in the British press. Echoing Churchill's June 22 comments, but adding new twists of his own, Temple declared that the Soviet "cause is ours, and our cause is theirs." He tried to anticipate possible objections by claiming that "Russia has not of late been an aggressive power." As for the Soviet invasion of Finland, "though we cannot justify it, [the attack] was based on a strategy of defense." Temple declared that "I for one look forward to close cooperation" with Moscow in the postwar world, on economic and political matters. "[Y]et this association inevitably brings problems which it would be foolish and wrong to ignore." These problems sprang from the Communists' "atheist philosophy," but even here things were changing for the better: "The form of Communism which [Lenin] first established was incompatible with that value of persons on which Christianity insists." Temple believed, however, that this had improved under Stalin: the "pressure of experience" had caused Lenin's successor to modify the Communist system to the point where the archbishop could claim: "I see little or nothing in it with which a Christian needs to quarrel." The Soviet system, he repeated, "does not seem open to condemnation as unChristian." Although one might quibble with such things as Moscow's ban on religious education for the young, the archbishop said, this was something about which reasonable men might disagree. Addressing the finer qualities of Stalin and his lieutenants, Temple said: "The leaders of Russia are clear-sighted, sincere, and very able men. They do not expect us to pretend that their principles are other than they are."[39]

To the British public, Temple's extraordinary speech appeared to be the product of his own unaided reason, but this was not the case. In a letter to Smollett four days after the speech, the Reverend Williams of the Ministry of Information's Religions Division wrote: "Personally, I thought it was a useful speech, and I of course remembered the source of the suggestion!"[40] Smollett had done more than merely suggest the topic to Archbishop Temple; working through the World Council of Churches' Reverend William Paton, he apparently exercised a significant influence on the argument, Paton supplying Temple with a memorandum that "underlay" the latter's remarks.[41] Paton had, in turn, imbibed many of his ideas from Smollett.

It might be wondered how an Anglican archbishop could be induced to issue such fatuous remarks about a Communist dictatorship. The answer to the apparent paradox lies partly in the emerging spirit of the alliance and the machinations of Smollett but more importantly in Temple's own background and developments in British religious opinion during the interwar years. Temple represented a recognizable type of modern Anglican bishop, much more common in the postwar era than before the war, when the church was often referred to as the "Conservative Party at prayer." A scion of the English elite, educated at Rugby and Oxford, Temple displayed impressive intellectual talents at an early age, becoming the president of the Oxford Union. While still at university, he also exhibited what would become a lifelong devotion to social questions, especially the plight of the poor, visiting the university settlements in London's impoverished East End, for instance.

Curiously enough, although he would later become Britain's foremost clergyman and a popular writer, famous for his explication of contemporary Christian thought, Temple was at first, in 1906, refused ordination by the bishop of Oxford. The latter wrote that he could not accept as an Anglican priest a man who could say nothing stronger than that he was "inclined, very tentatively, to accept the doctrine of the Virgin Birth, and with rather more confidence, that of the Bodily Resurrection of Our Lord."[42] Temple's inability to believe unquestioningly in the central tenets of the Christian faith was symptomatic of his general intellectual makeup: he shared with many modern theologians a disinclination to reject alternative beliefs, even when they clashed with his own. In a private letter of 1944, Temple admitted this, referring to his "habitual tendency to discover that everybody is quite right."[43] While many people saw Temple's temporizing as a refreshing attribute in a cleric, others interpreted it as a sign of intellectual incoherence.

If Temple could not bring himself to reject rival religious beliefs, he was more zealous in his denunciations of what he viewed as the depredations of capitalism. Indeed, it would not be far wrong to say that socialism supplied something of the moral certainties otherwise lacking in the archbishop's outlook. Becoming a member of the Labour Party in 1918, like many of his generation, Temple came to identify capitalism as responsible for the First World War, a view only strengthened by the onset of the Great Depression. A large portion of the Anglican clergy, like most intellectuals during the 1930s, was shocked by what it regarded as the systemic failure of capitalism; and it saw the prevention of another depression, with its long unemployment lines and blighted lives, as a moral and religious, as well as political, imperative. Temple was already predisposed to such a view, and so he became a leading light of those within his church arguing for a new social gospel.

In a book he published in 1942, entitled *The Hope of a New World*, Temple outlined his views on the economic and political problems of the day. The root cause of Britain's economic troubles, Temple argued, was a falling away from "God and his Laws." God, Temple informed his readers, wished mankind to devote industry to "the supply of men's wants"; instead, however, "in our world goods are produced, not primarily to satisfy the consumer, but to enrich the producer." "We have to recognise that democracy, as we have known it, displays some of the characteristics for which the totalitarian States denounce it," he scolded—the primary flaw being the individual's freedom to pursue narrow personal, material self-interest at the expense of the collective good. "It is easy to infer from this that some form of Communism or State Socialism is the ideal system," he admitted, though he explained rather feebly—and none too clearly—that Communism might underrate man's "activity as a producer and not only as a consumer." The archbishop proposed a sure and certain remedy: "[T]he State, as the representative of the whole community and, therefore, of the consumer, must undertake the planning of our economic life." Only state planning could lead to "the fullest attainable combination of order or planning with freedom or personal initiative." Socialism, in this reading, was Christianity transferred to the political plane.[44]

Temple was not writing about the Soviet Union; indeed, he knew very little about it. That was part of the problem. Like so many educated, left-leaning—but non-Communist—intellectuals in the West during the 1930s and early 1940s, he combined a near total ignorance of Soviet reality with an almost childlike enthusiasm for Soviet economic "planning." The marvels of state control over industry beckoned from afar and seemed to proffer the solution for the manifest ills of the West. This enthusiasm was fed by the flood of books purporting to be "academic" studies of the Soviet political and economic system, books by such authors as Sidney and Beatrice Webb, Maurice Dobb, and Anglicanism's own Hewlett Johnson.[45] These works portrayed the Stalinist USSR as a collectivist Disneyland, with something for everyone and enough for all. They ignored the darker side of Stalinist economic planning, the mass deportations, slave labor, and even the mammoth flaws in the great Stalinist industrial projects, much of which was known at the time for those willing to review the evidence dispassionately.[46]

The archbishop knew vaguely that reality for Christians in the USSR was grimmer than apologist authors let on; he certainly knew more than he was prepared to say in public. Almost a year and a half after announcing to the world that he saw no essential conflict between Christianity and Stalinist Communism, Temple, by this time archbishop of Canterbury, sounded a markedly different note in a private letter to the Ministry of Information. The Reverend Hugh Martin had asked Temple to lend his name to a declaration condemning fascism, to be issued jointly with the Russian Orthodox Church. "I do not think that there need be any difficulty about this," the archbishop wrote, "apart from my difficulty of distinguishing between Fascism and Communism!"[47] Temple's intellectual dishonesty about the nature of Communism and the suffering of his fellow Christians in the USSR undercuts to a large degree the sympathy one might otherwise feel for him, mired as he was in the complex moral dilemmas of wartime.

Despite his reservations about Communism—only expressed when he was safely outside the public view—Temple would play a significant role in moderating the image of the USSR as persecutor of religion. The most prominent such occasion arose as a consequence of the visit by Metropolitan Nikolai to the British embassy in Kuibyshev in September 1942.[48] During this visit, it will be remembered, Nikolai had proposed an exchange between the hierarchs of the Russian Orthodox and Anglican churches; he had also asked that the archbishop of Canterbury write an introduction to the translation of *Pravda o religii v Rossii*. Clearly these ideas were supported by the Soviet government, or else Nikolai would never have conveyed them; but the British Foreign Office was at first cool to the notion of an exchange of ecclesiastical visits. The reaction of Permanent Under Secretary for Foreign Affairs Alexander Cadogan was typical: "I am rather chary of all this," he wrote; "deathbed conversions are not very convincing."[49]

Despite such negative initial assessments, the British nevertheless finally agreed to the exchange, though they insisted that an Anglican delegation make the first visit. The decision was made by Foreign Minister Anthony Eden, who at that time still cherished hopes of capitalizing on the rising prestige of the Soviet Union by appearing as the sane and sober champion within the British government of aid to Russia. Eden explained his reasoning to Lord Halifax, the British ambassador in Washington. He was, he said, "inclined not to rebuff [the] Metropolitan's proposal." Eden admitted that "we realise that . . . [the] probable purpose [of the exchange] is to pull the wool over [the] eyes of Church people in Great Britain and [the] United States of America." But, the message continued: "[The] very fact that [the] Soviet Government feel it desirable to propitiate churches is a sign of grace which we feel ought not to be discouraged, so long as it is made quite clear to church leaders that [the] gesture is a political one and does not necessarily represent any change of attitude in policy toward religion on the part of [the] Soviet Government."[50]

The Ministry of Information agreed with Eden that the exchange should go ahead, though the Reverend H. M. Waddams of the Religious Section cautioned that "Everything must be done to minimise the impression of a propaganda stunt." Waddams had no wish to see Anglican clergymen made into water carriers for Soviet propaganda: "To say the least, it would be possible that the Soviet Government would blazon the visit round the world as a proof that religion was in fine fettle in the Soviet Union, and that normal relations existed between the Russian and Anglican Churches."[51] As time would show, Waddams had less cause to worry about Soviet than about British propaganda.

Notwithstanding these concerns, a meeting at the Ministry of Information, with Smollett present, decided that the exchange must go ahead. In light of his personal acquaintance with the archbishop of Canterbury, the Reverend Hugh Martin agreed to try and persuade Temple to approve the idea.[52] Significantly, although all the government officials involved in these deliberations stated repeatedly that everything must be done to avoid the impression that the Anglican Church was being exploited in a "propaganda stunt," neither the Foreign Office nor the Ministry of Information had bothered to consult officials in the Church of England before deciding to proceed with the exchange.

On November 26, Martin met with Archbishop Temple to discuss Metropolitan Nikolai's two proposals: that Temple write an introduction to *The Truth about Religion in Russia*, and that an exchange take place between the Anglican and Russian Orthodox churches. According to Martin's record of the meeting, Temple "[w]as greatly interested and much impressed" by the prospect of an exchange of visits. "While keenly alive to the dangers and difficulties," the archbishop thought that such a visit, if handled carefully, would be a salutary thing. Temple asked to be given a little time to reflect on the matter. Martin later told the Foreign Office that "we ought, I am sure, to await his reply before taking any action on it."[53]

As for the proposed introduction that the Soviets wanted Temple to write, Martin did not record the archbishop's exact words, providing instead a summary of what the two men supposedly decided between themselves. On this point, however, the account seems to be somewhat misleading. According to Martin, Temple's first reaction was reserved; the archbishop supposedly said "not only that he could not write a preface which would be satisfactory to the Soviet authorities, but that [the book's] publication at all in this country would be likely to do harm to Anglo-Soviet relationships." He did not question the sincerity of the Russian church leaders' support for the war against the Nazis, but the book "appears to suggest that the Orthodox Church is not suffering from any oppressive measures in Russia and that the stories of religious persecution are entirely unfounded." If such a book were to be translated into English, it would "inevitably provoke a very unhelpful controversy." British Christians were generally "friendly disposed" toward the Soviets, but "If they do not feel it appropriate just now to say much in public about the past and present record of the Soviet Government in relation to religion that is not because they have forgotten or do not care." Martin closed his account by recommending to the Foreign Office that they decline the Soviet request to publish an English edition of *Pravda o religii* "on the grounds that it would be bad propaganda.... [O]ur advice would be based entirely upon the conviction that the publication would not promote more friendly feelings, but the reverse."[54] In another note, Martin warned that to claim more freedom for religion in the USSR than actually existed would backfire on the British: "[N]o subject in the world . . . is capable of arousing stronger feeling in, say, Latin America, or Spain, or Sweden, than this, even on the part of many folk who never darken the door of any church."[55]

There is good reason to believe that Martin was putting his own words into Temple's mouth in his account of their talk. Martin was one of the more restrained officials in the Ministry of Information when it came to evaluating the degree of religious freedom in the USSR.[56] Judging from subsequent correspondence, however, far from agreeing with Martin that publication of an English translation would be counterproductive, Temple had evidently argued, and continued to believe, that it would be both useful and desirable. A couple of weeks after their meeting, in a letter to Martin dated 8 December 1942, Temple was still pressing his case: "You are a better judge of this question than I am, because you are in closer touch with the movements of opinion. It is quite true that if this book is published, it will provoke a considerable amount of hostile comment of the kind you mention. I should not expect this to become very public or to go on very long. The public mind is too full of other things." Temple believed that the appearance of the book in the USSR "is an indication of a new attitude" on the part of the Kremlin, and he clearly remained unpersuaded by Martin's view that a translation into English would be ill-advised. He wrote: "I think that people who know anything of the history of the relations between the Government and the Church would be greatly impressed at the thought that the Government had permitted the preparation of such a book." Furthermore, although in his opinion the Soviets had eased their repression of the church only owing to the demands of war, they might find it hard to clamp down again in peacetime: "[T]he main thing is to get the thin edge of the wedge in, and I think the issue of the book will do that." He continued unambiguously: "All this no doubt refers more to the publication in Russia than to the publication of an English translation here; but here [in Britain] also I think that it should be available, and on balance I think that it would do more good than harm"[57]

Eight days later Martin enlisted the skills of Sir Archibald Clark Kerr, the British ambassador to Moscow and a skeptic about religious freedom in Russia who was temporarily back in London, to try once again to dissuade Temple from advocating a translation, or from having his name "in any way associated with the book if he were asked." Had *Pravda o religii* actually been available to Soviet readers, Martin might have taken a different view, but it was not, and he did not wish to abet Soviet efforts to "whitewash" its record on religion.[58]

The archbishop was not about to be dissuaded. One day before Christmas, he wrote to Martin, telling him that he "should strongly support" publication of the book.[59] As before, he did not specify precisely what benefits would spring from the publication; but on January 21, he wrote once again in favor of a translation, this time having been reinforced in his views by Canon Douglas, who headed the Church of England's Committee of Foreign Relations. Douglas "seems very clear on two points," Temple wrote: "First, there ought to be an English translation of [*Pravda o religii*] published. He is sure that the balance of advantage is on that side. And secondly, he thinks that whoever holds my office ought not to be involved in it."[60]

Temple admitted that *Pravda o religii* was packed with half-truths and outright lies, he knew that it was almost entirely unavailable to Soviet readers, and he understood that it would convey a misleading impression to Western readers about the state of religion in the USSR. Yet he advocated that the Ministry of Information publish an English-language edition at the government's expense, arguing that "it would do more good than harm." While he was willing to press for the book's publication, however, he did not want to have his name or office associated with it in the public mind; he was thus careful to protect himself from any adverse side effects of the project.

In large part owing to Archbishop Temple's covert advocacy, the Ministry of Information would ultimately arrange the translation of *Pravda o religii* and its publication. In the meantime, Temple also approved sending a British ecclesiastical delegation to the USSR. It only remained to select an appropriate clergyman of sufficient rank to undertake what would be a grueling journey in wartime conditions. Temple persuaded his successor as archbishop of York, Cyril Garbett, who professed himself "very keen to go" despite the fact that he was sixty-seven years old and in poor health.[61] The archbishop was to have two traveling companions, both of whom were Anglican ministers: Herbert Waddams and Francis House. The former was a high-ranking official in the Ministry of Information's Religious Division and the latter was a wartime employee of the BBC. To forestall the impression that the journey was a "propaganda visit," government officials sought to conceal these institutional affiliations from the public, were annoyed when the press uncovered them, and tried to prevent publication of the news.[62] None of the three travelers spoke Russian, which placed them entirely at the mercy of interpreters and guides supplied by the Soviet government.

In correspondence with the Ministry of Information during the run-up to Garbett's journey, Temple wrote that "from the standpoint of the Russian Government," the visit would certainly be "primarily political." "But," he continued, "there must be no doubt about the fact that *our* interest in it is primarily religious; this would have to be made quite clear" both to the public and to the Soviet authorities.[63] As for the Orthodox Church, however, Temple snidely suggested that his brother Russian clerics had lower standards than his own: "I expect the Russian Church is not very sensitive about the avoidance of its own utilisation for genuinely political ends!" Martin agreed, writing back that the British must be "on our guard against the attempts that will no doubt be made by the Soviet Government to use the visit for political purposes." He then seemed to backtrack: "This political purpose is to a large extent, I think you will agree, entirely legitimate. They are anxious to promote friendship between the two countries and to make something of a demonstration of it."[64] Despite Temple's concerns about being seen as a tool of government propaganda, when the Foreign Office suggested that the church might pay for the forthcoming mission to Moscow to avoid giving any pretext for just such an accusation, the archbishop dismissed the idea—and took the money.[65]

Before sending the archbishop of York to Moscow, it only remained to devise an acceptable communique condemning Nazism, for the Russian Orthodox and Anglican churches to issue jointly. This proved trickier than anyone expected. One draft stated that:

> We unite in condemning the brutal system of Fascism, and the horrors and destruction with which it is associated. In seeking to absorb the individual into the State, Fascism changes men and women who were created by God as children into mere tools of a national State. Thus by its brutal oppression and misdirection of the young it both frustrates spiritual aspiration and undermines the mutual trust on which all healthy society depends. We also unite in looking forward in hope and faith to the firm establishment of a world order in which the Christian principles of right may prevail, and in which the Christian Churches may develop in freedom and prosperity.[66]

This document might seem innocuous enough. The Ministry of Information had drafted it after all, and the archbishops of York and Canterbury quickly approved it. But the ministry later reconsidered on the advice of the Foreign Office. Its reasoning speaks volumes about the transformation in religious propaganda since the summer of 1941. Martin wrote apologetically to the archbishop of York: "I expect that I ought to go down on my bended knees before suggesting that any statement approved by two Archbishops is not really suitable . . . though of course we have no quarrel with what it says." Martin then came to the point: "There is the further difficulty that at some points it would be deplorably easy to substitute the word 'Bolshevism' for 'Fascism'! . . . I am sure neither of you will mind my being so frank. I fully realise of course that it has to be your statement."[67] As neither of the archbishops objected, the draft was quietly dropped.

The second-ranking cleric of the world's Anglicans thus readied himself to lead the first ecclesiastical delegation to visit the USSR since the Bolshevik Revolution. The visit was certain to place the weight of the British government and the moral authority of England's state church behind the Soviets' efforts to rehabilitate their sordid international image. These shepherds of the Anglican flock, a delegation whose members were almost as ignorant of Russian history and Soviet society as they were of the Russian language, recoiled even from calling on their brother Russian clergymen to work for a world where "Christian principles of right may prevail," for fear of drawing unwonted public attention to the uncomfortable similarity between Nazi totalitarianism and the nature of their Soviet ally's regime. Yet Archbishop Temple could write sarcastically and dismissively (in private correspondence, of course) about how Russian Orthodox bishops, unlike himself, were prepared to let themselves be used in a politically driven "propaganda stunt." At least the Russian clerics could plead powerlessness in the face of the secret police; the Anglican hierarchs had no such excuse.

An Innocent Abroad

The archbishop of York, Dr. Cyril Garbett, and his two companions arrived in Moscow on Sunday, September 19, remaining in the USSR for only ten days. The Kremlin made the most of the propaganda opportunities provided by the visit. On September 4, only two weeks before the arrival of the Anglican delegation, Stalin and Molotov met in the Kremlin with the leaders of the Russian Orthodox Church and granted them permission to convene a Holy Synod to select a new patriarch. The *sobor'* duly met on September 8, and on the 12th it elevated Sergii to the patriarchal throne, just in time to meet the Anglican visitors. The British ambassador, Sir Archibald Clark Kerr, informed the Foreign Office that more than 2,000 people attended the synod, either as participants or observers, "including a fair number of Red Army officers and soldiers." But he also noted that, other than a "brief announcement" in the foreign-language *Moscow News* of September 11, there had been "no public mention" of the new patriarch's election, or of the *Sobor's* meeting.[68]

This is by no means to suggest that Stalin chose to breathe new life into the Moscow Patriarchate solely for the effect that this would have on the visiting British archbishop; Soviet motives were, of course, far more complex and driven at least as much by domestic need as by the demands of international propaganda. Nonetheless, the selection of the patriarch less than a week before the arrival of Dr. Garbett was no mere coincidence; Sergii's return from Ulianovsk to Moscow had been timed so that he would be in the capital when the Anglican delegation arrived, and Stalin had urged Sergii to arrange his *sobor'* quickly so that he could greet his visitors as patriarch.[69] Curiously, although many historians have discussed the Soviets' reasons for reviving the Patriarchate, few even note the near simultaneous tour of the Anglican delegation to Moscow, and yet this was the weightiest foreign religious group to visit the USSR since the revolution of 1917.[70] The presence of the Anglicans in the Soviet Union just after the election of a new patriarch would focus world attention on religious matters and would enable Soviet propaganda organs to blazon its message around the globe that the USSR was the defender of freedom of conscience against the onslaught of Godless Nazism. Even more important, since the visiting clergymen were British, the more widely trusted BBC and the British press would act as a megaphone to give greater publicity to, and confer greater credibility on, the resurrection of the Patriarchate than it could hope to receive from Soviet propaganda alone.

The British government was happy to oblige; in a secret memorandum circulated to British newspaper editors, the Press and Censorship Division of the Ministry of Information stated that "His Majesty's Government attach considerable importance to the successful outcome" of the tour.[71] Furthermore, the fact that the other two members of the archbishop's delegation traveling to Moscow, Waddams and House, though clergy members, were in fact also representatives of the Ministry of Information and the BBC, ensured that the visit would get high-profile treatment. Finally, of course, the archbishop's very presence in the USSR, and his meetings with Patriarch Sergii, quite apart from anything Dr. Garbett might say, would convey the impression that the Anglican Church recognized and applauded as genuine this latest twist in Soviet religious policy.

Garbett's group pursued an active schedule during its brief stay in Moscow, visiting with the new patriarch and discussing wartime charity work of the two churches. Sergii noted the huge outpouring of gifts given by simple Russians to the Orthodox Church's fund-raising drives and said that "Many citizens brought valuables but many of the donors did not want their names to be known." Without being unduly cynical, one might think of several explanations for such modesty. Metropolitan Nikolai, always more overtly political than his superior, "delicately raised the question of the second front" over one lunch and later treated his guests to a sumptuous tea where, as the Reverend Waddams noted acidly, the group consumed a "very rich chocolate cake of a quality which has not appeared in England since before the war."[72]

In addition to two church services at the Bogoiavlenskii Cathedral, where the archbishop observed Russian Orthodox ceremonies, the group made an excursion to the New Jerusalem Monastery at Istra, not far from Moscow. The Soviets claimed that the Germans had desecrated the monastery, though some believed that it may also have been a victim of earlier Soviet atheist campaigns —the Soviets had certainly shut the monastery and used it as an anti-God museum at one time.[73] Whoever was responsible for the destruction, the walls of the monastery were daubed with Cyrillic slogans. According to Waddams's diary: "In several places on the wall there were quotations from Lenin. I asked [a Russian-speaking British diplomat] to discover what they said, and he was later surprised while reading them, by the bishop of Riazan. Riazan made a depreciating [sic] gesture, shrugging his shoulders as he looked towards the inscription, clearly signifying that of course we all agreed to look upon such things as nonsense." Unfortunately, owing to the interruption, Waddams was unable to have many of the slogans translated, and he recorded none of them in his diary; but he claimed that "The translations which I happened to get were not particularly anti-religious."[74]

The delegation did not confine its activities to religious ceremonies; Garbett had also stipulated before leaving Britain that he wished to tour a collective farm. As one Ministry of Information official put it, "The Archbishop is, of course, intensely interested in social matters."[75] The Soviets duly swept their visitors through a model collective farm, and, judging from Garbett's later statements, their efforts were well spent. At no time, according to the British records, did any member of the delegation so much as meet an ordinary Russian; all their contacts were with Soviet officials or trustworthy Russian Orthodox clergy, and their itinerary was strictly limited to those places the Communist authorities deemed safe for foreign eyes. Even had they been able to circulate freely about the Soviet capital, however, none of them could speak Russian, and at any rate the average Soviet citizen in Stalin's time was properly wary of contacts with foreigners.[76]

Some people might have been reluctant to issue sweeping judgments regarding a foreign country about which so little was known following a lightning tour during which the agents of the ruling dictatorial regime carefully managed the schedule. The archbishop of York, however, was not such a person; he apparently lacked this elementary sense of caution, or humility. Following his return to Britain, he held a press conference, seated next to Brendan Bracken, Britain's minister of information. Bracken's presence testified to the high degree of importance the British government attached to propaganda generated by the tour.

With only modest disclaimers, Garbett pronounced his opinions on various aspects of Soviet religion and life. After recounting the outlines of his tour and praising Russian hospitality, the archbishop declared that, based on his observations during his visits to churches in the Soviet capital (he had visited only two that were in operation), "There can be no doubts that worship within the churches is fully allowed [in the USSR]. The Orthodox prelates were emphatic about this." "I have never seen such a vast congregation," he continued; he estimated that 10,000 Russians were present in the cathedral or in the square outside during the service, and he recounted the enthusiastic greeting he had received from the throng. Garbett seemed anxious to refute the notion that only older Russians would risk government displeasure by attending church. Based on his observation of this unique instance of open worship, the archbishop declared confidently that most Russian believers were middle-aged or younger: "To say that congregations consist chiefly of the aged is sheer nonsense." He said that the number of open churches was increasing—which was true, though a very recent and complex development—and said that, although "there are large numbers [of Soviets] who conscientiously reject all belief in God," he detected a revival of interest in religion.

Garbett explained the reasons, as he saw them, for the Soviet government's new course on religious matters:

> Premier Stalin is a wise statesman, who recognises that religion is inherent in the majority of the Russian people; he has had to take from them in the national cause much that they value, but he feels that he can give them something in making it plain that there is no hindrance to their worship, and secondly, and I think this is important, the church is no longer the supporter of the old regime. It accepts loyally the present constitution. It has thrown itself heart and soul into the national cause.

In more direct words, the regime's letup on religion was Stalin's generous reward to an obedient population and a repentant church.

The archbishop noted that Soviet children "looked happy and healthy" and deduced from this that the Soviets took great care of the young. He admitted that he "was very interested in finding that the [Soviet] people are allowed to possess personal property of their own." He evidently had subscribed to the widely held, but mistaken, belief that in the USSR even such personal items as bicycles were collective property. But, having newly discovered that this was not the case, Garbett enthusiastically explained Soviet-Marxist theory in terms that might have been lifted from the works of Hewlett Johnson: "Russia is at its present stage a socialist, rather than a communist state," he said, "that is[,] while the means of production and distribution belong to the State, the individual may keep for his own use or dispose of as he thinks fit, whatever he has himself earned."

In the final words of his opening statement, the archbishop said that "However much we may condemn some of the methods used during and after the Revolution, and I think we should all condemn some of them, we should now watch with sympathy the working out of a great social and economic experiment [in the USSR], even though we may feel that much of it may be inapplicable to our own country." He did not, of course, elaborate what these objectionable methods were, though the clear implication of his remarks was that these unnamed abuses were now in the past.

Bracken then opened the floor to questions from the press, and Garbett misleadingly explained, among other things, that "Before the Revolution the Church was completely under the control of the State. With the Revolution the Church was both disestablished and disendowed and it now has the right to appoint its own Patriarch, its Bishops and to hold its own Council." He did not mention that for the first twenty years following the revolution the church did not enjoy these 'rights.' As for non-Orthodox denominations, Garbett claimed, dubiously and with no proof, that "The State is neutral and allows freedom to all other denominations." When asked "how . . . they treat the coloured question in Russia," Garbett at first responded frankly: "I am afraid I do not know the answer to that." Ignorance did not stop him, however; he continued, "but I believe that there is no discrimination of any sort or kind."

Closing the press conference, the minister of information thanked the archbishop for his remarks and for his services to the nation. Bracken, who was also a Conservative MP, a longtime friend of Churchill, and a major shareholder in the robustly capitalist *Financial Times*, said that "I believe myself that no better representative of England could have gone to Russia, no more sympathetic spirit could have approached that amazing new experiment." Garbett thanked the press and, having delivered his view on the whole range of Soviet questions, said humbly that "After all I was only ten days in Russia, I do not know the language and Russia is so vast that it needs several years."[77]

The archbishop's humility regarding the limits to his knowledge of Soviet life did not, however, prevent him from writing a long article for Lord Beaverbrook's *Daily Express*, in which he repeated most of his remarks from the press conference.[78] Nor did it stop him from issuing a news release through the Press Bureau of the Church of England in which he added a few further observations: once again noting that average Soviet citizens owned some personal property, he said, "The position has been well summed up when it was said 'there are many Russians who own motor cars, but there is no one who owns a share in a motor car company.'" (In fact, very few Russians owned automobiles. The production of motorcars in the USSR had begun less than ten years earlier, and almost all were owned by high-ranking officials, who might well be said to have controlled the factories.) Garbett gushed about the degree of economic equality supposedly attained in the Soviet Union. Although he allowed that "Neither in Russia nor anywhere else will we find everyone equal," he claimed that in the USSR "neither birth nor lack of money stand in the way of a man advancing to the highest posts. There is equality in educational opportunities, and there is no recognition of class distinctions." Clearly, in Garbett's mind these conditions stood in glaring contrast to the situation in Great Britain.

Although this had been the archbishop's first visit to the USSR, he judged that, so far as the lives of ordinary Russians was concerned, "from what I have read and seen and heard, I think there has been undoubted improvement, and if there had been no war it would have been still more marked." The USSR, he closed, "has great leaders, notable scientists, capable organisers, engineers and architects surpassed by no other country; brilliant writers and thinkers; and behind them a great mass of youthful people ready to live or die for their country as circumstances may require." The future of the world would depend on British "co-operation with this great and remarkable nation"; therefore, it was incumbent upon those who hoped for a better world to seek greater "understanding and friendship" with the Soviets "notwithstanding our deep divergencies on many questions."[79]

In view of Archbishop Garbett's almost complete ignorance of Soviet conditions before his visit, and given the short length of his stay in that country, he evidently believed himself to be a quick study. Nonetheless, the British press took the archbishop's remarks at face value, giving him high marks for acuity and judgment. The editors of the *Times* for instance (whose leader articles on Russia were for the most part penned by E. H. Carr), congratulated Garbett on his journey and linked his reception in the USSR to the resurrection of the Moscow Patriarchate. Speculating on the reasons for Stalin's new warmth toward the church, the article claimed that, "It will not be unfair to assume that one of the motives inspiring the decision . . . was a desire to remove a glaring discrepancy between the attitude of the Russian Government and that of its principal allies toward religion. . . . [I]t demonstrates the strength and sincerity of Russian purpose to sweep aside ancient prejudices and draw closer the bonds of friendship between" the USSR and the Western democracies. The article allowed that "some commentators" had argued that the revival of the Patriarchate had foreign policy undertones; Moscow might hope to tap Balkan Orthodox and Pan-Slav emotions in advance of the Red Army's approach to the peninsula. But the *Times*, seeing nothing malevolent here, viewed it as reassuring: "It may help to allay some anxieties," the article continued, "that Russian interest in countries with which her future relations must necessarily be close and intimate should be expressing itself through other than Communist channels," the unstated assumption being that the Russian church was somehow independent of the Soviet state. In the view of the *Times*, Soviet Communism was no longer so threatening as it had been during the early days of the revolution: "In the past seven or eight years the Soviet leaders have undertaken a sifting process in the ideas which became the accepted dogmas of the 1917 revolution." Thankfully, "Nothing that has happened precludes any modification in the social and economic principles of the revolution. But the lapse of time has established the distinction between these [essential] principles and the incidental accretions which adhered to them in the period of ferment and innovation." That hostility to religion, or to "metaphysics" of any sort, could be seen as an "incidental accretion" to materialist Marxism would have surprised Lenin or Stalin (to say nothing of Marx himself), but many other British papers, as well as the BBC, repeated the *Times* argument in its essentials.[80]

Following his return from the USSR, the archbishop of York visited the United States to spread the word about the resurrection of religion in the USSR and to discuss the role of the church in the war against Germany. He reached a wider audience than the average ecclesiastical visitor, speaking over a "nationwide radio hookup." He also made speeches and delivered lectures both in churches and at secular gatherings. "The Russian Church," he told Americans, "is enjoying a freedom such as it has not possessed for centuries."[81]

The Voice of London

The propaganda impact of the archbishop of York's visit to Moscow, and of the naming of a new Moscow patriarch, is difficult to estimate, because public impressions of the Soviet Union and the Russian church were, as always, being shaped simultaneously by a host of factors. Furthermore, the propaganda was directed at different target audiences: not only at citizens of Great Britain and the United States, but also—and perhaps even more urgently at this time—at people in Nazi-occupied East and Southeast Europe, which lay in the path of the advancing Red Army. London was central to the dispersal of this propaganda, owing to the vast British information network and the critical position of Peter Smollett. Absent the British role in publicizing the Moscow events, the revival of Russian Orthodoxy in the autumn of 1943 would have had a much more limited political impact.

In Britain itself, the people by and large viewed these events as one more piece of evidence that their Soviet ally was changing its ways, or perhaps even that these ways had never really been all that malevolent in the first place. The Ministry of Information's regional officers reported that the public "variously interpreted" religious developments in the USSR. Many people saw them as a sign that the Russians had "'gone back on religion.'" "[S]ome ask if [the apparent liberalization] is genuine," the weekly confidential government report of public opinion noted, "while others are puzzled as to its meaning, and ask if there is religious freedom in Russia. Whether regarded as genuine or due to 'expediency', however, the move is widely welcomed as 'the answer to the many who still regard Russia as godless.'" The archbishop's tour of Moscow "has caused little comment," the report concluded. "Some are pleased, as his visit is thought likely to help in dispelling the 'bogey that our Ally is anti-religious.'"[82]

It is little wonder that average British subjects came to believe that Soviet religious persecution was merely a "bogey," because this is what their propaganda mandarins were tirelessly telling them. Things had come a long way since the days of the Nazi-Soviet Pact, when the Ministry of Information routinely portrayed the Soviet Union as the earthly equivalent of Hades. Now, owing in large part to the persistent behind-the-scenes efforts of Smollett, the magnificent informational apparatus of the British government was mobilized to spread politically expedient misinformation in a manner that Moscow's propagandists could only dream about.

As ever, the most important propaganda tool was the BBC, which gave religious developments in Moscow the highest priority. Soviet intelligence highly estimated the power and reach of British broadcasting; consequently, as Smollett's NKVD superior noted, "naturally the BBC was among [Smollett's] favourite targets."[83] Following the archbishop's visit to Moscow, Smollett encouraged the BBC to broadcast a series of programs in English, as well as the languages of Eastern Europe and the Balkans, explaining the ostensible significance of the Russian Orthodox Church's resurrection. These broadcasts gave the Moscow events a political spin that could scarcely have been more suited to Soviet political needs had they been composed in the Lubianka itself.

According to this new interpretation, since the times of Peter I in the early eighteenth century the tsarist state had entirely subordinated the church to secular authority. Early Bolshevik revolutionaries—now recast by British broadcasters as moderate reformers—had been compelled to attack the church, not because of any atheist impulse on their part, but rather owing to the church's close association with the old monarchical, exploitative order: "When the Church was the biggest landowner in Russia it met the fate of other landowners in the early days of Bolshevik reform. But when the Soviet reorganisation was completed, and the Constitution was set up in 1936, one of the provisions was freedom of worship—freedom for all religious faiths."[84] "The war," the broadcast continued, "has speeded up the reabsorption of the Church into the main stream of Russian national life." The BBC then quoted the international mouthpiece of the Russian church, Metropolitan Nikolai, who gave European Christians their marching orders: "'I have seen the terrible traces of Fascism's satanic struggle against the Church,' he stated. 'Hitler is the grimmest enemy of Christianity. Hundreds of Russian churches have been desecrated by the Germans. The fight against these enemies is the most sacred duty of every Christian.'" Even Stalin was recast as a leader of democratic sensibilities, responsive to the desires of his people. The reestablishment of the Holy Synod, the BBC continued, was "[a]bove all . . . a sign of Soviet stability and strength. Stalin is practising toleration in the spirit of the four freedoms [of Roosevelt]. He recognises the trend of public opinion in Russia, the genuine religious revival. In the period of total effort by all the forces of the Russian nation, the Church is again taking its place, both in the national struggle against the country's enemies, and in the work of reconstruction."[85] In a broadcast beamed to Yugoslavia the following day, the BBC labeled Stalin's apparent reconciliation with the church "a decisive act not only of toleration but of sympathy."[86]

In yet another broadcast to the Balkans, the BBC quoted Hewlett Johnson, the "Red Dean" of Canterbury. At the outset of the Soviet-German war, it will be recalled, the Ministry of Information had shunned Johnson as a pariah, owing to his shameless apologetics for Stalinism. Now he was being quoted as a serious authority on Soviet affairs, demonstrating just how far two years of alliance with the USSR had shifted the rules of the game. According to the Dean, the rebirth of Russian Orthodoxy was "in line with the whole of Soviet policy. . . . As they get stronger they can give wider liberties." British broadcasters picked up Johnson's theme, apparently eager to dispel any notion that Stalin had been forced by circumstances beyond his control to make concessions to the public or the church. The Soviet government had undertaken "the final cessation of all interference with religious worship," the BBC assured its listeners at home and on the continent. "Today the Orthodox priest no longer feels himself an outlaw in his own country. There is room for him too and for the contribution of his church in the new Russia." "Tolerance," the BBC declared authoritatively, "springs from confidence. . . . It springs from [the] feeling that the Soviet regime has finally proved its political stability." Moscow's newly visible spirit of religious tolerance was not dictated by the exigencies of war but rather had been growing steadily since 1934 at least. "The new Constitution of 1936 with its more liberal provisions was a landmark in this process of development; the abolition of the Comintern earlier this year was another." The resurrection of the church was "the latest sign of renaissance of the Russian people who are emerging from the testing time of the past 25 years with a deepened appreciation of life and an unshakeable confidence in their own strength," the BBC concluded bathetically.[87]

For the Soviets, these BBC broadcasts, targeted at both the domestic and the wider European audience, constituted propaganda beyond price. Throughout Nazi-occupied Europe, people who distrusted broadcasts from the totalitarian regimes in Berlin and Moscow instead tuned in to the BBC, the voice of democratic Britain, often risking the death penalty at the hands of the Nazis should they be discovered doing so. In the instances cited here, popular trust in the BBC's devotion to truth was sadly misplaced. The BBC's paroting of the latest Soviet propaganda line on religion amounted to little more than a litany of half-truths and lies, and British broadcasters knew this perfectly well. They had willingly exploited the legacy of Soviet religious repression when it suited their political purposes to do so; now, through the wizardry of radio, they transformed the Bolsheviks and Stalin into moderate democrats, securely in control of a loyal people, responsive to their subjects' needs.

The message of such broadcasts for Eastern Europe and the Balkans was very clear: the inhabitants of the region had no reason to fear that the advancing Red Army would export Communism and atheism. According to the BBC, in the Soviet Union itself Stalin was hard at work curbing the excesses he had inherited from the early days of the revolution, negotiating a modus vivendi with the church, and closing the revolutionary Comintern. The Soviet dictator was quickly becoming less a Communist than a traditional Russian leader—albeit an authoritarian, tough-minded, avuncular one.

The effectiveness of such propaganda varied from person to person, but there can be no doubt that it had a significant impact. Jozsef Cardinal Mindszenty later wrote that, as the Red Army swept into Eastern Europe, he debated Soviet intentions with his fellow Catholic clergy, a group that one might have thought would be nearly unanimous in its distrust of the USSR. This was not the case, however. Mindszenty himself had firsthand experience of the Communists from the closing period of the Great War and did not trust them at all, but his friend, Bishop Janos Mikes, was more optimistic:

> Bishop Mikes had listened to foreign radio broadcasts and believed that Russian communism had changed and no longer threatened the Church. His remarks at the time were proof of the unfortunate fact that responsible leaders of our people did not know how to judge Soviet intentions correctly. They naively believed that the western allies of the Soviet Union had the power to prevent ideological and territorial expansion of bolshevism. Such a hope was natural enough, for at the moment the country was suffering under Nazi rule and longing for liberation from it.[88]

The importance of British broadcasts to Eastern Europe must not be underestimated. The final years of the war brought a bewildering rush of events. As

Czeslaw Milosz has written of East Central Europe: "Th[e] war was much more devastating there than in the countries of Western Europe. It destroyed not only their economies, but also a great many values that had seemed till then unshakeable."[89] Oppressed by the hated Nazis, frightened by advancing Stalinism, cut loose from the moorings of traditional institutions and discredited domestic political authorities, which were being swept away by the war, Eastern Europeans looked toward the Western Allies in "despair mixed with a residue of hope."[90] Amid of this confusing situation, when the seemingly authoritative radio voice of Britain announced that the USSR was changing its ways, many people believed this—or at least wanted to believe it. As the example of Mindszenty demonstrates, not everyone was convinced, but pro-Soviet propaganda drove wedges into the population, forestalling the coalescence of groups that might otherwise have resisted Soviet power and persuading many people that might have been reluctant to collaborate with Communist parties that the risk of doing so had abated.

As for the propagators of these broadcasts, not everyone in the Ministry of Information was comfortable with the transmission of such falsehoods. The Reverend Herbert Waddams, who had accompanied the archbishop of York to Moscow and was not himself averse to a certain level of wishful thinking about religion in the USSR, wrote to an associate that "Quite frankly these B.B.C. broadcasts on the subject of the election of the Patriarch & Holy Synod make me sick." The broadcasts' description of the synod as " 'the Governing body of the Russian Orthodox Church,' " when the atheist Soviet authorities clearly remained in control, "gives an entirely misleading impression." The portrayals of the Soviet system as friendly to religious faith, he concluded, "are ill-judged and badly balanced."[91]

Waddams, and others in the know who deplored the falsification of the Soviet record on religion, reserved their qualms for confidential correspondence with fellow officials. At the same time, Smollett continued to push the propaganda bounds to their limit, all the while working to convey the impression that he, too, was appalled by the excesses of overly pro-Soviet propaganda. He countered complaints from his colleagues about the BBC by writing disingenuously: "I agree, but a) have we any real power over the proper authority inside B.B.C.? b) who is the proper authority & is there one? c) will it be of lasting value if we check?"[92] Although he promised to pursue the matter at a later date, Smollett clearly did nothing to restrain the BBC.[93]

In fact, the Ministry of Information was never reticent about restraining the BBC when it was determined to do so; in the summer of 1941, for instance, it had insisted on the removal of the BBC Moscow correspondent when he had suggested that Stalin's voice sounded tremulous during the dictator's first radio address to the Soviet people following the Nazi invasion.[94] Far from reining in enthusiastic broadcasters, Smollett was eager to spur them on. A month after the selection of Patriarch Sergii, he was again at work. The BBC's director of European broadcasts asked Smollett to "get in touch with Orthodox dignitaries in the Near East" to obtain statements in support of the Russian Orthodox Church and its new head. "The Nazis," he continued, "are clearly, frightened by this event and are trying to cause doubt in Orthodox Communities." In the BBC's view, however, only certain religious leaders should be asked to express their opinions: "Unfortunately the Roman Catholic circles are not very pleased about the Moscow Patriarch, so that their cooperation in the Near East is not to be expected."[95]

Smollett immediately ordered his subordinates to track down "information about Orthodox dignitaries in the Near or Middle East, who can be expected to express themselves favourably."[96] He then informed the BBC that "I am finding out who among [Orthodox hierarchs] would be most likely to say the right thing, and will then ask our Middle East office to obtain the material you require. . . . I personally think this an important matter and will give every support."[97] This was, of course, more than Smollett's mere personal preference; his Moscow superiors were working hard to exploit the Russian Orthodox Church's political capital in the Balkans and Eastern Mediterranean, motivated in part by a desire to counter Catholic influence.[98]

Unfortunately for Smollett, Eastern Orthodox hierarchs were properly cautious about events in Moscow. While supportive expressions were easily obtained from Patriarch Christophoros of Alexandria, who could be pressured since he resided in British-occupied Egypt, British officials worried that "it will not be an easy thing to obtain appropriate statements from the other Greek Orthodox Patriarchs in the Middle East. The Patriarch of Constantinople is virtually under Turkish control, which means that he cannot be approached in the matter. The Patriarch of Antioch and the Patriarch of Jerusalem have so far not given any evidence of their friendly sentiments towards Moscow."[99] Britain's propagandists were not about to be deterred: instead, they issued Christophoros's misleading statement that "It must not be thought that the restoration of the Holy Synod is a political device imposed by circumstances. On the contrary it is due to an outspoken declaration of the national faith. Long before the dissolution of the Third International [the Comintern] the Orthodox Church had assumed its rightful place."[100] The BBC soon broadcast the patriarch of Alexandria's remarks, which were also circulated to newspapers, conveying the incorrect impression that the Eastern Orthodox world stood four-square behind the decisions of the Moscow *sobor'*, when in fact it remained divided.[101]

Four months later, and with Smollett's promises to restrain exuberant broadcasters a distant memory, the BBC was still transmitting breathless commentary on Russian Orthodoxy. Timed to coincide with Orthodox Easter celebrations, British radio aired a program, complete with melodramatic instrumental and choral music as well as earnest quotations from the Orthodox liturgy, Fedor Dostoevskii, and the Russian religious philosopher Sergei Bul'gakov. The announcer, Robert Speaight, proclaimed that the Russian Orthodox Church had "compromised its independence" before the revolution. With the church in thrall to the state, the Russian people's mystical "hunger for community and thirst for social justice turned into what we know as 'Communism,' and denied the faith that had once sanctioned it." Bolshevism had thus been the fruit of the church's own moral failures. With Orwellian logic, Speaight said that "the militant atheists of the Russian Revolution, by the very act of proscribing the Church, set it free. The cost was terrible, but the Church of Russia stood revealed in the nakedness and poverty of the Gospel."

"We do not want to exaggerate," Speaight said—rather late in the game in light of the backstage maneuverings between the BBC and the Ministry of Information. "The freedom of the Church in Russia is only a relative freedom; it is not free as the Christian churches are free in Britain and America." Nonetheless, all the signs from Moscow pointed in a hopeful direction. "It is a fact, and a fact of profound political importance, that a common allegiance to the Christian faith is the strongest link between the representatives of the Western European countries and the half-Asiatic power of Russia."[102] Thus, one of the principal dividing lines separating the USSR from its Western Allies—their radically opposed attitudes toward religion and freedom of conscience—was miraculously transformed into the "strongest link" connecting the supposedly semi-Asiatic Russian masses with their brethren in the West.

It would be simplistic to argue that Smollett had somehow singlehandedly hijacked British radio and transformed it into a mouthpiece for Soviet propaganda. His game was much more subtle, and the system within which he worked much too complex, for that. Instead, Smollett was always careful to mask his own views, sympathetically clucking his tongue when his associates objected to specific instances where the press or radio had indulged in excessive flattery of the USSR, or outright factual misstatement. In such cases, he invariably shrugged his shoulders and pretended that very little could be done, or argued that not much harm had resulted from this or that instance of misinformation.

All the while, he continued to probe for soft spots within the system, playing on the very real urgency to counter German propaganda, using people who were favorably disposed toward the Soviet Union, or who were overworked, naive, or uncritically enthusiastic about the alliance. His chief asset was the ineffable spirit of the wartime alliance, which fostered admiration of the Soviet peoples' martial achievements and suppressed critical thinking about the Stalinist system—or at least stifled its public expression. In this extraordinary milieu, Smollett was able to hide in plain view, even managing to appear rather moderate compared to some of his colleagues in the Ministry of Information.

Although allegations that Smollett was a Soviet mole began to appear in print many years before the end of the Cold War and the opening of Soviet archives finally confirmed his secret role, he has never attracted the attention of scholars or popular writers on espionage.[103] Instead, he has always been overshadowed by his more notorious contemporaries, the so-called Cambridge Five—Guy Burgess, Anthony Blunt, Donald McLean, John Cairncross, and Kim Philby. These better-known spies have the enhanced attraction of being native Britons and having betrayed their backgrounds of privilege and education. Their espionage was also of a more traditional kind: Burgess gave suitcases bulging with pilfered Foreign Office documents to his handlers, Philby betrayed covert operations against the Albanians, McLean revealed Anglo-American cable traffic, Cairncross assisted Soviet atomic espionage, and Blunt performed as a recruiter, only to retire from espionage, accepting a cushy post as the queen's art adviser.

Smollett, by contrast, sprang from obscure, continental origins; he was not even born British, and he certainly betrayed no privileged class background. His life and career lack entirely the romantic, antiheroic patina of the Cambridge spies. Indeed, it might even be questioned whether his activities amounted to actual espionage and treason at all. Although a number of purloined top-secret British documents that lie in the Soviet archives passed over his desk before winding up in Moscow, the documents do not reveal who stole them, and no proof has yet emerged that Smollett was the person who did so; another person, perhaps Burgess, may have been the culprit. Although he concealed his Communist affiliations, most of what Smollett achieved within the Ministry of Information was the product of open argument and was done with the consent and agreement of his colleagues.

Of Smollett, it is fair to ask the blunt historiographical question: so what? Even though he was a Soviet mole, did he actually change the trajectory of events (a question often asked of espionage in general)? Given the fact that Smollett had no power to enforce his will, and for the most part had to carry the day through force of argument, how significant were his efforts? One of the very few historians to look at Smollett has concluded that the wave of pro-Soviet enthusiasm that swept over Britain and the United States was much too large a phenomenon to be traced to the work of an obscure Austrian Communist mole, and so he dismisses Smollett in a few pages of an otherwise detailed study.[104]

Cast in such apocalyptic terms, the conclusion is obvious. Absent Smollett, there would still have been a wartime "red romance." But the same diminishing, almost Tolstoian, standard could be applied to virtually all but the most towering historical figures; at most, individuals are only capable of giving great events a shove in a certain direction. This Smollett certainly did. One person whose judgment on such matters deserves a hearing believes Smollett to have been a most effective agent indeed. Oleg Gordievskii, who defected from the Soviet KGB to the British in the early 1980s, believes that Smollett—for all his obscurity—was actually a more significant agent than the Cambridge spies.[105] This could be dismissed as just another instance among many of an intelligence officer misunderstanding the culture of the target country and overestimating the importance and impact of his own profession. In this case, however, there is every reason to believe that Gordievskii is correct. Smollett operated in highly favorable circumstances, perhaps even unique ones for a mole. He was able to visit the Soviet embassy openly and without embarrassment and, once there, to confer in secrecy with his masters. He could thus receive or pass on sensitive material almost at will. And he worked indefatigably. Such large-scale propaganda stunts as the 1943 visit of the archbishop of York to Moscow, or the mass rally in London's Albert Hall celebrating the twenty-fifth anniversary of the Bolshevik Revolution, would most probably not have occurred at all but for his dogged advocacy within the British government. After Archbishop Nikolai suggested an exchange of ecclesiastical visits in September 1942,[106] even with Smollett's pushing, the visit took a year to plan and organize. Certainly, had Smollett's office been occupied by a skeptic about the USSR, the exchanges would not have received the critical publicity throughout Europe that they did. Orders might come from on high, from the prime minister on down, to cease overly indulgent propaganda about the USSR, but Smollett always managed to appear to be enforcing these instructions while in fact flouting them whenever possible. By no means did Smollett ignite the fires of wartime popular enthusiasm for the USSR, but he stoked them constantly, and, whenever his superiors' attention was diverted, he surreptitiously squirted gasoline on the coals. The flame thus flared much higher, brighter, and longer than it would have without his careful tending.[107]

In wartime, every objective reporter should be shot.

— Ilia Ehrenburg

I explained to him [Stalin], what doubtlessly he already knew better than I, that the press was owned by millionaires and reflected very largely their attitude and directed public opinion in the channels they desired.

— Hewlett Johnson, dean of Canterbury, August, 1945

Guardians of the Truth

From the likes of Britain's Lord Beaverbrook and America's William Randolph Hearst to the Australian Rupert Murdoch, millionaire press barons wielded enormous power throughout the twentieth century, shaping news coverage to suit their political and economic interests, or simply to boost readership. Hewlett Johnson's comments to Stalin, quoted in an epigraph to this chapter, were not entirely off the mark. What the dean did not know, or more likely chose to ignore, was that the man to whom he was speaking, Stalin, headed a regime that manipulated the press in ways that made Western newspaper tycoons look like amateurs in comparison. Soviet publications, such as *Pravda* and *Izvestiia*, both of which had millions of readers, were, of course, completely controlled by Communist political authorities and reflected only those glimpses of reality that the Kremlin judged suitable for the eyes of common Soviet readers; the rest was pure fiction. The impact of these publications outside the USSR was minimal, but the Soviets did not only control their own domestic press. During the war, they were able to influence greatly the coverage of news in Western newspapers and on the radio as well.

Members of the press like to see themselves as watchdogs of the truth, as guardians of the public interest against the excesses and distortions of government. In this romanticized view, the function of the so-called fourth estate is to provide the voting public with a clear picture of reality, enabling it to judge soberly the actions of government and to make informed decisions. The truth has seldom been so clear-cut, least of all during wartime. By and large, press reporting during the war was of high quality when compared with that of previous wars, but then that is not much of a claim. The eastern front was another matter entirely. Without the check that might have been supplied by accurate reporting, the power of Soviet propaganda was enhanced tremendously, because it poured into an information vacuum. The blame for this cannot all be laid at the door of Soviet censorship. A variety of factors shaped press coverage of the Soviet Union during the war. American and British reporters' commitment to the war effort, and their realization that the bulk of the German army was engaged in the East, meant that they had no desire to dwell on the negative aspects of Stalinism for fear of undermining the Soviet war effort. Ideological sympathy for Soviet socialism clouded some reporters' perceptions or caused them to ignore unpleasant realities. Finally, blackmail, venality, careerism, and simple slothfulness were also significant factors shaping the coverage of the eastern front.

"Use Foreign Correspondents"

Konstantin Umanskii had told his fellow propagandists and diplomats that they must try to "use foreign correspondents" as much as possible to get their message across to the Western public. In the era before television, few sources of information were more potent than the weekly photo magazines. Therefore, the arrival of one of America's great photojournalists in the USSR was the propaganda equivalent of manna from heaven. In the spring of 1941, more than three months before the Nazi invasion of the USSR, the editors of the American magazine *Life* agreed to send one of their star photographers, Margaret Bourke-White, to the USSR, believing "that Russia was the coming key country in the march of the war."[1] Bourke-White had visited the Soviet Union eleven years before, but Soviet censors had then prevented her from taking any photographs in the country. Nonetheless, she wrote a book about her visit that was positive in tone to the first five-year plan then unfolding in Stalin's empire.[2]

More than six decades on, this book seems a rather favorable, even uncritical, treatment of the USSR in which many of the darker aspects of Soviet collectivization and industrialization go unmentioned, perhaps even unnoticed. Curiously enough, the Soviets were less than satisfied. A VOKS official would

Metropolitan Aleksandr Vvedenskii, of the Obnovlencheskii, or Renovationist, Church. (Photograph by Margaret Bourke-White, first published in Margaret Bourke-White, *Shooting the Russian War*; reprinted with permission of the heirs of Margaret Bourke-White.)

Metropolitan Vvedenskii giving the benediction, summer 1941. (Photograph by Margaret Bourke-White, first published in Margaret Bourke-White, *Shooting the Russian War*; reprinted with permission of the heirs of Margaret Bourke-White.)

Soviet soldiers pose in front of the war-damaged cathedral in Yelnia, near Smolensk. (Photograph by Margaret Bourke-White, first published in Margaret Bourke-White, *Shooting the Russian War*; reprinted with permission of the heirs of Margaret Bourke-White.)

Worshipers in the Obnovlencheskaia Sobor'. (Photograph by Margaret Bourke-White, first published in Margaret Bourke-White, *Shooting the Russian War*; reprinted with permission of the heirs of Margaret Bourke-White.)

Orthodox bishops, including Acting Patriarch Sergii, conduct a service, Bogoiavlenskaia Sobor' (Cathedral of the Epiphany), Moscow, summer 1941. (Photograph by Margaret Bourke-White, first published in Margaret Bourke-White, *Shooting the Russian War*; reprinted with permission of the heirs of Margaret Bourke-White.)

later write dismissively that Bourke-White was a "typical middle American." This was supposedly proved by her focus on the food, clothing, and living standards of Soviet citizens. "Only this is for her a criterion of a progressive society." According to Bourke-White, the USSR was a country of "great surprises, of a great experiment." Although she showed a certain sympathy for the Soviet Union, according to VOKS she treated it almost as though it were some island to which civilization was only then arriving.[3]

Despite their reservations about her work, Soviet authorities allowed her to return in 1941, and this time they permitted her to bring her camera equipment—weighing in at six-hundred pounds. It was a good decision. Bourke-White arrived in Moscow at the beginning of May, and as fate would have it she was still there when Barbarossa erupted, staying for the first four months of the Soviet-German war. With her magnificent photographic talents, and her clear sympathy for the "Soviet experiment," Bourke-White would provide propaganda beyond price, first in *Life* magazine and later in a book entitled *Shoot-*

ing the Russian War. Unlike many other war correspondents, she would be allowed to make a visit near the front line, to a region that would soon fall to the Nazis. All the while she recorded her experiences in a series of striking pictures.

Her writing has a breathless, quasi-anthropological cast to it, as though the author is visiting some strange land peopled by curious anthropoids. "Red Army soldiers," she writes for instance, "have that healthy, red-blooded look that comes from having plenty of meat to eat. . . . These Russian soldiers are tough and come from hardy peasant stock. The Russian peasant loves his land, and therefore winning back the land from the invader has a deep and sacred meaning."[4] One would never get the impression from reading Bourke-White that, during the months of her stay, the Red Army was reeling in one of history's great retreats, with millions of Soviet soldiers already captive to the Nazi invaders.

Bourke-White's book contains a pertinent chapter on religion, entitled "God in Russia."[5] She reprints her portraits of the leading figures of Russian Orthodoxy, including both Metropolitan Sergii as well as Metropolitan Aleksandr Vvedenskii, then still the head of the so-called Living Church. "When I heard that the priests of Moscow were praying for victory," Bourke-White wrote, "I decided the time had come to go to church." There she witnessed Sergii delivering a sermon in support of the war: " 'If our Mother Church is dear to us,' intoned Sergei, 'do we not hold equally dear our mother country—a country where people are building life on the basis of truth and good will!' " Bourke-White witnessed funerals and baptisms, wondering "whether these youngsters would ever even hear that they had started their lives with a bath in a font," since "the young rarely go to church these days, even in other parts of the world."

Although she noted the incongruity of Orthodox priests praying for the victory of an atheist state, Bourke-White was easily satisfied on this score:

> When we found the Dean of the Cathedral I tried to draw him out on this seeming inconsistency. "No one interferes with us," he told me; "we are quite free. The Church receives a license from the government and, within church walls, the [acting] Patriarch and the archbishops are supreme." As we talked it became plain that he believed if Hitler won the war, the Church would be obliterated altogether, so that a Soviet victory was vital.

The American visitor then met the aged Sergii, who, she assured the reader, "at close range looked quite real," as though she had feared that he was some sort of waxwork. Having tea with the bishops, Bourke-White noted that "Patriarch

Sergei was as deaf and jolly as anybody's great-grandfather." Nothing seemed to shake the photographer's determination to see only the bright side. When one Soviet militiaman saw her photographing a church, for instance, he "telephoned police headquarters to see if I had a permit." This did not trouble her: "It is a proof of the authority of the Church over its own affairs that he was instructed that within church walls it was for the bishops and not the militia to say whether I might take photographs." Thus reassured, she saw no contradiction when she noted that, following this incident, the Foreign Commissariat thought it necessary to issue special instructions on religious questions to foreign correspondents, "an unprecedented procedure for the Soviet Foreign Office," she wrote proudly.

Not limiting herself to the majority church, Bourke-White also visited Pastor Mikhail Orlov, President of the All-Union Council of Evangelists and a Baptist minister. The American cut right to the heart of the matter, asking Orlov what he thought of Lenin. Replying through the ever present state-supplied translator (for Bourke-White knew no Russian), Orlov replied that "'We consider the social program of Lenin [to be] very close to that of the Bible.'" "The Baptists and evangelists have the strongest possible reasons for working to further a Soviet victory," Bourke White wrote, because they were freer under Stalin's rule than they had ever been under the tsars. Only after the disestablishment of the Orthodox Church by the Bolsheviks did "singing Baptists, armed with hymnbooks, begin spreading their faith through the land"—surely a unique view of Lenin and Stalin's USSR.

Visiting an antireligious museum (shortly before these were shut down for the war's duration), Bourke-White noted that, in addition to being told how religion had impeded scientific progress throughout the ages, Soviet children guided through the museum were also shown "many fine examples of religious paintings [which are] kept there for study." Ending on a positive note, she wrote, "The People's Commissariat for Education believes that religion will eventually die out; but in the meantime no one persecutes or interferes with whatever worshippers wish to go to church, for the Soviet Constitution adheres strictly to its provision which ensures to citizens freedom of conscience."

Relying on Bourke-White's account, a reader would never know the sad history of Soviet religious persecution, nor that a widespread revival of religious faith was at that very time underway in the USSR, despite the continuing state-imposed barriers. Rather, the impression she conveyed was that religion was a relic of the past and that the Soviet state looked on it rather bemusedly as an antiscientific, empty doctrine that would inevitably disappear as modern youth imbibed the correct understanding of the material world. The Soviets could happily tolerate religion, an insignificant and unthreatening remnant of an unlamented past.

Little wonder, then, that Soviet officials were satisfied with Bourke-White's second book about their country. They found the tone to be "completely different" from her first effort. "The chief object in this second book," a Central Committee figure wrote, "is the correct representation of the role and significance of the Soviet people in the struggle for democracy and progress, a correct understanding of the people, a recognition of their power and unity." Furthermore, "A comparison of Bourke-White's two books shows how the role of the USSR in world events of the last decade and, most importantly, its participation in the second world war, has changed the consciousness of the middle American, teaching her feelings of respect [and] admiration in relation to our country and its people."[6]

Margaret Bourke-White's striking photographs of the USSR would reach hundreds of thousands of viewers via *Life* magazine and her book, and they constituted the strongest visual image many people had at that time of Soviet life. If Bourke-White's was the earliest and most influential Western photographic record of the USSR at war, her counterpart in print and over the air waves was Alexander Werth. Werth, unlike so many of his fellow Moscow correspondents, including Bourke-White, spoke fluent Russian; he wrote for Reuter's news service, later in the war for London's *Sunday Times,* and, most important, he wrote regular broadcast texts from Moscow for the BBC. Werth himself estimated that, quite apart from his wire service writing, his broadcasts reached a huge audience of between 15 and 20 million.[7] His impact on the Western understanding of the war in the East is arguably more significant than that of any other writer, since, in addition to his wartime journalism, he would later author a best-selling account of the Soviet-German war, entitled *Russia at War*— part memoir, part history—which remains in print more than thirty years after its publication. An extraordinarily vivid and readable account, it remains a very useful historical source. Nonetheless, his book, like his wartime reporting, is selective.

Throughout the war, in his broadcasts and writing, Alexander Werth took an indulgent view of the Stalinist regime's many shortcomings. He justified Stalin's prewar purges as a necessary preparation for war.[8] He downplayed the Red Army's headlong retreat from western Ukraine, guessing that it was planned "to avoid a pitched battle on the unfavourable terrain of the Western Ukraine; where, by the way, in the absence of woods, there aren't many opportunities for partisan activity."[9] In fact, as Werth well knew, Ukraine becomes both flatter

and less wooded the further *east* one goes; and partisan activity would flour-
ish in this very area—first against the Nazis and later against the returning
Soviets.

When, in September 1941, the Soviets deported to Uzbekistan about 600,000
"Volga Germans,"[10] fearing that they might constitute a "fifth column," Werth
was unbothered by this particular instance of Soviet cruelty. The deportations
were "a realistic approach," he wrote. "No doubt, it's going to be hard on a lot of
innocent people, but still _____ [*sic*]." The fact that Western correspondents reported the deportations, by contrast, disturbed him far more: "[Philip] Jordan
has made a big story of what he called 'the greatest forced migration in history';
and the *News Chronicle* have naturally splashed it all over the place. Very unwise, I think. It'll only encourage the anti-Reds and also our more tender-
hearted Liberals to talk about Soviet brutality."[11]

In all his wartime reporting, Werth routinely downplayed the significance of
ethnic or religious tensions in the USSR. When word reached Moscow that
many people in the Baltic states welcomed the Germans, for instance, he wrote
that "Estonia and Latvia aren't really *countries*" anyway. In mid-August, when
the Germans arranged the reopening of Smolensk Cathedral, long since closed
by the Soviets, Werth dismissed the whole affair contemptuously as nothing
more than a propaganda stunt.[12] The Nazis had indeed arranged the event for
its propaganda value, and they did not give a fig for the Russian people's interests; but Werth was doing his readers and listeners no service by refusing to explain why the Germans were able to exploit the genuine beliefs of the Russian
population under their control. Rather than assuming a modicum of intelligence among his audience, he and other correspondents like him, stooped to
producing counterpropaganda.

Werth did more than that. In July 1941 he actually composed a memorandum, which he sent to the Foreign Office and Ministry of Information, entitled
"possible propaganda points in dealing with Russia." In this remarkable document, he repeated many of the assertions just quoted, but the point he returned
to time and again was that British propaganda must "be essentially realistic" by
downplaying the differences between the Soviet Union and Britain: "The Russians don't talk of us as capitalists, still less as imperialists; nor should we emphasize Bolshevism and Communism." At any rate, he continued, "Russia is a
Communist country only in name," having long since become "a national en-
tity, rather than . . . the fountain-head of the Communist revolution." He acknowledged that "Awkward questions may of course arise, in connexion with
Stalin's past record. Regarding the [purge] trials, it may be well to suggest that,
inexcusable as they are from a liberal point of view, they represent an aspect of

Stalin's 'realism,'" since by this means he cleansed his country of radical Communists as well as potential quislings. The best way to overcome British popular suspicions of Communism was to concentrate on the riches of Russian culture, especially music—Mussorgsky, Borodin, Rimsky-Korsakov, and Tchaikovsky. "It is also very important that this kind of propaganda," Werth wrote, "which may seem childish in some ways, should not be sabotaged by certain White Russian elements in the Monitoring service of the BBC, or by Nazi or semi-Nazi agents like certain 'Ukrainian nationalists.'" Apparently, Werth favored a purge of his own in the BBC. Finally, he insisted that the British press should stifle the urge to register surprise at Soviet staying power and that it should censor itself: "[W]e should, if possible, refrain, for the time being, from indulging in the luxury of making jokes about the Ogpu [predecessor of the NKVD], points of similarity between the soviet and nazi regimes and the like" because the Soviets "are very touchy people" and "[w]ithout the Russians the victory could only have been a very slow one, perhaps an infinitely slow one."[13]

The decision to overlook differences between the Soviet regime and the democracies, the grim determination to insist, in the face of the facts, that Stalin's government "has raised (or reduced) Russia to the condition of a *country*, with nationalism as the keynote, not very different from other countries," foreordained, of course, that Werth and other reporters who subscribed to his notions of wartime journalism would not report the full truth about the Soviet Union. By failing to do so, they fostered Western public misconceptions about their Soviet ally, conferred on Soviet propaganda much greater credibility than it otherwise would have had, and helped to create unrealistic expectations about Stalin and his regime that would come crashing down after the war.

The behavior of Werth in his reporting from Moscow makes a mockery of the claim that the BBC was independent of the government, a mantra repeated endlessly when it wished to dodge responsibility. In reality, it worked hand-in-glove with the authorities when it chose to do so, but it always tried to hide this.[14] The Soviets were fully aware of these cozy arrangements through their espionage network and could only have been confirmed in their opinion that Western protestations of press freedom were a sham, merely masking the hidden levers of government and class control.

Not all reporters in Moscow adopted Werth's methods. If they did not, however, they soon found that they had little news to report, and Soviet censors would regularly shred their stories. American and British editors understood the restrictions on honest reporting from the USSR, but the lure of having a Moscow correspondent, purportedly delivering news hot from the scene of action, proved almost impossible for many of them to resist. The Moscow byline conferred a degree of spurious legitimacy to stories about the eastern front; but in truth journalists stationed in the Soviet capital often knew less about political, military, diplomatic, and even social developments on their own doorstep than did their counterparts stationed many thousands of miles away from the USSR. Certainly, the Moscow press corps was not free to report everything it did know.

In September 1944 Paul Winterton, the Moscow correspondent for the British *News Chronicle* and a regular broadcaster for the BBC,[15] wrote two lengthy, fascinating letters to his employers back in London, in which he poured out his heart about the tribulations of Western reporters trying to practice their craft in the wartime Soviet Union. These letters are probably the most insightful description of the restrictions under which Western reporters labored in the Soviet capital. Winterton wrote that Soviet authorities rarely allowed reporters to visit areas near the front line, and "our only news source is the Soviet press, and this is colourless, vague and always out of date." The "dim intelligence" of Soviet censors delayed the filing of even those stories that reflected well on the USSR. Members of the press had tried "individually and collectively" to improve the situation, even writing to Andrei Vyshinskii and Viacheslav Molotov, "but we have never had even an acknowledgement of our letters." "We have absolutely *no means* of getting any sort of satisfaction whatsoever," he wrote, "or even of getting our complaints heard. You can imagine the state of frustration in which we live."

Although he doubted that these vexing conditions were the product of a clearly thought-out Soviet policy, nonetheless, Winterton wrote, "The sinister thing about all this (the Russians are quite clever)" was that this policy forced Western correspondents to "justify our existence here by re-writing the tripe which the Soviet newspapers print, dressing it up attractively, and sending that. The Russians are more than satisfied that we should do this, for news thus served has the desired flavour and they find they get (or in the past have got) just as good a show in the world's press, or almost as good." The only remedy, he argued, would be to restrict Soviet journalists in Western Europe in similar ways, or else to withdraw Western reporters from Moscow.

But neither is professionally possible—we're a very mixed bunch; we have our yesmen, and we have people working on space whose living depends on regular filing, and the agencies feel that they must file and would get no backing from their offices if they didn't. As to [pulling reporters out of the USSR], correspondents are always leaving Moscow, mostly American and all sadder and wiser men, but new ones keep coming—and Russia being an ally and the war still being on, I suppose the truth is never told at home about news gathering conditions here, even if anyone were interested.

Perhaps, Winterton wrote, Western correspondents could visit the USSR, then return home to file their honest stories. "If the Russians prevent that by refusing visas to a man who's written frankly on his return to London, that'll merely prove that the right method has been adopted."[16]

In his second letter, Winterton complained about the shoddy quality of Soviet reporting, which, given the heavy reliance of Western reporters on the Moscow press for source material, was a serious problem. "Shortly after I came here," he wrote, "Ilya Ehrenberg [sic] said to me during a discussion 'In wartime every objective reporter should be shot.' I don't suppose most Russian journalists would put their attitude quite as bluntly as that, but it's a fact that Russian newspapers care nothing for fact if it clashes with policy."

Whereas Alexander Werth had censored himself when reporting about Soviet religious and nationalities issues, Winterton found that the Soviets could do the job just as well. For instance, when he and several other reporters visited the Estonian capital, recently retaken by the Red Army,

> I discovered that the bulk of the people of Tallin were extremely hostile to the Soviet Union, had no desire to be part of it, feared that the Russians would deport large numbers of them into the interior of Russia as was done in 1940, and had been if anything rather relieved by the German occupation. I tried to write a part of this, but of course the censor stopped it all—even though I put the whole thing in an objective setting and emphasised the strategic importance of the Baltic States to Russia's security.[17]

Instead of conveying the ambiguous truth about Soviet advances into the western borderlands, reporting from Moscow consistently portrayed the Red Army as liberators and the locals as uniformly grateful for the return of Soviet power.

Stalinist conditions made basic news gathering impossible, because average Russians wisely shunned foreigners, and especially reporters, fearing the political consequences. "In spite of all the talky-talky about friendship and cooperation, most Russians are scared to have anything to do with us direct," Winterton wrote. "We know 'tame Russians', of course—writers, artists, poets, film actresses, musicians whose relations with us are approved from on high because they create the illusion of contact." But most ordinary Russians regarded Western reporters as agents of infection.

This isolation from average Russians, combined with the "political censorship," have "made it virtually impossible for a single critical word to leave the

Soviet Union and . . . has left in the minds of readers abroad an impression about this country which is hopelessly onesided." If the Soviet authorities were responsible for thus distorting the news, however, Western correspondents were not innocents either:

> One of the most sinister things about reporting from here—and this will apply after the war too—is that there are always plenty of correspondents whom the Russians can blackmail. About half the correspondents here at the present time are people whose personal wellbeing or financial position depends on their being good boys and so retaining the right to live in Russia or come and go freely. Some have domestic ties which make it impossible for them to break with the Russians—and to write honestly would be to break with them. Some are writers and journalists whose whole lifetime has been spent in writing about Russia and who would not be employed by any paper to write about anything else.[18]

Winterton warned: "Visa-appeal smells to heaven in an enormous number of articles and books written about Russia. I wasn't wholly innocent myself when I returned to London last summer. I swear I'll never sin that way again."[19]

Making his most serious point, Winterton predicted that these sins of omission and commission would eventually produce grave consequences: "One of the things that worries me is the reaction that is likely to occur in Britain and America when those of us who know Russia and have been gagged for so long become free again to write the facts. . . . The reaction will probably go far beyond what is necessary or desirable and may endanger the cooperation with the Soviet Union which I firmly believe is essential if we are to avoid another war."[20] The circumstances about which Winterton complained had not arisen accidentally. Soviet authorities had made some small efforts in the summer of 1941 to win over foreign correspondents and shape their news coverage, and they would continue to use their visa weapon for this purpose. They soon realized, however, that too many Western reporters simply could not be controlled to the degree Moscow desired. Not everybody could be bribed, threatened, or won over as Bourke-White and Werth had been. Instead, the Soviets decided to cultivate certain correspondents, while freezing out those, like Winterton, whom they could not control or direct.

Occasionally, of course, Moscow correspondents filed negative reports, but they generally did so, as Winterton had mentioned, only after returning to the West. Even many of the articles deemed to be critical appear rather mild in retrospect. The Soviets' last line of defense in such cases was to file sharp complaints with the appropriate American or British authority, suggesting that great damage was being done to the alliance. If the Soviet ambassador himself did not personally issue the objection, then one of the embassy's secretaries did so; or, in Britain, one of the Soviets' friends in Parliament—frequently D. N. Pritt, MP—would ask a hostile question in the House.

In January 1945, for instance, Walter Graebner of the *Daily Mail* published a three-part article following his return from the USSR. For the most part, the pieces were laudatory of the Soviet war effort; they stressed the tremendous suffering being endured by the people, their near-starvation rations, their support for the war, and their Russian patriotism. He even wrote that "Russians . . . vehemently deny that there is not religious freedom in the country. The regulated Press, they say, exists only for the time being while enemies inside the country are being eliminated." Graebner waded into deeper waters, however, when he wrote that Soviet bureaucrats constituted a separate class "every bit as distinct from the masses as the English nobility is from the Cockneys." Even worse, he wrote that the "No. 1 Bureaucrat, of course, is Stalin. He is above criticism." Furthermore, "there is an unmistakable heaviness in the Russian atmosphere. One constantly has the feeling that one is being watched or followed . . . that telephones are being tapped, and so on." Average Russians "fear that they will be accused of being agents if they are seen too much in the company of foreigners."[21]

This all made the gallant Soviet ally look uncomfortably like the Nazi enemy—police state and all. After the first article, which had dwelt on food issues—political questions had to wait for the third installment—Zinchenko immediately rushed to the Foreign Office to complain, saying that there was "no need to rub in the difficulties" of food shortages, and so forth. When the third article appeared, with its references to Stalin and to popular fears, one Foreign Office official wrote that "Much of all this might be true, but to blurt it out like this does not make matters any easier for Mr. Graebner's successors . . . or for the journalists & diplomats still in the country." He continued: "It's exactly the kind of thing that complicates our relations with the Russians in every way."[22]

It was one thing for Soviet officials to prevent bad news from leaking out of the USSR, or to protest if it did; it was quite another to propagate the Soviet view of the world. In late 1943 V. Fin, an officer of Informbiuro, complained to Lozovskii that the Soviet message was not reaching the foreign audience in the desired way.[23] Official Soviet news was transmitted to the United States and Great Britain via two routes, he wrote: Informbiuro releases and foreign correspondents. "Both these sources of information, if it might be so expressed," Fin wrote, "are not of full value." The problem lay in the prejudices of Western readers: "Readers of foreign newspapers very frequently relate with distrust toward the first source [Informbiuro]. First, [because] it is a Soviet source, and, second, [because] it is official." The Western public generally trusted its foreign correspondents, but in the Soviet estimation American and British reporters did not place events in the proper political context, since their "information is, truly, tendentious." Fin had a proposal to solve this conundrum: "It would be ideal if we could present our information (the type of information of the Sovinformbiuro) to the foreign reader under some sort of foreign screen [*vyveska*]. The problem is complex, but attempts are being made to solve it. Now, as things happen, a possibility presents itself in this relation."

A low-ranking press officer at the British embassy, Wright Miller, a subordinate of the head of the British press section John Lawrence, had approached the Informbiuro with a curious proposition. "The thing is," Fin continued, "that a number of powerful English newspapers and especially the British Broadcasting Corporation are dissatisfied (if one can believe the assurances of Mister Miller . . .) by the materials coming from Informbiuro. They consider these materials to be crudely propagandistic, of little interest," as well as being one-sided and containing few original ideas. " 'The vital pulse of underlying life is not felt' states Miller. 'There is no color in them and nothing specifically Russian, Soviet.' " Miller suggested that, if the Soviets could supply more colorful, lively materials, these would gain "wide distribution in England." But copy of this sort must be written to suit British tastes.

Apparently, Fin had spoken to Miller several times about this dilemma: "These conversations led me to an idea *about the creation among the editors of 'B[ritanskii] S[oiuznik] of a small and unofficial center to organize dispatches of our materials.*" Acting on Miller's suggestion, Fin proposed that Informbiuro arrange for Soviet writers to compose pieces that could then be translated into English before "send[ing] them abroad *in the name of the Press section of the British embassy through the NKID*" (emphases in original). Before transmitting these articles back to London, the British would have to submit them to NKID censors, as was the case with all foreign reporting. This would give Soviet authorities a final opportunity to guarantee that the British had not rewritten the materials in an unapproved manner.

Fin realized that Lozovskii might be suspicious of this scheme; it seemed almost too good to be true. "A question arises naturally: why, strictly speaking, do Lawrence and company need all this? Does their agreement to dispatch materials about the USSR, approved by the NKID, not signify the presence of some long-undertaken plan, connected with the machinations of espionage?" Considering this possibility, Fin rejected it: "After my conversation with Miller,

I already 'felt' the ground on this. Miller stated that he considers that the supply of materials about the USSR to the foreign press would raise the authority of the English employees of 'Britanskii soiuznik' and their prestige in the British Ministry of Information. 'We would,' [Miller] stated, 'easily score off those foreign correspondents who frequently write about things they don't know.'" Rather than the product of deep plotting by British intelligence, Miller's approach could easily be explained by personal ambition: "It seems to me," Fin wrote, "that this wish to strut about before the Ministry of Information, to show their 'talents' plays, possibly, a big part" in Miller's agreement to send reworked materials, written by Soviet authors, out of Moscow "*under his name.*" Fin concluded, "personal interestedness and ambition of the clerks and petty journalists working on the editing of 'Britanskii soiuznik' . . .—that is a powerful lever." Fin thought that "an experiment should be risked in this relation." A "trusted person from Informbiuro" ought to compose a few articles, feed them to Miller, then "We will watch how this will turn out. After that, much will become clear."[24]

Unfortunately, Soviet records do not reveal what became of Miller's intriguing approach, and it is impossible to tell from the despatches of the British embassy's press section whether he eventually engaged in such a cover operation. Naturally, if Miller had gone through with his scheme, he would have done everything possible to hide his trail. Nonetheless, the incident shows how frustrated Western correspondents and press officers were by the restrictions on their work in Moscow, and how far some of them were prepared to go in their hunt for headlines—and to advance their careers. It also demonstrates how Moscow was able to use the careerism and sheer boredom of allied reporters to further its own ends.

More common than Miller's dishonest scheme were attempts by reporters to ingratiate themselves with Soviet officials—the "visa appeal" that Winterton had identified. In April 1944, for instance, the Moscow correspondent for NBC, Robert Magidoff, met with Lozovskii to discuss his first visit to the United States since his assignment to Moscow four years earlier.[25] Lozovskii thought the meeting important enough to relay copies of his notes to Molotov, Shcherbakov, Andrei Vyshinskii, and Vladimir Dekanozov. Magidoff tried to portray himself as the voice of moderation and friendship toward the Soviet Union in an otherwise hostile, capitalist world. The United States, he said, hardly even appeared to be a country at war; Americans worked hard, to be sure, but then this had been the case even before Pearl Harbor. As for opinion about the USSR, when one listened to certain radio broadcasts or some newspapers, then one had to ask: "Against whom is the USA fighting: against Germany or against the USSR?"

Magidoff then contradicted himself by allowing that most broadcasts were "objective and neutral" about the Soviet Union. But, like Hewlett Johnson, he said that radio shows were sponsored by companies and therefore reflected business interests. He claimed that there were "a number of reactionaries" on the governing board of NBC. The head of that network's parent company, RCA, however, was David Sarnoff, himself an immigrant from Minsk who, according to Magidoff, was favorably inclined toward the USSR and looked forward to postwar commercial possibilities in the Soviet Union.

Lozovskii inquired about the sources of anti-Soviet opinion in the American press; the MacCormack and Patterson papers were not the only "guilty" parties in this respect, he claimed. "They are without doubt tools," Lozovskii said, "but in whose hands?" Magidoff explained that there were "many fascist and semifascist" groups in the United States; these included ethnic Germans, reactionaries of various hues, as well as "white-guard Russians." Certain "powerful capitalists" also harbored anti-Soviet views. Magidoff told Lozovskii that one vice-president of NBC had even said to him that it made no sense to arm the Soviets, since the United States would only have to fight them in the future. "Various departments" of the government also sheltered people with "anti-Soviet opinions," he claimed. He cited "the civil servants of the State Department in general and the Russian section . . . in particular." This supposedly applied as well to many officials in the War and Navy Departments.

Having thus demonstrated his friendly orientation, Magidoff then made his pitch: he was one of the few remaining old Moscow hands from the prewar press corps, and yet he had not thus far been granted an exclusive story. He asked to be allowed to visit the Soviet Far East and broadcast to America from Khabarovsk or Vladivostok. He realized that getting permission for such a trip would be difficult, but, Lozovskii recorded, "if we allowed him to go, then he would use this trip in a manner that would be very useful for us." Magidoff even promised to write a follow-up series of favorable articles for the American wire services. His second request was for permission to visit the front line. He complained that Alexander Werth, his former boss Henry Cassidy of Associated Press, and Henry Shapiro of United Press International had all made such visits, but he had not yet been allowed to do so, which undercut his authority with his bosses back in America who were asking why he was denied similar favors from the Kremlin.

This conversation was a fine illustration of the dynamics about which Win-

terton had complained. By denying official favors to some reporters while dol-
ing them out sparingly to others who toed the Kremlin line, the Soviets allowed
market forces to work to their advantage. Editors in the West pressed their correspondents for better stories, pointed to articles by the likes of Werth, and
asked why their own men were unable to file comparable pieces. Magidoff had
been forced to plead for access, promising to write favorable stories in exchange. Given this state of affairs, it was little wonder that Moscow reporters
did not file honest stories about ethnic, political, and religious tensions in the
USSR, or about the nature of the Soviet police state.

None of this is to claim that the Kremlin had a perfect record in managing
foreign guests, as would become clear during the visit of Leo Gruliow to the
USSR in January and February 1944. Gruliow had worked as a journalist on the
New York Democrat until losing that job with the onset of the great depression.
Like a handful of other left-leaning Americans at that time, he had been drawn
to the USSR of the first five-year plan. Once in the Soviet capital, he resumed
his journalistic profession, writing for the English-language publication *Moscow News* until 1938, when Stalin's purges made further residence in Moscow
highly hazardous for foreigners.[26] Although not himself a Communist, Gruliow remained favorably inclined toward the USSR despite his experience with
the Terror, and so, after the Nazis attacked the Soviet Union, he naturally became involved in American efforts to assist the Soviet war effort. In 1942, he became the research director of Russian War Relief (RWR), an organization designed to mobilize political and financial support throughout the United States
for the Soviet war effort.

After arriving in Moscow, Gruliow conveyed a lengthy memorandum to Lozovskii explaining the work of RWR in the United States.[27] There were organizations collecting funds for other Allied countries, such as China and Greece,
Gruliow explained, but these groups raised most of their money from a few
very rich contributors; by contrast, RWR received most of its donations from
families with annual incomes of under $5,000. RWR had set up "committees to
aid Russia" in 413 American cities, staffed entirely by volunteers; these people
made speeches, radio addresses, established contact with local newspapers, and
distributed postcards, emblems, posters, and the like, all "with Soviet themes."
Gruliow's group had also created "men's and women's youth organizations" as
well as an "All-American religious organization, which carries out its work
chiefly in the Protestant and Jewish churches [*sic*], and receives, by the way,
great support from the Baptists in the southern states of the USA." They also
worked among Americans with Russian and other Slavic ethnic backgrounds.

The USSR had benefited greatly from RWR's fund raising. By the beginning of 1944, the group had already sent $12-million worth of equipment to the Soviet Union, and none of this had been lost in transit; furthermore, overhead was less than 5 percent, a very good record for any charitable group, which could be explained by the widespread use of volunteers as administrators. Another advantage of RWR assistance, Gruliow explained, was that it came in addition to Lend-Lease aid, not being subtracted from that total.

To advertise its work, RWR had placed more than 10,000 articles in papers throughout the United States in the first ten months of 1943 alone. Some of these had appeared in leading national newspapers and journals, such as the *New York Times* and the Scripps-Howard chain. RWR's lecturers' bureau had organized 600 big rallies throughout America, most notably in Chicago stadium, the Hollywood Bowl, and Madison Square Garden, where Harry Hopkins and Maksim Litvinov had spoken, the latter making an impassioned plea for an early "second front." They planned a further series of meetings in thousands of small towns and large cities across the United States.

The work of RWR had not been universally popular: the Hearst press had opposed them, as had "certain sections of the Catholic Church." So far, however, RWR had not encountered any opposition that it could not handle. People were always accusing RWR of being a Communist front group, but the organization was quick to defend itself from this charge. "If other means do not help," Gruliow explained, "then the threat of legal proceedings for slander gets quick action." In fact, so far they had not yet been forced to go to court, because the threat of lawsuits had to date proven sufficient to scare away slanderers. Instead of outright hostility, RWR had instead met "passive opposition"; the Patterson press, for instance, refused to publish anything about the group's work.

Gruliow had come to the USSR to improve his organization's fund-raising propaganda in the United States. So far, RWR had relied on articles taken from the English-language *Moscow News*, materials supplied by VOKS, Informbiuro bulletins, and Soviet publications from the Library of the American-Russian Institute. Although such materials had sufficed so far, Gruliow wrote, "they do not entirely correspond to our needs." American public tastes were not the same as those of Soviet readers', being shaped by "completely different surroundings, history, culture and national characteristics." In particular, he wrote of Soviet propaganda, "this material is insufficiently connected with our specific work" in the United States. For example, he said that Americans were not yet sufficiently antagonistic to the German people to appreciate Soviet materials highlighting Nazi atrocities. It would be both more positive and effective to show how Soviet children used American aid. When Gruliow explained this to V. Kemenov, the head of VOKS, however, the latter angrily replied that Engels had shown how all aspects of life were interconnected. Gruliow said honestly enough: "[U]nfortunately, very few Americans read Engels." Americans might not immediately understand the link between German atrocities and the need to assist Soviet children, he argued.

Gruliow made several excellent suggestions designed to improve the effectiveness of RWR propaganda. He proposed that Soviet authors should write pieces tailored to American tastes; he offered to consult with VOKS on this and to screen any such articles. To show Americans how their donations were being used, he suggested that Soviet authorities arrange for members of the Moscow press corps to visit hospitals and children's homes where RWR assistance was making a difference; this would "grease" the wheels for more aid in the future. The Soviets might also make short documentary films showing German destruction, illustrating "the debt of thanks of the American people to the Soviet people who are giving America time to prepare" for a more active role in the war. Gruliow also requested Soviet photographs, posters, and dramatic and musical material for use in radio broadcasts back in the United States. In a particularly sentimental American touch, Gruliow suggested that VOKS arrange for personal correspondence between Soviet recipients of aid and American donors: "This is very important," he wrote, "because nothing makes such an impression on Americans as 'personal' letters writing about wartime life." He also suggested that it might help if RWR's work were to receive some supportive mention in the Soviet domestic press.

On the face of things, Gruliow's proposals seem to make a great deal of sense, and indeed Maksim Litvinov, who had been the Soviet ambassador in Washington from December 1941 until the summer of 1943, supported him wholeheartedly. Although he did "not know [Gruliow] personally . . .," Litvinov wrote, "he was sent here in the capacity of an organization working exclusively for the extension of monetary and material assistance to our Union. To help this organization is to help ourselves." He continued: "Gruliow supports what I often wrote from Washington: namely, that the material sent by VOKS and Informbiuro is completely unsuitable and is not adapted to local conditions." Gruliow's offer to collect effective propaganda material himself "would save us a large sum of Soviet and foreign hard currency being wasted on unhelpful shipments of unneeded materials being sent to America." Litvinov argued that "it is extraordinarily important" to demonstrate to American donors how their money was being used. He also endorsed the idea of soliciting letters from aid recipients. In addition, he wrote: "Sending lecturers to the USA would be very expedient, not only from the point of view of receiving material assistance, but also [political] propaganda. I know, however, that this proposition is almost unrealizable." Throughout the war, the Kremlin would consistently oppose such an idea, apparently for fear of losing tight, central control over the formation and flow of propaganda. In closing, Litvinov argued that, at the very least, VOKS or the NKID ought to pay Gruliow's living expenses in Moscow, since the more money RWR spent on Gruliow, "the less we will receive from it."[28]

Both Gruliow and Litvinov would run into a political and cultural wall. Kemenov composed a vitriolic attack on RWR as an organization and on Gruliow personally, which he sent to Shcherbakov.[29] Although it would be easy enough to dismiss this letter as just another example of Stalinist myopia, in fact it reflected the deep cultural gulf separating Americans and Russians; it also demonstrated the abiding political suspicions that were never very far below the surface of the wartime alliance.

Kemenov argued that RWR had been a useful organization when formed in August 1941, and he admitted that it had already raised millions of dollars for the USSR and planned to collect even more in the future. But, Kemenov wrote, RWR's character had changed in the succeeding two and one-half years. Without providing any hard evidence for his allegations, Kemenov claimed that the American government was now "making use of the sympathy of the American people for the USSR" in order to funnel money supposedly raised for the Red Army into the hands of other allied governments, such as those of Britain and China. "The main goal" of RWR had long since become "self-advertisement and the exaggeration of the aid given by America to the USSR." (This last sentence apparently caught Shcherbakov's eye, since it was underlined by hand.) As for RWR's recent activities, "things were far from alright."

A clandestine capitalist conspiracy had hijacked the organization, Kemenov argued, again providing no concrete proof. The "outward" appearance of the group still seemed favorable to the USSR, but American officials had gradually assumed control, "at first in a covert way, later in ever more open form." People trusted by the U.S. government, such as Edward Carter, had taken over the leadership and appointed "passive" or even "reactionary" people in subordinate posts. VOKS had tried to circumvent RWR's leaders by sending propaganda resources directly to local RWR groups, rather than the national organization, and Moscow had received assurances that these materials were highly appreciated. "Despite that—or precisely thanks to that," Kemenov warned darkly, "the Central Council of RWR issued a secret directive banning direct contacts of departments with the USSR."

The aid being sent by RWR was also second-rate, according to Kemenov, including goods that had lain on store shelves for a long time, as well as "dirty shoes" and so forth. This was no accident but rather a capitalist effort to dump surplus or shoddy goods: "By such means, the sympathy of the [American] population for the USSR and its efforts to give assistance to our people are being used for the strengthening of financial bases either of the War Department or groups of capitalists connected with the leadership of RWR."

Kemenov's most heated complaints concerned the nature of RWR's fundraising propaganda, and here it is clear that differing cultural perceptions were at play. Soviet officialdom was uncomfortable with American salesmanship. Evaluating RWR's propaganda, Kemenov accused the organization's leaders of "wrecking tendencies." Their most serious sin in his eyes was that, rather than highlighting the heroic deeds of the Red Army and Soviet people, RWR devoted 99 percent of its materials "exclusively to advertisement of RWR itself." Kemenov thought he understood the ulterior motive for this: RWR's leaders wanted to defuse popular demands for a "second front" in Europe by demonstrating "American 'goodwill' toward the Soviet people." He cited several examples from American radio broadcasts, which claimed that Russians admired American industrial methods and that American engineers had helped to build the Soviet industrial infrastructure during the five-year plans of the 1930s. Even worse, RWR broadcasts slandered Russian history by asserting that Muscovites had always borrowed ideas and methods from the West—from the time of the semimythical Viking king Riurik through Peter the Great, up to Stalin himself.

The boastfulness and informality of American PR methods also offended Kemenov, who recounted how RWR broadcasts often asserted that American supplies "Mean very much to them [the Soviets]—they mean the difference between life and death." RWR radio advertisements referred to Soviet generals by their first names, or by invented, shortened nicknames—Marshal Timoshenko thus became "Tim," for example—and they composed fake dialogue where these real-life characters supposedly engaged in conversations designed to drum up support for RWR, complete with hokey Hollywood-Russian accents. VOKS tried to supply appropriately sober Russian propaganda, but Americans endlessly replied that these materials had to be reworked for "American tastes." "However," Kemenov wrote suspiciously, "experience shows that RWR protests not against the form, but against the contents of materials, trying to receive from us articles that will answer *their* propaganda line." RWR's leaders simply refused to recognize that Moscow knew best.

In retaliation, VOKS reduced its shipments of propaganda to the United States and refused to collaborate with RWR to create an exhibit showing how the Soviet people used American aid. Gruliow had come to Moscow, in part, in order to persuade VOKS to reconsider, but he had failed. Rather, Kemenov despised RWR's emissary: "From the first day of his trip to the USSR Gruliow has conducted himself in a pushy and insolent manner." Owing to his prewar experiences in the USSR, the American refused to take VOKS's no for an answer; when he met resistance from one agency, he used his contacts to try another, exploiting Soviet institutional redundancy. "Having met a sufficiently cold welcome at VOKS," Kemenov wrote, "Gruliow turned to Sovinformbiuro and comrade Lozovskii." There, Gruliow complained that VOKS simply did not understand American conditions and was uncooperative. He told Lozovskii: "'These remarks are, of course, confidential and are said between us as people. I know that I can be completely open with you and don't have to resort to diplomatic methods of speech. You understand me.'" Lozovskii may indeed have understood Gruliow, but he promptly passed his letter on to VOKS nonetheless.

Kemenov was especially annoyed when Gruliow visited the Chalakhovskii children's home in the town of Malakhovka, attempting afterward to send a telegram to RWR describing his experiences. VOKS refused his request, but Gruliow circumvented that agency and sent his message via the American section of Informbiuro. VOKS objected to the tone of the telegram, which claimed that the Russian orphans who had been helped by RWR supplies sent their greetings and thanks to their American benefactors.

To set matters straight, Kemenov drafted an angry letter to Edward Carter, the head of RWR, laying out Soviet grievances against both Gruliow and the organization itself. Although he admitted that the work of VOKS and RWR "runs together" in many ways, the American group should cease singing its own praises and instead stress the deeds of the Soviet Army and people. As regards radio broadcasts, Kemenov complained that they gave an "incorrect representation" of Soviet life and made the unacceptable claim that American assistance was of life-or-death importance to the Soviet people. Furthermore, such broadcasts were "offending the feelings of national pride" by stressing Russia's historical debt to the more advanced West. He also singled out one broadcast where the announcer had said that a Russian boy spoke Russian "just like a real person." "Of course, Mr. Carter," Kemenov wrote in high dudgeon, "you do not believe that a real person should speak only in English. But how did the author and editor of the broadcast allow such words?"[30]

Most seriously, Kemenov wrote that the USSR had suffered unheard of destruction and immeasurable human losses during the war. "Americans should know the truth of these occurrences," he wrote, and above all they should realize that the Soviet people owed no debt to the Americans for their material aid; rather, the reverse was true. Soviet sacrifices in blood more than made up for any material assistance RWR might supply. Finally, the lighthearted, disrespectful tone of "American publicity" was out of place in such serious matters and, Kemenov claimed, it had wounded the feelings of Soviet leaders.[31]

The RWR affair reveals the cultural and political chasm separating American and Soviet approaches to information and propaganda. For Gruliow and the RWR, the task seemed blindingly clear and simple: the USSR needed material assistance to bolster its war effort and to feed and clothe its hungry people. If Americans were going to be persuaded to dig deep in their pockets for the cause, then the full bag of commercial tricks had to be employed. The dictates of salesmanship meant playing down the sinister aspects of Soviet history, "humanizing" the Soviet leaders and people, and stressing individual stories to show potential donors that real people received and used American aid. If propaganda broadcasts referred to Soviet leaders in overly familiar ways, then this was only designed to soften their otherwise forbidding image. The plight of Russian children, especially orphans, was especially emotive and could be expected to yield the greatest results; this might be viewed as somewhat exploitative, but if it helped defeat the Nazis, then the end justified the means. Gruliow and his bosses were less concerned with moral issues than they were with the concrete task at hand—increasing American donations. They asked themselves the questions any marketer might ask: what will move potential donors to part with their money?

VOKS, by contrast, was quintessentially Stalinist in its approach: propaganda must serve an "educative" function. There was a correct propaganda "line," and any deviation from it constituted "wrecking." Kemenov distrusted any claim that American tastes differed from Soviets'. The American working class could be relied upon—as a class—to support the workers' state. In this view, the gimcrackery of American commercial advertising was both demeaning and designed to obscure the genuine issues at stake in the war. Marketing technique was embedded in the DNA of the culture in which Gruliow and the RWR operated; the Russian culture, however, had an even longer tradition in which the authorities determined orthodoxy and then expected the common people to conform and obey. To Kemenov, Gruliow's repeated pleas that he was simply trying to cater to the tastes of his target audience made no sense whatsoever. To a Stalinist, or indeed a tsarist, bureaucrat, the notion that propaganda could be shaped from the bottom up—in other words, market analysis—was virtually incomprehensible. Gruliow's arguments merely served to feed Kemenov's suspicions that the bourgeois Americans were distorting the war in the East to serve their own political and class ends, and even to harm Soviet interests.

Despite Litvinov's spirited defense of RWR, this affair served as one of a myriad of instances where Soviet diplomats with experience abroad proved unable to overcome the political and cultural incomprehension of Moscow-based oligarchs whose perceptions of the outside world were determined and distorted by their cultural and ideological preconceptions. Another revealing instance occurred in March 1943, when the BBC requested permission to station a permanent correspondent in Moscow. A Soviet embassy official in London, Rostovskii, advocated accepting the suggestion on the grounds that "millions of people listen" to the BBC; broadcast scripts could be vetted in advance by Soviet authorities, and cooperation with British broadcasting "gives us the opportunity to spread information useful to our government among wide strata of populations abroad."[32] Rather than welcoming a proposal that would no doubt have given the Soviet message a much wider airing abroad, Molotov angrily wrote: "Nobody from *Soviet* [underlined twice by hand] organs empowered comrade Rostovskii to plead for the BBC."[33] Given the fact that arrests on trumped-up charges of espionage were commonplace in Stalin's regime, Molotov's icy note must have chilled Rostovskii's heart. It also showed just how out of touch members of the politbiuro could be.

As Maiskii admitted to Smollett, "It was his perennial problem to make Soviet leaders accept his explanations of English political life."[34] Soviet propaganda was extraordinarily effective when it was left in the hands of people who understood the West and knew how to exploit the openness of the American and British societies. With propaganda, as with the economy, however, rigid centralized planning had its glaring flaws—unresponsiveness, clumsiness, and a near complete disregard for the needs and wishes of the consumer.

"What a Problem Russia Is to Us All"

Many Western clergymen were among the very least reliable sources about Soviet reality. On May 5, only days before the end of the war in Europe, the dean of Canterbury, Hewlett Johnson, author of the laudatory book, *The Socialist Sixth of the World*, vice-chairman of the Society for Cultural Relations with the USSR, and chairman of the Joint Committee for Aid to the Soviet Union, responsible for raising thousands of pounds for Red Army relief and for spreading the gospel of Soviet Communism far and wide, received his just reward for services rendered: he arrived for a victory lap through the Soviet imperium.[35]

Johnson toured outlying portions of the USSR, as well as flying to Prague and traveling through Poland, but the supreme moment of his journey came on July 6, when he met with Stalin and Molotov for fifty minutes, with only a translator present. This was an extraordinary sign of grace and favor; any number of ambassadors had completed entire stints in the Soviet capital without catching more than a glimpse of these two busy titans atop Lenin's tomb during public festivities. We have only Johnson's account of this strange session, and, according to him, he raised only a few issues, "the religious question" being the most prominent. Johnson also told Stalin that he had visited his birthplace in Gori, in the Republic of Georgia, where Lavrenty Beria had only recently placed the dictator's humble boyhood home in a ghastly, totalitarian-kitsch marble shrine (Johnson found it "beautifully designed"). He also described a visit to the Orthodox seminary in Tbilisi, where the young Iosif Vissarionovich had—according to Stalinist lore—operated an illegal printing press. "It was clever work," Johnson gushed to Stalin—a churchman ironically congratulating the dictator on outfoxing his priest-teachers. This unreal exchange then followed:

> [Johnson] "Finally I stood bareheaded before the tomb of your mother in a church up the steep hill."
> [Stalin] "My mother was a simple woman."
> [Johnson] "She was a good woman," I replied, and added: "I can generally see the portrait of the mother in the character of the son."

Johnson explained that before the war the British had been suspicious about the USSR, but, in a testament to the impact of wartime propaganda, he said that his "countrymen . . . are more inclined now than formerly to believe my statements about Russia." He continued: "[L]argely false and exaggerated" information "as to the treatment of the Church by the Soviet Government" had frightened the English, who "are a religious people." Stalin patiently explained that the leaders of the Russian Orthodox Church had "pronounced an anathema on the new Soviet Government," so the Soviets "were obliged to defend ourselves. The State had to act." Stalin continued:

> "Doubtless," he said, "in the time of war and tension there were excesses on both sides," and he smiled a half-amused, half-sad smile as he said it. "The war, however," he went on to add, "had created a new and different situation." The war had shown the Church how essentially patriotic the Soviet Government was. It had also revealed the patriotism of the Church.

When Stalin spoke of the close ties that had existed between the Russian Orthodox Church and the tsarist state, Johnson eagerly agreed:

"Yes," I added, "perhaps sometimes closer to the Tsar than to the Head of the Church, Jesus Christ." I personally, I went on, have seen in so many things that the Soviet Government has done for the common man something that was very much in accord with my concept of Christian teaching and morality. I fear that there have often been grounds for the charge that those who say they believe in a God of Justice and Love act as if they did not believe it, while many who deny such belief act as if they did. Stalin and Molotov smiled slightly.

The Soviet dictator made one last comment on the church, repeating himself catechistically to make sure the dean understood the point: "Religion . . . cannot be stopped. Conscience cannot be stilled. Religion is a matter of conscience. Conscience is free. Worship and religion are free."[36]

The attention lavished on Johnson paid propaganda dividends. He was awarded the Soviet Red Banner of Labor, and his tour, especially the visit with Stalin, received prominent press treatment in the USSR and abroad. In return, Johnson attended the enthronement of the Armenian Catholicos, which, as the British visitor noted, "was of course used to promote the idea of the union of the other Christian Churches in opposition to a reactionary and anti-Soviet Vatican." Following this occasion, the dean expressed the view that Turkish Armenia "should be returned to [Soviet] Armenia," of which it had never been part. Later, while visiting Tashkent, he declared that "The foundations of the Soviet State seem to me profoundly moral and scientific; therefore that which takes place in Russia satisfies me as a man, as a scholar, and as a Christian." Johnson also expressed his support for the Communist-dominated Polish government, which, he said, was "as stable as any government in any country." Finally, in Leningrad Johnson told a TASS writer that "In Britain the opinion may be heard in certain circles that the Soviet Government persecute believers. I shall be happy in returning to my country to tell my countrymen that these statements are without foundation. I shall be happy to tell the truth about everything I have seen in the Soviet Union."

In fact, Johnson freely acknowledged to a British reporter—in private, to be sure—that he was intending to do anything but tell the whole truth about the USSR: "[W]hen Miss Marjorie Shaw, the Moscow correspondent of the *New Statesman*, asked him if he intended to deal in his book on Russia with the unfavourable as well as with the favourable aspects of Soviet life," Frank Roberts reported, "the Dean replied that after the hospitality he had received he did not think that it would be fair to say very much about the bad features of the regime."

British officials, who regarded the dean as one specimen of a species deemed relatively harmless and eccentric when confined to its domestic habitat, were mildly disturbed by Johnson's inanities, but they were puzzled as to why the Soviets set so much store in him. Roberts guessed that the explanation must "either [be] that the Soviet authorities are unusually grateful to friends who were faithful in hard times, or that the true position of such persons at home is misunderstood here, that the Soviet people still require to be convinced that they have friends abroad or that the propaganda value of such visits is over-estimated. Perhaps all four motives are present in the Soviet mind, which is not prone to careful discrimination."[37]

In fact, the Soviets knew perfectly well what they were doing, Roberts's con-descension aside. Although it was certainly true that, in Britain itself, the prop-aganda value of Johnson's tour was limited by the fact that the dean's uncritical admiration for the USSR was widely known, the scope of Soviet religious poli-cies was much more all-encompassing than Roberts could have suspected. The visit placed a significant foreign stamp of approval on Stalin's entire wartime approach to religion, reinforcing the message of the *sobor'* and the visit of the Eastern Orthodox hierarchs to Moscow earlier in the year, when Aleksii had been elevated to the patriarchal throne. Religion was healthy in the USSR; the Catholic Church was the enemy of progressive peoples everywhere; no Chris-tian need fear the expansion of the Soviet political sphere—even Christian leaders in the Western democracies understood these things and were ready to testify to them. As Roberts himself acknowledged, many people in the United States, the USSR, and especially Eastern Europe, were ignorant of the dean's relatively modest position, confusing him with the much more consequential archbishop of Canterbury. In fact, the dean was a minor figure in the church, being responsible only for the cathedral in the city of Canterbury, but his title evoked misleading images of Thomas Becket and other great archbishops. Thus, when Johnson declaimed his views on a wide range of political issues, a great many people naturally believed that his remarks were backed by the full authority of the Anglican Church and, more important, of the British govern-ment. The views the dean expressed also seemed only one modest step further on a course already charted by archbishops Temple and Garbett.

This course reached its terminus during the summer of 1945, when the Rus-sian Orthodox Church returned the honor of Archbishop Garbett's 1943 visit —even as Johnson was bouncing around the USSR. The reciprocal visit by the Russian hierarchs had been scheduled for the summer of 1944, but the deaths that spring of Archbishop Temple and Patriarch Sergii, in addition to the dis-location of transport occasioned by the invasion of Normandy in June 1944, postponed the journey until the following summer.[38] As it happened, this meant that the visit would be more in the nature of a triumphal victory tour than a wartime propaganda exchange.

The aura surrounding the visit in June 1945 was entirely different from Archbishop Garbett's visit to Moscow in 1943. At that time, although the Red Army was on the advance following a series of stunning victories, the Germans were still deep in the USSR, and the outcome of the war remained in doubt. Soviet soldiers were dying in the millions, and the Western Allies had not yet landed in France. In 1945, by contrast, the war in Europe had been won; the Eastern and Western Allies had met on the Elbe, and the Hitlerite glue holding the "Grand Alliance" together was rapidly coming unstuck. Stalin's forces had already started to impose their order in Eastern Europe. Red Army men had begun to look less like distant and mysterious heroes and rescuers than as the harbingers of a new, red totalitarianism almost as threatening as the brown version.

One sign of the mood change came from none other than Archbishop Garbett, who, in private correspondence, was much more guarded in his evaluation of the Soviet order than he had been in his very public praise of Stalin and his regime in 1943. In June 1945 he wrote Christopher Warner of the Foreign Office:

> I have always been afraid that with the close of the war the Communist Party would renew to some degree its activities against the Church. On the other hand I am hopeful that the considerable breathing space the Church has had will have enabled it to secure its position against any actual persecution. I feel hopeful that the kind of reception that the Russian Church delegation will receive here will help to strengthen it, provided of course that we are very careful not to do or say anything which looks as if we were supporting the Church by criticising the State.

Garbett professed himself "glad" that "Archbishop Nikolai" would be heading the Russian delegation to London, since "He is the statesman of the party." True enough, but he was also the man who had spearheaded the suppression of rival churches in the western borderlands before the war and again at its close, and Nikolai had solemnly assured the world that the Katyn murders were the work of the Nazis. Garbett chose to ignore these things; instead, he believed: "The more closely we can keep the Russian Church in contact with the rest of Christendom, the more cautious the [Communist] Party will be about actual persecution. But what a problem Russia is to us all."[39]

By the time of Nikolai's arrival in London, Anglican Church leaders had known for months that not all was well for clergy and believers behind Soviet lines. The church had a "Deportees Welfare Committee" looking into the issue of Soviet religious-political repression in the USSR, and it reported the sad truth: that deportations were a prominent and integral feature of the reestablishment of Soviet power in the formerly German-occupied regions. In the autumn of 1944, the group composed a letter, which it proposed to hand to the Soviet Embassy in London, asking for reassurances about the fate of known deportees. When the Ministry of Information and the Foreign Office learned of the idea, however, they quickly quashed it, assisted by cautious figures within the church itself. Reverend Waddams, of the ministry's Religions Division, wrote that "If such a letter were sent it would receive a rude reply, and might prejudice the chances of further developments in Anglican–Russian Orthodox relations."[40] Church leaders were also concerned, especially if, as was being suggested, the new archbishop of Canterbury, Geoffrey Lloyd, were to put his name to the letter. A clergyman in Lambeth Palace wrote that "The Archbishop is most anxious not to take any action which might in any way upset relations between ourselves and the Russians, yet many people feel that unless some action is taken the deportations will continue." "Speaking frankly," he continued, "I think that it would be disastrous if the Archbishop and others took any action which might tend to muddy the political waters, but at the same time if a great wrong is being committed someone ought to speak."[41]

As ever, of course, few volunteers were prepared to speak out, and a thousand good-sounding reasons abounded for not doing so. Nonetheless, there seems to have been some dissent within the Church of England against giving the Russian delegation an uncritical welcome; but the Ministry of Information circumvented "certain very difficult members of the Church of England Committee" by securing government money to cover the visit's costs. As the Reverend Williams wrote: "If we are in fact paying a good part of the bill we can guide the course of events very much more wisely and profitably than if we are not." "I have mentioned the matter to Mr. Smollett," Williams continued, "and understand that he is in full agreement."[42] Just to make sure that events stayed on track, the Ministry of Information made sure that the Reverend Waddams, who had accompanied the archbishop of York to Moscow in 1943, and whose affiliation with the government propaganda agency was not widely known, would be in charge of the visit's arrangements. "We are in a rather favorable position," Williams wrote to Smollett. "We shall thus have an excellent link with the body which is effectively controlling the delegation in this country."[43]

The run-up to the arrival of the Russian Orthodox delegation neatly outlines the intractable dilemma faced by Western Church leaders: to speak out about known Soviet outrages would leave the church vulnerable to the charge of endangering the alliance; after the war, any public protests could likewise be condemned for complicating international relations in the delicate postwar European situation. The time was never right. Furthermore, public protest might actually have the effect of worsening the conditions of the very people being repressed. To stay silent, however, was in some way to condone crimes on a vast scale. Unfortunately, Anglican Church leaders chose neither to stay silent nor to condemn publicly Stalinist atrocities. Instead, they convinced themselves that if they continued to act in public as though nothing untoward was happening, while at the same time actually praising the USSR, its leaders and system, then perhaps the Soviets could be drawn into a cooperative net that might one day cause them to mend their ways. Although this was a comforting delusion, in practice it was a rationale for inaction and for prolonging the deceptive wartime propaganda into the early postwar. As for ties between the Russian Orthodox and Anglican churches, rather than becoming a means of softening the Stalinist regime, or of assuring better treatment of church people in the USSR as Anglican hierarchs hoped, the connection was quickly becoming one more hostage to fortune. To condemn renewed Soviet religious repression would not only harm East-West diplomatic ties, the argument now ran, but it would also threaten the newly restored religious links.

London was not the only foreign destination of Orthodox dignitaries in the spring and summer of 1945. In early March, Nikolai attended a Pan-Slav meeting in Sofia, Bulgaria, now occupied by the Red Army. The Bulgarian Orthodox Church had been in schism from the rest of the Orthodox world since 1872, when the Ottomans had bestowed on Bulgaria its own exarchate with the aim of driving wedges between the Turkish Empire's Orthodox subjects. The tactic had worked, with the largely Greek leadership of the Orthodox Church refusing to recognize Bulgarian autonomy. In 1945, following persistent coaxing from the Moscow Patriarchate, backed of course by the presence of the Red Army in that country, the ecumenical patriarch finally accepted Bulgarian autocephaly. A Divine Liturgy held in Sofia and attended by Russian clerics and members of the Soviet diplomatic corps celebrated the healing of the schism.[44] The move clearly served Soviet interests—in the same way that the original split had benefited Ottoman imperialism—because Bulgaria was under Soviet political control, and therefore the recognition of the Bulgarian Church's autocephaly separated that church from fellow Orthodox in Greece and Turkey, both of which groups remained outside the Soviet sphere. Perhaps in recognition of these new realities of power, Metropolitan Stefan of Sofia bowed his head and spoke glowingly of the USSR at the Pan-Slav Conference:

Karl Marx had failed to find followers in Germany or Great Britain* who would put his theories into practice. It was the Russian spirit that had discovered the solution of the social problem, according to which all men would become brothers. Russian Communism . . . had achieved real equality and had abolished the chains of slavery, of poverty, and of social restriction. It had solved not only the problems of the Russian muzhik (peasant) and the great Russian land, but also of the whole world.[45]

An impressive testament to the triumph of Moscow's religious offensive: an Orthodox cleric, whose country and church lay at the feet of the Red Army, claiming that Karl Marx had been the first thinker to discover the key to universal brotherhood.

Two months later, at the end of May, a delegation of Russian clergymen, headed by Patriarch Aleksii and Metropolitan Nikolai, left the USSR and, traveling via Teheran, visited Damascus, Beirut, Palestine, Jordan, and Egypt, in each place conspicuously being greeted by local Orthodox clergy.[46] On June 10, Nikolai and two priests parted from Aleksii in Cairo and traveled to London. The British interpreted the unusual scope of the tour as a strong assertion of the newly revived Soviet interest in the Mediterranean region: "It looks very much as if the Soviet Government were intending to encourage the Russian Orthodox Church in attempts again to become the centre of the Orthodox world. This will not be difficult with the Balkans under the thumb of Soviet influence and only Greece standing outside." "It will appear to the countries concerned as a revival of the interests of Imperial Russia in these parts." Moscow had already begun to make noises about its interests in Turkish Armenia; now, along with the Russian Orthodox Church, Soviet Moslems might be drawn into foreign policy work. "Thus the Soviet authorities will be able to make use of the religious strings of their bow without their Government being identified with exclusively Orthodox interests, which was the case under the Tsars."[47]

Just as significant as the places the Russian churchmen chose to visit were the centers of Orthodoxy they conspicuously circumvented. The Russians had avoided Greece, and they were not welcomed by the government of Turkey. The leaders of the Greek church were highly skeptical about the Soviets' new-found interest in religion, and they no doubt saw the tour of the Balkans as one

---

*It is interesting, and reflective of the growing tensions between Soviet and British interests in the Balkans (over Yugoslavia and Greece, in particular), that Britain and Germany were being paired in such a derogatory manner at a conference sponsored by the Soviets.

way of undercutting any Pan-Orthodox sympathy that might have welled up on behalf of the non-Communist forces in Greece's simmering civil war. As for the patriarch of Constantinople, whatever his personal beliefs about Soviet sincerity, the Turkish government had no wish to see him used as a tool in Moscow's territorial claims against them.

Commenting on the Russian hierarchs' swing through the Near East, another British diplomat, Frank Roberts, who had an excellent sense of history, shrewdly noted a parallel: "[T]he irreligious Communist State," he told Anthony Eden, "is using for its own political purposes the Orthodox Church in much the same way as the irreligious French Republic of the late nineteenth and early twentieth centuries used the religious orders for its own purposes in the Near East and throughout the French colonial empire."[48] Roberts felt that the archbishop of Canterbury and other Anglican hierarchs should be warned in advance of the Russian visit to London that there was both more and less than met the eye in the Soviet use of the Orthodox Church. Russian Orthodoxy, Roberts predicted accurately, might have reached its high water mark under Stalin; its future looked bleaker. He noted that the schools and the press were already resuming a campaign of materialist education designed to counter the growth of religious belief, especially among the young,[49] and from this he concluded: "It seems probable that, now that the Soviet State is no longer in mortal peril . . . the Orthodox Church will be mainly used for external propaganda purposes and that a determined attempt will be made to prevent the revival of religion inside Russia gaining any further ground." As for the resumption of antireligious themes in the Soviet press, Roberts wrote: "This education campaign, together with the difficulties of giving religious teaching and of training an effective body of priests, is likely to ensure that the Orthodox Church in Russia will remain little more than a museum piece inside the country, although it will no doubt be increasingly used for extending Russian influence outside the Soviet Union."[50]

The Foreign Office largely agreed with Roberts's assessment of Soviet motives, though significantly they gutted his strongest arguments in their own summary analysis which they conveyed to the archbishop of Canterbury: "The Communist Party," they told the archbishop, "will always insist on being the senior partner in this rather odd ideological alliance, but the patriotism preached by the Orthodox Church is of much political use and may prevent the Church ever becoming a 'museum piece.'" This ran exactly counter to Roberts's well founded pessimism, of course, but the archbishop already knew through his own sources that the situation of the Russian Orthodox Church was not all it appeared to be on the surface.

None of these swinish doubts, well-founded though they might be, would be allowed to poke their rude snouts into the gala party being devised to celebrate the ostensible spirit of alliance amity that was set to sweep Nikolai through his eleven-day visit to London. As far as the public was concerned, nothing was to be allowed to upset the happy image of a revived and self-confident Russian Orthodox Church, the harbinger of a new, less threatening Soviet reality. As ever, Smollett was at his station, writing that "There is no doubt that this event will yield very colourful pictorial as well as acoustic material which the newsreel cameras should be glad to have"—and which he was glad to supply.[51] The itinerary of the Russian guests was impressive and testified to the importance the British government attached to the success of the visit. Not only did they meet the new archbishop of Canterbury and tour Lambeth Palace, they also visited Windsor and were greeted by King George VI at Buckingham Palace.[52] At a joint service in Westminster Abbey on June 19—a dream setting for Smollett's newsreel cameras—the archbishop of Canterbury gave thanks that "by the mercy of God, we are delivered from the perils which beset our homelands and from the false and evil doctrines which degraded human life and sought to destroy the foundations of Christian faith." The Soviet past, and the memory of its sins, were thus wiped away. Employing a turn of phrase not much in vogue since 1938, the archbishop said that "Peace in our time depends on a continuation and strengthening of that comradeship which so gloriously sustained us through the war."[53] Metropolitan Nikolai responded in like terms, intoning that "our common struggle against the foe of civilisation and Christianity [has] brought our peoples very close to a feeling of mutual friendship."[54] Earlier, Nikolai had read out a message from Patriarch Aleksii, in which the latter said the victory over fascism "assumes a sacred significance as the defence of Christian principles from the barbaric foes of our Christian Civilisation."[55]

Warm as such phrases might have been, the tone of the visit was quite different than when the archbishop of York journeyed to Moscow in 1943. The introductory speeches by British political leaders, academics, and politicians were even blander and more noncommittal than usual. The end of the war had sapped the religious question of its urgency, and East-West political tensions had already begun to emerge into the open. Sensing that the shifting winds were starting to blow away from the East, political figures with sensitive meteorological antennae detected that it might no longer be a political asset to be too closely linked in the public mind with wartime Russophilia. At least on the British side, there had been little enthusiasm for the visit, but it had gone ahead anyway owing in part to inertia as well as to the fact that there was simply no polite way to refuse Nikolai and his fellow clerics once the British delegation had been to Moscow.[56]

Nikolai's visit to London, as well as Hewlett Johnson's strange session with Stalin, constituted the capstone to the selling of the Holy Alliance between Moscow and the West. During the early summer of 1941, it would have been impossible to predict that within only four years a metropolitan of the Russian Orthodox Church would travel to the British capital, with the full approval of his Communist masters, there to be feted by the archbishop of Canterbury and by the king himself. Only a few years hence, as the Cold War grew and became hot, it would be almost as hard to recall such scenes as well as the warmth that had once characterized relations between Moscow and its Western Allies—at least at a superficial level. For a brief and critical time, however, when power relationships remained in flux throughout Europe, both sides shared a common interest in pretending that religion was in fine fettle throughout the USSR, that all the Allied powers together sought to defend "Christian Civilisation," and that Western churches could enjoy full fellowship with their seemingly free Russian brethren.

The world is still deceiv'd with ornament.

In law, what plea so tainted and corrupt

But, being season'd with a gracious voice,

Obscures the show of evil? In religion,

What damned error, but some sober brow

Will bless it and approve it with a text,

Hiding the grossness with fair ornament?

There is no vice so simple but assumes

Some mark of virtue on its outward parts.

—William Shakespeare, *The Merchant of Venice*

If we look to our clergymen to be more than men, we shall
probably teach ourselves to think that they are less.

—Anthony Trollope, *Barchester Towers*

Conclusion

The sinking of the Titanic, the most infamous disaster
in maritime history, continues to foster wide-ranging speculation that shows
no sign of abating almost a century after the event. Numerous theories circulate purporting to explain why the huge, supposedly "unsinkable" ship failed so
catastrophically on her maiden voyage. One hypothesis holds that the iron of
the ship's hull, though extraordinarily strong under everyday conditions, contained impurities that caused it to lose its resiliency and become brittle when
cooled by the icy waters of the North Atlantic in the frigid spring of 1912. When
the ship struck an iceberg, the theory goes, rather than rebounding or crushing
the ice, the iron—or perhaps only the iron rivets—"cracked," causing a long,
narrow gash under the waterline.

Popular fascination with the Titanic has never primarily centered on the attraction of solving technical puzzles, however; rather, what draws readers as
well as film and television viewers is the metaphorical power of the Titanic
image. The ship can be viewed as representing the condition of humanity at
the dawn of the twentieth century. The sinking of the oceangoing Leviathan
raises questions about man's attempts to dominate nature, about the hubris of

industrial society, and about the frailties of Western civilization on the eve of the First World War. With the drama of its rich and poor passengers, it also raises issues of class and privilege that have become commonplaces of intellectual discourse throughout the succeeding decades.

The collapse of the USSR, coming as it did nearly at the opposite end of the violent twentieth century, bears more than a passing similarity to the sinking of the Titanic. The Bolshevik regime came into existence only five years after the destruction of the great ship. Like the liner, the "Soviet experiment," as it used to be called, represented a Promethean attempt to dominate nature, harness the power of industry, and create a gigantic monument to human ingenuity and might. Bolshevism was part of the same European milieu that produced the Titanic. Early Communists, much like British maritime architects, had a nearly religious faith in the transformational powers of science and industry. One can still find evidence of this belief scattered throughout the former USSR: an early Bolshevik graveyard in St. Petersburg, for instance, contains headstones featuring gears, rotors, and propeller blades in place of traditional Russian Orthodox crosses. The symbolism is clear: religion had been supplanted by a belief that science and planning would yield secular salvation. Emelian Iaroslavskii, the head of the League of Militant Godless, best expressed the Bolsheviks' new socialist-materialist creed:

> A person cannot act correctly, cannot act in an organized manner as a Communist, as a Leninist, if his brain is poisoned by religion. In order to overcome the tremendous difficulties which confront us; in order to remold the world as the working class and the peasantry want it to be; in order to subjugate all the forces of nature and compel them to work for the welfare of mankind; in order to change social relationships from top to bottom; in order to eradicate war between nations, to exterminate poverty from the face of the earth—it is necessary *that every person, that every peasant and worker sees things as they are, without the intervention of gods*, saints, angels, fiends, goblins, were-wolves, and other spirits, good or evil.[1]

The Bolsheviks' goals—to refashion the human condition in its entirety—were nothing if not ambitious, but, notwithstanding their zeal, their new faith was built on sand. Like the Titanic, the USSR, for all its gargantuan size and apparent power, would break and then crumble all at once, the victim of external and internal pressures as well as inherent design flaws.

In many ways, the Stalinist state was extraordinarily powerful. It had the capacity to eliminate rival domestic centers of power and overwhelm internal dissent; it would also prove vital enough to replicate itself in Eastern Europe and elsewhere, all the while protecting the expanding Communist empire with mighty armed forces and a ubiquitous police network. Yet, just as iron can withstand great pressures and strains, only to shatter in response to a smaller force applied under specific conditions, so too the Soviet Union withstood the Nazi onslaught, only to implode in peacetime. The Soviet system was indeed very powerful; it was also strangely brittle.

Seen in retrospect, the war years provided a preview of the forces that, when unleashed decades later, would sweep the USSR away. Nationalism, much of it inextricably mixed with religious faith, would prove the Achilles' heel of the Soviet Union. Less than a year after his fall from power, Mikhail Gorbachev himself acknowledged this when he said that "the nationalities issue" was the single greatest cause of the USSR's collapse.[2] Religion and nationalism are not identical, of course, but especially in Eastern Europe they often run together, posing insurmountable challenges to unstable, multinational regimes.[3] If one comprehends the religious and national fault lines that emerged, or reemerged, during the war, surfacing again in the 1980s, then post-Soviet realities become much clearer. In the western borderlands, the very same religious schisms and factions that rent the Russian Orthodox Church following the Nazi invasion returned in force as Moscow's power and control ebbed. The Ukrainian Autocephalous Church, the Ukrainian Autonomous Church, and Orthodox Church in Moldova all vie over disposition of church property given by Stalin to the Moscow Patriarchate.[4] The sharpest conflict is between the now restored Greek Catholic Church and the Russian Orthodoxy.[5] A dispute has even erupted between the Estonian Orthodox Church and the Moscow Patriarchate over the former's declaration of autocephaly, echoing the wartime battles between Moscow and Archbishop Sergii (Voskresenskii).[6]

Soviet history was, in large measure, a war against the past, against the historical legacy of tsarist Russia and the Russian Empire, which the Communists sought to bury in order to give birth to a "new Soviet man." Recurrent campaigns against religion were central to the whole Soviet enterprise. As Dostoevskii had predicted, the Orthodox God first had to be toppled from His throne before Man, in the guise of the new party-state, could assume His place. The Bolsheviks were the bearers of the Russian intelligentsia's abiding faith in materialist socialism; not all members of the prerevolutionary intelligentsia became Bolsheviks, to be sure, but the overwhelming number rejected religious belief entirely.[7] For Russian radical *intelligenty*, Orthodoxy represented everything they dreamed of uprooting in Russia: traditionalism, backwardness, and the dark life of the Russian peasantry with its superstitions and self-enslaving rituals. Clouds of Orthodox incense only served to obscure the bright future promised by science and industry.

Soviet Communism offered an alternative religion, which, despite its "scientific" pretensions, was every bit as ritualistic and unverifiable as the Orthodox faith that the Soviets derided as a remnant of the dismal past—and, if anything, Communism was even more intolerant of rival beliefs than Orthodoxy had been for many generations. Walled in as they were by their own set of dogmas, Soviet leaders could never really understand the reasons for the persistence of religious faith; they assumed that every rational, educated person would naturally discard religious superstitions just as a baby outgrows its rattle. Trotskii, for instance, wrote that religion provided nothing more than a tawdry spectacle and that, like vodka, it befuddled the "masses." In his view, Bolshevik cinema could easily replace the "Meaningless ritual" of the church, because film provided a better, more varied "drama." "The cinema," he wrote, "amuses, educates, strikes the imagination by images, and liberates you from the need of crossing the clerical door. The cinema is a great competitor not only of the tavern but also of the church."[8]

Despite being bitter enemies, Trotskii and Stalin shared this contemptuous view of religion. In the autumn of 1941, when W. Averell Harriman conveyed President Roosevelt's concerns about religious liberty to Stalin, the dictator responded quizzically: "He asked me," Harriman recalled, "whether the President, being such an intelligent man, really was as religious as he appeared or whether his professions were for political purposes."[9] Like Trotskii, Stalin assumed that religion was a fraud and that all clergymen were charlatans, manipulating the uneducated people for their own selfish ends. His was a view simultaneously contemptuous of the clergy, for its supposedly cynical exploitation of human weakness, and of the laity, for its ignorance and backwardness. (It causes one to wonder just what scenes he had witnessed as a young man in Tbilisi's Orthodox seminary to implant so firmly such a misanthropic and limited view of religion and of human nature.)

Many observers have seen the Soviet system as a logical outgrowth of tsarist traditions, part of a "Russian Syndrome," or "Russian Tradition" of statism.[10] In this view, the Soviet regime was little more than a modernized and more technically sophisticated variant of the Russian autocracy, and Stalin was simply a "Red tsar," or Genghiz Khan with a telegraph; the vast maw of the Russian autocratic tradition had swallowed Marxism whole—humanistic impulses and all—regurgitating it as Stalinism. The history of relations between the Orthodox Church and the Soviet state during the war is perhaps the single best test case of this proposition; for here the atheist regime found itself forced by circumstances to employ as an ally a cast-off relic of the old regime, an ideological enemy that it had hitherto repressed savagely. Superficially then, the Kremlin's wartime resurrection of the church would seem to support the contention that the USSR was little more than the Russian Empire recast and updated. Certainly a great many people during the war—including a large number of ordinary Russians—assumed that the return of the church and the general wartime revival of Russian nationalist themes indicated that Stalin had at long last jettisoned Bolshevik radicalism in favor of a reversion to traditional norms of governance.

While it would be wrong to deny that significant continuities link Soviet practice with Russian cultural customs, mores, and attitudes, Stalin's remarks to Harriman, as well as the hidden history of wartime relations between the Soviet regime and the Russian Orthodox Church, demonstrate that it is simplistic to draw a straight line between the tsarist and Soviet systems. Stalin and his underlings had by no means abandoned Communism, and ideology remained an important determinant in governing both during and after the war. Most important, ideology shaped the perceptions of Soviet rulers: they knew religion was an enemy, but they could not comprehend its lasting appeal.[11]

Aleksandr Solzhenitsyn famously compared Communism to a cancer, by which he meant that the disease's cells masquerade as healthy tissue only ultimately to kill their host. So Communist regimes appear to possess national characteristics while in fact they are destructive of nationality. Solzhenitsyn's analogy applies well to wartime church-state relations. The Kremlin faced domestic and foreign policy challenges very similar to those that had confronted its tsarist predecessors during the previous three centuries: the centrifugal forces of religion and nationalism threatened Moscow's control over its western borders. To deal with these, the Communists resorted to similar methods and tools, including the Russian Orthodox Church. But they did so in a vastly different spirit. For Stalin, religion was an instrument of social control, nothing more, and he would use it as such to manage the "simple people." The Soviet dictator was prepared to use religion as a tool of statecraft, but in his view he was only beating the priests at their own game—countermanipulating the manipulators. Tsars and their officials may have used the church to further their own secular political ends, even as Stalin did, but they did not simultaneously order their underlings to regard the church as an enemy, arrest and shoot its priests, deride its doctrines as unfit for intelligent adults, work to restrict its growth, and educate the young to reject its tenets—all the while pretending to guarantee freedom of conscience and religion.

Contrary to many accounts, what took place during the war was a mass revival of religion, not of the church. The distinction is important, because the revival of religion erupted spontaneously from below as a response to mass death in wartime and the temporary loosening of Communist atheist bonds. This revival was politically volatile, and so Stalin sanctioned the restoration of the Moscow Patriarchate in hopes of restoring order and stability. Among ethnic Russians, the religious revival took the form of increased grass-roots demands for the reopening of churches, the restoration of church property, and the activation of small religious groups and sects that were often hostile to Soviet power and suspicious of the Moscow Patriarchate, or frankly hostile to it, and thus were beyond state control. It is also important to remember that there were differences of opinion between the hierarchy of the Russian Orthodox Church and many of its lower clergy. Not all of the latter were prepared to play the role assigned to them by their political masters and apparently condoned by many of their own ecclesiastical superiors. They sought to minister to believers' needs, rather than serve as agents of their erstwhile tormentors, the Communists. Rejecting the authority of pliant church hierarchs, and salted throughout the union, these independently minded priests posed a very real political and social threat to the Soviet order.

The Soviet regime made the Moscow Patriarchate its agent, not to assuage the public's thirst for religion, but rather to control and defuse unwelcome popular religious and national enthusiasms, rendering them politically manageable. In this sense, the church's resurrection—so visible to the outside world —was designed to deal with the religious revival, which was considerably less apparent. By portraying the reappearance of the Moscow Patriarchate as an instance of the Kremlin's benevolent grace and favor, rather than the product of dire necessity, the Soviet religious-propaganda campaign was a resounding success. Like a parasitic cancer, the Stalinist regime masked itself under the camouflage of nationalism and religious freedom in order to stalk and kill spontaneous religious practice; the church, which in different circumstances might have been an agent of Russian civil society, thus became a weapon for its extinction. Stalin's state was not entirely insensitive to mass public opinion; on this, traditionalist historians who argue that totalitarian states are immune to public pressure have long been wrong. The Kremlin was well aware that a great many of its people were restive or disloyal. It could scarcely have been otherwise, after so many Soviet citizens had collaborated with the invader, fought against the reassertion of Soviet power, or flocked to unofficial churches, flounting regime values. At the same time, however, it would be very wrong to conclude from the history of church-state relations that the Soviets "negotiated" with believers, or that the regime was genuinely responsive to the public will. As every classified high-level Soviet document attests, the regime maintained its determination ultimately to extirpate religious belief; in the minds of Soviet leaders, the collaboration with the Moscow Patriarchate was nothing but a tactic in this long game.

Orthodox churches remained open well after the war, during the remainder of Stalin's life and for half a decade thereafter; the Soviet state would not resume its offensive against the Russian Orthodox Church until Khrushchev's time. The fact that Stalin refrained from moving against the church so long as he lived has persuaded many historians that this was one instance where the aging dictator kept his word, sticking to his part of the September 1943 bargain with church hierarchs—another testament to how successful Soviet propaganda had been in masking the true nature of church-state relations. On the surface, the situation seemed paradoxical: even as the rest of Soviet culture and society was crammed into an ever tightening intellectual and political straitjacket during the postwar years, the church seemed to be an exception. In fact, the paradox is more apparent than real. The regime allowed churches under the control of the Moscow Patriarchate to remain open precisely because it still required the services of the official church to sort out the massive chaos in religious and national affairs spawned by that conflict. Thus, the fact that Russian Orthodox churches remained open did not testify to a newfound tolerance for religion but to the reverse: it showed that the Kremlin had still not tamed this hostile force. A functioning Moscow Patriarchate was no indicator of religious freedom, any more than the thoroughly Stalinized Soviet Writers' Union demonstrated that Soviet authors enjoyed freedom of expression.

The cancer analogy has a second aspect that Solzhenitsyn did not develop: by killing its host, the disease dooms itself as well. Ideas have consequences; so do their deaths. If a country as disparate as the USSR is to be held together, it must have a unifying mythology. The USSR won the war, but, notwithstanding the shrill claims of Soviet propaganda, its Bolshevik foundation myths were deeply wounded in the process. In this respect, the war against Hitler was a turning point in Soviet history every bit as profound as the 1917 revolution. The unprecedented demands of the war had forced the Kremlin to go to the well of Russian history, but the manipulation of potent traditional symbols and institutions exacted long-term costs. Governments cannot switch religion and nationalism on, then off, as one would a faucet. For the masters in the Kremlin, Communism may still have been the ultimate goal, but for many Soviet subjects, and indeed for a good many state bureaucrats as well, the war seemed to be an affirmation of Russian nationalism.

Among minority nationalities—especially in the western borderlands—the war, German occupation, and the limited restoration of religious life in the Soviet public sphere actually reinforced the dangerous, and ultimately fatal, bond between religious faith and anti-Soviet nationalism that the NKVD-NKGB tried so hard to sever. In the short term, the subjection of independent churches to the power of the Moscow Patriarchate—and, through that body, to Stalin's Kremlin—facilitated the Soviet reoccupation of the western borderlands; but the policy left people of the region sullenly resentful of Soviet power and of its ecclesiastical surrogates. As each successive parish in the western borderlands was handed over to newly minted priests from Moscow, while this helped to break up the networks of civil society that enabled the locals to resist Soviet power, it did nothing to win the people's hearts and minds. The role of Russian nationalism in the victorious war effort made Soviet rule look to non-Russians ever more like traditional tsarist imperialism, and the prominent role accorded to the Russian Orthodox Church only reinforced this impression. Stalin was no "Red Tsar," but many of his alienated subjects saw him as one—only modernized and equipped with the latest horrors of perverted police-state science. During the Bolshevik Revolution, Latvians and other Balts had served as bodyguards for Lenin, believing that Bolshevik internationalism would free minority peoples from the yoke of tsarist-Russian domination; by 1945, their sons were fighting against the reimposition of Communist rule.

From 1945 until the collapse of Soviet power, the Communist regime would draw on new myths of the Great Patriotic War for legitimization. The Soviet regime, it was claimed, had saved human civilization from fascism, conclusively demonstrating its superiority over such decadent capitalist countries as France by surviving the Nazi onslaught, by mobilizing the country's resources through socialist planning, and above all else by showing that the supposed "union of free peoples" within the Soviet order could defeat any enemy. The reality had been quite different; it had been, as the duke of Wellington said of Waterloo, "The nearest run thing you ever saw in your life."

The war had forced the regime to rely on the Russian core to an extent not visible to outside observers at the time or for many years afterward. By grafting Russian nationalism onto the trunk of internationalist Communism as Stalin did during the war, however, the Kremlin gave birth to a sickly new hybrid— a species neither entirely national nor internationalist in nature. Non-Russian Soviet subjects increasingly saw the union as an alien, totalitarian force, a Russian-manned prison house of nations. At the same time, the Russians themselves were split: a great many, best exemplified by Solzhenitsyn, were willing to fight for Mother Russia but rejected the remaining internationalist elements of Soviet Communism as corrosive of Russia's national health, and they believed Russia itself to be the first victim of Communism and empire. A second set of Russian nationalists, the so-called national Bolsheviks—many of whom clustered round the church—did, and do, see the USSR as the fulfillment of Russia's national mission and guarantor of its greatness. The regime's own servitors became less certain whether they were Communists first and Russians second, or vice versa. This confusion at so many levels of society helped further to expose the increasingly apparent falsity of Soviet Communist pretensions.[12] The Soviet Titanic had struck its nationalist iceberg, but it would take many years for the commanders and crew to realize that it was slowly sinking.

Sergii's Choice

The collaboration of Sergii and his fellow bishops with the Stalinist state raises a number of questions. Why did Sergii decide to cooperate, and did he make a wise—or even moral—decision in doing so? Did he save the Russian church, or, by his actions, did he enter into a fatal marriage with the Kremlin, imperiling the future of Russian Orthodoxy in exchange for a temporary respite from state-sponsored persecution? What real choice did he have at all? There can be no definitive answer to such questions, but, in order to address them, one has to keep in mind not only the two-decades-long history of Soviet religious persecution but also the traditions of Russian Orthodoxy, which differ markedly in so many ways from those of Western Christianity.

By the end of the 1930s, the Russian church lay at the feet of the Communist state, almost extinct as an institution. Although the large majority of Russians retained their religious beliefs in the face of official disapproval, they did so in private, with the Soviets slowly but inexorably strangling public worship. The withered tree of the Russian church still stood above ground, but its branches were rotten, its trunk riddled with parasites, and its roots cut. The church seemed to have no future: the authorities had closed all seminaries, preventing the education and ordination of new priests; the Soviets had banned public or group religious education of children, and they had forbidden the raising of money for the maintenance of church buildings or for the sustenance of the dwindling remnant of priests. With no new ordinations, it looked as though the apostolic succession of the Russian priesthood might actually be broken after the passing of a generation.

Following the outbreak of the Nazi-Soviet war, a dim ray of sunshine revived the few remaining leaves on the tree of the Russian church. The war seemed to promise a slim hope for Russian Orthodoxy's resurrection. When the Soviet authorities approached Sergii to bless the cause of the Red Army, he complied. Had he refused, of course, the full weight of NKVD repression would have fallen squarely on the Russian Orthodox Church. But there is no reason to believe that threats alone explain the willingness of Orthodox hierarchs to support the war against Hitler. Throughout its history, as Russian Orthodox leaders averred time and again, the church had stood beside the people in times of foreign threat: during the Mongol invasions of the thirteenth century, when the Poles threatened to extinguish Russian independence during the "Time of Troubles" of the seventeenth century, at the time of Napoleon's invasion in 1812, and so forth.

To have refused support for the Soviet state in 1941, even as the Russian people faced the most determined and lethal—even genocidal—enemy in their history, would have been almost unthinkable, and, win or lose, the populace might never have forgiven priests making such a choice. Stalin may have been a devil, but he was the Soviets' own devil. Whereas the Communist state sought to stifle religious belief, the Nazis' "crusade" would have enslaved the entire Russian people—along with their church. That some Orthodox hierarchs in the occupied regions nonetheless chose to collaborate with the Nazis is eloquent testimony to just how brutal the prewar Stalinist regime had been, and how deep hatreds ran. Of course, the full extent of Hitler's plans for the East only unfolded over time, and people on both sides of the fighting line made their choices based on incomplete information.

Having decided to cooperate with Stalin and the Communist government as early as 1927, Sergii could console himself with the gradual restoration of limited religious freedoms as the war progressed. Soviet power exacted a price in exchange for the partial restoration of the church, of course. Above all, Sergii and his fellow hierarchs both denied the history of Soviet religious persecution—the shutting of churches and the torture, imprisonment, and execution of their fellow priests and believers—and also sanctioned Stalin's rule as divinely ordained. In November 1942, for instance, on the anniversary of the Bolshevik Revolution, Sergii issued a treacly open letter to Stalin: "[I]n the name of our clergy and all believers of the Russian Orthodox Church, the faithful children of our homeland, I cordially and prayerfully welcome in your person the God-chosen leader of our military and cultural forces. . . . May God bless with success and glory Your great deed for the motherland."[13] Such paeans of praise to the Great Leader, coming from the pen of the head of the Russian church, certainly stick in the throat of any reader familiar with the history of the USSR.

Whether the Faustian bargain between church and state was ultimately a wise one, from the church's point of view, can be disputed endlessly, and any judgment on such a matter will inevitably reflect one's individual values and preconceptions. From the strictly secular point of view, there can be little doubt that Russian church leaders made the right choice in 1941. Had they not decided to collaborate with Stalin, their church might well have disappeared, hounded into oblivion by the combined forces of the Soviet repressive organs and the outrage of many average Russians. Had the Nazis won, the situation would have been even more dire.

The Russian Orthodox Church was not, however, simply a secular institution, and the activities of its clergy must be interpreted, and judged, within Christian, and specifically Orthodox, traditions. During the Stalin era and ever since, the collaboration of Russian Orthodox clergy with the Stalinist regime has drawn criticism from religious writers. If support for the Soviet war effort is understandable, given the nature of the enemy, the Patriarchate's collaboration in the taming of domestic religion, its participation in dishonest international propaganda, and especially its role in the dismantling of rival churches and sects were all more dubious and controversial. One Jesuit historian, for instance, writes that Sergii's wartime "vision did not coincide with the traditions of Christians in the West."[14] If the alternative to collaboration with the Stalinist regime was martyrdom, this argument implies, then so be it. Just as it would have been unconscionable for early Christians to sing the praises of Nero, Sergii should have resisted the worldly temptations Stalin dangled in front of him.

In assessing such an argument, one must always remember that, for Sergii, individual martyrdom was never an option; his choices determined the fate of thousands of Orthodox priests and believers as well as his own. A further problem with such criticisms of Sergii lies in the fact that the Russian Orthodox Church did not share "the traditions of Christians in the West." It had its own history and practices, and many of these pointed along the path Sergii ultimately chose to follow. Not since the eighteenth century, when Peter I transformed the patriarchal church into virtually another branch of the secular government, had Russian Orthodox leaders seriously challenged the political power of the state. Theology and tradition, as well as economic dependency, all pushed the church into the arms of the secular powers.

Throughout its near millennium-long history, the Russian Orthodox Church had never before faced a Russian state that was opposed to religion as such. To be sure, certain tsars, such as Peter I, had been either indifferent or even hostile to some aspects of church doctrine or practice, but they had never set out to destroy the church root and branch.[15] With the advent of Bolshevism, Russian Orthodoxy experienced a threat unprecedented in its history, and nothing in its past gave it the theological, intellectual, or material resources to challenge state power—even if that power was fundamentally atheist. Unlike the Vatican, the Russian church was largely limited to one country; it did not have the luxury of being able to sacrifice its institutions inside Russia, secure in the knowledge that the church would live on elsewhere. And one should remember that even the Western Church did not lightheartedly confront hostile regimes. Pope Pius XII was notoriously too cautious in challenging Hitler for fear of harming Germany's Catholics.[16] If the wartime situation of Catholicism was delicate enough, the dilemmas of the Moscow patriarch were far more desperate. The survival of a Russian Orthodox Church severed from Russia itself is as improbable as a tropical rain forest flourishing in Antarctica.

None of this is to apologize for Sergii's embrace of the Stalinist state—if apology is needed. Rather, it is enough to understand his anguished circumstances, as well as the range and consequences of the options open to him. Certainly not all Orthodox thinkers have uncritically accepted the logic of his choices. Twenty years after the war, under the conditions of degenerating Brezhnevian totalitarianism, a new generation of Orthodox writers and priests emerged to question the wisdom of the church's collaboration with the Soviet state. In 1965, two priests, Nikolai Eshliman and Gleb Iakunin, issued open letters to the patriarch asking, "Does not the sacred duty of a bishop command him to lay down his life for the sake of the sheep of Christ's flock?" The compliance of the patriarch and other hierarchs with the Soviet state had borne bitter fruit: "[T]he mass closure of churches, monasteries and church schools undeniably testifies to the unconditional submission of the Moscow Patriarchate to the secret dictates of atheist-officials."[17]

Seven years later, in March 1972, Aleksandr Solzhenitsyn, whose own political dissidence was grounded in his Orthodox faith, followed the priests' open letter with his own even sharper *Lenten Letter to Patriarch Pimen'*. "The past half century has already been lost beyond hope," Solzhenitsyn wrote. Acknowledging the disastrous embrace of the state by the Russian church under the tsars, he continued: "The study of Russian history during the last few centuries convinces one that the whole of our history would have taken a far more humane and harmonious course if the Church had not renounced her independence and if the people had heeded her voice in a way comparable, for instance, to Poland. Alas, in our country it has long been otherwise."[18] It was futile to complain of history, but Solzhenitsyn directly attacked the collaborationist policies of the Moscow Patriarchate and called church leaders to return to the spirit of early Christian martyrs.

Not everyone shared Solzhenitsyn's personal courage, nor did they accept his political and moral analysis. Although Pimen' could not respond directly to his critics, owing to his delicate political position, the patriarch had his defenders. One of the most important was Father Sergei Zheludkov of Pskov', himself no lapdog of the Soviet state. A supporter of religious and secular dissidents, and the editor of underground religious publications, Zheludkov admitted that the situation of Russian Orthodoxy under a totalitarian regime was far from ideal.[19] But, he asked: "What remains for us to do in such a situation?" As for the patriarchal collaboration with Communist authorities, "*there was no other choice.*"[20]

Arguments about the relation of the church to the secular order were never finally settled before the collapse of the USSR and have persisted into the post-Soviet era, remaining both bitter and unresolved. While some clergy, such as Iakunin, demanded an honest reckoning with the Soviet past and openness about the history of clergy collaboration with Soviet secret police, the bulk of the clergy was far too deeply implicated with the Communist authorities to favor airing the church's dirty laundry. In early 1997, the council of bishops excommunicated the bothersome Iakunin, in part as a message to other overly insistent critics.[21]

For better or worse, the actions and statements of Sergii and his fellow bishops during the Stalin years tied Russian Orthodoxy's fate to that of the USSR and to a peculiarly virulent form of Soviet-imperialist nationalism. In his public statements, Sergii's successor, Patriarch Aleksii, often drew no dividing line whatsoever between the interests of the church and those of the nation, leaving little or no space for the claims of individual conscience. "Serving the Holy Russian Orthodox Church," Aleksii declared, "is inseparable from serving our Fatherland." "Nobody can be a good Christian who is not a good and faithful son of his Motherland, ready to sacrifice everything for her glory and flourishing."[22] These were not idle words; throughout the Cold War, the Moscow Patriarchate would slavishly endorse Soviet foreign policy, even in its most dubious adventures, such as the invasions of Hungary, Czechoslovakia, and Afghanistan. So deeply enmeshed in Soviet foreign policy was official Russian Orthodoxy that the personnel of its Department of External Church Affairs outnumbered that of all its other departments combined.[23]

Soviet authorities were well aware that this bond between the Orthodox Church and the Communist state, forged in the heat of the war and carried on afterward, remained a valuable asset, as a member of Gorbachev's Presidential Council Anatoly Lukianov averred when he met with Orthodox hierarchs in the waning days of the Soviet empire. "I want to stress once again," Lukianov stated, "that our relations with the Russian Orthodox Church have not changed.

All of its [the church's] activities, especially during the war and postwar years, have demonstrated that we can work together well."[24] These assembled higher clergy actually took Gorbachev's reformist government to task for insufficiently suppressing the non-Russian nationalism that was dissolving the bonds of empire and undermining the church's position in the western borderlands. Thus, as the Communist state disintegrated, high-ranking clerics proved more ardent than the Soviet leadership, actually mourning the passing of the Soviet state that had done so much harm to their church.

Stalin's grand wartime confidence trick, whereby he appeared to resurrect the Orthodox Church while in fact co-opting its hierarchs into restricting religion's growth and sapping it of its vitality, had bequeathed a bitter legacy. Not only did the church become an uncritical cheerleader for Soviet foreign policy, but also domestically Russian Orthodoxy's center of gravity shifted away from Russia itself to the western borderlands, especially Ukraine, where the vast proportion of its open churches were located. The church thus had a great stake in maintaining the Soviet-imperial order, and so it was forced even more deeply into the arms of the state; this also explains why, even in the post-Soviet era, Communist politicians and Orthodox Church leaders are often to be found in the same camp. Absent the imperial system, held together by Soviet might, the church faced ruinous loss.

By 1945 the Russian Orthodox Church's relations with the Soviet state resembled those between a falcon and its master. Like the invisible ties linking the hunting-bird with its trainer, those bonding the Russian church to the Kremlin were, to some extent, symbiotic. Master and bird were hunting the same game: anti-Russian nationalists, religious schismatics beyond Moscow's grip, overly enthusiastic believers. The well-trained bird soared upward, swooped down, seized and dispatched its prey; to the unknowing passerby it even appeared like a bird in free flight. But the falcon continued to hunt only so long as the master retained his taste for the sport.

The Consequences of the Holy Alliance

Three years after the end of the war, the year of the Berlin airlift and the Czech Communist coup, the archbishop of York, Cyril Garbett, delivered a sermon entitled "Communism and Christianity." Following his visit to Moscow five years earlier, Archbishop Garbett had called Stalin a "wise statesman," praising the creativity and egalitarianism of the Soviet system and calling on his fellow Britons to learn from Soviet central planning. During the intervening years, he seemed to have changed his mind—or at least, in the new climate of East-West tension, he had decided to air his reservations about the Stalinist regime with a frankness that he had believed to be inconsistent with the spirit of the wartime alliance.

Although Garbett said that "the ideal [of Communism] is not un-Christian, and ought not to be condemned as such," he drew a distinction between the supposedly lofty ideal and its "Marxian" reality (what Eastern Europeans who actually had to live under Communist regimes would later grimly call "real, existing socialism"). "There are many Christians who are convinced that there is much more in common between Christianity and Communism than between Christianity and Capitalism," he claimed. Having said this, however, the archbishop was unsparing in his criticism of the same Stalinist reality in which he had earlier found so much to admire. With words that might have fallen from the lips of John Foster Dulles, Garbett declaimed that Marxism was "a denial of all the ethical and moral values which have helped to form Christian civilisation." Christianity and real-world Communism were "opposed on matters of faith and ethics on which there can be no compromise." The USSR, which Garbett had earlier called "this great and remarkable nation" that Britons should view "with sympathy," now posed a dire threat to human civilization:

> By a gigantic system of spies and informers it removes by imprisonment, exile or death any who venture to criticise its policy or actions. By complete control of education, the press, and the wireless, the dominant party gradually moulds the opinions and actions of the people into conformity with its own. It becomes a ruthless tyranny under which liberty is impossible. It establishes a reign of terror. The lights of freedom are extinguished and darkness spreads over the land.[25]

Given the European situation in 1948, and the squalid reality of Soviet police-state terror, Garbett's sermon was scarcely remarkable and passed largely without notice amid the general East-West exchanges of abuse at that time.

The Stalinist system decried by Garbett had not undergone a radical change in the intervening five years since his visit to Moscow. It had been a police state then, and so it remained. No miraculous transformation had occurred in the USSR, but a significant change had taken place in the intellectual and political climate of the West. Things once unutterable had become commonplaces. For a public figure such as the archbishop to have wallowed in the dark side of Stalinism in midwar would have required political courage—or recklessness. In the words of one historian, "any politician who dared break that taboo found shot and shell flying round his head."[26]

It is harder to explain the moral flexibility that enabled clerics such as Garbett to shift nimbly between praise of the USSR one year and the harshest condemnation the next than it is to understand Patriarch Sergii's difficult position. Unlike their Russian counterparts, Western clergymen did not have the deadly pressure of the NKVD at their backs to blame for their moral compromises. The need to prosecute the war against Hitler excused a great many sins, to be sure, but much of Western wartime propaganda crossed an important line: refraining from unnecessarily attacking the USSR when it was carrying the weight of the fighting against the Wehrmacht may have been one thing, but actually singing the praises of the Soviet system, even inventing virtues that it supposedly exemplified, was quite another. Like Archbishop Garbett, when in public, Archbishop Temple was prepared to describe "the leaders of Russia" as "clear-sighted, sincere, and very able men" who "do not expect us to pretend that their principles are other than they are." And he could declaim that Stalinist Communism "does not seem open to condemnation as unChristian." Yet, writing in private, he freely confessed that he saw no essential difference between Nazism and Communism, and a Church of England Committee quietly monitored the fate of clerics being arrested and deported within the USSR.

Government propagandists do these sorts of things routinely, and they could be expected to put the demands of the war ahead those of the truth, but religious leaders at least claim to stand for something more than political expediency. The leadership of the Catholic Church, and Pius XII in particular, have rightly drawn criticism for its insufficient condemnation of Nazi horrors. One wonders what historians would have said had the pope actually described Hitler as "sincere," or said he was a "wise statesman"? Perhaps because they were on the winning side, these Western clerics have been spared the same level of historical scrutiny.

During the war, Western clergymen consoled themselves by arguing that it was not the right time, so long as Nazism remained undefeated, to press the Kremlin to honor human or religious rights; and they deluded themselves with the pious hope that the Western Allies' moral example would somehow magically moderate the Soviet system, without anyone ever having to brave public opprobrium and speak out. In fact, these proved to be nothing more than arguments for an expedient silence. Clerics such as Garbett were perfectly willing to condemn the very real evils of the Soviet system in 1948, at a time when doing so promised no chance whatsoever of actually inducing change within the USSR, and when such condemnations had become both routine and politically and socially acceptable. The failure to use their special position of influence and moral authority during the time of the alliance to say at least something about the gulag, police terror, and mass deportations—of which they were aware—was a serious failure of moral nerve; their silence was also unnecessary. It is hard to imagine how the Soviet war effort could have been harmed had Western clergy leaders been willing to follow Churchill's June 1941 lead and make a sober case for aid to Russia, while maintaining their principled opposition to the evils of the Stalinist system.

Western churchmen were only bit players in the much wider drama of pro-Soviet wartime propaganda, the tools of people with much greater political savvy. This larger selling of the alliance had important short- and long-term consequences. Soviet propagandists were adept at seizing on statements made by Western politicians or clergymen to the effect that the Soviet people enjoyed religious freedom. They quickly recycled such statements and circulated them throughout the USSR itself as well as Eastern Europe and the Balkans. For Soviet believers, a great many of whom attributed the very limited wartime reappearance of religion in the USSR to Western pressure, such statements must have been uniquely disheartening.

Even more critical, in political terms, was the impact of Soviet religious policy and propaganda in the Balkans and Eastern Europe. In the wake of the German defeat, political parties and structures throughout this region were in complete disarray; trade unions and other civil groups had been smashed by prewar or wartime authoritarian rightist regimes (some under Nazi influence or control), or were scattered by the advancing Communists. Generally, by default, churches were the most powerful extant civil groups in the region. Through their cleverly devised religious policies, the Soviets were able to neutralize or isolate hostile groupings within these churches. Among Orthodox believers, the reappearance of the Moscow Patriarchate conferred a spurious gloss of religious tolerance on Soviet policy. In countries and regions with large Orthodox populations, such as Romania, Bulgaria, Sub-Carpathian Rus' and to a lesser degree Serbia, Communists co-opted church hierarchies, isolating or removing obstinate, nationalist, or anti-Communist clergy, and branding all resisters as "fascists." At the same time, the Moscow Patriarchate, as handmaid of Soviet foreign policy, plausibly denounced the other major religious force in the region —the Vatican—as the defender of the defeated and discredited fascists. The Patriarchate stoked ancient suspicions and hatreds between the Orthodox East and Latin West, all the better to divide and conquer.

Historians who only look at Soviet religious propaganda as being directed at the Western public overlook a much wider story. Friendly statements issued by Western clerics, praising the ostensible freedom of religion in the USSR, may not have entirely eradicated religious suspicions of Soviet Communism among the believing public of the Western democracies; but these very same statements, reissued via Moscow's own propaganda organs or through the remarkably compliant BBC World Service, convinced a great many clerics throughout the new Soviet imperium either that Moscow had indeed changed its atheist ways, or, at the very least, that they were entirely alone in their resistance to the establishment of Soviet power in their countries, unable to rely on the support of Western church leaders or governments. These underlying dynamics explain the otherwise inexplicable praise of Marxism issued by nervous Orthodox Christian hierarchs throughout the Balkans in 1945. By co-opting or isolating hostile Balkan religious organizations—one of the very few social forces that was capable of rallying some form of collective resistance to the imposition of Soviet-Communist political authority—Moscow's religious wartime program must be judged a significant success and a major contributor to the Kremlin's policy of establishing satellite regimes in the area. Religious policy was a significant, yet largely unnoticed, element of the notorious "salami tactics" adopted by the Soviet occupiers to impose Communist control gradually and by degree.

If the most significant successes of the Soviet religious-propaganda effort came in Eastern Europe, however, the impact in the Western democracies cannot be dismissed as unimportant. Hostile clerics were silenced by the growing spirit of the alliance, itself partly a spontaneous reaction to the heroism of the Soviet people, but also of behind-the-scenes manipulation. In the end, the American government approved Lend-Lease assistance for the USSR in the autumn of 1941 in the absence of any significant resistance from the churches. Indeed, some churches, especially American Protestants, became conduits for grassroots aid to the Soviet Union, through such agencies as Russian War Relief.

One historian of the twists and turns in American public opinion toward the USSR during the war argues that, throughout the conflict, "most Americans were anticommunist but pro-Russian." In his opinion, this apparent contradiction created "cognitive dissonance," which the public tended to resolve by "(1) insisting that Russia was evolving away from communism; (2) avoiding information contrary to this new view of Russia; and (3) repressing information which tended to 'play the Axis game' of undermining Allied Unity."[27] In fact, this is to get things the wrong way around: Western opinion was not suffering from a mass psychosis of psychological denial; instead, the three points listed above reflect what official propagandists were telling the public during the war. These points conform remarkably to the guidelines for propaganda secretly suggested by Alexander Werth to the Foreign Office in 1941. The American and British publics had no need to repress or avoid information that might suggest that their Communist ally retained its totalitarian system; this service was being provided for them gratis—by the Soviets themselves, by newspaper reporters who were censored or eager to ingratiate themselves with the Soviet authorities, by American and British leaders who suppressed information about atrocities such as Katyn and mass deportations, or by clerics who refused to reveal in public what they knew to be true about continuing religious and political repression in the USSR. There was no vast, unified conspiracy to hide the truth about Stalin's empire; rather, for a host of widely varying reasons—from ideological commitment to reasons of state, from careerism to fear of public censure, or from simple intellectual slothfulness—people of various political or personal convictions had their own, often very different reasons for suppressing or denying the truth about the USSR.

Ultimately, this larger campaign of whitewashing Soviet reality may have been too successful for the Soviets' own good. Throughout the war, Red Army soldiers and Soviet citizens were routinely portrayed in grand terms, their very real heroic deeds magnified to superhuman proportions, and the shortcomings and weaknesses of the Soviet system hidden from view. By the end of the fighting, the USSR had lost more than 25 million of its citizens, its towns and cities lay in ruins, its economy was shattered, and its people were starving.[28] The Red Army was victorious, but neither it nor the country behind it was in any state to face new conflicts. The vice-lock of Soviet censorship, the propaganda machine, and the hermetic seal of the border all conspired to mask Soviet weaknesses from view. There is reason to believe that, just as he did in his atomic diplomacy, Stalin acted belligerently in Europe and elsewhere in part to hide the vast damage done to Soviet power during the war, and the enormous weaknesses of Soviet society.[29] By concealing their weaknesses while behaving aggressive internationally, however, the Soviets contributed to the postwar fear of Soviet power in the West that was almost certainly out of proportion to any genuine threat posed by the weakened Soviet armed forces. Furthermore, as the selling of the alliance ended, and the American and British governments began eagerly to supply the dirty details of Soviet rule that they had once downplayed or repressed, the inevitable public backlash contributed to the growth of the near hysterical anti-Communist wave that contributed so greatly to the rise of McCarthyism.[30]

Ever since the end of the war, and the onset of the Cold War, historians have argued over where to place the blame for the postwar falling out among the Allies. One school—the so-called traditionalists—has pointed to Stalin's personal responsibility for the Cold War, seeing the dictator as aggressive and as unbound by the sorts of domestic constraints that restrict the power of Western leaders. Historians of this persuasion tend to emphasize Stalin's relative political and diplomatic autonomy and the role played by his dictatorial will.[31] A rival school—self-styled "revisionists"—has blamed U.S. leadership, claiming that American postwar diplomacy sought to remake the world in its own image, one safe for American interests, especially market capitalism. In this view, Soviet diplomacy was primarily reactive to American initiatives; the United States enjoyed the more powerful position, and thus it had the luxury, which it did not exercise, of refraining from a confrontation with the USSR.[32]

This study of religion and nationalism in the Soviet Union during the war suggests an alternative view, one that does not entirely vindicate either of the established positions just outlined, but one that places Soviet foreign relations in their domestic context. Stalin was indeed aggressive—few people can doubt that anymore—and the regime he led was brutal beyond the powers of description. But the USSR was also much weaker than anyone outside the Soviet leadership could have known at the time. Moscow's control over its outlying provinces was very tenuous, and the war had taught the Soviet oligarchs a bitter lesson: that only the truly terrible nature of the Nazi invader, combined with massive doses of repression, had prevented many of their subjects from deserting the Soviet cause. Disloyalty remained a genuine problem, and it was at its most acute in precisely the regions most vulnerable to hostile penetration: the western borderlands.

Given this domestic situation, it is difficult to imagine how any Soviet leaders, not just Stalin himself, could have hazarded genuinely open intercourse with the non-Communist world following the war without fatally undermining their own power. The Soviets were busily exiling or shooting Soviet POWs as they returned from German camps, precisely to minimize the danger that they might spread foreign contamination to other subjects.[33] Had Soviet borders been porous after the war, this would almost certainly have led to a massive hemorrhaging of Soviet subjects fleeing material shortage, police terror, and political and national repression. Stalin and his government were aware of public opinion, and they could not ignore it with impunity. Soviet leaders determined that, to save their police-state dictatorship, and perhaps even their lives, they needed to wall off their dominion from the outside world.

Until the collapse of the Soviet bloc, the internal instability and political illegitimacy of Communist regimes remained one of the chief sources of East-West tensions, and religion's persistence remained near to the heart of this problem. Historians of the Cold War and international relations have generally relegated religious questions to the margins of their larger story of East-West conflict, often not mentioning them at all. Yet it is becoming increasingly clear that this was never the view from Moscow itself. Soviet authorities always regarded religion as one of their most dangerous opponents. As an alternative belief system, linked so strongly with national identity, it was omnipresent throughout the Communist world and impossible to eradicate, and it was the area where foreign and domestic threats intersected most hazardously. As late as 1984, only seven years before the collapse of the USSR, the KGB was still fighting the religious wars, and, as ever, one of the most dangerous flashpoints was in the western borderlands. The KGB "Center" in Moscow warned its *residents* abroad that the Catholic Church under the Polish Pope John Paul II represented a "subversive" threat to "socialist countries": "The Vatican is at present putting the main emphasis in its so-called 'Eastern policy' on practical steps to revive the activity of Catholic and Uniate parishes." The KGB called on its agents abroad to work to "discredit [Pope] John Paul II" and to "make more systematic use of existing agent resources and to create new ones in Catholic centres and organizations and, above all, in the Vatican."[34]

The Soviet empire would crack and begin to crumble in Poland, in large part owing to the powerful combination of religion and nationalism that the KGB so rightly feared. The disintegration would then spread to the USSR's own western borderlands, the Baltic states and Ukraine. Of course, religion was not the sole force in this massive systemic breakdown; technological failure, heavy military expenditure, economic crisis, poor consumer goods, the erosion of faith in Communism even among the elites—all these were fundamental. The collapse of East European Communism was too vast to lay at the feet of a single cause. Nonetheless, Soviet leaders from Trotskii to the KGB of the mid-1980s were right to see religion as a mortal rival. As much as any other force, it can justly claim to be the "grave-digger of the revolution."

NOTES

Introduction

1. Fukuyama, *The End of History and the Last Man*. Fukuyama argues that, if one accepts the Hegelian dialectical view of history as being defined by clashes between contending organizing principles of human civilization, then we have come to the end of this process with the elimination of rivals to the Western liberal-capitalist model. He does qualify his argument somewhat in relation to religion; see pp. 216–17. In an article that has attracted a great deal of controversy, Samuel P. Huntington has argued that, in the post–Cold War world, civilizations defined by religious demarcations have replaced the Soviet-Western rivalry as the locus of international conflict. Huntington, "The Clash of Civilizations?," pp. 22–49.

2. See Vorontsova and Filatov, "Freedom of Conscience in Russia," pp. 375–81. By 1997 the Russian Orthodox Church had been edged out of first place as the most trusted institution in Russia by the army—even in the wake of the disastrous Chechen War: 48 percent of Russians listed the armed forces, and 44 percent the church as the group most trusted. *Economist*, August 2, 1997, p. 38.

3. Two students of current Russian religious opinion conclude that most Russians regard themselves as " 'Christians in general,' " and that "Russian religious feeling today is spontaneously anarchic and, even if unconsciously, ecumenical." Vorontsova and Filatov, "Freedom of Conscience in Russia," p. 380.

4. In September 1997 the church was able to convince an overwhelming number of Duma deputies to pass legislation severely restricting rival churches and religious sects from owning property, publishing literature, and evangelizing. Gordon, "Irking U.S., Yeltsin Signs Law Protecting Orthodox Church," pp. 1 and 5. For an exploration of many of the more important early results of the new law, see Uzzell, "Letter from Moscow," pp. 17–19.

5. A recent example of a popular author vastly overstating Stalin's control over events is Radzinsky, *Stalin*.

6. In 1972 John Gaddis, a historian of the Cold War (and a personal friend and former colleague at Ohio University), wrote that "The Russian dictator was immune from pressures of Congress, public opinion, or the press. Even ideology did not restrict him: Stalin was the master of communist doctrine, not a prisoner of it, and could modify or suspend Marxism-Leninism whenever it suited him to do so." *The United States and the Origin of the Cold War*, p. 360. Gaddis has changed his views considerably since he wrote these lines, especially concerning the role of ideology. See his *Now We Know*. Nonetheless, the view he expressed is still widely held and frequently even affected Western policy toward the USSR during the Cold War.

7. For such revisionist arguments, see Getty, *Origins of the Great Purges*. An even more extreme, and recent view is Thurston, *Life and Terror in Stalin's Russia*; Lih, Naumov, and Klevniuk, *Stalin's Letters to Molotov*. In a passage from his introduction to these documents, Lih outlines one common revisionist view of the great dictator: "Stalin was caught up in

events beyond his comprehension (we are still struggling to understand them today), and his conceptual equipment was plainly inadequate for grasping the real causes of his problems or the effects of his actions. His ignorance and anger, amplified by his sincerity and his leadership skills, led to crimes of horrifying dimensions. It would take the powers of a Dostoevsky to fully describe the combination of cynicism and belief, of manipulation and sincerity, that resulted in the tragedy of Stalin and his times" (p. 63). With the collapse of the USSR, certain revisionist historians have sought to backtrack somewhat, admitting that Stalin was, after all, the single indispensible figure of his era. See the introduction in Getty and Manning, *Stalinist Terror*, pp. 1–18.

8. The focus of this work is overwhelmingly on the role of the Christian churches, and especially the Russian Orthodox Church, during the war. Judaism, Islam, and Buddhism are mentioned, though infrequently. This is not because these other religions were unimportant in Soviet life, but rather because they did not play as large a role in Soviet wartime policy, domestic and international, as did Russian Orthodoxy, the religion of the Russian majority. Although Jewish issues were very important during the war, of course, and the Soviets created the Jewish Antifascist Committee to mobilize international Jewish opinion in favor of the war effort, specifically religious questions played a relatively small part in the committee's efforts. The committee's work was almost entirely secular. Furthermore, the Nazis' genocidal anti-Semitic program meant that Soviet Jews were less conflicted in their loyalties than were many Christians. As for Islam and Buddhism, although Moscow obtained declarations of support for the Soviet war effort from the domestic leaders of these religions, they did not take on the same degree of urgency as did issues related to Christianity, largely because the USSR was not at war with a state able to make full use of Pan-Islamic or Pan-Buddhist appeals.

9. The citation is from what was for many years one of the most widely used texts on Russian and Soviet history, Riasanovsky, *A History of Russia*, p. 642.

10. One of the most recently published such histories typifies this tendency. A chapter on culture and society—including a section entitled "Mind, Body, and Soul"—contains no discussion of religion. The Orthodox Church's role during the war is dismissed in a single sentence. Suny, *The Soviet Experiment*, pp. 269–90 and 327. Keep, *Last of the Empires*, pp. 168–71, devotes fewer than three pages to the Orthodox Church in a chapter on dissent. Although he makes several good points, he too sees the church as essentially a passive victim of state power.

11. Weigel, *The Final Revolution*, argues that the Christian religion brought down Communism, largely through its moral example. But he says scarcely a word about the role of the Orthodox Church, focusing almost exclusively on Catholicism.

12. This point is made by Pipes, *Russia under the Bolshevik Regime*, p. 337.

13. The most recent history of the USSR during the war, for instance, devotes fewer than two pages to the subject of religion and rather oddly explains Orthodoxy's revival in part by asserting that "Stalin, the ex-seminarian, may never have lost entirely his faith." The author also briefly mentions the importance of religion in mobilizing nationalist sentiment. Overy, *Russia's War*, p. 203. One notable exception to the neglect of religion is Alexander Werth, who has an insightful, though short, discussion of the church's wartime role in his *Russia at War*, pp. 429–38. Nonetheless, even he largely misses the international context of Soviet religious policy and entirely overlooks the role of international propaganda.

14. Cited in Fitzpatrick, *Stalin's Peasants*, p. 204. Fitzpatrick's work is an exception, giving as it does a good deal of space to the exploration of religion among the peasantry.

15. Stites, *Culture and Entertainment in Wartime Russia*. Nor does Stites discuss wartime religion in his *Russian Popular Culture*.

16. Barber and Harrison, *The Soviet Home Front*, p. 70.

17. See, for example, Kondakova and Main, *Intelligentsia Rossii 1941–1945 gg.*, especially chaps. III/1, and V/1 and 2, which purport to examine such things as the "rebirth of spiritual life" in purely secular terms. As this manuscript was going to press, Shkarovskii, *Russkaia Pravoslavnaia Tserkov' pri Staline i Khrushcheve* appeared. Although it contains a good, short survey of the period covered by this study, it does not examine the international context.

18. There is no mention at all of religious issues in such standard works on Soviet foreign relations as Mastny, *Russia's Road to the Cold War*, and Taubman, *Stalin's American Policy*.

19. The best history of the Russian Orthodox Church during the Soviet era as a whole remains Pospielovsky, *The Russian Church under the Soviet Regime*. Although written before the opening of the Soviet archives, this excellent study is sensitive to the complex nuances of religion in the USSR and remains enormously valuable. Pospielovsky's focus is entirely on the church itself; he is less interested in the international context of Soviet religious policy, and he tends to downplay those occasions when the interests of church and state ran together. Following the opening of the Soviet archives, Pospielovsy published a short article on the Russian Orthodox Church during the war, "The 'Best Years' of Stalin's Church Policy (1942–1948) in the Light of Archival Documents," pp. 139–62. There are, of course, other fine studies of the church in more recent times, which contain historical reviews, but these mention the war years only in passing. See Davis, *A Long Walk to Church*; and Ellis, *The Russian Orthodox Church*.

20. Perhaps this is because many of the historians drawn to the study of the Orthodox Church are either themselves members of that church or at least understandably empathetic to its members' sufferings, and so overlook the degree to which Orthodox clergy often cooperated with Soviet power.

21. See Fireside, *Icon and Swastika*; and Alexeev and Stavrou, *The Great Revival*; Dallin, *German Rule in Russia* devotes a chapter to religious questions in the German-held regions. Fletcher, *The Russian Orthodox Church Underground* has an excellent chapter on the war and outlines many of the church-state dynamics examined in this work. Writing in 1971, Fletcher did not, however, have access to Soviet records, nor did he examine the international, propaganda aspect of religion in its totality. Bociurkiw, *The Ukrainian Greek Catholic Church and the Soviet State (1939–1950)*. This latter book, which appeared while the current study was being written, makes great use of Soviet sources, but its subject is restricted to Soviet Uniates.

22. Fletcher, *Religion and Soviet Foreign Policy*. Fletcher focuses exclusively on activities of church hierarchs and does not look at the state's advocacy of religious propaganda or at the work of Soviet propagandists and agents abroad. Alexeev, *The Foreign Policy of the Moscow Patriarchate* vol. 2. Despite Alexeev's title, his work devotes only a few pages to foreign policy matters before 1945; given the time at which he wrote (1955), it is also inevitably based almost entirely on published Soviet sources.

23. This view was expressed most clearly by Britain's archbishop of York following his visit to the USSR in September 1943. "Notes of a Press Conference Held at the Ministry of Information on Monday, 11th October, 1943," PRO INF 1/792. See chapter 7.

24. *Izvestiia*, August 18, 1927.

25. One exception is Matthew Spinka, who in most cases is very sensitive to Kremlin ma-

nipulation of the church. He writes: "[E]ven Stalin acknowledged the very great services rendered to the patriotic cause by the Church. He rewarded Sergei by allowing him to be elevated to the patriarchal throne." Spinka, *The Church in Soviet Russia*, p. x. Dear and Foot, *The Oxford Companion to World War II*, p. 943, also view Stalin's actions as an "official reward" for the church's loyalty.

26. Solzhenitsyn, *Letter to the Soviet Leaders*, p. 17. See also Pospielovsky, *A History of Soviet Atheism in Theory and Practice, and the Believer*, 2: p. 91. Dunlop, *The Faces of Contemporary Russian Nationalism*, pp. 14–16. Dunlop also sees the relaxation of religious repression as a concession to internal forces.

27. The Orthodox historian Nicolas Zernov, writing in 1945, subscribed to this view, writing that "the great sufferings which the [Russian] nation experienced during the German invasion forged a new sense of national unity." The church's support for the war effort "impressed the Government and secured for the Church a greater freedom of action." *The Russians and Their Church*, pp. 165–66. This is also the view propagated by the Moscow Patriarchate in recent years. "World War II forced Stalin to mobilize all the national resources for defense, including the Russian Orthodox Church as the people's moral force." Department for External Church Relations of the Patriarchate of Moscow, "Russian Orthodox Church (Historical Background)," Moscow Patriarchate web site ‹russian-orthodox-church.org.ru/hist_en.htm›, accessed January 7, 1999.

28. See the discussion of this question in chapter 2.

29. As the Jesuit historian Robert A. Graham has pointed out, the Nazis claimed to be defending "Western civilization," not specifically "Christian" civilization, because Nazism was, at heart, opposed to religious belief no less than Soviet Communism. This was one of the major reasons why the Germans proved to be so inept at capitalizing on the religious question in the regions they occupied. Robert A, Graham, *The Vatican and Communism during World War II*, p. 26.

30. Fireside, *Icon and Swastika*, p. 133.

31. Ware, *The Orthodox Church*, p. 155; Pospielovsky also sees competition with the Germans as the determining factor in Stalin's shift in religious policy, *The Russian Church under the Soviet Regime*, 1:196.

32. Unfortunately, Medvedev does not document this interesting claim. Medvedev, *All Stalin's Men*, pp. 93–94. Medvedev's unwillingness to entertain the notion that the Soviets needed the prestige and nationalist appeal of the church may owe something to his own faith in the appeal of Leninism.

33. Volkogonov, *Triumf i tragediia*, pp. 382–83.

34. In fact, the suggestion for an exchange of visits between the Anglican and Russian Orthodox churches was a Soviet, not a British one. But this was not known at the time, or until now. See chapter 7.

35. Gordun, "Russkaia Pravoslavnaia Tserkov' v period s 1943 po 1970 god," pp. 39–40. Although Gordun's article was based on church and Soviet documents, the section explaining Soviet motives for the restoration of the Patriarchate appears not to have been. Rather, it draws heavily on Alekseev, "Neozhidannyi dialog," p. 42. The decision to invite an Anglican delegation was made more than a year before the autumn of 1943; see the discussion in chapter 7.

36. Since the beginning of the war, the Soviets had allowed clergy to publish articles in

journals and newspapers directed at foreign readers, such as *Moscow News* and *Soviet War News*.

37. This uneven distribution of open churches has long been known by historians, even before reliable numbers were revealed from closed Soviet sources. See, for example, Bohdan R. Bociurkiw, "Religion and Atheism in Soviet Society," in Marshall, *Aspects of Religion in the Soviet Union*, p. 54. By far the majority of wartime church reopenings occurred in Ukraine, which in 1939 had a total population of 30,946,218, of which 23,667,509 were ethnic Ukrainians while only 4,175,299 were ethnic Russians. Rossiiskaia akademiia nauk, *Vsesoiuznaia perepis' naseleniia 1939 goda: Osnovnye itogi*, pp. 56 and 68.

38. Not to be confused with Metropolitan Sergii, patriarch *locum tenens*.

39. Pospielovsky, *The Russian Church under the Soviet Regime* 1:194. The Soviets seemed most concerned at this time to place the Ukrainian nationalist Greek Catholic Church under the more obedient Russian Orthodox Church. See Dennis J. Dunn, "The Catholic Church and the Soviet Government in Soviet Occupied East Europe, 1939–1940," in De George and Scanlan, *Marxism and Religion in Eastern Europe*, pp. 107–18. For a discussion of this period, see chapter 1.

40. The only exception being Alexeev, *Foreign Policy of the Moscow Patriarchate*, whose history was privately published, in Russian, and did not use Soviet records, these being unavailable at the time. Fletcher, *Religion and Soviet Foreign Policy*, has only a few remarks on wartime diplomacy.

41. See Dunlop, *The Faces of Contemporary Russian Nationalism*, pp. 3–28. Writing in 1946, and watching signs of the restoration of Russian national themes, Nicholas S. Timasheff believed that the Communist system was slowly reverting to traditional Russianism. Timasheff *The Great Retreat*.

42. Paleologue, *An Ambassador's Memoirs*, 1:213–14.

43. Ibid.

44. This point is well made by Dennis J. Dunn, "Nationalism and Religion in Eastern Europe," in Dunn, *Religion and Nationalism in Eastern Europe and the Soviet Union*, pp. 1–14. Sabrina Ramet uses the term "ecclesiastical nationalism": "Ecclesiastical nationalism consists in several distinct aspects of church activity: in the church's preservation and development of the cultural heritage, in the church's usage of a specific language for liturgy and instruction, in the advancement of specific territorial claims on putative ethnic grounds, and in the cultivation of the social idea itself, that is, the idea that a given people, united by faith and culture, constitute a nation." Pedro Ramet, "Autocephaly and National Identity in Church-State Relations in Eastern Christianity," in Ramet, *Eastern Christians and Politics in the Twentieth Century*, 1:10.

45. "The equation of religious unity with political unity and later with national identity became the raison d'etre for autocephaly in the Orthodox world. Especially with the growth of nationalism in the nineteenth century, to be a nation meant to have a church of one's own, and to be entitled to one's own state." Ibid., p. 4.

46. Dimitri Obolensky argues that Russia, and other nations that adopted Orthodoxy from Byzantium, in fact magnified church-state unity, in excess of the original model, owing to "native traditions of kingship" and the fact that such states as Russia were ethnically more homogeneous than the more heterogeneous Byzantine Empire. Obolensky, *The Byzantine Commonwealth: Eastern Europe*, p. 398.

47. John Meyendorff, *Byzantium and the Rise of Russia*, pp. 11–12.

48. See, for example, Ware, *The Orthodox Church*, pp. 15–16.

49. Aleksandr Solzhenitsyn writes that, following the Great Schism, "never again during [the] . . . three hundred years to come, did Orthodoxy in Russia regain its vigorous dynamism." This is also a recurring theme in his fiction. Solzhenitsyn, *The Russian Question at the End of the Twentieth Century*, p. 9.

50. One of the foremost scholars of the Russian church, Gregory Freeze, argues vigorously that the degree of church submission to the state in tsarist Russia has been greatly exaggerated, at least in purely ecclesiastical matters. Freeze, "Handmaiden of the State? The Church in Imperial Russia Reconsidered," pp. 82–102. Nonetheless, Freeze allows that "the Church's political clout and specific sphere of authority declined in the course of the eighteenth and nineteenth centuries" and that "its worldly functions and competence . . . were drastically diminished" (pp. 89 and 90). In one of the most recent reexaminations of Peter I's church policy, Lindsey Hughes declares the tsar "the clear winner" in his struggle with church power. *Russia in the Age of Peter the Great*, pp. 332–56.

51. In the words of Peter I's ukaz of May 17, 1722, "If during confession someone discloses to the spiritual father an uncommitted but still intended crime, especially treason or rebellion against the Sovereign or the State, or an evil design against the honour or health of the Sovereign and his Family, and in declaring such an evil intent shows that he does not repent of it . . . then the confessor must not only withhold absolution and remission from the sinner, but most promptly report him to the appropriate place." The historian Geoffrey Hosking notes that, with Peter's church regulations, priests became "in short, spiritual administrators and grass-roots agents of the autocratic state." Hosking, *Russia*, p. 228.

52. Freeze, *The Parish Clergy in Nineteenth-Century Russia*, esp. pp. 450–58.

53. One prokurator of the Holy Synod, Konstantin Pobedonostsev, who was most active in Russification, wrote that "Russia and Orthodoxy are Synonymous." See Byrnes, *Pobedonostsev*, pp. 188–208.

54. B. H. Sumner, an Oxford scholar of Russian history, who worked for the British Foreign Office Research Department during the war, wrote an excellent short study of the role of the Russian church in Pan-Slavism, which highlights each of its functions in this endeavor. "The Russian Orthodox Church and Pan-Slavism," October 15, 1943, B. H. Sumner, PRO FO 371/36962.

55. For an excellent exploration of early Soviet antireligious campaigns, which conclusively demonstrates their ineffectuality, see Peris, *Storming the Heavens*.

56. Lenin to Molotov and members of the Politburo, March 19, 1922, in Pipes, *The Unknown Lenin*, pp. 152–54.

57. Luukkanen, *The Party of Unbelief*, p. 84. Sabrina Ramet claims that the Bolsheviks killed 28 bishops and 1,215 priests between 1917 and 1922. Ramet, *Cross and Commissar*, p. 24.

58. Peris, *Storming the Heavens*, p. 27.

59. Ramet, *Cross and Commissar*, p. 40.

60. Conquest, *The Harvest of Sorrow*, pp. 199–213.

61. Pospielovsky, *A History of Soviet Atheism in Theory and Practice, and the Believer*, 2:ix.

62. The figure for the number of open churches is from Karpov to Aleksandrov, August 30, 1945, RTsKhIDNI, f.17, op.125, r.1408. The figure for priests is taken from Gordun, "Russkaia Pravoslavnaia Tserkov' v period s 1943 po 1970 god," p. 40. Ramet estimates that

"a mere 500" churches remained open on the eve of the German invasion. Ramet, *Cross and Commissar*, p. 24.

63. See discussion of this issue in chapter 4.

64. Fletcher, *The Russian Orthodox Church Underground*, p. 50.

65. Ibid., p. 51.

66. Fletcher shrewdly notes: "A subtle distinction exists in the Russian phrasing of this statement, for the word 'motherland' is feminine in gender, while 'Soviet Union' is masculine. The possessive pronoun in "The joys and successes *of which*" is feminine, and therefore the exact meaning of the phrase is that it is the joys and successes of the motherland, not of the Soviet Union, with which the Church identifies." Ibid., p. 54.

67. Ibid., p. 52.

68. Dunn, *The Catholic Church and the Soviet Government*, p. 39.

69. Papal Encyclical, *Divini Redemptoris*, March 19, 1937.

Chapter 1

1. Conquest, *Stalin*, pp. 166–67. Although Conquest's work is built on a lifetime of careful research, he completed this biography before the opening of Soviet archives.

2. Ronald Grigor Suny, "Stalin and His Stalinism: Power and Authority in the Soviet Union, 1930–53," in Kershaw and Moshe Lewin, *Stalinism and Nazism*, p. 26.

3. Thurston, *Life and Terror in Stalin's Russia*, pp. xix, 232 (emphasis added).

4. Stalin, *Sochineniia*, vol. 3, pt. xvi, p. 24.

5. Institut Marksizma-Leninizma, *Istoriia Velikoi otechestvennoi voiny Sovetskogo Soiuza*.

6. For a useful discussion of Khrushchev-era military memoirs, see Bialer, *Stalin and His Generals*, pp. 15–44.

7. Tumarkin, *The Living and the Dead*. In an otherwise brilliant and moving study of the creation and use of myths about World War II, Tumarkin unfortunately focuses almost exclusively on Russia and ethnic Russians, and so largely ignores the issues of nationality and the role of wartime myth in perpetuating Soviet rule in the Union republics.

8. "Gorbachev Speech to GOSR Meeting," *Foreign Broadcast Information Service*, November 3, 1987, p. 47.

9. Tumarkin, *The Living and the Dead*, p. 35.

10. Letter of I. S. Fed'ko, in Samsonov, *Znat' i pomnit'*, p. 103.

11. Letter from D. A. Shchetinkin, in ibid., p. 101.

12. Volkogonov, *Triumf i tragediia*, book II, part 2, pp. 12–31.

13. It has been estimated that in the Russian countryside during the 1860s only 6 percent of the population was literate; by 1921 in European Russia this figure had grown to 71 percent among boys and 52 percent among girls. Brooks, *When Russia Learned to Read*, p. 4. By 1936 Soviet authorities claimed that illiteracy had been entirely eliminated in the USSR, but students of Soviet education long believed that this overstated the level of progress. Holmes et al., *Russian Education*, p. 8. When the long-suppressed Soviet census of 1939 was finally published, it revealed that 58 percent of ethnic Russians were literate, whereas most Soviet nationalities had lower levels. Rossiiskaia akademia nauk, *Vsesoiuznaia perepis' naseleniia 1939 goda*, p. 83.

14. Grossman, *Life and Fate*, p. 196. He is writing here about a character named Sofya Os-

ipovna Levinton, based on Grossman's own mother who perished in the Holocaust. In the process of being arrested, deported, and eventually murdered by the Nazis, Levinton, an assimilated Jew, rediscovered her connection with the Jewish people.

15. Fitzpatrick, *Stalin's Peasants*, p. 312.

16. Ibid., p. 320.

17. Tumarkin, *The Living and the Dead*, pp. 64–65.

18. Fitzpatrick, *Stalin's Peasants*, p. 204.

19. Fireside, *Icon and Swastika*, pp. 160–65. Soviet authorities were also highly aware of this phenomenon. See Karpov to Aleksandrov, August 30, 1945, "Sovershenno sekretno," RTsKhIDNI, f.17 op.125 r.1408.

20. Soviet-era figures estimate more than 2,200,000 deaths from a prewar Belorussian population of 9,046,000. Kozlov et al., *Velikaia otechestvennaia voina 1941–1945*, p. 86.

21. For a long NKGB analysis of Ukrainian anti-Soviet nationalist and religious groups, including Jewish organizations, see "Iz orientirovki tret'ego upravleniia NKGB SSSR," Ivan Shevelev, May 31, 1941, *OGB*, vol. I, book 2, pp. 172–87.

22. One historian estimates the number of Jewish victims during Khmel'nitskii's uprising at "tens of thousands" and as "one of the most traumatic events in [Jewish] history." Subtelny, *Ukraine*, pp. 127–28. See also Magosci, *A History of Ukraine*, pp. 200–202.

23. Chuev, *Sto sorok besed s Molotovym*, p. 390.

24. "Dokladnaia zapiska NKGB USSR Sekretariu TsK KP (b) Ukrainy N. S. Khrushchevu," undated, but not earlier than April 15, 1941, *OGB*, vol. I, book 2, p. 99.

25. Chuev, *Molotov Remembers*, pp. 257–58.

26. Russian published documents are relatively sparse on this question, and they do not explain Moscow's motives—merely revealing the Kremlin's methods. For the annexations of the Baltic states, the relevant diplomatic documents are published in Ministerstvo inostrannykh del Rossiiskoi federatsii, *Dokumenty vneshnei politiki 1940–22 iiunia 1941*. In a disturbing return to Soviet-era practice, this collection has clearly been carefully edited and contains only two documents relating to the annexations of these three countries, neither one revealing Moscow's reasons for seizing them.

27. In my own work, I have argued for the more aggressive interpretation of Soviet motives. Miner, *Between Churchill and Stalin*. See also Tucker, *Stalin in Power*, pp. 223–28, 592–607; Rozanov, *Stalin Gitler*. For a very different interpretation of Soviet motives, see Geoffrey K. Roberts, *The Soviet Union and the Origins of the Second World War*.

28. Chuev, *Sto sorok besed s Molotovym*, p. 14.

29. Misiunas and Taagepera, *The Baltic States*.

30. Kulik to Stalin, Molotov, and Voroshilov, September 21, 1939, in Pikhoia, et al., *Katyn'*, pp. 83–85.

31. Ibid.

32. Kagan and Cohen, *Surviving the Holocaust with the Russian Jewish Partisans*, pp. 135 and 139.

33. Quoted in Gross, *Revolution from Abroad*, p. 35.

34. This is Gross's conclusion in ibid., p. 34.

35. Ibid. Although Gross's book, which is based largely on a treasure trove of first-person accounts from Polish soldiers, appeared before the opening of Soviet archives, it has held up well. In his otherwise thorough treatment, however, he almost entirely ignores the question

of the churches. Another analysis of Stalin's war against the Polish population that retains its value even following the opening of Soviet archives is Zawodny, *Death in the Forest.*

36. In February 1941, the Soviet politbiuro ordered the division of the secret police into the NKVD and NKGB, the latter dealt with Soviet espionage abroad, with the activities of foreign espionage services, and with the liquidation of organized opposition within the USSR. The NKVD was given the remaining security tasks. "Postanovlenie politbiuro Ts K VKP(b)," February 3, 1941, *OGB* vol. I, book 2, pp. 24–25.

37. Vardys and Sedaitis, *Lithuania*, pp. 28–29.

38. Interestingly, in light of Soviet unpreparedness when Barbarossa finally erupted, Soviet intelligence services had plenty of information about German preparations for the invasion. They also seemed to assume that it would come in due course. For a fascinating collection of such intelligence warnings, published by the Russian successor to the KGB, see Federal'naia sluzhba bezopasnosti rossii, sluzhba vneshnei razvedki rossii, and Moskovskoe gorodskoe ob"edinenie arkhivov, *Sekrety Gitlera na stole Stalina.*

39. Merkulov to TsK VKP(b) SNK SSSR and NKVD SSSR, April 8, 1941, *OGB*, vol. I, book 2, pp. 79–81.

40. *OGB*, vol. I, book 2, p. 141n.

41. Kobulov to NKGB BSSR, "Iz ukazaniia NKGB SSSR No. 1996/M," May 30, 1941, *OGB*, vol. I, book 2, pp. 166–170.

42. For numbers of those deported from the Baltic states and Bessarabia at this time, totaling 85,000, see memorandum by Konradkov, Volobuev, and Goriachev, "Sovershenno sekretno," June 11, 1941, in *TSIM*, pp. 154–56. No reason is given in the documents why deportees from western Ukraine were tabulated separately.

43. Merkulov, "Dokladnaia zapiska NKGB SSSR" to TsK VKP(b), *OGB*, vol. I, book 2, pp. 144–46.

44. Thurston also writes astonishingly of "the close connections between police and society." *Life and Terror in Stalin's Russia*, pp. 84–85, 98, and 107.

45. The account given here and below contrasts sharply with the view expressed by one recent historian that "The colossal and costly destruction that [Stalin] brought on the country on the eve and in the early days of the Second World War gave rise to no organized opposition." Ronald Grigor Suny, "Stalin and His Stalinism: Power and Authority in the Soviet Union, 1930–53," in Kershaw and Lewin, *Stalinism and Nazism*, p. 26.

46. Still in many ways the most thorough history of the OUN is Armstrong, *Ukrainian Nationalism.*

47. Meshchik, "Iz tsirkuliara narodnogo komissariata gosudarstvennoi bezopasnosti USSR," April 10, 1941, *OGB*, vol. I, book 2, pp. 85–87.

48. Meshchik, "Dokladnaia zapiska NKGB USSR" to Khrushchev, April 15, 1941, *OGB*, vol. I, book 2, pp. 99–100.

49. Losev and Mastitskii, "Iz direktivy upravlenii NKVD i NKGB USSR po Rovenskii Oblasti," *OGB*, vol. I, book 2, pp. 118–20.

50. Ibid.

51. Beria, "Iz direktivy NKVD SSSR," to NKVD and NKGB in Ukraine, April 29, 1941; and "Postanovlenie TsK VKP(b) i SNK SSSR," May 14, 1941, *OGB*, vol. I, book 2, pp. 121 and 139–40.

52. Lavreny Beria to "all heads the the UNKGB," May 21, 1941, in *TSIM*, p. 146.

53. Merkulov, "Iz dokladnoi zapiski NKGB SSSR No. 1832/M," to Ts K VKP(b) and SNK SSSR, May 23, 1941; and Merkulov, "Dokladnaia zapiska NKGB SSSR No. 1843/M" to Ts K VKP(b), SNK, and NKVD SSSR, *OGB*, vol. I, book 2, pp. 154–56.

54. Memorandum of Konrakov, head of the department of Labor and Special Exile, June 11, 1941, in *TSIM*, pp. 154–56.

55. Merkulov, "Direktiva NKGB SSSR No. 126," 21 June, 1941, *OGB*, vol. I, book 2, p. 297.

56. *OGB*, vol. I, book 1, p. 73n. Bandera, by then in emigration, would be assassinated by the Soviets in 1959.

57. Shevelev, "Iz orientirovki tret'ego upravleniia NKGB SSSR," May 31, 1941, *OGB*, vol. I, book 2, pp. 172–87.

58. Ciszek with Flaherty, *He Leadeth Me*, p. 18.

59. Bociurkiw, *The Ukrainian Greek Catholic Church and the Soviet State (1939–1950)*, pp. 34–37.

60. Shevelev, "Iz orientirovki tret'ego upravleniia NKGB SSSR," May 31, 1941, *OGB*, vol. I, book 2, pp. 172–87.

61. Ibid.

62. Simon Petliura was a leader of leftist-nationalist Ukrainian forces during the Russian civil war, who in December 1918 briefly created a Ukrainian national government in the wake of the German defeat in the First World War and before Bolsheviks forces could consolidate their power in Ukraine. Ever afterward, Soviet Communists used Petliura's name as a pejorative, labeling all "bourgeois nationalist" Ukrainian forces to be "Petliurist." Following his political defeat, and when in exile, Soviet agents assassinated him in 1926. Mawdsley, *The Russian Civil War*, p. 119.

63. See chapter 2 for a discussion of this issue.

64. Ivan Serov, "Iz ukazaniia NKGB SSSR," to UNKGB-UNKVD, May 17, 1941, *OGB*, vol. I, book 2, pp. 147–48.

65. Fletcher, *Nikolai*, p. 33.

66. Pospielovsky, *The Russian Church under the Soviet Regime* 1:194.

67. For Nicholas's dismantling of the Greek Catholic Church, with its important parallels with Stalin's policies from 1943 to 1944, see Lencyk, "The Eastern Catholic Church and Czar Nicholas I."

68. Fletcher, *Nikolai*, pp. 12–13.

69. Fireside, *Icon and Swastika*, p. 134.

70. Fletcher, *Nikolai*, p. 34.

71. Ibid., pp. 35 and 52.

72. Quoted in Urban, *Stalinism*, p. 42.

73. Robert Conquest has argued forcefully that Stalin's collectivization policies in Ukraine, in combination with his war against the Ukrainian intelligentsia and church, amounted to genocide. If one accepts an expansive definition of the term, implying a campaign to destroy national identity and the ability of a people to resist outside powers, then perhaps Conquest is correct. If one uses the term "genocide" in its more restrictive sense, as a war to destroy an entire people physically, then the collectivization—although homicidal—does not match the definition. Conquest, *The Harvest of Sorrow*.

74. Ibid., pp. 199–213.

Chapter 2

1. By April 1939 the Germans had noticed the changed tone of the Soviet press. See "Memorandum by the State Secretary in the German Foreign Office (Weizsacker)," April 17, 1939, in Sontag and Beddie, *Nazi-Soviet Relations*, pp. 1–2.

2. N. Pal'gunov to Upravlenie propagandy i agitatsii TsK VKP(b) A. A. Puzin, May 10, 1941, RTsKhINI, f.5, op.6, r.1354.

3. Harlow Robinson, "Composing for Victory," in Stites, *Culture and Entertainment in Wartime Russia*, pp. 65–66. Robinson calls "Nevskii" "cartoonish, almost operatic." True, perhaps, but it was also visually striking and very effective cinema, having a long-term effect on the art and shaping such later hits as George Lucas's *Star Wars*.

4. As late as June 14, the Soviet telegraph agency, TASS, issued an infamous communiqué, published in all the major Soviet newspapers, denouncing "widespread rumors" about German preparations for an invasion of the USSR, calling these "a clumsy propaganda maneuver of the forces arrayed against the Soviet Union and Germany." See "The German Ambassador in the Soviet Union (Schulenburg) to the German Foreign Office," June 14, 1941, in Sontag and Beddie, *Nazi-Soviet Relations*, pp. 345–46.

5. Kravchenko, *I Chose Freedom*, p. 353.

6. Ibid., p. 365 (emphasis in original).

7. Markovna, *Nina's Journey*, pp. 156–57. Even the more mature Dov Cohen, who in 1941 would join the Jewish partisans and survive the war, wrote later that on the eve of the German invasion "The horror stories simply didn't make sense. We went on with our lives, deluding ourselves that it was impossible for such murderous atrocities actually to be approved and perpetuated by the authorities. The Germans were considered a civilized nation." Kagan and Cohen, *Surviving the Holocaust with the Russian Jewish Partisans*, p. 36.

8. For the account of one person thus deported, who nonetheless willingly fought in the Red Army during the war, see Karol, *Between Two Worlds*. On the question of espionage, see I. Serov (People's Commissar for Internal Affairs of the Ukrainian SSR) to Sazykin, Sedov, Martynov, and Veretennikov, August 21, 1940, in *TSIM*, pp. 88–90.

9. See, for example, Ivan Serov to Moldavian NKVD, August 21, 1940, in *TSIM*, pp. 88–90.

10. Many of the Polish victims shot by the NKVD in 1940 in the so-called Katyn Forest Massacre were condemned because they were "refugees" from the German-occupied zone of Poland. See discussion in chapter 3, especially notes 44 and 47.

11. German radio from Zeesen, quoted in *The Spiritual Issues of the War*, no. 92 (August 7, 1941), PRO INF 1/790.

12. Fireside, *Icon and Swastika*, p. 120.

13. Dallin, *German Rule in Russia*, p. 472.

14. Ibid., pp. 476–77.

15. Cited in ibid., p. 473.

16. Notes of Hasso von Etzdorf quoted in Graham, *The Vatican and Communism*, p. 122.

17. Fireside, *Icon and Swastika*, p. 119.

18. Graham, *The Vatican and Communism*, p. 121.

19. Cited in Dallin, *German Rule*, p. 143.

20. Fireside, *Icon and Swastika*.

21. Through their espionage in Germany, the Soviet leadership was aware that the German

High Command assessed the Red Army as being very weak following its poor showing in the war against Finland. See especially "Zapiska narkoma gosbezopasnosti SSSR V. N. Merkulova I. V. Stalinu, V. M. Molotovu i L. I. Beriia s tekstom besedy, poluchennym agenturnym putem, o germanskikh planakh voiny s sovetskim soiuzom," in Federal'naia sluzhba bezopasnosti Rossii, *Sekrety Gitlera na stole u Stalina*, pp. 124–27.

22. G. Kumanev, "V ogne tiazhelykh ispytanii (iiun'–noiabr' 1942 g.)," p. 5.

23. The seige of Brest-Litovsk became the subject of one of the most famous of all Soviet-era wartime paintings, a sort of Soviet Alamo. The painting, *Zashchitniki Brestskoi kreposti*, by P. A. Krivonogov is reproduced in most official Soviet histories of the war, including, in part, in M. M. Kozlov et al., *Velikaia otechestvennaia voina 1941–1945*, following p. 416.

24. Summaries of Red Army shortcomings are provided in the standard histories: Seaton, *The Russo-German War, 1941–1945*; Erickson, *The Road to Stalingrad*.

25. A good summary of these military problems is in David Glantz, *When Titans Clashed*.

26. According to German sources, 5,754,000 Soviet soldiers were taken as POWs during the war. Dallin, *German Rule in Russia*, p. 427.

27. Volkogonov, *Stalin*, p. 429; Overy, *Russia's War*, p. 124.

28. Herwarth, *Against Two Evils*, p. 198–99.

29. Quoted in Volkogonov, *Stalin*, p. 427.

30. Quoted in Tolstoy, *The Secret Betrayal*, p. 34. The Gorbachev-era Russian biographer of Stalin, Dmitrii Volkogonov, attributes these merciless orders solely to Stalin's well-known brutality. Volkogonov, *Stalin*, p. 427. Another historian calls the holding of soldiers' families hostage "unique" and "not founded on Soviet, or any other law." Sella, *The Value of Human Life in Soviet Warfare*, p. 101. Although these were Stalin's personal orders, however, they had firm Leninist roots. During the Russian civil war of 1918–20, the first Soviet commissar of war, Leon Trotskii, had likewise held officers' families hostage, doing so with Lenin's full approval. In his memoirs, Leon Trotsky was frank about the need for terror in the new Red Army, writing: "An army cannot be built without reprisals." Trotsky, *My Life*, p. 427. Although most dictatorial regimes—including the Nazis, of course—have always used terror to ensure loyalty within their armies, the Soviets were unusual, though not unique, in using the threat of imprisonment and violence against the families of those suspected of insufficient loyalty. From the earliest days of the Bolshevik regime, the Soviets extended the use of hostage-taking, terror, and execution even to the economic arena. An "economic specialist" who worked closely with Lenin on matters related to the supply of timber, for instance, recalls how Lenin ordered the seizure of hostages and executions to ensure the prompt delivery of wood, as well as the clearance of snowdrifts from rail lines. Liberman, *Building Lenin's Russia*, p. 14. Stalin did not issue his orders in the throes of an irrational blood frenzy; facing the very real threat of mass disloyalty, he acted squarely in the Bolshevik tradition.

31. Andreev-Khomiakov, *Bitter Waters*, p. 170.

32. Cited in ibid., p. 428. In addition to those shot, an additional 442,000 were sentenced to serve in "penal battalions" and a further 436,000 to terms of imprisonment. Overy, *Russia's War*, p. 200. By way of comparison, one American soldier, Private Eddie Slovik, was executed for desertion during World War II.

33. Interview with Harriman in Urban, *Stalinism*, p. 43.

34. Stalin issued orders for the creation of such units to Beria on July 20. Overy, *Russia's War*, p. 108.

35. Volkogonov, *The Rise and Fall of the Soviet Empire*, p. 118.

36. Herwarth, *Against Two Evils*, p. 198.

37. "Russia's War: Blood upon the Snow," Public Broadcasting System documentary, 1997. Kravchenko also relates personally witnessing such NKVD units in action. *I Chose Freedom*, p. 369.

38. Avrich, *Kronstadt 1921*, p. 153.

39. Historians have been overly diffident about exploring the lavish use of terror in the Red Army, perhaps for fear of being accused of denigrating the genuine heroism and achievement of Soviet soldiers. This has led to some odd contortions. Sella, for instance, writes that "only an army that was basically highly motivated, well organized and disciplined" could have survived the ferocious German attack. *The Value of Human Life in Soviet Warfare*, p. 99.

40. Fitzpatrick, *Stalin's Peasants*, p. 314.

41. Markovna, *Nina's Journey*, p. 178.

42. Strik-Strikfeldt, *Against Stalin and Hitler*, p. 25.

43. Herwarth, *Against Two Evils*, p. 201.

44. Andreev-Khomiakov, *Bitter Waters*, p. 170.

45. On Belorussia, where such things occurred in a number of towns, see Zaprudnik, *Belarus*, p. 95. It is estimated that, in Galicia and western Volhynia alone, the Soviets thus murdered between 15,000 and 40,000 people. Magocsi, *A History of Ukraine*, p. 624.

46. On the deportation of ethnic Germans, see Bugai, *L. Beriia-I. Stalinu*.

47. Leonhard, *Child of the Revolution*, pp.137–38. Despite their imprisonment, many inmates of the gulag reacted with patriotic outrage to the Nazi invasion.

48. During his meetings with British foreign secretary Anthony Eden in December 1941, Stalin told his guest that "The German Army is not so strong after all," and predicted that the USSR would be able to enter the war against Japan in the spring of 1942. See Miner, *Between Churchill and Stalin*, p. 188.

49. Zhukov on Stalin's overconfidence. John Erickson, *The Road to Stalingrad*, p. 347.

50. Ibid., p. 349.

51. Kosiba, *Stalin's Great Game*, explores the sensitivity of the Soviets regarding their "soft underbelly" in the Black Sea and their oil-rich regions around the Caspian Sea.

52. The number for 1942, in round numbers, was 1,653,000 Soviet POWs. Dallin, *German Rule in Russia*, p. 427.

53. This may also have been in part the result of more effective, harsh disciplinary measures. See Overy, *Russia's War*, pp. 194–201.

54. Kravchenko, *I Chose Freedom*, p. 366.

55. Leonov to orginstruktorskii otdel, "Vypiska Politicheskogo Upravleniia Severo-Kavkazskogo fronta," June 28, 1942, RTsKhIDNI, f.5, op.6, r.1358.

56. "Sekretno," "Vypiska Politotdela primorskoi armii," June 8, 1942, RTsKhIDNI, f.5, op.6, r.1358.

57. Ibid.

58. Stavskii (Ruk. grupp brigadnyi komissar) to Shikin (zam. nach. glavnogo politicheskogo upravleniia RKKA divizionomu komissaru), December 5, 1942, RTsKhIDNI, f.17 op.125 r.1409.

59. On these deportations, see Conquest, *The Nation Killers*; Nekrich, *The Punished Peoples*; Bugai, *L. Beriia-I. Stalinu*.

60. Chuev, *Molotov Remembers*, p. 195.

61. See Subtelny, *Ukraine*, chap. 23; and Armstrong, *Ukrainian Nationalism*.

62. For the politics of the OUN, see Subtelny, *Ukraine*, pp. 459–60.

63. Captured German SS document from Khar'kov oblast', August 8, 1942, RTsKhIDNI, f.17, op.125, r.1376.

64. This tallies with the testimony of Pavel Sudoplatov, who during the war headed an NKVD death squad targeting Ukrainian nationalist leaders. "The bulk of guerilla commanders," he writes, "came from the families of Ukrainian clergymen." Sudoplatov, *Special Tasks*, p. 251.

65. Captured SS document, August 8, 1942, RTsKhIDNI, f.17, op.125, r.1376.

66. *OGB*, vol. I, book 2, p. 181n.

67. Hansjakob Stehle, "Sheptyt'sky and the German Regime," in Magocsi, *Morality and Reality*, pp. 125–44. Stehle claims that Sheptyt'sky approved the creation of the "Galicia" SS division because he believed the Germans were losing the war and that an armed Ukrainian force was needed to prevent widespread disorder as Nazi authority collapsed and before the Soviets arrived. For a more detailed discussion of Sheptyt'sky and the Greek Catholic Church, see chapter 5.

68. Kozlov et al., *Velikaia otechestvennaia voina*, p. 741.

69. Zaprudnik, *Belarus*, p. 97.

70. Kozlov, et al., *Velikaia otechestvennaia voina*, p. 533.

71. Leonov memorandum, "Sovershenno sekretno," "Spravka o faktakh izmeny rodine v chastiakh deistvuiushchei Krasnoi Armii," July 15, 1942, RTsKhIDNI, f.5, op.6, r.1358.

72. Ibid.

73. Leonov, "Vypiska Iugovo-zapadnogo fronta," July 15, 1942, RTsKhIDNI, f.5, op.6, r.1358.

74. Shikin to Shcherbakov, September 28, 1942, f.5, op.6, r.1358.

75. Stavskii to Shikin, December 5, 1942, RTsKhIDNI, f.17, op.125, r.1409.

76. In his novel *Life and Fate*, Vasilii Grossman, who had been a front-line correspondent for the Red Army newspaper *Krasnaia zvezda*, had one of his less appealing characters, the political commissar Getmanov, express these widely held views: "A frown suddenly appeared on his face. 'Quite frankly,' he went on angrily, 'all this [talk of national amity] makes me want to vomit. In the name of the friendship of nations we keep sacrificing the Russians. A member of a national minority barely needs to know the alphabet to be appointed a people's commissar, while our Ivan, no matter if he's a genius, has to "yield place to the minorities." The great Russian people's becoming a national minority itself. I'm all for the friendship of nations, but not on these terms. I'm sick of it!' " Grossman, *Life and Fate*, p. 221.

77. Stavskii to Shikin, December 5, 1942, RTsKhIDNI, f.17, op.125, r.1409.

78. On Vlasov's motivation, see Andreyev, *Vlasov and the Russian Liberation Movement*, pp. 37–61. Andreyev's view of Vlasov's motives are not universally shared; some continue to view him as nothing more than a traitor. We may never know for certain.

79. Solzhenitsyn, *The Gulag Archipelago*, pp. 261–62.

80. Werth, *Russia at War*, p. 411.

81. Quoted in Anatol Goldberg, *Ilya Ehrenburg*, p. 197.

82. Urban, *Stalinism*, p. 41.

83. Werth, *Russia at War*, p. 415–16.

84. One must constantly remember that we are forced to rely on Soviet documents to

paint the picture of loyalty patterns in the Red Army. Whether the official documents portray the actual state of affairs, or merely reflect the prejudices of Soviet officials, may be impossible to determine. Nonetheless, the Kremlin was reading these reports and forming policy based on their analysis.

85. Werth, *Russia at War*, p. 177.

86. Timasheff, *The Great Retreat*, p. 230.

87. These are references to historical invaders of Russia, respectively, the Mongols in the mid-thirteenth century; the Germanic crusading order of the Teutonic Knights of the same time; the Swedish invasion of the early eighteenth century; and the French invasion of 1912.

88. "Pastyriam i pastvam khristovoi pravoslavnoi tserkvi," Moscow, June 22, 1941, *RPTsIVOV*, pp. 3–5.

89. Pospielovsky, *The Russian Church under the Soviet Regime*, 1:194–95. William C. Fletcher makes the excellent point that Sergii may have been eager to make his appeal for another reason: had he not done so, he might be arrested as a security threat (or a possible collaborator with the invaders) and his church closed. Fletcher, *The Russian Orthodox Church Underground*, p. 154.

90. A handful of such approvals can be found in the former party archive. Soviet archivists seem not to have saved all such approvals, and I can discern no particular pattern in the ones they chose to file away. Kobulov to Shcherbakov, April 11, 1944; Fedotov to Shcherbakov, June 6, 1944; Karpov to Shcherbakov, June 16, 1944; Polianskii to Molotov, July 5, 1944; Kobulov to Shcherbakov, July 15, 1944; Zhukov to Shcherbakov, July 25, 1944; Polianskii to Malenkov, February 12, 1945, RTsKhIDNI, f.17 op.125 r.1408. Generally far more copies seem to have been authorized for publication in foreign languages and for distribution abroad than for the Soviet domestic audience.

91. This question is explored in depth in chapter 3.

92. Those histories that mention the wartime restoration of the Russian Orthodox Church generally point to Sergii's June 22 statement as the beginning of this development. See, for instance, Overy, *Russia's War*, p. 203.

93. See headings for documents in *RPTsIVOV*, which detail where such clergy statements appeared.

94. Declaration of Metropolitan Sergii, October 14, 1941, *RPTsIVOV*.

95. For one such warning, see "Pod zheleznym natiskom voinov-bogatyrei," "To Believers in the Ukraine, November 7, 1943," in Nikolai, *Slova, rechi, poslaniia (1941–1946 gg.)*, pp. 251–53.

96. "Head of Russian Orthodox Church Denounces Traitors," *Soviet War News*, no. 192 (February 1942): 4.

97. For a discussion of the role of Sergii (Voskresenskii), see chapter 1.

98. Fireside, *Icon and Swastika*, p. 134.

99. Fireside seems to have things in reverse. He argues that Sergii "did not renounce his allegiance to the Church head in Moscow until his September 1942 denunciation by the Patriarchy made a rupture unavoidable." While true, this ignores the reason for the rupture: Sergii had accused the Patriarchate of being a Soviet tool, therefore compelling Moscow to make the break. Ibid., p. 134. See also Dallin, *German Rule in Russia*, pp. 489–90.

100. "Osnovnye voprosy nemetskoi propagandy v Estonii," September 5, 1941, RTsKhIDNI, f.17 op.125, r.1359.

101. "Po delu mitropolita Sergiia Voskresenskogo s drugimi," Sergii (Stragorodskii), September 22, 1942, *RPTsIVOV*, pp. 35–36.

102. Nikolai, *The Russian Church and the War against Fascism*, p. 18.

103. Kobulov to Shcherbakov, October 11, 1941, RTsKhIDNI, f.17 op.125 r.1360.

104. "Po delu mitropolita Sergiia Voskresenskogo s drugimi," Sergii (Stragorodskii), September 22, 1941, *RPTsIVOV*, pp. 37–38.

105. "Vozliublennym o-khriste vsem vernym chadam nashei sviatoi pravoslavnoi russkoi tserkvi, v osobennosti obitaiushchim v Litve, Latvii i Estonii," Metropolitan Sergii, September 22, 1942, *RPTsIVOV*, pp. 32–34.

106. Fireside, *Icon and Swastika*, p. 138.

107. Graham, *The Vatican and Communism during World War II*, pp. 51–52.

108. For a memoir by one of the leaders of such forces, see Sudoplatov, *Special Tasks*, p. 251.

109. Metropolitan Sergii, in Ulianovsk, to believers behind German lines, June 22, 1942, *RPTsIVOV*, pp. 29–31.

110. "Preosviashchennym arkhipastyriam, pastyriam i vsem vernym chadam sviatoi nashei tserkvi v oblastiakh SSSR, eshche ne osvobozhdennykh ot nemetskoi okkupatsii," Sergii (Stragorodskii), *RPTsIVOV*, pp. 39–40.

111. "Tserkov' zovet k zashchite rodiny," Metropolitan Aleksii, *RPTsIVOV* pp. 51–54.

112. See, for example, "Obrashchenie Mitropolita Sergiia s prizyvom k sboru na obshche-tserkovnuiu tankovuiu kolonnu," *RPTsIVOV*, pp. 41–42.

113. "Decree of January 23, 1918, 'On Freedom of Conscience and Religious Sovieties,' " in Hecker, *Religion and Communism*, pp. 289–93.

114. Message from Sergii, patriarch *locum tenens*, June 22, 1942, *RPTsIVOV*, pp. 26–28.

115. Kozlov, *Velikaia otechestvennaia voina*, p. 624.

116. Sergii message, June 22, 1942, *RPTsIVOV*, pp. 26–28.

117. "Blizok chas nashei pobedy," *RPTIsVOV*, pp. 8–10.

118. Both sides in the war seemed to favor this particular accusation, that the other had converted churches into stables. The image appears constantly in both Nazi and Soviet propaganda. See Fireside, *Icon and Swastika*, pp. 116 and 122.

119. Ibid.

120. Sergii's Easter message, April 2, 1942, *RPTsIVOV*, pp. 24–25.

121. Yaroslavsky, *Religion in the U.S.S.R.*, pp. 50–51.

122. See chapter 4, note 3.

123. G. Aleksandrov to Andreev, Malenkov, and Shcherbakov, January 19, 1942, RTsKhINI, f.17 op.125 e.kh.104.

124. Cripps to Ministry of Information, July 30, 1941, PRO INF 1/790.

125. Cripps to Foreign Office, August 23, 1941, PRO FO 371/29468.

126. S. Gaselee to Reverend A. C. Don, undated, though probably late August 1941, PRO FO 371/29468. For a discussion of the "Living Church," see chapter 4. Ian H. White-Thomson to Gaselee, September 11, 1941, PRO FO 371/29468.

127. Moscow Chancery to Foreign Office, September 30, 1941, PRO FO 371/119663. A copy of Cripps's cable was relayed to the Ministry of Information, PRO INF 1/790.

128. "Notes of a Conversation with Sir Stafford Cripps," October 30, 1942. PRO INF 1/769.

129. Waddams memorandum, June 25, 1942, PRO INF 1/769.

130. Werth, *Russia at War*, pp. 433–34.

131. Kudriavtsev to Malenkov, Shcherbakov, and Aleksandrov, October 22, 1942, RTsKhIDSI, f.17 op.125 r.1364 e.kh.118.

132. Georgievskii, "Easter, 1942, in Moscow," in Patriarchate of Moscow, *Pravda o religii v Rossii*, p. 216.

133. Ibid. p. 217.

134. "Postal intercept letter from Morriss, Hornsey, to Greer, Dublin," April 21, 1942, PRO FO 371/32949.

135. Sir A. Clark Kerr to Mr. Eden, July 8, 1942, PRO FO 371/32949.

136. "Postal intercept letter from Morriss, Hornsey, to Greer, Dublin," April 21, 1942, PRO FO 371/32949.

137. This was a sufficiently widespread belief greatly to worry Soviet leaders. G. Aleksandrov, in a major Central Committee guidance document on propaganda, fretted that "lying rumors" were circulating among the people that the church had been restored as "a result of the influence of the allies. See Aleksandrov to Fedoseev, undated but 1944, RTsKhIDNI, f.17 op.125 r.1392. For a discussion of this document, see chapter 4.

138. Quoted in Dallin, *German Rule in Russia*, p. 163.

139. A. J. P. Taylor famously argued that Hitler was a German statesman in the traditional mode rather than an ideologue. A. J. P. Taylor, *The Origins of the Second World War*.

140. Tucker, *The Lenin Anthology*, pp. 654–58, quotations from pp. 657 and 654.

141. Declaration of the Russian clergy, November 24, 1941, *RPTsIVOV* (Moscow, 1943), p. 9.

142. Grossman, *Life and Fate*, p. 223.

143. Chuev, *Molotov Remembers*, pp. 187–88.

144. Dostoevskii quoted in Walicki, *The Slavophile Controversy*, p. 536.

145. The most recent Russian estimate of the number of people imprisoned in the gulag at the outset of the war suggests a figure of 2.3 million people, which had been reduced at war's end to about 1.2 million. Much of that reduction was owing to mortality, which is estimated to have reached a total of 3.4 million people between June 1941 and December 1944, or in fact significantly more people than were originally imprisoned. This figure includes only those who were imprisoned in camps and "corrective labor colonies"; it does not include those who were simply deported to places of exile within the USSR. V. N. Zemskov, "Smertnost' zakliuchennykh v 1941–1945 gg.," in Institut rossiiskoi istorii RAN, *Liudskie poteri SSSR v period vtoroi mirovoi voiny*, p. 174. See also Bacon, *The Gulag at War*.

Chapter 3

1. Complete figures for open churches, province-by-province, are contained in G. Karpov to G. Aleksandrov, "Sovershenno sekretno," August 30, 1945, RTsKhIDNI, f.17, op.125, r.1408, e.kh.131. For a fuller discussion of church openings, see chapter 4.

2. Significant exceptions had been greetings from Patriarch *locum tenens* Sergii and Metropolitan Nikolai to Stalin on the occasion of the USSR's twenty-fifth anniversary, printed in *Izvestiia*, November 10, 1942.

3. Two Russian Orthodox appeals to Romanian soldiers were broadcast over Soviet radio on November 22 and December 9, 1942: "Brat'ia po vere! Soldaty Rumynskoi armii!," and "K Rumynskim pastyriam i pastve," *RPTsIVOV*, pp. 77–79 and 80–82. Also see Sergii, *Patriarkh Sergii i ego Nasledstvo*, pp. 135–36.

4. Weinberg, *A World at Arms*, pp. 408–70.

5. Bohdan Bociurkiw, the most recent historian of the Uniate Church, writes that "In Galicia —which experienced less oppression than other German-occupied parts of Ukraine—most Ukrainians, having experienced Soviet rule in the years 1939–1942, considered German occipation a lesser evil than Soviet reannexation." *The Ukrainian Greek Catholic Church and the Soviet State (1939–1950)*, p. 65. According to a post-Soviet historian of Moldavia, "that portion of the population of Moldavia that related more or less loyally to Soviet power, changed its position after the realization of the campaign of deportations." V. I. Pasat, "Poteri Respubliki Moldova v gody vtoroi mirovoi voiny," in Rossiiskaia akademiia nauk, *Liudskie poteri SSSR v period vtoroi mirovoi voiny*, p. 120.

6. Cited in Miner, *Between Churchill and Stalin*, pp. 186–90.

7. In May 1942 the British had been willing to recognize by treaty the Soviet claim to the three Baltic states if Moscow would in turn compromise on the border with Poland. When the Soviets refused to make this quid pro quo, London backed down and would not sign any treaty with territorial provisions. Roosevelt, by contrast, would not sign any public deal concerning frontier changes, but he told the Soviet ambassador, Maksim Litvinov, that the United States could not, and would not, contest Soviet control over these states after the war. Ibid., pp. 184–251.

8. *DPSR*, 1:141.

9. Miner, *Between Churchill and Stalin*, p. 240.

10. Litvinov to Molotov, June 2, 1943, printed in full in Perlmutter, *FDR and Stalin*, pp. 230–46.

11. Lacy Baggallay (Kuibyshev) to Foreign Office, "The Metropolitan of Kiev," September 20, 1942, PRO, FO 371/32950.

12. First Secretary of Soviet Embassy (Graur?) to Foreign Office, December 1, 1942, PRO FO 371/32950.

13. Baggallay to Foreign Office, September 20, 1942, PRO FO 371/32950.

14. Baggallay to Foreign Office, "The Metropolitan of Kiev," September 20, 1942, PRO FO 371/32950.

15. Interestingly, the records of Nikolai's approach to the British are not contained in the Central Committee files of those agencies normally charged with propaganda abroad— VOKS and the Informbiuro. In itself, this is not sufficient proof that Nikolai was working directly for the Soviet secret police, but it does little to allay such suspicions. Fletcher, *Nikolai*.

16. Foreign Office memorandum by "J.L.R.," February 17, 1943, PRO FO 371/36961; Pospielovsky, *The Russian Church under the Soviet Regime*, 1:197.

17. One source indicates that a small printing of the Bible in Russian was allowed in the 1920s. Foreign Office memorandum, "The Position of the Orthodox Church in the Soviet Union," G. W. Berry and G. Reavey, September 20, 1942, PRO FO 371/32950; Anderson, *People, Church and State in Modern Russia*, 17.

18. Foreign Office memorandum by "J.L.R.," February 17, 1943, PRO FO 371/32961.

19. Baggallay (Kuibyshev) to Warner (London), October 3, 1942, PRO FO 371/32950; also PRO INF 1/792.

20. Moscow Embassy to Foreign Office, "The Truth about Religion in Russia," September 20, 1942, PRO FO 371/32950.

21. Armine Dew memorandum, February 27, 1943, PRO FO 371/36961. An American cor-

respondent in Moscow wrote that "I heard that a people's commissar—in other words, a member of the cabinet—sent his secretary out to purchase a copy of the book on religion, and was told it was intended only for circulation abroad." Cassidy, *Moscow Dateline*, p. 355.

22. Thus, in a series of important broadcasts to the world during 1943 and 1944, the BBC would echo this theme. A broadcast to occupied Europe in 1944 would claim that "the militant atheists of the Russian Revolution, by the very act of proscribing the church, set it free." "The Russian Church," BBC script, April 9, 1944, PRO INF 1/791. See discussion in chapter 7.

23. Pospielovsky, *The Russian Church under the Soviet Regime*, 1:198–99.

24. Sergii himself had briefly belonged to the *obnovlentsy* before rejoining the mainstream church. Whether he did so in order to inject the patriarchal church with the Renovationist bacillus, as his critics believe, is very hard to say. At any rate, by 1942 Sergii clearly preferred to end the *obnovlencheskii* schism and bring all Russian Orthodox back under the control of the Moscow Patriarchate. The Soviet state had come to want the same thing. See discussion of Vvedenskii, introductory chapter and chapter 4.

25. Veniamin was a fiery character at the center of several lawsuits in the American courts, which he filed on behalf of the Russian Orthodox Church, to reclaim property that had been taken over by American Orthodox groups in rebellion against the Moscow Patriarchate. Waddams to Martin, "Proposed Exchange of Visits between the Russian Church and the Church of England," October 22, 1942, PRO INF 1/790.

26. Veniamin, Metropolitan of the Aleutians and North America, Patriarchal Exarch in America, "Poslanie ko vsem russkim liudiam v Amerike," first published October 16, 1941, in *Novoe Russkoe Slovo*. Citations in the text are from Patriarchate of Moscow, *Pravda o religii v rossii*, pp. 283–88.

27. Sir A. Clark Kerr to Foreign Office, October 8, 1942, PRO FO 371/32950.

28. Baggallay to Eden, September 20, 1942, PRO FO 371/32950.

29. These issues are explored in chapter 7.

30. Although initially created to reach the native Slavic populations of Eastern Europe, to the surprise of the Soviet authorities, as D. Polikarpov noted three years after the committee's formation, "It is turning out that the main attention of the All-Slav Committee is being directed at American Slavs." Polikarpov to Shcherbakov, September 19, 1944, RTsKhIDNI, f. 17, op. 125, r. 1393. At war's end, the Soviets judged the work of the All-Slav Committee to have been the most effective of the five antifascist committees. Lozovskii to Malenkov, July 25, 1945, RTsKhIDNI, f.17, op.125, r.1409.

31. Jelavich, *St. Petersburg and Moscow*, pp. 20–21.

32. Jelavich, *Russia's Balkan Entanglements*, p. 208.

33. The history of these regions, and of the religious feuds that have marked their history, is naturally quite an emotional one, sparking a deeply divided, and often polemical historiography. See Zernov, *The Russians and Their Church*, pp. 82–92; for background on Russian hostility toward the Uniate Church and St. Petersburg's attempts to use Orthodoxy to cement political control during the early nineteenth century, see Wasyl Lencyk, "The Eastern Catholic Church and Czar Nicholas I."

34. Subtelny, *Ukraine*, pp. 425–52.

35. Polish Research Centre, *The Orthodox Eastern Church in Poland*, p. 38.

36. Ibid., p. 33.

37. Subtelny, *Ukraine*, p. 441. Although Subtelny's is undoubtedly one of the best histories

of Ukraine, he wrongly dates the declaration of Polish autocephaly to 1924. Sabrina Ramet claims that "some 150 Orthodox Churches were either closed or destroyed" by the Polish government between the wars. Ramet, "Autocephaly and National Identity in Church-State Relations in Eastern Christinity," in Ramet, *Eastern Christians and Politics in the Twentieth Century*, 1:10.

38. Polish Research Centre, *The Orthodox Eastern Church in Poland*, p. 33.

39. Ibid., p. 34.

40. See the examination of this process in chapter 1.

41. O'Malley to Eden, April 29, 1943, PRO FO 371/34571. This is a fascinating, and remarkably accurate lengthy review written in the wake of Moscow's decision to break off relations with the Polish government-in-exile in London.

42. Ibid. These estimates have been largely confirmed by recent scholarship. Jan T. Gross estimates that the Soviets deported about 1.25 million people from eastern Poland, or roughly 9 percent of the prewar civil population. Gross, *Revolution from Abroad*, p. xiii.

43. The relevant remaining documents, plus a short history, with supporting materials, of the Soviet government's attempts from Khrushchev's time through the Gorbachev period were first published in *Voennye arkhivy Rossii* no. 1 (1993). A more complete set of documents appeared in *OGB*, I:152–61, and 165–71. A more complete collection of documents was published by the Russian government, which adds little beyond some extra detail, to the key documents published earlier. Pikhoia et al., *Katyn'*.

44. This was the thesis of the best book written on the Katyn massacre before the availability of Soviet records. Zawodny, *Death in the Forest*.

45. Dokladnaia zapiska narkoma vnutrennikh del SSSR No. 794/B v TsK VKP(b), undated, but no later than March 5, 1940, *OGB*, I:153–55. The execution order was signed personally by Stalin, V. M. Molotov, A. I. Mikoian, M. I. Kalinin, K. E. Voroshilov, and L. M. Kaganovich. The politbiuro order for the shootings is dated March 5, *ibid.*, p. 156. The exact total of those killed seems to have been 21,957, Shelepin to Khrushchev, March 3, 1959, *Voennye arkhivy Rossii*, no. 1 (1993):127–28. Before the murders, the Soviets arranged an especially chilling operation: prior to shooting their prisoners, when the victims were still unaware that their fate had been determined, the NKVD ordered the Polish POWs to list their closest relations and others who lived with them before the war. Following the mass executions, the NKVD arranged for the deportation to Soviet Central Asia of these people, numbering between 75,000 and 100,000. Lavrenty Beria, "Ukazanie NKVD SSSR No. 892/B," *OGB*, I:158–61.

46. Record of a Conversation between Ambassador Kot and M. Stalin, November 14, 1941, *DPSR*, 1:210.

47. Minute of Conversation between General Sikorski and M. Stalin, December 3, 1941, *DSPR*, 1:233.

48. Communiqué issued by Berlin Broadcasting Station, April 13, 1943, *DSPR*, 1:523–24.

49. Following the German revelations, the Soviets changed their story, claiming that the men had been released from Soviet imprisonment in 1940 and had been on construction work details west of Smolensk when they had fallen into German hands. Moscow further claimed that the site named by the Germans as a mass grave was in fact a well-known archaeological dig, a historical burial ground. Informbiuro communiqué, April 15, 1943, reprinted in *Soviet War News*, no. 541 (April 17, 1943).

50. Ibid.

51. "At the same time, however," they stipulated, "the Polish Government, on behalf of the Polish nation, denies to the Germans the right to draw from a crime which they ascribe to others arguments in their own defence." "Statement of the Polish Government," April 17, 1943, PRO FO 371/34571.

52. O'Malley to Eden, April 29, 1943, PRO FO 371/34572.

53. D. Allen memorandum, April 30, 1943, PRO FO 371/34571.

54. Churchill to Stalin, April 28, 1943, PRO FO 371/34572.

55. Churchill to Eden, April 28, 1943, PRO FO 371/34571.

56. Note from Commissar Molotov, April 25, 1943, *DPSR*, 1:533–34.

57. D. Allen memorandum, April 30, 1943, PRO FO 371/34571.

58. Lenin wrote: "Only Comrade Kalinin should publicly undertake measures of any kind—Comrade Trotsky should at no time and under no circumstances speak out [on this matter] in the press or before the public in any other manner." Lenin to Molotov and polit-biuro members, March 19, 1922, in Pipes, *The Unknown Lenin*, pp. 152–54. Pipes writes: "Although Trotsky played a critical role in the 1922 antichurch campaign and may have even been its instigator, he was kept in the background throughout, in order not to feed rumors that the campaign was a Jewish plot against Christianity" (p. 155).

59. *Sputnik agitatora*, no. 10 (May 1943). Reported with somewhat different wording in *Soviet Monitor* [radio bulletins from the USSR issued by TASS], May 19, 1943, PRO, FO 371 36961. Curtiss, *The Soviet State and the Russian Church*, p. 292, quotes Kalinin as saying "that he did not feel that it was outrageous for young men in the army to laugh at middle-aged recruits who wore crosses, although he warned against outright abuse in such cases." Although Curtiss is a careful scholar, I have been unable to find the original source for such wording.

60. See *Pravda*, May 22, 1943. The news was also broadcast on Radio Moscow.

61. Such was the opinion of Leonhard, *Child of the Revolution*, p. 226. Leonhard recounts the belief of those in the Comintern school at the time of the dissolution, himself included, that this was being done to placate the British and the Americans.

62. "Marshal Stalin on Dissolution of Communist International," May 31, 1943, PRO FO 371/120964.

63. Communists were still expected to toe Moscow's line. The director of the Comintern School in Ufa told his charges: "The tasks of the Communists in England and America today is [sic] to support the efforts of the their countries in the war. The Communists of Germany and Italy, on the other hand, have to do everything they can to bring about the destruction of Fascism. The Communists in the occupied countries have another task again—to set themselves at the head of a national patriotic anti-Fascist front and to liberate their countries from Fascist oppression." Leonhard, *Child of the Revolution*, p. 221.

64. On the American Communist Party at this time, see Klehr, *The Heyday of American Communism*; even before the dissolution of the Comintern, Moscow had attempted to restrain Tito's overt expressions of Communism. See Banac, *With Stalin against Tito*, pp. 9–11.

65. Cited in Robert A. Graham, *The Vatican and Communism during World War II*, p. 106.

66. Neither the Hungarians nor the Romanians are Slavic peoples, although historically the latter are Orthodox. The citation is from Polikarpov to Aleksandrov, July 1942, RTsKhIDNI, f.17 op.125 e.kh.125.

67. Patriarch *locum tenens* Sergii and Metropolitan Nikolai, "Brat'ia po vere! Soldaty rumynskoi armii!," November 22, 1942, *RPTsIVOV*, pp. 77–79. Much the same themes were

repeated by the same authors in "K rumynskim pastyriam i pastve," December 9, 1942, *RPTsIVOV*, pp. 80–82.

68. Sir A. Clark Kerr to Mr. Eden, May 14, 1943, "An Eyewitness Account of the Pan-Slavonic Meeting in Moscow on the 9th May, 1943," PRO FO 371/36961.

69. Metropolitan Nikolai, "Budem ediny: Rech' na vseslavianskom mitinge v Moskve, 9 Maia 1943 goda," *Slova, rechi, poslaniia*, pp. 182–86.

70. Clerk Kerr to Eden, May 14, 1943, PRO FO 371/36961.

71. "The Russian Orthodox Church as a Factor of the Russian Policy towards Poland," M. Wyaznski (Polish Ministry of Information) to Warner, September 24, 1943, PRO FO 371/36962.

72. Questions concerning schismatic Ukrainian churches are dealt with in chapters 4 and 5.

73. Polish Research Centre, *The Orthodox Eastern Church in Poland*, p. 36.

74. "The Present Policy of the Moscow Patriarchy towards the Polish Orthodox Church," translation of Sergii's message, a copy of which was conveyed to the British Foreign Office by the Polish government-in-exile. PRO FO 371/36962.

75. By 1948 the Moscow Patriarchate would finally recognize the autocephalous status of the Polish Orthodox Church. By that time, the number of Orthodox believers in Poland had been drastically reduced and the church was in no position to act as a center of Ukrainian disaffection with the USSR. Department for External Church Relations of the Moscow Patriarchate, "Visit of the Primate of the Polish Orthodox Church," September 1998, Moscow Patriarchate web site ‹www.russian-orthodox-church.org.ru/nc081283.htm›, accessed January 5, 1999.

76. M. Wyaznski (Polish Ministry of Information) to Warner (British Foreign Office), September 24, 1943, PRO FO 371/36962.

77. "The All Soviet Communist Party's Attitude towards Religion," Polish Ministry of Information, London, September 1943.

78. H. Martin (MOI) to J. H. Oldham, August 23, 1943, PRO INF 1/790.

79. Many of these legal restrictions were outlined in "Answers to questions on the Church in the U.S.S.R.," A. B. Elkin (MOI) to Thomas Hall (OSS), undated, but probably February 1944, PRO INF 1/769.

Chapter 4

1. Polish Ministry of Foreign Affairs Circular, September 10, 1943, *DPSR*, 2:50–51.

2. Gordun, "Russkaia Pravoslavnaia Tserkov' v period s 1943 po 1970 god," p. 39.

3. Merkulov to Central Committee and Shcherbakov, July 3, 1943, in Corley, *Religion in the Soviet Union*, p. 138. Merkulov gave a further reason: "given the mood of the church leaders, as well as the visit of the delegation from England of the English [Anglican] church expected in September of this year, I consider it desirable to permit the transfer of the church centres ... from Ulyanovsk to the town of Moscow." In addition to Sergii, Merkulov also suggested returning to Moscow Archbishop Aleksandr Vvedenskii of the Obnovlencheskii Church and the leaders of the "All-Union Council of Evangelical Christians." (The visit of the Anglican delegation to Moscow is discussed in chapter 7.)

4. The bishops had been away from Moscow for two years. "Vpechatlenie uchastnika Sob-

ora episkopov pravoslavnoi tserkvi v Moskve 8 Sentiabria 1943 goda," *ZhMP*, no. 2 (October 15, 1943); pp. 16–17.

5. Fletcher, *Nikolai*, p. 50.

6. Davis, *A Long Walk to Church*, pp. 18 and 234.

7. Karpov's notes of his meeting with Stalin, September 4, 1943, in Corley, *Religion in the Soviet Union*, pp. 139–40. By placing church affairs in the hands of the state apparatus, rather than that of the Communist Party, Stalin no doubt hoped to foster the impression that Communist officials would not be giving orders to the church. It was all pretense, of course. The supposed division between party and state authorities was largely fictional; church affairs continued to be largely directed by the NKGB.

8. Ibid., p. 141.

9. This account, by A. Levitin-Krasnov, an Orthodox figure who drew on Sergii's own reminiscences, is quoted at length in Medvedev, *All Stalin's Men*, pp. 95–96. The same text is quoted in Pospielovsky, *The Russian Church under the Soviet Regime*, 1:201–03. Levitin-Krasnov's account of the meeting was the only reliable one until the publication of Karpov's notes; they are still useful, however, because they provide some dialogue missing from Karpov's schematic account.

10. Karpov notes, Corley, *Religion in the Soviet Union*, p. 143.

11. Krasnov-Levitin mistakenly claims that the meeting lasted six hours. Karpov, who was present, notes the time precisely.

12. Pospielovsky, *The Russian Church under the Soviet Regime*, 1:202n. Although Pospielovsky rightly doubts certain details provided by this source, and believes that its author was hostile to the church, this remark by Stalin certainly has the ring of authenticity; it also reflects the scope of the plans the Kremlin had for the church, as well as the exaggerated notions Soviet leaders had always held about the Vatican's powers.

13. Karpov notes, Corley, *Religion in the Soviet Union*, p. 144.

14. Ibid.

15. Levitin-Krasnov quoted in Medvedev, *All Stalin's Men*, pp. 95–96.

16. Inexplicably, Ronald Grigor Suny describes this meeting between Stalin and the patriarch as "a long and friendly talk." Suny, *The Soviet Experiment*, p. 327.

17. Standley to Secretary of State, September 9, 1943, *FRUS* 3:856, "The British Commonwealth, Eastern Europe, and the Far East."

18. *Soviet Monitor*, September 9, 1943, PRO FO 371/36962.

19. Fletcher, *Nikolai*, p. 50.

20. Ware, *The Orthodox Church*, p. 125.

21. Whose name, interestingly, is omitted from the declarations published following the *sobor'*. One can safely assume, however, that the NKGB planted informants in the *sobor'*.

22. Karpov to Aleksandrov, August 30, 1945, RTsKhIDNI, f.17 op.125 r.1408 e.kh.131.

23. Gordun, "Russkaia Pravoslavnaia Tserkov' v period s 1943 po 1970 god," p. 46.

24. "Lozh' fashistov i pravda o pravoslavnoi tserkvi v SSSR," *ZhMP*, no. 2 (February 1944): 29–30. The same terms were used in "Rech' sviateishego Patriarkha Sergiia v Kafedral'nom Bogoiavlenskom Sobora g. Moskvy, v den' intronizatsii, 12 Sentiabria 1943 g.," *ZhMP*, no. 2 (October 15, 1943): 8; and "Izvestitel'nye gramoty Patriarkha Sergiia vostochnym Patriarkham," ibid., pp. 6–7.

25. *Soviet Monitor*, September 9, 1943, PRO FO 371/36962; *ZhMP*, no. 1, p. 14; Alexeev, *The Foreign Policy of the Moscow Patriarchate*, 2:5.

26. Gordun, "Russkaia Pravoslavnaia Tserkov' v period s 1943 po 1970 god," p. 42.

27. Moscow Embassy to Foreign Office, October 7, 1943, PRO FO 371 36963; and Hamilton to Secretary of State, October 9, 1943, *FRUS*, 3:859.

28. Karpov would continue to head the Soviet for the Affairs of the Russian Orthodox Church until his dismissal in 1960, during Khrushchev's de-Stalinization. At that time, he would be accused of having "flagrantly violated socialist legality, conducted mass arrests of completely innocent citizens, deployed perverted methods of conducting investigations and also falsified records of the interrogation of those arrested." Report to the Committee for Party Control Attached to the CPSU CC for the Period, March 1, 1956 to March 1, 1957, in Corley, *Religion in the Soviet Union*, p. 204. Interestingly, Karpov seems not to have been attacked specifically for his activities relating to the Russian Orthodox Church, and he remained in charge of his soviet for three more years after this damning indictment.

29. Fletcher, *Nikolai*, p. 51.

30. A much fuller discussion of this visit is in chapter 7.

31. Letter from the archbishop of Tambov to the head of the Moscow eparkhii, intercepted by Soviet censors and relayed by G. Aleksandrov to G. Malenkov, August 1944, RTsKhIDNI, f.17 op.125 r1391 e.kh.235.

32. "Lozh'fashistov i pravda o pravoslavnoi tserkvi v SSSR," *ZhMP*, no. 2 (February 1944): 29–30. The Soviet government clearly favored the recentralization of authority under the Moscow Patriarchate. Karpov informed his subordinates in the Soviet for the Affairs of the Russian Orthodox Church: "[I]n those cases where renovationist clergy transfer at their own request from the renovationist tendency to the patriarchal sergyite church, they are not to be obstructed. Similarly there are to be no obstacles to the transfer of groups of believers or of parishes as a whole from the renovationist to the Sergyite church at the request of the believers." Karpov circular, October 16, 1943, in Corley, *Religion in the Soviet Union*, p. 147.

33. Bourke-White, *Shooting the Russian War*, p. 149, photo caption. High-ranking clergy in mainstream Russian Orthodoxy are forbidden to marry.

34. Balfour to Warner, December 14, 1943, PRO FO 371/43338.

35. "Vosoedinenie obnovlencheskikh sviashchennosluzhitelei s pravoslavnoi tserkoviu," *ZhMP*, no. 1 (January 1944): 7–8.

36. "Vossoeddinenie obnovlencheskikh sviashchennosluzhitelei s pravoslavnoi tserkoviu," *ZhMP*, no.4 (April 1944): 9.

37. "Dioceses of the Orthodox Church of the U.S.S.R., 1944," Foreign Office Research Department, undated, PRO INF 1/769 119975.

38. When Churchill visited Moscow for the second time, in October 1944, Stalin said: "'There are lots of things that happen even here in Russia which our Secret Service do not necessarily tell me about.'" "I let it go at that," Churchill replied. Churchill, *The Second World War*, 3; 55.

39. For a discussion of wartime disloyalty, see chapter 2.

40. I. Fomina to G. F. Aleksandrov, undated, but probably November 1943, RTsKhIDNI, f.17 op.125 r.1378 e.kh.181.

41. Aleksandrov and M. Iovchuk to Zhdanov, January 19, 1944; relating questions from Stavropol, Krasnogvardskii krai, Kiev, Kharkov, Stalinsk, Sumskoi, Poltavskoi, and Cherni-

govskoi oblast's of Ukraine, and Kalinin, Orlov, Smolensk, Kursk, Rostov, and Stalingrad oblast's of the RSFSR. RTsKHIDNI, f.17 op.125 r.1392.

42. Aleksandrov to Zhdanov, May 11, 1943, questions asked between April and May 1944, in Kiev, Zhitomir, Zaporozhe, Dnepropetrovsk, Kirovograd, Vinnitsa, Stalinsk, and Rovensk oblast's of Ukraine; Polessk, Mogilev, Vitebsk, and Gomel of Belorussia; Krasnodar, Stavropol krais from the RSFSR; also from Astrakhan, Penzensk, Chitinsk and Ul'ianovsk oblast's. RTsKhIDNI, f.17 op.125 r.1392 e.kh.242.

43. V. Zolotukhin to Shcherbakov, September 15, 1944, RTsKhIDNI, f.17 op.125 r.1391 e.kh.235.

44. Karpov to Aleksandrov, August 30, 1945, "Sovershenno sekretno," RTsKhIDNI, f.17 op.125 r.1408 e.kh.131.

45. Sudoplatov, *Special Tasks*, p. 251.

46. "Po linii borby s antisovetskimi elementami iz chisla tserkovnikov i sektantov," "sovershenno sekretno," June 1946, in *TSIM*, pp. 583–85.

47. The NKGB also targeted smaller non-Orthodox religious groups, such as the minuscule *Innokent'evsky* sect. Moldavian NKGB reported that, "On the territory of Moldavia there is a widespread dissemination of sectarian underground formations, chiefly monarchical sects of *Innokent'evtsy*. During the period from April 1944 through May 1946 agents and operatives liquidated 17 anti-Soviet organizations and groups, with the arrest of 71 people"—a small operation by Stalinist standards but significant given the small numbers in the sect. *Innokent'evsky* were followers of the early twentieth-century Orthodox cleric Innokenty Levizor, who believed that Innokenty himself was the earthly incorporation of the Holy Spirit and prophesied the imminent end of the world followed by a harsh Judgment Day. Centered in Moldavia, Bessarabia, and Ukraine, this sect was condemned as anti-Soviet and promonarchist, and its leaders were tried by the Soviets. For the Soviet version of events, see Novikov, *Ateisticheskii slovar'*, pp. 174–75. "Po linii borby s antisovetskimi elementami iz chisla tserkovnikov i sektantov," "sovershenno sekretno," June 1946, in *TSIM*, pp. 583–85.

48. Moscow Embassy to Foreign Office, September 8, 1943, FO 371/43339. The references to schismatics are, respectively: "Renovators," members of the "Living Church," who argued that the Soviet regime was, through its supposed communitarianism and egalitarianism, enacting Christian principles in the social world; the "Gregorians" were followers of Archbishop Grigorii of Ekaterinoslav, who called a synod of bishops in 1925 to challenge Sergii's authority and questioned the latter's decision in the next year to make peace with Soviet power; the "Josephians" were followers of Metropolitan Iosif, who led a schismatic movement in Leningrad, beginning in 1927, also questioning Sergii's authority and resisting his call to accept Soviet power. See Fletcher, *The Russian Orthodox Church Underground*, pp. 46–49 and 62–69.

49. Metropolitan Nikolai, "Pod zheleznym natiskom voinov-bogatyrei," *Slova, rechi, poslaniia*, pp. 251–53.

50. *ZhMP*, no. 2, p. 3.

51. Karpov to Aleksandrov, August 30, 1945, RTsKhIDNI, f.17 op.125 r.1408 e.kh131.

52. "Po linii borby s antisovetskii elementami iz chisla tserkovnikov i sektantov," "sovershenno sekretno," June 1946, in *TSIM*, pp. 583–85.

53. Karpov to Aleksandrov, "sovershenno sekretno," August 30, 1945, RTsKhIDNI, f.17 op.125 r.1408 e.kh.131.

54. Ibid.

55. "Dioceses of the Orthodox Church of the U.S.S.R., 1944," Foreign Office Research Department, undated, PRO FO 371/119975.

56. L. D. Wilgress to Secretary of State for External Affairs of Canada, February 8, 1945, PRO FO 371/47929.

57. Gordun, "Russkaia Pravoslavnaia Tserkov' v period s 1943 po 1970 god," p. 40.

58. Pospielovsky, *The Russian Church under the Soviet Regime* 1:204. Pospielovsky says that by 1945 there were only forty-one bishops under the Moscow Patriarchate.

59. Whereas higher theological education had taken between six and seven years in the past, the new course would be cut to only three. In addition to seminary training, each bishopric would institute a lower form of theological education lasting only two years. Training in both programs involved extensive reading in church history, scriptures, patristics, and the church Slavonic language. Both would also include education in "the canonical code and the Constitution of the U.S.S.R." Bishop Grigory of Saratov, "Theological Education in Russia," *Soviet War News*, no. 801 (March 2, 1944).

60. "Religious Communities in the Soviet Union," unsigned, *Soviet War News*, August 22, 1941.

61. Gordun, "Russkaia Pravoslavnaia Tserkov' v period s 1943 po 1970 god," p. 46.

62. The Cheka was the precursor of the NKVD-NKGB, and throughout the Soviet era political police were routinely referred to as "Chekists." "Report on Informational and Agent Work of the Cheka among the Clergy," 1921, in Corly, *Religion in the Soviet Union*, p. 25. Chekists were also ordered to search priests' living quarters to find correspondence that might provide material for blackmail. A document smuggled out of the USSR during the 1970s, written by Deputy Chairman of the Soviet for Religious Affairs V. Furov, revealed that "There is no consecration of a bishop, no transfer without thorough investigation of the candidate by appropriate officials of the Council in close cooperation with the commission, local organs, and corresponding interested organs." Quoted in Sabrina Ramet, *Eastern Christians and Politics in the Twentieth Century*, 1:11.

63. Pospielovsky, *The Russian Church under the Soviet Regime*, 1:204n.

64. Karpov to Aleksandrov, "sovershenno sekretno," August 30, 1945, RTsKhIDNI, f.17 op.125 r.1408 e.kh.131.

65. I. Polianskii to Aleksandrov, August 31, 1945, RTsKhIDNI, f.17 op.125 r.1408 e.kh.313.

66. E. Novosel'tsev to Khodov, relays a copy of a document labeled "sovershenno sekretno" from Colonel G. B. Nikolaev of Ukrainian People's Commissariat State Security (UNKGB) in Penza oblast', June 28, 1943, RTsKhIDNI, f.17 op.125 r.1378 e.kh.181.

67. E. Novosel'tsev to Khodov, relays "sovershenno sekretno" report from Colonel Nikolaev of UNKGB in Penza, June 28, 1943, RTsKhIDNI, f.17 op.125 r.1378 e.kh.181.

68. Extract from a 1945 NKVD document, in Corley, *Religion in the Soviet Union*, p. 155. Unfortunately, the editor of this exceedingly useful documentary collection does not in this case supply the name of the document's author.

69. I. Polianskii to Aleksandrov, August 31, 1945, RTsKhIDNI, f.17 op.125 r.1408 e.kh.313.

70. *ZhMP*, no. 2, p. 3.

71. I. Polianskii to Aleksandrov, August 31, 1945, RTsKhIDNI, f.17 op.125 r.1408 e.kh313.

72. Ibid.

73. M. Kuznetsov and V. V. Chernyshev to L. Beria, January 15, 1945, in N. F. Bugai, "Pub-

likatsii: 'Pogruzheny v eshelony i otpravleny k mestam poselenii . . .'; L. Beria–I. Stalinu," *Istoriia SSSR*, no. 1 (January–February 1991): 155.

74. "Spravka Otdela spetsposelenii NKVD SSSR o kolichestve spetsposelentsev po oktiabr' 1946 g.," in ibid.

75. Novosel'tsev to Khodov, June 28, 1943; and Potogin to Secretary of Penza Obkom, undated, RTsKhIDNI, f.17 op.125 r.1378 e.kh.181.

76. Ibid.

77. Pentecostals, with roots in the United States. The USSR government deemed this sect to have an "antisocial character," and what remained of it was herded into the officially registered Baptist Church in 1945. For the Soviet version of this sect, see Novikov, *Ateisticheskii slovar'*, p. 375.

78. I. Polianskii to Aleksandrov, August 31, 1945, RTsKhIDNI f.17 op.125 r.1408 e.kh.313. This documents the retribution these people received from the authorities.

79. Kozachenko (deputy minister of state security of Moldavian SSR) to Butov, October 17, 1946, in *TSIM*, pp. 591–93.

80. Ibid. Although the section of the document containing this material has been cut by the collection's editor, he summarizes the content in n. 2, p. 591.

81. I. Polianskii to Aleksandrov, August 31, 1945. Lithuanian Catholic clergy and the armed anti-Soviet resistance were deeply intertwined. One historian writes: "At least 250 of Lithuania's 1,300 Catholic clergy are said to have been actively involved in the anti-Soviet resistance movement of 1944–53, with two of them (Ylius and Lelesius) serving as brigade leaders. In retribution, the Soviets deported about 30 percent of the priests, four bishops, and almost all monks and nuns to forced labor camps. Ramet, *Cross and Commissar*, p. 34.

82. Karpov to Aleksandrov, August 30, 1945.

83. Ibid.

84. Batyrov to Aleksandrov, December 7, 1943, RTsKhIDNI, f.17 op.125 r.1378 e.kh.184.

85. Aleksandrov to Malenkov, August 2, 1944, relaying the intercepted letter, which Aleksandrov wrote was "of very great political interest." RTsKhIDNI, f.17 op.125 r.1391 e.kh.235.

86. Merkulov to Shcherbakov, March 1, 1944, RTsKhIDNI f.17 op.125 r.1394 e.kh.251. The astonishing thing, testifying to the extreme centralization of Stalinist Russia, is that such a matter should be decided by high-ranking members of the Central Committee.

87. The preceding examples are all taken from Karpov to Aleksandrov, August 30, 1945.

88. Aleksandrov and P. Fedoseev to Zhdanov, undated, but 1944, RTsKhDNI, f.17 op.125 r.1392.

89. The Central Committee documents are printed in Institut Marksizma-Leninizma, *Kommunisticheskaia Partiia sovetskogo soiuza v resoliutsiiakh i resheniiahk s"ezdov konferentsii i plenumov Ts K*, vol. 7; these were, respectively, for Moldavia, "Postanovlenie TsK VKP(b)," June 14, 1944, pp. 501–4; for Belorussia, "Postanovlenie TsK VKP(b)," August 9, 1944, pp. 506–12, and "Postanovlenie TsK VKP(b)," January 20, 1945, pp. 533–36; for Ukraine, "Postanovlenie TsK VKP(b)," September 27, 1944, pp. 524–25, and "Postanovlenie TsK VKP(b)," September 27, 1944, pp. 526–31.

90. "Postanovlenie TsK VKP(b)," June 14, 1944, ibid., pp. 501–04.

91. "Postanovlenie TsK VKP(b)," August 9, 1944, ibid., pp. 506–12.

92. "Postanovlenie TsK VKP(b)," January 20, 1945, ibid., pp. 533–36.

93. "Postanovlenie TsK VKP(b)," January 20, 1945, ibid., pp.533–36.

94. "Postanovlenie TsK VKP(b) ob organizatsii nauchno-prosvetitel'noi propagandy," September 27, 1944, ibid., pp. 521–23.

95. Frank Roberts, *Dealing with Dictators*, pp. 80–81.

96. Roberts to Eden, April 21, 1945, PRO FO 371/47929.

97. memorandum of I. Kovalev (zam. zav. otdelom propagandy i agitatsii Dorogobych-skogo obkoma KP(b)U), February 26, 1945, RTsKhIDNI, f.17 op.125 r.1408.

98. All citations are from ibid.

99. Slepov to G. I. Malenkov, April 16, 1945, RTsKhIDNI, f.17 op.125 r.1408. e.kh.313.

100. For a recent Russian account of church history during this period, see Vostryshev, *Bozhii izbrannik: Krestnyi put' sviatitelia Tikhona Patriarkha Moskovskogo i vseia Rossii*, pp. 94–118. Also see Solzhenitsyn, *The Gulag Archipelago*, 1:342–52.

101. The account was relayed by the British ambassador, Clark Kerr, to the Foreign Office, August 9, 1944, PRO FO 371/43340.

102. Harriman to Secretary of State, January 13, 1944, *FRUS*, 3:864. Of course, the very presence of Harriman could well explain the heavy police presence.

Chapter 5

1. Bugai, *L. Beriia-I. Stalinu*.

2. Klehr, Haynes, and Firsov, *The Secret World of American Communism*, pp. 98–106.

3. The Hoover Institution in Stanford, California, has files on the American Slavic Congress, dealing with its activities during the war.

4. Polikarpov to Shcherbakov, September 19, 1944, RTsKhIDNI, f.17 op.125 r.1393 e.kh.246.

5. Gundorov to Malenkov, October 26, 1945, RTsKhIDNI, f.17 op.125 r.1409 e.kh.317 (emphasis in original).

6. Gaddis, *The United States and the Origins of the Cold War*, p. 145n.

7. "Soviet Monitor: Radio Bulletins from the U.S.S.R.," May 3, 1943, PRO FO 371/34573.

8. Harriman to Secretary of State, January 18, 1944, "The British Commonwealth and Europe," *FRUS* 3:1230–32.

9. Secretary of State to Harriman, January 24, 1944, ibid., pp. 1398–99.

10. Memorandum of Stettinius to Roosevelt, March 8, 1944, ibid., p. 1402.

11. "Record of a Conversation between I. V. Stalin and the Roman Catholic Priest St. Orlemanski," April 28, 1944, in Murashko et al., *Vostochnaia Evropa v dokumentakh rossiskhikh arkhivov*, 1:36–42.

12. Hamilton to Secretary of State, May 7, 1944, "The British Commonwealth and Europe," *FRUS* 3:1407–9. A fuller account of Orlemanski's radio remarks is in S. Orlemanski, "My Visit to Moscow," *Soviet War News*, no. 853 (May 9, 1944).

13. *Soviet War News*, no. 853 (May 9, 1944).

14. Hamilton to Seceretary of State, May 9, 1944, *FRUS*, vol. 4, *Europe*.

15. Ciechanowski to Romer, June 14, 1944, *DPSR*, 3:267.

16. Polish Ministry of Foreign Affairs Circular, September 10, 1943, *DPSR*, 2:50–51.

17. Gaddis, *United States and the Origins of the Cold War*, p. 145; Walter Kolarz calls Stalin's meeting with Orlemanski "the nearest approach to an offer of peace made to the Vatican during Stalin's lifetime." Kolarz, *The Soviet Union and the Catholic Church*, p. 194.

18. Dennis J. Dunn believes that the Soviets themselves spread that rumor that the Vatican

was preparing to engage in mutual diplomatic relations, but that the Holy See was not interested. Dunn, *The Catholic Church and the Soviet Government* (Boulder, 1977), p. 88.

19. "Russia as a factor in Political Warfare," Political Warfare Executive, February 4, 1944, PRO FO 371/43326.

20. Lozovskii to Shcherbakov, "Sekretno," August 8, 1944; Shcherbakov to Stalin, "Sovershenno sekretno," undated but August 1944; the text of the pilfered British Political Warfare Executive document is May 6, 1944, RTsKhIDNI, f.17 op.125 r.1393 e.kh.244. The documents passed over the desk of Peter Smollett, a Soviet mole in the British Ministry of Information. Whether he, or someone else, passed on the secret documents to the Soviets is not revealed by the copy in the Russian archives. On Smollett, see chapter 7.

21. "Polish-Soviet Agreement," July 30, 1941, *DPSR*, 1:141–42. See also Anders, *An Army in Exile*.

22. See discussion in chapter 6.

23. Translation of a postal intercept to an American bishop, August 11, 1942, PRO INF 1/769.

24. Stehle, *Eastern Politics of the Vatican*, pp. 128ff. Robert A. Graham, *The Vatican and Communism during World War II*, p. 131–32.

25. Ciszek, with Flaherty, *With God in Russia*. Citations from pp. 84 and 85. Also, Ciszek, with Flaherty, *He Leadeth Me*, pp. 74 and 80–81.

26. For an instance of Soviet trust in Orlemanski, see Gundorov to Malenkov, October 26, 1945, RTsKhIDNI, f.17 op.125 r.1409 e.kh.317.

27. Pravdin was central to the widespread prewar and wartime Soviet spy ring in the United States. See Weinstein and Vassiliev, *The Haunted Wood*, p. 104; also Klehr and Haynes, *Venona*, p. 53.

28. Bohlen to Mathews, May 24, 1944. *FRUS*, 4:1224.

29. "Mezhdunarodnoe polozhenie sovetskogo soiuza," March 25, 1944, RTsKhIDNI, f.17 op.125 r.1391 e.kh236. This line echoed what was already being told to members of the public by propagandists. On July 11, 1943, for instance, one British diplomat reported that he witnessed an agitator in Moscow's Central Park of Culture and Rest say that "The Pope did not want a complete German victory as the Nazis oppressed the Catholic Church. On the other hand, he did not want a complete defeat of the Axis, as a strong Russia would mean a strong orthodox Church, particularly in the small Slav countries which would cling to Russia in the event of an Axis defeat. It was to the interest of the Vatican to bring about a compromise peace." "Consultation on Foreign Affairs," T. Brimelow, July 11, 1943, PRO FO 371/121047.

30. Harriman to Secretary of State, July 1, 1944, *FRUS*, 4:1215–16; Kerr to Foreign Office, July 3, 1944, PRO FO 371 43340. "Council for Religious Creeds," *Soviet War News*, no. 900 (July 4, 1944).

31. Cited in Northern Department to Moscow Embassy, July 8, 1944, PRO FO 371/43340.

32. Bociurkiw, *The Ukrainian Greek Catholic Church and the Soviet State (1939–1950)*, p. 69. Bociurkiw writes that K. A. Zaitsev was briefly named as the head of the organization.

33. Kerr to Foreign Office, July 28, 1944, PRO FO 371/43340.

34. Bohlen memorandum, July 5, 1944, *FRUS*, 4:1215–16.

35. Beria to Stalin, Molotov, and Antonov, July 18, 1944, in Rossiiskaia akademiia nauk, *NKVD i pol'skoe podpol'e 1944–1945 (Po "Osobym papkam" I. V. Stalina)*, pp. 35–37.

36. I. A. Serov to L. Beria, October 16, 1944, in ibid., pp. 38–43.

37. Ciechanowski, *The Warsaw Rising of 1944*; Zawodny, *Nothing but Honour.*

38. Such, at any rate, was the contention of Valentin Berezhkov, at that time still a high-ranking member of the Soviet Foreign Ministry, in a personal interview with the author. Richard Overy declares, both assuredly and equivocally at the same time, that the answer to the question as to whether Soviet forces could have rescued the Polish insurgents "seems unambiguously negative." In his account, however, Overy does not mention that Soviet radio called on the Poles to rise up in front of the Red Army's advance, nor does he detail Stalin's refusal to allow Anglo-American parachute drops, or his denial of Soviet airfields for use by American and British aircraft until the uprising was almost defeated. Overy writes, confusingly: "There can be no question that Allied air drops could not have sustained Polish resistance in Warsaw for long." Overy, *Russia's War*, pp. 297–98.

39. "Zapis' besedy I. V. Stalin s F. Ruzvel'tom," December 1, 1943, Ministerstvo inostrannykh del SSSR, *Tegeranskaia konferentsiia rukovoditelei trekh soiuznykh derzhav*, p. 151.

40. Taylor to Roosevelt, July 17, 1944, box 11, 1944–45, Myron Taylor Papers, Franklin D. Roosevelt Library, Hyde Park, New York.

41. Taylor to Roosevelt, July 17, 1944, *FRUS*, 4:1217–21.

42. Taylor to Roosevelt, July 17, 1944, Taylor Papers.

43. Ibid.

44. Standley memorandum for Taylor, August 12, 1944, box 11, 1944–45, Taylor Papers.

45. These figures were printed in "Religious Communities in the Soviet Union," *Soviet War News*, no. 27 (August 22, 1941). See discussion in chapter 6.

46. Tardini memorandum in Taylor to Roosevelt, July 17, 1944, *FRUS*, 4:1217–21.

47. "Soobshchenie rezidentury NKGB SSSR v Italii o peregovorakh predstavitelei nemetskhikh voennykh krugov s soiuznikami o zakliuchenii separatnogo mira," in Moskovskoe gorodskoe ob'edinenie arkhivov, *Neizvestnaia Rossiia*, p. 301.

48. August 27, ibid.

49. Sudoplatov, *Special Tasks*, p. 250. Involved as he was in Ukrainian affairs, Sudoplatov may have seen only part of the picture; the Vatican was also worried about the fate of Catholics in the Baltic states, Poland, and the portions of Europe that might fall into Red Army hands.

50. There is no record in the otherwise exhaustive Churchill biography by Martin Gilbert. *Winston S. Churchill* 7:887–922.

51. Cited in Aarons and Loftus, *Unholy Trinity*, p. 17.

52. Litvin (Secretary TsK KP(b)U po propagande i agitatsii) to Aleksandrov, April 15, 1945, RTsKhIDNI, f.17 op.125 r.1408 e.kh.313.

53. Subtelny, *Ukraine*, p. 488.

54. See discussion in chapter 1.

55. Conquest, *Harvest of Sorrow.*

56. Quoted in Stehle, *Eastern Politics of the Vatican*, p. 199.

57. Ibid. See discussion in chapter 1.

58. Cited in Stehle, *Eastern Politics of the Vatican*, p. 220.

59. Walter Kolarz claimed that Nikita Khrushchev attended Sheptyt'sky's funeral, but this seems not to have been the case. Kolarz, *Religion in the Soviet Union*, p. 231. Bociurkiw, *The Ukrainian Greek Catholic Church and the Soviet State*, pp. 82–83.

60. Bociurkiw, *The Ukrainian Greek Catholic Church and the Soviet State*, p. 87.

61. *OGB*, vol. 1, book 2, p. 181n.

62. The Russian Orthodox Church still views Kostel'nik and his part in the destruction of Uniatism positively. Patriarch Aleksii II issued a message on the fiftieth anniversary of Kostel'nik's "martyrdom," saying that, although "church state relations" at war's end "were run over in our country by the authoritarian atheist regime," this had merely "distorted to a certain degree the essentially organic process" of the Uniate Church's absorption into Russian Orthodoxy. Department for External Church Relations of the Moscow Patriarchate, "Message from His Holiness Patriarch Alexy II of Moscow and All Russia," September 20, 1998, Moscow Patriarchate web site ‹www.russian-orthodox-church.org.ru›.

63. Sudoplatov, *Special Tasks*, pp. 24–29 and 37–38.

64. Sudoplatov claims that his forces inflicted a suspiciously large number of casualties on Nazi and anti-Soviet forces during the war: "[We] annihilated 137,000 German officers and soldiers, killed 87 high-ranking German officials by individual terrorist operations, and liquidated 2,045 agents and police officers who were Soviet collaborators in the service of the Germans." Ibid., p. 129.

65. Ibid., p. 251. Unfortunately, Sudoplatov does not provide the date for this meeting, although it must have been in autumn 1944, before the death of Sheptyt'sky.

66. Bociurkiw, *The Ukrainian Catholic Church and the Soviet State*, pp. 97 and 104.

67. Ibid., pp. 100 and 102.

68. Litvin (Secretary TsK KP(b)U[krainy] po propagande i agitatsii) to Aleksandrov, April 15 (?), 1945, TsK Upravlenie propagandy i agitatsii, RTsKhIDNI, f.17 op.125 r.1408 e.kh.313.

69. All citations about public reactions are from ibid.

70. The other two were Dr. Mikhail Ivanovich Mel'nik, senior priest of the church in Nizhankovichii, vicar of the Peremyshl'skii eparkhii, of the Drogobychskii oblast', and president of the Peremyshlskii eparkhii; and Anton Andreevich Pel'vetskii, senior priest of the church in Kopychintskii, deacon of the Gusiatinskii dekanat, and representative of the Stanislavskii eparkhii.

71. Quoted in Bociurkiw, *The Ukrainian Greek Catholic Church and the Soviet State*, p. 132.

72. N. Khrushchev to Stalin, undated but late May 1945, RTsKhIDNI, f.17 op.125 r.1408 e.kh.313.

73. Unfortunately, as with so many Soviet records, this document was not in the files. High-level documents are all too often either missing or not retained in the Central Committee records.

74. "Initiating group" to the Soviet of People's Commissars, May 28, 1945, enclosed in Khrushchev to Stalin, ibid.

75. Gordun, "Russkaia Pravoslavnaia tserkov' v period s 1943 po 1970 god," Zhurnal Moskovskoi Patriarkhii, p. 48.

76. Conquest, *Harvest of Sorrow*, pp. 212–13.

77. The question of clergy collaboration with Soviet security organs remains a contentious issue in post-Soviet lands. The extent of such collaboration varied priest to priest, but it remained a fact of Soviet life until the end of the regime. Archbishop Khrizostom of Vilnius and Lithuania admitted in a 1993 interview that "We [clergymen] had to keep contact open with all those who had authority in one sphere or another. There was no other

way." Mikhail Pozdnyayev, "'I Cooperated with the KGB . . . but I Was Not an Informer': An Interview with Archbishop Khrizostom of Vilnius and Lithuania," *Religion, State and Society*, 21, nos. 3–4 (1993).

78. Sudoplatov, *Special Tasks*, p. 251.

79. Ware, *The Orthodox Church*, p. 165.

80. For a study of this phenomenon, see Fletcher, *The Russian Orthodox Church Underground*.

81. Gordun, "Russkaia Pravoslavnaia Tserkov' v period 1943 po 1970 god," p. 48.

82. Kerr to Foreign Office, May 17, 1944, PRO FO 371/43339.

83. Henry Cassidy radio broadcast, NBC, May 16, 1944, monitored in PRO FO 371/43339.

84. Informbiuro communiqué, May 19,1944, PRO FO 371/43339.

85. Novikov, *Ateisticheskii slovar'*, p. 12. Although this source provides the basic biographical information about Aleksii, its obvious antireligious slant prevents it from mentioning Aleksii's receipt of the Medal for the Defense of Leningrad.

86. "Soviet Home Service, 22.30, 20.5.44 [radio intercept]," PRO FO 371/43339.

87. "Soviet Home Service, 6.00 21.5.44. [radio intercept]," PRO FO 371/43339.

88. Pospielovsky, *The Russian Church under the Soviet Regime*, p. 208.

89. TASS report, November 21, 1944.

90. Despite the importance and unusual nature of this gathering, the event has attracted almost no attention from historians, and those who have noted it have often misunderstood it. One otherwise authoritative account wrongly claims that "The enthronement [of Aleksii] . . . was attended even by some foreign dignitaries, such as Cyril Garbett (1875–1955), the Archbishop of York, who undertook the hazardous journey to demonstrate his church's solidarity." Dear and Foot, *The Oxford Companion to World War II*, p. 943. In fact, Archbishop Garbett visited the USSR almost a year and a half earlier, in September 1943, days after the enthronement of Aleksii's predecessor, Patriarch Sergii. The authors do not explore the great political, ecclesiastical, and propaganda significance of the gathering of the patriarchs and their representatives.

91. Memorandum by B. Miller, February 16, 1945, PRO FO 371/47929. Theophilus, "leader of the rival faction, whose position has hitherto been ambiguous, also sent a delegation."

92. Field Marshal Viscount Gore (Palestine) to Secretary of State for the Colonies, 12 January, 1945, PRO FO 371/47929.

93. *Soviet Monitor*, undated, though almost certainly February 1945, ibid.

94. See discussion in chapter 4.

95. J. H. Watson (Moscow) to Eden, February 8, 1945, PRO FO 371/47929.

96. On famine in the USSR at war's end, based on newly opened Soviet materials, see Zima, *Golod v SSSR*, especially pt. 1, pp. 4–37.

97. L. D. Wilgress to Secretary of State for External Affairs of Canada, copy given to British Foreign Office, February 8, 1945, PRO FO 371/47929.

98. J. H. Watson (Moscow) to Eden, February 8, 1945, PRO FO 371/47929.

99. One concern was the disposition of tsarist-era church property in Jerusalem. L. D. Wilgress to Secretary of State for External Affairs of Canada, PRO FO 371/47929.

100. "Russian Orthodox Church Appeal," *Soviet War News*, no. 1081 (February 9, 1945).

101. Wilgress to Secretary of State for External Affairs of Canada, February 8, 1943, PRO FO 371/47929.

102. Undated memorandum quoted in Bociurkiw, *The Ukrainian Greek Catholic Church and the Soviet State*, p. 99.

103. Pospielovsky, *The Russian Church under the Soviet Regime*, 1:212–13.

104. Interestingly, Pospielovsky later writes that *samizdat* publications of the late Soviet period criticized the centralized system created by the 1945 *sobor'* on the grounds that it enhanced state control of the church. A more decentralized structure might, they argued, have responded more creatively to local challenges and threats. Ibid., 214.

105. Karpov to N. S. Khrushchev, July 24, 1953, in Koenker, *Revelations from the Russian Archives*, p. 469.

106. Ibid.

107. N. Golubev to V. S. Abakumov, July 16, 1946, in *TSIM*, pp. 585–87. The concern with Jewish and Zionist groups is especially puzzling, given that the number of Jews still living in Moldavia following the Holocaust must have been small indeed—and therefore only a political threat under the very broadest of definitions.

108. Ibid.

109. Zima, *Golod v SSSr*, p. 17.

110. Ibid., p. 167.

111. Letter of L. F. Kucheriavyi, intercepted by the MGB MSSR, in *TSIM*, pp. 593–96.

112. Kozachenko (deputy minister of state security MSSR), "Iz spravki MGB MSSR o vrazhdebnoi deiatel'nosti tserkovno-sektantskikh elementov na teritorii moldavskoi SSR," in ibid.

113. Pol'ianskii memorandum, "Council for the Affairs of Religious Cults," Moscow, November 19, 1952, in Corley, *Religion in the Soviet Union*, p. 182.

Chapter 6

1. Oliver Harvey to Eden, July 10, 1941; War Cabinet Conclusions 68 (41), July 10, 1941, PRO FO 371/29602. The moderator of the Church of Scotland, the Reverend Cockburn, was also eager to prevent the playing of the "Internationale," sending a telegram to the Ministry of Information's Hugh Martin: "[P]lease impress on government that playing Internationale would [*sic*] seriously weaken defence of Russian alliance stressing Communistic aspect." Cockburn to Martin, June 1941, PRO INF 1/790.

2. Duff Cooper to Eden, July 12, 1941, PRO FO 371/29602.

3. *London Evening Standard*. Ultimately, the British government would reverse itself and allow the playing of the Soviet national anthem, but this was only after Moscow had replaced the revolutionary "Internationale" with its more Russian-nationalist successor.

4. "Proekt rezoliutsii o KP SShA," May 5, 1941, in Institut Vseobshchei Istorii, *Komintern i vtoraia mirovaia voina*, pp. 528–34.

5. "Shifrogramma M. Toreza i A. Marti Parizhskomu rukovodstvu FKP ot 26 Aprelia 1941 g.," in ibid., pp. 526–27.

6. For a discussion of this issue, see "Religious Reaction to the British Cooperation with Russia," contained in Martin to Parker, July 5, 1941, PRO INF 1/790.

7. Cited in Bell, *John Bull and the Bear*, p. 93.

8. BBC broadcast text to Poland and Greece, January 1, 1940, PRO INF 1/783. For what it is worth, Stalin was not a member of the League of Militant Godless, though of course the

organization could scarcely have continued to function had he not approved its broad activities.

9. BBC broadcast text, January 10, 1940, ibid.

10. Quoted in Flint, "English Catholics and the Proposed Soviet Alliance, 1939," p. 480. I thank Professor Bruce Steiner for bringing this article to my attention.

11. See the discussion of this issue in chapter 2.

12. For a history of domestic British wartime propaganda, which also supplies organizational details of the Ministry of Information, see McLaine, *Ministry of Morale*. See especially, the organizational chart on p. 5.

13. I. Kirkpatrick (BBC) to F. Maclean (Foreign Office), February 13, 1941, PRO FO 371/29463.

14. F. W. Ogilvie to Duff Cooper, June 28, 1941; Cooper to Ogilvie, June 30, 1941; Foreign Office to Cripps (Moscow), June 30, 1941, PRO INF 1/913.

15. Smollett to H. Grisewood (BBC), February 14, 1944, PRO FO 371/43326. "Overseas Planning Committee Plan of Propaganda to U.S.S.R. Draft Supplement to Appreciation," February 3, 1944, PRO FO 371/43326.

16. Ministry of Information, memorandum, October 10.

17. D.D.G. to the Minister, October 3, 1941, PRO INF 1/147.

18. R. H. Parker to D.D.G, August 21, 1941, PRO INF 1/147.

19. Smollett's role is explored in greater depth in chapter 7.

20. "Religious Reaction to the British Cooperation with Russia," in Martin to Clark and Parker, July 5, 1941, PRO INF 1/790.

21. Churchill, *The Second World War*, 2:371.

22. "Religious Reaction to the British Cooperation with Russia," contained in Martin to Clark and Parker, July 5, 1941, PRO INF 1/790.

23. Undated telegram from Ministry of Information to Cockburn, undated, PRO INF 1/790.

24. "Church of Scotland Moderator on British-Russian Alliance," July 17, 1941, reprinted in the *Spiritual Issues of the War*, no. 90 (July 24, 1941), PRO INF 1/790.

25. R. R. Williams to Major Hamilton, June 28, 1941, PRO INF 1/790.

26. Dr. William Paton, "Can the Nazis Defend Christianity?" Text suggested for French-language broadcast to Europe, PRO INF 1/790.

27. D. Randall (Foreign Office) to Richard Hope (MOI), June 24, 1941, PRO INF 1/790.

28. For the attempts at persuasion, see Moloney, *Westminster, Whitehall, and the Vatican*, pp. 223–26.

29. Cardinal Hinsley response to unnamed Catholic member of Parliament, June 28, 1941, PRO INF 1/790.

30. Chadwick, *Britain and the Vatican during the Second World War*, p. 193.

31. From Hope (Catholic Division) to Leigh Ashton (Foreign Division), June 30, 1941, PRO INF 1/790.

32. Gates memorandum, July 3, 1941, PRO INF 1/790.

33. Ryan (BBC) to Director General of Ministry of Information, September 4, 1941, PRO INF 1/676.

34. Ibid.

35. Ibid.

36. Unsigned Ministry of Information memorandum, July 16, 1941, PRO INF 1/790.

37. R. R. Williams (Protestant Section) to Hill July 24, 1941, PRO INF 1/790.

38. Ministry of Information draft telegram to Moscow, July 26, 1941, PRO INF 1/790.

39. Soviet Statement on religion in Russia, undated, but received July 28, 1941, PRO INF 1/790.

40. See chapter 2.

41. "Iz telegrammy posla SSSR v SShA v Narodnyi kommissariat inostrannykh del SSSR," June 22, 1941, Ministerstvo inostrannykh del SSSR, *Sovetskie-amerikanskie otnosheniia*, 1:42–44.

42. A poll of American opinion in 1942 ranked Russians twelfth among nations most admired, behind the English, Canadians, South Americans (as one category), and, most surprisingly, the Germans (who ranked seventh). Levering, *American Opinion*.

43. Gallup figures in British Ministry of Information, July 13, 1941, memorandum, PRO INF 1/790.

44. Welles to Steinhardt, June 23, 1941, *FRUS*, 1941, 1:767–68.

45. Cited in Hamby, *Man of the People*, p. 270.

46. "The Ambassador in Italy (Phillips) to the Secretary of State," July 24, 1941, *FRUS*, 1941, 1:999.

47. "The Acting Secretary of State to the Ambassador in Italy (Phillips)," ibid., p. 999.

48. Quoted in Flint, "English Catholics and the Proposed Soviet Alliance, 1939," p. 483.

49. Unsigned editorial, *Commonweal*, July 18, 1941.

50. Helen Iswolski, "Russia at War: Russian Needs and the Russian Future," *Commonweal*, July 25, 1941.

51. Both British and American military experts assumed that the USSR would be defeated within weeks, or at most months. These estimates are summarized in Beaumont, *Comrades at Arms*, pp. 26–27.

52. For a recent discussion of this question, see Warren F. Kimball, *The Juggler*, pp. 22–28. As Kimball notes, Soviet-era historians widely resented these estimates, but because they denied the now well-established scope of the military purges, their objections carry very little weight. Rzheshevsky, *World War II*, pp. 108–18.

53. Kimball, *The Juggler*, p. 22.

54. Harriman and Abel, *Special Envoy to Churchill and Stalin*, p. 103.

55. Robert Grant to Roosevelt, July 1, 1941, OF 220a, Russia 1941, Franklin Roosevelt Papers, Franklin D. Roosevelt Library, Hyde Park, New York.

56. Roosevelt to Grant, July 1, 1941, ibid.

57. "Memorandum by the Assistant Chief of the Division of European Affairs (Henderson) to the Assistant Secretary of State (Berle)," *FRUS*, 1941, 1:1003–4.

58. "Letter from President Roosevelt to His Holiness," September 3, 1941, in Myron Taylor, *Wartime Correspondence between President Roosevelt and Pope Pius XII*, pp. 61–62.

59. Ibid., "Reply of His Holiness to President Roosevelt," September 20, 1941. In his accompanying message, Myron Taylor told Roosevelt that in their meeting the pope had outlined his views and that he, Taylor, would report these to the president when he returned to Washington. No record of the Taylor-Roosevelt meeting seems to have been preserved, either in State Department records or in the Roosevelt Papers at Hyde Park, New York. The president was not, of course, a good record keeper, and he was prone at times to conduct diplomacy through unofficial channels, without keeping the State Department informed.

60. James MacGregor Burns claims that "The Vatican did respond to Roosevelt a bit by re-stating doctrine in such a way as to enable Catholics to make a distinction between aiding Russians and aiding Communism. Roosevelt also tried to induce Moscow to relax its anti-religious posture, but with little effect." *Roosevelt*, p. 152. Unfortunately, Burns does not cite any evidence to prove that the pope changed his position at all. As for the claim that the president tried to get Moscow to change its "posture" this seems dubious. Stalin did indeed change the Soviet "posture," when it came to propaganda, but there is no evidence whatso-ever that Roosevelt ever seriously tried to persuade Moscow to change its actual antireligious practices, as opposed to its publicity. In his study of Vatican-Soviet relations, Dennis J. Dunn argues that Rome did drop its earlier regular denunciations of Communism following Bar-barossa, and it no longer called as frequently for an immediate peace. If Dunn is correct, these were highly guarded signals indeed. Dunn, *The Catholic Church and the Soviet Gov-ernment*, p. 89.

61. A. L. Perkovskii, "Istochniki po natsional'nomu sostavu naseleniia Ukrainy v 1939–1944 gg.," in Rossiiskaia akademiia nauk, *Liudskie poteri SSSR v period vtoroi mirovoi voiny*, p. 50.

62. Stehle, *Eastern Politics of the Vatican*, p. 201.

63. See discussion in chapter 1.

64. Stehle, *Eastern Politics of the Vatican*, p. 199.

65. "Memorandum of Conversation, by the Secretary of State," *FRUS*, 1941, 1:832–34.

66. "Telegramma posla SSSR v SShA Predsedateliu Soveta Narodnykh Kommissarov SSSR," Ministerstvo inostrannylah del SSSR, *Sovetsko-Amerikanskie otnoshenie* 1:107–9.

67. President's remarks to the press, cited in "The Secretary of State to the Ambassador in the Soviet Union (Steinhardt)," *FRUS*, 1941, 1:1000–1001.

68. Sherwood, *Roosevelt and Hopkins*, p. 384.

69. Gaddis, *The United States and the Origins of the Cold War*, p. 41.

70. See discussion of this phenomenon, and the official Soviet reaction to it, in chapter 4.

71. Dies to Roosevelt, October 10, 1941, OF 220a Russia 1941, Roosevelt Papers.

72. Burns, *Roosevelt*, p. 152.

73. Mathew Spinka to Roosevelt, October 9, 1941, OF 220a Russia 1941, Roosevelt Papers.

74. Ruth O'Keefe, "New Letter to Catholics Interested in Social Progress," October 30, 1941, OF 76b Catholic, 1940–41, Roosevelt Papers.

75. Ibid.

76. Harriman and Abel, *Special Envoy*, p. 103.

77. *Times* (London), "Religious Freedom in the U.S.S.R.," PRO INF 1/769.

78. Steinhardt to Secretary of State, October 4, 1941, *FRUS*, 1941, 1:1002–3.

79. Ibid.

80. Harriman and Abel, *Special Envoy*, p. 103.

81. Ibid., p. 104.

82. The British government had been especially concerned about the impact of Soviet propaganda in the empire, most particularly in India. On this question, see White, *Britain and the Bolshevik Revolution*, pp. 89–109.

83. Cited in Baer, *A Question of Trust*, p. 247.

84. For the best evidence of Comintern activities before the war, which details numerous violations of Litvinov's pledge to refrain from interference in American internal affairs, see Klehr, Haynes, and Firsov, *The Secret World of American Communism*.

85. V. Kemenov to G. Malenkov, December 26, 1940, RTsKhIDNI, f.5 op.6 r.1357 e.kh.76. Subsequent citations are from this document.

86. Ibid.

87. Lozovskii to Shcherbakov, "Tri goda raboty SOVINFORMBIURO (24 June 1941 g.–24 June 1944)," "Sekretno," RTsKhIDNI, f.17 op.125 r.1393 e.kh.244.

88. Conquest, *The Great Terror*, p. 215.

89. Gromyko, *Diplomatecheskii slovar'*, 2:152.

90. "The German Ambassador in the Soviet Union to the German Foreign Office," November 25, 1940, in Sontag and Beddie, *Nazi-Soviet Relations*, pp. 258–59.

91. To a very great extent, this inability to reach the public in the USSR can be explained by remoteness and by the ability of the dictatorial regime to wall out foreign influences. The Americans, and to a greater extent the British, did make some efforts to influence Soviet opinion. The U.S. Embassy printed a bulletin that was widely circulated, and the British published a journal, *Britanskii soiuznik* (British ally) that became quite influential among the educated public. At the same time, however, fear of offending the Soviet government prevented the Western Allies from pressing too hard on this front. For instance, the British considered, before rejecting as too provocative, the idea of direct shortwave radio broadcasts in Russian.

92. Tocqueville, *The Ancien Regime and the French Revolution*, pp. 41 and 42.

93. For the appeal of the Soviet state for Western intellectuals, see Caute, *The Fellow Travelers*, and Hollander, *Political Pilgrims*.

94. Cited in Caute, *The Fellow Travelers*, p. 188.

95. N. Pal'gunov to Upravlenie propagandy i agitatsii TsK VKP(b) A. A. Puzin, May 10, 1941, RTsKhIDNI, f.5 op.6 r.1354.

96. Ibid.

97. Maiskii, *Before the Storm*.

98. Gromyko et al., *Diplomatechiskii slovar'*, 2:172.

99. The courtship had begun in the 1930s, but it was not always clear who was courting whom. In June 1935, for instance, Maiskii wrote to Beaverbrook, mentioning a discussion the two had had the previous day about Russian literature and sending him of a copy of the ambassador's address on the subject at a meeting of the Society for Cultural Relations with Russia. Beaverbrook's secretary summarized the talk for the busy press lord by saying "There is nothing very profound or original about the article." Nonetheless, Beaverbrook wrote to Maiskii: "Will you allow me to congratulate you on it. You have, if I may say so, a clear and interesting viewpoint and you express it with vigor." Maiskii to Beaverbrook, June 21, 1935, and Beaverbrook to Maiskii, June 25, 1935, BBK. C/238, Lord Beaverbrook Papers, House of Lords.

100. Quoted in Miner, "Soviet Ambassadors from Maiskii to Dobrynin," in Craig and Loewenheim, *The Diplomats*, pp. 614–15.

101. "Extract from a Conversation: Mr. Eden and Mr. Maisky," June 26, 1941, PRO INF 1/913.

102. See discussion earlier in this chapter.

103. Zinchenko to Elizabeth Hill (MOI) with enclosure "Religious Toleration," July 28, 1941, PRO INF 1/790.

104. Zinchenko to Hill, August 26, 1941, PRO INF 1/790.

105. "Religious Toleration."

106. G. Saksin (London embassy) to Lozovskii, November 17, 1944, RTsKhIDNI, f.17 op.125 r.1393 e.kh.244.

107. "Religious Communities in the Soviet Union," unsigned, *Soviet War News*, August 22, 1941. For the number of clergy at the *sobor'*, see discussion in chapter 4.

108. Brokgauz and Efron, *Rossiia'*, p.168. I have been unable to find reliable figures for the number of working churches in the USSR in 1941. Still, even at the end of the war against Hitler, during which Soviet officials themselves admitted that "a massive opening of churches" had taken place, there were only 10,243 open Orthodox churches in the USSR; only 2,297 were in the RSFSR. In short, the *Soviet War News* figures seem inflated. Karpov to Aleksandrov, August 30, 1945, RTsKhIDNI, f.17 op.125 r.1408 e.kh.131.

109. Davis, *A Long Walk to Church*, p. 16.

110. Perkovskii, "Istochniki po natsional'nomu sostavu naseleniia Ukrainy 1939–1944 gg.," p. 50.

111. PRO FO 371/36961.

112. Hill to Zinchenko, August 29, 1941, PRO INF 1/790.

113. Williams to Dunning, January 14, 1942, PRO INF 1/790.

114. M. Burskii to Shcherbakov, September 4, 1941, RTsKhIDNI, f.5 op.6 r.1352.

115. Burskii to Shcherbakov, undated but probably September 22, 1941, RTsKhIDNI, f.5 op.6 r.1352.

116. Perhaps Burskii offended his immediate superior, Lozovskii, by going directly to Shcherbakov.

117. All following citations from the meeting are drawn from "Stenogramma soveshchaniia u tov. Lozovskogo," October 2, 1941, RTsKhIDNI, f.5 op.6 r.1352.

118. From the receiving end, Henry Cassidy of Associated Press confirms that Lozovskii's humor was effective at first, but over time it proved no substitute for hard information. He wrote that Lozovskii's "quips were to become famous in the short time his conferences lasted," but "Eventually his flippancy became a nuisance. It grew more and more difficult to draw a serious answer from him." Even the Soviets eventually learned that to hold news briefings only to provide no serious news was not worthwhile, and so Lozovskii suspended his daily briefings. Cassidy, *Moscow Dateline*, p. 60.

119. Umanskii was not specific, though it would seem that he was referring to Spencer Williams and Albert Rhys-Williams.

120. Koppes and Black, *Hollywood Goes to War*, p. 190.

121. Interestingly, German intelligence also believed that Roosevelt exercised great financial influence over the Vatican. Less than a month after the outbreak of Barbarossa, German agents citing sources in the Vatican noted that "the largest contributors of money [to the Holy See]—the Netherlands, Belgium, France, Austria, Spain—have dropped out. Consequently, since the beginning of the War the Vatican has regularly received a considerable sum from the U.S.A. which is described as money collected by American Catholics but which, in reality, is drawn from secret funds held by Roosevelt." Memorandum of Amt Ausland/Abw. III, July 12, 1941, in Friedlander, *Pius XII and the Third Reich*, pp. 74–75. Friedlander cautions that "this report must be read with the greatest circumspection." True enough, but it is nonetheless interesting that both the Nazis and the Soviets believed that Roosevelt wielded some form of strong financial power over the Vatican through secret means, and that the

Soviets seem to have gained this idea from Roosevelt himself. Steven Merritt Miner, "Why the Vatican Condoned U.S. Aid to Stalin's Army," *Los Angeles Times*, November 9, 1997.

Chapter 7

1. "Stenogramma soveshchaniia u tov. Lozovskogo," October 2, 1941, RTsKhIDNI, f.15 op.6 r.1352.

2. For an interesting, if breezy, portrait of the capital at this time, see Brinkley, *Washington Goes to War*. Brinkley repeatedly, and entertainingly, makes the point that Washington retained the characteristics of a small town during much of the war.

3. "Organizatsii angliiskoi vneshnei propagandy," "Sekretno," undated but certainly 1945, RTsKhIDNI, f.17 op.125 r.1409.

4. Smollett to Sinclair, June 27, 1942, PRO INF 1/84.

5. Before gaining a post in the Ministry of Information, Smollett had first tried unsucessfully to enter the British secret services. Andrew and Gordievsky, *KGB*, pp. 334–35.

6. R. H. Parker to D.D.G., 21 August, 1941, PRO INF 1/147.

7. Smollett to Christopher Warner (Foreign Office), November 5, 1941, PRO FO 371/29470. Even before this time, Smollett had been functioning in the capacity of liaison; Bracken's authorization was simply the codification of practice. Interestingly, I can find no reference to Zinchenko in Soviet sources about the diplomatic corps, such as *Diplomatecheskii slovar'*. Either he would later be disgraced, and his name consequently erased from the official record, or else—an equally likely possibility—he was working for one of the Soviet intelligence services rather than for the Foreign Ministry. In the latter case, Zinchenko may not even have been his actual name.

8. Grubb to Heald, decisions of a Ministry of Information meeting of November 11, 1941, PRO INF 1/147.

9. In the only full-scale history of British propaganda and the Anglo-Soviet alliance, Phillip Bell almost completely ignores the critical role of Smollett, and he does not mention that he was a Soviet mole; indeed, Bell has only three references to Smollett in an otherwise comprehensive and informative study of the subject—in itself odd given the fact that Smollett was so central to propaganda decisions on the USSR. Perhaps this can be explained by the fact that, although Anthony Blunt had exposed Smollett's secret role and Chapman Pincher had had revealed this in print by 1981, Bell may have judged that insufficient corroboration had yet emerged when he published his book. Bell, *John Bull and the Bear*. Another study of Britain's wartime Ministry of Information, which devotes a chapter to the Soviet question, is McLaine, *Ministry of Morale*, pp. 186–216. McLaine's study appeared a year before Blunt revealed Smollett's role. Although both histories are excellent and insightful studies of the formation of British wartime propaganda, neither uses Russian sources, and, because they both misunderstood Smollett's key activities, they tend to take at face value the Ministry of Information's claim that it was "stealing the thunder of the Left," without realizing the extent to which Smollett was working behind the scenes to undermine this very policy.

10. Smollett was also eager to assert that the suggestion to exclude "white Russians," came from the Soviet embassy, not from "me personally." Smollett to Parker, November 22, 1941, PRO INF 1/676. Both McLaine and Bell see the ministry's role in "Anglo-Soviet Weeks" as

being directed at *restricting* pro-Communist propaganda and seizing control of such events from the British Communist Party (BCP). They both judge this policy to have been largely successful, since the CP, after initiating such events, generally backed off and allowed the ministry to run them. McLaine even claims that British Communists "responded with docility to the intrigues of the Ministry." This view takes the British documentary record at face value and certainly misunderstands Smollett's role. It also largely misses the point: even at its peak, the BCP was minuscule and could not hope to manage a large number of rallies. Far better to set such rallies in motion, then leave the heavy lifting to the Ministry of Information, which, thanks in large measure to Smollett, was selling the USSR far more effectively than the marginalized BCP ever could. McLaine, *Ministry of Morale*, p. 205. Bell is more circumspect, admitting that "It may well be that the traffic in arranging and exploiting Soviet Weeks was not as one-way as the files of the Ministry of Information would indicate." Indeed it was not. Bell, *John Bull and the Bear*, p. 46.

11. "Conversation with M. Zinchenco 20. 10. 41," H. P. Smollett, October 20, 1941, PRO INF 1/676. This is an instance where Philip Bell's unawareness of Smollett's double role has led him into misjudgment. Bell writes, correctly, that ministry officials sought to persuade Soviet Embassy figures to appear at British rallies in uniform, and that the Soviets refused for fear of being seen as interfering in British domestic policies. In fact, however, Maiskii himself did appear at such rallies, and the Soviets' refusal to field other, lower-ranking official speakers can be explained by a number of factors. First, Foreign Commissar Molotov was reluctant to allow speakers to address rallies for fear either that they might spontaneously follow an "incorrect" line, or that they might be drawn into public disputes, perhaps occasioned by "provocateurs." Second, there was no reason to field such speakers, or offer such tempting targets for anti-Soviet intrigues, when Smollett could be relied upon to vet speakers behind the scenes. Bell, *John Bull and the Bear*, p. 46.

12. G. M. Vevers (editor of the *Anglo-Soviet Journal*), to G. Meara, October 1941, PRO INF 1/676. The ministry even asked that the government-regulated paper quota be increased for the journal.

13. Draft letter of the minister of information to Foreign Minister Anthony Eden, October 22, 1941, PRO INF 1/676. McLaine claims that the SCR "was recognised but received no cooperation." *Ministry of Morale*, p. 204. Again, this relies overly on the British documentary record, where this was indeed policy; but Smollett made certain that practice was entirely different.

14. V. Kemenov to Aleksandrov, August 20, 1942, RTsKhIDNI, f.17 op.125 r.1364. Interestingly, the argument of this letter was that VOKS was being hampered in its ability to control such organizations because it was not being given timely copies of their journals; it lacked sufficient funds to pay for imports of key publications, and it was having trouble gaining sufficiently swift security clearance.

15. Unsigned memorandum, October 1941, PRO INF 1/676. The British Council was distinctly cool to the idea of cooperating with the SCR. Sir Malcom Robertson wrote to Alexander Cadogan, listing the well-known pro-Soviet figures associated with the SCR, and said "I should prefer that the Council should have nothing to do with it." Robertson to Cadogan, November 26, 1941, PRO FO 371/29603.

16. Policy Committee notes, September 4, 1941, PRO INF 1/676.

17. BBC (name illegible) to Duff Cooper, July 11, 1941, PRO INF 1/913.

18. V. I. Pasat, "Poteri Respubliki Moldova v gody vtoroi mirovoi voiny," in Institut rosi-iskoi istorii RAN, *Liudskie poteri SSSR v period vtoroi mirovoi voiny*, p. 119. The figure of deportees does not include the nearly 100,000 ethnic Germans "repatriated" to the Reich while Moscow and Berlin were still partners. Pasat therefore places the total number of "human losses" in Moldavia during the first period of Soviet occupation at 150,000.

19. "Talk on 'Current Affairs' for Schools Department of B.B.C. prepared by A. Rothstein at request of that Department for delivery on 26.6.1941, and rejected by them as 'unobjective,'" PRO INF 1/913.

20. Later in the war, the British allowed Rothstein to compose and deliver his own TASS broadcasts to the Soviet audience in Moscow. PRO FO 371/36919. It must be remembered that the idea of the British themselves broadcasting in Russian had been rejected as being likely to cause offense in the Kremlin.

21. "Broadcasts to Schools: Travel Talks," November 17, 1941; Sargent to C. J. Radcliffe, November 24, 1941, PRO FO 371/29603.

22. The reading list included Hewlett Johnson's apologetic *Socialist Sixth of the World* as well as *Selected Works of Lenin* and Stalin's own *Foundations of Leninism*—certainly a candidate for one of the most falsified histories of this or any century. "Stalin's Text-Books for British Schoolchildren," *Daily Express*, August 25, 1942.

23. The first issue of *Britanskii soiuznik* was issued in August 1942, PRO FO 371/32891. On Smollett's suggestions for British propaganda in the USSR, see Smollett to Warner, August 7, 1943, PRO FO 371/36920.

24. Brendan Bracken to the Prime Minister, September 8, 1941, PRO INF 1/913.

25. Previous histories of the Ministry of Information have chosen to emphasize the restraining role, underplaying, in my view, the extent to which British propagandists in fact promoted enthusiasm for the USSR. McLaine *Ministry of Morale*, and Bell, *John Bull and the Bear*.

26. "Agreed Policy in Public," unsigned, October 1941, PRO INF 1/676.

27. Religion in the Soviet Union, guidelines prepared by the Religious Division, PRO INF 1/790.

28. "Some Comments on the Proposed Exchange of Visits between the Russian Church and the Church of England," H. M. Waddams, October 22, 1942, PRO INF 1/790.

29. "Boldness Pays," *Catholic Herald*, October 3, 1941. Similar articles appeared in the *Catholic Times* and the *Universe*; the Foreign office estimated the total circulation of these three papers to be 220,000. Memorandum from Armine Dew, October 22, 1941, PRO FO 371/29469.

30. "An Archbishop's Unhappy Lead," *Catholic Herald*, October 10, 1941.

31. Cripps to FO, October 11, 1941, PRO FO 371/29470. The offending articles about Soviet bureaucracy had appeared in the *Hertfordshire Mercury* and the *Edinburgh Evening News*.

32. Maiskii memorandum handed to the Foreign Office, October 18, 1941, PRO FO 371/29469.

33. Eden notes, October 30, 1941, PRO FO 371/29469.

34. Cripps to FO, October 11, 1941, PRO FO 371/29470.

35. Armine Dew memorandum, October 22, 1941, PRO FO 371/29469.

36. Christopher Warner memorandum, October 23, 1941, PRO FO 371/29469. Radcliffe believed that quiet pressure on religious editors was the wisest course. Smollett to Dew, October 25, 1941, PRO FO 371/29469. Radcliffe thought that there was no point speaking with the editors of the *Herald*, who were "beyond appeal anyway" in his judgment.

37. Smollett to Armine Dew, October 25, 1941, PRO FO 371/29469.

38. Coote to Smollett, November 25, and Smollett to Coote, November 26, 1941, PRO FO 371/29470.

39. "Russian Economic System: 'No Christian Need Quarrel with It,'" *Yorkshire Post*, November 14, 1941.

40. R. R. Williams to Smollett, November 17, 1941, PRO INF 1/790.

41. William Paton (World Council of Churches) to Smollett, November 25, 1941, PRO INF 1/790.

42. Wickham Legg and Williams, *Dictionary of National Biography*, p. 870.

43. Ibid.

44. Temple, *The Hope of a New World*, citations from pp. 9, 17, 22, 55, and 52.

45. Webb and Webb, *Soviet Communism*; Dobb, *Soviet Planning and Labour in Peace and War*; Dobb, *Russia To-day and To-morrow*; Johnson, *The Socialist Sixth of the World*.

46. For a brilliant, concise examination of the shortcomings of the great Stalinist showpiece projects, see Loren Graham, *The Ghost of the Executed Engineer*.

47. William Cantuar to Hugh Martin, April 20, 1943, PRO INF 1/792.

48. See discussion in chapter 3.

49. Of all the Foreign Office commentators on this suggestion, only one, Sir Orme Sargent, thought the idea had any real merit. "Exchange of Visits between Leaders of the Russian Church and Church of England," minutes by Wilson, Dew, Warner, Sargent, and Cadogan, September 1942, PRO FO 371/32949.

50. Eden to Halifax, October 12, 1942, PRO FO 371/32950.

51. "Some Comments on the Proposed Exchange of Visits between the Russian Church and the Church of England," the Reverend H. M. Waddams, PRO INF 1/790.

52. Memorandum of a November 13 meeting at the Foreign Office, unsigned, November 14, 1942, PRO FO 371/32950, and INF 1/792.

53. Martin to Warner, December 2, 1942, PRO INF 1/792, and FO 371/32950.

54. Ibid.

55. Hugh Martin to Hogben, February 23, 1943, PRO INF 1/790.

56. Martin had once written: "It would be better, in my judgement, not to suggest that all criticisms of the bolshevik attitude to religion are lies or that there is complete religious freedom in Russia. It is true that the Soviet Government provides for freedom of worship in the sense that you are not interfered with if you go to the few churches which have been allowed to remain open and if you can find one of the surviving priests, but there are all sorts of restrictions upon religious freedom as understood in other countries." Unfortunately, this sort of restrained argument rarely carried the day in ministry debates. Martin to Hogben, February 23, 1943, PRO INF 1/790.

57. William Cantuar to Martin, December 8, 1942, PRO FO 371/32950.

58. Hugh Martin to C. Warner, December 18, 1942, PRO INF 1/792. In fact, in this account Martin once again seemed to believe that he had brought Temple round to his point of view, but, as the archbishop's later correspondence shows, this was not the case. Perhaps Temple, who confessed himself to be incapable of disagreeing with any point of view, was the sort of person who always conveys to his partner in conversation that he agrees with what is being said.

59. William Cantuar to Hugh Martin, December 24, 1942, PRO FO 371/36961.

60. William Cantuar to Martin, January 21, 1943, PRO INF 1/792.

61. Ibid.; William Cantuar to Martin, 7 May 1943; record of a telephone conversation between Waddams and Warner (Foreign Office), June 23, 1943, PRO INF 1/792.

62. "[W]e have really carefully avoided mentioning House's connection with the B.B.C., and our Press Department has very definite instructions not to let the Press publicise this connection." Rev. J. W. Welsh to Williams, September 16, 1943, PRO INF 1/792.

63. William Cantuar to Hugh Martin, May 27, 1943, PRO INF 1/792.

64. Martin to Temple, May 28, 1942, PRO INF 1/792.

65. Hugh Martin to Archbishop of York, July 16, 1943; Hugh Martin to Christopher Warner (Foreign Office), July 19, 1943; Archbishop of York to Hugh Martin, July 17, 1943; Warner to Martin, July 17, 1943; Martin to Archbishop of York, July 19, 1943; Archbishop of York to Martin, July 20, 1943; Waddams memorandum of talk with archbishop of York, July 21, 1943; archbishop of York to Martin, July 22, 1943, PRO INF 1/792.

66. Draft of a joint statement to be issued jointly by the Russian Orthodox and Anglican churches, undated, PRO INF 1/792.

67. Martin to Temple, August 3, 1943, PRO INF 1/792.

68. Sir Archibald Clark Kerr to Anthony Eden, September 13, 1943, PRO FO 371/36963.

69. Merkulov to Central Committee and Shcherbakov, July 3, 1943; and Karpov's notes of his meeting with Stalin, September 4, 1943, in Corley, *Religion in the Soviet Union*, pp. 138 and 142.

70. Interestingly enough, since the collapse of Communism and the relative freeing of the historical profession in their country, Russian historians have noticed this coincidence whereas most of their Western counterparts have not. Volkogonov, *Triumf i tragediia*, book II, part 1, pp. 382–83; also see Gordun, "Russkaia Pravoslavnaia Tserkov' v period s 1943 po 1970 god," pp, 39–40.

71. G. P. Thomson, "Private and Confidential Memo to Editors," October 9, 1943, PRO INF 1/792.

72. Herbert M. Waddams, MOI, "An Account of the Visit to Moscow by the Delegation of the Church of England," September 24, 1943, PRO FO 371/36963; "Programme of Visit of the Church of England Delegation to Russia," undated, PRO FO 371/36963.

73. As Metropolitan Nikolai put it delicately, "In 1920 the New Jerusalem Monastery was converted into a museum." Nikolai, *The Russian Church and the War against Fascism*, p. 31.

74. Herbert M. Waddams, "An Account of the Visit to Moscow by a Delegation of the Church of England," September 24, 1943, PRO FO 371/36963.

75. Waddams, "Notes of a Conversation with the Archbishop of York on 26.6.43 with regard to the Proposed Visit of an Anglican Delegation to the Russian Orthodox Church," PRO INF 1/792.

76. For the Soviet method of managing foreign tourists, see Paul Hollander, *Political Pilgrims*.

77. "Notes of a Press Conference held at the Ministry of Information on Monday, October 11, 1943," PRO INF 1/792.

78. "Mission to Moscow, 1943, by the Archbishop of York," *Daily Express*, October 12, 1943.

79. Press Bureau of the Church of England, news release, November 26, 1943, PRO INF 1/792.

80. "The Russian Church," *Times* (London), September 17, 1943.

81. Quoted in Melish, *Religion Today in the USSR*, p. 17.

82. Ministry of Information Home Intelligence Weekly Report, September 23, 1943, PRO INF 1/792.

83. Modin, *My Five Cambridge Friends*, pp. 86–87.

84. BBC transcript, "English News Talk, Russian Church Commentary by H. W. Shirley Long," also broadcast in Bulgarian, Greek, Serbo-Croat, Magyar, Danish, Norwegian, and Swedish, September 5, 1943, PRO INF 1/791.

85. Ibid.

86. BBC broadcast to Yugoslavia, September 6, 1943, quoting an article in London's *Daily Telegraph*, PRO INF 1/791.

87. BBC broadcast in English and Greek, September 6, 1943, PRO INF 1/791.

88. Mindszenty, *Memoirs*, p. 22.

89. Milosz, *The Captive Mind*, p. 25.

90. Ibid.

91. Waddams to A. Elkin, September 13, 1943, PRO INF 1/791.

92. Handwritten comments by Smollett on a memorandum from Elkin September 15, 1943, PRO INF 1/791.

93. The Reverend R. R. Williams agreed that "no doubt" Waddams's complaints were correct but advised against "drastic action," writing strangely that "We must not be unreasonable as to what we expect of the B.B.C." "In spite of the technical criticisms I do not feel that the *general* impression created by the broadcasts is untrue or unfair." Smollett underlined the word "general," before minuting that he agreed with Williams. He then let the matter stand. Williams to Smollett, September 18, 1943, PRO INF 1/791.

94. Philip Bell, who has carefully studied the interrelation between the Ministry of Information and the BBC, shows that the Home Service was less enthusiastically pro-Soviet than was the World Service, though neither was critical of Moscow. He also writes that "the output of the BBC . . . was entirely under official control." Smollett's protestations to the contrary only serve to underline his double role. Bell, *John Bull and the Bear*, p. 47.

95. N. F. Newsome to Smollett, November 10, 1943, PRO INF 1/791.

96. Smollett to Elkin, November 11, 1943, PRO INF 1/791; also, Waddams to Hare, December 20, 1943, soliciting statements from the patriarchs of Constantinople, Antioch, Jerusalem, also suggesting that the Soviet embassy might provide suitable quotations.

97. Smollett to N. F. Newsome, November 11, 1943, PRO INF 1/791.

98. See discussion in chapter 5.

99. A. Elkin to Smollett, November 13, 1943, PRO INF 1/791.

100. Cited in ibid.

101. Waddams to Elkin, draft for BBC broadcast, November 28, 1943, PRO INF 1/791.

102. "The Russian Church," BBC script, April 9, 1944, PRO INF 1/791.

103. When Anthony Blunt was publicly revealed to have been a Soviet agent, he confirmed that Smollett had also been a mole. The first journalist to publish the accusation was Pincher, *Their Trade Is Treachery*, p. 114. Since that time, the Soviet KGB defector Oleg Gordievskii confirmed Smollett's role, based on his own work in KGB archives; Yuri Modin, who was one of Smollett's superiors during the time of his espionage, also testifies to Smollett's role. Although they identify Smollett as a Soviet spy, however, these writers only mention this in passing, not discussing his role in any detail. Modin, *My Cambridge Friends*, pp. 86–87.

104. Andrew and Gordievsky, *KGB*, pp. 334–39.

105. Interestingly, Gordievsky's fellow author, Christopher Andrew, disagrees. He writes: "Brilliantly ingenious though the 'active measures' orchestrated by Smollett and [Guy] Burgess were, they were less influential than the KGB believed." "The 'active measures' campaign orchestrated by Smollett at the Ministry of Information helped to blur the distinction between the heroism of the Russian people and the Stalinist regime, but by comparison with the victories and sacrifices of the Red Army its influence on British opinion was marginal." Andrew and Gordievsky, *KGB*, pp. 338 and 339. While admitting Andrew's point that Soviet victories were far more effective in evoking Western admiration of the USSR than anything Smollett did, the effective management of propaganda, as well as the fact that news of Soviet achievements was almost never counterbalanced by information about the genuine nature of the Stalinist regime, had an enormous impact on the nature of this admiration.

106. In fact, the entire idea for an Anglo-Soviet ecclesiastical exchange was originally urged by Smollett. In the autumn of 1941 he had suggested issuing an invitation to Metropolitan Sergii to visit Britain. Smollett to Radcliffe and Kenneth Grubb, October 7, 1941, PRO INF 1/147.

107. Ironically, according to Christopher Andrew, who bases his view on the KGB records purloined by Vasili Mitrokhin, Soviet intelligence distrusted Smollett, because he had been hired by Kim Philby, whose reliability it also doubted. Andrew and Mitrokhin, *The Sword and the Shield*, p. 120.

Chapter 8

1. Bourke-White, *Shooting the Russian War*, p. 5.

2. Bourke-White, *A Look at Russia*.

3. "Vnutrennii biuleten' VOKS no.11–12," unsigned, "sekretno," stamped May 1944, RTsKhIDNI, f.17 op.125 r.1394.

4. Bourke-White, *Shooting the Russian War*, photo caption, p. 253.

5. Ibid., pp. 136–57; all subsequent citations are from this chapter.

6. "Vnutrenii biuleten' VOKS no. 11–12," "sekretno," stamped May 13, 1944, RTsKhIDNI, f.17 op.125 r.1394.

7. Werth, *Moscow 1941*, p. 141. This book was little more than a compilation of his early wartime dispatches. In the broadcasts he composed, Werth often argued the Soviet case very forcefully, especially the question of the "second front," of which he became an ardent champion. Foreign Office officials regarded his broadcast texts on this subject to be nothing but "propaganda," and his radio reports to London were even debated angrily in the War Cabinet, where it was asked: "[W]as it reasonable that we should give facilities for the broadcasting in this country of statements belittling our military achievements?" War Cabinet Conclusions 118 (43), PRO FO 371/36921. The cabinet decided that any action against Werth would be counterproductive. Werth wrote the "Russian Commentary" that was broadcast over the BBC on Sunday evenings following the nine-o'clock news, one of the best time slots for heavy listening numbers. The texts were read by Joseph Macleod, "[a] highly respected news reader," Bell, *John Bull and the Bear*, p. 71.

8. Ibid., pp. 49–50 (emphasis in original).

9. Ibid., p. 128.

10. In the late eighteenth century, Catherine the Great had recruited ethnic Germans to farm in Russia, hoping that they would instill their more advanced agricultural methods among the Russian peasantry. The descendants of these people remained in Russia, and then the USSR, until Stalin deported them to Central Asia in the autumn of 1941.

11. Ibid., p.174.

12. Ibid., pp. 51 and 128.

13. Alexander Werth to Sir Stafford Cripps, July 16, 1941, with enclosure by Werth, "MEMORANDUM on possible Propaganda Points in dealing with Russia." Cripps forwarded the memorandum to the Foreign Office, which sent a copy to the Ministry of Information. In a cover letter Cripps commented: "I don't agree entirely with the views expressed but I do agree very largely with what he [Werth] says as to the presentation of the case in England," Cripps to Sargent, July 16, 1941, PRO INF 1/913.

14. In the cover note to Sir Stafford Cripps accompanying his memorandum on propaganda, Werth wrote that "Naturally, it would be better, from the point of view of our relations with the Moscow authorities, if our names were not disclosed to anyone except the most responsible people in London." Werth said that he had been assisted in composing his suggestions by Maurice Lovell; he also attributed some of his ideas to Cripps himself. Werth to Cripps, July 16, 1941, PRO INF 1/913.

15. The BBC did not have a regular broadcaster stationed in Moscow. Instead, it relied on several people, among them Winterton, Werth, and John Fisher.

16. Paul Winterton to Norman Cliff, September 14, 1944, PRO FO 371/43337.

17. Henry Cassidy had also learned of resistance to the Red Army during Barbarossa in 1941. "Men were sniping from the rooftops, women were stabbing in the streets, as the Red Army retreated." He could not, of course, report this while still in the USSR. Cassidy, *Moscow Dateline*, p. 56.

18. Winterton to Sir Walter Layton, November 5, 1944, PRO FO 371/43337.

19. Winterton to Cliff, September 14, 1944, ibid.

20. Winterton to to Layton, November 5, 1944, ibid.

21. Walter Graebner, "Shoe Leather for Bread," *Daily Mail*, January 12, 13, and 14.

22. Wilson memorandum, January 14, 1943, PRO FO 371/36923.

23. V. Fin to S. Lozovskii, December 30, 1943, RTsKhIDNI, f.17 op.125 r.1393 e.kh.244.

24. All citations are from ibid.

25. Lozovskii minutes of meeting with Magidoff, April 29, 1944, RTsKhIDNI, f.17 op.125 r.1394.

26. Obituary of Leo Gruliow, *Ohio Slavic and East European Newsletter* 26, no. 1 (September 1997): 1.

27. Leo Gruliow, "Voennaia pomosh' Rossii," January 18, 1944; Lozovskii to Shcherbakov, January 25, 1944, RTsKhIDNI, f.17 op.125 r.1393.

28. Litvinov to Lozovskii, January 31, 1944, RTsKhIDNI, f.17 op.125 r.1393.

29. V. Kemenov to Shcherbakov, February 22, 1944, RTsKhIDNI, f.17 op.125 r.1394.

30. Soviet propaganda was not immune from silly editorial mistakes when it came to dealing with USSR's allies. In April 1942 the editors of *Izvestiia*, through "criminal carelessness," published a photograph of a burning tank, captioned: "Western Front: The Inglorious End of a Fascist Tank." In fact, the picture was of a British Matilda. Lozovskii to Shcherbakov, April 31, 1942, and Pal'gunov to Lozovskii, May 31, 1942, RTsKhIDNI, f.17 op.125 r.1364.

31. Draft letter from V. Kemenov to Edward Carter, February 22, 1944, RTsKhIDNI, f.17 op.125 r.1394.

32. Aleksandrov to Molotov, relaying Rostovskii's proposal, March 1943, RTsKhIDNI, f.17 op.125 r.1385.

33. Molotov note, March 18, 1943, ibid.

34. Smollett memorandum of meeting with Maiskii, May 11, 1944, PRO FO 371/43327. This conversation occurred after Maiskii had been withdrawn from London as ambassador; the two met during Smollett's visit to Moscow.

35. Johnson's visit to Russia coincided with that of Clementine Churchill, the prime minister's wife. In a speech at a meeting honoring the two, Johnson declaimed that he had been happy when Churchill had brought Britain into the war "on the right side," as though Britain, not the USSR, were poised to ally with the Nazis in 1941. Frank Roberts to E. Bevin, August 11, 1945, PRO FO 371/47930.

36. "What Stalin Told Me," by the Dean of Canterbury, August 11, 1945, PRO FO 317/47930.

37. Ibid.

38. Clark Kerr to Foreign Office, June 26, 1944, PRO FO 371/43338.

39. Archbishop of York to Warner, June 11, 1945, PRO FO 371/47930.

40. Reverend H. M. Waddams to Foreign Office, October 10, 1944, PRO FO 371/43340.

41. Reverend I. H. White Thomson to Wilson (Foreign Office), October 12, 1944, FO 371/43340.

42. Williams to Campbell (Finance Division), May 5, 1945, PRO INF 1/793. Before his death, Archbishop Temple had already agreed, in late February 1944, that the Ministry of Information should subsidize the visit. The high degree of church cooperation with government propaganda was to be concealed from the public, however: "It was thought that it would be wiser not to have a lunch for the Delegation on Ministry of Information premises." "Note on a Meeting at the Foreign Office on 21st February, 1944," February 22, 1944, PRO INF 1/793. Although these arrangements were made when the visit was originally scheduled for 1944, they remained in force when it was rescheduled for 1945.

43. R. R. Williams to Smollett, March 3, 1944, PRO INF 1/793.

44. Memorandum by B. Miller, Foreign Office Research Department, June 1, 1945, PRO FO 371/47929.

45. Quoted in Graves, *A Record of the War*, p. 104.

46. A summary of this tour, based on the contemporary Soviet publications, can be found in Alexeev, *Foreign Policy of the Moscow Patriarchate*, pp. 24–25.

47. Waddams to Galsworthy (Northern Department of the Foreign Office), May 24, 1945, PRO FO 371/47930.

48. Roberts to Eden, April 21, 1945, PRO FO 371/47929.

49. See discussion in chapter 4.

50. Roberts to Eden, April 21, 1945, PRO FO 371/47929.

51. Smollett to Waddams, June 8, 1945, PRO INF 1/793.

52. "Visit of Russian Church Delegation: Programme," PRO INF 1/793.

53. "Addresses of Welcome to the Russian Orthodox Church Delegation by the Archbishop of Canterbury," June 19, 1945, PRO INF 1/793.

54. "The Reply of His Beatitude the Metropolitan Nikolai of Krutitsy [*sic*]," June 19, 1945, ibid.

55. Letter of Aleksii, delivered by Metropolitan Nikolai, June 12, 1945, ibid.

56. In spring of 1944 when it looked as though the Russian visit would take place that summer, Waddams had written: "I was recommending a policy of masterly inactivity as far as the Ministry was concerned in the matter of entry visa." R.R.W. minute, May 16, 1944, PRO INF 1/793.

Conclusion

1. Iaroslavskii, *Religion in the U.S.S.R.*, p. 31 (emphasis in original).

2. Gorbachev cited in Remnick, *Resurrection*, p. 17. Interestingly, Western leaders suffered from a similar lack of insight on this matter. Margaret Thatcher writes, for instance, that in assessing the state of the USSR in the early 1980s, "The one issue which, in retrospect, we underestimated . . . was the nationality question." *The Downing Street Years*, p. 451.

3. Dennis J. Dunn makes a spirited defense of this point in "Nationalism and Religion in Eastern Europe," in Dunn, *Religion and Nationalism in Eastern Europe and the Soviet Union*, pp. 1–14. He argues that because the peoples of this region so often lacked stable state structures, churches were the nuclei for nationalities. He writes: "[N]ationalism in Eastern Europe was and is essentially proreligious," p. 11.

4. Regarding the Russian and Romanian Orthodox churches, the Moscow Patriarchate writes: "As is known, their relations have been overshadowed by the unsettled issue concerning the future of the so-called 'Bessarabian Diocese.'" Department for External Church Relations of the Moscow Patriarchate, "The 12th International Meeting on People and Religions," September 1998, Moscow Patriarchate web site ‹www.russian-orthodox-church.org.ru›.

5. For a recent examination of these conflicts, see Joseph R. Gregory, "Ukraine: Christians in Conflict," *First Things*, no. 71 (March 1997): 24–27. The Moscow Patriarchate writes indignantly that "The years between late 80s and early 90s saw the worsening of the relations between the Orthodox and Catholic Churches. The main cause was the inadmissible violent methods employed by the Greek Catholic churches to restore their legal parish life after an 'underground' existence." It also notes ruefully that "world public opinion" sided with the Uniates, "believing that what was going in Western Ukraine was the reversal of historical injustice." Department for External Church Relations of the Moscow Patriarchate, "The Synodal Theological Commission Studies Issues Related to the Dialogue between the Orthodox and Roman Catholic Churches," April 1997, Moscow Patriarchate web site ‹www.russian-orthodox-church.org.ru/ve110771.htm›.

6. Communication service of the Department for External Church Relations of the Moscow Patriarchate, "Discussion on Church Situation in Estonia," November 30, 1998, Moscow Patriarchate web site ‹www.russian-orthodox-church.org.ru/ne81130.htm›.

7. In 1909 Sergei Bulgakov lamented that "it is well-known that there is no intelligentsia more atheistic than the Russian. Atheism is the common faith into which are baptized all who enter the bosom of the humanistic intelligentsia church." Bulgakov, "Heroism and Asceticism: Reflections on the Religious Nature of the Russian Intelligentsia," Shagrin and Todd, *Landmarks*, p. 29. There were, of course, a great many exceptions to this rule, the novelist Fedor Dostoevskii and the philosopher Vladimir Solov'iev, to name only two of the most prominent. For a good, short review of the Russian intelligentsia's antireligious beliefs as these evolved over time, see Luukkanen, *The Party of Unbelief*, pp. 39–45.

8. Trotskii, *Problems of Everyday Life and Other Writings on Culture and Science*, pp. 34–35.

9. Sherwood, *Roosevelt and Hopkins*, p. 392.

10. Notable examples are D'Encausse, *The Russian Syndrome*; and Szamuely, *The Russian Tradition*.

11. This remained true right up to the collapse of the USSR. A report to the Central Committee in 1974 sought to explain the bewildering, and disquieting, appeal of religion to young people: "Their interest in religion is quite often associated with errant moral and philosophical 'searchings' and at times with contrariness and the desire to stand out from the crowd. Misconceptions of religion as an effective regulator of moral behavior even now, under socialism, are common among certain students. Certain students believe that religion plays an important role in personal moral behavior by supposedly 'humanizing us,' 'establishing a framework for moral behavior,' 'restraining us from immoral acts,' and so forth. The persistance of these misconceptions has largely been facilitated by religious propaganda, which emphasizes that religion is the 'only repository of morality.' There have been cases where political nihilism, rejection of the Soviet way of life, nationalistic attitudes, and so forth are cloaked in the attraction to religion and heightened interest in religious antiquity." As ever, the only prescription to deal with these errant views was deemed to be more effective education in the "scientific and materialist outlook." "Report by Institute for Scientific Atheism, May 21, 1974, to the Central Committee on Increasing Effectiveness of Atheist Education among Youth," in Koenker, *Revelations from the Russian Archives*, pp. 493–95.

12. The confusion between imperial traditions and Russian nationalism is itself nothing new in Russian history. In an engaging new history, Geoffrey Hosking has argued that "in Russia state-building obstructed nation building." Hosking, *Russia*, p. xxiv. This is the principal thesis of his history. Just as this confusion over identity made the Russian Empire unstable at its core, despite its military power and geographic reach, so I would argue the Stalinist empire suffered from the same debilitating weakness.

13. Patriarch *locum tenens* Sergii, Metropolitan of Moscow and Kolomenskoe, November 9, 1942, *RPTsIVOV*, p. 93.

14. Robert A. Graham, *The Vatican and Communism during World War II*, p. 56.

15. For an excellent examination of Peter I and the Russian Orthodox Church, see Cracraft, *The Church Reform of Peter the Great*.

16. The historiography on Pius XII and the Nazis is voluminous. Perhaps the strongest attack on his role is still Falconi, *The Silence of Pius XII*. One attempt to defend Pius's legacy by a Jesuit historian is Robert A. Graham, *The Vatican and Communism during World War II*, esp. pp. 9–14. For evidence that Pius XII's wartime role remains controversial, see Robert S. Wistrich, "The Pope, the Church, and the Jews," *Commentary* 107, no. 4 (April 1999): pp. 22–28; and the contentious correspondence following its publication, "Letters," *Commentary* 108, no. 1 (July–August 1999): pp. 12–24. The most recent attack on Pius XII, based on certain Vatican archives, is Cornwell, *Hitler's Pope*.

17. Nikolai Eshliman and Gleb Iakunin, "Otkrytoe pis'mo sviashchennikov Nikolaia Eshlimana i Gleba Iakunina Patriarkhu Aleksiiu," *Grani* 61 (October 1966): 132.

18. Solzhenitsyn, *A Lenten Letter to Pimen, Patriarch of All Russia*, p. 6.

19. Scammell, *Solzhenitsyn*, pp. 766–67.

20. Cited in Evgeny Barabanov, "The Schism between the Church and the World," in Solzhenitsyn et al., *From under the Rubble*, p. 176 (emphasis in original).

21. "Orthodox Yes-Men," *Economist*, April 5, 1997, pp. 50–52.

22. Significantly, these remarks by Aleksii were quoted by his successor Pimen' when he was enthroned as patriarch on January 3, 1971. Quoted in Peter J. S. Duncan, "Orthodoxy and Russian Nationalism in the USSR, 1917–88," in Hosking, *Church, Nation and State in Russia and Ukraine*, p. 321.

23. Ramet, *Cross and Commissar*, p. 4.

24. Lukianov would ultimately also reject Gorbachev's relative liberalism, becoming one of the plotters of the failed August 1991 coup. A. Lukianov memorandum for TsK KPSS, February 7/9, 1990, TsKhSD f. 89, op. 8, d. 41.

25. Garbett (archbishop of York), *Christianity and Communism*, pp. 1–7.

26. Bell, *John Bull and the Bear*, p. 7.

27. Levering, *American Opinion and the Russian Alliance*, p. 203. Levering's book remains the best study of the shifts and characteristics of American opinion at this time, even though this portion of the conclusion is unconvincing.

28. For the most recent and comprehensive description of the aftermath of the war, see Zubkova, *Russia after the War*. On postwar famine, see Zima, *Golod v SSSR*.

29. On Stalin's belligerence in atomic diplomacy, see Holloway, *Stalin and the Atom Bomb*.

30. As did the early revelations about Soviet wartime espionage, fears that, as recent revelations from the Soviet archives have demonstrated, had a solid basis in fact. See Weinstein and Vassiliev, *The Haunted Wood*; and Haynes and Klehr, *Venona*.

31. John Lewis Gaddis most recently and explicitly recasts this view: "*As long as Stalin was running the Soviet Union a cold War was inevitable.*" *We Now Know*, p. 292 (emphasis in original).

32. Such is the argument of Leffler, *A Preponderance of Power*.

33. This mass Soviet purge, and the discreditable Western role in it, has long been known. Bethell, *The Last Secret: Forcible Repatriation to Russia*.

34. Svetlov [Gribin] to RESIDENTS and to Gornov [Gordievsky], December 19, 1984, in Andrew and Gordievsky, *More "Instructions from the Centre,"* pp. 46–52.

BIBLIOGRAPHY OF WORKS CITED

Aarons, Mark, and John Loftus. *Unholy Trinity: How the Vatican's Nazi Networks Betrayed Western Intelligence to the Soviets.* New York, 1991.

Alekseev, Wassilij. "Neozhidannyi dialog." *Agitator*, no. 6 (1989): 42.

Alexeev, Wassilij. *The Foreign Policy of the Moscow Patriarchate, 1939–1953.* Vol. 2, *Materials for the History of the Russian Orthodox Church in the U.S.S.R.* (in Russian). Moscow, 1955.

Alexeev, Wassilij and Theofanis G. Stavrou. *The Great Revival: The Russian Church under German Occupation.* Minneapolis, 1976.

Anders, Wladyslaw. *An Army in Exile.* London, 1981.

Anderson, Paul B. *People, Church and State in Modern Russia.* London, 1944.

Andreev-Khomiakov, Gennady. *Bitter Waters: Life and Work in Stalin's Russia.* Trans. Ann E. Healy. Boulder, 1977.

Andrew, Christopher, and Oleg Gordievsky. *KGB: The Inside Story of its Operations from Lenin to Gorbachev.* London, 1990.

———, eds. *More "Instructions from the Centre": Top Secret Soviet Files on Global Operations, 1975–1985.* London, 1992.

Andrew, Christopher, and Vasili Mitrokhin. *The Sword and the Shield: The Mitrokhin Archive and the Secret History of the KGB.* New York, 1999.

Andreyev, Catherine. *Vlasov and the Russian Liberation Movement: Soviet Reality and Emigre Theories.* Cambridge, 1987.

Armstrong, John. *Ukrainian Nationalism, 1939–1945.* New York, 1963.

Avrich, Paul. *Kronstadt 1921.* Princeton, 1970.

Bacon, Edward. *The Gulag at War: Stalin's Forced Labour System in the Light of the Archives.* New York, 1994.

Baer, George W., ed. *A Question of Trust: The Origins of U.S.-Soviet Relations: The Memoirs of Loy W. Henderson.* Stanford, 1986.

Banac, Ivo. *With Stalin against Tito: Cominformist Splits in Yugoslav Communism.* Ithaca, 1988.

Barber, John, and Mark Harrison. *The Soviet Home Front, 1941–1945: A Social and Economic History of the USSR in World War II.* London, 1991.

Beaumont, Joan. *Comrades in Arms: British Aid to Russia, 1941–1945.* London, 1980.

Bell, P. M. H. *John Bull and the Bear: British Public Opinion, Foreign Policy and the Soviet Union, 1941–1945.* London, 1990.

Bethell, Nicholas. *The Last Secret: Forcible Repatriation to Russia, 1944–7.* London, 1974.

Bialer, Seweryn. *Stalin and His Generals: Soviet Military Memoirs of World War II.* New York, 1969.

Bociurkiw, Bohdan R. *The Ukrainian Greek Catholic Church and the Soviet State (1939–1950).* Edmonton, 1996.

Bourke-White, Margaret. *A Look at Russia*. New York, 1934.

———. *Shooting the Russian War*. New York, 1942.

Brinkley, David. *Washington Goes to War*. London, 1989.

Brokgauz, F. A., and I. A. Efron, eds. *Rossiia: Entsiklopedicheskii slovar'*. Reprint. Petersburg, 1898.

Brooks, Jeffrey. *When Russia Learned to Read: Literacy and Popular Literature, 1861–1917*. Princeton, 1985.

Bugai, Nikolai F. *L. Beriia-I. Stalinu: "Soglasno Veshemu ukazaniiu."* Moscow, 1995.

Burns, James MacGregor. *Roosevelt, 1940–1945: The Soldier of Freedom*. New York, 1970.

Byrnes, Robert F. *Pobedonostsev: His Life and Thought*. Bloomington, 1968.

Cassidy, Henry C. *Moscow Dateline*. Boston, 1943.

Caute, David. *The Fellow Travelers: A Postscript to the Enlightenment*. New York, 1973.

Chadwick, Owen. *Britain and the Vatican during the Second World War*. Cambridge, 1986.

Chuev, Felix. *Molotov Remembers: Inside Kremlin Politics; Conversations with Felix Chuev*. Chicago, 1993.

———. *Sto sorok besed s Molotovym: Iz dnevnika F. Chueva*. Moscow, 1991.

Churchill, Winston Spencer. *The Second World War*. Boston, 1948–.

Ciechanowski, Jan. *The Warsaw Uprising of 1944*. Cambridge, 1974.

Ciszek, Walter J., with Daniel L. Flaherty. *With God in Russia*. New York, 1964.

———. *He Leadeth Me*. New York, 1973.

Conquest, Robert. *The Great Terror: A Reassessment*. New York, 1990.

———. *The Harvest of Sorrow: Soviet Collectivization and the Terror-Famine*. Oxford, 1986.

———. *The Nation Killers: The Soviet Deportation of Nationalities*. London, 1970.

———. *Stalin: Breaker of Nations*. New York, 1991.

Corley, Felix, ed. *Religion in the Soviet Union: An Archival Reader*. London, 1996.

Cornwell, John. *Hitler's Pope: The Secret History of Pius XII*. New York, 1999.

Cracraft, James. *The Church Reform of Peter the Great*. London, 1971.

Craig, Gordon A., and Francis L. Loewenheim, eds. *The Diplomats, 1939–1979*. Princeton, 1994.

Curtiss, John S. *The Soviet State and the Russian Church, 1917–1950*. Boston, 1953.

Dallin, Alexander. *German Rule in Russia, 1941–1945: A Study of Occupation Politics*. Reprint. New York, 1980.

Davis, Nathaniel. *A Long Walk to Church: A Contemporary History of Russian Orthodoxy*. Boulder, 1995.

Dear, I. C. B. and M. R. D. Foot, eds. *The Oxford Companion to World War II*. Oxford, 1995.

D'Encausse, Helene Carrere. *The Russian Syndrome: One Thousand Years of Political Murder*. New York, 1992.

De George, Richard T., and James P. Scanlan, eds. *Marxism and Religion in Eastern Europe*. Dordrecht, 1974.

Dobb, Maurice. *Russia To-day and To-morrow*. London, 1930.

———. *Soviet Planning and Labour in Peace and War: Four Studies*. London, 1942.

Dunlop, John B. *The Faces of Contemporary Russian Nationalism*. Princeton, 1983.

Dunn, Dennis J. *The Catholic Church and the Soviet Government, 1939–1949*. Boulder, 1977.

———, ed. *Religion and Nationalism in Eastern Europe and the Soviet Union*. Boulder, 1987.

Ellis, Jane. *The Russian Orthodox Church: A Contemporary History.* Bloomington, 1986.

Erickson, John. *The Road to Berlin: Continuing Stalin's War with Germany.* Boulder, 1983.

———. *The Road to Stalingrad: Stalin's War with Germany.* New York, 1984.

Eshliman, Nikolai, and Gleb Iakunin. "Otkrytoe pis'mo sviashchennikov Nikolaia Eshlimana i Gleba Iakunina Patriarkhu Aleksiiu," *Grani* 61 (October 1966).

Falconi, Carlo. *The Silence of Pius XII.* Boston, 1970.

Federal'naia sluzhba bezopasnosti rossii, slushba vneshnei razvedki rossii, and Moskovskoe ob"edinenie arkhivov. *Sekrety Gitlera na stole Stalina: Razvedka i kontrrazvedka o podgotovke germanskoi agressii protiv SSSR Mart-iiun' 1941 g.* Moscow, 1995.

Federal'naia sluzhba kontrrazvedki rossisskoi federatsii. *Organy gosudarstvennoi bezopasnosti SSSR v velikoi otechestvennoi voine: Sbornik dokumentov.* Vol. I and II. Moscow, 1995.

Fireside, Harvey. *Icon and Swastika: The Russian Orthodox Church under Nazi and Soviet Control.* Cambridge, 1971.

Fitzpatrick, Sheila. *Stalin's Peasants: Resistance and Survival in the Russian Village after Collectivization.* Oxford, 1994.

Fletcher, William C. *Nikolai: Portrait of a Dilemma.* New York, 1968.

———. *Religion and Soviet Foreign Policy, 1945–1970.* London, 1973.

———. *The Russian Orthodox Church Underground, 1917–1970.* London, 1971.

Flint, James. "English Catholics and the Proposed Soviet Alliance, 1939." *Journal of Ecclesiastical History* 48, no. 3 (July 1997).

Freeze, Gregory L. "Handmaiden of the State? The Church in Imperial Russia Reconsidered." *Journal of Ecclesiastical History* 36, no. 1 (1985): 82–102.

———. *The Parish Clergy in Nineteenth-Century Russia: Crisis, Reform, Counter-Reform.* Princeton, 1983.

Friedlander, Saul. *Pius XII and the Third Reich: A Documentation.* New York, 1966.

Fukuyama, Francis. *The End of History and the Last Man.* New York, 1992.

Gaddis, John . *The United States and the Origins of the Cold War, 1941–1947.* New York, 1972.

———. *We Now Know: Rethinking Cold War History.* Oxford, 1997.

Garbett, Cyril. *Christianity and Communism.* London, 1948.

General Sikorski Historical Institute. *Documents on Polish-Soviet Relations, 1939–1945.* 2 vols. London, 1961.

Getty, J. Arch. *Origins of the Great Purges: The Soviet Communist Party Reconsidered, 1933–1938.* Cambridge, 1985.

Getty, J. Arch, and Roberta Manning, eds. *Stalinist Terror: New Perspectives.* Cambridge, 1993.

Gilbert, Martin. *Winston S. Churchill.* Vol. 7, *Road to Victory, 1941–1945.* London, 1986.

Glantz, David. *When Titans Clashed: How the Red Army Stopped Hitler.* Lawrence, 1995.

Goldberg, Anatol. *Ilya Ehrenburg: Writing, Politics, and the Art of Survival.* London, 1984.

Gordon, Michael R. "Irking U.S., Yeltsin Signs Law Protecting Orthodox Church." *New York Times,* Saturday, September 27, 1997.

Gordun, Sergii. "Russkaia Pravoslavnaia Tserkov' v period s 1943 po 1970 god." *Zhurnal moskovskoi patriarkhii,* no. 1 (1993): 39–40.

Graham, Loren R. *The Ghost of the Executed Engineer: Technology and the Fall of the Soviet Union.* Cambridge, 1993.

Graham, Robert A. *The Vatican and Communism during World War II: What Really Happened?* San Francisco, 1996.

Graves, Philip. *A Record of the War: The Twenty-Second Quarter, January 1, 1945–March 31, 1945.* London, 1945.

Gregory, Joseph R. "Ukraine: Christians in Conflict." *First Things*, no. 71 (March 1997): 24–27.

Gromyko, A. A., et al., eds. *Diplomaticheskii slovar'.* 3 vols. Moscow, 1985.

Gross, Jan T. *Revolution from Abroad: The Soviet Conquest of Poland's Western Ukraine and Western Belorussia.* Princeton, 1988.

Grossman, V. *Life and Fate.* New York, 1985.

Hamby, Alonzo. *Man of the People: A Life of Harry S. Truman.* New York, 1995.

Harriman, W. Averell, and Elie Abel. *Special Envoy to Churchill and Stalin, 1941–1946.* New York, 1976.

Hecker, Julius F. *Religion and Communism: A Study of Religion and Atheism in Soviet Russia.* New York, 1934.

Herwarth, Johnnie von. *Against Two Evils: Memoirs of a Diplomat-Soldier during the Third Reich.* London, 1981.

Hollander, Paul. *Political Pilgrims: Travels of Western Intellectuals to the Soviet Union, China, and Cuba, 1928–1978.* New Brunswick, 1981.

Holloway, David. *Stalin and the Atom Bomb.* New Haven, 1994.

Holmes, Brian, et al. *Russian Education: Tradition and Transition.* New York, 1995.

Hosking, Geoffrey, ed. *Church, Nation and State in Russia and Ukraine.* London, 1991.

———. *Russia: People and Empire, 1552–1917.* Cambridge, 1997.

Hughes, Lindsey. *Russia in the Age of Peter the Great.* New Haven, 1998.

Huntington, Samuel. "The Clash of Civilizations?" *Foreign Affairs* 72, no. 3 (1993): 22–49.

Institut Marksizma-Leninizma. *Istoriia Velikoi otechestvennoi voiny Sovetskogo Soiuza.* Moscow, 1960–.

———. *Kommunisticheskaia Partiia sovetskogo soiuza v resoliutsiiakh i resheniiakh s'ezdov konferentsii i plenumov Ts K.* Vol. 7. Moscow, 1985.

Institut Vseobshchei Istorii. *Komintern i vtoraia mirovaia voina: Chast' I, do Iiunia 1941g.* Moscow, 1994.

Jelavich, Barbara. *Russia's Balkan Entanglements, 1806–1914.* Cambridge, 1991.

———. *St. Petersburg and Moscow: Tsarist and Soviet Foreign Policy, 1814–1974.* Bloomington, 1974.

Johnson, Hewlett. *The Socialist Sixth of the World.* London, 1939.

Kagan, Jack, and Dov Cohen. *Surviving the Holocaust with the Russian Jewish Partisans.* Portland, 1998.

Karol, K. S. *Between Two Worlds: The Life of a Young Pole in Russia, 1939–46.* New York, 1986.

Keep, John. *The Last of the Empires: A History of the Soviet Union, 1945–1991.* Oxford, 1995.

Kershaw, Ian, and Moshe Lewin, eds. *Stalinism and Nazism: Dictatorships in Comparison.* Cambridge, 1997.

Kimball, Warren F. *The Juggler: Franklin Roosevelt as Wartime Statesman.* Princeton, 1991.

Klehr, Harvey. *The Heyday of American Communism.* New York, 1984.

Klehr, Harvey, and John Earl Haynes. *Venona: Decoding Soviet Espionage in America.* New Haven, 1999.

Klehr, Harvey, John Earl Haynes, and Fridrikh Firson, eds. *The Secret World of American Communism.* New Haven, 1995.

Koenker, Diane, ed. *Revelations from the Russian Archives.* Washington, D.C., 1992.

Kolarz, Walter. *Religion in the Soviet Union.* London, 1966.

——. *The Soviet Union and the Catholic Church.* London, 1962.

Kondakova, N. I., and V. N. Main. *Intelligentsia Rossii 1941–1945 gg.* Moscow, 1995.

Koppes, Clayton, and Gregory D. Black. *Hollywood Goes to War: How Politics, Profits and Propaganda Shaped World War II Movies.* New York, 1987.

Kosiba, Harold J. *Stalin's Great Game: Anglo-Soviet Relations in the Near East, 1939–1943.* Ann Arbor, 1991.

Kozlov, M. M., et al., eds. *Velikaia otechestvennaia voina 1941–1945: Entsiklopedia.* Moscow, 1985.

Kravchenko, Victor. *I Chose Freedom: The Personal and Political Life of a Soviet Official.* New York, 1946.

Leffler, Melvin. *A Preponderance of Power: National Security, the Truman Administration, and the Cold War.* Stanford, 1992.

Lencyk, Wasyl. "The Eastern Catholic Church and Czar Nicholas I." Ph.D. dissertation, Fordham University, 1961.

Leonhard, Wolfgang. *Child of the Revolution.* Chicago, 1958.

Levering, Ralph. *American Opinion and the Russian Alliance, 1941–1945.* Chapel Hill, 1976.

Liberman, Simon. *Building Lenin's Russia.* Chicago, 1945.

Lih, Lars T., Oleg V. Naumov, and Oleg V. Klevniuk, eds. *Stalin's Letters to Molotov, 1925–1936.* New Haven, 1995.

Luukkanen, Arto. *The Party of Unbelief: The Religious Policies of the Bolshevik Party, 1917–1929.* Helsinki, 1994.

Magosci, Robert. *A History of Ukraine.* Seattle, 1996.

——, ed. *Morality and Reality: The Life and Times of Andrei Sheptyt'sky.* Edmonton, 1989.

Maiskii, Ivan. *Before the Storm: Recollections by I. M. Maiskii.* London, 1944.

Markovna, Nina. *Nina's Journey: A Memoir of Stalin's Russia and the Second World War.* Washington, D.C., 1989.

Marshall, Richard H., Jr., ed. *Aspects of Religion in the Soviet Union, 1917–1967.* Chicago, 1971.

Mastny, Vojtech. *Russia's Road to the Cold War: Diplomacy, Warfare, and the Politics of Communism, 1941–1945.* New York, 1979.

McLaine, Ian. *Ministry of Morale: Home Front Morale and the Ministry of Information in World War II.* London, 1979.

Mawdsley, Evan. *The Russian Civil War.* Boston, 1987.

Medvedev, Roy. *All Stalin's Men: Six Who Carried out the Bloody Policies.* Trans. Harold Shakman. New York, 1984.

Melish, William Howard. *Religion Today in the USSR.* New York, 1945.

Meyendorff, John. *Byzantium and the Rise of Russia: A Study in Byzanto-Russian Relations in the Fourteenth Century.* Cambridge, 1981.

Milosz, Czeslaw. *The Captive Mind.* Reprint. London, 1985.

Mindszenty, Joszef Cardinal. *Memoirs.* New York, 1974.

Miner, Steven Merritt. *Between Churchill and Stalin: The USSR, Great Britain, and the Origins of the Grand Alliance.* Chapel Hill, 1989.

Ministerstvo inostrannykh del Rossiiskoi federatsii. *Dokumenty vneshnei politiki 1940–22 iiunia 1941.* Moscow, 1995.

Ministerstvo inostrannykh del SSSR. *Tegeranskaia konferentsia rukovoditelei trekh soiuznykh derzhav—SSSR, SShA i Velikobritanii (28 noiabra–dekabria 1943 g.): Sbornik dokumentov.* Moscow, 1984.

———. *Sovetskie-Amerikanskie otnosheniia v velikoi otechestvennoi voine 1941–1945.* Moscow, 1984.

Misiunas, Romuald, and Rein Taagepera. *The Baltic States: Years of Dependence, 1940–1990.* Berkeley, 1993.

Modin, Yuri. *My Five Cambridge Friends: Burgess, Maclean, Philby, Blunt, and Cairncross by their KGB Controller.* New York, 1994.

Moloney, Thomas. *Westminster, Whitehall, and the Vatican: The Role of Cardinal Hinsley, 1935–1943.* Tunbridge Wells, 1985.

Moskovskoe gorodskoe ob"edinenie arkhivov. *Neisvestnaia Rossia.* Moscow, 1992.

Murashko, G. P. et al., eds. *Vostochnaia Evropa v dokumentakh rossiiskikh arkhivov.* 2 vols. Moscow, 1997.

Nekrich, Aleksandr. *The Punished Peoples: The Deportation and Fate of Soviet Minorities at the End of the Second World War.* New York, 1978.

Nikolai, Metropolitan. *The Russian Church and the War against Fascism.*

———. *Slova, rechi, poslaniia (1941–1946 gg.).* Moscow, 1947.

Novikov, M. P., ed. *Ateisticheskii slovar'.* 2d ed. Moscow, 1986.

Obolensky, Dimitri. *The Byzantine Commonwealth: Eastern Europe, 500–1453.* New York, 1971.

Overy, Richard. *Russia's War: Blood upon the Snow.* New York, 1997.

Paleologue, Maurice. *An Ambassador's Memoirs.* Trans. F. A. Holt. 3 vols. New York, 1925.

Papal Encyclical. *Divini Redemptoris.* March 19, 1937.

Pasat, V. I. *Trudnye stranitsii istorii Moldovii 1940–1950.* Moscow, 1994.

Patriarchate of Moscow. *Pravda o religii v Rossii.* Moscow, 1942.

———. *Russkaia pravoslavnaia tserkov' i velikaia otechestvennaia voina.* Moscow, 1943.

Peris, Daniel. *Storming the Heavens: The Soviet League of the Militant Godless.* Ithaca, 1998.

Perlmutter, Amos. *FDR and Stalin: A Not So Grand Alliance, 1943–1945.* Columbia, 1993.

Pikhoia, P. G., et al., eds. *Katyn': Plenniki neob'iavlennoi voiny.* Moscow, 1997.

Pincher, Chapman. *Their Trade Is Treachery.* London, 1981.

Pipes, Richard. *Russia under the Bolshevik Regime.* New York, 1993.

———. *The Unknown Lenin: From the Secret Archives.* New Haven, 1996.

Polish Research Centre. *The Orthodox Eastern Church in Poland, Past and Present.* London, 1940.

Popov, N. V., ed. *Arkhivy raskryvaiut tainy: Mezhdunarodnye voprosy; Sobytiia i liudi.* Moscow, 1991.

Pospielovsky, Dimitry. "The 'Best Years' of Stalin's Church Policy (1942–1948) in the Light of Archival Documents." *Religion, State, and Society* 25, no. 2 (1997): 139–62.

———. *A History of Soviet Atheism in Theory and Practice, and the Believer.* 2 vols. New York, 1988.

———. *The Russian Church under the Soviet Regime, 1917–1982.* 2 vols. Crestwood, 1984.

Radzinsky, Edvard. *Stalin.* New York, 1996.

Ramet, Pedro (Sabrina) ed. *Eastern Christians and Politics in the Twentieth Century.* Durham, 1988.

———. *Cross and Commissar: The Politics of Religion in Eastern Europe and the USSR.* Bloomington, 1987.

Remnick, David. *Resurrection: The Struggle for a New Russia.* New York, 1977.

Riasanovsky, Nicholas V. *A History of Russia.* 2d ed. New York, 1969.

Roberts, Frank. *Dealing with Dictators: The Destruction and Revival of Europe, 1930–70.* London, 1981.

Roberts, Geoffrey K. *The Soviet Union and the Origins of the Second World War: Russo-German Relations and the Road to War, 1933–1941.* New York, 1995.

Rossiiskaia Akademiia nauk. *Liudskie poteri SSRR v period vtoroi mirovoi voiny: Sbornik statei.* St. Petersburg, 1995.

———. *NKVD i pol'skoe podpol'e 1944–1945 (Po "Osobym papkam" I. V. Stalina.* Moscow, 1994.

———. *Vsesoiuznaia perepis' naseleniia 1939 goda: Osnovnye itogi.* Moscow, 1992.

Rozanov, G. L. *Stalin Gitler: Dokumental'nyi ocherk sovetsko-germanskikh diplomatich-eskikh otnoshenii 1939–1941 gg.* Moscow, 1991.

Rzheshevsky, Oleg. *World War II: Myths and the Realities.* Moscow, 1984.

Samsonov, A. M. *Znat' i pomnit': Dialog istorika s chitatelem.* Moscow, 1988.

Scammell, Michael. *Solzhenitsyn: A Biography.* New York, 1984.

Seaton, Albert. *The Russo-German War, 1941–1945.* New York, 1972.

Sella, Amnon. *The Value of Human Life in Soviet Warfare.* London, 1992.

Sergii (Stragorodskii). *Patriarkh Sergii i ego Nasledstvo.* [1946?].

Shagrin, Boris, and Albert Todd, eds. *Landmarks.* New York, 1977.

Sherwood, Robert E. *Roosevelt and Hopkins: An Intimate History.* New York, 1950.

Shkarovskii, M. V. *Russkaia Pravoslavnaia Tserkov' pri Staline i Khrushcheve.* Moscow, 1999.

Solzhenitsyn, Aleksandr. *The Gulag Archipelago, 1918–1956: An Experiment in Literary Investigation.* 3 vols. London, 1973.

———. *A Lenten Letter to Pimen, Patriarch of All Russia.* Minneapolis, 1972.

———. *Letter to the Soviet Leaders.* New York, 1974.

———. *The Russian Question at the End of the Twentieth Century.* New York, 1995.

Solzhenitsyn, Aleksandr, et al. *From under the Rubble.* Chicago, 1974.

Sontag, Raymond James, and Jams Stuart Beddie, eds. *Nazi-Soviet Relations, 1939–1941: Documents from the Archives of the German Foreign Office.* Reprint. Westport, 1976.

Spinka, Matthew. *The Church in Soviet Russia.* New York, 1956.

Stalin, I. V. *Sochineniia.* Stanford, 1967.

Stehle, Hansjakob. *The Eastern Politics of the Vatican, 1917–1979.* Athens, 1980.

Stites, Richard. *Russian Popular Culture: Entertainment and Society since 1900.* Cambridge, 1992.

———, ed. *Culture and Entertainment in Wartime Russia.* Bloomington, 1995.

Strik-Strikfeldt, Wilfried. *Against Stalin and Hitler: Memoir of the Russian Liberation Movement, 1944–1945.* London, 1970.

Subtelny, Orest. *Ukraine: A History.* Toronto, 1988.

Sudoplatov, Pavel. *Special Tasks: The Memoirs of an Unwanted Witness—a Soviet Spymaster.* Boston, 1994.

Suny, Ronald Grigor. *The Soviet Experiment: Russia, the USSR, and the Successor States.* Oxford, 1998.

Szamuely, Tibor. *The Russian Tradition.* London, 1974.

Taubman, William. *Stalin's American Policy: From Entente to Detente, to Cold War.* New York, 1982.

Taylor, A. J. P. *The Origins of the Second World War.* Reprint. London, 1991.

Taylor, Myron C., ed. *Wartime Correspondence between President Roosevelt and Pope Pius XII.* New York, 1947.

Temple, William. *The Hope of a New World.* London, 1942.

Thatcher, Margaret. *The Downing Street Years.* New York, 1993.

Thurston, Robert W. *Life and Terror in Stalin's Russia, 1934–1941.* New Haven, 1996.

Timasheff, Nicholas S. *The Great Retreat: The Growth and Decline of Communism in Russia.* New York, 1946.

Tocqueville, Alexis de. *The Ancien Regime and the French Revolution.* London, 1976.

Tolstoy, Nikolai. *The Secret Betrayal.* New York, 1978.

Trotsky, Leon. *My Life: An Attempt at Autobiography.* Reprint. London, 1970.

———. *Problems of Everyday Life and Other Writings on Culture and Science.* New York, 1973.

Tucker, Robert. *The Lenin Anthology.* New York, 1975.

———. *Stalin in Power: The Revolution from Above, 1928–1941.* New York, 1990.

Tumarkin, Nina. *The Living and the Dead: The Rise and Fall of the Cult of World War II in Russia.* New York, 1994.

Urban, George R. *Stalinism: Its Impact on Russia and the World.* Aldershot, 1982.

Uzzell, Lawrence A. "Letter from Moscow." *First Things,* no. 79 (January 1998): 17–19.

Vardyis, Stanley, and Judith B Sedaitis. *Lithuania: The Rebel Nation.* Boulder, 1997.

Volkogonov, Dmitrii. *The Rise and Fall of the Soviet Empire: Political Leaders from Lenin to Gorbachev.* London, 1998.

———. *Stalin: Triumph and Tragedy.* Trans. Harold Shukman. New York, 1988.

———. *Triumf i tragediia: I. V. Stalin; Politicheskii portret.* Moscow, 1989.

Vorontsova, Lyudmila, and Sergei Filatov. "Freedom of Conscience in Russia: What the Opinion Polls Show." *Religion, State, and Society* 21, nos. 3–4 (1993): 375–81.

Vostryshev, Mikhail. *Bozhii izbrannik: Krestnyi put' sviatitelia Tikhona Patriarkha Moskovskogo i vseia Rossii.* Moscow, 1990.

Walicki, Andrzej. *The Slavophile Controversy: History of a Conservative Utopia in Nineteenth-Century Russian Thought.* Oxford, 1975.

Ware, Timothy. *The Orthodox Church.* Rev. ed. London, 1993.

Webb, Sidney, and Beatrice Webb. *Soviet Communism: A New Civilisation?* New York, 1936.

Weigel, George. *The Final Revolution: The Resistance Church and the Collapse of Communism.* New York, 1992.

Weinberg, Gerhard. *A World at Arms: A Global History of World War II.* Cambridge, 1994.

Weinstein, Allen, and Alexander Vassiliev. *The Haunted Wood: Soviet Espionage in America —the Stalin Era.* New York, 1999.

Werth, Alexander. *Moscow, 1941.* London, 1942.

————. *Russia at War, 1941–1945.* New York, 1964.

White, Stephen. *Britain and the Bolshevik Revolution: A Study in the Politics of Diplomacy, 1920–1924.* London, 1979.

Wickham Legg, L. G., and Williams, E. T. *Dictionary of National Biography, 1941–1950.* Oxford, 1959.

Wistrich, Robert S. "The Pope, the Church, and the Jews." *Commentary* 107, no. 4 (1999): 22–28.

Yaroslavskii, Emelian. *Religion in the U.S.S.R.* New York, 1934.

Zaprudnik, Jan. *Belarus: At a Crossroads in History.* Boulder, 1993.

Zawodny, J. K. *Death in the Forest: The Story of the Katyn Forest Massacre.* New York, 1962.

————. *Nothing but Honour: The Story of the Warsaw Uprising, 1944.* London, 1978.

Zernov, Nicolas. *The Russians and Their Church.* London, 1945.

Zima, V. F. *Golod v SSSR, 1946–1947 godov: Proiskhozhdenie i posledstviia.* Moscow, 1996.

Zubkova, Elena. *Russia after the War: Hopes, Illusions, and Disappointments, 1945–1957.* New York, 1998.

INDEX

Adrian, Patriarch, 123

Aleksandr II (tsar of Russia), 19

Aleksandr III (tsar of Russia), 19

Aleksandrov, G., 79–80, 157; memorandum on controlling religion, 150–54

Aleksii, Patriarch, 76, 125, 127, 327; background, 191; elevation to patriarchate, 191, 306; letter to Stalin, 191–92; tour of 1945, 310–13

All-Slav Antifascist Committee, 103, 164

American Communist Party, 110, 219, 242

American Slavic Congress, 164

Anders, Wladyslaw, 169, 173, 176

Anders Army. *See* Anders, Wladyslaw

Anglican Church, 8, 97, 130, 259; joint communique with Russian Orthodox Church, 263; relations with Orthodoxy, 97, 308; silence about Soviet atrocities, 308–9

Antichrist, 24, 77

Anti-God museums, xii–xiii, 285; closing of, 69

Anti-Hitler coalition, 10, 96, 208–9, 214, 307; strains in, 174

Anti-Semitism, 41

Archbishop of Canterbury, xiii, 20n, 80, 97, 247, 259–60, 311–12

Armenians, 64

Atheism, xiv, 2, 7, 11–12, 68–69; Russian intelligentsia and, 317–18; Soviet, American distrust of, 220–21; Soviet campaigns promoting, 70

Atlantic Charter, 95

Austria-Hungary, 14–15

Azerbaijan, 64, 65

Bagallay, Lacy, 96–97, 99, 103

Bakhchiserai, 61

Balkans, xiv, 8, 19, 331

Balkhars, 62

Baltic Sea, 15

Baltic States, 10, 11n, 38, 49, 72, 94, 175, 287

Bandera, Stepan, 41, 44, 63, 189

Baptists, 135, 142, 285

Bartlett, Vernon, 211

Baty (khan), 69

BBC (British Broadcasting Corporation), 66, 69, 81, 207, 214, 246, 249, 270, 288, 293, 303, 332; broadcasts on Soviet religion, 271–76; broadcasts to occupied Europe, 271–76, 288; debates on broadcasts to USSR, 210; denunciations of Soviet atheism by, 205–6, 208–9; and Garbett's trip to Moscow, 265; sympathetic broadcasts about USSR, 249–50

Beaverbrook, Lord, 226, 233, 268, 279; on propaganda, 245

Belorussia, 17, 21, 38, 45, 49, 105

Berdiaev, Nikolai, 93

Beria, Lavrenty, 43, 144, 173, 182, 304; on restoration of Patriarchate, 124

Berle, Adolph, 217

Berling, Z., 114, 173

Bessarabia, 11n, 43, 47, 49, 94

Bezbozhnik, 69, 80–81

Big Three, 8

Black Sea, 15

Blunt, Anthony, 277

Bobrinskii, Vladimir, 14

Bogoiavlenskii Cathedral, 262

Bohlen, Charles, 172

Bolshevism, 13, 20, 24

Bormann, Martin, 53–54

Bourke-White, Margaret, 131, 280–86, 291

Bracken, Brendan, 246–47, 251; on Garbett's trip to Moscow, 266–68

Bradley, Omar, 67

Brauchitsch, Field Marshal Walter von, 178

Brest-Litovsk, 55, 104

Brezhnev, Leonid, 29–30

Britanskii soiuznik, 250

Buddhists, 33

Bukovina, 11n, 94

Bul'dovskii, Metropolitan Feofill, 137

Bulgaria, 19, 70, 111; Orthodox Church of, 309

Bullitt, William, 217–18

Burgess, Guy, 277

Burskii, M., 236–37

Byzantium, 16–17

Cadogan, Alexander, 258

Cairncross, John, 277

Callendar, Harold, 110–11

Capone, Al, 218

Carr, E. H., 268

Carter, Edward, 299, 301

Caspian Sea, 60

Cassidy, Henry, 295

Catherine II (empress of Russia), 18, 104, 145

Census of 1937, 5, 33

Central Committee (CPSU), xv, 43, 79; directives on propaganda, 230, 232; pleased with Bourke-White's book, 286; and popular disloyalty, 62, 73; religious policy of, 82, 171–72; renews campaign against religion, 149–61

Chaplin, Charles, 240

Chechens, 62

Cheka, 23

Chicago Tribune, 238

Chuev, Feliks, 93

Churchill, Winston, 8, 131, 246, 252, 268, 331; forbids broadcast of Soviet anthem, 206; June 22, 1941, speech, 211, 214, 255; on Katyn killings, 107–8; on Soviet territorial demands, 94–95; visits Vatican, 178; wary of Soviet propaganda, 249

Church Statute of 1945, 197–98

Ciechanowski, Jan, 167, 224

CIO (Congress of Industrial Organizations), 164

Ciszek, Walter, 169–71, 185

Civil War, Russian, 20

Clark Kerr, Sir Archibald, 83, 260

Cockburn, J. Hutchinson, 212

Cold War, xiii, 13, 333–34

Collectivization, 22, 32; legacy of, 34, 180, 188, 252

Comintern, xiv, 209, 232, 238, 275; attacks on Roosevelt, 206; directives to international Communists, 206–7; dissolution of, 110, 112, 177, 245

Commonweal, 219

Communism, 7, 12, 33; as alternative religion, 318; front groups, 23; international appeal of, 231–32; transformed by war, 322–23

Communist Party of the Soviet Union, xiii, 7; public opinion on, 31; Twentieth Congress (1956), 29

Constantinople, 17

Cooper, Duff, 213, 246–47

Council for the Affairs of Religious Cults, 172

Council for the Affairs of the Russian Orthodox Church, 172; control of patriarch, 198; creation of, 125, 129; and petitions for reopening churches, 147–49

Crimea, 60–61

Cripps, Sir Stafford, 83, 215–16, 233, 253; assesses religion in USSR, 80–81

Curzon Line, 174–75

Czechs, 70

Daily Express, 268

Daily Mail, 292

Daniil, Bishop, 73

Darwin, Charles, 2

Davies, Joseph, 240

Dekanozov, Vladimir, 294

Democratic Party (United States), 216

Department of State (United States), 217, 218–19, 232

Deportations: from western borderlands, 39, 41–44, 106; from within USSR, 144

Dies, Martin, 225

Dimtrii Donskoi, 69; tank unit named after, 76, 114

Divini Redemptoris, 23–24, 213

Dobb, Maurice, 258

Dostoevskii, Fedor, 88, 276

Drogobych, 134

Easter: Soviets' open celebration of, 82–83

Eastern Europe, xiv, 1–2, 12, 14–15, 33, 110, 331; Christians in, 171

Eastern Orthodoxy, 15–17, 19

East Germany, 59

Eden, Anthony, 94, 108, 233, 259

Ehrenburg, Ilia, 66, 237–38, 279; on American religious opinion, 241; on wartime journalism, 290

Eisenstein, Sergii, 51, 240

Engels, Friedrich, 297–98

Eshliman, Nikolai, 326

Estonia, 11n, 40, 43, 47, 72, 176, 287; hostility to return of Soviets, 290; Orthodox Church of, 317

Evangelicals, 142

Evening Standard, 206

Fierlinger, Z., 114

Filaret, Patriarch, 17

Fin, V., 292–93

Finland, 81, 94

Fish, Hamilton, 225

Fomina, I., 132

Foreign Commissariat (USSR), 216, 228, 230, 285, 293, 299

Foreign Office (Great Britain), 205

Four Freedoms, 225

Galan, Iaroslav, 179, 183, 185

Galicia, 14

Gallup Poll, 217

Garbett, Cyril (archbishop of York), 9, 130, 306–7; changes views of USSR, 328–30; impact on public opinion of tour, 270–71; trip to Moscow, 1943, 262–70, 308, 312; views of Stalin, 267

Gefter, Mikhail, 32

Genghiz Khan, 318

George VI (king of England), 312

Georgians, 64–65

Germany, 13; invasion of USSR by, 7, 9, 13, 21, 32, 34, 36, 38, 43, 48–49, 52, 55, 68–69, 76, 205–6, 210, 216, 232

Gerontsi, Archbishop, 160–61

Gestapo, 52

Goebbels, Josef, 108

Gollancz, Victor, 231–32

Gorbachev, Mikhail, xii–xiii, 30, 190, 316, 327–28

Gordievskii, Oleg, 278

Gordun, Sergii, 8

Graebner, Walter, 292

Grand Alliance. *See* Anti-Hitler coalition

Grant, Robert A., 220

Great Britain, xiii, 3, 8

Great Patriotic War, 29

Greek Catholic Church. *See* Uniate Church

Greeks, Soviet, 60–61

Gregory VII (patriarch of Constantinople), 106

Grigorii, Archbishop of Saratov, 137

Grigulevich, Joseph, 178

Grossman, Vasilii: *Life and Fate*, 32, 51, 87

GRU (Glavnoe Razvedyvatel' noe Upravlenik; Chief Espionage Directorate), 63

Gruliow, Leo, 296–302

Gulag, xii, 59; clergy in, 126, 128, 142–43, 170; prisoners' view of German invasion, 59

Gusev, Fedor, 252–53

Habsburgs, 15

Halifax, Lord, 259

Harriman, Averell, 57, 67, 161, 164, 226–27, 318–19; on importance of religion, 220; skepticism about Soviet religion, 227

Herwarth, Johnnie von, 57–58

Heydrich, Reinhardt, 53–54

Hill, Elizabeth, 234–36

Hinsley, Cardinal, 213

Hitler, Adolf, 24, 28, 51, 53–55, 59, 66, 72–73, 77, 111, 129, 132, 158, 170, 211, 219, 251, 321, 330; contempt for religion, 53–54

Hollywood: Soviet penetration of, 240
Holy Synod, 17
Hoover, Herbert, 216
Hopkins, Harry, 217, 223, 297
Hull, Cordell, 174, 223
Hungary, 15
Huxley, Julian, 211

Iakunin, Gleb, 326
Iaroslavskii, Emelian, 69, 78, 316
Ickes, Harold, 217
Informbiuro, 107, 226, 292–93, 301; created, 230; establishes policy on Western propaganda, 237–43
Ingersoll, Ralph, 239
Ingush, 62
"Internationale," 28, 205–6
Islam/Moslems, 1, 15, 33, 169; and national dissent, 62
Ivan III (grand prince of Russia), 157, 188
Ivan IV (tsar of Russia), 157
Izvestiia, 23, 196, 279

Jews
—American: opinions of, 240
—Polish, 38; and reception of Red Army, 1939, 38
—Soviet, 33–35, 44, 142; and German invasion, 52; repression of, 34–35
John Paul II (pope), 335
Johnson, Hewlett (dean of Canterbury), 8, 258, 279, 295, 313; and BBC broadcasts, 272; tour of Soviet Union, 303–6
Judaism, 14

Kabardintsy, 62
Kagan, Jack, 35, 38
Kalinin, I. V., 142
Kalinin, Mikhail, 109, 125n
Karaganda, 59
Karelia, 81
Karlowitz Synod, 106
Karpov, Georgii, 130, 172; addresses *sobor'* of 1945, 193–94; and death of Sergii, 191; named president of Council, 129; on reli-

gious revival, 199; and restoration of Patriarchate, 125–29
Katyn massacre, 106–8, 165, 173, 307, 333
Kazakh, 59, 65
Kazan' Cathedral, xii
Keitel, Field Marshal Wilhelm, 178
Kemenov, V., 228–30, 297, 299–301
Khachaturian, Aram, 240
Khar'kov, 63; political opinions in, 132–33; religious incidents in, 143–44; Soviets reoccupy, 132
Kherson, 149
Khmel'nitskii, Bohdan, 35
Kholm, 46
Khrushchev, Nikita, 29, 41, 170, 188, 321; antireligious program of, 190; denounces Stalin, 163; and dissolution of Uniate Church, 186
Kiev, 56, 143
King, Harold, 110
Kirovograd, 149
Kobulov, Bogdan, 73–75
Koch, Erich, 54
Kollontai, Aleksandra, 229
Komsomolskaia pravda, 156
Konovalets, Yevghen: assassination of, 182
Kosciuszko League, 165
Kostel'nik, Havryil, 163, 184–85; goes to Moscow, 182; on history of Uniate Church, 186–88; motives of, 186
Kotiv, Ivan, 182
Kovalev, I.: memorandum on religion, 156–59
Krasnaia zvezda, 32
Kravchenko, Viktor, 52
Kronstadt, 57
Krzycki, Leo, 164–65
Kuibyshev, 96, 98
Kulik, G. I., 38
Kursk, battle of, 9, 94

Labour Party (Great Britain), 257
Lang, Cosmo Gordon (archbishop of Canterbury), 23, 252, 255
Lange, Oscar, 164–65

Latvia, 11n, 39, 43, 53, 72, 222, 287
Lawrence, John, 293
League of Militant Godless, 93, 99, 172, 316
Left Book Club, 231
Lend-Lease, 10, 67, 95, 208, 216, 220, 223, 226, 297, 332; congressional debate over extension to USSR, 224–25, 252; extended to USSR, 227
Lenin, Vladimir Ilych (Ulianov), 13, 20, 93, 96, 109, 176, 255, 265, 270, 285; and cannibalism, 20; on Clausewitz, 232; murder of clergy, 20–21; persecution of the church, 20–21, 159; on religion, 86
Leningrad, xi–xii, xiv, 72
Leonhard, Wolfgang, 59
Lezgins, 64
Life, 283, 286
Lindbergh, Charles, 216
Lithuania, 11n, 40, 43, 46, 72, 104, 222; Catholics in demand religious freedom, 146; Christian Democratic Party of, 46
Litvinov, Maksim, 95–96, 228, 237, 297–99, 303
Lloyd, Geoffrey (archbishop of Canterbury), 308
Lozovskii, Solomon, 230, 238–40, 292, 294–95; on Soviet religious rights, 226–27
Luk'ianov, Anatoly, 327
Lutheran Church, 23
L'vov, 134, 179, 181, 183

Magidoff, Robert, 294–96
Maiskii, Ivan, 174, 206, 229, 237, 239, 250, 303; complains about Catholic press, 253–54; as effective ambassador, 233–34; on Soviet religious record, 252
Malenkov, Georgii: on restoration of Patriarchate, 124
Maly, Teodor, 246
Mamulian, Rouben, 240
Mamulov Stephan, 182
Markovna, Nina, 52, 58
Martin, Hugh, 123, 212, 258, 260–61, 263
Marx, Karl, 2, 310
Marxism, xii, 19

McCarthy, Joseph, 225
McCarthyism, xiii, 333
McLean, Donald, 277
Medvedev, Roy, 7–8, 10
Merkulov, Vsevolod, 44; suggests restoring Patriarchate, 124
Meshchik, Pavel, 36, 42
Mikes, Janos, 273
Mikhail, Bishop of Kherson, 128
Mikhail (tsar of Russia), 17
Miller, Wright, 293–94
Milosz, Czeslaw, 274
Mindszenty, Jozsef Cardinal: and impact of British propaganda, 273–74
Ministry of Information (Great Britain), 80–81, 206, 209, 211, 232, 234; agrees to clergy exchange, 259; and Catholic opinion, 213; crafts Soviet policy, 251–52; creation of Soviet Relations Branch, 210–11, 247; problems with religious policy of, 213–15; on public views of Soviet religion, 270–71; Soviet penetration of, 246–50; structure of, 209–10
Ministry of Information (Poland), 118
Minsk, 53, 104
Mission to Moscow, 240
Molotov, Viacheslav, 20, 38, 40, 165, 186, 226, 289, 303; complains about London Poles, 164; denies Soviet complicity in Katyn massacre, 108; and deportations, 62; justification of terror, 35–36; meets with archbishop of York, 264; meets with Hewlett Johnson, 303–5; meets with Orlemanski, 166; meets patriarch, 129; on restoration of Patriarchate, 124; signs Katyn death order, 108; on Stalin, 88, 93
Mongols, 69; invasion of Russia by, 324
Morgenthau, Hans, 217
Moscow, xiv, 20, 27
Moscow News, 99, 296–97
Moscow Patriarchate, xiv, 8, 11–12, 16–18, 34, 47, 71–72, 102–3, 105, 181, 317, 320–21; appeals to East European Christians, 196; attacks on Vatican, 194–96; and closure of Uniate Church, 183; excommunication

of collaborationist clergy, 136; and Polish
Orthodox believers, 106; reasons for collaboration with Kremlin, 130–31; as tool
for political control, 144, 198, 320–22; as
tool of Soviet foreign policy, 327, 331
Moscow Radio, 10, 111, 123, 165–66, 191, 238;
poor quality of broadcasts, 229
Moslems, Soviet, 64
Mussolini, Benito, 171, 253

Napoleon (emperor of France), 69, 160,
176, 324
Nationalities, non-Russian, 11, 14–15, 21,
35–37, 39–41, 44; dissension among,
61–66; Soviet attempts to control, 12;
Soviet misunderstanding of, 39
Nazis/Nazism, xi, xiv, 2–4, 23–24, 29, 33, 51;
barbarism of, 7, 34–35, 52, 55, 60–61, 87–
88, 132, 220, 324; collaboration with, 33,
73; invasion of Poland by, 41; occupation
of USSR, 34
Nazi-Soviet Pact, 10, 47, 51, 69, 206, 208, 233
NBC (National Broadcasting Company),
191, 294–95
Nevskii, Aleksandr, 51, 69; air squadron
named after, 76
New Jerusalem Monastery, 265
New Republic, 238
News Chronicle, 289
New Statesman, 305
New York Daily News, 238
New York Democrat, 296
New York Post, 238
New York Times, 110, 297
Nikolai (Iarushevich), Metropolitan, 10, 48,
51, 103, 125, 127, 307; addresses Ukrainian
believers, 137; appeals to international
Christians, 111, 272–72; appointed to
Commission to Investigate Fascist
Crimes, 151–52, 156; approaches British
in 1942, 96–99, 258–59; as archbishop,
277; on Katyn massacre, 113; meets arch-
bishop of York, 265; at Pan-Slavic Con-
ference (1943), 112–15; tour of 1945, 307–
13

Nikolai I (tsar of Russia), xii, 19, 48
Nikolai II (tsar of Russia), 13
Nikolai Nikolaevich, Grand Duke, 14
Nikol'skii Sobor', xi
Nikon, Patriarch, 17, 192
NKGB (Narodnyi Kommissariat Gosudarstvennoi Bezopasnosti; People's
Commissariat of State Security), 39,
42–44, 46, 52, 86, 142, 145, 171, 182, 189;
agents in Rome, 177–78
NKVD (Narodnyi Kommissariat Vnutren-
nykh Del; People's Commissariat of Internal Affairs), 39, 41, 43–44, 47–49, 52,
56, 60, 70, 72, 98, 125, 127, 144, 170, 173,
186, 228, 324, 330; compromises clergy,
140–41; deportations, 86; and manipulation of churches, 73–74; monitoring of
church activities, 160–61; numbers shot
for desertion, 57, 59; reporting of public
opinion, 131–32
Novodevichyi monastery: reopened, 140

Obnovlentsii (Renovationists), 21, 101, 130;
dissolution of, 196; schism ended, 131
Ogienko, I. I., 46
Old Believers, 18, 160–61
Orlemanski, Stanislaus, 164–67, 169, 172, 185
Orlov, Mikhail, 285
OSS (Office of Strategic Services), 178
Ossetes, 62
Ottoman Empire, 15, 17, 104, 192, 309
OUN (Organization of Ukrainian Nation-
alists), 41–44, 47, 63, 184

Paleologue, Maurice, 14, 19, 24
Pal'gunov, Nikolai, 232–33
Pan-Slavic Congress (1943), 111–13
Pan-Slavism, 19, 70, 96, 103–4, 269, 309;
Russian Church appeals to, 129
Partisans: anti-Soviet, 61–63, 134–35; So-
viet, 61
Paton, William, 212, 256
Patriarchs, Eastern Orthodox, 16, 17n, 106,
115, 119, 125, 275–76, 309–10; 1945 *Sobor'*,
190–98; suspicions of Soviets, 193–94

Patton, George, 67
Pentecostals, 145
Penza, 142, 145
People's Commissariat of Education: campaign against religion, 156
Peter I (tsar of Russia), 17–18, 157, 271, 300, 325
Philby, Harold ("Kim"), 246, 277
Pimen', Patriarch, 236–27
Pius XI (pope), 23; denunciation of Communism, 213; establishes Russicum, 170
Pius XII (pope), 224, 326, 330; on religion in Eastern Europe, 174–76, 221–22
PM, 239
Poland, 5, 11n, 15, 17–18, 38, 41, 70, 94, 104, 175, 303; Communists of, 38, 164–65, 305; London exile government of, 95, 106–7, 115, 123, 164–65, 173–74; Orthodox Church of, 105, 116, 118; Orthodox population of, 105; partition of, 10; religious freedom demanded by, 169; tensions with Soviet occupiers of, 172–74; treatment of Ukrainians in, 38
Pol'ianskii, I. V., 172
Polish Home Army, 173
Polish-Soviet Agreement (1941), 95
Politbiuro (USSR), xv
Political Warfare Executive (Great Britain), 168
Pravda, 82, 279
Pravda o religii v rossii, 97–103, 130, 177, 258, 260–61; translation into English, 260–62
Priestley, J. B., 211
Pritt, D. N., 292
Profittlich, Archbishop Edward, 176
Prokofiev, Sergii, 240
Propaganda
—British: and dilemma of alliance with USSR, 205–9
—German, 7, 9–10, 46–47, 212; religious, 53, 68–71
—Soviet, 7–8, 12–13, 29, 31, 46–47, 52–53, 60, 70–71, 93–94; anti-Catholic, 178; anti-religious, 154–56; appeals to occupied Europe, 230–31; difficulties reaching

Western audience, 231; difficulties working in United States, 238–39; directorate of, 132; ease of operation in Britain, 238–39, 245–47; emulates British methods, 229, 246; explains defeat of France, 232–33; and German invasion, 52–53; impact in Balkans, 331; religious, 10, 45, 177; shortcomings of, 228–31; toward West after German invasion, 228–43
Prosvita, 63
Protestantism, 2; American, 217, 332
Pravdin, Vladimir, 171
Pugachevshchina: Soviet fears of, 145

Rakosi, Matyas, 240
RCA (Radio Corporation of America), 295
Reagan, Ronald, xiii
Red Army, xiv, 8, 10–12, 28, 38, 55, 76, 95, 114; believers in, 93–94; desertions from, 173; enters Balkans, 269; enters Belorussia, 172; enters Eastern Europe, 168; enters L'vov, 181; enters Poland, 164; and executions, 57, 65–66; international underestimation of, 55, 220; loyalty/disloyalty of soldiers, 56–57, 59–62, 64–65; nationalist dissension within, 62; numbers of prisoners, 56–57, 60; partisan resistance to, 145; popular reception in western borderlands, 38; recruitment into, 134–35; reoccupies Ukraine, 131–32; and tensions with local populations, 62
Red Square (Moscow), 27
Religion: Balkan Christians, 98; comparison of Nazi and Soviet approaches to, 84–89; conflicts over church property, 146–47; continuities between tsarist and Soviet policies, 11–12, 14–24, 196; German manipulation of, 7, 46, 53–55, 73, 75–76, 287; international opinion on, 72, 74, 76–79, 80–81, 83, 93–94, 96, 103–4; and nationalism in western borderlands, 44–49; number of open churches, 47, 199; popular belief in, 33; repression of, 45, 47; Russo-Polish rivalry related to, 104–7, 115–21, 124, 167–68, 179–80; So-

viet destruction of icons, 147; Soviet incomprehension of, 35, 155; Soviet manipulation of, 79–83, 87–89, 142–43; wartime closure of churches, 80; wartime revival of, 6, 33–35, 78–83, 141–49

Renovationists. *See* Obnovlentsii

Republican Party (United States), 216

Reuters, 110

Riga Cathedral, 48

Riga Declaration, 75

ROA (Russkaia osvoboditel'naia armiia; Russian Liberation Army), 66

Roberts, Frank, 155–56, 305–6, 311

Roman Catholicism, 2, 14–16, 19, 23, 33, 44–45, 47, 88, 104, 165–67; American hierarchy, 174–75; American reaction to Roosevelt's policy, 226; American suspicions of USSR, 217, 219, 221, 223–25, 242; Americans urged to support USSR, 221; and anti-Soviet resistance, 45–46; hostility to USSR, 207; Soviet arrest of clergy, 176; Soviet attempts to split, 241

Romania, 15, 93, 104; Soviet propaganda toward, 111–12

Roosevelt, Franklin D., 8, 102, 165, 178, 206; advocates aid to USSR, 221; and American Catholics, 241; attempts to mediate Russo-Polish tension, 174–78; belief in Soviet victory, 220; correspondence with Pius XII, 221–23; exaggerates Soviet religious freedom, 223–28; on Katyn killings, 107–8; meets with Umanskii, 223–24; on Orlemanski incident, 167–68; on religious question, 168; and Soviet territorial demands, 94–95; Umanskii assesses position of, 217

Rosenberg, Alfred, 53

Russian Empire (tsarist), 15, 18, 33

Russian nationalism, 9, 11, 13, 27–28; wartime revival of, 67–68

Russian Orthodox Church, xi–xv, 2–3, 5–11, 14, 17–22, 24, 44, 46–47, 319–20; alternative Vatican, 189–90; appeals to Balkan Christians, 111; appeals to East European Christians, 168; appeals to international

opinion, 111–12; attacks on Vatican, 171; clergy's distrust of Soviets, 127–28; continuing wartime restrictions on, 121; fundraising of, 76–77, 159; importance of in Soviet policymaking, 4–6, 9–11; joint communique with Anglican Church, 263; as national symbol, 68–69; number of clergy, 22, 140; number of open churches, 22, 138–39; persistence of, 4; political manipulation of, 46–50; reopening of seminaries, 138–41; as tool for occupation, 96, 105–6, 115, 118–19, 124, 131, 136–41; as tool for political control, 320; wartime change in circumstances of, 93–94

Russian War Relief, 296–302, 332

Russification, 12, 14, 18, 68, 158

Ryan, A. P., 214–15

St. Isaac's Cathedral, xii–xiii

St. Petersburg, xii, 11, 14, 20, 316

Samsonov, A. M., 30

Sargent, Sir Orme, 250

Sarnoff, David, 295

Sazonov, Sergii, 14

Schulenburg, Count von der, 126

Scripps-Howard newspapers, 217, 297

Sergii (Voskresenskii), Bishop, 10, 48, 317; collaboration with Germans, 72–74; murder of, 75–76

Sergii (Stragorodskii), Patriarch, 6, 9, 22–23, 47, 70, 73, 115, 141, 284–85, 330; appeals to international Christians, 111; attacks Poles, 116–19; death of, 190, 306; elected patriarch, 127, 275; meets with archbishop of York (1943), 264–65; meets with Stalin (1943), 123–27; and Nazi invasion, 69–70; and *Pravda o religii*, 97–103; reasons for collaboration with Soviet state, 323–28; recants opposition to Soviet state, 23, 101–2; wartime proclamations of, 71–72, 74–79, 121

Serov, Ivan, 173

Seventh-Day Adventists, 142, 144

Shakespeare, William, 315

Shapiro, Henry, 295
Shaw, Marjorie, 305
Shcherbakov, A. S., 74, 124, 236–37, 299;
  named director of Informbiuro, 230
Sheptyt'sky, Metropolitan Klymentii, 44–
  45, 182, 189; attacked in Soviet press, 179,
  183–85; disillusioned with Germans,
  180–81; and letter to Hitler, 63–64; and
  letter to Stalin, 181; and Soviet occupa-
  tion, 180
Shevelev, Ivan, 44
Shostakovich, Dmitrii, 240
Sigismund III (king of Poland), 19
Sikorski, General Wladyslaw, 107
Sikorskii, Bishop Polykarp, 71–72, 98, 137
Slavophiles, 88
Slipyi, Metropolitan, 181, 185; arrested, 189;
  calls to cease resistance to Soviet power,
  181–82; and dissolution of Uniate
  Church, 186
Slovakia, 15, 70
SMERSH (*Smert' shpionam*; "death to
  spies"), 134
Smolensk, 53
Smollett (Smolka), Peter, 270–71, 303, 308,
  312; assessment as Soviet mole, 277–78;
  manipulation of BBC, 271, 274–77; ma-
  nipulation of press, 253–54; named di-
  rector of Foreign Ministry's Soviet Rela-
  tions Branch, 211; role as Soviet mole,
  245–50; ties with archbishop of Canterbury, 259–60
Sobor' of 1943, 126, 141, 147–48, 161, 172, 192,
  264; appeals to international Christians,
  128–29; consequences of, 149; convening
  of, 127
Sobor' of 1945, 190–98, 276, 306
Society for Cultural Relations with the
  USSR, 248–49, 303
Solzhenitsyn, Aleksandr, 1, 7, 319, 321–22,
  326–27; on Vlasov Army, 64; works of, 1
Soviet-Finnish War (1939–40), 220, 255
Soviet ideology, 4, 7, 13
Soviet population: loyalty/disloyalty of, 7,
  49–50, 70

Soviet religious policy: confusion over,
  154–60; destruction of churches, 22, 123;
  mid-war change in, 109–11; murder of
  clergy, 21–22; resumption of antireligious campaigns, 311; shutting of seminaries, 22; splitting of churches, 230
Soviet War News, 72, 234
Spanish Inquisition, xii, 23
Speaight, Robert, 276
Spinka, Matthew: letter to Roosevelt,
  225–26
SS (Schutzstaffel; elite guard), 63
Stalin, Iosef Vissarionovich, xii, xiv, 3, 6, 7,
  11, 13, 21, 28, 37, 44, 60, 112, 114, 119, 151–52,
  172, 174–75, 196, 270, 279, 292, 300, 319–
  20, 322, 324, 334; contempt for religion,
  318; decides to dissolve Uniate Church,
  183, 186, 190; and deportations, 62; on
  desertions, 57; on dissolution of Comintern, 110; fanning racial hatred, 67;
  greetings to Sobor' of 1943, 151–52; "Holy
  War" of, 3, 11–12; on Katyn massacre, 107;
  meets with archbishop of York, 264;
  meets with Harriman and Beaverbrook,
  226; meets with Hewlett Johnson, 303–5;
  meets with Hopkins, 223; meets Metropolitan Sergii, 123–27; meets with Orlemanski, 166–67; military misjudgments,
  30; as national icon, 27, 29; and occupation of western borderlands, 38; and
  Order Number 270 (1941), 56; orders
  "scorched earth," 58; and public opinion,
  30–31, 131–32; purges, 220, 240, 296; restoration of Patriarchate, 124; on Russian
  people, 67, 88; singing voice of, 93; Temple views as sincere, 256; and Ukraine,
  163; war aims of, 94–96, 165; and Warsaw
  Uprising, 173–74. *See also* Stalinist terror
Stalingrad, battle of, xiv, 9, 32, 60, 64, 73, 94,
  112
Stalinist terror, 20, 28, 33–35, 41, 55
Standley, Admiral William H., 176
Stanislavyv, 38
Stankevich, Adam, 46
Steinhardt, Laurence, 227

Stettinius, Edward, 165
Strik-Strikfeld, Wilfried, 58
Sudoplatov, Pavel, 136; campaign against Ukrainian nationalism, 182–83; on dissolution of Uniate Church, 189
Suslov, Mikhail, 156
Swoboda, L., 114

Tallin, 176, 290
Tardini, 174, 177
TASS, 171, 228, 238
Tatars, 59, 61; collaboration with Germans, 61–62
Taylor, Myron: mission to Vatican, 174–78, 221, 224
Teheran Conference, 8–9
Temple, Archbishop William, 255, 330; agrees to translation of *Pravda o religii*, 259–62; death of, 306; and exchange of clergy visits, 262–64; intellectual dishonesty of, 258; views of alliance with USSR, 255–58
Teutonic Knights, 69
Tevias Sargs, 39–40
Third Rome: Moscow as, 17
Tikhon, Patriarch, 115–16, 123, 127, 190, 192
Timasheff, Nicholas, 205
Time of Troubles, 17
Times (London), 269–70
Timoshenko, Marshal Semyon, 300
Tito, Josip Broz, 110
Tocqueville, Alexis de, 231
Tolstoi, Aleksii, 237
Treaty of Riga (1921), 105, 119
Trinity Monastery, 166
Trollope, Anthony, 315
Trotskii, Leon, 1, 57, 109, 335; on religion, 318
Truman, Harry S., 218
Tumarkin, Nina, 32

Uchitel'skaia gazeta, 156
Ukraine, 8–9, 17, 21–22, 34, 41, 54, 63, 105; and arrival of Germans, 58; and Nazi occupation, 64; Orthodox believers in, 9, 63, 105; religious opinion in, 71, 184–85;

resistance to Soviet occupation, 181; Slavic nationalism in, 21, 64; Slavic patriotism in, 67–68; SS in, 64; western, 15, 38, 41, 47
Ukrainian Autocephalous Church, 21, 34, 317; repressed, 136–37
Ukrainian Autonomous Church, 21, 34, 317; repressed, 136–37
Ukrainian Central Committee: attempts to limit religious influence, 195–96; dissolution of Uniate Church, 183
Ulianovsk, 124, 264
Umanskii, Konstantin, 216–17, 219, 226–27, 245, 280; meets with Roosevelt, 223–24; on propaganda in West, 238–42
Uniate (Greek Catholic) Church, 2, 9, 14–15, 19, 34, 39, 44, 46, 48, 104, 130, 158; and anti-Soviet underground, 44–47; arrest and deportation of clergy, 189; clergy of, 159; persecution of, 29; Soviet suppression of, 179–90
Union of Brest (1596), 19
United States, xiii, 3, 8; ethnic Poles in, 165
USSR (Union of Soviet Socialist Republics), xi, xiii–xv, 4–6, 12, 15, 23–24, 27, 44; collapse of, 27–28; national anthem, 28; popular loyalty/disloyalty to, 27–31, 70, 334; postwar famine in, 200–201; public opinion of Nazis, 51–53
Uzbeks, 65

Vatican, 12, 19, 88, 111, 123, 126, 158, 179, 183, 219, 253–54, 326, 335; concern for Soviet mistreatment of Catholics, 222–23; fears of Soviet expansion, 168–69, 171, 178, 221
Veniamin, Metropolitan, 102, 241
Vilnius, 39, 46
Vinnitsa, 148
Vlasov, General Andrei, 66
VOKS (Vsesoiuznoe Obshchestvo Kul'turnykh Sviazei s zagranitsei; propaganda agency), 228–30, 234, 240, 248, 280–83, 297–302
Volga Germans, deportation of, 59, 287
Volhynia, 48

Volkogonov, Dmitrii, 8, 31
Volokitin, Kh. T., 142
Voroshilov, Marshal K. I., 38
Vvedenskii, Archbishop Aleksandr, 21,
    101, 284; reenters Moscow Patriarchal
    Church, 130–31
Vyshinskii, Andrei, 289, 294

Waddams, Herbert, 81, 259, 274, 308; ac-
    companies Garbett to Moscow, 265–66
Warner, Christopher, 205, 245, 307
Warsaw Uprising (August 1944), 173
Wassilewska, Wanda, 114
Webb, Sidney and Beatrice, 233, 258
Wehrmacht, 10, 53, 60, 95, 330; casualties,
    55; and Soviet POWs, 56
Weizsäcker, E., 178
Welles, Sumner, 217–18
Werth, Alexander, 66–67, 69, 290–91, 295–
    96, 332; recommendations on propa-
    ganda, 287–88; reporting from Moscow,
    286–88; on Soviet religion, 81–82
Western Allies, xiii, 3; ignorance of USSR,
    215; opinion of USSR, 207–8, 214, 216,
    220–21, 251–52, 332–33; Soviet public
    opinion of, 132–33, 201–2; and Soviet
    religious repression, 10, 12, 24, 70; and
    war effort, 94
Western borderlands, xiv, 11–12, 32–34, 39;
    clergy's collaboration with resistance in,
    136, 154; German occupation of, 53, 124;
    Jews in, 105; public opinion in, 132–36;

199–202; religious fault lines in, 317, 322,
    335; resistance to Soviet occupation, 94,
    131–41, 145, 149, 158, 199–200; Soviet oc-
    cupation of (1939–40), 35–44, 47–50,
    235; Soviet reoccupation of, 39–44, 134–
    36
Western Christians: aid to Soviets from, 24
Williams, R. R., 215, 256, 308; skepticism of
    Soviet information, 236
Williams, Spencer, 240
Wilson, Hugh, 176
Winterton, Paul: on reporting from
    Moscow, 288–91, 295–96
World Council of Churches, 212, 256
World War I, 14, 19, 58
World War II, 24; Soviet memories of,
    27–31
Wyaznski, M., 118–19

Yakov, Archbishop, 73
Yalta Conference, 155

Zhdanovshchina, 133
Zheludkov, Sergei, 327
Zhitomir, 144
Zhukov, Marshal Georgii, 29
Zhurnal moskovskoi patriarkhii: resumes
    printing, 129
Zinchenko, G., 215–16, 292; liaison with
    Smollett, 247; supplies figures on religion
    in USSR, 216, 234–36
Zolotukhin, V., 134–35